JOHN KEVIN NEWMAN
FRANCES STICKNEY NEWMAN

Troy's Children

Lost Generations in Virgil's *Aeneid*

2005

GEORG OLMS VERLAG HILDESHEIM · ZÜRICH · NEW YORK

This work and all articles and pictures involved are protected by copyright.
Application outside the strict limits of copyright law without consent
having been obtained from the publishing firm is inadmissible and punishable.
These regulations are meant especially for copies,translations and micropublishings
as well as for storing and editing in electronic systems.

Das Werk ist urheberrechtlich geschützt. Jede Verwertung außerhalb der engen Grenzen
des Urheberrechtsgesetzes ist ohne Zustimmung des Verlages unzulässig und strafbar.
Das gilt insbesondere für Vervielfältigungen, Übersetzungen, Mikroverfilmungen und
die Einspeicherung und Verarbeitung in elektronischen Systemen.

Bibliografische Information Der Deutschen Bibliothek
Die Deutsche Bibliothek verzeichnet diese Publikation
in der Deutschen Nationalbibliografie; detaillierte bibliografische Daten
sind im Internet über http://dnb.ddb.de abrufbar.

Bibliographic information published by Die Deutsche Bibliothek
Die Deutsche Bibliothek lists this publication in the
Deutsche Nationalbibliografie; detailed bibliographic data are available
in the Internet at http://dnb.ddb.de.

∞ ISO 9706
© Georg Olms Verlag AG, Hildesheim 2005
www.olms.de
Alle Rechte vorbehalten
Printed in Germany
Umschlagentwurf: Irina Rasimus, Köln
Gedruckt auf säurefreiem und alterungsbeständigem Papier
Herstellung: KM-Druck, 64823 Groß-Umstadt
ISSN 0548-9705
ISBN 3-487-12810-1

Discipulis quotquot ubicumque
fuerunt, sunt, erunt,
dedicamus auctores.

Et vos praecipue, Gregoriani,
Sexta quos camera diu docebam
Tantorum studiorum amans amantes,
Servatos animo memor iocoso
Numquam depositurus hic recordor.

CONTENTS

	Preface	ix
I.	Lost Generations	3
II.	The Declining Mode	27
III.	Children and Virgil's Epic Technique—I	55
IV.	Children and Virgil's Epic Technique—II	75
V.	The Rhetoric of Virgil's Women—I	101
VI.	The Rhetoric of Virgil's Women—II	121
VII.	Dido	138
VIII.	Dido and Virgilian Nightmares	167
IX.	Women and Children: The Supporting Cast	189
X.	The Men Characters—I: The Supporting Cast	207
XI.	The Men Characters—II: Aeneas	241
XII.	The Men Characters—III: Anchises and Iulus/Ascanius	265
XIII.	The Future	278
XIV.	The *Vates*	306
	Appendix: The *Aeneid* as *Heracleid*	329
	Glossary of Critical Terms	341
	Booklist	346
	Index Locorum Vergilianorum	356
	Index Locorum Ceterorum	373
	Index Rerum et Nominum	383

PREFACE

In the last fifty years the interpretation of the *Aeneid* has swung between opposite poles. Aesthetically, this oscillation has spun off perhaps from that "pathetic structure" which Sergei Eisenstein found at the nucleus of all great art. But it has also occurred on moral grounds, in revulsion against the horrors of war and the tyrants usually thought to engender them. The darkness visible of at least certain features of Virgil's imagination has been thrown into relief, and there has been an effort even to suggest that the poem blurs and devalues the whole Augustan enterprise. More subtly, attention has been called to the poem's "two voices," "further voices," its "public and private" aspects. All these criticisms afforded valuable but necessarily partial insights. To change the metaphor, they recorded acute hearings of some of the poem's many harmonies, that polyphony which it shares with the whole Classical tradition of epic.

Countervailing cries have also been heard, emphasising the Roman, imperial, even cosmic dimensions of the *Aeneid*. These are in their way also true to form. Historically speaking, it hardly makes sense to suppose that the emperor would have followed with such interest or made such efforts to preserve an epic which had exhausted its own author, if he had himself concluded that it served no purpose useful to the republic. But he did take the most careful pains to save it from the flames. We are left then with the choice that either the poem's principal listener (a native speaker of Latin) was tone-deaf to discords audible even in today's noisy classrooms, or that he was by no means the steely counterpart of those totalitarian engineers of the soul with which the twentieth century made us familiar. *Vissi a Roma, sotto 'l buono Augusto....* As Augustus (in Eduard Meyer's revisionary insight) becomes a new Pompey, Dante is suddenly up to date. It turns out that we moderns cannot after all comfort ourselves in our cruel age with the thought that it was even worse before. It was not. This truth is slowly beginning to make itself apparent yet again.

Augustan Virgil has been thought to tell a tale in which history's losers, the Trojans, somehow at Laurentum, in spite of Juno, became history's winners, the Romans. But there is one troubling feature of the poem which seems to negate such optimism: to tell against the bias of the emperor's hopeful moral reforms and even more largely against the basis of any society which aims to survive, and that is its attitude to children. For although children play such an affecting role on the Ara Pacis Augustae, the *Aeneid* offers as its only collective, cosmic image of the living and growing generation the labyrinthine, in that sense "Cretan," lying, *Lusus Troiae*, led by Iulus / Ascanius. In a later book, by an extraordinary breach of epic etiquette, emphasising the sacredness of his status, and elevating him beyond any merely historical calculus, Iulus / Ascanius is even described. But Iulus had been invented for dynastic reasons. If he was Ascanius, who was Ascanius? "Pompeian" Livy is not sure. Such promise, and such elusiveness?

Yet paradoxically this is where Ascanius most resembles his great descendant, Augustus, who is not identifiable with any of the *Aeneid*'s protagonists, and certainly not, for the most part, with Aeneas. Rather, he is a prophesied figure, "one who is to come," as yet largely beyond the horizons of the *Aeneid*'s world, the salvific servant and avatar of priestly Apollo, rather than the iron minister of savage Mars.

Such irresolution would fit well with the Virgilian technique of half-assertion, but where in the poet's own mind did those haunting echoes rise? *Tusco de sanguine vires* he says of his native Mantua, described by the Elder Pliny as still in his day the last Etruscan outpost north of the Po. What if, in fact, like his admirer Propertius, like his patron Maecenas, Vergilius Maro was Etruscan? *Mar / maru* was the title given to holders of an Etruscan magistracy perhaps comparable with the Roman aedileship. *Marones*, in Martial (VIII. 55. 5) "poets such as Virgil," are assigned in an Umbrian inscription the duties of building a wall. Virgil was not an Umbrian. The connecting link is Etruria.

If so, the poet would perhaps have shared collective memories of the arrival from Asia Minor of an immigrant people with high hopes; of initial successes followed by long decline and defeat, of which Perusia illustrated the final debacle; of the waning of a tradition and a language in the face of the hard reality of Martian Rome: *occidit, occideritque sinas ... faciamque omnis uno ore Latinos*. Did this awareness colour his appreciation of "Asiatic" Aeneas' mission and its fading aftermath? Is it this "poetology" which influences his epic?

Maurice Bowra said that the *Aeneid* was the poetry of defeat written from the standpoint of the defeated. For an Etruscan, this would perhaps have been true in a special sense. But the Tuscan *vates* could rescue something from the shadows, a moral lesson perhaps about the dangers of endless iteration, a hope that the Apollo / Alexander of Falerii Veteres might come to outshine the Mars of Todi, and that is what his *Aeneid* does.

There is something to be said then for both poles of interpretation mentioned at the outset here, and our modest study hopes to promote this eirenical, Hegelian *Aufhebung*.

* * *

The passages adduced as supporting examples in our text have usually been translated into simple prose for the convenience of students and by way of implicit *prise de position*. How much Virgil's own allusive, impressionistic language defies this assault upon its lurking places is best known to his admirers.

During 1999–2000 J. K. Newman was kindly granted a sabbatical leave by the University of Illinois to advance his share of the long-laboured book, which, as our dedications suggest, is based on ideas adumbrated in class over many years. We would both like to thank all those who helped in any way with our task, and in particular Professor Dr. Ulrich Köpf of the University of Tübingen and Dr. Gottfried Kiefner, Gymnasialprofessor, Altsprachliches Gymnasium, Tübingen, both of whom generously read over our manuscript and recommended its publication.

The impressive resources of the University of Illinois Library, in particular of its Classics Library, presided over by Dr. Bruce Swann, have always been most courteously set at our disposal.

The museums and archaeological sites we have visited, notably those of Italy and England, have visibly influenced our interpretations and understanding of what the *Aeneid* is trying to say.

The book is offered as a contribution to *literae humaniores*. Dean Swift once presented a work to His Royal Highness Prince Posterity. In commending our efforts here to our students and former students, we mean with fitting humility to do the same.

Urbana 2004 J. K. Newman, F. S. Newman

Troy's Children

Lost Generations in Virgil's *Aeneid*

I

LOST GENERATIONS[1]

Quin occidit una / Sarpedon, mea progenies ...
Aen. X. 70–71
Filios meos, quos iuvenes mihi eripuit fortuna ...
Augustus, *Res Gestae* 14

The Aims of the Aeneid

Theophrastus, successor of Aristotle as head of the Lyceum, defined epic as a genre embracing the troubles[2] of gods, heroes and humans: περιοχὴ θείων τε καὶ ἡρωικῶν καὶ ἀνθρωπίνων πραγμάτων (Diom. gramm. apud Keil I, p. 484, 1–2). The *Aeneid* obviously fits this definition, but its narrower focus was perhaps originally more that of a Pindaric epinician than of epic *per se*. Pindar is concerned with putting his patron's modern achievement both into the timeless perspective of myth and the timed series of his family. He does not tell tales simply to impress or divert, even though he is not only a masterly narrator but also an exponent of a theory of narratology which would later be picked up by the Alexandrians.

In exactly the same way, the overt task of the *Aeneid* was not to recount a story for its own sake, but to link a modern victory, Actium (commemorated by the *Ludi Actiaci*), and its victor, Augustus, with a mythical tale, the establishment in Italy of the followers of Aeneas, the ancestors of Augustus' family. The proem to Lucretius, like the researches of Varro (*de Familiis Troianis*), shows that such ideas generally were in the air. In the event however, just as the Suda-lexicon reports that Pindar wrote "tragic songs,"[3] Virgil too developed his theme obliquely, religiously, tragically, as

---

[1] This is a different book, but we would like to begin with an acknowledgment of M. Owen Lee, *Fathers and Sons in Virgil's* Aeneid (Albany 1979). His title is reminiscent of Turgenev, "on the eve" of another revolution. — Valuable insights uniting two great poets are found in M. Petrini, *The Child and the Hero: Coming of Age in Catullus and Vergil* (Ann Arbor 1997).

[2] This translation of πραγμάτων is clearly superior to the flaccid "affairs." It gives a more Aristotelian turn to the definition, and uses a sense of the noun found both in the Classical and Hellenistic periods.

[3] Τραγικὰ ᾄσματα: cf. Modern Greek τραγούδια, "songs." The poet's interest in Pindar is illustrated already by the proem to *Georgics* III.

Dante saw (*l'alta mia tragedia*, *Inf.* 20. 113). Aeneas became the paradigm of the failures of Rome to find a satisfactory way of living with its Italian neighbours. Augustus was not so much his worthy descendant in any encomiastic mode as a messianic figure transcending all the ghastly history of previous mistakes, in that sense surpassing his ancestry.[4]

To catch the mood of his audience, the poet had to tack between the Scylla of unconvincing eulogy and the Charybdis of despairing dissent. Art hates compromisers, but his compromise became the national statement of Roman purpose, still painstakingly copied by some officer's child on one of the Vindolanda tablets in rainy Durham, by another in scorching Egypt. How did he carry out his extraordinary mission with such success?

The Lusus Troiae *as Paradigm*

Lost generations, Troy's children: childless Horace is unexpectedly sensitive to their fate.[5] Within the universe of Greek epic and tragedy their falling star was Astyanax. The *Aeneid* speaks of him too, as of dead Troilus and Polydorus. Do we now encounter those who survived most poignantly in their dumb-show at the Funeral Games of Anchises, wheeling and turning, as if on some carnival unmerry-go-round, in what was called, though Virgil avoids that precise phrase, the *Lusus Troiae* (V. 545 ff.)?[6] This Etruscan *truia* takes place in an Etruscan locale, a *circus* (551), a version perhaps of the Circus Maximus, itself a model of the wheeling cosmos.[7]

For the Romans, and for Virgil, this was no ordinary place. Tertullian (*De Spectaculis* 8) links the first circus races with Circe (Latinus' ancestress, *Aen.* VII. 189), honouring her charioteering father, the Sun (cf. *Aen.* XII. 164, Latinus / Augustus). Augustus' interest in the Circus and its Sun obviously tallied with the inspiration his regime drew from its patron Apollo.

---

[4] Indeed, if his personal propaganda made him a new Pompey, in some sense he even repudiated it. This is the thesis of E. Meyer in *Caesars Monarchie und das Principat des Pompejus* (Stuttgart / Berlin³ 1922). See also now Ya. Yu. Mezheritsky, «Республиканская Монархия» (Moscow 1994).

[5] *Odes* IV. 6. 18–20: cf. *Il.* VI. 57–60, XXII. 62–64; Aeschylus *Sept.* 348–50.

[6] The contrast with Pindar's programmatic dance of the Hyperboreans (*Py.* 10. 31–44) is instructive: cf. *Py.* 10. 38, χοροί; *choris*, *Aen.* V. 581. That is a scene of wild revelry, accompanied by lyres, flutes and the braying of asses, presided over by a laughing Apollo (see Newmans, *Pindar's Art*, pp. 81–82). How much Virgil mutes all this, even though he is portraying children. At the cosmic level, Dante, *Par.* 12. 1 ff.; 28. 13 ff., may also be compared (both with music).

[7] So R. D. Williams ad 288–89; cf. John H. Humphrey, *Roman Circuses* (London 1986), p. 64; on Nero, A. Alföldi, *Die Kontorniaten* (Budapest 1943), pp. 61–62: in general, H. F. Soveri, *De ludorum memoria praecipue Tertullianea capita selecta* (diss. Helsinki 1912).

And the sun also rises. The theme of resurrection was clearly alive for Maxentius, whose Circus among the tombs along the Appian Way recalled his dead son, just as Christos Helios is seen ascending in his chariot on a ceiling mosaic among the tombs under St. Peter's on the site of the Circus of Caius and Nero, and Nero / Apollo himself is found on fourth-century *contorniati*. Augustus, following his adoptive father's example (Suet., *Jul.* 39), was then at the *Lusus Troiae* engaged, like Aeneas, like Maxentius, in an act of cosmic resurrection. After the objections of the conservative Asinius Pollio (Suet., *Aug.* 43), even he let the practice die.

On the epicene faces of Virgil's children, generations blend (V. 576). Yet here too the poet is in declining mode. The fraught silence of his scene is broken only by the applause of the audience (575), the crack of a ringmaster's whip (*flagello*, 579), a sound the poet associates with vengeance and war.[8] In this passage of key importance to his whole epic concept, Virgil has seized the universal in the particular. This is his *danse des Heures* (*choris*, 581),[9] his whirligig of time, his apocalyptic, even cosmic vision, contradicting Cicero (*De Rep.* VI. 18–19), of the unmusical cycle of Roman history. Where were all these young riders until now? Where afterwards (like the son of Epytus himself [547, 579]) do they vanish? What is the significance of this Cretan labyrinth (588) within the poem as a whole? Shortly it will recur on the doors of Apollo's temple at Cumae (*error*, V. 591; VI. 27), where enough deaths of children are noted. At the end, it will be the deadly *pas de deux* executed by Aeneas in pursuit of childless Turnus.[10]

Iulus shows his paces on a horse provided by Dido (571), whose haunting gifts are so ill-omened for the young (IX. 266; XI. 74).[11] Whatever promise for the future is offered here, Virgil overlays his scene with such shifting, even sombre colours that we can hardly separate out a dominant pattern of hope. Some Romans perhaps tried. Did Augustus try? How long? After his experience of *fortuna*, he ended with Tiberius.

The Ara Pacis

He tried at least as late as the side panels of the Ara Pacis Augustae

---

[8] Cf. VI. 570, Tisiphone; VII. 731, mustering for (civil) war against the Trojans; VIII. 703, Bellona. Pindar's Hyperboreans, by contrast, have escaped from ὑπέρδικος Νέμεσις (*Py.* 10. 44).

[9] An Augustan motif? A column with three dancing Hours, found near the Ara Pacis, is now in the Vatican Gallery of Busts, Museo Pio Clementino.

[10] Cf. *orbibus orbis*, V. 584 and VIII. 448; *orbis*, XII. 763; *orbibus* earlier of the serpents that will entwine Laocoon's children, II. 204.

[11] Cf. V. 572 ~ V. 538, Cisseus / Cisseis [Hecuba] theme.

(13–9 B.C.), with their charming vignettes of the imperial children among their graver elders. These children seem so natural, and are in fact so revolutionary in public art of this kind.[12] The visitor has customarily entered their museum to confront immediately the two end panels (1 and 2) on the west, flanking the steps which lead inside. One, on the right, shows Aeneas sacrificing the sow (*Aen.* VIII. 84–85). A figure at the back with a spear may have been Achates. A smaller, hardly visible figure in front was perhaps Ascanius, though a youthful head which used to be added here has since been removed on the grounds that its ringlets make it more suitable as a personification of Honos, and that therefore its proper place is elsewhere.[13]

Panel 2, on the left, shows the suckling of Romulus and Remus by the wolf (VIII. 630–34). Mars and Faustulus look on. The longer side panels are structured in such a way that this is their culmination. The Augustan present is thus validated by its Martial past, a risky stratagem, as Horace knew (*Epodes* 7), and Virgil himself, replacing Apollo with Mars, confirms.

The rear panels to the east (3 and 4) display on the right what was perhaps Dea Roma seated on a trophy. On the left sits Earth / Italy, with two playful children (Karpoi?) in her lap. She is joined with air and water. Fire would have come from the sacrifice, thus restoring a Golden Age of fruitful harmony—though such immutable gold breeds its own problems.

A modern scholar has commented eloquently on the natural implications of this iconography:

> Non va d'altra parte dimenticato l'aspetto politico, propagandistico, che questi monumenti dell' arte ufficiale rivestivano. La simbologia che ricollega il nome di Augusto alla Pace; questa al rifiorire dell' Italia e della Terra, sotto il dominio universale di Roma (pannelli 3 e 4); città la cui origine è d'altra parte ricollegata alla stirpe di Enea (pannelli 1 e 2), e quindi di nuovo ad Augusto (entrato per adozione nella gente Giulia, discendente da Enea) è evidente; la storia di Roma e del mondo vengono così provvidenzialmente ricollegate al nome di Augusto. La stessa operazione sarà condotta a termine, nella storiografia, da Tito Livio, nella poesia, da Virgilio, legati ambedue alla corte imperiale. Così si concludeva in chiave aulica, la vicenda che aveva gradualmente trasformato il giovane Ottaviano nel divo Augusto, il fondatore dell' Impero. (Filippo Coarelli)

On the other side, the political and propaganda purpose served by these

---

[12] One may point to the daughters of Akhenaten (*Egyptian Painting* [Skira 1954], p. 116; before 1358 B.C.). Interestingly, in an "official" room in the Gonzaga Palace in Mantua (Camera degli Sposi, completed 1474), with painted busts of emperors on the ceiling, Mantegna, so careful an imitator of Roman antiquity, has put on the walls wonderfully natural pictures of the ducal children among their elders. How did he sense that this could be official too?

[13] Maria Laura Cafiero, *Ara Pacis Augustae* (Rome 1996), p. 19 with fig. 10 on p. 20.

memorials of official art should not be forgotten. An obvious symbolism links the name of Augustus to Peace, and Peace to the rebirth of Italy and Earth, under the universal sway of Rome (panels 3 and 4), a city whose origin is on the other side joined with the family of Aeneas (panels 1 and 2) and therefore again to Augustus, who had been adopted into the Julian house. The history of Rome and of the world is thus providentially linked with the name of Augustus. The same process will be taken to its culmination, in history by Livy, in poetry by Virgil—both authors with ties to the imperial circle. This was the courtly conclusion of the changes which had step by step transformed the young Octavian into the Divine Augustus, founder of the Empire.

Perhaps, and notably in their last volumes, Propertius and Horace did their courtly best to serve this programme. But how far is that true of Livy and Virgil? Livy, called *Pompeianus* by Augustus (Tacitus, *Ann*. IV. 34), is not sure who Ascanius' mother was (I. 3. 2), and wondered whether Rome would have benefited more if Julius Caesar had never been born.[14] Caesar himself, eager though he was to introduce an Iulus among Aeneas' children, found it difficult, to judge by a denarius of his now in the Armenian Historical Museum at Erevan (inv. 17824 / 115), to satisfy all claims. His coin shows the flight of Aeneas from Troy. Yet, though the hero is seen carrying Anchises, and holding the palladium in his right hand, no Creusa is visible—and no Ascanius / Iulus.[15]

The painted frieze from the Esquiline columbarium now in Room V of the Palazzo Massimo, tentatively dated to the beginning of the Augustan period, is also interpreted, in the light of Dionysius of Halicarnassus, as if Augustan propaganda spoke with one voice about the origins of Rome.[16] Evidently this is received opinion. But there was in fact conflict and ambiguity. What place does the *Aeneid* claim in these high dynastic debates?

[14] Apud Sen., *Nat. Quaest*. V. 18. 4: *in incerto esse, utrum illum magis nasci reipublicae profuerit an non nasci*. For Livy's doubts about Ascanius below, p. 272.

[15] Great soldiers meet over the centuries. A similar scene (Aeneas with Anchises only) is found on a relief from the portal of Eugene of Savoy's palace in Vienna (1695, Fischer von Erlach). Evidently at some stage the question of succession is secondary, though, as Marie Tanner's *The Last Descendant of Aeneas* (New Haven 1993) shows, succession did have its importance. More on this below, pp. 235, 244.

[16] *Museo Nazionale Romano: Palazzo Massimo alle Terme* (Rome 1998), pp. 51–58 (Rosanna Capelli). The contrasts and parallels with the (marble) narrative Telephus frieze from Pergamum (begun 165 B.C.), now in Berlin, are instructive. Telephus, son of Heracles and Auge, ancestor of the Attalid kings, is suckled by a lioness (panel 12). In the fresco of the same subject in Naples (*Oxford History of Classical Art* [1993] no. 167), he is suckled by a hind. There is much that is pastoral here, and no god of war. Lycophron (*Alex*. 1248) speaks of the sons of Telephus (allies of Aeneas) as αἴθωνες λύκοι, but is this more than epic ornament?

The Aeneid's Women and their Role

No women, no children. But what women in the *Aeneid* have children? Virgil's invention here, notably in the so-called "Iliadic" half of the poem, is astonishing (and obscured by too much tracing of parallels). Childless Dido, to give her due pride of place, is no doubt a blend of many surviving originals, though not of course reducible to the sum of her parts. What however are we to say of the horrible Allecto? On the other side of Camilla, Juturna, even Lavinia? Characteristically, when it comes to women, possibly when it comes to any sort of sexuality, the poet's imagination slides between extremes without finding any sure hold in between. Perhaps he was a closer observer of royal and imperial women than has been thought. The pages of the historians—Livy on Tanaquil, Tacitus on Nero's mother—supply us in some atemporal sense with his models. But as a creating artist he introduced these creatures into his heroic epic for several purposes. One of them was to provide a voice for the irrational, alogical, for all the painful oddities of experience so often dulled by the anaesthetic combativeness of the male. Another was to signpost the road to hell. This aspect of his genius deserves attention.

Musa, mihi causas memora ... / Κῶς δέ, θεαί.... The *Aeneid* is nothing if not learned ("allusive"), here harking back to the first book of Callimachus' *Aetia* (fr. 7. 19) with its tale of the Argonauts; and, by grace of Mnemosyne, poets also remember their tradition by other than discursive means.[17] It is necessary to begin then from the *Aeneid*'s beginnings.

Gilgamesh establishes for Classical epic a typical pattern, repeated, for example, in the Book of Genesis. A superhuman hero, by the mediation or intervention of the feminine, comes to terms with the divine, and with its opposite, his own mortality. In a final tablet of the story, the dead Enkidu tells Gilgamesh of the dreary underworld, anticipating Achilles (*Od.* XI. 489–93). Achilles would ask after his son, and Enkidu urges that the only remedy for the fate in store is to beget children—as many as possible, who will make offerings to the dead of food and drink.[18]

With the bias which Nietzsche diagnosed in the Greek genius, the *Iliad* reshapes this model in tragic form. Achilles is projected towards his destiny by his goddess-mother who, with Eos, will become an archetypical *mater*

---

[17] Cf. M. Bakhtin's theory of the remembering genre: Проблемы Поэтики Достоевского (Moscow 1963), p. 162: cf. Critical Terms, below, p. 341.

[18] *The Oxford Companion to the Bible* (1993), *s.v.* "Gilgamesh Epic," p. 254 (C. H. Gordon): cf. *The Epic of Gilgamesh*, ed. Andrew George (Penguin Classics 1999), pp. 177, 187–88.

dolorosa;[19] and, in talking with Priam about the human condition, he recalls (of all things) the story of ultimately childless Niobe (*Il.* XXIV. 602; cf. Dido, *Aen.* VI. 471).

The antiquity of the *Odyssey*'s premises is observed in its *spoudogeloion*, although there too the hero must recognise his limitations. With comic exaggeration, the poem enlarges the traditional frame (yet not by incorporating Telemachus' siblings), as its galaxy of women characters attests. Among them Circe, a version of Shiduri / Ishtar, directs Odysseus to the underworld.

Dido, the *Aeneid*'s Circe, herself a kind of *mater dolorosa* as she cradles Ascanius / Cupid (I. 718–19), will not do that; or rather, she will direct the hero to a hell of her own choosing. She has her own apocalypse (IV. 612–20), and her Temple of Juno has another (I. 456–93). When Aeneas arrives in Italy, his guide to a different Avernus will be the Sibyl, though Circe lurks here too (VI. 557a ~ VII. 15a).

Women in the *Aeneid* are usually important in this way, as vessels of revelation of one sort or another, not as mothers of children, unless those children are dead or doomed or fantasised. The Sibyl is a *virgo*, and the offspring of her chaste intercourse with Apollo is her prophecy (VI. 77–80). Dido reveals Hannibal—but as the progeny of her bones rather than her flesh (IV. 625). The dissonance of these two female voices, one Apolline, one fired by the Furies (IV. 376), determines the atonality of Virgil's modern tragic song. In the end, the Furies win (XII. 913–14, 946)—and they (but by what father?) are Dido's children (IV. 474).

Dead Ends

About to recount his adventures to Dido at the start of Book II, Aeneas is certainly like Odysseus, addressing Arete at the court of Alcinous—

'Infandum, regina, iubes renovare dolorem ... ' (II. 3)
ἀργαλέον, βασίλεια, διηνεκέως ἀγορεῦσαι
κήδε' ... (VII. 241–42)

—and ultimately angling to leave both her and Nausicaa. But he is also the husband restored who tells an edited version of his tale to Penelope at the end of his wanderings (ἤρξατο, XXIII. 310; *incipiam*, II. 13). Virgil—typically—blends, in cinematographic language, "mixes," these two occasions, enhancing their pathos. For Homer's married couple and their son, reunion; for Dido and Aeneas, the beginning of a barren, impossible affair

---

[19] Cf. μάτηρ, Pindar, *Ol.* 2. 80: *Memnona si mater, mater ploravit Achillem*, Ovid, *Am.* III. 9. 1. Virgil pairs Aeneas / Memnon (I. 488–89): below, p. 196.

10 Chapter One

predestined to failure: *infelix Dido, nunc te facta impia tangunt?* ... (IV. 596).

In the last scene of the *Aeneid*, the sight of Turnus' belt causes Aeneas to lose control and sacrifice (*immolat*, XII. 949) his surrendering rival. Fired by the Furies (XII. 946), like Turnus himself (VII. 456–57; contrast I. 291–97 and V. 461–62), he loses his chance to be a Roman by Augustan standards (*prior ... parce*, addressed to Julius, VI. 834; *Romane ... parcere*, VI. 851, 853; cf. *iacentem lenis in hostem*, Hor., *Carm. Saec.* 51–52). Jupiter's first word in the poem is *parce* (I. 257).[20] The poem's first simile (I. 148) praises the power of the word to quell *furor*. Aeneas will not hear that word.

This belt is also described by the same telling epithet, *infelix*, which occurs 50 times[21] (XII. 941–42):

> infelix umero cum apparuit alto
> balteus et notis fulserunt cingula bullis ...
>
> ... when the ill-starred belt caught his gaze, set high on the shoulder, the studs he knew so well flashing on its straps ...

The scene engraved on the belt is described earlier, when Turnus seizes it from the young and mortally wounded Pallas (X. 496–98):

> rapiens immania pondera baltei
> impressumque nefas: una sub nocte iugali
> caesa manus iuvenum foede thalamique cruenti ...
>
> He snatched the belt for all its vast weight and its deep imprint of horror. In a single wedding night, a host of young bridegrooms was foully murdered, the bed-chambers running with blood ...

Clearly this subsumes aspects of Troy's and Pallas' own fate. Horace shows us (*Odes* III. 11. 35) that what was remembered about this story was how one of the wives, *splendide mendax*, proved unable to commit the crime. Propertius notes her innocence (IV. 7. 67–68). Virgil is not interested in that exception.[22]

---

[20] *Parce metu*, the sacral μηδὲν φοβηθῇς, *Prometheus Vinctus*, 128; cf. אל־תּיחר ודאל, OT Dan. 10:12; μὴ φοβοῦ, Ζαχαρία, NT Lk. 1:13; μὴ φοβοῦ, Μαριάμ, ibid. 1:30. See *Theologisches Wörterbuch zum Alten Testament* (= *TWAT*), ed. G. J. Botterweck *et al.*, III, col. 884, *infra* (H. F. Fuhs).

[21] Below, pp. 49 ff.

[22] The Danaids were already shown on a series of bronze statues in Piso's villa at Herculaneum, now preserved in Naples (Museo Archeologico, invv. 5604–05, 5619-20-21). Later they occur (in nero antico marble herms) as part of the decorations of the Temple of the Palatine Apollo, and are interpreted in the Palatine Antiquarium (Room V, invv. 1048, 1053, 1056) as symbolic of Augustus' defeat of his Egyptian foes. Yet Virgil calls their crime *nefas*. Could he then have accepted so naively univocal an interpretation? (It would anyway have run the risk of suggesting that Augustus was an Argive.) Could it have survived a

But in the *Aeneid thalami* are rarely if ever normal or happy.[23] Ruined (and no doubt bloody) *thalami* were one of the signs of Troy's own doom (II. 503). *Reginam thalamo cunctantem* (IV. 133) began the day of Dido's fatal error. And in Italy what awaits (VI. 93–94)?

> 'causa mali tanti coniunx iterum hospita Teucris
> externique iterum thalami.'

> 'The cause of such great suffering is once again a foreign bride among Teucer's children, and once again a union with an outsider.'

Iterum .... Chronologically, the poem is interwoven in this way with the promise of happy fruition repeatedly gone awry. That is the curious and unexpected aspect of its sensibility which too triumphal an interpretation neglects. This is what Maphaeus Vegius' corrective *Supplementum* ("Book XIII"), written to fill up the gaps felt by a normal sensibility, attests.[24]

Augustus and Children[25]

Conubio iungam stabili propriamque dicabo (I. 73 = IV. 126). Augustus' social policy, encouraging stable family life, is illustrated by the popularity in his day of scenes of the playing infant Dionysus.[26] It is celebrated by both Horace and Propertius at the end of their poetic careers (*Odes* IV. 15; *Elegies* IV. 11), suggesting the continuing concern shortly to be visible in the legislation of 9 B.C. In an earlier manifestation, its puritanical rigours had provoked trouble (*nec vitia nostra nec remedia pati possumus*, Livy, *Pref.* 9). Yet the emperor's practice was less idealistic. Himself the divorced husband of a divorced wife, he used divorce ruthlessly to further dynastic ends, as Agrippa and Tiberius both had occasion to discover.

He had ordered the execution of Caesar's son by Cleopatra.[27] His

---

reading of Greek tragedy? The poet is interested in Io / Dido / Cleopatra (below, p. 71), but perhaps the Palatine iconography more broadly represented a rejected barbarism. If Turnus' belt was meant to recall the foundress of his city of Ardea (VII. 410), why link a descendant of Hypermestra with the guilt of that crime?

[23] See H. Merguet's *Lexikon zu Vergilius*, *s.v.* There are 20 examples, too many to detail here. VI. 94 (ominous) and VII. 253 allude to the marriage of Lavinia and Aeneas; X. 649 is bitterly sarcastic about the same prospect. Deiphobus' *infelix thalamus* (VI. 521) is typical, but cf. also VI. 623 and X. 389 (incest). See the similar range of *hymenaei*, below, p. 286.

[24] Vegio, showing uninhibited normality, is quite emphatic about exactly the themes of fruitfulness which Virgil himself declines or denies. Below, p. 278.

[25] Cf. Beth Severy, *Augustus and the Family* (London 2003).

[26] An example is the sardonyx-agate cameo now in Naples (inv. 25880).

[27] A coin in the British Museum (Room 72, Case 7, no. 51) is said to show "Cleopatra VII and her baby Caesarion, son of Julius Caesar." A date of 35 B.C. is

experience with his own child and her children was chequered. He forbade a great-grandson to be reared. Others he confined (Suet., *Aug.* 65):

> Ex nepte Iulia post damnationem editum infantem agnosci alique vetuit.... atque ad omnem et eius [*sc.* Postumi Agrippae] et Iuliarum mentionem ingemiscens proclamare etiam solebat:
>
> Αἴθ' ὄφελον ἄγαμός τ' ἔμεναι, ἄγονός τ' ἀπολέσθαι.
>
> nec aliter eos appellare, quam tres vomicas ac tria carcinomata sua.
>
> The child born to his granddaughter Julia after her condemnation he would neither have acknowledged nor reared.... Every time the names came up of either Postumus Agrippa or his two Julias he would groan and declaim a Greek tag about his wish to have stayed unmarried and to have died without issue. He never referred to them except as his three wens, even three running sores.

The elder Julia in fact is described on a Priene inscription of 15–12 B.C. as both a goddess and "the mother of many children,"[28] "daughter of Augustus Caesar;" and indeed, at that time, she was the mother of four, including Caius and Lucius. But the emperor, who came to judge differently, was adapting a Homeric line (*Iliad* III. 40) with an irony at his own expense which Virgil would have found satisfying.[29]

Postumus Agrippa was ultimately disposed of without ceremony (Tac., *Ann.* I. 6). Whether any of these troubles were in view before Virgil's death or not, it is this sick reality rather than the glitter of public pomp and pious aspiration which the vatic poet has chosen to depict in his epic. This did not diminish his devotion to the ideals of Augustus and Rome. Indeed, it would make those ideals more than ever necessary and sacred.

Certainly Virgil was alive to commemorate the death of Marcellus, token

---

given, though 45 would be more likely. By 35 Caesarion was at least 11 years old. See the basalt statue now in Cairo (Egyptian Museum, inv. 13/3/15/3), perhaps from Karnak, dated 35–30 B.C., reproduced in *Cleopatra of Egypt*, edd. Walker and Higgs (British Museum Press 2001), p. 172. Was the baby perhaps Antony's? His daughter Selene at least was spared. A pathetic light is shed on this by the new interpretation of P. Bingen 45 (Berolinensis 25.239), dated to 33 B.C., in which the queen authorises with the imperious γινέσθω certain tax concessions to Antony's lieutenant Publius Canidius (Crassus) on behalf of "ourselves and the children": Peter van Minnen, "An official act of Cleopatra," *Ancient Society* 30 (2000), 29–34: *Cleopatra of Egypt*, p. 180.

[28] BM Inscr. 428 (GR 1870.3-20.104). See case 15 of Room 70. In the third line . . .]ΑΛΛΙΤΕΚΝΟΝ may perhaps be restored as ΑΤΙΤ]ΑΛΛΙΤΕΚΝΟΝ (ἀτιτάλλω, "nurse"). For ἀτιτάλλω / Dido, p. 138, below.

[29] He was assuming the *persona* of Paris, a role Aeneas himself is at times forced to play (IV. 215; cf. VII. 321, X. 705). But in the epic's characteristic blending Turnus is also Paris: *Aen.* XI. 492 = Apollonius, *Arg.* III. 1259 = *Il.* VI. 506 (Turnus / Jason / Paris). Aeneas too is Jason (below, p. 34). *Senseram enim quam idem essent*, Cicero, *ad Att.* X. 8. 5.

of the children on whom the emperor fixed his hopes, only to see them swept off by *atrox fortuna* (Suet., *Tib.* 23). On both occasions the line quoted at the start of this section describes promises of Juno (to Aeolus and about Dido) which were left unrealised.

Women and Children on Troy's Last Night

Hic Iuno Scaeas saevissima portas / prima tenet (II. 612–13). Virgil chooses (I. 9–11) to assimilate his labouring hero to the model already established by Hercules, which entailed enmity with Juno. Her unrelenting hostility to Troy and its survivors in the poem means that, during its action, the goddess of marriage is on the wrong side—and not passively either, but recklessly ready to destroy in pursuit of her vendetta all that normally she should foster and protect. She inherits, it seems, the child-eating cruelty of her father Saturn. To Juturna, she recommends abortion (*conceptumque excute foedus*, XII. 158). This is the metaphysical background.[30]

Chronologically, Virgil's story opens with the collapse of a society brought low by its perjuries (IV. 542, V. 811) and pride (III. 2), its materialism (II. 504), its royal adultery (X. 92)—the last offence recently recalled by Horace (*Odes* I. 15). Sexuality is despoiled, as Helen disfigures Deiphobus (VI. 495). Sexuality's fruits are perverted. Troy's walls are overleapt (VI. 515) by a monstrous Horse pregnant with arms (*feta armis*, II. 238), which Capys has vainly tried to abort (*terebrare cavas uteri et temptare latebras*, II. 38).[31] As he begins his tale (II. 19–20), Aeneas recalls that in fact the Horse's womb (*uterumque*, 20; cf. *uteroque*, 52; *utero*, 243, 258) was filled with armed soldiery. Its brood will wreak destruction.

On that last night of fire and horror, Aeneas witnesses the group of terrified women and children seized by the Greeks (II. 766), dead now to Troy. Earlier, dazed and demoralised, Panthus, Apollo's priest, is seen pulling along his toddler grandson (320). But later Panthus is killed (429), and we are left to guess at his grandson's fate. The virgin Cassandra, Apollo's priestess, is dragged off, her frustrated suitor slain (403, 424). Mutilated

---

[30] Uni and Astarte are identified on the bilingual gold tablets recovered from Pyrgi and now in the Villa Giulia (Room 22). If Dido's Juno is the counterpart of Astarte, particularly worshipped at Sidon, the change Virgil has wrought to serve his own purposes in this goddess of fertility is manifest. See *TWAT* VI, cols. 453–63, *s.v.* עשתרת (H.-P. Müller).

[31] With this horse may be compared the horse's head which at Carthage marked the site of Juno's temple (I. 444). Cf. Silius, *Pun.* II. 410–11, the Thracian sacrifices mentioned below (pp. 18–19), and *TWAT* V, cols. 782–91, *s.v.* סוס, II. 2 (F. J. Stendebach).

Hector, once Troy's hope and bulwark, has appeared in a vision to recommend only flight (II. 270). Aeneas climbs to the roof of Priam's palace by a rear stair used in happier times by *infelix Andromache*, bringing Hector's son Astyanax to see his grandparents (II. 455–57). The epithet tells and negates all—and if Priam's palace sheltered fifty couples (II. 503), what has become now of their children? He is present when Queen Hecuba and King Priam, themselves decrepit, look on at the symbolic killing of their son Polites, "the citizen" (526), to be followed by tottering Priam's own death and decapitation—all this at the hands of one who clearly is the degenerate (549) son of his famous father. And whatever other anonymous Trojan women survive to join his expedition (*matres*, 797), for him the departure from his homeland begins with the loss of his wife Creusa (738).[32] The Homeric analogue makes her like Odysseus' dead mother Anticleia (*Aen.* II. 792–94 ~ *Od.* XI. 206–08). Where is now the promise of the virginal *pueri ... innuptaeque puellae* who vied to touch the rope pulling the Horse into Troy (II. 238), as once the Israelites escorted the Ark into Jerusalem (II Samuel 6)? There Uzzah came to grief, and Virgil's religious phrase recurs like a desolating leitmotif in more than this poem (cf. VI. 307 = *Geo.* IV. 476).[33]

Dido, listening to Aeneas' tale, is herself childless (*infelix*, I. 712), and even the victim of a malicious trick played by Venus on her maternal feelings. The Iulus she dandles on her lap is, for her, a changeling, the god of an infertile love kindling the flame of a crazy passion which, though at first it may save Aeneas and his men, ultimately will ignite her pyre—and in that offer the paradigm of what one day the Romans would inflict on Carthage (IV. 669–71).[34] *Urbem quam statuo vestra est* (I. 573). How truly she spoke, and how cruelly—though after the intervention of her equally cruel *ultor*—her impulsive generosity would be repaid.

[32] Yet a black-figure amphora in London (BM GR 1836.2.24.138; 490–80 B.C., "said to be from Vulci") has Aeneas escaping from Troy carrying Anchises with Creusa at his side. There is no trace of Ascanius. An earlier black-figure amphora in the Vatican (no. 34532, late 6th c.) shows on side A Aeneas carrying Anchises without companions of any sort. This is like the picture found on Caesar's denarius (above, p. 7). The legend evidently varied, as Lycophron and Naevius indicate. See below, p. 265. Virgil chose the version without the mother.

[33] On a mural from the House of Menander at Pompeii, now in Naples, the Horse is dragged along by four Trojan young men. Two dancers are visible, not however touching the rope that pulls the Horse. The miniature at Vat. Reg. Lat. 1505, fol. 197v, interpreting Dictys Cretensis and Dares Phrygius, shows "the Greeks offering the Horse to the Trojans." Virgil enlarges and alters to suit his own suggestive purposes a scene variously preserved in the tradition.

[34] See *The Classical Epic Tradition* (Madison 1986), pp. 176–77.

Troy the Image of Rome

A too rich, too mighty city, brought down by public vice and public lies, its doom encapsulated in missing children.... But, as Virgil recited his story to Roman listeners, what city was this? Merely Troy or Carthage?[35] The echo of I. 12 (*urbs antiqua fuit*) in II. 363 (*urbs antiqua ruit*) certainly suggests this parallel. But what about the Urbs, which already by the time of Ennius had become a kind of Troy (*Ann.* 344–45, Sk.)? Virgil himself traces the link in the Roman bloodline, in naming the *Lusus Troiae* of his day: *Troiaque nunc pueri, Troianum dicitur agmen* (V. 602).

This was not a legacy to be assumed too lightly. *Suis et ipsa Roma viribus ruit* (Horace, *Epodes* 16. 2) became an Augustan topos (Prop. III. 13. 60), still echoing in Seneca (*Const. Sap.* 2. 2) and Lucan (I. 72). Catullus had branded the sins of the dying Republic (64. 397–408). These criticisms were equally the stuff of later satirists. *Quid Romae faciam? mentiri nescio* ... (Juvenal III. 41). Was Rome then Troy (*Ucalegon, ibid.* 199), its only hope a saviour? This too is one of Juvenal's themes (*spes* ... *in Caesare tantum,...* VII. 1).

The concept of the emperor as specially linked with the City was already of course Augustan, as Varius attests.[36] But this Caesar / saviour would be different from Aeneas. Aeneas was *Laomedontius heros* (VIII. 18; cf. *Laomedontia pubes* of the Aeneadae, VII. 105), the heir of a cheat. An escape was needed from this guilty cycle. Virgil had drawn the moral—and the contrast—already in the *Georgics* (I. 501–04):

> ... satis iam pridem sanguine nostro
> Laomedonteae luimus periuria Troiae.
> Iam pridem nobis caeli te regia, Caesar,
> invidet ...

> For too long in our own blood we have been atoning for the perjury of Laomedon's Troy. For too long, Caesar, heaven's palace has been begrudging you to us ...

501. *iam satis*, Horace, *Odes* I. 2. 1.

503. *Regia* here hints that the emperor is already (long before Lepidus' death) a sort of pontifex maximus in waiting.

503–04. *serus in caelum redeas*, Horace, *loc. cit.*, 45.

Augustus brings salvation from Laomedon's original sin. Rome would burn

---

[35] Or fratricidal Thebes? Aeschylus, *Septem* 345–68: M. L. West, *The East Face of Helicon* (Oxford 1997), pp. 553–55.

[36] *Tene magis salvum populus velit, an populum tu, / servet in ambiguo qui consulit et tibi et Urbi / Iuppiter* ... (5, Buechner = Hor., *Epp.* I. 16. 27–29); cf. *vix timeat salvo Caesare Roma Iovem*, Prop. III. 11. 66.

16   Chapter One

in the days of an emperor who could not live up to his legacy.[37] Still burdened with that sin, ultimately the *Aeneid*'s hero was a dangerous model.

He is already someone stripped of normality, *fato profugus*, a missionary, for whom there will be no solace with obliging nymphs, and certainly in this version no children on the side; one who, because of this isolation, will dally bemusedly with Dido and be ready for a *mariage dynastique* with Lavinia, and its ambiguous progeny.

Young Ascanius / Iulus is noted as *magnae spes altera Troiae* (XII. 168). Yet there had obviously to be more than this single slender thread, and the poet from time to time hints that others apart from Iulus would leave their children to the future (cf. V. 121, 123). But there was an "economic" dilemma. In an *Aeneid*, the focus is naturally and consistently on the leadership of Aeneas, his father Anchises, and ultimately his son. To secure this prominence, other figures are necessarily cast in subordinate roles. This means that it is difficult to take them seriously as family men. For the most part, whatever *matres* survived Troy are left behind in Sicily (V. 715–18). Again the reader feels the centrality of the *Lusus Troiae*. Its young participants may, in that resurrecting context, recall the features of their old parents (V. 576). But their silent, funereal gyration already seems that of some old home movie, found again years too late, or a dream.

In any case, Rome is *not* to be Troy. It is *not* to be filled with Orientals. Augustus himself warned Tiberius against the foreign influx (παντοδαπὸς ὄχλος, Dio Cassius LVI. 33. 3). Europe and Asia are opposites throughout (cf. VII. 224; X. 91; XI. 268). Here, the dutiful poet seems to give best to Iarbas (*Maeonia mentum mitra crinemque madentem / subnixus*, IV. 216–17) and Turnus (*semiviri Phrygis*, XII. 99; cf. *desertorem Asiae* of Aeneas, XII. 15 ~ *regnatorem Asiae* of dead Priam, II. 557). Rutulian Numanus' insults are especially offensive (IX. 616)—but their own "laus Italiae" (603–13) must have struck a responsive note in Roman hearts. The reader has already noted the intrusive air of exotic affluence (*Troia gaza*, I. 119, II. 763; *barbarico*[38] *postes auro spoliisque superbi*, II. 504; *Troiaeve*

---

[37] And then Nero, the ape of Augustus, would draw the parallel with Troy (Tacitus, *Ann.* XV. 39). But ultimately Augustus cannot be Aeneas. Asian Aeneas, *nimium pius* (cf. Hor., *Odes* III. 3. 58), continues the old patterns of iterated (*iterabitur, loc. cit.* 62), Iliadic violence, already noted in the Sibyl's language at *Aen.* VI. 94. Roman Augustus is called to break out of them. See below, p. 281.

[38] Cf. *ope barbarica*, borrowed from Ennius' Cassandra on Troy (*Andromacha* 89, Jocelyn) for Mark Antony, VIII. 685. Milton borrows it for (Pope) Satan (*P. L.* II. 4). With *gaza* cf. Farsi *ganj*, "treasure." Dante still notes Troy's pride: *Purg.* 12. 61–63.

opulentia, VII. 262) which seems to hang about this "Asian" Troy, its link with perjured Laomedon which made its revival in any sense a moral impossibility for Augustans (Horace, *Odes* III. 3. 22). Even if all this signalled the repudiation of Julian hankerings,[39] there is an insistent, anachronistic, un-Homeric racism in the poem of this sort.[40] And eventually, whatever posterity Troy is to bequeath will be absorbed by the Latins (XII. 835–37), although as late as Book X (27, 58, 74) it has seemed even to the gods (even to Jupiter) that the aim of Trojan settlement in Italy is precisely to refound Troy.

The Aeneid *and the Civil Wars*

And, in a way, Troy was refounded there. In the end, Juno's plea (*sit Romana potens Itala virtute propago*, XII. 827), and Augustus' warnings, failed. Satiric Juvenal knew as much: *iam pridem Syrus in Tiberim defluxit Orontes* (III. 62). His adverbs sound like an ironic echo of the finale to *Georgics* I noted above.[41] Already epic Lucan, avid student of the *Aeneid*, points (*Phars.* VII. 389–408) to a city teeming with humanity's offscourings on the one hand, and a countryside deserted and devastated by war on the other. No longer any family farms, nor any sturdy ploughboys who might have filled the ranks of the legions. Again, these are Horatian themes. In Virgil, they had been heard in the *Georgics*. Do they vanish from the *Aeneid* (cf. VII. 635–36; VIII. 8)? Is there not rather, inspired perhaps by a Catullan passage (64. 38–42) very much in this vein (cf. *Pharsaliam, Pharsalia, ibid.* 37), a horrible counterpoint filling the "Iliadic" half of the poem, between the conventional heroic demand for gory deeds of valour, ἀριστεῖαι, which may yet somehow include the prophecy of future heirs (*Il.* XX. 307–08; Catullus 64. 338); and, on the other side, the ethnic

---

[39] See below, p. 247. Meyer (*Caesars Monarchie*, p. 521) details Julius' rumoured plans to move his capital to a rebuilt Ilion (= "Julion": cf. *Iulius, a magno demissum nomen Iulo, Aen.* I. 288). He compares Constantine / Constantinople. In 63 Cicero had professed apprehension that Rullus might be planning to found a rival to Rome at Capua (*Leg. Agr.* I. §§18–19, II. §§86–87). Horace hints that such ideas were in the air (*Epodes* 16, *Odes* III. 3. 57 ff.). Their day would come.

[40] Of the sort obstinately excluding Turkey from the Common Market. Rome here is made to borrow later Greek popular sentiments. Compare Aeschylus, *Persae* 181–89, and the tit-for-tat kidnappings already adduced by Herodotus (I. 1–5) as the cause of the friction between East and West, in an account which he attributes to "Persian" sources. The contention between the continents is a theme still alive for Lycophron (*Alex.* 1291 ff.) and Moschus (*Europe* 8 ff.).

[41] The combination *iam pridem* occurs three other times in the poet, according to *TLL* V. 1², col. 2175, *supra*.

cleansings preceding and even following Virgil's own birth? Sallust alludes to the *vastitas Italiae* (*Jug.* 5. 2). Livy said of Sulla that he had filled Rome and all Italy to the brim with blood (*Urbem ac totam Italiam caedibus replevit, Epit.* lxxxviii). His interpretation of the Social War as a Civil War may be reflected in Florus (*Epit.* II. 6). Sulla's treatment of the Italian towns is notorious[42]—and his massacre of the Samnites (Strabo V. 4. 11) might well seem to encapsulate the Italian experience at Rome's hands. Octavian at Perusia continued the pattern for Etruscans. By the time of Actium, the history of Italy had been laden for a century with brutal civil and social strife. Is it this reality which the second half of the poem mirrors, ostensibly talking about the heroic past while in fact addressing the gruesome murders—including that of mutilated Cicero—still fresh in memory? Aeneas, an *improbus advena* (XII. 261; cf. *Ecl.* 9. 2), with his *advena ... exercitus* (VII. 38–39), bursts on the Italian scene to renew death and destruction: *quam multa sub undas / scuta virum galeasque et fortia corpora volves, / Thybri pater!* (VIII. 538–40; cf. I. 100–01). He may be called *causa mali tanti* just as much as Lavinia. No doubt a manifest destiny drove him and his Aeneadae on, past Nisus and Euryalus and their massacre, past Lausus and Mezentius, past Camilla, and Pallas, finally past Turnus. But what a trail of blood led to his throne!

And yet both sides followed this trail, since that is the nature of civil wars. Turnus, who bedizens his chariot with his enemies' heads (XII. 512), was Latium's Achilles (VI. 89; IX. 742). His name is Etruscan, and an Etruscan bronze mirror[43] shows Achilles holding the severed head of Troilus above a fallen horse. Historically, Turnus' decapitation both of Amycus and Diores and of Nisus and Euryalus (IX. 465–67), which has little corresponding to it in Homer,[44] finds a parallel in Marius' fate (Appian, *Bell. Civ.* I. 94, τὴν κεφαλὴν ἐκτεμών) and Sulla's maltreatment of the Praenestine prisoners (τὰς κεφαλὰς τοῦ τε Δαμασίππου καὶ τῶν συνεξετασθέντων αὐτῷ πρὸς τὸ Πραινέστε πέμψας ἀνεσκολόπισε, Dio Cassius, fr. 105. 4).

But the vatic poet was also attuned to older practices. According to the catalogue of a recent exhibition of treasures from Bulgaria[45] "several appliqués from Letnitsa show horse or human heads suspended behind the backs

---

[42] *Illa Sullani temporis messis*, Cic., *Parad.* VI. 2. 46; Appian, *Bell. Civ.* I. 96. 6.

[43] BM GR 1873.8–20.108 (= Bronzes 625), 300–200 B.C.

[44] Cf. *Il.* XVIII. 176–77: West, *op. cit.*, p. 388.

[45] *Ancient Gold. The Wealth of the Thracians*, ed. Ivan Marazov (New York 1998), p. 62.

of horsemen.... Suggestions of human and equine sacrifice in Thrace, usually linked to royal rites, can be found in the written sources as well." The writer cites Florus (*Epit.* II. 26, *immolato equo*). Thrace was the home of Mars (*Aen.* XII. 335), and Mars was the Romans' ancestor. Virgil understands what all this implies at a more urgent level perhaps than the optimism of the Ara Pacis. Our chapter XIII will take up this point.

Evander had saluted Aeneas as *o Teucrum atque Italum fortissime ductor* (VIII. 513) in offering the aid of his doomed son. But what *Itali* are these? How could a coalition of Trojans, Arcadians and Etruscans fighting such adversaries as Turnus and Camilla represent Italy or Rome? And, if they do, is that not Civil War?

A puzzled question put by the poet himself seems to favour this interpretation, since (like Florus / Livy) he views the fighting of Book XII at least as some kind of Social and even Civil War (XII. 503–04):

> tanton placuit concurrere motu,
> Iuppiter, aeterna gentis in pace futuras?

Was it your will, Jupiter, that such great strife should embroil peoples destined to live together in everlasting peace?

Just after this he mentions the fate of Amycus and Diores: *curruque abscisa duorum / suspendit capita et rorantia sanguine portat* [sc. Turnus] (511–12).

Pax here is the *pax Augusta*, after the Civil Wars were over. Contrast VII. 317, the start of hostilities, where *gener atque socer* gives the clue:

> 'hac gener atque socer coeant mercede suorum ...'

'Let this be the price paid by their kin as son-in-law and father-in-law meet ...'

Jupiter himself had protested. *Discordia*, in Ennius invoked at the start of war against a *foreign* foe (*Ann.* 225–26, Sk.), here is the familiar term for the civil strife at Rome:[46]

> 'abnueram bello Italiam concurrere Teucris.
> quae contra vetitum Discordia?' (X. 8–9)

'I had refused permission for any warlike challenge by Italy to Teucer's sons. What is this civil strife in defiance of my ban?'

This was certainly to write history poetry[47] of the most relevant kind. The poet borrows a phrase from Catullus (*socer / gener*, Cat. 29. 24 ~ *Aen.* VI. 830–31), which became stereotyped in reference to civil war,[48] to emphasise ahead of time Lucan's point that the Civil Wars between Pompey and Caesar

---

[46] *Discordia cives*, *Ecl.* 1. 71, *Aen.* XII. 583; Prop. I. 22. 5: below, p. 295.

[47] The expression is parallel with the art historian's "history painting."

[48] E.g. Ovid, *Met.* I. 145; more in *Roman Catullus*, p. 181, note 108.

were *plus quam civilia*. Eventually in Book VI this passes into the theme of the cruelty of fate, sweeping away at so young an age the peerless Marcellus, posthumously enrolled by Augustus in the service of *res publica restituta*. His athletic funeral statue, now in the Louvre,[49] was adapted from that of Hermes Psychopompus keeping watch over the Athenians who died at Chaeronea defending their city's freedom against Philip.[50] Cleopatra was of Philip's blood (Propertius III. 11. 40), and Augustus himself had been seen by Horace as a youthful Mercury in this very year (*Odes* I. 2. 41–44). Horace (*Epodes* 9) and Propertius (IV. 6. 62, *libera signa*) celebrate his defence of freedom at Actium. Quite early in his reign, his iconography would equip Pax with Mercury's caduceus.[51] But martial Aeneas is no Mercury of this sort. One of his offers of peace (*paciferaeque manu ramum praetendit olivae*, VIII. 116) is the prelude to Pallas' recruitment and death.

Children in the Aeneid

Indeed, in all this epic history and horror, it is particularly the fate of the young which attracts Virgil's attention. In Book VII, when snake-haired Allecto summons the shepherds to war ("hollow pastoral" motif), she does it with a blast which makes mothers in panic hug their children to their breasts (518). The line is modelled on Apollonius' description of the effect of the serpent's hoarse and terrifying call (cf. *anguem, Aen.* VII. 346; *anguibus,* 561) as Jason and Medea approach to rob it of the Fleece (*Arg.* IV. 136–38). There it anticipates, like so much of that poem's language throughout, a deadly future in which one day Medea's frightened children will smile in vain at a mother bent on murder (Eur., *Medea* 1041).

The boys performing the *lusus Troiae* in Book V flitted in and out of the poem without any substance. Virgil has a habit of using κωφὰ πρόσωπα, "dumb characters," supernumeraries conjured into existence for a momentary effect (*multis cum milibus ibat*, V. 75) and then vanishing. This is quite unlike the care Apollonius takes with Medea's twelve handmaidens (*Arg.* IV. 1221, 1296–97, 1521–22, 1722–24).[52] Virgil's use of this technique is

---

[49] Inv. no. MA 1207, sculpted by Cleomenes of Athens, dated to 23 B.C.

[50] Milton, servant of Cromwell / Augustus, nobly enlists Isocrates on freedom's side (*Sonnets* X. 8).

[51] James Hutton, *Themes of Peace in Renaissance Poetry* (Ithaca 1984), notes a silver coin from 28 B.C. (p. 30).

[52] The largely anonymous ἑταῖροι of the *Odyssey* offer some parallel, and there Apollonius does follow old models. He never mentions again 21 out of 54 of the heroes he catalogues (cf. Pindar, *Py.* 4. 171–83). More on the quirky etiquette of these lists, below, pp. 207–13.

evidently borrowed from or reinforced by the contemporary stage.[53] Latinus' city too has such young "extras" (VII. 162):

ante urbem pueri et primaevo flore iuventus ...

Where do they disappear? Children need peace. What were the chances of peace with the Italians? How long would the feud go on? In confirming the treaty between himself and Aeneas (XII. 207), King Latinus uses a simile—that of a bough destined never to bear leaves again—borrowed from Achilles' oath never to rejoin the fight against the Trojans, whatever the cost in suffering to his own side (*Il.* I. 234). What relevance has this parallel? How can old Latinus εἰρηνοποιός be matched with the young hero of the Iliad, *impiger, iracundus, inexorabilis, acer* (Horace, *A.P.* 121), whose compounded error would ultimately lead to the death of Patroclus and, in revenge, that of Hector? The *tertium comparationis* is evidently the suffering. Camilla / Patroclus was dead. Latinus, already, like Augustus, bereft of direct male heirs (VII. 50–51), would now lose Amata / Hecuba and Turnus / Hector. Perhaps the venomous hatred of the Iliadic quarrel is meant to be reversed. But it is unfortunate that the leafless, lifeless wood was not reversed. What a barren figure! How quickly in the event the promise of peace in the *Aeneid* fades! Later, Aeneas plucks from the wild olive (*oleaster*, XII. 766; cf. *infelix ... oleaster, Geo.* II. 314) a spear (Polydorus motif). In its last scene, the hero, reminded of a dead son by a vision of murderous wives, is led on by the Furies and his anger to rob another father of his son.

Too much optimism would have jarred. Family strife, childlessness were now and Rome, now and Italy. *Squalent abductis arva colonis (Geo.* I. 507 ~ *latos vastant cultoribus agros, Aen.* VIII. 8). Sexuality is disruptive (*Geo.* III. 209–10; cf. IV. 198–99, the contrasting case; *illum turbat amor, Aen.* XII. 70; *apes*, XII. 588). The *Aeneid* is not a different poem from the *Georgics*, but universalises the processes there described by raising them to the mythical and heroic. Similes owed to the Hesiodic (*Ascraeum*, II. 176) *Georgics* hem in the whole "Iliadic" action of the second half of the poem.[54]

Yet, whatever the binocular squint of their poetry, the origin of the *Georgics* lay in a reaction against civil war. After the land confiscations and upsets noted in the very first *Eclogue*, Italy and its farmers needed a respite. At Rome, many of Augustus' reforms were necessarily concerned to foster the revival of the great families, following the appalling casualties of civil war and proscription. Some years before, in urging Tullus, his former

---

[53] Hor., *Epp.* II. 1. 189–93.
[54] *The Classical Epic Tradition*, pp. 131–35. See pp. 68–69, below.

patron, with verses recalling the *Georgics' laudes Italiae*, to return home (and precisely from Asia), Propertius notes in an epic phrase (*ampla nepotum / spes*, III. 22. 41–42) that it is here that he will find the chance of marriage and children.

This cheery optimism is not the tone of the *Aeneid*! Virgil ironically reverses a similar (or perhaps the same) phrase. Aeneas witnesses the fates of Hecuba, of the hundred brides (*centumque nurus*, II. 501) in the royal palace, and of Priam. The line that seemed so well secured vanishes in a night. In the first verse here *thalami* has the deadly connotation already noted (*Aen*. II. 503–05):

> quinquaginta illi thalami, spes tanta nepotum,
> barbarico postes auro spoliisque superbi,
> procubuere; tenent Danai qua deficit ignis.

> Those fifty bedchambers, with all their great hope of children, those door-posts made proud by Eastern gold and trophies taken, came crashing down. The Greeks are masters where the fire leaves off.

503. *spes am* ..., P; *tanta*, M, Mynors; *ampla*, codex Gudianus, Austin.

Asian Troy has no future (*Aen*. III. 1 and 11; XII. 828). Homer knew this (*Il*. IV. 164–65 = VI. 448–49):

> ἔσσεται ἦμαρ ὅτ' ἄν ποτ' ὀλώλῃ Ἴλιος ἱρή,
> καὶ Πρίαμος, καὶ λαὸς ἐυμμελίω Πριάμοιο.

> The day shall come when sacred Troy will perish, and Priam, and the people of Priam, for all his stout spear of ash.

Virgil mirrors this Homeric scene in Book XII, where Lavinia's changing complexion is illustrated by a borrowed simile (XII. 67–69 ~ *Il*. IV. 141–47). This certainly tells the reader that the truce between Latinus and Aeneas is to be shortlived. But what city will fall, to correspond to Menelaus' prophecy of doom for Troy? Within the heroic action, perhaps Laurentum—and what a paltry parallel that would be! But suppose we shift to historical time. Will the parallel be Rome? What had been meant by Scipio, friend of satiric Lucilius and stern critic of Rome's moral decline, when he famously quoted Homer's lines to Polybius?

At the domestic level, Augustus' official composer of lyric (*Romanae fidicen lyrae*, *Odes* IV. 3. 23) illustrates the dissociation of sensibility between the public commitment and the private misgiving. Although, in his epithalamial poem 61, Catullus had celebrated the marriage of Manlius Torquatus and Vinia, and looked forward to a *Torquatus parvulus*, Horace, in an ode from his fourth book, which in some ways offers a commentary on the *Aeneid*, advises another Torquatus to indulge himself in order to keep his legacy out of the hands of an heir (7. 19; cf. *heres*, II. 14. 25). Father

Aeneas, Rome's kings, are dust and shadow (15–16). Whatever the promises about the future in other odes, this was an extraordinary—and yet tolerated—denial of natural feeling and of official Augustan policy.[55] Horace, who thinks of *pater Aeneas* in this passage (15), was close here to Virgil, whose Dido reverses Catullus' epithalamial *parvulus* (IV. 328).

Of course the *Aeneid* does not speak with one voice. What music can? Romulus is to be reconciled with Remus. That is part of the new (Augustan) future prophesied to Venus by Jupiter (I. 292), and illustrated, for example, on an Augustan intaglio now in Florence (NMA inv. 14914) showing Caius and Lucius Caesar, with the wolf and her twin nurslings on the reverse. Even so, historically speaking, the Roman life remembered in the poem had often been ruthless, notably to women as mothers. At either end of it, the Shield of Aeneas canonises the Rape of the Sabines (VIII. 635), and Cleopatra's suicide (697).

Monsters

Some of the *Aeneid*'s children might better have been left unborn. Much in the poem is inspired by the theme of impermissible or monstrous love. Scylla (Catullus 60. 2) and Charybdis (Horace, *Odes* I. 27. 19) erotically lurk at the approach to Book IV (III. 684; cf. VII. 302). The blazing, Cyclopean fires of Etna already realise the dangers of Dido's passion,[56] erupting as she listens to Aeneas' tale. Times blend. What was chronologically prior is rekindled in the one hearing of it now. *Aetnaei ignes* eventually burn on mad Turnus' helmet with its horrible (Lycian / Etruscan) Chimaera (VII. 786).[57] The one-eyed Etnaean Cyclopes are inevitably associated with this nightmarish creature, and Dido borrows the Cyclops' curse from the *Odyssey* (*Aen* IV. 612–20 ~ *Od*. IX. 528–35). The rebellious

---

[55] And of Roman values, since the same word (χῆρος / *heres*) has such negative connotations in Greek, such positive meaning in Latin. See below, pp. 54, 326.

[56] Cf. Horace, *Epodes* 17. 32–33; Ovid, *Rem. Am*. 491, *Her*. 15. 12, *Met*. XIII. 868; Seneca, *Hipp*. 101–03; Boethius, *Cons. Phil*. II, m. V. 25; Petrarch, *Africa* V. 399 and 405; J. Sannazaro, *Epigrammaton liber primus. Opera omnia latine scripta*, Aldine ed., 1535, p. 43, v. 3; Byron, *The Giaour* (1813: Penguin ed. by A. S. B. Glover [1954], p. 88); A. S. F. Gow on Theocritus II. 133 and XI. 51 ff. Virgil makes the image real. S. Eisenstein (who is thinking of the "King's Eye" and so on) calls such concrete realisation of metaphors the "Aristophanes effect" (Теоретические Исследования [Moscow 1945–48], III, p. 219).

[57] Every visitor to Florence will have noted its (restored) bronze image in the Museo Archeologico there. Homer finds it in Lycia (*Il*. VI. 179), and evidently, like him, the Etruscans remembered one of the bizarre creatures of Hittite and Middle Eastern fantasy, of the sort we find also in the Apocalypse of St. John.

Giant Enceladus is buried under Etna (III. 578, IV. 179). In his first occurrence, we have a rehearsal for the perilous meeting with rescuing Dido. In the second, the danger her Etnaean passion presents to Aeneas is in full flame. The uncomprehended, fiery cause persists (III. 584; V. 5).

The Cretan (!), cannibalistic Minotaur, met at the start of the vatic Book VI, enjoys a special place in this complex. The bronze gates of Apollo's temple at Cumae relate a triple tale of death. Androgeos, Minos' son, was killed, and the Athenians were ordered to sacrifice their children in requital. Daedalus had aided the queen in the effort to gratify the unnatural lust that gave birth to the Minotaur, now locked in a labyrinth, later to die. Yet, in fleeing from so perverted a world, he had lost his own son. The "orbs" of this labyrinth haunt the poem to the end (XII. 763).

But Theseus, slayer of the Minotaur, even so does not come off too well. Although for Euripides, as later for Statius (and Chaucer) he is a hero of Attic enlightenment, we bid farewell to him in hell as *infelix* (VI. 618). In the myth, told as recently as Catullus 64, he had crowned his triumph on Crete by abandoning Ariadne and causing the death of his own father.

There are other horrific births. Grotesque Fama (IV. 173 ff.), daughter of Mother Earth, counterpart of Homer's Eris, is the centrepiece of a display of surreal Hellenistic bravura.[58] Allecto disgusts her own father and sisters (VII. 327). Another Fury, sister of Megaera (and therefore of Allecto) and daughter of Night, is sent to harass Turnus to his death (XII. 843 ff.).

Like the Cyclops Polyphemus in Sicily, monstrous Cacus, at the very site of Rome, is a cannibal (VIII. 197)—not so in Livy. Even Aeneas is turned by Dido into a monster, suckled by tigers (IV. 366–67). When the poet himself compares his *pius* hero with the rebellious giant Aegaeon (X. 565), we have some inkling of what his encounter with her has cost.

---

[58] Quite different from the often beautiful Fame with her two trumpets familiar in Renaissance iconography. She is found, for example, on the front of the stage overhang in the newly rebuilt Globe Theatre in London; on a fresco from the main floor of the Palazzo Odescalchi at Bassano Romano, reproduced in M. Fagiolo, *Roman Gardens* (Eng. tr. New York 1997), p. 192; on a fresco by F. Salviati in the Sala dei Fasti Farnesiani in the Palazzo Farnese, Rome, honouring Paul III, facing a fresco whose central figure is Aeneas; and in the painting by Bernardo Strozzi in the National Gallery, London (NG 6321). Pietro da Cortona put her on the ceiling of the Sala Grande of the Palazzo Barberini, where Milton must have seen her in 1639; and Tiepolo on the ceiling of the Palazzo Canossa, Verona (1761?). A late 18th-century English clock in the Gilbert Collection, Somerset House, London (inv. 1999.37) has a female figure with double trumpets apparently celebrating the sacrifice of a lamb at the altar of Apollo. *Los clarines de la Fama* (Góngora on the death of El Greco) has a long history. The Virgilian *Fama melior* (IV. 221), contrasted with the grotesque who is *tam ficti pravique tenax quam nuntia veri* (IV. 188), may have contributed to it.

Ascanius / Augustus

Could this Hallowe'en blend easily with the proclamation of the emperor's All Saints (VI. 787)? In the passage earlier adduced from the end of Book I, the *Georgics* found no difficulty with this contradiction (500–01):

> hunc saltem everso iuvenem succurrere saeclo
> ne prohibete.
> At least do not forbid this young hero to rescue our age of turmoil.

500. *Iuvenis* is a code-word for Octavian in lines of Horace echoing some source now unknown: *iuvenis ... ab alto / demissum genus Aenea* (*Satires* II. 5. 62–63); cf. *Odes* I. 2. 41, a similar locus to that in the *Georgics*. Calpurnius Siculus picks it up for Nero (*Ecl.* 1. 44). In his note on the passage from the *Satires* here Heinze suggests a reminiscence of one of the innumerable (Greek) oracles in circulation at the time, but *demissum* (cf. *Iulius, a magno demissum nomen Iulo, Aen.* I. 288) is not explained by this.

Using religious language, which will become, centuries later, that of St. Ambrose's *felix culpa*, Lucan explains in his proem that the cost of Civil War was worth paying if it was to prepare the way for the coming of Nero (another youthful ruler).[59] Was he (again) merely interpreting the *Aeneid*? The Shield of Aeneas displays in its central panel *Augustus agens Italos in proelia Caesar*, locked in combat with Antony and his foreign spouse (VIII. 678). For the first and only time in the poem the Italians, under constructive leadership, are on the winning side, in defence of what our age has come to call "Western values." Perhaps we are to understand that whatever paradoxes and horrors had preceded Octavian were to be accepted (though not approved!) as the fated price of the new, "august" saviour of the Roman state, and of what the *Georgics* had already named (II. 176) the *Romana oppida* of Italy. But Octavian had his own Italian atrocities (*Perusina fames*, Lucan I. 41; cf. Prop. I. 21 and 22; Seneca, *Clem.* I. 11) to atone for. *Purpureos spargam flores....* Aeneas had to tread on a scarlet carpet unless his relevance to Octavian's revolution was to be invisible.

Yet the one person who is permitted progeny is Aeneas: Ascanius, hailed by Apollo as *dis genite et geniture deos* (IX. 642), his son by Creusa; and Silvius (VI. 756 ff), his prophesied son by Lavinia.[60] *Geniture deos* looks ahead to Julius and Augustus. *Nec te Troia capit* (IX. 644), said by Apollo of Ascanius, is Virgil's anticipation of Propertius' *Hectoreis cognite maior avis* (IV. 6. 38), said by Apollo of Augustus. When Anchises foretells Silvius' birth to Aeneas he thinks too of Romulus, destined to enclose

---

[59] *Venturo fata Neroni*, Lucan I. 33; below, p. 30.

[60] There are problems however with this lineage: below, p. 279.

within a wall glorious Rome (*incluta Roma*, VI. 781), happy in her offspring of men (*felix prole virum*, 784). "Romulus" however was a title *discarded* by the emperor (Suet., *Aug*. 7. 2), even if Propertius still plays with it perhaps as late as 13 B.C. (*Teucro ... Quirino*, IV. 6. 21).

Virgil's eulogy in Book VI climaxes with Augustus Caesar, the restorer of a Golden Age, a topos to which each of the poet's three major works alludes. He will advance the empire over Africa and Asia (794–95). But, even to Mars' Rome, a Golden Age must by definition in the end bring peace, not war, an embarrassment which the poet had already encountered in *Ecl.* 4 (31–36). Inevitably such a mythical peace, when it comes, freezes time in an eternal present, and in that sense tends to turn children—the future—into decoration, *putti*. Marcellus grew up—and died. *Marmoream reliqui*. Now his marble image would never alter.[61] The praise of the Golden Age in *Aeneid* VI fades away with him.

Virgil could not know of the deaths of Caius and Lucius Caesar. To two other young soldiers who have died prematurely, in their case pointlessly, the poet later promises immortality: *dum domus Aeneae Capitoli immobile saxum / accolet imperiumque pater Romanus habebit* (IX. 448–49). *Immobile* is well chosen. As Augustus Caesar looked around him in Rome, did he reflect that his Golden Age was offset by a barrenness more than physical? The statue of the veiled emperor found in 1910 in the Via Labicana (Palazzo Massimo inv. 56230), attributed to the later part of his reign, perhaps completed shortly after the Ara Pacis, perhaps after the emperor's death, is one of the profoundest statements of Augustan religious humanism, still finding a place in the iconography of Maxentius, as a statue identified as his in the Museum at Ostia may show. The absorbed intensity ("pensosa e distaccata intensitá") of the expression anticipates the enraptured saints of Bernini, and recalls Dido: *quam si dura silex aut stet Marpesia cautes*. Yet men are not marble. No mortal can dispense with the future. Augustus' lament for his (adopted) sons which forms the second epigraph to this chapter is one of the few personal touches in the *Res Gestae*. Perhaps at this point he had come to understand what the vatic author of the *Aeneid* had already foreseen and enshrined in his poem.

---

[61] Nor that of the children / Karpoi on the Ara Pacis (Cafiero, p. 16). The new fragment possibly from the *Dionysalexandros* of Cratinus makes fun of the point. The unnatural suspension of time characteristic of the Golden Age will ultimately be forced to incorporate sexually active children (a theme satirised in Aldous Huxley's *Brave New World*) and eventually, as time accelerates, will lead to a perpetually present orgy, though not of course to any new children.

II

THE DECLINING MODE

> Les poèmes se font des mots ...
> Stéphane Mallarmé

The *Iliad* and the *Odyssey* look back to a vanished heroic age. Always aware of its disappearance, they make no use of the "historic present." Nor does Pindar. Apollonius' *Argonautica* followed this precedent, which is universal in Greek epic. At Rome it was rejected already by Livius Andronicus; and, in this tradition, Virgil makes liberal use of such present tenses. His epic, dissolving time, announcing the metamorphosis of Troy into Rome, looks to and comprehends the future, prophesied in its first book to Venus by Jupiter himself. That future was necessarily glorious, since its herald after all was under an obligation to Maecenas and therefore to Augustus (which does not of course in Roman aesthetics impede the authenticity of the artistic and patriotic voice). The poem had also to solve a chronological problem. The long gap between the fall of Troy in the twelfth century and the foundation of Rome in the eighth had to be filled by inheritance passing securely from one generation to another. Both these were pressing reasons why the *Aeneid* should, if not tell, at least forecast a story of children successfully born and raised over four hundred years to fulfil divine expectation.

Anchises essays to do this in the vision offered by Book VI (756–886), but even that ends with the death of Marcellus, the heir in whom Augustus had placed his earliest hopes—and with an exit from the Ivory Gate. The Shield of Book VIII, with a second vision, is in the end an *imago* (730), what Apollonius in the case of another shield calls a δείκηλον (*Arg.* I. 746; cf. IV. 1672, Crete). It is forged at night. Perhaps in that case Herodotus' δείκηλα τῶν παθέων (II. 171), referring to the nocturnal re-enactment by the Egyptians of the sufferings of Osiris, is even more appropriate to the Virgilian context. They however were "mysteries."

The *Aeneid*, itself so mysterious, is not on any fair reading a propaganda piece. It blows two different trumpets (cf. IV. 188). A recurrent habit of its author's mind is to be in "declining," diminuendo, minor mode. Some of its bias is illustrated by a characteristic yet unexpected use of words referring to birth and family.[1]

One aspect of this habit, though not of course the only one, may be designated by the term "hollow pastoral." A motif which ought to be developed "idyllically" somehow frustrates that anticipation. The fourth *Eclogue*, for example, salutes the inauguration of a new Golden Age to be brought about by the birth of a child (*Eclogue* 4. 5–10):

> magnus ab integro saeclorum nascitur ordo.
> iam redit et Virgo, redeunt Saturnia regna,
> iam nova progenies caelo demittitur alto.
> tu modo nascenti puero, quo ferrea primum
> desinet ac toto surget gens aurea mundo,
> casta, fave, Lucina.
>
> The great sequence of the ages is born anew. Now the Virgin returns, and Saturn's Age. Now a new child is sent down from high heaven. You only, chaste Diana, bless that child in his birth, with whom the race of iron will first cease, and a golden people rise throughout the world.

This is a magnificent fanfare—in an eclogue. What happens in the *Aeneid* to *nascitur ordo*, to *nascenti* and to *progenies*?

At the start of its second half, the Trojans have completed their wanderings and are to establish themselves in Italy, to begin the long process of history which will lead to the walls of lofty Rome (VII. 41–44):

> tu vatem, tu, diva, mone. dicam horrida bella,
> dicam acies actosque animis in funera reges,
> Tyrrhenamque manum totamque sub arma coactam
> Hesperiam. maior rerum mihi nascitur ordo.
>
> You, goddess, you must inspire the prophetic poet. Dread wars will be my theme, battle lines and princes driven by anger to their deaths, Etruria's band and all Italy forced under arms. Greater is the sequence of events now coming to birth for me.

Magnus ab integro saeclorum nascitur ordo from *Eclogue* 4 is picked up here by *maior rerum mihi nascitur ordo*. But, in the event, the second, "Iliadic" half of the epic will be filled with war and death, often the deaths of the young. *Horrida bella* (41) were already on the lips of the vatic Sibyl (VI. 86), whose heir vatic Virgil is; and *eadem horrida belli fata* (XI. 96–97) will later move Aeneas to tears. The revelation of battle and death heralded in Book VII turns out therefore to be a ghastly reversal of the earlier promise

---

[1] The items considered here are: *nascor, progenies, filius / filia, proles, stirps, pario, parens, infans, puella / puer, pater, mater, genitor, genetrix, coniu(n)x, felix / infelix*. For *thalamus* and *hymenaeus* see above, p. 11 and below, p. 286. Even so, only a selection of the poet's vocabulary could be examined. The curious student will collect and scrutinise any too obvious omissions.

of the "Messianic" eclogue, only to be endured because it prepares the way for Augustus' Golden Age, prophesied in Book VI. This is the argument which Lucan puts forward less ambiguously on behalf of his new Augustus in the proem to the *Pharsalia*. There, it is laughed at.

After the fourth *Eclogue*, *nascenti* (*Ecl.* 4. 8) recurs only once in Virgil (and certainly not with *puero*). Evander uses it (VIII. 564) when he boasts of having sent Erulus to hell, even though "at his birth" his mother had granted him three lives.

Nothing in fact "is born" at all in the first half of the *Aeneid*, and in the second the two things born are metaphorical, inhuman. One we met (VII. 44). In Book X, we hear of fiery Sirius, whose baleful heat is also felt at *Geo*. IV. 425 (the advent of vatic Proteus) and *Aen*. III. 141 (the misconceived settlement in Crete).[2] The context reads (X. 273–75):

>   aut Sirius ardor
> ille sitim morbosque ferens mortalibus aegris
> nascitur et laevo contristat lumine caelum.

Or burning Sirius, laden with thirst and sickness for ailing mankind, comes to birth and with his ill-omened light makes gloomy the sky.

275. Cf. *Auster / nascitur et pluvio contristat frigore caelum* (*Geo.* III. 278–79), cited below, p. 199. *Contristat* occurs only in these two places in all Virgil.

This is principally adapted from *Il.* XXII. 26b–31,[3] where Priam espies the advance of Achilles to the final duel with his son Hector. It is used here by Virgil to describe the Shield of Aeneas, returning with his Etruscan and other allies, as it catches the rays of the sun. Birth is usually a cause for joy. Here, the Italian Achilles (VI. 89) has evidently met his match, though (since the Trojans are themselves originally from Italy) how much in the poet's mind this engenders a fratricidal strife of twins!

As the passage quoted already shows, *progenies* starts off splendidly in *Eclogue* 4 (7–10):

> iam nova progenies caelo demittitur alto.
> tu modo nascenti puero, quo ferrea primum
> desinet ac toto surget gens aurea mundo,
> casta, fave, Lucina. tuus iam regnat Apollo.

---

[2] Crete is a recurrent symbol of deception in the poem: see Index Rerum et Nominum, *s.v.*

[3] Cf. *Il.* XVIII. 207–13 (return of Achilles to battle). Other parallels are adduced by G. N. Knauer *ad loc*.: *Die Aeneis und Homer* (Göttingen 1964), p. 415. D. Nelis, *Vergil's Aeneid and the Argonautica of Apollonius Rhodius* (Leeds 2001), adds (p. 90) Apollonius, *Arg.* III. 956–61, Jason as he appears to Medea. This is one of those hints of Dido's presence ("Dido motif") which haunt the later books of the *Aeneid*.

In the *Aeneid*, this high promise is maintained in certain contexts. Anchises uses *progenies* to prophesy Caesar and the glory of Iulus' line (VI. 789–90):

> 'hic Caesar et omnis Iuli
> progenies magnum caeli ventura sub axem.'

'Here is Caesar, and all that generation sprung from Iulus destined to emerge beneath the turning sky.'

790. *ventura* is eschatological. Cf. *venturo fata Neroni*, Lucan I. 33; *quando iudex est venturus* in the *Dies Irae* (saec. xiii?). The concept of "the one who is to come," ὁ ἐρχόμενος, is shared by both Greek and Hebrew: cf. σὲ δ' ἐρχόμενον ἐν δίκᾳ πολὺς ὄλβος ἀμφινέμεται, Pindar, *Py*. 5. 14; εὐλογημένος ὁ ἐρχόμενος ἐν ὀνόματι Κυρίου, LXX Ps. 118:26 (= *benedictus qui venit in nomine Domini* in the *Sanctus*); σὺ εἶ ὁ ἐρχόμενος, ἢ ἄλλον προσδοκῶμεν; Luke 7:19; יֹב, בֹּא in *TWAT* I, cols. 536 ff. (H. Preuß), 808 ff. (J. Scharbert).

This directly introduces the praises of Augustus Caesar himself.

With this may be associated the allusion to the children of Lavinia and Aeneas in Book VII (257–58):

> huic progeniem virtute futuram
> egregiam et totum quae viribus occupet orbem.

She should be mother of a generation marked out by its manly courage, destined to seize by its power the whole world.

—and the earlier mention of a young Priam, child of dead Polites, at V. 565 *progenies, auctura Italos*.

But, if part of Augustus' Golden Age is peace (I. 291–96), already at I. 19–20, for example, a less peaceful note intrudes. Within the economy of the poem, Dido intrudes:

> progeniem sed enim Troiano a sanguine duci
> audierat Tyrias olim quae verteret arces.

But indeed Juno had heard that a generation was to come from Trojan blood which one day should overthrow the citadels of Carthage.

And clear promise is to be overcast. As with *nascitur*, Book X again seems to mark a turning point. At X. 30, the imperial *progenies*, once used by coaxing Venus in her address to Jupiter (I. 250), turns into a wholly selfish allusion. She is no longer thinking forwards, but back to a silly incident in the *Iliad* (V. 330b–40). Book X also brings before us *Phorci progenies* (328–29), the seven brothers whose mortal challenge to Aeneas is so futile.

The last occurrence of the noun in this book and in the whole poem (X. 471) is fraught with doom. Jupiter explains to Hercules that he cannot save Pallas. Even his own son, Sarpedon, had to die (X. 469–72):

> 'Troiae sub moenibus altis
> tot gnati cecidere deum. quin occidit una
> Sarpedon, mea progenies; etiam sua Turnum
> fata vocant, metasque dati pervenit ad aevi.'

'Beneath Troy's high walls so many children of the gods have fallen. And with them fell Sarpedon, my own child. Turnus too hears the call of his destiny, and he has reached the finishing post of the time given to him.'

The tragic significance of Sarpedon in the *Aeneid*, where he occurs as early as Book I (100) has been emphasised by Knauer.[4] The theme of Troy's lost children seems to acquire special emphasis in Jupiter's words here. It is as if in Book X the term *progenies* winds down to end in mortality, not with a bang, but a whimper.

* * *

Some of this language may now be investigated in greater detail.

Nascor. The two examples in the *Aeneid* of the present tense (VII. 44; X. 275) were noted already. The future of *nascor* is found in the fourth *Eclogue*'s list of signs greeting its new age (*Assyrium vulgo nascetur amomum*, 25). In the epic it is used in Jupiter's splendid prophecy to Venus of the birth of Caesar (*nascetur pulchra Troianus origine Caesar*, I. 286), which itself will herald a new age. This wonderful passage (I. 283–96) stands however outside the time-scale of the *Aeneid* (*olim*, 289 = the prophetic ביום ההוא, "on that day"). Ambiguity is appropriate to such distant fulfilments. What Caesar is this? *Troianus* and *Iulius / Iulo* here suggest Julius and his propaganda, but quite obviously Augustus cannot be excluded from the promises made. In any case, this is a prophecy made among gods. The mortals who first heard it were Augustans, with Augustan expectations. An important point is established. Augustus' presence in the *Aeneid* is that of a saviour / champion who waits as yet on the threshold (*limine*, VIII. 720).[5]

A similar passage of Apolline prophecy, this time made directly to the Trojans, also shows the future (III. 97–98; noted below, p. 287):

'hic domus Aeneae cunctis dominabitur oris,
et nati natorum, et qui nascentur ab illis.'

'Here Aeneas' house will lord it over every shore, with their children's children, and those to be born of them.'

Again, this alludes to a distant and hardly understood time. Anchises interprets the god in the immediate present as referring to ill-omened Crete.

These are the only examples in the *Aeneid* of the finite verb. Three other instances of the present participle (in addition to VIII. 564) are listed: IV. 515 (love charm collected by suicidal Dido); X. 27 and 75 (*Troia nascens*).

---

[4] *Op. cit.*, pp. 298 ff.

[5] Cf. the religious *adventus*, *Aen*. VI. 798 (= ἀπάντησις; cf. ὑπάντησις, NT John 12:13).

The last two occurrences, again from Book X, seem notably deluded, since Troy will not in fact be "born" again in Italy (*occidit*, XII. 828).

The instances of *natus / nata* do not substantially alter the chequered mosaic already assembled. They are too many to enumerate here in detail, but these occurrences may be mentioned.

Nate is found in 35 examples, 27 of them directed to Aeneas; and in the poem, all such dialogic usages of *nate* look back. The person concerned is addressed, not as part of a future yet to unfold, but as already "born" here and now. Virgil addresses no visionary "son" yet to come.

The required future aspect of *natus* is more fittingly sought in the nominative. It is here one may look for agents who are the subjects of finite and transitive verbs, doing things.

This is the aspect which in an *Aeneid* one expects to have pride of place —one such occurrence was just noted, when Apollo prophesied the glorious future of Aeneas' house (III. 97–98). Later, *Teucrum nati* take part in the *Lusus Troiae* (V. 592–93):

> Teucrum nati vestigia cursu
> impediunt texuntque fugas et proelia ludo.

The Trojans' children confound their own tracks in their quick manoeuvres, interweave flight and skirmish, though only in sport.

If that spectacle blends over the centuries with the ceremony revived by Julius and Augustus, perhaps Apollo's words find their confirmation here.

Yet *fugas et proelia* give pause for thought, and the *Lusus Troiae* has its labyrinthine, Cretan ambiguities (V. 588), to be noted later. Other uses of the nominative plural do not echo the trumpet blast of Book III, which in any case Anchises heard as a signal to settle in an untenable Crete. In book V (285), Sergestus receives the prize of a Cretan slave woman with suckling twins, *gemini ... nati*. At V. 621 Iris turns herself into pathetic Beroe, "who had once had family, name and children." (And it will be pathetic Pyrgo, "the royal nurse of so many sons of Priam," who sees through her disguise, 645). In Book VI (649), Aeneas finds among the dead *magnanimi heroes, nati melioribus annis*. The last example of this form (cited above) was in Book X (470): *tot gnati cecidere deum*.[6]

Elsewhere, *albi nati* are twice (III. 392, VIII. 45) the piglets at the udders of the prophetic sow marking the safe arrival of the Aeneadae at their destination. This is bathos.

---

[6] *Gnatus*, the old-fashioned orthography, is said by Norden to show greater emotion than the later *natus* (ed. of *Aeneid* VI, repr. Stuttgart 1957, p. 157, ad v. 116). He notes VI. 868, leading into the death of Marcellus.

Dulces is the adjective used by the Romans with *nati* when they are in sentimental mood (Lucretius III. 895; cf. *Aen.* V. 214, *dulces ... nidi*). The adjective occurs twice in the *Aeneid* with *natos* in this way:

'nec mihi ... spes ulla videndi
nec dulcis natos exoptatumque parentem,...' (II. 137–38)

'nec dulcis natos Veneris nec praemia noris?' (IV. 33)

These are pretences. How jarring that the first speaker here is Sinon, and the second Anna, Dido's sister!

Turning from these plurals to the singular, and recalling that the desiderated case is the *nominativus agentis* with a transitive verb, one is surprised to discover that *natus* is found in the nominative masculine singular only once. The Sibyl grimly prophesies the bloody future awaiting the Aeneadae in Italy (VI. 89–90):

'alius Latio iam partus Achilles,
natus et ipse dea.'

Pario as well as *nascor* are employed here, but the result is not a triumphant trumpet blast.

Polites, *unus natorum Priami*, may appear to be an agent in Book II (527). *Unus* at least is in the nominative here! He is in fact running away from the Greek who will catch and kill him. Following a long established pictorial tradition, the poet extracts the maximum pathos from this murderous encounter of Priam with Pyrrhus. The participle occurs another three times, appropriately now in an oblique case: *nati ... letum* (Priam to Pyrrhus, 538); *sanguine nati* (again Priam to Pyrrhus, 551). Later, Aeneas threatens his stubborn father that Pyrrhus will burst in at any moment, *natum ante ora patris, patrem qui obtruncat ad aras* (663).

Creusa, prevented by the great Mother from accompanying her husband, sadly commends Ascanius to his care: *nati serva communis amorem* (789). Aeneas, no doubt a devoted father, is however singularly undemonstrative in carrying out this injunction. The most striking example of mutual affection between a heroic father and his youthful son in the poem is perhaps that set by Lausus, who (like a second Antilochus) sacrifices his life on the battlefield in a vain attempt to save Mezentius / Nestor from Aeneas / Memnon (cf. Pindar, *Py.* 6. 28 ff.). Lausus is twice *nati* (X. 800, 906).

The reader is shocked by ruthless Pyrrhus in Book II, and such enemies drive home bad lessons. Clearly Aeneas' own character does not improve on closer acquaintance. In Book X, Magus' plea to him *hanc animam serves gnatoque patrique* (525) falls on deaf ears (and Aeneas picks up the emotional form in his last taunt [*gnatis*, 532]). In Book XI (178–79),

34   Chapter Two

insistent on revenge, Evander demands satisfaction from Aeneas. He uses a similar phrase:

> 'dextera causa tua est, Turnum gnatoque patrique
> quam debere vides.'
>
> 'Your right hand is my excuse (for living on), a hand which so evidently owes Turnus to a father and a son.'

Trojan claims to Italian lineage descend from the Etruscan town of Corythus (III. 170, VII. 209), and, true to type,[7] Aeneas believes in human sacrifice (XI. 81–82). The poem will end with this motif (*immolat*, XII. 949).

The last example of *natus* in the poem is in Book XII, where Venus descends with a Cretan herb to heal her son's wound and ready him for his last combat with Turnus (411–12):

> Hic Venus indigno nati concussa dolore
> dictamnum genetrix Cretaea carpit ab Ida,...
>
> At this point Venus, her maternal heart shaken by her son's undeserved suffering, plucked dittany from Cretan Ida.

This is a profoundly ambiguous passage. Venus is intervening in a situation where Apollo has withheld his aid, and unsurprisingly her help is not wholly efficacious (XII. 746–47).[8] Medea's drug had itself lasted only for a day (*Arg.* III. 850).

Do the *Aeneid*'s daughters fare better than its sons? The Trojans' future in Italy depends on the marriage between Lavinia and Aeneas, commended by the oracle of Faunus himself. Yet, in the operative Book VII, *nata* (with one exception always in oblique cases) is used of the destined bride in strange contexts. Latinus naturally ponders over his daughter's marriage (VII. 253; cf. *est mihi nata*, 268). But Amata sheds tears over the prospect of a wedding to a Phrygian (358). She accuses Latinus of showing no pity to his daughter (360): indeed she hides her to prevent any match with Trojans (387). Finally, driven crazy (*furorem*, 386), she sings the pretend marriage song of her daughter and Turnus (398). But we know that Turnus himself is soon to be as crazy (*amens*, VII. 460).

The last examples of *natam* fade away in Book XII (27, 42). Latinus attempts vainly to dissuade Turnus from his futile plans to marry a Lavinia now forever beyond his grasp. The marriage which did take place, between

---

[7] S. Haynes, *Etruscan Civilization. A Cultural History* (Los Angeles 2000), p. 306.

[8] A hero receiving a drug, thanks to the intervention of a deity of love, as preparation for a supreme ordeal is a second Jason, assisted by a Medea (Dido motif). See also below, pp. 317 ff.

Lavinia and Aeneas, was however celebrated by another poet.[9]

Filius is found 14 times. Metrical reasons hinder the use of certain cases of this noun in hexameters, though not of the vocative singular. Virgil uses only the nominative singular.

We begin with a formally structured line (I. 325)

    Sic Venus, et Veneris contra sic filius orsus.

But the repetition smoothes over a deception. Aeneas is unwittingly in flirtatious conversation with his disguised mother.

We go on in Book I to *Aurorae ... filius* (751), the doomed Memnon (Pindar, *Ol*. 2. 83) who, on the pictures in Dido's temple at Carthage, directly precedes Aeneas himself (I. 489; cf. VIII. 384, noted below, where the parallel is made explicit). In this vein, Aeneas later asks about a *filius* who turns out to be Marcellus (VI. 864). In Book VII, *filius* is the lost son (or sons?) of Latinus (50–51):

    filius huic fato divum prolesque virilis
    nulla fuit, primaque oriens erepta iuventa est.

Destiny had decreed that he should have no son, no male stock. Even as it sprang up, it was snatched away in its early bloom.

This is one of those times when Latinus seems very close to Augustus.

Later in Book VII doomed Lausus rides as *filius* at his father Mezentius' side (649). Twice in Book VIII, doomed Pallas is *filius* (104, 466).

A number of instances (VII. 736, Oebalus; VII. 781, Virbius; IX. 581, the son of Arcens; X. 194, Cupavo) allude to lesser heroes. No doubt the poet was particularly proud of Ocnus (X. 199), sprung from Manto, of his native Mantua. These are all decoration.

Jupiter is described as *filius* when he respectfully listened to his mother as she asked for Aeneas' ships to be spared (IX. 93).

The last instance describes the son of Aunus (XI. 700). He is one of Camilla's victims, mentioned to be killed.

Filia is found four times, again always in the nominative singular. At the opening of Book VII (11), the *Solis filia* is Circe. Twice *filia* describes Circe's descendant (via Picus) Lavinia (VII. 52, XII. 605). In the first example, she is the lone child keeping her father's palace. In the second, she leads the lament for her suicidal mother.

Filia Nerei (VIII. 383) is Thetis. Venus evokes both her and Eos in appealing to Vulcan for new arms for Aeneas. But Thetis and Eos were

---

[9] Maffeo Vegio, in his *Libri XII Aeneidos Supplementum* (ed. Venice 1471 [British Library Cat. No. IB. 19536. a.]): below, pp. 278–79.

normally united as examples of sorrowing mothers, who in their different ways sought immortality for their dead hero-sons.[10] Virgil's readers knew that (Ovid, *Am*. III. 9. 1). What extraordinary parallels on Venus' lips! Achilles killed and was killed. What are we to conclude about the arms which eventually Vulcan supplies?

Proles first occurs in Virgil in the *Georgics* (III. 35–36):

> Assaraci proles demissaeque ab Iove gentis
> nomina....

Assaracus' stock, and the names of a clan descending from Jupiter.

It is also part of the stirring prophecy of Anchises in Book VI (781–87):

> 'en huius, nate, auspiciis illa incluta Roma
> imperium terris, animos aequabit Olympo,
> septemque una sibi muro circumdabit arces,
> felix prole virum: qualis Berecyntia mater
> invehitur curru Phrygias turrita per urbes
> laeta deum partu, centum complexa nepotes,
> omnis caelicolas, omnis supera alta tenentis.'

'See, my son! Under his sacred sway glorious Rome shall bound its empire by the world, its spirit by high heaven. Though but one, it will enclose with its walls seven citadels, blessed in its brood of warriors. So the Great Mother advances in her chariot, turret-crowned, through the cities of Asia, rejoicing in her divine children, embracing her hundred grandsons, all dwellers in heaven, all denizens of the lofty realms above.'

With this may be joined *genus antiquum Teucri, pulcherrima proles* (VI. 648), *Dardaniam prolem* (VI. 756). *Prolem Ausoniam* was earlier part of Jupiter's message to Mercury (IV. 236).

But already in the *Georgics proles* (used twice only) had recurred in an unhappy context (IV. 281):

> sed si quem proles subito defecerit omnis ...

But if perchance anyone shall suddenly have lost all his stock ...

In the *Aeneid*, with Silvius in Book VI (*tua postuma proles*, VI. 763) we enter on the ambiguous history of Aeneas' immediate descendants, and even earlier (with Romulus and Remus, I. 274) on the ambiguous history of Rome itself (Horace, *Epodes* 7. 17–20). In some sense this is reinforced when we find *proles* applied both to Aeneas and then to Hercules:

> 'Anchisa generate, deum certissima proles,...' (VI. 322)
> 'Scion of Anchises, most evident child of the gods,...'

---

[10] See, for example, K. Schefold, *Götter- und Heldensagen der Griechen in der spätarchaischen Kunst* (Munich 1978), pp. 241 ff.

The Declining Mode 37

'salve, vera Iovis proles, decus addite divis,...' (VIII. 301)
'Hail true son of Jove, glory enhancing the gods!...'

Hercules has two sides, saviour and madman, and so has Aeneas.[11]

Elsewhere, *Neptunia proles* of Messapus becomes a mannerism (VII. 691; IX. 523; X. 353; XII. 128). Mercury is *Cyllenia proles* (IV. 258). These are flaccid instances. *Prolesque biformis* of the Minotaur (VI. 25) is ominous, and signals the man / bull transformations which ring the poem's second half.[12] As the epic progresses, the noun seems to run out of energy. What is the resonance, for example, of *prolem Dolichaonis Hebrum* (X. 696), one of Mezentius' victims, the last occurrence of the word in the poem? Once more Book X seems to crush hopes previously so high.

Stirps occurs 19 times in the *Aeneid*. Not all of these examples need detain us (I. 626, Teucer; III. 326, Neoptolemus; V. 711, Acestes; X. 543, Caeculus). But already in Book V we are reminded that "royal" Diores is "from Priam's chosen stock" (*egregia Priami de stirpe*, 297). This is the stock that is of concern.

In that connection, the noun perhaps shines most brilliantly from Vulcan's workmanship on Aeneas' new Shield. Again (627) we find the eschatological *venturus* (VIII. 626–29):

> illic res Italas Romanorumque triumphos
> haud vatum ignarus venturique inscius aevi
> fecerat ignipotens, illic genus omne futurae
> stirpis ab Ascanio pugnataque in ordine bella.
>
> There the lord of fire had crafted the story of Italy and the Romans' triumphs, fully aware of prophetic lore and of the age to come. There he had set all the race of that future stock to be descended from Ascanius, and the battles fought in their due course.

Haud vatum ignarus contrasts sharply with Dido and Anna, whose minds were "ignorant of the seers" (*vatum ignarae*, IV. 65). Aeneas himself here is *ignarus* (VIII. 730). For him, what is on the Shield is god-talk.

Vulcan is repeatedly in this episode *ignipotens* (414, 423, 628, 710). Here, he directs his energies to crafting weapons of war. Even so, can one forget the violent, uncontrollable side of Fire throughout the poem, most visible perhaps in the monstrous Cacus, Vulcan's own son, of this same Book VIII? In any case, the reader notes that, on the Shield, the future of Rome's relations with Italy is linked with a series of wars.

With this may be compared a similar passage in Book XII (166–69):

---

[11] See Appendix, below, pp. 329–38.
[12] Below, p. 68.

> hinc pater Aeneas, Romanae stirpis origo,
> sidereo flagrans clipeo et caelestibus armis,
> et iuxta Ascanius, magnae spes altera Romae,
> procedunt castris....
>
> On this side prince Aeneas, the author of Rome's stock, his starry shield and heavenly armour all ablaze, with Ascanius at his side, great Rome's second hope, came forth from the camp.

Yet the splendid appearance of *pater* Aeneas and his son heralds nothing genuine. The peace so solemnly ratified will be aborted (*excute*, 158) a hundred lines later (cf. *hostis*, 266).

In Book VII, Faunus had warned Latinus not to seek a Latin husband for his daughter, but to look rather for a foreign groom. From such a union, he prophesies imperial children (96–101):

> 'ne pete conubiis natam sociare Latinis,
> o mea progenies, thalamis neu crede paratis;
> externi venient generi, qui sanguine nostrum
> nomen in astra ferant, quorumque a stirpe nepotes
> omnia sub pedibus, qua sol utrumque recurrens   100
> aspicit Oceanum, vertique regique videbunt.'
>
> 'Do not seek to unite your daughter to a Latin suitor, my child, and trust not a match ready to hand. Sons-in-law will come from foreign parts to carry with their blood our name to the stars, and from their stock your descendants will see, where the sun in his course views both east and west, all things beneath their feet swayed and ruled.'

This declaration is in fact a two-edged sword. The Trojans may well give their blood. But, in the outcome, as a result of Jupiter's final concessions to Juno (*commixti corpore tantum / subsident Teucri*, XII. 835–36), will they have served as anything except breeding stock to ensure Latin glory? Faunus certainly hails coming worldwide empire, but his *sub pedibus* (v. 100; of the *calcatio colli*) is somewhat troubling. Perhaps the Romans did once view their subjects in that way. They had notoriously maltreated the Italians, as C. Gracchus complained. Is this then yet the *pacique imponere morem* of Anchises' commission to Augustan Rome (VI. 852)?[13]

A stirpe nepotes in Book VII here (v. 99) is an echo from an earlier passage, in which Aeneas had wondered about the identity of a young soldier glimpsed in Hades (VI. 863–66):

> 'quis, pater, ille, virum qui sic comitatur euntem?
> filius, anne aliquis magna de stirpe nepotum?
> qui strepitus circa comitum! quantum instar in ipso!   865
> sed nox atra caput tristi circumvolat umbra.'

---

[13] See E. Fraenkel's note, *Horace* (Oxford 1957), pp. 160–61: *modestiam apud socios* of Augustus' reforms, Tac., *Ann.* I. 9.

'Who, father is he who accompanies the hero in that way? Is it his son, or someone from the mighty stock of his descendants? What hubbub from his thronging comrades! What dignity in the young prince! Yet dark night with its gloomy shadow broods about his head.'

863: *sic* is once again the idiomatic οὕτως εἰκῇ, "without ceremony": cf. *sic o sic positum, Aen.* II. 644. Here almost perhaps "in that dejected manner."

865: *instar* is כֹּבֶד ("weight"); *ipse* as often refers to someone of consequence, in Tacitus, for example, "the emperor" (*postremus ipse scaenam incedit, Ann.* XIV. 15): cf. *per ipsum et cum ipso et in ipso* at the end of the Canon in the Tridentine Mass.

This is of course the doomed Marcellus, honoured perhaps at v. 866 with a reminiscence from Ennius (hence Horace's heroics at *Sat.* II. 1. 58).

His fate was one dark spot. There was another. Apollo had assured the Trojans that their "ancient mother" would welcome them back (III. 94–96):

'...quae vos a stirpe parentum
prima tulit tellus, eadem vos ubere laeto
accipiet reduces. antiquam exquirite matrem.'

'That same land which first bore you from the stock of your parents will now with her generous breast receive you on your return. Seek out your mother of old.'

Anchises immediately deduces that the god is speaking of Crete. That inevitably turns out to be a false hope, since Crete is a symbol of lying and deceit throughout the poem. The *stirps* carried by the Trojans is evidently ambivalent (*prolem ambiguam*, III. 180). Elsewhere this ambivalence is signalled—and traced to Troy itself—by allusions to cheating Laomedon.[14]

There is thus a systematic difficulty in the effort to trace a clear line between the *stirps* of the Trojans and the Romans of Virgil's day. Augustan policy, as is visible from the *Georgics* and indeed Horace, rejected eastern decadence, and exalted instead the sturdy virtues of the Italian farmer.[15] This note is also sounded in the *Aeneid*. The *locus classicus* (using *propago*) is at XII. 827–28, but what about the gibes of both Turnus and his brother-in-law Remulus, both of whom use *stirps*? Turnus makes this point first (VII. 578–79):

Teucros in regna vocari,
stirpem admisceri Phrygiam, se limine pelli.

The Trojans were to take over the kingdom, Phrygian stock was to be imported, while he was shown the door.

[14] See below, pp. 253–54. Homer's Aineias by contrast is not directly descended from Laomedon.

[15] The *Laudes Italiae* (*Geo.* II. 136–76) stress that Italy is superior to the East. Propertius repeats the claim (III. 22). See also below, pp. 251–52, where Juno's diatribe against Troy in Horace (*Odes* III. 3. 18–68) is quoted.

Remulus develops a long indictment (IX. 602–04; 607–10; 614–20):

> 'non hic Atridae nec fandi fictor Ulixes:
> durum a s t i r p e genus natos ad flumina primum
> deferimus saevoque gelu duramus et undis ...
> at patiens operum parvoque adsueta iuventus
> aut rastris terram domat aut quatit oppida bello.
> omne aevum ferro teritur, versaque iuvencum
> terga fatigamus hasta ...
> vobis picta croco et fulgenti murice vestis,
> desidiae cordi, iuvat indulgere choreis,
> et tunicae manicas et habent redimicula mitrae.
> o vere Phrygiae, neque enim Phryges, ite per alta
> Dindyma, ubi adsuetis biforem dat tibia cantum.
> tympana vos buxusque vocat Berecyntia Matris
> Idaeae; sinite arma viris et cedite ferro.'

'No sons of Atreus here, no Ulysses with glib tongue. We are a people hardy of stock who begin by carrying our children to the stream and hardening them in the icy waters. Our young men are used to toil, used to short commons, busied with hoeing the ground into submission or shaking towns with war. Our whole life is honed by the iron, we ply even our steers' backs with the butts of spears. You Trojans like to dress in saffron and purple, you like your holidays, and relaxing in your dances. Your undershirts have long sleeves, your party hats long streamers. To speak the truth, you are women from Phrygia, not men! Off with you to run over high Dindyma, where the twin-stopped flute plays the tune you know so well. The drum calls you and the boxwood pipe of the Berecyntian Mother of Mount Ida. Leave weapons to men, give way to our blades.'

At patiens operum parvoque adsueta iuventus...: this is the spirit of the *Georgics*. There is something too here of Catullus' poem on the fate of Attis. The general anti-eastern tone anticipates that of Lucan's epic, or Juvenal's satire.

Elsewhere, *stirps* may be used more cruelly. Dido urges her Tyrians to harry with hate Aeneas' whole stock and race to come (*stirpem et genus omne futurum*, IV. 622), and in Book VII her puppet-mistress Juno refers to them as *stirpem invisam* (293).

Later, her puppet Turnus is annoyed by Drances' barbs (XI. 392–95):

> 'pulsus ego? aut quisquam merito, foedissime, pulsum
> arguet, Iliaco tumidum qui crescere Thybrim
> sanguine et Euandri totam cum s t i r p e videbit
> procubuisse domum atque exutos Arcadas armis?'

'Am I routed? Or will anyone, you craven wretch, rightly accuse me of that, who sees the swelling Tiber in spate with Trojan blood, and the utter ruin of Evander's house together with his line, and his Arcadians stripped of their weapons?'

The dreadful reality behind these arrogant words is all too plain.

At the frustrated ratifying of peace in Book XII Latinus is carrying a sceptre borrowed from the *Iliad* (I. 234–38). The king's words are a curious repetition of Achilles' in that passage (206–10):

> '...ut sceptrum hoc' (dextra sceptrum nam forte gerebat)
> 'numquam fronde levi fundet virgulta nec umbras,
> cum semel in silvis imo de s t i rp e recisum
> matre caret posuitque comas et bracchia ferro,
> olim arbos ...'

'...just as this sceptre' (he was wielding a sceptre in his right hand as he spoke) 'will never bring forth light leaves on branches to give shade, now that it has been cut once and for all in the forest from the root of its stock, now that, robbed of its mother, it has shed its locks and arms under the blade, though once it was a tree.'

208: the gender of *stirps* astonishes (cf. 781 below). Presumably the archaism is explained by an allusion to some lost passage from Republican literature.

Achilles however had been ratifying, not a peace, but his resolve to stay out of the battle until Agamemnon makes satisfaction to him for taking Briseis. In the *Aeneid*, Aeneas / Agamemnon is to take Lavinia. Involuntarily, Latinus is putting into words the resentments of Turnus / Achilles. This "shift" (in Formalist parlance, сдвиг) assures the listener that the peace will wither. Meanwhile, the barren sceptre takes on a quasi-human status. We could be hearing of some dead warrior, youthful because of the allusion to a mother. Turnus has lost his mother. Is this already Turnus' corpse?

As with so many of these terms, *stirps* winds down in a version of the hollow pastoral. As if they were farmers clearing a piece of ground for cultivation, in preparing the lists for the last combat of Turnus and Aeneas, the Trojans had cut down a wild olive. *Nullo discrimine* here, echoed from v. 498 (*nullo discrimine caedem*), is ominous (XII. 770–71):

> sed stirpem Teucri nullo discrimine sacrum
> sustulerant, puro ut possent concurrere campo.

The Trojans, making no allowance, had removed the stock, to clear the ground for the combat.

But the country god Faunus, whose tree this was, will not be treated so unceremoniously. In answer to Turnus' desperate prayer, when Aeneas' spear lodges in the stump still left, it cannot be dislodged. The scene is a reprise of the plucking of the Golden Bough (and of Polydorus at the start of Book III), except that the hero was able to seize the Golden Bough after an effort. Here, as he struggles in vain to wrench his spear free (*lentoque in stirpe moratus*, 781), the delay gives Juturna a chance to restore to her brother his lost sword. Venus then pulls Aeneas' spear out for him, and the champions can start afresh. Is it not unfortunate that their combat, over which "breathless Mars" (790) presides, must end in death? Aeneas and

Turnus are both Italians in some degree. Are not Romulus and Remus here proleptically at work? Is the *Aeneid*—or at least does it imply?—a *Thebaid*, as perhaps its admirer Statius sensed?

Pario is found in finite tenses only six times. Two of these have the dead as their subjects (VI. 434–35, *letum ... peperere* of innocent suicides, in a violent oxymoron; XI. 25, *patriam peperere*, the heroic war dead). Elsewhere, *alius Latio iam partus Achilles* (VI. 89) is threatening enough. At II. 783–84, Creusa alludes broken-heartedly to Lavinia (*illic ... regia coniunx / parta tibi*). *Vobis parta quies* denotes the dead calm of Buthrotum (III. 495). *Parta quies* on the lips of Latinus (VII. 598) betrays his consciousness of imminent death.

Some form of *parens* meets us in the *Aeneid* 67 times. Of these, the feminine singular provides 13 instances (vs. 35 of the masculine singular). Seven of these allude to Venus, three to Cybele, one to Terra. One, also showing *puer*, recalls Creusa: *ecqua tamen puero est amissae cura parentis?* (III. 341), pathetically on the lips of Andromache, who is referring directly to Ascanius, but clearly embracing too a remembered Astyanax. One refers (inevitably!) to the mother of Euryalus (IX. 289).

There seems to be no instance where a male *parens* is seen taking decisive action to secure the future of the Trojan line in Italy. The noun is found in the masculine nominative singular only twice. In Book VI (*pulsatusve parens*, 609) the reference is to criminal assault, punishable by the pains of hell; in Book X, Turnus is cynically wishing that a *parens* (his? his victim's?) might be on hand, as if at some gladiatorial combat, to view Pallas' death: *cuperem ipse parens spectator adesset* (443). In the oblique cases, Anchises is *parens* 14 times. Aeneas similarly is *parens* only in oblique cases, and only twice (I. 646; IX. 261). Evander, destined to lose Pallas, is *parens* certainly four times; Daunus, Turnus' father, four times, his ancestor Pilumnus, once. The last occurrence of a singular oblique case in the poem is part of defeated Turnus' appeal to Aeneas (XII. 932). This may be his cringing reversal of the brutal bravado at X. 443, just noted. In any case, he is not heard (cf. X. 597).

Among the plural forms, the recurrent *ante ora parentum* perhaps deserves most notice. Polites is cut down "before his parents' gaze" (II. 531; cf. *ante ora patris*, II. 663). In Hades, *iuvenes* set upon the pyre "before their parents' gaze" crowd to the bank of Styx (VI. 308). In a variant of this, on Camilla's death, the routed Italians are slain *ante oculos lacrimantumque ora parentum* (XI. 887). These associations inevitably lend a certain ambiguity to the *Lusus Troiae*, where the young riders parade to the crack of a whip *ante ora parentum* (V. 553). In Book II, the miraculous flame appearing on Iulus' head *manus inter maestorumque ora parentum* (681) portends a glorious future. But can this single episode make up for all the cruel losses sustained elsewhere? When and how?

Infans. In spite of the tender parting of Hector with Andromache and his son Astyanax in the *Iliad*, though even there with a presage of Troy's doom; in spite of the pressure exercised on the *Aeneid* by a future which would give rise to Rome, some deep reluctance apparently forbids Virgil to write about babies in any convincing way. In one of his typical acts of declension, and as another part of his "hollow pastoral," the poet uses *infans* to sentimentalise the fanciful upbringing of ill-fated Camilla (XI. 541, 549, 573; cf. 578, *puerilia*). Elsewhere, in the plural, the word refers to the wailing, untimely dead children of hell (VI. 427), the sound that greets Aeneas as he enters the place of apocalypse, just as untimely dead *puer* Marcellus will end his visit (882). There is no more.

Puella is found only twice (II. 238; VI. 307), both times in the quasi-formulaic *pueri innuptaeque puellae*, the doomed and barren. No doubt the pretty little elegiac *puella* in the singular is beneath the dignity of epic, but obviously once again some *Keimentschluß*[16] is at work too. Virgil tells us plainly that most of the *matres* who set out from Troy (II. 797) are left behind in Sicily (V. 715, 750). Must we deduce that the Trojan *puellae* are also abandoned somewhere (to what fate?), to free the men to take Italian wives (*genus ... mixtum*, XII. 838)?

There are 53 instances of *puer* (not all detailed here). *Puer Ascanius* becomes itself a sort of formula (I. 267; II. 598; III. 339; IV. 156, 354; V. 74; X. 236, 605: cf. I. 678, 684; III. 341, 487; V. 569 [Iulus], 599; X. 70, 133; XII. 435); and the noun is sentimentally applied to him by Apollo in Book IX (641, 656) even when it may contradict the picture so carefully drawn of advancing maturity. Perhaps these repetitions of *puer*, which extend to the *Lusus Troiae* (V. 553, 561, 569, 602; cf. V. 548), are meant to convey the impression of a youthful, even thronging generation. But *puer* also describes Troilus (I. 475), Astyanax (II. 457), raped Ganymede (V. 252), dead Marcellus (VI. 875, 882), the sons of Tyrrhus (VII. 484), slain Almo (VII. 575), Pallas (VIII. 581; XI. 42; XII. 943), Lausus (X. 825), Romulus and Remus (VIII. 632), Caesar and Pompey (VI. 832). *Puer* also describes tricky Cupid (I. 684). Elsewhere, along with mothers, daughters-

---

[16] "Seminal decision": the term was coined for aesthetics by F. Schleiermacher: see Glossary of Critical Terms, *s.v.*, p. 342.

in-law and sisters, *pueri parentibus orbi* "curse" (*exsecrantur*) Turnus' war and "marriage plans" (XI. 215–17, another example of ill-starred *hymenaei*[17]). Can Ascanius / Iulus and his silent, vanishing cohorts in Book V counterbalance all this weight of sorrow?

Puer also sentimentalises Euryalus (V. 296, 349; IX. 181, 217, 276). His misadventure with Nisus in Book IX, at the start of the *Aeneid*'s last quartet, clearly mirrors his misadventure in the footrace in Book V, at the start of the *Aeneid*'s second quartet. British imperialism used to see games as some sort of preparation for the battlefield. Now, as if in some gross pre-parody of the Duke of Wellington (or Sir Henry Newbolt!), the playing fields of Sicily metamorphose into the killing fields of Rutulia. Virgil milks these episodes unashamedly for all the tears they will deliver. In Book IX particularly, he has on hand Euryalus' aged mother, to give exaggerated expression to her hopeless grief for her dead son. It would however be quite uncharacteristic of the poet merely to want us to indulge in sentiment. The laughter (181, 182, 358) and games (113, 593, 605, 674) of Book V are discovered after all to be a poor preparation (on both sides) for the game of war in IX (cf. 335–38; 606). This old motif, seen in the depiction by Greek vase-painters of Ajax losing to Achilles at draughts, has been re-explored in our own day.[18] It will be noted below that Dido lends an astringent flavour to both books.[19] Her absence would make their cloying aroma intolerable.

Pater is found 171 times in the poem. Of these, Jupiter is *pater* 26 times, Anchises 27, Aeneas 33. A difficulty is presented to the interpreter looking for proof of kinship by the fact that, in Latin usage (as in Hebrew), the term is a title of respect given to someone senior, whether by rank or merely by age (e.g. Horace, *Sat*. II. 1. 12). Jupiter clearly earns this title as "almighty" (*pater omnipotens*, 10 times) or as "lord of the gods" (*divum pater*, 4 times; cf. *magne pater divum*, IX. 495; *pater ille deum*, X. 875),

---

[17] We already noted VII. 398. See also below, p. 286.

[18] The motif is treated on a number of vases, of which the most moving is the black-figure amphora in the Vatican signed by Exekias (Arias and Hirmer, *A History of Greek Vase Painting*, London 1962, no. XVII with commentary; J. Boardman, ed., *The Oxford History of Classical Art*, Oxford 1993, no. 70). The vase, found at Vulci, and therefore bought by an Etruscan patron, illustrates the Lydian / Etruscan taste for gambling (Herodotus I. 94; *lusum it Maecenas*, Hor., *Sat*. I. 5. 48). "In our own day": Paul Fussell, *The Great War and Modern Memory* (New York 1975), esp. pp. 191 ff. Theatre-goers will remember Joan Littlewood's adaptation (1963) of Charles Chilton's play "The Long, Long Trail," later turned into a film ("Oh! What a Lovely War!" Paramount 1969).

[19] Dido motif: it is she who is recalled by the "Amazonian" quiver and *balteus* of V. 311–13 and who offers (*dat*) a bowl at IX. 266.

without emphasis on his physical relationship in any given case. Other gods are variously introduced as *pater*: Apollo, Neptune, Mars, Quirinus among others. Here it is a substitute for "king," "lord."

When Virgil therefore writes (II. 2):

> inde toro pater Aeneas sic orsus ab alto ...

can there be anything intended except the equivalent of "Lord" ("Prince," even "Sir") Aeneas? And so at XII. 697–98:

> At pater Aeneas audito nomine Turni
> deserit et muros et summas deserit arces ...
>
> Hearing the name of Turnus, Prince Aeneas leaves the walls and towering citadels of Laurentum ...

Even if we press this to mean that Aeneas is now exercising a fatherly responsibility, he does not thereby become his people's biological "father."

Something similar is meant by *pater Romanus* at IX. 448–49:

> dum domus Aeneae Capitoli immobile saxum
> accolet imperiumque pater Romanus habebit.
>
> ...so long as the house of Aeneas shall live near the steadfast rock of the Capitol, and the father at Rome keep his authority.

The Roman emperor was certainly father of his people (*pater atque princeps*, Horace, *Odes* I. 2. 50; *pater patriae*, Suet., *Aug.* 58), just as his successor the Pope is "papa," or his successor the Czar / Caesar was "father of all the Russias." There is no necessary link by blood. What is to be commemorated here in the *Aeneid* are the pointless deaths of two young Trojan soldiers.[20]

There is a link by blood with Anchises and Ascanius. That with Anchises inevitably looks back. The forward relationship with Ascanius / Iulus is on the whole muted. One touching scene in *Aeneid* II (674) is discussed below; and, again in *Aeneid* II, as little Ascanius trots *non passibus aequis* by his heroic father's side (724), the reader smiles. Ascanius refers to his father when he is holding the fort during Aeneas' absence (*patri*, IX. 312). But we must offset against these familial moments the stark fact that Aeneas speaks directly to his son only in Book XII (cf. *pater*, 440), when he thinks he may lose his life in the last combat. Here, exchanging identities with mad Turnus / Ajax, he borrows language from Sophocles' mad Ajax (πατρός, 550), and on this unique occasion the son is too grief-stricken to reply.

Latinus is *pater* ten times, and Evander seven. In this, the reader may well find pathos. Latinus will lose in Turnus both his nephew and his

---

[20] On this passage also below, p. 223.

son(s) already dead. Evander loses in Pallas what Zeus lost in Sarpedon (see on *progenies*, above).

Patres (22 examples) is normally a retrospective word, meaning "ancestors," "elders." It lends a notion of immemorial antiquity stretching back through time (*religione patrum*, II. 715; *more ... patrum*, XI. 186; *Albanique patres*, I. 7). It describes Dido's ancestors (I. 641); Turnus' ancestors (VII. 372; cf. X. 282); ancestral kinship between Evander's line and Aeneas' (VIII. 132). Sometimes it alludes to a senate (V. 758; VII. 611; IX. 192; XI. 379), even at Carthage (IV. 682).

The most striking "Roman" instance is that where Augustus leads the Italians to battle (VIII. 679):

> cum patribus populoque, penatibus et magnis dis.

This is the SPQR of the legionary standards. Its spirit is not sustained.

The last instance of the plural occurs at XII. 211. The ominous sceptre which Latinus wielded in making his frustrated prayer for peace was borne by the "sires of Latium." There is a sense in which Latinus here is again Augustus, particularly visible in the diadem which he wears (162–64). Later, the king is forced to withdraw from the erupting violence (285–86). This certainly fits the picture of an Augustus waiting in the poem on the threshold, disengaged from its bloody and often ruthless action.

"May you share the prosperity of Jerusalem ... and live to see your children's children" sang the Psalmist (128:5–6 NEB). It is hard to distinguish any passage in which the *Aeneid* looks forward to "fathers of fathers" or where we hear of any new father greeting with delight a son or daughter who will guarantee the future of his clan. Virgil evidently can write stirringly about ancient lineage continued through the generations: *multosque per annos / stat fortuna domus et avi numerantur avorum* (*Geo.* IV. 208–09). Why does he confine his skill to sexless bees?

Matres in the plural is found 31 times. In Sicily, in a rare pro-active mood, they try to burn the fleet (V. 654); but the usual role of these ladies is to provide a choric backdrop to enhance the pathos of the events described. This is primarily what interests Virgil about mothers. The term is a freely manipulable prop; to change the metaphor, Tchaikovskian wind.

In this regard, precisely because it shows no use of *mater*, a negative conclusion may be drawn from the passage in which Aeneas' family resolves to leave Troy (II. 634 ff.). Creusa, her claim as mother unmentioned, makes no positive contribution to the family council, but is allowed to throw herself on the threshold at her husband's feet, holding up her young son to his father (*parvumque patri tendebat Iulum*) in a desperate appeal to him to remember his responsibilities (673–78). *Talia vociferans gemitu tectum omne replebat* (679) describes the conclusion. *Gemens ... tectum omne replebat* is used of Silvia's wounded deer (VII. 501–02)—hit of course by the same Iulus in a reprise of his father's treatment of Dido (IV. 69).[21] *Vociferans*, always in the *Aeneid* in the dramatic nominative singular present participle like this,[22] is irrational. It is next used of frenzied Amata (VII. 390). Elsewhere, we find it of brash Remulus, the husband of Turnus' younger sister (IX. 596), and crazed Turnus (X. 651; XII. 95).

Ut pictura poesis: one may well imagine some Victorian painting of this scene in Book II.[23] But, given the importance here of inchoate sound, the operatic / pantomimic sensibility also seems very close. Virgil is seeking pathos as he defines it. He uses *pater* (674, 678) and *parvus* (674, 677). But it is not in the end so much the fact that Creusa is a mother which he chooses to emphasise, as that she is a *coniunx* whose tenure is to be so short lived (II. 597, 651, 673, 678, 711, 725, 738; cf. 783). In earlier poetry, Aeneas' wife was Eurydica (Ennius, *Ann.* 36 Sk.), and it is that parallel with Orpheus' Eurydice which interests the poet (cf. *Geo.* IV. 499–502: *volentem, Geo.* IV. 501; *Aen.* II. 790; IV. 390 [ita M]). There is also a contrast with Anchises (*Aen.* II. 792–94 ~ VI. 700–02) to provide the necessary foil. In this pre-Roman family, *patria potestas* is all. This is what Dido found out (*patris Anchisae*, IV. 351, 427).

Mater is found in the singular 51 times. Sometimes the reference is to animals (IV. 516; VII. 283 and 484; VIII. 632; IX. 565, 628: cf. *matribus* in this sense, I. 635; IX. 61). It may even refer to a tree (XII. 209). Italy (III. 96) and Tellus (XI. 71), in a conjunction which reminds us of the Ara Pacis, are called *mater*. Eight cases refer to Venus (I. 314, 382, 405, 585, 720; III. 19; VIII. 370; XII. 52). Some quirks of her maternal behaviour will be discussed later.[24] Five refer to Cybele (III. 111; VI. 784; VII. 139; IX. 108 and 619). Leda is the mother of immoral Helen (I. 652), whose finery Aeneas bestows on Dido. Many instances fill in some mythological detail: the mother of the Nereids (III. 74), of Acestes (V. 38), *mater Aricia* (VII. 762), *Feronia mater* (VIII. 564), *Populonia mater* (X. 172), the

---

[21] Cf. Ovid, *Met.* V. 153; *Alcestis Barcinonensis* 22.

[22] Cicero's nocturnal visit to Heraclea may be compared, when he was met by a long line of torch-bearing *matres*, whose leader *me suam salutem appellans, te suum carnificem nominans, fili nomen implorans, mihi ad pedes misera iacuit ...* (*Verrine* V §129). This is virtually out of some stage performance. They were not at the trial.

[23] Tennyson's Guinevere offers some parallel: *Idylls of the King*, "Guinevere," 602–03.

[24] Below, p. 59.

48 Chapter Two

mothers of Antiphates (IX. 697), Ocnus (X. 200), Lichas (X. 315), of Tarquitus (X. 557), Camilla (XI. 542), Onites (XII. 515). Carmentis is the mother of Evander (VIII. 335-36). Even Ilia may be added to this list (VI. 778). No effort is made to play up Turnus' mother (X. 76), or Lausus' (X. 818), though Pallas' (VIII. 510) again adds pathos. Turnus in fact uses the emotion-laden *o mater* twice (to demonic Allecto and unstable Amata; see below), in neither case to his real mother. Was she dead?

Euryalus' mother by contrast is exploited for pantomimic effect in the tragic vein (IX. 216-17, 302, 474, 484, 486), and with more melodrama than Creusa. So in Book VII (361) is Amata. Later, her emotional speech to Turnus (XII. 56-63), with its echoes of Dido, betrays this (*matris*, 64) and Turnus uses the fraught *o mater* to her at 74. Elsewhere, Clytaemnestra pursues Orestes as a *mater* (IV. 472). The "mother of the Eumenides" (VI. 250) adds terror and solemnity to Aeneas' sacrifice before his descent into Hades. Virgin Allecto (VII. 331), denizen of hell, is also addressed as *o mater* (VII. 441). The listener can apprehend this only as savage irony.

Genitor occurs 57 times, always in the singular. Of these occurrences, 19 describe Anchises, and again therefore look essentially to the past. Some uses are "pathetic." At II. 560, for example, Aeneas is reminded that he is neglecting his family at home: *subiit cari genitoris imago*. At VI. 108, *cari genitoris* again evokes Anchises.

Eleven examples refer to Jupiter. His brother Neptune is twice *genitor* (I. 155; V. 817). The Tiber is *genitor* (VIII. 72).

Six instances refer to Aeneas. Three times (IX. 257, 264, 272) Ascanius, in commissioning the doomed Nisus and Euryalus, speaks of the absent Aeneas as *genitor / genitore*. Evidently he is a proud son. But Aeneas never does anything in the role of *genitor*. Elsewhere, the noun is applied to him only in the genitive: Venus, talking to Cupid, alludes to him as *cari genitoris* (I. 677). At I. 716 he is the suppositious father (*falsi ... genitoris*) of Cupid / Ascanius. Dido, nursing an impostor on her lap, is as it were big with a lie. Later she is *genitoris imagine capta* (IV. 84), "ensnared by the semblance of a father."

What relevance does all this have to the future? Again perhaps Lausus tells us something. At X. 789, Mezentius, soon to die along with his noble son, is also *cari genitoris*, the phrase already recorded for Anchises and Aeneas. Later in this passage, he is *genitor* (in the nominative) three times in rapid succession (800, 833, 848). Ascanius' language in Book IX may be compared. On this evidence, Virgil enjoys the pathos more than the humdrum possibility of engendered survival.

Evander, who loses Pallas, is *genitor* twice (VIII. 583, Pallas leaves for war; XI. 161, Pallas' corpse is brought back home). The most affecting example is perhaps at X. 466, where Jupiter, unable to rescue Pallas / Sarpedon, addresses his son Hercules (*genitor natum*) on the unforgiving brevity of human life. Perhaps this carries a lesson for the poem's audience. It is not the future but the duty of the here and now which is the concern of men.

The last occurrence is at XII. 933–34. Turnus, on the verge of death, appeals in the name of his father Daunus, reminding Aeneas that he too had such a father: *fuit et tibi talis / Anchises genitor*. Anchises had actually preached *parcere subiectis* (VI. 853). But at the end no reference to a life-giver is able to save Turnus from death.

Genetrix occurs 13 times. Six of these refer to Venus, five to Cybele. At IX. 284, Euryalus is making arrangements for his mother to be looked after in case of his death. In answer (IX. 297), Ascanius declares that he will treat her like his lost mother Creusa, who did not merit the title in Book II. Both examples are used to enhance the pathos of Euryalus' death. There is nothing that could be called normal human intercourse.

There are 60 uses of *coniu(n)x*, 10 of *coniugium* and 14 of *conubium*. Dido's pretence at *coniugium* (IV. 172) is offset by *Lavinia coniunx* (VI. 764; VII. 314; XII. 17, 80, 937), pathetic enough on the lips of Creusa (*regia coniunx*, II. 783), tragic enough in its implications for Turnus, and surely for the Aeneas who kills him.

Felix / infelix also merit treatment here. These two adjectives, "fruitful" and "barren," are linked by etymology with *fellare*, the action of babies at the breast, and *filius / filia*. They might well then be expected to play some balanced part in an epic whose theme compels it to describe a fresh start following a series of what may be called "dead ends." The evidence is not quite so straightforward.

At the very outset of the Republic, death is inflicted by a father (Brutus) on his sons. *Infelix* here (VI. 822) signals a leitmotif in the poem. Childless Dido even applies it to herself (IV. 596). Amata, in some ways Dido's double, and certainly also destined for suicide, describes herself as *infelix* at the moment when she senses she is to lose her daughter to Aeneas (VII. 401). What should have been cause for rejoicing—the prospect of marriage and family continuance—leads on to death (*infelix*, XII. 598). Turnus, rejected by history, *impar* (XII. 216), despising his adversary as a lurking *latro* (XII. 7), loses his menace to become an echo of ambushed Troilus, *infelix puer atque impar congressus Achilli* (I. 475).[25] *Infelix*

---

[25] These are the only two examples of *impar* in this form in the *Aeneid*.

simulacrum atque ipsius umbra Creusae (II. 772) struck a chord in the heart of St. Augustine. Creusa was not merely "unhappy" in some sentimental sense (although she was that too). From now on, she was barren, because she had lost her son and husband for ever. Yet it is the Great Mother who presides over this alteration in her state.

It is not as if Virgil was incapable of picturing children's often maddening charm. The passage in the second book (453 ff.) where Aeneas describes his efforts to drive back the Greeks from Priam's palace may be recalled. He mentions the private passage, often used while Troy still stood, which Andromache would follow to visit her parents-in-law, "dragging along" the boy Astyanax.[26] Every mother who has firmly encouraged a reluctant and curious toddler to move on will recognise the scene.

Yet it is just here that Andromache is described as *infelix* (455–56). There should be no puzzlement.[27] The poem operates with a multi-layered, prophetic ("vertical") time, and the adjective *infelix* is an example of prolepsis. Book II is narrated by Aeneas, who has earlier been at Buthrotum. Even when he is talking about a Troy still standing, Andromache's then coming (and now come) sorrow and barrenness are registered in his memory. For him, she has already lost her son, as is noted later (III. 482 ff.), when Andromache presents gifts to Ascanius, the sole surviving "image"— another leitmotif in the poem—of Astyanax (*o mihi sola mei super Astyanactis imago*, 489).

There are wider implications still. The passage echoes the *Odyssey*, where however it is Helen who remarks on Telemachus' resemblance to Odysseus (IV. 141 ff.). Later, she makes Telemachus a similar gift (XV. 125 ff.). She has no son of her own. Telemachus is just about to return to Ithaca to be reunited with his father. Dido / Helen, giver of gifts (*Aen.* V. 571–72), about to lose Ascanius for the attractions of Italy (IV. 234, 275, 355), may think she is hearing a story about Andromache, but in fact this is her own plight.

In this scene from Book III, as she begins to answer Aeneas' questions, Andromache has congratulated Polyxena, sacrificed at the tomb of Achilles by the departing Greeks (321–24):

> 'o felix una ante alias Priameia virgo,
> hostilem ad tumulum Troiae sub moenibus altis

---

[26] *Trahebat*, 457: cf. *trahit* at v. 321 of doomed Panthus with his grandson.

[27] The words *dum regna manebant* (455) "would seem rather a stopgap here, unless they are meant to stress the contrast between Andromache's present fate (*infelix*) and her former happy domesticity": R. G. Austin, *Commentary*, pp. 181–82.

> iussa mori, quae sortitus non pertulit ullos
> nec victoris heri tetigit captiva cubile!'

'Happy beyond all others the maiden daughter of Priam, for she was bidden to die at her enemy's tomb beneath the lofty walls of Troy. No lots were cast for her, she never laid a prisoner's hand on the bed of a conquering master!'

321. *Priameia virgo*, II. 403, Cassandra.

By the standards of the Virgilian universe, this paradox seems quite appropriate. But how can a *virgo* executed before marriage be *felix*?[28] We accept this *Umwertung* only because the whole un-Euclidean geometry of the poem skews our sensibilities. This is why we are so often taken inside the characters' perceptions. The poet's Gygean *videre* becomes a window, not to outside, but to within. *Cor ad cor loquitur.*[29] In this aesthetic, even the "pathetic half lines" (another of Newman's phrases) have a part to play.

As Aeneas bids Andromache and the other Trojans farewell, he says *vivite felices* (III. 493).[30] This is tragic irony, for although Andromache mentions those Trojan women who had borne children in slavery (*servitio enixae*, 327), there is no suggestion in the *Aeneid* that she herself found any consolation for the death of Astyanax, even though eventually she came to be married to Trojan Helenus. She could not have done so in the imperial economy of the poem, any more than in the imperial economy of real life there was any room for Caesarion.[31]

Dido too is *infelix*. In IV. 68, when she vainly seeks encouragement before the altars, Virgil says: *uritur infelix Dido*. But the *Georgics* (I. 84–85) had recommended that barren fields (*sterilis ... agros*) should be set on fire, and that "light straw" be burnt out (*crepitantibus urere flammis*). This is exactly what the poet will do with his heroine as she ascends the pyre at the end of the book. In 450–51, again by the altars, *infelix ... Dido / mortem orat*. Her pregnancy is with the Furies (474). They are fiery enough (*Allecto ... exarsit in iras*, VII. 445; cf. *Furiis accensus et ira* of Aeneas, XII. 946). She has been bullied here, like so many women over the ages, like Iphigenia (II. 116), like Medea predestined to kill Pelias (Apoll., *Arg.* III. 64), into accepting a fate (a marriage with Hades?) already ordained for her, and bearing its brood. This is the union arranged for her by the goddess

---

[28] In the parallel at I. 94, Aeneas uses *beati*, a passage adapted by Chateaubriand: "Pourquoi ne suis-je pas tombé avec mes contemporains, les derniers d'une race épuisée?" (*Mémoires d'Outre-Tombe*, edd. E. Bire and P. Moreau [Paris 1947], III, vi, pp. 90–91).

[29] J. H. Newman's cardinalitian motto, Augustinian / Pascalian in tone, but in fact from St. Francis de Sales.

[30] On this idiom, *Roman Catullus*, pp. 242–45.

[31] See p. 11, above.

of marriage, malevolent, "Saturnian" Juno.[32]

Earlier, as Dido looked out from her watch-tower upon the departing fleet (IV. 584 ff.), in a theatrical tirade she had castigated herself for not scattering Aeneas' dismembered body over the waves, or serving up Ascanius to his father. She is thinking of what Medea did to her brother, Apsyrtus, and Atreus did to Thyestes' sons. Like Hector, she could have carried fire into his camp. Her words, which echo those of Apollonius' Medea (*Arg.* IV. 392–93), are wild:

> 'faces in castra tulissem
> implessemque foros flammis natumque patremque   605
> cum genere exstinxem, memet super ipsa dedissem.'

'I should have carried firebrands into his camp, filled his gangways with flames, wiped out father and son with the whole tribe, and then hurled myself on top.'

But Carthage had its own tradition of fiery child-murder, and sacred infanticide seems to have spread to Etruria.[33] Is Dido its priestess? Is Virgil interpreting Ennius (*Poeni soliti suos sacrificare puellos, Ann.* 214 Sk.)?

Inevitably therefore, after all this, as Aeneas looks back (V. 3–4) toward Carthage, he sees the walls glowing with the funeral flames *infelicis Elissae*, "childless Liz." They would haunt him.

At the entrance to the underworld are found the souls of infants torn from their mothers' breasts (VI. 426 ff.). When Aeneas reaches the Fields of Grief, *Lugentes Campi*, he meets Dido, now reunited with Sychaeus, but still unhappy, unlucky, barren (*infelix*, 456). Later (521), Deiphobus ruefully speaks of his *infelix ... thalamus*, quite appropriately, since his union with Helen had fostered death for himself and his whole city. But so had *infelix Dido* foreshadowed the death of her whole city (IV. 330, 670). Virgil's Roman listeners knew what Scipio had done in 146 B.C.

Andromache is *infelix*, "infertile," Dido is *infelix*, yet sterility and barrenness are more than they imply in the poem. Il y a des fleurs du mal, a negative fruitfulness of evil (*Ergo ubi concepit Furias*, IV. 474). *Infelix* is also used of the Trojan Horse (II. 245), in the sense that it has a curse to spread to everything around it. This pregnant Horse is *lignum* (II. 45), "a piece of firewood," quite literally, since (like Paris) it will burn down Troy. It is a gift to the *virgin* goddess Minerva and around it *unwed* girls sing (238). It seems like the carefully chosen choir of *virgines puerique* that would celebrate the *Carmen Saeculare*. Horace foresees marriage for his girls (*nupta, Odes* IV. 6. 41). But will these girls in Virgil ever live to marry?

---

[32] Cf. *pronuba*, IV. 166, VII. 319, the only occurrences in the poem.

[33] Haynes, *Etruscan Civilization*, p. 28.

The Declining Mode 53

We have already been reminded of the blood of the slain virgin Iphigenia in II. 116. The death of Laocoon's two sons (213–15) presaged the end of Troy.

Sinon, who lets the soldiers out of the Horse's womb (*inclusos utero Danaos et pinea furtim / laxat claustra*, 258–59), evidently acts as a sort of monstrous midwife. Since Machaon was a doctor, the puzzling *primusque Machaon* (263) is perhaps meant to hint at his important role in the medical procedure. The Trojan temptation to "bore into" the Horse's womb (II. 38) is therefore to commit a kind of abortion. It seems strange that such an operation would have been the means to safeguard Troy's future.

The Trojans do however bore into at least one womb (VII. 496–99):

> ipse etiam eximiae laudis succensus amore
> Ascanius curvo derexit spicula cornu;
> nec dextrae erranti deus afuit, actaque multo
> perque uterum sonitu perque ilia venit harundo.

> Prince Ascanius, on fire with longing for distinction and praise, let fly pointed arrows from his curving bow. Whatever the unsteadiness of his hand, a god intervened, and the shaft, loudly hissing, pierced the womb and flanks.

What deity was this? The deadly outcome is linked with the imagery showing Aeneas as a huntsman from the very opening of the poem (I. 184–93), which then passes into simile and metaphor (*letalis harundo*, IV. 73; cf. *more ferae*, 551).

Similarly, in Book VII, we heard the story that Hecuba, when she was to bear Paris, was pregnant with a firebrand (320). The language of Juno's terrifying curse (*gener atque socer*, 317) extends this prophetically to the Civil War at Rome (cf. VI. 830–31). Catullus' *socer generque* (29. 24) was stereotypical in such contexts. *Iterum* here also attracts attention (322). The story is picked up in Book X (704–05), when Mimas is killed by Mezentius. Juno's prophecy is thus working out exactly.

Any analysis of particular turns of phrase in Virgil is bound to kindle lines of thought likely to explode into dissertations. It remains true that the poet, in an epic which has somehow to bridge the four centuries between the sack of Troy and the foundation of Rome, shows remarkably little concern with any general escape from the closed world he presents in such sombre colours. Indeed, for him birth is too often ambiguous (III. 180) and even, as was noted, monstrous (*prolesque biformis* of the Minotaur, VI. 25). Promise for the future is apprehended only dimly by his heroes, and fulfilled mainly in an extra-temporal Augustus.

In the late 20's, as Virgil pondered the final shape of his epic, Propertius prayed to Venus for the emperor's welfare as Aeneas' descendant (*ipsa tuam serva prolem, Venus: hoc sit in aevum, / cernis ab Aenea quod superesse caput*: III. 4. 19–20). Even as Virgil was dying, Cupid, Venus' child, was shown with a heroic Augustus on the original of the Prima Porta statue now in the Vatican (inv. 2290: shortly after 20 B.C.). But the *Georgics* had already questioned the whole Trojan legacy (I. 502). Horace would later choose even Aeneas to illustrate his favourite theme of transitoriness (*Odes* IV. 7. 14–16).

Could the *Aeneid* then reclaim what Troy lost? The following chapters will explore the nature and lesson of this poem of dead ends (Marcellus), false starts (Crete, Carthage) and lost generations.

III

CHILDREN AND VIRGIL'S EPIC TECHNIQUE—I

Vagitus et ingens / infantumque animae flentes (Aen. VI. 426–27) at the entrance to Hades; *nati melioribus annis* (VI. 649) of Troy's dead heroes. Who does not recognise the characteristic notes of Virgilian pathos? In both cases here they colour and depress the hope of children. What are some graver notes of Virgil's epic technique? Can children expect to survive their bias?

Binocular Vision

Rome began with the birth of twins to Ilia. They quarrelled, and settled their differences by fratricide. Every Roman, including Horace (*Epode* 7), learned the tale from Ennius. That was too strong meat for Augustus, and, in the spirit of the intaglio of Caius and Lucius Caesar mentioned earlier, the *Aeneid* emphasises their reconciliation: *Remo cum fratre Quirinus* (I. 292; cf. *Geo.* II. 533). As these twins are reconciled, they become doubles of each other, what a later poet will call *geminos ... Quirinos* (Juvenal XI. 105).[1] By an opposite turn of affairs, Julius and Pompey are in harmony in the world below: *concordes animae nunc et dum nocte prementur* (VI. 827). Eventually, in life, they will be deadly enemies, picking up the bloody mantle which Romulus and Remus have discarded, feeding Discordia's ugly appetite.

Dead Pompey is also dead Priam (II. 557–58). Priam's heir Ascanius, withdrawn from the fray by Apollo (IX. 649 ff.), is, we saw, a kind of pre-Augustus. The children in the *Lusus Troiae* look like their parents, and anticipate their Roman descendants. No doubt propaganda reasons govern these particular transformations, but such pairings also corresponded to something within Virgil's own psyche, which here we may call "binocular vision," a tic aided by and yet often quite over and above the continually implied pairings with Homeric or other originals. Dido's dream offers an

---

[1] Propertius (IV. 1. 9) can use *Remi* for the metrically intractable *Romuli*. Again Cicero's *senseram ... quam idem essent* (*ad Att.* X. 8. 5) is relevant.

extreme instance. Here, the insight is into a mind awry: *videt ... solem geminum et duplices se ostendere Thebas* (IV. 469–70).[2] But the characteristic feature of his epic imagination in general is "twinning." A French critic has called this *dédoublement*, but this is a *dédoublement des inégaux*.[3] To focus on one image inevitably blurs its twin. By way of anticipation, we may again look back to the *Georgics*. A Renaissance painting in the National Gallery (London) depicts their final episode.[4] There is a shore. Beyond the action taking place there, the viewer sees a blue city (one thinks of nostalgic Housman's "blue remembered hills"). It hints perhaps at the city and palace of Cyrene and her nymphs, paysage sousmarin, englouti. This other, translittoral world (*tendebantque manus ripae ulterioris amore*), of shadows, of a different or no time, of the transrational and divine, is what continually haunts the poet's sensibility, as it had haunted that of the Etruscans.[5] It finds a supreme illustration in the simile used as Dido is glimpsed in the centre of *Aeneid* VI (453–54): *aut videt aut vidisse putat*.

It has consequences for the poet's apprehension of the role of children in the scheme of things. If children are physical pledges of continuance, and assert their mission by the boisterous, seemingly rule-free behaviour every parent knows too well, they cannot easily be fitted into the unreal, the half-glimpsed or half-heard, unless of course they are ill or suffering or mourned. Virgil is bound by the very nature of his vatic vision to denature the child. His children become lost possibilities, of whom Dido's *parvulus Aeneas* is the most obvious, walk-ons (*pueri innuptaeque puellae*), doomed youths (Marcellus, Pallas, Lausus). So powerful is this paradigm that murderous Turnus, paired in any case with innocent, beautiful, loving Juturna (XII. 142–60), eventually regresses to become a Troilus, laid low by a lurking Achilles (cf. *latronis*, XII. 7).[6] Ascanius / Iulus, who is (perhaps!) to

---

[2] This typically Virgilian, subjective *videt*, not so much looking "out there," as looking into the disordered imagination within, may be called the "Gyges perspective" (cf. Plato, *Rep.* II 359d). Leo Spitzer notes it of Racine's *voir*: "Die klassische Dämpfung in Racines Stil," *Archivum Romanicum* XII (1928), 394.

[3] Twinning: M. Bakhtin, Проблемы Поэтики Достоевского, pp. 38–39 and *passim*; *dédoublement*: J. Heurgon, "Un exemple peu connu de la *Retractatio* Virgilienne," *Revue des Études latines* 9 (1931), 261; cf. Knauer, p. 137, note 1.

[4] Niccolò dell' Abate (born 1509), *The Death of Eurydice* (inv. no. 5283), probably from the artist's French period (1552–71). Heurgon (above, n. 3) parallels (263–66) the disappearance of Eurydice in *Geo.* IV and of Creusa (known to the cyclic epics as Eurydice and in Ennius' version of the myth as Eurydica) in *Aen.* II.

[5] See *Augustan Propertius*, pp. 89–90. The *Aeneid* uses *caerul(e)us* 21 times.

[6] Above, p. 18. The scene is found in the Tomb of the Bulls, Tarquinia (about 530 B.C.). Cf. nos. 15, 89, 100, 131 in the Museo Archeologico, Perugia.

survive, and to whose role the poet has evidently devoted some thought, is described (X. 132-38), not to make him more vivid as a person, but because that is the sign of his generic relegation to the unreal.[7] Why otherwise are such flattering descriptions most familiar from the Greek novel?

The same is true of those vessels and guardians of the future, women, exemplified at their opposites in the human economy of the poem by Dido and Lavinia. Lavinia never speaks and Dido says too much. But Dido acquires her ultimate dimensions by passing into the realm of the Furies, persecuting her lover from beyond. Coy Lavinia is absurdly blended into one of Dido's avatars (I. 650), vindictive, capering Helen (VI. 517).[8] And, in this beyond, other women too are usually unreal; hapless or withered virgins, witches, what Lucilius and Horace would call *lamiae*, hating anything which could foster life. This transmutation affects even Juno, who, as goddess of marriage, ought on any normal calculus to represent a force for good. In Book XIV of the *Iliad*, as Hera, she can still play on her sexual charms. But in the *Aeneid* she has become *la femme d'un certain âge*, old hat verging on old hag, a characterisation picked up by Ovid (*Met.* II. 466 ff.). In the first lines of the poem we read about her motives: *et genus invisum et rapti Ganymedis honores* (I. 28). The thought of generation, the sight of youthful beauty, fires her with jealous resentment. Venus herself, even if she is no longer the spoiled brat seen in Homer's Aphrodite, shuttles uneasily between the roles of guardian of Rome's destiny and minx. It is the token of a dissociation of sensibility in the poet's own mind.

Through a glass darkly

Ἀρχόμενος σέο, Φοῖβε, παλαιγενέων κλέα φωτῶν.... Κλέος however is ambiguous, like Virgil's Fama / Eris (IV. 173-88). Epic poetry exalted for good *and* ill, as the student of Apollonius' hero still understands. At Rome, by a natural, though morally irresponsible, simplification, it had come to seem (to Cicero, for example, in the *Pro Archia*) propaganda for the glorious deeds of old heroes, and the modern patrons who were described as their successors. Yet the *Aeneid*, for all its allusions to contemporary events, is a poem of reservations, disappointments, darkness; and Vegio's *Supplementum* is the token of that. Only in it do we find Turnus fittingly memorialised, and the contrasting wedding, with its glorious promise for the

---

[7] See further below, pp. 273-77. The use of *describo* repays study: *TLL* V. 1, cols. 659-60 (lines 65 left—25 right).

[8] This is what *causa mali tanti coniunx iterum hospita* implies (VI. 93); cf. *causa mali tanti* (XI. 480), with its Homeric parallel (*Il.* XXII. 116).

58   *Chapter Three*

future, of Aeneas and Lavinia. Virgil himself, whose last word is *umbras*, "shadows," leaves all that out.

The artist needs his own space. Already at the end of the *Georgics*, Virgil was torn ("twinned") between Proteus (who tells it as it is) and Orpheus (who feels its injustice), and this split sensibility affects his manner of speaking. Just as much therefore as Ovid, also an exponent of the telling omission, of the intruded parenthesis,[9] Virgil is a master of irony. What the *Aeneid* may say is always more than it says. Since in both poets this irony affects what we hear about women and children, this is part of the poetic we must impossibly define.

Is Virgil disqualified *ab initio*? Donatus states (*Vita* §9) that he was *libidinis in pueros pronioris*, but that he rejected a liaison suggested by Varius with Plotia Hieria. Where women are concerned, he has indeed seemed sexually naive, especially if contrasted with epic Ovid. Already in Naples, by an obvious pun on the orthography "Virgilius," he was nicknamed "Parthenias" (*Vita* §11); and, in a Byzantine epigram echoing this, Dido asks why the Muses armed against her ἁγνὸν ... Μάρωνα (*App. Plan.* 151. 9), "virginal Virgil." But to extrapolate from this impression of the private man to his poetic imagination is quite wrong. Ovid and Virgil, *l'allegro* and *il penseroso*, mocker and melancholiac, are much closer in sensibility than is often acknowledged.

Some instances of this perception as it affects women and their sexuality in the *Aeneid* may be noted. What is meant, for example, by the scene in Book I (407–10) where Aeneas realises he has been talking to his own mother in disguise? *Imago* / δείκηλον (cf. Ap. Rhod., *Arg.* I. 746) is telling:

> 'quid natum totiens, crudelis tu quoque, falsis
> ludis i m a g i n i b u s ? cur dextrae iungere dextram
> non datur ac v e r a s audire et reddere voces?'
> talibus incusat ...

'Why do you so often trick your son with deceit and illusions? You are as cruel as all the others! Why may I not clasp your right hand in mine, and listen to and return voices of truth?' These reproofs he utters ...

These are the cries of the modern existentialist, the sensibility of a disappointed Orpheus.

Aeneas has landed on Scheria / Aeaea, as well as on Ithaca (Knauer). There is already a hint of an erotic *frisson*. When Odysseus arrives home, Athene appears to him modestly disguised as a young prince (*Od.* XIII.

---

[9] M. von Albrecht, *Die Parenthese in Ovids* Metamorphosen *und ihre dichterische Funktion* (Hildesheim 1964).

222). Anticipating Camilla (*Aen.* XI. 649), Venus has appeared to Aeneas as a Spartan or Thracian *virgo* in fetching hunting garb, *nuda genu* (I. 320), and in what he says we hear echoes of naked Odysseus' greeting to nubile Nausicaa (*Od.* VI. 149).

But Nausicaa and Odysseus were after all strangers. Like the knowing listener, Venus was no doubt amused when, in superfluously proffering his identity card (378–79), her Aeneas brashly outdid his Homeric model (*Od.* IX. 19–20). The whole episode is beset with these ambiguities, if not clumsinesses. Later, nettled by his implied criticism of her maternal care, Venus is enough of a mother to drop her mask and interrupt his complaints with an injunction, in essence, to stop whining (385 ff.). But then she leaves him to visit her favourite shrines in the way in which Homer's Aphrodite withdraws in embarrassment after being caught out in her affair with Ares (I. 415–17 ~ *Od.* VIII. 362–66). Aeneas of course is "Martial" enough. A mother flirting with her own son? What is the sexuality of all this?[10]

Another example, again involving *imago*, is provided by *rerumque ignarus imagine gaudet* (VIII. 730).[11] Here, Aeneas' tricky (*laeta dolis*, 393) mother has given him new arms.[12] She has coaxed them out of her husband Vulcan in return for a (rare?) bout of sex; there is the proverbial *coup de foudre* at VIII. 391–92.[13] Vulcan rises to his task *medio iam noctis abactae* (407)[14] like a woman to her weaving. Whatever it owes to the *Iliad* (XII. 433), this comparison has been modified with the aid of Apollonius (III. 291 ff.), in whose epic Medea has seen Jason for the first time and been smitten by the arrow of Eros. This is part of the technique of vertical time whereby the Alexandrian poet sometimes appears rather ineptly to compare A with B because the real and apt comparison is with an unspoken Z in the

---

[10] Knauer speaks of "epic irony" (p. 162, note 2). What of Agrippina (Tac., *Ann.* XIV. 2)?

[11] See the remarks of E. Fraenkel, *Kleine Beiträge zur klassischen Philologie* II (Rome 1964), p. 224.

[12] *Arma* is also sexual, as Ovid knew, citing *arma virumque* (*Tr.* II. 533–34); cf. Propertius' sly *in armis / qualemcumque Parim*, III. 1. 29–30. Aeneas, we saw, is sometimes Paris, stealing Dido from Iarbas, and then Lavinia from Turnus. Only a Paris could slay the Achilles of VI. 89. What does Dido have in the back of her mind at IV. 11: *quam forti pectore et armis*? The intimate conversation there between two women is after all about Aeneas' eligibility as a husband and father.

[13] The scene is modelled on *Iliad* XIV. 292 ff., where Hera *distracts* Zeus from the events on the battlefield. The simile is linked by Knauer with *Il.* XVI. 297–300. These are curious and thought-provoking parallels.

[14] What is the semantic suggestion underlying *abactae* here? Cf. *partum sibi ... abegisset*, Cicero, *Pro Cluentio* §32; *TLL s.v.*, cols. 96–97.

background (*tertium comparationis*): in this case with a Medea also to be bereft, from now on, of normal family support, and eventually stressed into becoming the murderer of her own children.

What have Jason and Vulcan, Vulcan and Medea, in common? Whatever may be his amatory stirrings, the transference in the *Aeneid* is quite inapposite to the grim god of the smithy. Yet a more powerful passion looms. It is just in the smithy that the "ignipotent" (414) god rouses the "Etnaean" Cyclopes to action (440). "My love is like the fires of Etna" was a topos suggested earlier in the poem.[15] There the volcano, coming just before Book IV, anticipated Dido's deadly fires (*exoriare aliquis nostris ex ossibus ultor / qui face Dardanios* ... 625–26; *hauriat hunc oculis ignem*, 661), later to be found on Turnus' helmet (*Aetnaeos ... ignis*, VII. 786). Here then in Book VIII is another scene shot through with quasi-Ovidian sexuality. For what sort of future will Aeneas *advena*, stealer of another man's bride, fight with these Etnaean "arms"? How will he fight? Whom will he kill? In this sensibility, love and nastiness seem inextricably mixed.

A similar instance starts with sexuality and leads on to fighting and death. When her mother Amata, recalling Hecuba's pleas to Hector in *Iliad* XXII, tries to persuade Turnus to avoid combat with the Trojans, Lavinia's face is covered with maidenly blushes (XII. 64–69):

> accepit vocem lacrimis Lavinia matris
> flagrantis perfusa genas, cui plurimus ignem   65
> subiecit rubor et calefacta per ora cucurrit.
> Indum sanguineo veluti violaverit ostro
> si quis ebur, aut mixta rubent ubi lilia multa
> alba rosa, talis virgo dabat ore colores.

> Lavinia heard her mother's protest, her burning cheeks wet with tears. A deep blush kindled fire, and suffused her hot face, like the blood-red crimson that despoiles Indian ivory or bunches of white lilies set among banks of roses. Such were the colours coming and going in her girlish face.

67. *violaverit* must be given its full, brutal force. Eight other instances of the verb from the *Aeneid* are listed in the concordances, of which four cluster in Book XI (255, 277, 591, 848), the last three followed by *vulnere*.
68–69. Cf. Horace's *breve lilium*, *Odes* I. 36. 16; *brevis ... rosa*, II. 3. 13–14. Lilies in particular have ominous associations: Norden on *Aen*. VI. 883.

In the *Iliad*, Pandarus has shot off an arrow, breaking the agreement that Menelaus and Paris will fight in single combat for Helen. It wounds Menelaus, and the blood pours down his leg, like crimson dye over ivory (IV. 141 ff.). His brother Agamemnon is led on to prophesy Troy's ultimate

---

[15] III. 639 ff.: see above, p. 23. Dido's curses (IV. 612–20) are borrowed from the *Odyssey*'s Cyclops (IX. 528–35). This links the passion of *Aeneid* IV with the end of III.

doom (164–65). In Book XII of the *Aeneid*, Tolumnius *augur* will play exactly the same part (258). Aeneas is wounded, also by an arrow and in the leg (318 ff., 384 ff.).[16] The truce which might have resolved the quarrel of Latins and Trojans is over, and the stage is now set for Turnus' death—with the eventual destruction of what city?[17] But already, even as we listen to the interchange between Turnus and Amata, and take note of Lavinia's silent blushes, all this is ineluctably determined. Personal feeling may be implied, but it is irrelevant. How heavily such destinies droop on girlish cheeks!

The supreme example of this irrelevance to Virgil's epic of the personal is recorded at I. 482. In a picture in Juno's temple at Carthage, the women of Troy are seen approaching Pallas with a robe and offering their prayers for deliverance. The goddess is obdurate:

diva solo fixos oculos aversa tenebat.

In Book VI, Dido is equally obdurate to Aeneas' entreaties (469):

illa solo fixos oculos aversa tenebat.

Diva / illa: only two syllables distinguish the two lines. Even before Dido and Aeneas have met, the stony gaze (VI. 471) is already fixed. What hope of children here? The context of the original (*Il.* VI. 286 ff.) unites many refracted aspects of the *Aeneid*.[18] When this scene is actually imitated more literally ("iterated") in Book XI (477–85), there is no need for Virgil even to mention that the petition was in vain.

In such a looking-glass, refraction takes many shapes. At the end of Book I (753) Aeneas is challenged by Dido to tell his tale. At the start of II (8–9), he points out that the late hour leaves little time for stories. He is quoting from *Odyssey* XI (330–34), where Odysseus (who will not linger on Scheria any longer than he has to) says the same thing, but in the *middle* of the narrative of his κατάβασις, just after his catalogue of fair women. The heroines he has met in Hades, who include abandoned Ariadne, are clearly in parallel with the heroines Aeneas will later meet (*Od.* XI. 326 ~ *Aen.* VI. 445), all victims of love's disease, whose culmination is Dido (450). Two

---

[16] The painting of the scene in Naples from Pompeii (House of Siricus, inv. 9009) deserves a mention, even though its quality is dismissed as "mediocre." Its fourth style dates it to the Neronian or Flavian period.

[17] Above, p. 14, Scipio to Polybius on Carthage / Rome.

[18] The Trojan women offer, for example, a *Sidonian* robe (291; cf. *Aen.* XI. 74, funeral of Pallas), and it is here that Homer tells us about the fifty bedchambers in Priam's palace (244; cf. *Aen.* II. 503). At the end of the book, Hector will take leave of his son and his wife, Andromache, δακρυόεν γελάσασα, never to speak to either again. The next mention of Astyanax will be at XXII. 500, after his father's death.

times mingle, ours and hers. For us, even before the story of Troy's fall is under way, there is a premonition, if at this stage no more, of Aeneas' *descensus Averno*, of his prior inevitable *discessus* (VI. 464) and Dido's subsequent brutal death. When that has happened, as so often, Callimachus' comedy will become Virgil's tragedy (VI. 460 ~ Catullus 66. 39). Later in VI, Virgil's Deiphobus, hacked about by Menelaus at Helen's instigation (*infelix habuit thalamus*, 521), affords a muffled reminder of Dido's fate at Aeneas' hands, and of the repeated monstrous frustrations in the poem of the *thalamus*.[19]

Odysseus, induced by Queen Arete to continue his tale, had not known that his mother Anticleia was dead (*Od.* XI. 171–73). Aeneas was not sure that Dido was dead (VI. 456–57). Dido's refusal to speak to Aeneas is like Ajax's refusal to speak to Odysseus (XI. 563). Dido therefore, switching from Arete to Anticleia to Ajax, is Nausicaa's mother, and Odysseus' mother, and Odysseus' suicidal rival. Nausicaa's own encounter with Odysseus provided a parallel for Venus' encounter with her son and for Dido's (I. 314–20 and 498–502 ~ *Od.* VI. 102 ff.). What tensions this narrative acquires if we view it as in some way like one transparency laid on top of another: in other words, as an unstable metamorphosis oscillating between different realities: *vel scaena ut versis discedat frontibus* (*Geo.* III. 24). But where does this labyrinthine sensibility leave the normality of children?

Allusion / Illusion

We hear much about Virgil's *arte allusiva*, but what about his *arte illusoria*?

Apollonius set the example of "inept" Homeric borrowings. The *Aeneid* seems often to repeat Homeric contexts in this way only to perplex and confuse. Why should Ascanius, for example, promising gifts to the already eager Nisus and Euryalus (IX. 263), be like Agamemnon, vainly promising them to the sulking Achilles (*Il.* IX. 121 ff.; cf. *Il.* X. 304 ff.)? What need of bribes here? Certainly, their lives will be cut short, like Achilles' (*Il.* XVIII. 95–96). But what can such a pair do at best except act as messengers? What in fact do they accomplish to rival the Δολωνεία, or the capture of the Palladium? Is Ascanius Agamemnon (*Il.* IX. 121–56) or Hector (*Il.* X. 328–31) here? Heroic Aeneas may have shouldered his father and his Shield, but, as with Lavinia, how weightily such identities press upon the young!

---

[19] Knauer, pp. 114–17. On *thalamus*, above, p. 11, note 23. This is another instance of the musical / cinematic mixing or scrambling of motifs.

Often the Homeric analogue is evoked obliquely, suggestively. A complex of Homeric ideas may be re-arranged in a different way by Virgil, mixed or reshuffled among his characters. This was just noted at the beginning of *Aeneid* II, which already looked ahead to the catabasis of VI; and in Book VI, mangled Deiphobus (494–95) offered a parallel to mangled Dido, *recens a vulnere* (450). Individual roles may be interchanged. In the centre of Book VI, Dido is Ajax. But is Aeneas Ajax, as he urges his son, on the only occasion when he speaks directly to him throughout the entire poem, to learn valour and true endurance from him, but his fortune from others (XII. 435–36)?[20] Is Turnus rather Ajax, defending the city against Aeneas as Ajax defends the Greek ships against the assaults of Hector in *Iliad* XV (674 ff.)? Virgil throws these confusions at us because the world and experience throw up similar confusions. This is the poetry of an imperial people who often had to make rough choices on slim evidence. One sees the soldiers and administrators in a new light. "Between the motion / And the act / Falls the Shadow" (Eliot). Theirs was a world of shadows.

The device may also be used on other epic material. When Dido describes the priestess who, she alleges, has shown her a charm to make or break her love for Aeneas, she speaks of her as lulling to sleep the serpent guarding the apples of the Hesperides (IV. 486). Why would she do that? The epithet *soporiferum* is another piece of "ineptitude," and the motif is set in play because it is to remind us of Medea (*Arg*. IV. 156 ff.). Later, contradicting other versions of the myth, Apollonius says that the apples of the Hesperides were taken, not by Atlas, but directly by Heracles (IV. 1432 ff.),[21] and Virgil borrowed a simile from that episode for Dido. But it is Aeneas who is Hercules! We will see that Dido is certainly Deianeira ("husband destroyer") as she dies.[22]

---

[20] According to Macrobius (VI. 1. 58), this was an echo of the words used by Sophocles' Ajax (vv. 550–51 = Accius, fr. 123, W.) as he goes off to commit suicide.

[21] The vase painted by Asteas of Paestum, now in Naples (4th c., inv. 81847), shows a Hesperid actually distracting the serpent with some sort of *offa* while another collects apples for Heracles. How different the gentle humour of this charming picture from the horror which Apollonius describes! Similarly, an Athenian red-figure hydria (370–360 B.C.) in the British Museum (GR 1866.4-18.243, Vase E 227) shows a Heracles seated among the Hesperides while Eros, standing on his shoulder, hands him the golden apples. A small statue also in the BM (GR 1805.7-3.38, Bronze 827) from Byblos (Lebanon), dated to the first century A.D., shows Heracles at the tree holding three apples with the serpent behind still apparently unharmed, and many apples still in place. Apollonius chose a violent rendering of the incident, and it is he whom Virgil follows.

[22] Below, p. 129.

The *Aeneid* thus becomes a poem of allusion *and* illusion, both sides of the same coin.

It is a poem of allusion, because, as has been noted since antiquity, it depends for its full understanding on a knowledge of Homer's and Apollonius' epics, although of more Greek poetry than that; and too on acquaintance with Roman Republican poetry, both epic and dramatic.

It is a poem of illusion because such dependence immediately magnifies the polyphony (peralogicality) inherent in any great work of art. If Virgil uses Attic tragedy, for example, as a sounding box, how can we suppose that even the most attentive ear now catches all his notes? Or that some caught notes are not imposed by the undulating contours of the baffle board, irrational or transrational echoes (Roiron)?

Greek epic in particular lends a complexity of reference to the *Aeneid* by which there is constant blending ("contamination") of contexts and characters. If Virgil points back to the Homeric mirror,[23] in his new creation the once gleaming surface is found cracked and fissured. A Miltonic comparison might be to "storied windows richly dight," whose Roman colours absorb the clear Greek sunlight and break it into a thousand patterns, like rainbow Iris, *mille trahens varios adverso sole colores*. It is evidence of the Roman desire to fashion and control an inner space.

And it is here that Virgil's tragic irony finds particular scope. Propertius' boastful *maius Iliade* (II. 34. 66), meant as a compliment, is true only if *maius* implies more room for the gap between promise and fulfilment. Sometimes this irony of implied comparisons is devastating. At the death of Camilla / Patroclus, for example, her skulking assassin Arruns, in imploring the gods to guide his weapon to its target, echoes the prayer with which Homer's Achilles prays for his Patroclus' *safe* return from the battle.[24] Whatever the Alexandrian precedent for this use of contrasting contexts, perhaps it is Virgil's own temperament which lends to it throughout the *Aeneid* such sad bias.

The *Aeneid* is made even more convoluted by its trick of *internal* allusion, also something which the poet (like his admired Lucretius) could have learned from Homer. A striking example is *solvuntur frigore membra* (only I. 92 and XII. 951). The first time the phrase occurs it introduces Aeneas' name, and describes his panic-stricken reaction to the storm

---

[23] Pindar's ἔσοπτρον tellingly occurs in an ode (*Nem.* 7. 14) debating Homer's "lies." No one will suppose that Pindar offers a univocal alternative. Cf. "Pindar Through the Looking-Glass," *Eos* LXXXIX (2002), 233–53.

[24] Knauer, pp. 310–14.

unleashed by Aeolus.[25] From that he will be rescued, since history has a use for him. At the end, the phrase describes dying Turnus, for whom history has no use, any more than it has for Dido or Camilla or Juturna or, in the last analysis, for the Pallas whom Aeneas is so determined to avenge. Turnus is discarded, like Camilla (XI. 831 = XII. 952), not because of epic necessity, and not because of any crime of his (which at worst in this *alta tragedia* would be a ἁμαρτία[26]), but because on Virgil's reading Jupiter and the Fates will it so. Pallas dies—it is the final end of the pastoral world prefigured by Meliboeus in the first eclogue—because Rome's empire can find no room for Arcadian shepherds. Equally, it can find no room for pastoral Carthage.[27]

Metamorphosis

It has been said that the only worthwhile criticism of poetry is made by poets. In that case, Ovid's reading of the *Aeneid*, and more largely the commentary on epic method which his own epic offers, gains in relevance.[28]

Varium et mutabile semper femina. Cheating Mercury applies to women a sensibility governing much of the *Aeneid*. If Aristaeus had struggled with a metamorphosing adversary in the *Georgics* (IV. 406-11), right at the end, Aeneas seems to expect Turnus to resort to something similar (*verte omnis tete in facies* etc., XII. 891-93; cf. *quae memet in omnia verti* of Juno, VII. 309). Earlier, Diomedes, advising the Latins not to meddle with the Trojans, notes the transformation endured by his men, which he traces to his own assault on Venus (XI. 271-77).[29] If then critics are embarrassed by the episode of the transformation of Aeneas' ships into sea-nymphs in book IX, absurd on any realistic calculus, perhaps we have merely an example of what Formalist critics call "la dénudation du procédé," the "laying bare" of a device which elsewhere is used less obtrusively, but still is pervasive. Ovid felt no such embarrassment (*Met.* XIV. 546 ff.).

---

[25] The relevant parallel however is not so much to be found in *Odyssey* X as in *Il.* XV. 24-28. This adaptation introduces the *Aeneid's* Hercules theme (below, Appendix, pp. 329 ff.).

[26] Below, p. 227 ff.

[27] It can play with pastoral motifs (even on the Ara Pacis) nostalgically, artificially. That is a different thing. Messalla and Tibullus felt this gap. — On pastoral Carthage, below, p. 102.

[28] Gianluigi Baldo, *Dall' Eneide alle* Metamorfosi*: il codice epico di Ovidio* (Studi, testi, documenti 7, Padova 1995). See further "Ovid's Epic, Picasso's Art," *Latomus* LXII (2003), 362-72.

[29] Lycophron associates this episode with the theatre: θεατρομόρφῳ πρὸς κλίτει γεωλόφῳ, *Alexandra*, 602.

Metamorphosis was biological. It was religious. The Greek Church celebrates a metamorphosis as one of its twelve principal feasts.[30] To question another world with rigid instruments, calibrated according to a previously defined "logical" scale, is to ensure that the only answers received will be equally rigid, equally pre-defined. The readiness to allow that other to dictate its response, signalled by the wearing of masks, vestments, even the toga at the Ludi publici (of which Victorian "Sunday best" was a last survival), the use of a liturgical language *vix sacerdotibus suis satis intellecta*,[31] the resort to any kind of estrangement, prepares at least for the peralogical, uncanny, transrational, שׁרד.

Metamorphosis was a feature of the Roman imagination at least from the days of Plautus, whose braggart slaves slip into and out of a motley array of mythological identifications; and in the Augustan age perhaps the greatest metamorphosis of all was that of youthful Octavian first into Caesar / Alexander, then into Pompey and the venerable, "august" Father of his Country.

It was another device with which the Hellenistic poets had toyed. Parthenius, Virgil's adviser *in Graecis* (Macrobius, *Sat.* V. 17. 18), was himself the author of a *Metamorphoses*.[32] Virgil had signalled his own interest in metamorphosis as early as the sixth eclogue (41 ff.), a blueprint of his future poetic ambitions. It is there, for example, that he pays homage to Callimachus (3–5), who in the Preface to the *Aetia* had expressed his disdain for the homerising pastiche written to glorify kings and heroes which in his day passed for the continuance of the epic tradition—and whose first book of *Aetia*, anticipating the path which Virgil himself would tread, found the poet speaking rather of "georgic" Hesiod and his dream.

Callimachus did not mean to abandon Homer. The *Hecale* adumbrates a different technique of using the Homeric analogue.[33] In this sort of *dédoublement* there is more than mere borrowing. When, in the course of the story, young prince Theseus, whose first adventure this is, comes to the hut of old Hecale, he is like both Odysseus and Telemachus coming to the hut of the swineherd Eumaeus. The parallel with the youthful Telemachus is obvious enough. That between the fresh-faced stripling and the wily,

---

[30] Μετεμορφώθη ἔμπροσθεν αὐτῶν, NT Matthew 17:2. For the artistic tradition, James Elkins, *Pictures of the Body: Pain and Metamorphosis* (Stanford 1999); Nigel Spivey, *Enduring Creation: Art, Pain and Fortitude* (London 2000).

[31] Quintilian I. 6. 40: cf. "Thou art a scholar—speak to it, Horatio." *Hamlet* I. 1. 40

[32] H. Lloyd-Jones and P. Parsons, *Supplementum Hellenisticum* (Berlin–New York 1983), p. 304, no. 636–37.

[33] See Pfeiffer ad frr. 239, 241 = Hollis frr. 28, 30. Hollis has an interesting appendix on "The Hospitality Theme" (pp. 341 ff.).

grizzled Odysseus must raise a smile. But what would Theseus become in the course of his heroic career, as he abandoned Ariadne, involuntarily brought about the death of his own father—and ended in hell (*Aen*. VI. 618)? Callimachus raises these contrasting possibilities about the heroic by the simple trick of blending, with Homer's aid, one hero into another; in other words, by metamorphosis.

Virgil's sixth eclogue already shows this Callimachean technique. Gallus receives Linus' pipes, with which Hesiod, the *Ascraeus senex*, "drew ungainly ash-trees down from the mountainside" (71). Hesiod certainly has programmatic, Callimachean significance here. But it was not Hesiod who used to captivate trees. That was Orpheus, as the third eclogue already told us (*silvasque sequentis*, 46). So Apollonius, *Arg*. I. 28–32, 34:

φηγοὶ δ'ἀγριάδες κείνης ἔτι σήματα μολπῆς
ἀκτῇ Θρηικίῃ Ζώνης ἔπι τηλεθόωσαι
ἑξείης στιχόωσιν ἐπήτριμοι, ἅς ὅγ' ἐπιπρό
θελγομένας φόρμιγγι κατήγαγε Πιερίηθεν.
Ὀρφέα μὲν δὴ τοῖον ἑῶν ἐπαρωγὸν ἀέθλων...
δέξατο....

And even now, as a sign of that singing, wild oaks still grow along the shore of Thracian Zone, in serried ranks, which of old time were spellbound by his lyre and brought down from Pieria. Such was Orpheus, whose aid in his contest Jason welcomed.

Horace echoes the motif (*Odes* I. 12. 7–12; cf. Calpurnius Siculus, *Ecl*. 4. 64 ff.), and, for all his small Latin and less Greek, Shakespeare still perhaps knew it.[34]

In the eclogue, there is an implied hint about the sort of poet Gallus strove to be: Hesiodic (in Callimachus' and Euphorion's sense) yes, but also Orphic: lyrical, musical and even perhaps vatic, given that, for Horace (*A.P.* 392–400), Orpheus is eventually the principal *vates*. Scholars treat with reserve the report that, at the end of the *Georgics*, the story of Orpheus and Eurydice, told by vatic, metamorphosing Proteus, replaced some sort of *laudes Galli*, but we may at least ask whether, in the tragic downfall of Orpheus, Virgil noted some sort of poetic parallel to Gallus' own fall from grace, and suicide. Had he foreseen this right from *Eclogue* 6? But, unless a highly-strung Gallus had already chosen (and meant to act out?) this identity for himself, how? At the very least, Orpheus' loss of Eurydice continued to influence Aeneas's loss of Creusa / Eurydica.[35]

---

[34] "Orpheus with his lute made trees / And the mountain tops that freeze / Bow themselves when he did sing ... " (*All is True* III. 1. 3).

[35] Above, p. 56, n. 4.

Metamorphosis and Eros[36]

Virgil has been called the greatest of the Augustan love-poets and, because of his *Eoae* or *Catalogue of Fair Women*, Hesiod has been taken as the ancestor of this sort of poetry. The *Georgics*, themselves Hesiodic, offer extraordinary insights into the erotic world. While ostensibly reporting the fate of the farmer's animals, Virgil dwells on the universality of the sexual impulse, enigmatically and distortingly alluding to the human while he does so. An instance is offered by the hinted tale of Hero and Leander in Book III (258 ff.), where the names of the lovers in this famous story are not used.[37]

This sensibility persists. In the *Aeneid*, Virgil actually links Books VII and XII with reminiscences drawn from the same passage in the *Georgics*. The real bulls of the *Georgics*, fighting over a beautiful heifer,[38] metamorphose into Aeneas and Turnus, fighting over Lavinia, whose sacrificial status is thus guaranteed.

The connection is made, partly by repeated language, and partly by repeated imagery. In book VII of the *Aeneid*, the peaceful relations between the Trojans and the Latins are ruptured by Ascanius' chance slaying of a pet deer (Iphigenia motif). Resentment is fanned by Juno, and at last serious fighting breaks out between the two sides. It is just like a small wave, growing into a huge breaker (*Aen.* VII. 528–30):

> fluctus uti primo coepit cum albescere vento,
> paulatim sese tollit mare et altius undas
> erigit, inde imo consurgit ad aethera fundo.

> As when a wave begins to grow white before the first puff of wind: slowly the sea swells, thrusting its waters higher. Then it surges from its lowest depths to high heaven.

But this is the simile which in the *Georgics* described the surprise onslaught on his unsuspecting rival by the bull at first defeated (III. 219–23, 237–41):

---

[36] "Ce qui est en jeu dans l'érotisme est toujours une dissolution des formes constituées," Georges Bataille, *L'Érotisme* (Paris 1957), p. 25. But Eros may be deadly. The same author notes (p. 17): "En effet, bien que l'activité érotique soit d'abord une exubérance de la vie, l'objet de cette recherche psychologique indépendante ... du souci de reproduction de la vie, n'est pas étranger à la mort." And if Virgil has suppressed or muffled this *souci*?

[37] Nor by Byron: "When Love, who sent, forgot to save / The young, the beautiful, the brave, / The lonely hope of Sestos' daughter": *The Bride of Abydos* (1813), canto II. 3–5.

[38] The transference of this image to the human is presupposed in the story of Io (cf. Bacchylides 19 [18]. 24; Eur., *Supp.* 629). See Fraenkel's note on *Aga.* 1125 ("oracular language"); OT Amos 4:1 פרות, and πόρτις / πόρις in Lycophron (*Alex.* 102, 184, 320).

pascitur in magna Sila formosa iuvenca:
illi alternantes multa vi proelia miscent   220
vulneribus crebris; lavit ater corpora sanguis,
versaque in obnixos urgentur cornua vasto
cum gemitu; reboant silvaeque et longus Olympus ...

fluctus uti medio coepit cum albescere ponto,
longius ex altoque sinum trahit, utque volutus
ad terras immane sonat per saxa neque ipso
monte minor procumbit, at ima exaestuat unda   240
verticibus nigramque alte subiectat harenam.

A fair heifer grazes on tall Sila. Turn and turn about, the bulls ply their combat with all their strength, inflicting many a wound. The crimson blood bathes their bodies, their horns push against their confronting foe amid desolating groans, re-echoed by the woods and broad sky ...

As when a wave out at sea begins to grow white: far out on the deep it ruffles the surface, then rolling ashore crashes on the rocks, and is tall as a mountain when it falls. It boils up from the depths as it crests, and tosses high the black sand.

And in *Aeneid* XII (715–22):

ac velut ingenti Sila summove Taburno
cum duo conversis inimica in proelia tauri
frontibus incurrunt, pavidi cessere magistri,
stat pecus omne metu mutum, mussantque iuvencae
quis nemori imperitet, quem tota armenta sequantur;
illi inter sese magna vi vulnera miscent
cornuaque obnixi infigunt et sanguine largo
colla armosque lavant, gemitu nemus omne remugit.

And as when on tall Sila or Taburnus' top two bulls rush, heads lowered, into the bitter fray, the herdsmen retreating in panic, all the herd dumb with fear, the heifers lowing—who is to be the new master of the pasture, leader of all the herds? They with mighty force join in their gory combat, pushing hard and sinking in their horns, a bloody tide awash on their necks and shoulders, while all the forest echoes to their groaning.

The poet has mined his own work for structural props. Once again, everything is fore-ordained. Even as the fight begins in Book VII, with the help of the *Georgics* we are reminded of its predestined end in XII. Externally, the simile is certainly borrowed from the *Iliad* (IV. 422). But Virgil's self-borrowings help to make over his ostensibly military epic into a poem about love—but love seen as blind, demeaning, "infuriating," and for women, deadly. *Nunc age, qui reges, Erato*....

Metamorphosis in the *Aeneid* is continually associated in this way with *eros*. Diomedes' bird–followers (XI. 273) were remarked. Cupavo (X. 186), with swan feathers in his crest, is the son of Cycnus. Love is to blame for his father's fate (X. 187–93):

Chapter Three

> cuius olorinae surgunt de vertice pennae
> (crimen, Amor, vestrum) formaeque insigne paternae.
> namque ferunt luctu Cycnum Phaethontis amati,
> populeas inter frondes umbramque sororum
> dum canit et maestum Musa solatur amorem,
> canentem molli pluma duxisse senectam
> linquentem terras et sidera voce sequentem.

Swan feathers spring from his head—Love's guilty mark, and the token of his father's beauty. Story tells that Cycnus, the Swan Prince, grieving for his beloved Phaethon, sang among the leafy poplars and the shade cast by the transformed sisters, consoling his love with sad lament. So he drew upon himself the white down of old age, and soared above the earth on wings of song to the stars.

Apollonius had handled the fall of Phaethon with romantic suggestivity (IV. 596 ff.). The virtuosity of Virgil's passage, its allusivity, its rhetoric, its verbal music and word-play, its pastoral fantasy—and its assertion of Love's guilt—are the product of a quasi-Alexandrian taste which Ovid's *Metamorphoses* will relish.

Elsewhere, the element of the erotic returns in more suggestive guise. An instance is Amata's snake, and its sexual foreplay. An ambivalent, even healthful symbol (שחנ, ןושחנ) is interpreted *in malam partem* (VII. 349–53):

> ille inter vestis et levia pectora lapsus
> volvitur attactu nullo, fallitque furentem
> vipeream inspirans animam; fit tortile collo
> aurum ingens coluber, fit longae taenia vittae
> innectitque comas et membris lubricus errat ...

The snake glided between her robes and smooth breasts, moving without touching and, unnoticed by the mad queen, breathed into her the spirit of the viper. It changed itself into the gold necklace hanging big about her neck, into the braids of her long garland; it wound around her hair and traced a slippery path over her limbs.

In the continuation at v. 356 we should perhaps therefore read *concepit* (R):

> necdum animus toto concepit pectore flammam.

Her spirit through all her breast was not yet pregnant with flame.

percepit Mynors pudibundus.

The child of this nightmare union is fire (*ignem*, 355; Vulcan / Cacus theme). Later, Turnus, as was remarked, has an "Etnaean," surreal device on his helmet. Is it still alive (VII. 785–88)?

> cui triplici crinita iuba galea alta Chimaeram
> sustinet Aetnaeos efflantem faucibus ignis;
> tam magis illa fremens et tristibus effera flammis
> quam magis effuso crudescunt sanguine pugnae.

His tall helmet had a triple crest, surmounted by a chimera breathing Etna's fires from its jaws. The noisier its scream, the deadlier its wild flames, the more the combat grows fresh with flowing blood.

He also carries a metamorphosed Io on his shield (789–92), a version perhaps of Dido / Diana—and of *Aegyptia coniunx* (VIII. 688). She was the ancestress of the Danaids, seen on the belt he took from Pallas, and in that act closed about himself the circle of myth. For Aeschylus' (or his son Euphorion's?) Prometheus, she was the living proof of how far Zeus' lust and cruel indifference to human suffering could go.

In all these cases, there is a primitive coalescence of the human individual with the totemic animal, sometimes with an ugly, even loathsome creature. Turnus' *Aetnaeus* in particular was a loaded epithet within the economy of the poem. But Amata's snakes are also part of a recurrent pattern.[39] Both these allusions are erotic.

The poem indeed begins with metamorphosis: Venus as a Spartan or Tyrian hunting maid, Cupid as Ascanius—so that while the childless queen Dido fondles him on her lap she may drink in the fires of passion. How incredibly heartless it is to play like this on the queen's maternal instincts so as to destroy her, and how much even in these early lines the theme of erotic deception and cheating (cf. *falsi ... genitoris*, I. 716), which will dominate Book IV, is already heard.

We are the clothes we wear. By his gift of finery once worn by Helen (I. 650), unfaithful to Menelaus, Aeneas changes Dido into someone unfaithful to Sychaeus (*Aen.* IV. 552; Dante, *Inf.* 5. 61–62)—and changes himself into Paris (IV. 215). How else could he kill his Achilles (VI. 57, 89)?

Homer's Circe was an expert at ringing changes. She is found in the *Aeneid* more often than appears.[40] One of the most extraordinary moments comes at the very beginning of Aeneas' relationship with the Latins. King Latinus presents him with horses (VII. 280–83):

>absenti Aeneae currum geminosque iugalis
>semine ab aetherio spirantis naribus ignem,
>illorum de gente patri quos daedala Circe
>supposita de matre nothos furata creavit.

For absent Aeneas he gave a chariot, and twin horses, of heavenly stock, breathing fire from their nostrils, from that bastard line which crafty Circe stole by breeding to their sire a substitute dam.

---

[39] See above, p. 70.

[40] The effect of her charms had long been allegorised (Xenophon, *Mem.* I. 3. 7; cf. Horace, *Epp.* I. 2. 23). Vatic (III. 358) Helenus mentions her (III. 386), which explains why he does not mention Dido. See below, pp. 145 ff.

281. *haec loca non tauri spirantes naribus ignem*, Geo. II. 140.

Daedala, nothos: these Greek words verge on satire.

The Aeneadae ostensibly sail by her island (VII. 10). In fact they were already on it when they landed in Africa, as parallels with *Odyssey* X in *Aeneid* I show (Knauer). Dido is no one Greek heroine, but among her guises is that of Circe, and her first words to Aeneas are adapted from Circe's surprised words to Odysseus in Homer (*Aen.* I. 617 ~ *Od.* X. 330).

It transpires that Circe is an ancestress of King Latinus via her marriage to Picus. In a story later appealing to Ovid (*Met.* XIV. 320 ff.), she had turned (*versum, Aen.* VII. 190) her husband into a magpie (189–91):

> quem capta cupidine coniunx
> aurea percussum virga versumque venenis
> fecit avem Circe sparsitque coloribus alas.

Under love's sway his wife all-golden struck him with her wand after she had transmuted him with her potions, turning him into a bird, and spangling his wings with her hues.

190: The motif is obviously old. Gilgamesh VI may be compared (Ishtar and the *allallu*-bird, George, p. 49).
190: *aurea* here is a nominative. Circe does not have a golden wand in the *Odyssey*. For *aurea* in erotic language, cf. *Venus aurea*, X. 16; Horace's Pyrrha, *Odes* I. 5. 9 with Nisbet and Hubbard's note.; *thalamo ... aureo, Aen.* VIII. 372. Circe has the added claim of being the Sun's daughter: *aureus sol* is as old as Ennius (*Ann.* 87, Sk. He notes Ovid, *Met.* VII. 663).

In marrying Lavinia therefore Aeneas is uniting his lineage with Circe's. It was a *liaison dangéreuse*, since her transformations were dehumanising (VII. 15–20; translation below, p. 147):

> hinc exaudiri gemitus iraeque leonum
> vincla recusantum et saeva sub nocte rudentum,
> saetigerique sues atque in praesepibus ursi
> saevire ac formae magnorum ululare luporum,
> quos hominum ex facie dea saeva potentibus herbis
> induerat Circe in vultus ac terga ferarum.

But the Circean poet will use all these animal comparisons—lions, boars, bears, wolves—for his own heroes, locked in Italian combat! *Hinc exaudiri gemitus* (15) is from the torments of hell (VI. 557). This passage, with its repeated *saev-*, prepares the way for the *saevus* used of Aeneas at the end of the poem (*saevo ... pectore*, 888; *saevi monimenta doloris*, 945).[41]

The *Aeneid* actually invents a metamorphosis which appealed not only to

---

[41] J. W. Mackail notes (on X. 813) *saevus* as a leitmotif for Aeneas introduced after the death of Pallas. However, its earlier uses in the poem repay study (61 examples *in toto*). When Aeneas applies it to Hector (I. 99), it perhaps echoes the ἀνδροφόνοιο of *Il.* VI. 498 and other passages.

Dante (*Inf.* 13. 31 ff.) but also to Ariosto (*O. F.* VI. 51 ff.). At the start of his travels, Aeneas lands in Thrace, and is engaged in sacrifice on the shore when he plucks a branch from a cornel bush growing there ("Golden Bough" motif: cf. VI. 210; XII. 208, 787). Blood oozes from the wound, and a voice from the thicket tells him that this clump of trees is growing over the body of young prince Polydorus, sent by Priam to the care of his supposed friend Polymestor when it looked as if the war was going against the Trojans—and treacherously murdered for the treasure he brought with him. This is another littoral death, like that of Priam. The copse has sprung up from the spear shafts planted and left in the child's body. There is nothing here that would not have delighted Ovid (cf. *Met.* II. 360), but whereas Ovid inclines to the comic, Virgil inevitably tends to the tragic. The grotesque, so innate to the Roman imagination, has been turned towards the ominous and even horrifying. When Seneca does this, we are inclined to regard it as proof of the "decadent taste" of his age. What we have to understand is that it is a recurrent feature of an aesthetic which both modifies the conventional picture of the Romans as lawyers and soldiers, and puts their taste into a menu for which our age has found a particular relish, that of "black comedy" (*comédie noire*), or the theatre of cruelty. Scholars are slowly coming to terms with these insights. The Romans were not Victorians.[42]

Polydorus, murdered for gold like Sychaeus, is taken from Book III, often regarded as one of the most tedious of the poem, but in fact one of the liveliest—if the principle of metamorphosis is understood. If the topos "my love is like the fires of Etna" is already found, as we saw, in Horace's *Epodes* (17. 33), the whole final episode, with its mysterious noises (584; cf. *causa latet*, V. 5) and lurking moon (587), may be seen as a preparation for the hidden fires of Dido's Carthage (*caeco carpitur igni*, IV. 2; *Dianae*, I. 499, IV. 511). Achaemenides, whom editors have wanted to expel as a poor duplicate of Sinon in II, reinforces the example of what happens if one is too kind to strangers. That is a lesson which Dido was also to learn in real life. For her, Aeneas was a hapless Sinon whose armies would however one day burn her city. But what was Aeneas' point of view? Thanks to that same Achaemenides, the Aeneadae nearly fall foul of the ominous Cyclops, whose kin could only be harnessed to more Roman ends in Book VIII (440) by his mother's ardours. Aeneas' subsequent encounter with a metaphorical

---

[42] If one thinks of Charles Dickens and his grotesque figures, perhaps the Victorians were not Victorians either. His interest in the theatre is repeatedly emphasised by Peter Ackroyd, *Dickens* (London 1990). Angus Wilson cites "O! the Mask!" from the recurring nightmares of Dickens' childhood: *The World of Charles Dickens* (Harmondsworth 1972), p. 9.

Etna in the passionate queen, and his misplaced generosity, are just as much a threat to his hopes for some kind of Italian Troy as Sinon was to the burned and doomed Troy he has left, or as Achaemenides unwittingly was to his fleet. Eventually, Dido threatens Aeneas with an *ultor*, whom in hindsight the Romans knew to have been Hannibal. But the one-eyed marauder[43] who had come over the Alps was in his way a Cyclops as grim as any that haunted Etna. Can the beautiful queen ultimately have posed such a danger to the Aeneadae? For all her courtesy, the answer for them must be "Yes." The writing is like one of those puzzle pictures in which the figures alter as one alters one's point of view.

"I laughed till I cried" is familiar enough. But does Homer's Andromache with her baby by her side prove that I also cry till I laugh? Certainly, metamorphosis can never be final, for that would be to deny its nature. *Feret haec aliquam tibi fama salutem* (I. 463). This is said by an Aeneas contemplating the record of Trojan suffering found on the wall of Juno's temple at Carthage. That is both past and future. The goddess may plot those iterations, but the disasters of one age can in fact provide a vatic warning for another. There is need of a "leap into another dimension" (перескок в другое измерение, Eisenstein) to escape from the Homeric paradigm. Augustus furnished that escape. But, when it came, which of Troy's children was at his side?

---

[43] *Ipse Hannibal aeger oculis ... altero oculo capitur*, Livy, XXII. 2. 10–11.

IV

CHILDREN AND VIRGIL'S EPIC TECHNIQUE–II

The Aeneid *and Music*

There is no adequate understanding of the *Aeneid* unless we bear in mind all the time that Virgil is taking for granted in his listeners knowledge of the vast Homeric corpus, and playing modern variations on it. But he does not write Homeric pastiche, or crudely adapt (as has been said of Ennius) the deeds and speeches of gods and heroes to consuls and tribunes. He alters and implicitly comments on his material in such a way as to betray the artificial nature of what he is doing (the tone which in Ovid manifests itself as fauxnaïf). He lives in two worlds. He tells a heroic story while preserving a sensibility for unheroic, unspectacular values, the chief of which is his sympathy with *mortales aegri* (*Geo.* I. 237; *Aen.* II. 268, X. 274, XII. 850) or *miseri* (*Geo.* III. 66; *Aen.* XI. 182) as the often unwitting instruments of the gods.

This complexity includes, as we saw, sexual awareness. The first time we hear of her (I. 344, 351), widowed Dido is *misera* and *aegra*, "Gygean," introspective terms. It is this tension between the martial story told and the poet's modern ("Parthenian," feminine?) sensibilities which makes him akin to the Alexandrians, and intrudes the emotive element which forces one all the time to look for musical analogies to his techniques.[1]

Numeros memini, si verba tenerem. The *Eclogues'* Lycidas spoke for his creator. The music is secure. It is the words which are elusive, spinning away from finite rationality. In the *Aeneid*'s first line *cano* already points to music. The first person surprises,[2] since Homer had used the second. But

---

[1] Cf. *Augustus and the New Poetry*, p. 259.

[2] Cf. *cantabo* in Horace's parody, *A.P.* 137. Callimachus' κλείω is equally sarcastic (*Epigr.* 6. 2). But here one must think rather of Hesiod's ἀρχώμεθ' ἀείδειν (*Theog.* 1) and of Apollonius' hymnic Φοῖβε ... μνήσομαι (*Arg.* I. 1–2); cf. ᾄσομαι, *Hom. hy.* 32 (Εἰς Σελήνην), 19. The Sumerian version of *Bilgames and the Bull of Heaven* appears to start with the first person (*Epic of Gilgamesh*, ed. George, p. 169. Further examples in West, *East Face*, pp. 593 ff.). — Ennius who (surprisingly, in view of the Homeric paradigm) does not use

cano is Apolline, Augustan: vatic / prophetic as well as musical (*augurium citharamque dabat*, XII. 394). Such connotations are unsettling. The *vates* cannot live only here and now, and music anyway is "systematic ambiguity" (*die Zweideutigkeit als System*, Thomas Mann). The *Aeneid's* prophecies incongruously join the mythical past with the revolutionary present. Its music, always famous (*Vita Verg. Don.* §29), may swell to the operatic, even melodramatic. Every listener knows its arias and recitatives. The question is: did an epic technique of this sort—polysemous, polychronous, "polyprosopic,"[3]—make it difficult or impossible for the poet to write convincingly about children?

The Aeneid *and Theatre*

When we try to define more precisely what that technique was, "classicising" answers of the kind already developing in later antiquity, and once again becoming fashionable, are not helpful. Both Virgil's *Aeneid* and Ovid's *Metamorphoses* have to be seen as related instances of Augustan and Roman art. Ovid, who compares his exilic poetry, deprived of its Roman audience, with dancing in the dark,[4] points our first efforts to come to terms with that art towards theatre, masque, altered states. In the Roman aesthetic, these were not disparate concepts.

The Augustans had naturally preserved the profound interest of their Republican ancestors in the stage, which at Rome had always been linked with the fortunes of the great, that is, with politics.[5] Pompey, aware of this, and of the political importance of theatricals in the Hellenistic world, had built Rome's first permanent theatre (Lucan I. 132–33; VII. 13–19). Julius had planned a grandiose theatre at the foot of the Mons Tarpeius (Suet., *Jul.* 44). Augustus, who is reported to have spoken of his own life as a mime (Suet., *Aug.* 99),[6] for the same reasons both repaired Pompey's Theatre and built the Theatre of Marcellus (*Vita Verg. Don.* §26), completed

canere of himself, refers the verb instead to the despised *Faunei vatesque* (*Ann.* 207, Sk.), whence vatic Virgil rescues it. See *Roman Catullus*, pp. 432–34.

[3] Πολυπρόσωπος of Pylades, Plutarch, *quaest. conv.* II. 711F: Athenaeus I. 20e; cf. *solusque per omnis / ibit personas, et turbam reddet in uno*, Manilius V. 482–83. Here is where Laevius' curious composite *Protesilaudamia* from his *Erotopaegnia* may fit. Παίγνιον is a t.t. for a kind of mime (Plut., *loc. cit.* 712E). On the historical plane, Cicero's *senseram ... quam idem essent* (above, p. 12, n. 29) is again relevant.

[4] *Ex Ponto* IV. 2. 33–36; contrast *Tristia* II. 519.

[5] T. Bollinger, *Theatralis Licentia* (Winterthur 1969).

[6] For the "Room of the Masks" in his house cf. Erika Simon, *Augustus. Kunst und Leben in Rom um die Zeitenwende* (Munich 1986), p. 218.

about 13 B.C. That same year he also allowed L. Cornelius Balbus to inaugurate the theatre again being uncovered by archaeologists.[7] Virgil attended the theatre (Tac., *Dial*. 13. 2), and his *Eclogues* were performed there (*Vita Don.*, *loc. cit.*), actually, if we may believe Servius (ad *Ecl*. 6. 11), by Gallus' old flame, the mime-actress Lycoris. Among the works of his contemporaries, Varius' *Thyestes* and Ovid's *Medea*, both plays with murdered children, are singled out for praise (Tac., *Dial*. 12). Yet Varius, like Ovid, was also an epic poet (Hor., *Sat*. I. 10. 43–44; *Odes* I. 6).

This Roman stage was more than Attic. Horace, vainly on guard against the grotesque at the very start of his *Ars Poetica*,[8] also warns his contemporaries against gross theatrical excess. Were these warnings "academic"? What would have been the point of that? In fact, the year 22 B.C. has particular importance at Rome, not for the conventional theatre, but for the pantomime (see below). This was the year when Horace may have been working on the *Ars*, after putting out *Odes* I–III.[9] His remarks represent a curious effort to adapt Callimachus to contemporary Roman realities—realities which, it is argued below, have much to do with the *Aeneid* (*A.P.* 185–88):

> ne pueros coram populo Medea trucidet,
> aut humana palam coquat exta nefarius Atreus,
> aut in avem Procne vertatur, Cadmus in anguem.
> quodcumque ostendis mihi sic, incredulus odi.

> No Medea must butcher her children in front of the throng, no vicious Atreus publicly cook human entrails. Procne must not change into a bird, nor Cadmus into a snake. Whatever you show me in that way, I find unconvincing and a waste of time.

185. *Populus* renders Callimachus' πολλοί (*Epigr*. 28. 2; cf. σικχαίνω πάντα τὰ δημόσια, v. 4) and similar expressions: cf. *Epigr*. 7 on Theaetetus' theatrical (?) experiments. At *populus tumido gaudeat Antimacho*, Catullus 95. 10; *pingui nil mihi cum populo*, Catalepton 9. 64: *Roman Catullus*, pp. 265, 371.

187. With *vertatur* cf. Virgil's *versis*, *Geo*. III. 24, quoted below; *vertuntur* in Turnus' last confusions, XII. 915. The verb occurs 74 (72?) times in the *Aeneid*.

188. *Ostendis* is a technical term of the pantomime: Jerome, *Epp*. 43; Cassiodorus, *Var*. IV. 51. 8. It corresponds to δεικνύναι: O. Weinreich, *Epigramm und Pantomimus* (Heidelberg 1948), pp. 73, 116. — In general, L. Friedlaender, *Darstellungen aus der Sittengeschichte Roms*[10] (Leipzig 1922), II, pp. 125 ff.

188. *Sic* ("in such a crude fashion") = οὕτως εἰκῇ as so often (above, p. 39).

---

[7] In the Via delle Botteghe Oscure: D. Manacorda, *Crypta Balbi* (Rome 2000).

[8] Augustan fascination with the grotesque is attested by Vitruvius (*De Arch*. VII. 5. 3–4).

[9] This is suggested by the extraordinary exaltation of the *vates* at *A.P.* 391 ff., who later, in works securely dated after Virgil's death, is confounded with the mere *poeta* (*Vergilius Variusque poetae*, *Epp*. II. 1. 247): *Augustus and the New Poetry*, pp. 160–65.

188. *Odi* recurs in *Odes* III. 1. 1, again denoting a (semi-)literary tenet (= Callimachus' μισῶ and σικχαίνω, *Epigr.* 28. 3, 4). Cf. *qui Bavium non odit, amet tua carmina, Maevi*, Virgil, *Ecl.* 3. 90, another literary edict. One has to remember however how much Horace practised what he preached against: *album mutor in alitem, Odes* II. 20. 10; *ursus ... hirudo, A.P.* 472, 476.

And later (*A.P.* 340):
> neu pransae Lamiae vivum puerum extrahat alvo.
> Nor pull a living child out of the belly of a Lamia who has dined too well.

A child drawn living from a witch's belly! What *théâtre de la cruauté* is this![10] And, in the earlier quotation here, what befell mutating Procne's child, mutating Cadmus' grandson? Attic theatre *narrated* horrors of this sort. Actually to *show* them, if only with the aid of gesticulating hands (χειρονομία), demanded a different kind of art.

Seneca rhetor is vexed by the pantomimic libretti of the gifted Silo (*Suas.* II. 19), though later such texts were composed by epic poets who included Lucan and Statius. Augustans liked the pantomime. If then it is a commonplace that Virgil wrote a "dramatic" epic, at Rome, in an Augustan context, the Aristotelian adjective is visibly too staid. The proem to *Georgics* III, already sketching a poetic for the *Aeneid*, suggests that what he was to write would be *theatrical* (III. 24–25):

> vel scaena ut versis discedat frontibus utque
> purpurea intexti tollant aulaea Britanni.
> Even as a scene vanishes when the background changes, and as embroidered Britons remove the shimmering curtain.

24. *Scaena, Aen.* I. 164; *scaenis*, I. 429, IV. 471, all part of Dido's world. *Versis frontibus* recalls the *theatra duo ... cardinum singulorum versatili suspensa libramento*, devised by Caesar's partisan Curio for his father's funeral, with their back-to-back stages, mentioned by Pliny (*N. H.* XXXVI §117), and intriguing to Leonardo, who made a sketch, now in Madrid, of his impression of them. Bernini actually experimented in real life in this line (I. Lavin, ed., *Gianlorenzo Bernini: New Aspects of his Life and Thought* [University Park, Pennsylvania 1985]).

25. The divide between the two worlds disappears, as in M. Bakhtin's "show without footlights" (Проблемы Поэтики Достоевского [Moscow, 1963], p. 163; Творчество Франсуа Рабле [Moscow 1965], p. 10).

Again we find *verto*. Doubling the illusion, the stage itself here seems to revolve like a carousel. What bias does that later lend to the entire *Aeneid*? Children and families certainly enjoy carousels. But if there is nothing else?

---

[10] At least if *fabula* (339) means "dramatic plot" more than "tall story" (as Brink interprets, following Kiessling–Heinze). At vv. 341–42 we are still in the theatre. Clearly whatever sort of poem is meant would have had a strong element of Grand Guignol.

Did the "versatile" medium Virgil chose for his epic, in the colouring he inevitably gave it as a Roman and Augustan, obscure or even exclude any effort to depict settled domestic normality? Hecale and her *moretum* were a whimsical exception. What kitchen does the Cumaean Sibyl keep?

The Sousse Mosaic

Whatever its commandments to the Roman tribe, the *Aeneid* was not set in stone. Antiquity itself did not take uniformly a "classicising," statuesque view of the poem. *Ut magus* is used by Horace of the playwright (*Epp.* II. 1. 213). If Virgil too eventually became a *magus* (and originally in Italy, as Comparetti documents), this perhaps pointed back to something transrational, mobile ("Protean") in his poetic posture divined quite early.

He was remembered, for example, as a superlative performer of his own work, famous in Nero's day and before for his *vox et os et hypocrisis* (*Vita Verg. Don.* §29). These are theatrical and histrionic attributes. The third-century mosaic often assumed to portray the poet, found in 1895 at Sousse in Tunisia, may throw light on this aspect of his art. It shows him seated, holding on his lap a papyrus scroll inscribed with words from the eighth and ninth verses of *Aeneid* I, in which *causas* is both Callimachean (αἴτια), historical (*hae ... causae*, Lucan I. 158) and religious, as the many aetiologies in the Hebrew Bible prove.[11] On his right stands a female figure grasping a scroll in both hands, identified sometimes as Calliope, normally regarded as the Muse of Epic, sometimes as Clio, eventually the Muse of history.[12] On the left is what must be Melpomene, holding a tragic mask.[13]

---

[11] It uses aetiology constantly, usually in explaining proper names: see *TWAT* VIII, *s.v.* אוֹת, cols. 142–45 (Reiterer, Fabry). Here is where a link with the work of J. J. O'Hara and others is possible (below, p. 208).

[12] A Muse with a scroll is certainly described as Clio in the "Room of the Muses" in the Vatican Museum (inv. 55). See however Margherita Albertoni *et al.*, *The Capitoline Museums* (Rome 2000), p. 201, where a female figure perhaps originally grasping a scroll, an Antonine copy from the group created by Philiscus of Rhodes in the second century B.C., is said to be Polyhymnia, though why a scroll rather than a *barbitos* (Hor., *Odes* I. 1. 34) would be the "symbol of her art" is not made clear.

[13] See *Mosaics of Roman Africa* by Michèle Blanchard–Lemée and others (Eng. tr. K. D. Whitehead, British Museum Press 1996), c. IX, pp. 219 ff. The entire nine Muses with individual attributes appear in a mosaic discovered in 1961 at El Djem (*op. cit.*, fig. 168: before A.D. 150?), and this assignment to separate genres may be already implied by Plato at *Phaedrus* 259b–d (and by the Priene relief?). See also the statues from the Roman theatre at Ferentium, now in the Museo Archeologico, Viterbo (later 2nd c. A.D), where there is a clear effort at discrimination of function. The earliest effort to distinguish the Muses by name and attribute is said however to be in a fresco from the Villa of Julia Felix at

Chapter Four

This presents a remarkable contrast both with other African mosaics and with the familiar marble relief signed by Archelaos of Priene, found at Bovillae along the Appian Way, but possibly originating from Alexandria.[14] At its foot Homer is crowned by Ptolemy IV Philopator and his consort in the guise of Time and the World. In the upper registers, a seated Zeus and standing Mnemosyne preside over a gathering of their offspring, the Nine Muses, amongst whom there is some effort at differentiation. The picture thus offered is crowded, and its claim is large. The Sousse mosaic, using a technique often thought characteristic of Virgil himself, has simplified, humanised and refined. There are three figures only. Seven of the Muses, like their divine parents, have been eliminated.[15] The two who are left must have unusual significance.

Dixit Dominus domino meo: sede a dextris meis. Sitting (יֵשׁב) is sacral already in Egyptian iconography. A poet seated between standing Muses assumes an official posture (*sella curulis*), even that of the religious teacher (*ex cathedra*). On this showing, the epic *Aeneid* is likely to be a (selective) religious (aetiological / vatic) amalgam of theatre and (especially if the right-hand Muse is Clio) history—exactly the programme of the proem to *Georgics* III: *purpurea intexti tollant aulaea Britanni*. But *what* tragic theatre

---

Pompeii now in the Louvre (P 4: A.D. 62–79): see *Louvre: Guide to the Collections* (Paris 1991), pp. 200–01. This leaves aside the claims of Philiscus' Muses. At a later date, a silver ewer from a burial in Russia (Kursk region), now in Moscow (Kremlin Museum: inv. M3 1153) has all nine Muses with their Greek names and with individual attributes (about A.D. 400). Among the poets, Horace appeals to Melpomene for a song of mourning (*Odes* I. 24. 3); Callimachus had made Clio in some sense the Muse of record (*Aet*. 43. 56, Pf.); Virgil thinks of Thalia as appropriate to his eclogues (6. 2) and (in Apollonius' wake) of Erato as matching the love interest of the second half of the *Aeneid* (VII. 37); Propertius already slyly asserts that he could tell Calliope from her sisters *a facie* (III. 3. 38), and argues that his quasi-epic eulogy of Augustus deserves her particular attention (IV. 6. 12).

[14] BM GR 1819.8.12.1 (Sculpture 2191): 225–205 B.C. A lively interpretation, suggesting a date of 150 B.C., in Lucilla Burn, *The British Museum Book of Greek and Roman Art* (British Museum Press, 1991), pp. 137–38, with illustration 118. A later silver calathus from Pompeii, now in Naples (inv. 24301), shows the poet being taken up to heaven by an eagle escorted by swans. Two female figures on either side represent the *Iliad* and *Odyssey*.

[15] An Attic red-figure hydria from Vulci (Vatican inv. 16506: 480–50 B.C.) had already reduced their number to six. A pavement at Trier (post 350) has five. The silver Muse Casket from the Esquiline Treasure (BM M & LA 66.12-29.2, also post 350), has eight (not Virgil's Erato), apparently with separate attributes. Eight Muses were perhaps also found at Ferentium, and are seen as late as a mid-17[th]c. *scrigno* in the Sala dei Paesaggi of the Palazzo Colonna, Rome (Safarik, p. 260). As individuals, they became popular on sarcophagi: e.g. BM GR 1805.7-3.120, A.D. 275–300; Palazzo Massimo, inv. 8071, A.D. 280–290.

does Melpomene represent? Again, the pantomime intrudes. Nero himself had wanted to dance Turnus (Suet., *Nero* 54). Later, Virgil's Dido became a favourite of the pantomime artist (Macrobius, *Sat.* V. 17. 5).

The Tragic Pantomime

The theatre of Virgil's day in fact was already sliding towards pantomime, which underwent such changes then that it was (wrongly) believed to have first found its way to Italy under Augustus.[16] There were amazing performers (*histriones*). Alexandrian Bathyllus, the comic actor, was a particular favourite of Maecenas. Evidently he borrowed his name from the lyrics of convivial Anacreon, court-poet to (among others) the Athenian Pisistratids, who was also celebrated by Horace (*Odes* IV. 9. 9; cf. *Epodes* 14. 9–12; *Odes* I. 17. 18). The tragedian Pylades of Cilicia seems to have been a more intense character, lecturing the emperor on the value of the theatre to despots, perhaps at some stage exiled for making an obscene gesture at an offensive spectator, composing a book on his art. His reforms included the enlargement of the orchestra accompanying his dances. Asked to define his innovations, he summarised them in a Homeric line (*Il.* X. 13):

αὐλῶν συρίγγων τ' ἐνοπήν, ὅμαδόν τ' ἀνθρώπων.
The call of flutes and pipes, and the hubbub of humankind.

The ὅμαδος was presumably that of his appreciative audience, imaginatively collaborating in and sympathising with the artistic construct. He felt then (and communicated) an excitement like that of Homer's own martial and heroic verses, another reason why it is foolish to argue that Augustan interest in Homer evinces a classicising repudiation of contemporary ("Alexandrian") aesthetics. His choice of "Pylades" for a stage name—that of the companion and "shadow" of mad Orestes, *scaenis agitatus* (*Aen.* IV. 471)—hints that he claimed a place, even if subordinate, in the heroic world.

This tragic pantomime, which at Rome eventually came to prevail over its comic counterpart, singled out particular highly charged episodes rather than told a connected story. A sung narrative accompanied the actor's studied dance. Some of the remarks about their use of stylised gesture perhaps hint that the best modern analogy to these performances would be the Kabuki theatre of Japan, though, since in their purest and strictest version words and dance in them were separated, essential differences would still remain.

---

[16] In 22 B.C., as noted earlier. Cf. Suetonius, *Reliquiae*, ed. A. Reifferscheid, p. 22. no. 4, *s.v.* "AUC 732."

From these episodes, the tragic pantomime extracted the maximum pathos. To judge from the surviving titles,[17] there was a preference for characters caught at liminal moments, in crisis and collapse, fluttering on the borderlines of sanity and madness, of one world and another. The plots might even be drawn from history (and hence what may be Clio at Sousse): Polycrates and his daughter; Seleucus' love for Stratonice (his father's mistress); Cleopatra's death. There were perhaps also Roman themes.

It is evident that these fraught and feverishly enacted scenes could not accommodate the slow rhythms of family life, its humdrum cycle of successes and disappointments, its patient waits for nature. A father might devour his children on the Roman stage. A mother might murder hers. A crucifixion could occur (Juv. VIII. 187-88; Suet., *Cal.* 57. 4). There was no scope for a nativity.

Such art, biased towards the unnatural, violent and frenzied, so popular at Rome, inevitably influenced more formal literature. The "dramatic" *Aeneid* may not as such offer a tragic, pantomimic libretto. But it is the product of an age which both relished such tastes and asserted that they had borrowed something from epic Homer; and it could be adapted to suit them. And, if this is the case, it may also be judged to some degree by criteria relevant to such a theatre. Here is where bleeding, metamorphosed Polydorus, cannibal Polyphemus and Cacus, Allecto and her monstrous congeners—Fama, the Dirae and so on, even Juno—take their place. If there is a side of the poem best understood as a candidate for the Festspielhaus at Bayreuth,[18] there is another reeking of the gory world of *Macbeth*.[19]

Rome as Theatre and Circus: the Circus Aesthetic

Sunt ceterae [sc. Caesaris virtutes] *maioribus quasi theatris propositae et paene populares* (Cic., *Rab. Post.* §42); σκηνὴ πᾶς ὁ βίος

---

[17] L. Friedlaender, *op. cit.* II, p. 127, lists *inter alia*: "Atreus and Thyestes"; "Ajax Mad"; "Hercules Mad"; "Niobe"; "Hector"; "Aphrodite and Adonis"; "Aphrodite and Ares"; "Apollo and Daphne"; "Phaedra and Hippolytus"; "Meleager and Atalante"; "Jason and Medea."

[18] This would make Wagner's theoretical writings about the *Gesamtkunstwerk* of the greatest relevance to the student of the *Aeneid*, as M. Owen Lee has seen. — The relevance of the Etruscan aesthetic to all this (since *ister* is after all an Etruscan word, according to Livy) is a separate study. See p. 91, n. 42, below.

[19] The play's attitude to children is encapsulated in the "bloody child" indicated by the stage directions before IV. 1. 93: cf. Cleanth Brooks, "The Naked Babe and the Cloak of Manliness," *The Well Wrought Urn* (New York 1947), pp. 22–49, esp. 39 ff. Macbeth of course ultimately determines that "Life's but a walking shadow, a poor player / that struts and frets his hour upon the stage" (V. 5. 23–24).

καὶ παίγνιον ... (*A.P.* X. 72). In New Rome, Palladas still echoes the traditions of the Old. "All the world's a stage"—but at Rome a particular sort of stage.[20] Παίγνιον was already noted as a kind of mime, and the Roman aesthetic is essentially carnivalesque, theatrical, pantomimic, musical, lyrical. M. Bakhtin spoke of "show without footlights," and this describes Roman life. Everyone is acting a role. But this may turn sinister. It is not a good world for children, easily frightened by bogeymen, too innocent to ignore the void, the nakedness behind the pretence.[21] The children of the Ara Pacis, and the Cupid of the Prima Porta statue, turn out to be magnificent exceptions.

A basic, though not exhaustive, list of principles of this circus aesthetic, inherited by Roman Virgil, would include:

Vertical time: everything is here now. The future in any creative sense is unnecessary; it can only replicate the idealised present. Yet what is here now has value only as a σύμβολον, the other half of a whole to which the listener must fit a second half from his own psyche and memory and apprehension before sense is attained or completed. Nothing therefore immediately presented is concrete or specific, if that means self-limiting;

The related *appetite for outdoing all that has gone before* (*fama s u p e r aethera notus*; *nescioquid m a i u s nascitur Iliade*). This means borrowing from the past as a way of making it contribute to a present already subsuming the future (the worst of Aeneas' world enlarged into Rome's Civil Wars, the best into the Golden Age of a greater Augustus), and is linked with

Contaminatio, the annihilation of serial sequence by the combination of different stages and models of the past in the present, particularly clear in Virgil's imitation of Homer's two epics in *both* halves of his *Aeneid*;

The use of form to transcend form ("leap into another dimension"). Since the Roman imagination was so profoundly theatrical and pantomimic, in

---

[20] Philistion (Martial II. 41. 15), active under Augustus, a native of Nicaea in Bithynia, appears to have been completely forgotten. Yet his serio-comedy, if we may extricate him from a confused notice in the Suda, *s.v.* "Philistion" (apud A. Westermann, *Biographoi, Vitarum Scriptores Graeci Minores*, p. 172, end), is symptomatic of the aesthetic of his time. Cf. ὁ τὸν πολυστένακτον ἀνθρώπων βίον / γέλωτι κεράσας Νικαιεὺς Φιλιστίων (*A.P.* VII. 155). The false quantity in the second line here sounds like the prosody of a Latin speaker. E. R. Curtius traces the topos in general as far back as Plato: *Europäische Literatur und lateinisches Mittelalter* (Bern 1948), p. 146, §5. The parable of the cave at the start of Book VII of the *Republic* implies indeed that life is a puppet show. See in general *Roman Catullus*, pp. 367 ff.

[21] *Eripitur persona*, Lucr. III. 58. Cf. Dickens' "O! the Mask!" (above, p. 73).

Roman poets what looks like (but rarely is) plain narrative tends to dissolve and resolve into the stagy / scenic, involving both sight and sound. *Tum silvis scaena coruscis* (I. 164) occurs even as the Aeneadae land in Africa, where they will find Dido building a theatre at Carthage (I. 427-29; cf. *scaenis*, IV. 471). But the Funeral Games for Anchises take place in a *theatrum* (V. 664), even a *theatri circus* (V. 288-89). The Rape of the Sabines is another Circus turn (VIII. 636). Hence also the prominence of rhetorically presented speeches, and the entrusting of what actors call "business"—the added details intended to flesh out the performance—ideally to the professional reciter ("hypocrite") and readers trained like him.[22] To Virgil's celebrated music must be joined his imprecise ("inexakt") key words such as *umbra* and *imago*.[23] One thinks of sarcastic Plato's σκιαγραφία, "scene-painting," transmitted by him to Aristotle.

Σκιαγραφία is allied to

The use of chiaroscuro, "darkness visible," part of

The control of inner space, with which may also be associated the fondness for the colossal and

The Gygean Vision, in which observers perceive the external world via the *camera obscura* of their own minds. See also "vertical time" above.

In the *Aeneid*, heroic combat itself becomes a spectator sport (*spectator*, X. 443), something gladiatorial, Etruscan. We note the poem's prophetic anticipations of Augustus' Rome;[24] its "symbolic" recall of and simultaneously promised "eternal" (XII. 504) solution to the Civil Wars; its *imperium sine fine*; the multiplication of un-Homeric, non-referential and also therefore "symbolic" adjectives (*ingens, altus, medius*); the fascination with fires in the night (*funalia noctem, nubila lunam, atris ignibus*); the constant shift towards music, aided by an architectural structure of internal echoes. Dido and Turnus—both deranged, "furious," liminal—became, as was noted, favourite pantomime parts. The whole poem is "Homer" (and Apollonius) off key. A Menandrean technique[25] is tuned to tragic discords.

---

[22] Donatus' *vox et os et hypocrisis*, Callimachus' αὐτὸς ἐπιφράσσαιτο κτλ. (Pf. III, fr. 57. 1) are again in point. Silent reading was not the rule.

[23] Cf. Fred Mench's pioneering attempt to apply Eisenstein's theories to Virgil's art: "Film Sense in the *Aeneid*," repr. in *Classical Myth and Culture in the Cinema*, ed. M. M. Winkler (Oxford 2001), pp. 219-32. — "Inexakt" here is quoted from F. Dornseiff's *Pindars Stil*, cited more fully below, p. 120.

[24] Even in details. Latinus' quite unrealistic palace is a good instance, VII. 170-191 (= Statius, *Silvae* IV. 2. 18 ff.).

[25] E. Handley, ed. *Dyskolos*, pp. 5-7; A. G. Katsouris, *Tragic Patterns in Menander* (Athens 1975); "Memini Me Fiere Pavum," *ICS* VIII (1983), 177.

But, for those who now live in a Golden Age, the reverse of all this is that to demand a future, if that brings change of any kind, is to demand the inevitably worse. And, in this universe, children are superfluous except as celebrators of the reiterated present, as Horace suggests at the end of *Odes* IV. The implications of the *Carmen Saeculare*, the supreme example of such recurring celebration, may also be studied.

The literary appreciation of such a fantastic world demands broader horizons than those of classicism. Perhaps classicism itself needs better definition. *Graecia capta ferum* .... surely, but Greece itself had changed. The Roman Alexandrianising poets were *cantores Euphorionis*, none perhaps more than Virgil's admired Gallus (*Chalcidico ... versu, Ecl.* 10. 50).[26] Euphorion finds his niche in the second generation of what literary historians call "Hellenistic" poetry. But, as with "Hellenistic" (plastic) art, said to show its typical features already in the middle of the fourth century, the present grows out of the past.[27] The Hellenistic world took a special pleasure in Euripides because his violent, emotional and yet oddly reflective manner seemed to mirror their own "sentimental" tastes. Thoughtful critics such as Callimachus (Pfeiffer on fr. 383. 1) saw in the compressed lyric narrative of musical Pindar (*Py.* 4. 247–48) the possibility of an alternative to the αὐτὰρ ἔπειτα of the hackneyed epic vein (*A.P.* XI. 130). Pindar's presence has already been discerned in the proem to *Georgics* III. It is this self-aware, self-constructing, "sentimental" classicism which is important, rather than that of the rhetorical textbook.

Hellenistic Epic

We must retrace at this point some old and sometimes weed-strewn paths (cf. *Geo.* III. 291–94). This Hellenistic world practised two sorts of epic: the eulogistic poem intended to glorify the martial deeds of some (royal) general of the day; and the more elusive poetry favoured by Callimachus and his admirers. The former sort, often given the title "cyclic," trailed along in Homer's wake, using his formulas to convey the impression that in the new champion the old heroes had found a worthy successor. Efforts have been made to defend this sort of poetry.[28] We now have very few specimens of it

---

[26] Cf. "Cantores Euphorionis," *Roman Catullus*, pp. 372 ff.; below, p. 108.

[27] J. Onians, *Art and Thought in the Hellenistic Age* (London 1979); G. Shipley, *The Greek World after Alexander* (London—New York 2000).

[28] By K. Ziegler, *Das hellenistische Epos*² (Leipzig 1966) and R. Häussler, *Das historische Epos der Griechen und Römer bis Vergil* (Heidelberg 1976) and *Das historische Epos von Lucan bis Silius und seine Theorie* (Heidelberg 1978). See *The Classical Epic Tradition*, index, *s.vv.* "cyclic epic," "history."

(though see below for some), and in a market so concerned to procure immortality that silence may be the loudest verdict on its quality—though not of course a proof of its non-existence. Helped perhaps by Etruscan, sympotic eulogies, it found a ready reception in Rome, as the epics of Naevius and Ennius show. It survived into Byzantine literature.[29]

In the Preface to his *Aetia*, Callimachus categorically rejected this style of writing. Yet he was interested in composing epic. Callimachean epic however is not easily categorised or even understood. The *Aetia* itself offered a sort of epic—in elegiacs. Homerising Ennius would paradoxically borrow for his hexameters its technique of the opening dream.

The patron of Callimachean epic, since Homer had been usurped by the propagandists, was Hesiod. This explains both Ἡσιόδῳ (I, fr. 2. 2, Pf.) in the proem to the *Aetia*, and the terms elsewhere of Callimachus' defence of Aratus against Praxiphanes (Ἡσιόδου, *epigr.* 27. 1). Aratus had written what nowadays (although not then) is called a "didactic" epic, where topics more appropriate to the prose textbook are presented in poetic dress. Horace's own *Ars Poetica* is a virtuoso, "lyrical" sally into this epic / didactic style.

Even the didactic epic might resort to narrative: Andromeda in Manilius, *Astr.* V, Orpheus in *Georgics* IV. And there was also—and more daringly—the fully narrative epic in hexameters, an effort to rescue the Homeric from the propagandist camp. In his *Hecale*, putting a woman in the title role (as also in his epic *Galatea*), Callimachus experimented with fresh ways of Homeric imitation (frr. 239, 240, Pf.). Just as in his twelfth *Iambos* he used the baby daughter of his friend Leon to find in the iambic something deeper and older than its conventional, male savagery,[30] the *Hecale* used the adolescence of Theseus to renew the concept of the heroic.

The Callimachean Poetic[31]

Euphorion, so popular at Rome, was himself an epic poet (Ὁμηρικός,

Defending it is even so better than disputing its reality, which is so clearly evidenced, for example, in the *Pro Archia*.

[29] Writers such as Corippus (*Iohannis*, *Laudes Iustini*) and Georgius Pisides (*Expeditio Persica*) are relevant to this debate: cf. Th. Nissen, "Historisches Epos und Panegyrikus in der Spätantike," *Hermes* LXXV (1940), 298 ff.

[30] By applying to her a eulogistic topos reserved normally for (male) grandees, a theme typically missing from Horace's *Iambi*: "Iambe / Iambos and the Rape of a Genre," *ICS* XXIII (1998), 101–20. —For the *Hecale*, above, p. 66.

[31] A *mise-au-point* in *Callimaque*, edd. F. Montanari and L. Lehnus, *Entretiens Hardt* 48 (Geneva 2002).

A.P. XI. 218. 4), tellingly the author, among other pieces, of a 'Ησίοδος (Powell, no. 22). The great rule of the Callimachean poetic and its adherents, owed to Aristotle, was to avoid trite and expected plots, loosely joined by chronology, "just stringing along." These were vices abundantly exemplified in the already noted αὐτὰρ ἔπειτα of the other side. A cardinal principle was the selection of climactic moments illustrating the law of ἀνάγκη (*Poetics* 1451a 27, quoted below, p. 243) and the consequent omission of less serviceable matter. Horace, who attributes such a procedure to Homer, is also describing the methods of the modern sophisticate (*A.P.* 148–50):

> semper ad eventum festinat et in medias res
> non secus ac notas auditorem rapit, et quae
> desperat tractata nitescere posse, relinquit.

Always in a hurry for a resolution, Homer plunges his listener into the middle of the story as into a familiar tale. What he sees holds no hope for polished craftsmanship, he abandons.

Summa sequar fastigia rerum shows that even Virgil's Venus accepted this narratological rule (I. 342).

Elsewhere, but within the same poetic, Horace counsels *brevitas* (*A.P.* 25, 335; cf. *est brevitate opus*, *Sat.* I. 10. 9). "Brevity" in narrative however, what Pindar calls his οἶμος βραχύς (*Py.* 4. 248), is not mechanical précis, but concentration of emotional impact. Since even Ennius strove to be "modern," *brevitas* of this sort was of concern to Roman epic poets separated by hundreds of years. In sacral language (*pulcer, amoena*) frightened Ilia relates her dream (Ennius, *Ann.* 38–39, Sk.):

> 'Nam me visus homo pulcer per amoena salicta
> Et ripas *raptare* locosque novos.'

'I dreamed some fair hero swept me past pleasing willow stands and river banks and strange haunts.'

This is all we get of the initial, for Rome so fateful, sexual encounter of god and maiden. Alexandrian Claudian uses this technique (though how much less patriotically!), abbreviating even further (*De Rapt. Pros.* II. 204–05):

> *rapitur* Proserpina curru
> imploratque deas ...

Proserpina is swept away by the chariot, calling on the nymphs.

This is all we get from him.[32] But this is not just a delight in puzzlement.

---

[32] J. B. Hall has an excellent note (p. 222 of his edition of the *De Raptu* [Cambridge 1969]) citing the "puerile" complaint of an earlier editor.

A longer examination of both passages would show them as pieces of theatre. In both of them (as in Venus' narrative of Dido's history in Book I) the device of brevity is used to intensify the feelings of women. But, in much of this theatricality, process is more important than result. Proserpina at least had no child. Where does Virgil take his stand?

Apollonius Rhodius[33]

Medea had children and murdered them. Aware enough of this consequence, Apollonius Rhodius' *Argonautica* abandoned Callimachus' good humour. Handling its Euripidean tale in the compass of the tragedies presented at a single sitting, as ordained for the modern epic by Aristotle (*Poetics* 1459b 21–22), it was perhaps the best known example, along with Pindar's fourth *Pythian*, before Catullus, of theatrical condensation applied to an ancient tale. Its tragic myth was used to explore the collapse of the heroic in the face of a nightmare world to which only the feminine was a wayward guide. It too intensified—and even in this case denatured—the feelings of a woman. The contrast with *Gilgamesh* may be pondered.

When Virgil was young, the *Argonautica* had recently been adapted at Rome by Varro Atacinus. It certainly influenced the *Aeneid*. But an Apollonian ἀμηχανίη ("helplessness") sat uneasily with Roman values, whether in narrative or didactic. In the hands of Varro's contemporary Lucretius, an Alexandrian enterprise, the rendering into Latin hexameters of the plain prose treatises of Epicurus, becomes the record of an extraordinary campaign of conquest; and the waspish, cautious philosopher of the Garden is turned into a skywalking hero. In the hands of Varro, the story of the Argonauts may well have become a tribute to the new master of Gaul and invader of Britain, already honoured in the *Bellum Sequanicum*, and his plans now to invade Parthia, just as the later treatment of this theme by Valerius Flaccus became a tribute to the Flavian conquest of Britain and Jerusalem.[34] *Tantae molis erat Romanam condere gentem*. The same smack of Roman *disciplina*, the everlasting will to victory (*A.P.* IX. 647), so evident in Julius Caesar, was bound to strike the *Aeneid*.

The astonishing thing is therefore that the *Aeneid* owes any debt at all to Apollonius' assault on the heroic ideal. Yet, with the help of Euripides,

---

[33] D. M. Nelis' already mentioned *Vergil's* Aeneid *and the* Argonautica *of Apollonius Rhodius* will naturally be at the reader's hand.

[34] See "The Golden Fleece. Imperial Dream" in *A Companion to Apollonius Rhodius*, edd. T. D. Papanghelis and A. Rengakos (Leiden 2001), pp. 320–21. Varro of Atax's innovations were perhaps inspired by the increasingly unacceptable nature of the sort of historical eulogy still appealing to Cicero.

Virgil enlarges, for example, his predecessor's critique of Heracles. He had sacrificed his children to his engagement with destiny. For the Caesars, he would be a dangerous model. The vatic poet saw that.

Part of the Augustan ethos was that women had little place at the side of warriors. Mark Antony's disgrace was to have forgotten this (*eheu*, Horace, *Epodes* 9. 11; *nefas, Aen.* VIII. 688). Accordingly, the reader of the *Aeneid* might have expected a champion more like Beowulf than Jason. No place there for woman except as adversary.

But Aeneas is much more intimately joined to women than this, whether to his mother or, on the human level, to Dido. He had to voyage, and a voyaging hero had a philogynous, tricky model: *sic notus Ulixes?* Like Odysseus, he visited the underworld though, unlike Odysseus, in the company of a woman. He would end in Italy by marrying into Circe's kin.

And Odysseus followed in Jason's wake (*Od.* XII. 70). Aeneas' Dido, able to offer a throne, is much more like Jason's Hypsipyle than any woman Odysseus encounters. The imitations extend even to details. We already noted in Apollonius the sinister implications of the Democritean δείκηλον (I. 746, IV. 1672). The first scene here, in which Aphrodite complacently views her own reflection in the shield of Ares, furnishes some parallel to Virgil's own Shield, the gift of Venus (*imagine*, VIII. 730). In Virgil's poem, there are 30 other uses of the slippery noun. As part of Juno's deception, Aeneas himself becomes an *imago* (X. 643, 661; cf. X. 82).[35]

Here, we return to the σκιαγραφία already listed as part of the Roman aesthetic. The poem ends with *umbras*. This sense of illusion and shadow is pervasive. It affects children. Why is the last hero Aeneas meets in the splendid line of Rome's future champions *aeris in campis latis* ("in the broad sublunar spaces") young Marcellus, dead prematurely, whose mother Octavia fainted (like Evander saying goodbye to Pallas, VIII. 584) as the "hypocritical" poet read the lines dedicated to her son (*umbra*, VI. 866)? This is not the *Hecale's* Prince Theseus. Certainly then the *Aeneid* eulogises, but it is not ultimately a eulogistic epic. Yet, if it is a Callimachean epic, the surprise is, that in rejecting pseudo-Homeric bombast for Callimachus, Virgil failed to respond to Callimachus' interest either in the adolescent or in the child. This is ultimately true even of the sublimation of Ascanius.

---

[35] Cf. νεφέλα at Pindar, *Py.* 2. 36. Juno's humiliating trickery provokes from Turnus a phrase (*aut quae iam satis ima dehiscat terra mihi*, X. 675–76) which is echoed by his sister Juturna at XII. 883. She has also been the victim of the goddess's inhuman machinations. More on *imago* in the poem, below, p. 179.

The Claim of History

The mirror–shield of Book VIII already faced us with certain ambiguities. If Clio is also present at Sousse, the *Aeneid*, cast in heroic time, is not about history in any immediate sense any more than its Greek models. Virgil's chief model, Homer, in spite of the Priene relief, in spite of the ambivalence of the scholiasts,[36] could not be in any real sense historical, since history as a genre is a late development even among the precocious Greeks; and, in Greek literary theory, history and poetry had an uneasy relationship. Aristotle had argued (*Poetics* 1451b 5–7) that philosophically poetry was superior to history by the simple fact of its freedom to concentrate on universals rather than particular trivialities. Driving the logic of his position to extremes, he had suggested that, even where history appeared to illustrate universal laws, that was mere coincidence, and could not mend the flaw inherent in its approach to the artistic medium.

But Aristotle's pupil Alexander had wept at the tomb of Achilles, who had so great a herald to proclaim his valour; and in spite of philosophical strictures, there were both poets eager for a fee to stanch the tears of the great and mighty, and admirers to supply justification for such trade. Especially at Rome the historical epic had been practised as soon as the Romans broke free from the influence of Livius Andronicus: by Naevius, by Ennius. In the already mentioned *Pro Archia*, Cicero reminds us of some of its achievements. In this vein, he himself composed three books of verse *De Consulatu Suo*. Pompey employed to tutor his sons a Greek who asserted that Homer had been a Roman.[37]

Intimate with Maecenas, favoured by Augustus, Virgil might at the new court of the new Alexander Magnus (*at magnus Caesar*, Prop. II. 7. 5: cf. Suet., *Aug.* 50) have made the obvious choice—to compose a (pseudo-) historical, eulogistic epic, of the kind notoriously written by Choerilus of Iasos. One wonders what place such poetry could have had for the child. A late Greek example praising the Roman commander Germanus as "breaker of men" (an epithet reserved in the *Iliad* for Achilles) perhaps serves to give an idea of what so conservative a genre purveyed. Simonides of Magnesia,

---

[36] "Homer's narrative was sharply contrasted with that of the historian.... Though the scholia do not doubt the historical truth of his tale, they regard the poet as its free manipulator": *The Classical Epic Tradition*, p. 48.

[37] Aristodemus of Nysa: F. Susemihl, *Geschichte der griechischen Literatur in der Alexandrinerzeit* (repr. Hildesheim 1965), II, pp. 183–85. The bias is clear. Cf. the Suda, *s.v.* Ἔννιος: φησὶ μόνον ἂν Ὅμηρον ἐπαξίους ἐπαίνους εἰπεῖν Σκιπίωνος.

who celebrated the elephants of Antiochus I, was another such practitioner.[38]

Roman epic poets were certainly open to the notion of the re-presentation of the past, since they had an acute sense of what was called above "vertical" time. This is why, unlike Homer, they favoured the "historic" present right from the days of Livius' *Odisia*.[39] But—though this was something too evanescent even for so subtle a palate as that of Cicero—such re-presentation could not now take the shape of crude eulogy. Under Callimachean influence, literary tastes among Roman *conoscenti* were changing. Pioneering Lucilius, urged to "sing" (trumpet?) the deeds of his patron Scipio (*facta Corneli cane*, 621, M.), had rejected that kind of epic for himself.[40] Parthenius of Nicaea, Virgil's adviser *in Graecis*, spurned conventional views of epic. Philodemus, who dedicated a treatise to Virgil, stoutly denied any essential connection between poetry and truth.[41] Callimachean Horace follows satiric Lucilius, either personally dismissing historical epic (*Epp.* II. 1. 257 *al.*), or pouring scorn altogether on whatever Choerilus produced (*A.P.* 357; *Epp.* II. 1. 232–34). If there have been attempts in our day to clothe the historical epic with respectability, and even a theory, these judgments by Virgil's closest literary friends and admirers must never be overlooked.

The *Aeneid* did not turn out to be a Choerilan poem, and yet it has historical links, as indeed at Rome it was bound to have. How can that be? We come back to the theatre. The *praetexta*, reviving memories of the achievements of the dead, was as old as Naevius. It may have had Greek, even Etruscan, antecedents.[42] There was then a genre which could deal with

[38] Page, *Greek Literary Papyri*, pp. 590–94; Lloyd–Jones / Parsons, *Supplementum Hellenisticum*, p. 349, no. 723. Cf. Plautus, *MG*, I. 1. 25–30.

[39] A bias they share with Sanskrit, though not with Old English. Livius *introduces* presents at fr. 15 (Warmington) = *Odyssey* IV. 495. For Sanskrit, cf. A. A. Macdonnell, *A Sanskrit Grammar for Beginners*² (London 1911), p. 205; for Old English, Randolph Quirk and C. L. Wren, *An Old English Grammar* (London 1955, repr. 1993), p. 77. Pindar, who retells so many epic tales, follows Homer in showing no historic presents.

[40] M. Puelma Piwonka, *Lucilius und Kallimachos* (Frankfurt 1949), is basic.

[41] Τὴν δ' ἀλήθειαν διὰ τί προσέθηκεν ὅμως ἀπορῶ, *De Poematis* V, ed. Mangoni, p. 137.

[42] Naevius was probably from Campania, where there was widespread Etruscan settlement. Capua is described as an Etruscan city (Livy IV. 37). Etruscan Persius wrote a youthful *praetexta* (*Vita* 8). For the Greek background, Susemihl, I, p. 273. The Gyges papyrus (E. Lobel, *Proc. British Acad.* 35 [1950]) is evidently a Hellenistic experiment in using the drama to get around the difficulties encountered by Choerilus of Samos, obliquely criticised by Aristotle in c. 9 of the *Poetics*.

history, sometimes overtly, as in the case of Phrynichus' Μιλήτου "Αλωσις and Aeschylus' *Persae*; and sometimes obliquely, as in the case of the *Eumenides* and the Areopagus, or the *Oedipus Rex* and its lofty, plague-ridden monarch, posturing even as another plague ravaged Periclean Athens.[43] Virgil could solve the dilemma which the *Poetics* had posed by borrowing from its already Platonic theory that epic tended towards drama. The "dramatic" epic might let in history by the back door; not in some crude effort to treat the modern hero as a reincarnation of Achilles, but by a re-evaluation and retro-application of the universality of myth. Through the gossamer curtain of old story could now shimmer the lights and shadows of modern reality. This was another technique which Pindar had pioneered. Roman audiences, quick to read contemporary allusion into actors' inherited words, showed how instinctively receptive they were to this.

Politics may have made some reform advisable. Julius Caesar's own account of his achievements, no doubt intended to show to good advantage in comparison with the hackwork of Pompey's Greeks, was ostensibly composed in what Cicero describes as unadorned prose, while Cicero himself, unable to absorb the lesson, celebrated his consulship in poetry which Juvenal later derides. It was part of Augustus' own pose as a simple citizen that, whatever his respect for the political legacies of Pompey and Cicero, in literature he exhibited some of Julius' fastidiousness (Suet., *Aug.* 89).

From his poets, he perhaps hardly knew what to expect. If indeed he looked for (without commanding) historical eulogy from the *ingenia* recommended to him by Maecenas, how poorly or circumspectly they performed by that standard! Horace and Propertius normally hand the task off to others, and hence the programmatic importance in those authors of the *recusatio*.[44] After his success with a tragic *Thyestes*, Varius Rufus promised great things: *forte epos acer / ut nemo Varius ducit* ... (Hor., *Sat.* I. 10. 43–44). But what in fact did Varius write? What was the *De Morte* about? No one knows for sure. After touching on so sensitive a topic as Julius' assassination, it seems to have ended with general reflections on mortality. If it lauded Augustus, what did it say about children?

---

[43] The political allusions in Attic tragedy are becoming more evident in recent studies. Cf. "Euripides' *Medea*: Structures of Estrangement," *Illinois Classical Studies* XXVI (2001), 53–76 (Pericles / Jason).

[44] Hans Lucas, in introducing this term to modern criticism ("Recusatio," *Festschrift für Johannes Vahlen* [Berlin 1900], XVIII, pp. 317-33), was of course able to call on such passages as Cic., *De Orat.* II. §26 and Hor., *Epp.* II. 1. 258–59. Hence the continuing relevance of W. Wimmel, *Kallimachos in Rom* (Wiesbaden 1960).

Virgil and Pastoral[45]

The most gifted of all Roman epic writers, who borrowed a line or two from Varius, might have been expected to answer the challenge with greater success. Indeed, if we can believe Donatus' *Vita* (§19), he may have begun with the simple notion that it was possible somehow to continue in the Ennian vein. It was not, and Virgil first presented himself to posterity, as Horace acutely re-emphasised (*Odes* IV. 12; cf. *Sat.* I. 10. 44–45), with so Alexandrian a genre as the pastoral, in the manner invented by Theocritus.

This was already to embrace a version of the mime, although a mime with masks, and we saw that, continuing this tradition, Virgil's own pastorals were performed on the stage. But there are important distinctions. The Theocritean corpus contains a *Heracliscus*, and the Alexandrian aesthetic thus claiming Virgil's allegiance is credited more largely with the discovery of the child. The epic / pastoral *Hecale* was about a hero's adolescence. For Virgil, however, the pastoral was hollow. It offered a downhill route, not towards the "idyllic," but to the discovery of his different artistic universe: its brokennesses, its exiles, its divided self, its shadows. How quickly the theme of unfulfilled promise makes its appearance! In the very first eclogue, Meliboeus is turned out of his paradise—and his goat has abandoned her twin kids on the bare rock (14–15). In the second, Corydon is his master's despairing rival for handsome Alexis. Dead Daphnis (*Ecl.* 5) had been love's victim. At the end, Gallus, the poet's alter ego, just because he has *lost* his Lycoris, will turn from Euphorion to pastoral (10. 50–51). Typically, birth will now be relegated to—hidden among—fantasy and prophecy (*Ecl.* 4). How soon the darkness falls (1. 83; 10. 76; cf. *Aen.* XII. 952)!

Yet the pastoral has never denied its awareness of the urban world. Writers as different as Boccaccio and Milton show this, and there is something of it even in Theocritus.[46] M. Valerius Messalla Corvinus, co-consul with Octavian in the year of Actium, may even have composed pastoral in Greek (*Catalepton* 9. 13–20). In any case, Virgil's most admired contacts in contemporary literature, Pollio and Gallus, celebrated in the *Eclogues* as poets, one of them "Sophoclean," like Messalla, were men of action in a sense completely different from anything known to Alexandria. Theocritus might appeal to Syracusan Hiero for largesse. Yet neither the king, nor whichever Sosibios the Callimachean Νίκη Σωσιβίου honours, was a

---

[45] Cf. "Semitic Aspects of the Greco-Roman Pastoral," *Studia Palaeophilologica*, ed. S. M. Bay (Champaign 2004), 53–69.

[46] Joan B. Burton, *Theocritus's Urban Mimes* (Berkeley 1995).

poet.[47] It was Rome's glory that its upper classes could unite both vocations.

Virgilian pastoral is not then a poetry divorced from the contemporary, something Calpurnius Siculus understood. The visit to a saving (messianic) *iuvenis* at Rome, the imminent birth of a divine child, however fancifully conceived, coming to restore a new Golden Age, are both the token of that, and simultaneously the illustration of Virgil's need to muffle fact, not so much in ornamental story, as in anthropology, religion, a myth that is felt more than used. It is in the *Eclogues* that the first allusions in his work to the *vates* are heard (7. 28; 9. 34). Rome (1. 19) and Helicon (*Aonas in montis*, 6. 65) are the two poles: is the *vates* the bridge which will enable the Apolline poet to join these disparate realms? How soon may one guess that Gallus had begun to speak among his admirers of the *vates*, and Octavian of his Palatine Temple?[48] But in the epic it turns out that Apollo cannot or will not heal Aeneas' wound (XII. 405–06). His son Ascanius looks on in grief (399).

Virgil and Callimachus

Callimachus had also written quasi-pastoral elegy, describing the idyllic love of Acontius and Cydippe (*Aetia* III. 67–75, Pf.). Virgil borrows a motif in the *Eclogues* (10. 53–54 = *Aetia* fr. 73). But Rome was too big or too ambitious for shepherds. Arcadian Evander mourns a son killed in war.

Horace, who could be both nostalgic and mocking about the countryside, was also aware of the pastoral as threat. He positioned *Pastor cum traheret*, with its warning against Paris' adultery and its public outcome, directed at contemporary Romans, immediately after an ode which Quintilian describes as an allegory of the ship of state, and the dangerous rocks which could wreck it (*Odes* I. 14 and 15). He was fulfilling the programme by which the *vates* was *utilis Urbi* (*Epp.* II. 1. 124).[49] Virgil too sensed the imperatives of civic *utilitas*. His epic *Aeneid*, which uses the vocatival and quite un-Homeric *cives* several times (cf. Lucan I. 8), was also in contact with history, aiming as much as Livy's prose narrative to afford Romans perspectives on their past. Some of this is directly reflected in the review of

---

[47] Hiero II apparently wrote technical treatises on agriculture. Ptolemy Soter was a historian. On Sosibius, Susemihl, I, pp. 603–05; Pfeiffer, *Callimachus* II, *Proleg.*, pp. xl–xli.

[48] Cf. the *aureus* perhaps from 36 B.C. noted in L. R. Taylor, *The Divinity of the Roman Emperor* (Middletown, Conn. 1931), p. 132 with fig. 20.

[49] *Civis ... utilis*, Lucan's Cato on Pompey, IX. 190–91. This is picked up from the Augustans: below, p. 307.

Rome's heroes to come in the Lower World, or on Aeneas' shield. Obliquely, we hear of Augustan projects: the Temple of the Palatine Apollo and its *XVviri sacris faciundis* (VI. 69); the Forum of Augustus (VII. 177). It was suggested above that the "Iliadic" story of the second half of the *Aeneid* presupposes Rome's Civil Wars.

But the historical epic at the level of propaganda, public relations, was *not* admissible. Virgil lived in an age where the most forward thinkers accepted Alexandrian ideas of how poetry should be written. The *Garland* and the poems of its editor, Meleager, who also ventured into Menippean satire, along with the poetry and prose treatises of Philodemus, offer the proof of that. Possibly Philodemus possessed copies of both Ennius and Lucretius.[50] But not perhaps because he relished in them any native uncouthness. We saw that even Homerising Ennius had felt obliged to adapt (and defiantly reverse) Callimachus' Hesiodic dream for the opening of his *Annales*; and, in Aratus' and Ennius' wake, Lucretius had composed that most Alexandrian of poems, a "didactic" epic.

The master himself, it was noted, had written epics, the *Hecale*, the *Galatea*. The "Acontius and Cydippe" claimed a historical source in Xenomedes. Apollonius' *Argonautica* "follows closely in Callimachus' footsteps."[51] And, within the same poetic as the didactic *Georgics*, the *Aeneid* is a Callimachean epic—though admittedly that is to say too much and too little: too much, because it suggests that the poem is a formalist experiment rather than a historical culmination; too little, because it ignores the poem's debt to a vast range of other authors and their ideas. The *Aeneid* is indeed an experiment in ultimately musical form, but it is more than that. Yet, if it is also involved with history, it is more than that.

War in Italy, for example, was historical enough. Virgil's narrative in Book VII (415 ff.) of its paradigm and αἴτια (*exordia*, 40) is not historical. The poet *declines* that challenge, turning instead to fancy.

The narrative is melodramatic. When Allecto appears to Turnus at Juno's behest to inflame his warlike passions, at first she takes the guise of the old priestess Calybe and warns the young prince not to ignore (as she interprets it) his duty. He laughs at her, and she replies by appearing in all her terrifying power, and ends by driving him insane.

The model for this episode is the appearance of Demeter to Erysichthon

---

[50] The Lucretius fragments have been published by K. Kleve, "Lucretius in Herculaneum," *Cronache Ercolanesi* 19 (1989), 5–28.

[51] "Apollonium Callimachi vestigia pressisse nunc constat, v. passim infra in commentario," Pfeiffer ad fr. 7, vol. I, p. 17.

in Callimachus' sixth hymn.[52] There are the same three elements: warning goddess disguised as old priestess; mocking rejection; epiphany and curse. But of course Callimachus' hymn is a comedy about a young blabbermouth condemned to eat his parents out of house and home, and Virgil's scene is profoundly tragic.

The development and final working-out of the theme is illumined by another Callimachean hymn, this time honouring a nativity. In the Greek poet (*Hy.* IV. 55 ff.), Hera, angry over Zeus' amours, seeks to hinder Leto from giving birth. The eventual shelter afforded by the starry island of Delos is reported to her by a lackey, compared to a hunting-dog (κύων ... θηρήτειρα, 228, 230; cf. *venator ... canis, Aen.* XII. 751) skulking beneath her throne (ὑπὸ χρύσειον ἐδέθλιον, 228; *Iovis ad solium*, XII. 849). Yet the tenor of the hymn is joyful. After some sarcastic remarks, Hera disappears, placated by Zeus (259). Artemis and Apollo were safely delivered. Their importance, with their mother Leto, in Augustan propaganda needs no emphasis.[53]

But Hera could be more sinister. In Euripides' *Heracles*, Iris had called on Lyssa to act in the goddess's service (823) by driving the hero to kill his own children. There were perhaps other tragic paradigms.[54] This is the complex genesis of the vengeful picture of Juno and her minions Allecto and Iris (quite different from Homer's Iris) in the *Aeneid*, where we find

---

[52] Vv. 40 ff.; Heinze, *Virgils epische Technik* (repr. Stuttgart 1957), p. 189.

[53] Propertius II. 31. 15. The relics of the Temple of Apollo Palatinus now on display in the Antiquario Palatino were noted above, p. 10. A fragmentary archaising relief in Pentelic marble from the Augustan period has a Nike with Apollo Citharoedus (Museo Barracco, Rome, inv. 188). A later marble relief (first or second century A.D.), showing Apollo Citharoedus standing in a temple frame and receiving a libation from a winged Nike, done in a classicising Attic style (BM GR 1776.11–8.6 = Sculpture 774), may also be relevant. A number of treatments of the theme were known: J. Winckelmann, *Geschichte der Kunst des Alterthums* (Dresden 1764), I, pp. 238–39. The one in the Torlonia collection (unlike that in the BM) shows what are now taken to be Leto and Artemis with Apollo (engraving in Winckelmann, p. ix). As late as the fourth century, a silver *lanx* recovered from Corbridge in Northumberland (BM PRB P.1993.4–1–1) has been thought to show Delos and its deities in some sort of imperial context.

[54] A red-figure calyx-krater from Apulia, now in London (BM GR 1849.6-23.48 = Vase F271, 350–40 B.C., ascribed to the Lycurgus Painter), shows the king of Thrace driven mad by Dionysus. He has killed his son Dryas. Above hovers Lyssa. At the bottom is seen an old retainer, "a stock figure in drama suggesting that the scene was inspired by Aeschylus' *Edonoi*." Heinze (p. 189, n. 2) refers also to Aeschylus' *Xantriae*, a play about Pentheus, in which Hera, in the guise of a priestess, tried to foster resistance to Dionysus. Lyssa was sent by Dionysus (not Hera!) to madden these unbelievers. There is some parallel with the action of *Aeneid* VII. 373 ff.

rather a poem of anti-birth. With the aid of Euripides, perhaps even of Aeschylus, Virgil takes Callimachus' nativity story and reverses it to refract the angry Juno and her death-dealing ministers throughout his epic, until there also at the end Jupiter placates (though at what cost to the Aeneadae!) his wife's resentments.

In this final scene, just like Callimachus' Hera, Virgil's Jupiter also has minions ὑπὸ ἐδέθλιον, by his throne. *Limen* too is noteworthy (XII. 845, 849-50):

> dicuntur geminae pestes cognomine Dirae ...
> hae Iovis ad solium saevique in limine regis
> apparent....

Twin plagues are told of, Dread Furies their name ... in attendance at Jupiter's throne, on the threshold of that ruthless lord....

Is the "ruthless lord" Jupiter or his brother Pluto? Does Jupiter make peace with his wife at the cost of assuming hellish attributes?

The whole secret of Virgil's art lies in this sort of conversion, which completely denies Ciceronian primness.[55] Originally comic (Dionysiac, "iambic," "carnival") devices, of which Virgilian irony is a particular case, are shifted from their hope and promise of rebirth, and instead depressed and intensified—concentrated—into tragedy. Aristotle's ὀψὲ ἀπεσεμνύνθη (*Poetics* 1449a 20-21), Bakhtin's редуцированный смех, find here their profoundest illustration. Dante's *Commedia*, exploring hell, purgatory and heaven, shows where the tradition lay; and, in resurrecting, reverses the *Aeneid* to which, in the first canto of the *Inferno*, it proclaims such a debt.

Catullus had set the example of adaptation. By the device of suppressed laughter, Alexandrian effects may be adapted, diverted, saddened, even ennobled. They become, for example, the world exploited for tragic ends in poem 63 (another denial of sexual normality).

Catullus had also composed in these central poems (61-68) a quasi-pantomimic cycle reflecting the many facets of *amor*.[56] In what is ostensibly a translation from Callimachus (66), he both exalts a happy marriage and hits out against *adulterium*. These were themes later dear to Augustus himself, finding echoes, for example, and diminuendos in Horace. One could be Alexandrian and engaged.

---

[55] *Itaque et in tragoedia comicum vitiosum est et in comoedia turpe tragicum*, *De Opt. Gen. Orat.* 1. Obviously Cicero, himself a master of tragi-comedy, is unthinkingly parroting rhetorical maxims of the day. Horace's qualifying remarks (*A.P.* 93 ff.) are apparently based on Callimachus (fr. 215, Pf.): below, p. 104. Andromache's δακρυόεν γελάσασα must never be forgotten, nor Servius on *Aeneid* IV init. (*paene comicus stilus est*, quoted below, p. 104).

[56] *Roman Catullus*, pp. 204 ff.

Virgil learned from his great Roman predecessor. In the event, he too wrote an Alexandrian, Callimachean epic, sharing Apollonius' mistrust of ἔρως, hoping, like Catullus, for ultimately better consequences.

The Aeneid as Tragedy

Callimachus commiserates with the failure of his friend Theaetetus, perhaps in dramatic competitions (*epigr.* 7), and Alexandria did have its tragic Pleiad. But when Dante makes Virgil refer to the *Aeneid* as "my high tragedy" (*Inf.* 20. 113), he has something more in mind. Plato had said that Homer was the "ring-leader" (ἡγεμών) of the modern tragedians (*Rep.* X. 595c), and Aristotle accepted the compliment on his behalf, happily combining in the first book of his *Poetics* with his discussion of tragedy allusions to the *Iliad* and *Odyssey*.

This tragic kinship has far-reaching consequences for our understanding of Virgil's own quasi-Homeric epic.[57] We may expect there the picture of an honourable (χρηστός) protagonist ("hero," though Aristotle does not use the word in the modern sense) who comes to grief because of a ἁμαρτία, some kind of flaw combining intellectual with moral misapprehension.[58] *Fallit te incautum pietas tua* says Aeneas to Lausus / Antilochus (X. 812), perhaps illustrating this very doctrine,[59] and anticipating his own ultimate fate. It was also the business of Aristotelian tragedy to evoke ἔλεος καὶ φόβος (*Poetics* 1449b 27). This in itself should protect the reader of the *Aeneid* from any conviction at the end of the satisfying rightness of things.

But Aristotle also enjoins the epic poet to imitate as little as possible in his own person, "for that is not where he is an imitator" (*Poetics* 1460a 7-8). He was writing for logical Greeks. Virgil however was a Roman, and he is not that kind of epic poet, any more than Ennius or Lucretius had been. He intervenes in the narrative of his poem a number of times.[60] This voice has (inevitably) been found challenging, baffling, ἄπορα πόριμος. And, quite apart from any considered views which the epic poet may express in his verses, there is also the lasting burden of outlook and attitude, psychology and mindset (*Keimentschluß*).

---

[57] See also below, pp. 241 ff.

[58] But stopping short of villainy: μὴ διὰ μοχθηρίαν ἀλλὰ δι' ἁμαρτίαν μεγάλην ἢ οἵου εἴρηται ἢ βελτίονος μᾶλλον ἢ χείρονος (1453a 15–17).

[59] It is Antigone's fault. Cf. Horace's *nimium pii, Odes* III. 3. 58.

[60] E.g. IX. 446–49. See also below, p. 324, for the implicit intervention at I. 456–93.

Orpheus / Proteus

The importance for the *Aeneid* of the poetic programme sketched in the proem to *Georgics* III was already noted. But we can also remark some of its author's tics in the story of Aristaeus at the end of IV. There, two sorts of reality clash. Orpheus, the singer, loses his wife Eurydice to divine yet quite amoral forces, whose submarine world is inaccessible to the ordinary mortal, even to a *numen* (IV. 453). Aristaeus is rescued from his guilty dilemma by a loving and unquestioning mother, whose instructions enable him to overcome a metamorphosing, vatic god. Leaving Hades, yet desolate after his too great love has betrayed him, Orpheus becomes a bacchic victim, and survives only by entering the waterworld which has proved superior, but as a grotesque, a singing head.

It seems at first strange that, in this episode, not Orpheus, as a reading of Horace would suggest (*Odes* I. 24. 13; cf. *A.P.* 392), but Proteus is the *vates*.[61] The reason is that, if there is need to enter and emerge from a waterworld, one must follow, not its victim, but its master. Here, it may be illuminating to think of the end of Plato's *Ion*. After poor Ion has been forced into the desperate expedient of claiming that he knows something about generalship, Socrates makes merry at his expense. "You are just like Proteus," he adds, "running the gamut of identities, twisting in every direction" (ἀτεχνῶς ὥσπερ ὁ Πρωτεὺς παντοδαπὸς γίγνῃ στρεφόμενος ἄνω καὶ κάτω, 541e 7-8).

Ion is seen as dodging the issue, and yet Socrates' own verbal magic (ἅπτει γάρ μου τοῖς λόγοις τῆς ψυχῆς, *Ion* 535a) and confessions of ignorance are evidence of the same attitude. Perhaps in Plato himself we have a recurrence of a frame of mind famously diagnosed for Tolstoy, in which a shifty fox continually masquerades as a stolid hedgehog. Virgil, another vulpine genius, in assuming the vatic, Protean mantle, was sketching at the end of the *Georgics* the chequered plan of his *Aeneid*. He is both Orpheus and Proteus, Ion and Socrates. But not to dodge! Rather, to skirt religiously, what earlier has been called "to decline," the central mysteries of his time.

What was the theme of Orpheus' last song? The question had already interested the Etruscans.[62] His fate is the model for Virgil's later epic, in which Eurydice becomes the Creusa of Book II (Heurgon). The normality of

---

[61] The passage contains three out of the four examples of the noun in the *Georgics* (387, 392, 450). The other instance is at III. 491.

[62] A mirror shows his decapitated head on the ground prophesying, while a young bystander takes careful notes: *Gli Etruschi. Una Nuova Immagine*, ed. M. Cristofani (Florence 1984, 1993), p. 149. For the Greek view of this, E. R. Dodds, *The Greeks and the Irrational* (Berkeley 1951), p. 168, note 78.

husband and wife—and *a fortiori* of children—is impossible in this heroic world. The gods of the *Aeneid*, though on a more imposing scale, are as amoral as Cyrene and Aristaeus, and the fate of Juturna offers proof. Aeneas has already lost his wife, and later himself descends to and returns from Hades like Orpheus (VI. 119). At the end he must surrender to a change which will rob him even of his Trojan tongue (*faciamque omnis uno ore Latinos*, XII. 837). His people at best will be *mixtum sanguine* (838). Turnus, also like Orpheus, loses his promised wife Lavinia, and (a failed Aristaeus) his battle with monstrous, metamorphosing forces. Aeneas, now Aristaeus, taunts his adversary with a challenge which makes him into a Proteus (*verte omnis tete in facies*, XII. 891). And, as in the *Georgics*, this is a sure signal of the poet's own imminent, Protean withdrawal from the moral conundrums he describes. To answer them plainly would have been to exaggerate the power of reason. "Hypocritical," polyprosopic, musical to the end—at what cost to his own Protean self?—Virgil vatically, bafflingly records the workings of fate with that tragic sense which has always been admired. *Horrendas canit ambages antroque remugit*.

But Virgil remains an Augustan poet. With his imperial art in general one might compare the chiaroscuro of Trajan's Basilica Ulpia, and perhaps the narrative manner of his Column; even facets of New Roman ("Byzantine") sensibility;[63] and this means that the *Aeneid* cannot be isolated from its successors—nor indeed, as for example its use of "contamination" shows, from its Republican predecessors. There *is* a Roman aesthetic—its rules were half-listed above—even though there is sometimes a tendency to deny the Romans aesthetic independence. This takes their own modesty far too literally. In spite of Virgil's *spirantia mollius aera*, it is absurd even in the plastic arts, and surely in painting or architecture. In spite of *orabunt causas melius*, it is no less absurd in judging their literature. But, if ultimately all this describes the labile world of the *Aeneid*, it is never wholly clear where its children come from, where they live or play or fidget during its whirligig, where its grieving mothers find rest for their spirits.

---

[63] Lelio Guidiccioni, *Latin Poems, Rome 1633 and 1639*, edd. Newmans (Hildesheim 1992), pp. 37 ff.

V

THE RHETORIC OF VIRGIL'S WOMEN—I

> *Poesis est ... fictio rethorica musicaque poita.*
> Dante, *Vulg. Eloq.* II. iv

Rhetorical Decorum

One of the great moments of Euripidean and European tragic art arrived when Medea's children were allowed to protest against their fate. Such dramatic licence infringed epic convention. No children speak in the *Iliad* or the *Argonautica*. This distinction carried over to Rome. Perhaps children spoke in Ennius' *Medea*.[1] In his epic *Annales*, the blare of *at tuba terribili sonitu taratantara dixit* (*Ann.* 451, Sk.; cf. *Aen.* IX. 503) drowns out such humble discourse. Even Virgilian young people, felt as young, speak most in the bloody adventure of Book IX. If we want to hear a different note—though not consistently different—we must listen to Virgil's women. Their voices are the instruments which open his orchestra's range into infinitude. They speak for their dumb children.

Ancient critical theory knew a doctrine of rhetorical decorum, the fitting of utterance to character. Augustan Horace retails its injunctions (*A.P.* 112–18). Accordingly, Aeneas is made to begin his relationship with Dido by mouthing *adynata* whose smooth structure and transparent glibness expose their poetic—and historical—falsity (I. 607–08). But there is more. His *montibus umbrae* (607), unique in the *Aeneid*, echoes the end of *Eclogue* 1 (83; cf. *Geo.* I. 342). Yet her answer is also telling. Libya was pastoral (*Geo.* III. 339); and Sicily, the birthplace of both Theocritus and his pastoral predecessor Stesichorus, is where Tyrian Carthage and Greco-

---

[1] Deiphilus / Polydorus in his nephew Pacuvius' *Iliona*, with his pathetic *mater, te appello*, was however a ghost (and indeed a young man before he was murdered). The tension even of this, attested by Cicero (*T. D.* I. §106), could already, as the anecdote in Horace, *Sat.* II. 3. 60 shows, become tragi-comic. See Warmington, *ROL* II, pp. 238–40. A terracotta tile in the Palazzo Massimo (inv. 34355 bis) may show a scene from Accius' *Astyanax* (based on a play of Sophocles?). A child is visible. He makes a fifth character on stage. What can he have said?

Roman civilisation met. Certainly earlier Greek authors (Homer, Pindar, Euripides, Plato) had shown a feeling for nature, and the Hellenistic period celebrated the "sacred landscape," in which rustic activities occur near some shrine.[2] But pastoral art as such is not Greek.[3] Was it, at least for Theocritus and the Romans, Semitic? At either end of a long time-scale, pastoral scenes are found, for example, on a Punic gold ring from Sardinia,[4] and persist on a silver bowl dating from the Roman period, with both pastoral and hunting scenes, discovered on the hill of St. Louis at Carthage.[5] How could Virgil, who used the *Georgics* to frame the second half of the *Aeneid*, fail to recall this tradition elsewhere in his epic? Phoenician Dido's first words in the poem, her greeting to the survivors from Aeneas' fleet, have a familiar rhythm:

> solvite corde metum, Teucri, secludite curas. (I. 562)
>
> pascite ut ante boves, pueri, summittite tauros. (*Ecl.* 1. 45)

This is what, listening from his mist, Aeneas had evidently sensed. Indeed, he had already sensed the pastoral in speaking on Libyan soil to his mother (*Vesper Olympo*, I. 374 ~ *Ecl.* 6. 86).

The rescuing queen speaks like the saving *iuvenis* Octavian. But the first eclogue, anticipating the finale of the *Aeneid*, ends, as we saw, with *umbrae* (cf. *Ecl.* 10. 76), and Moeris at least must still go into exile (cf. *sitientis*

---

[2] Cf. the opening of Menander's *Dyscolus*. A sacro-idyllic landscape from the Farnesina House (Rome, c. 20 B.C.) is illustrated in Henig, p. 101. Cf. a silver scyphos from the House of Menander (Naples inv. 145504); a painting in the Fourth Style with a shepherd and ram approaching a shrine (Naples inv. 9418).

[3] How long we have to wait, for example, for the beautiful silver dish with a goatherd and goats, now in the Hermitage, St. Petersburg (inv. ω 277), found in the province of Perm hoarded with other Byzantine and Sassanian objects, and bearing stamps from the reign of Justinian (A.D. 527–565)! Two other late pastoral scenes, one on tapestry, the other on glass, are noted *in Aurea Roma. Dalla Città Pagana alla Città Cristiana*, a cura di Serena Ensoli ed Eugenio La Rocca (Rome 2000), pp. 627 and 628. — To judge by his ecphrasis, Theocritus (I. 39, γριπεύς), like many poets of the *Anthology*, or indeed Neapolitan Sannazaro, seems to regard fishing as an element of pastoral. See the silver cup now in Milan catalogued in *Aurea Roma* (no. 326, p. 622), with the commentary of F. Baratte. Mantuan Virgil quite ignores this in the *Eclogues* (cf. 3. 36–43), but he revives it for the hollow pastoral of *Aeneid* XII (517–20).

[4] Tharros Tomb 12, inv. no. BM GR 1856.12-23-941. The golden bowl with cattle around its rim, found near Acragas (BM GR 1772.3-1470 = BM Jewellery 1574: cf. G. P. Caratelli, ed., *Megale Hellas* [Milan 1983], pp. 125–26, col. pl. 97), and thought to be Phoenician, is also relevant. The Book of Ruth is often called a pastoral. The songs of pastoral King David, including יהוה רעי, 'The Lord is my shepherd,' have changed civilisations.

[5] Late fourth–early fifth centuries A.D., British Museum M&LA AF 3276.

ibimus Afros, 1. 64). Exile, loss, a divided self, a temporary respite: an ear in tune with Virgil's pastoral might have already half caught in the allusive music of this first exchange hints of Dido's own flight (I. 357, 360) to Africa and subsequent fate at the hands of her *pastor agens telis ... nescius* (IV. 71–72), who is also an *advena* (IV. 591; cf. *Ecl.* 9. 2). Then she will plan to burn *exuvias ... omnis* (IV. 496) of her *perfidus* lover (IV. 305, 366), just as elsewhere in the *Eclogues* the heroine of Alphesiboeus' song sets *perfidus* Daphnis' *exuviae* on her threshold in an effort to regain his love (8. 90–92). Queen Dido in her hive (I. 430) surrenders (IV. 330) to an intruding shepherd (IV. 71; cf. XII. 587; *Il.* XIII. 493). This is the *Aeneid*'s "hollow" pastoral.

Obstipuit primo aspectu (I. 613). Dido falters here because she is looking to a future which for her never comes (cf. *quis tibi tum, Dido, cernenti talia sensus*, IV. 408; *vidit*, 587). The idea that epic women ordinarily "see" in this way and therefore speak differently from men is concretised in the notion of "feminine syntax" sometimes used to explicate the *Odyssey*.[6] There it is alleged to produce a comic effect. And when real-life ladies of distinction at Rome are complimented in the *De Oratore* on their pure Latinity, again this is language of a certain sort. The speaker is Crassus (III. §45):

Equidem cum audio socrum meam Laeliam ... eam sic audio, ut Plautum mihi aut Naevium videar audire....

The impression made on my ears by my mother-in-law Laelia is as if I were listening to Plautus or Naevius.

Presumably the allusion is to Naevius' comedies, and that poet certainly had a lively eye for a pretty girl (*Tarentilla*, 74–79, W.). But even in the *Bellum Punicum* we read *blande et docte percontat Aeneas quo pacto / Troiam urbem liquisset* (19–20, W.), and (because of the adverbs) this might have been Dido, using courtly, refined speech suited to her rank.[7]

Attention to character of this kind (ἠθοποιία) was thought by the ancients to be characteristic of comedy (Quint. VI. 2. 20). Menander's skill in using style to illustrate character is well known.[8] The pastoral itself, set

---

[6] The phrase is borrowed from B. L. Gildersleeve's review (*AJP* XXVIII [1907]) of M. Bréal, *Pour mieux connaître Homère* (Paris 1906).

[7] Latinus is suggested as the subject of *percontat*, but elsewhere, in an interchange between kings, the poet uses *comiter* (Warmington, *ROL*, II, p. 138, frr. 2-3). The historical present is noteworthy: above, p. 91.

[8] Cf. F. H. Sandbach, "Menander's Manipulation of Language for Dramatic Purposes" in *Ménandre*, Entretiens de la Fondation Hardt 16 (Vandoeuvres–Genève 1970), pp. 111–36, and the dissertation of J. S. Feneron, *Some Elements of Menander's Style* (Stanford 1976). The Menandrean use of a tragic

under the patronage of Thalia (*Ecl.* 6. 2), adapted for the stage, was also comic, even mimic. Servius was evidently aware that Book IV of the *Aeneid*—Dido's book—was not normal epic. He notes at its outset: *paene comicus stilus est.* Comedy / iambic is the woman's genre right from the start,[9] but the comedy he had in mind was presumably that of both Menander and his contemporaries, so beloved of Roman audiences, and so much influenced by certain plays of Euripides, who was nevertheless τραγικώτατος τῶν ποιητῶν (*Poetics* 1453a 29–30). Is there in general any evidence to sustain Servius' feeling either here or wherever else women figure in the *Aeneid*, and does it tell us something about how we are supposed to react to their characters?

Tragi-comedy

Whatever the predilection of Hellenistic critics for drawing distinctions between genres, Callimachean theory had understood, in Aristotle's wake, that at certain points tragedy and comedy touched.[10] Homer already exemplified this: his immortal δακρυόεν γελάσασα (*Il.* VI. 484) was cited above. Tragedy had seized and taken to extremes this gentle hint. Who but Euripides could have made a heroine out of Creusa in his sentimental *Ion*, or in his terrifying *Bacchae* have portrayed two old gentlemen on the verge of dancing, or a deluded mother brandishing the head of her own son, and then slowly realising the import of her behaviour?

Tragic Virgil's comedy is more restrained. Yet, although his dignified and decorous characters may display little of the broad humour found at the end of *Iliad* I, or of the sexual electricity between Paris and Helen of *Iliad* III, there is in him both a tendency to avoid or simplify the pretentious language of earlier Latin tragedy, intrusively evident in the fragments of Accius, and a sympathy (to be noted below) with the tragic pantomime. Like Homer (cf. Aristotle, *Poetics* 1448b 35), he was δραματικός, but in his age and in his Rome "dramatic" in a particular way. The stagy style, exaggerated and selective in its methods, of itself fosters in its audience a certain awareness of artificiality, the willing suspension of disbelief which at some moments may be strained to breaking point and anti-climax. How much more the antics of the *histrio*!

model as a subtext underlying the actions of his characters is noted above, p. 84. — For Greek tragedy, see Laura McClure, *Spoken like a Woman: Speech and Gender in Athenian Drama* (Princeton 1999). Clytaemnestra and Antigone are noted below (pp. 116, 155).

[9] Cf. "Iambe / Iambos and the Rape of a Genre," above, p. 86.

[10] *Interdum vocem comoedia tollit*, etc. Horace, *A.P.* 93 ff. Above, p. 97.

Tragedy supremely selects because it has to do with the unsustainable male effort to live alone on some peak of glory: αἰὲν ἀριστεύειν καὶ ὑπείροχον ἔμμεναι ἄλλων. No man can be a hero all the time. He must either surrender the struggle or die, go under the earth or come back to earth.

Women are not heroes in Achilles' sense. Their forte is endurance, their weapon is laughter in its various forms, and that is why their genre was the iambic, comedy. They are confronted by their very nature with realities —relationships, love, children, family—which explains why their comedies so often culminate in weddings or even births, their tragedies in the loss of precisely those felicities.

Virgil, who wrote a tragedy, also involved women in his heroic web, sometimes as spectators (his *matres* are the extreme case), but not always. Here too, on the human level at least, the listener notes a pattern of declension: Dido, Camilla, Juturna: a Herculean, suicidal queen; a woodland, fantasy figure; a lone chariot driver driven off the field in the end by a furious bird. This concession to the feminine meant however that he was always at risk of writing tragi-comedy, something the Renaissance Italian epicists gratefully took from him into their own Virgilian poems. The student of the *Aeneid* must be alert to this element of comedy both in its action and its speech.

The Rhetor's Rules

The *Aeneid* we read is the record of a recited, theatrical art, and Donatus reports that its author was a virtuoso performer, celebrated for his *vox et os et hypocrisis* (*Vita Verg.* §29). That simple premise must condition our reactions to his epic.

Reciting voices—even those of women—in so sophisticated a society as Virgil's Rome had to obey the rhetor's rules. Yet what most distinguishes the response to literature of moderns from that of their predecessors is said to be ignorance of and even contempt for rhetoric.[11] What about "sincerity"? But untutored sincerity, reflecting "real life," is not art (and *a fortiori* not superior to art). To argue so is rather like saying that canons and fugues are inferior to wild strumming on the electric guitar, or irrelevant to some structurally perfect ("artificial") masterpiece which nevertheless gives expression to humanity's innermost aspirations. Shelley's skylark poured

---

[11] Good remarks from a non-Classicist on rhetoric at the Renaissance in Peter Ackroyd's *Life of Thomas More* (New York 1998), pp. 25–26. The association with the stage is telling. James VI's youthful sonnet on the "perfyte poete" (1584), noting "Rhetorique" as part of his essential accomplishments, is quoted by Norman Davies, *The Isles. A History* (New York 1999), pp. 540–41.

her full heart in profuse strains of paradoxically unpremeditated art. At a given point, canons and fugues—internalised, moulded, transformed, "necessary" (in Aristotle's sense)—become a means to the sublimest end. When art acting on the receptive talent creates a second nature, these apparent opposites blend (Horace, *A.P.* 410-11). We cannot always now fruitfully separate them.

If then talk about poetic rhetoric raises hackles,[12] this is to forget that the very origins of rhetoric lay in the application to prose of the devices which had made poetry (like love) so eminently persuasive. Gorgias himself may be seen, not as abandoning philosophy after the impasse reached by his early enquiries into the possibility of communication, but as the explorer *par excellence* of a different way of communication, via transrational language.[13] Such language, because poetic, was bound to be musical, and this is why we find his disciple Isocrates championing the need μουσικῶς εἰπεῖν (*In Soph.* §16). His remarks, which owe some debt to lyric Pindar (*Ol.* 3. 8-9), may be paired with Philodemus' καὶ ἐπεὶ μάρτυρας ἐπισπᾶται τοὺς μουσικοὺς τοῦ λέγειν ἀληθῶς οὐδὲν συκοφαντεῖ (*De Poematis* V, Mangoni, p. 139). Philodemus dedicated a treatise to Virgil. Virgil's admirer Dante would still define poetry as "a fiction made from rhetoric and music." His remarks furnish the epigraph to this chapter.

Rhetoric in the *Aeneid* is both inevitable, and yet not the mechanical assemblage of discrete tricks to which objection is rightly raised. As the poet "pronounced" his verses (*Vita Don.* §29), they fused into a copious stream of sounding eloquence (*bene sonare, ibid.*) which must be imbibed as a unity. Its divisions are marked, not just by the arrangement of words within the line (though the argument about metathesis, noted below, shows how important that is), but by the impact of the paragraph, which thus becomes a liquescent element within a flowing whole. A presentation by French actors of one of Racine's tragedies may be the closest modern

---

[12] Even R. Heinze, the admirer of Eduard Norden, historian of rhetoric, is suspicious. *Virgils epische Technik* devotes a few paltry pages (431-35) to this essential topic. G. Highet, *The Speeches in Vergil's* Aeneid (Princeton 1972), concludes (pp. 277 ff.) that Virgil was a poet rather than an orator. Oratory is part of the world "of disorder and conflict and pain, inhabited by false dreams" (p. 290). The distinction is too sharply made. What other world does the *Aeneid* ordinarily inhabit? An older study by K. Billmayer (*Rhetorische Studien zu den Reden in Vergils* Aeneis, diss. Würzburg 1932) is carefully impartial. H. Belling, *Studien über die Compositionskunst in der* Aeneide (Leipzig 1899) argues for numerical balances as an organisational principle in the speeches too (here followed by Billmayer, pp. 84-87). Sven Lundström, *Acht Reden in der* Aeneis (Uppsala 1977), offers a discussion however of meaning rather than form.

[13] "Protagoras, Gorgias and the Dialogic Principle," *ICS* XI (1986), 43-61.

analogue to a Virgilian performance. Racine, in whose own dramaturgy a debt to comedy is observed, is noted for his women characters.[14]

Controversies

Post ubi digressi ... (IV. 80). Like Dido herself, we are often left to reconstruct silences. The hubbub has died away, and among the ruins of the feast drift a few floating leaves,[15] the fading remnants of discarded garlands, the token of voices now stilled. But the Rome of the Augustan Age was noisy, loud among other things with intense debate about the effective use of language, by orators and poets. Greeks arriving from the periphery of classical Hellas had much to say. Could word order make an essential contribution to meaning? Philodemus of Gadara and Dionysius of Halicarnassus, with Cicero, argued for the impossibility of metathesis.[16] Horace picks up these arguments, at first brashly contradicting Philodemus (*Sat.* I. 4. 60–62), then, with his doctrine of the *callida iunctura* (*A.P.* 46–48), ultimately accepting his view. The skilful use of prosaicisms[17] (allied with *curiosa felicitas*) offered an alternative to the old Roman (liturgical) notion that the only way to secure emphasis was by repetition of synonyms or synonymous phrases. A variation from expected idiom might be more effective. Perhaps Gallus had pioneered the technique.[18] Dido at least appears to borrow it. Her already noted *solvite corde metum* (I. 562), for the expected *solvite corda metu* (*solvite* replacing the metrically intractable *liberate*), is an inversion raising an ordinary turn of phrase to epic

---

[14] One might also listen to the recordings of James Joyce reading excerpts from *Finnegans Wake*. Molly's monologue at its finale is familiar.

[15] *Ac veluti folia arentes liquere corollas, / quae passim calathis strata natare vides*, Prop. II. 15. 51–52. The image lurks in the background of Horace, *Odes* I. 25. 19–20.

[16] Philodemus: P. Herc. 1676, tr. C [Sbordone]; Dionysius: *Comp. Verb.* ch. 4; Cicero: *Orator* 70, §§232–34. So also Quintilian (IX. 4)—and Tolstoy and Eisenstein. Dante's argument against translation may be compared (*Convivio* I. 7): "Nulla cosa per legame musaico armonizzata si può della sua loquela in altra trasmutare, senza rompere tutta sua dolcezza e armonia. E questa è la ragione per che Omero non si mutò di Greco in Latino...."

[17] Cf. κλέπτεται δ' εὖ, ἐάν τις ἐκ τῆς εἰωθυίας διαλέκτου ἐκλέγων συντιθῇ· ὅπερ Εὐριπίδης ποιεῖ καὶ ὑπέδειξε πρῶτος, Aristotle, *Rhetoric* III. 1404b 24–25. On older (and persistent) notions at Rome of poetic style, H. Haffter, *Untersuchungen zur altlateinischen Dichtersprache* (Berlin 1934).

[18] *Templa* ... *fixa* ... *spolieis* instead of *spolia (ad)fixa templis* in the new fragments: cf. *quae te* ... *sententia vertit* (I. 237) for *cur sententiam mutasti* and similar tricks.

dignity. This is how we must understand Agrippa's criticism.[19]

Not surprisingly, argument developed (already foreshadowed in Isocrates) about the scope of rhetorical rules in the creative ("poetic") process. It would of course have been impossible to urge their total irrelevance. Apollodorus of Pergamum, Augustus' teacher, urged strict compliance. Theodorus of Gadara, teacher of Tiberius, allowed genius to bend rules to its own needs. Tiberius was also, like Gallus, another soldier-poet, an admirer of Euphorion, court poet of the Syrian Seleucids, whose œuvre included a treatise on the *sambuca* (שׂבכא), rejected by Aristotle (*Politics* VIII. 1341b 1), and whose art may have exalted the power of music over rationality.[20] Certainly one feels that influence in the lush harmonies of yet another Gadarene, Meleager. And if Virgil is musical?

Rhetoric at Rome

It was the glory of Rome that literature—*belles lettres*—could re-assume there, notably under Augustus, a public role. Public figures even practised what they patronised. Tiberius, sceptical about rigid rules, actually modelled his own poems, not only on the work of Euphorion and Rhianus, but also on that of Parthenius of Nicaea, in Bithynia (Suet., *Tib.* 70. 2), the home of mimic, "ridiculous" Philistion (Martial II. 41. 15). But Parthenius, who dedicated the Ἐρωτικὰ Παθήματα to Gallus, had advised Virgil *in Graecis* (Macrobius). There is a curious contradiction. Scholars exalt Roman impatience in that Golden Age with the pettifogging minutiae of (Alexandrian) Greek pedants ("back to the Classics!"—as if the Alexandrian Library were not overflowing with Classical works at which we now only guess). But then, when we look beneath the surface, such "pedants" as Parthenius are found in the suites of Roman grandees, and in the company of the most creative Roman authors. Philodemus and Crinagoras are other examples.

Certainly, too much exegesis of ancient poetic rhetoric, parading its lists of schemes, has focused on the means and forgotten the music—and the ἠθοποιία—to serve which they were (and are) used.[21] Their very presence is

---

[19] Apud *Vita Verg. Don.* §44. *Ex communibus verbis* here is important.

[20] *Sambuca*: A. Meineke, *Analecta Alexandrina* (Berlin 1843), p. 67; OT Daniel c. 3 (Babylon). Euphorion's poetry and music: B. A. van Groningen, *La poésie verbale grecque* (Royal Netherlands Academy of Sciences, Letterkunde, N. R. 16 [1953], pp. 169–272). Hence Cicero's pointed *cantores Euphorionis*, T. D. III §45.

[21] Notoriously true, for example, of R. J. Getty's edition of Lucan I. — The idea that music has and affects character is fundamental to Plato (*Rep.* III) and Aristotle (*Politics* VIII).

sometimes thought by romantics to betoken a falling away from aschematic perfection. But we are in Rome, where tragic Pacuvius' *flexanima atque omnium regina rerum oratio* paid notable tribute to eloquence.[22] *Et tamen meas chartas revisitote* is the lingering farewell of the *Catalepton* to the *inanes ... rhetorum ampullae* of Virgil's youth (*Catal.* 5. 1, 13–14).[23] Macrobius regards the poet as a supreme rhetorician (V. 1. 1), just as the Greek critics saw Homer. Virgil is still described by Dante as a master of the *parola ornata* (*Inf.* 2. 67), and the entire *Aeneid* is full in that sense of rhetoric. Without its aid, would the ancients have thought effective speech possible?

If rhetoric is still suspect, this is in its way to assert that it is appropriate only to the high style, and that poetry (even epic poetry, if it hopes to be "sincere") must be written in some other vein. But why? In any case, Virgil, a master of all three of the *genera dicendi*, makes it clear at the outset of his epic that he is wholly committed to the power of rhetoric. The *Aeneid*'s system of similes opens with an arresting exaltation of this very theme. The turmoil of the unruly waters is settled by Neptune, just as an angry mob is quelled when public disorder threatens and *Furor* is busily supplying weapons of conflict.[24] It is then that some statesman, "weighty" (כבד) for his *pietas* and services to the commonwealth, is able to gain control of angry hearts (I. 153):

ille regit dictis animos et pectora mulcet.

Dictis is Ennian (*Ann.* 250, Sk.; cf. *dicti studiosus*, 209). In his eulogy of

---

[22] Warmington, *ROL* II, p. 232, no. 187 (from the *Hermiona*); cf. Euripides, *Hecuba* 816; Cicero, *De Oratore* II. §187; Quintilian I. 12. 18. *Flexanima* helps us to see that the rhetoricians' σχήματα διανοίας has been somewhat misunderstood. *Animus* is not νοῦς. The διάνοια of a poem is a *t.t.* for its imaginative range. Ion did not expound Homer in the classroom (διανοίας, *Ion* 530d).

[23] Cf. *an tragica desaevit et ampullatur in arte*, Horace, *Epp.* I. 3. 14; *ampullas*, *A.P.* 97: *hoc a Callimacho sustulit*, Porphyrio *ad loc*. Cf. *nosti illas* ληκύθους, Cic., *Att.* I. 14. 3 (Watt, p. 19) and Philodemus' λη]κύθων (P. Herc. 1081a fr. 41 = 39 Hausrath, overlooked in the Revised Supplement to LSJ⁹).

[24] Virgil is often criticised for this apparent incongruity, but the opening of Genesis shows that the victory of the creative word over the waters of chaos is an ancient topos in Near Eastern myth (cf. OT Job 38:11; NT Mark 4:39). A speech of this kind given to Thomas More in a play dealing with his life ("Ill May Day," *The Booke of Sir Thomas Moore*, BL, MS Harleian 7368, Addition II. D, "Hand D") preserves an imagery of angry mob ~ swelling sea ("o'er the bank" [45], "shark ... ravenous fishes" [95]). The passage is said to have been written out by Shakespeare himself. See *The Oxford Companion to Shakespeare* (2001), p. 434.

the *vir bonus dicendi peritus*, Quintilian glosses our passage (XII. 1. 27).

This is an Isocratean and Ciceronian ideal. Sallust, the historian of the Republic's decline, had already painted a picture of C. Memmius, addressing the people when they were in an ugly mood; as it turned out in those pre-Augustan days, futilely:

> dignitati quam irae magis consulens sedare motus et animos eorum mollire. (*Jug.* 33. 3)
>
> He put order ahead of anger, and tried to bring calm to their agitation, peace to their passions.

Virgil's simile in fact is a programmatic statement of the public purpose the vatic poem is meant to serve.[25] The *adlocutio* of the Prima Porta statue (after 20 B.C.?) may be put into this context.

Dido and Gaius Gracchus

But rhetoric may also work to stir the feelings of the crowd. Such rhetoric is not exclusively male, or perhaps rather male rhetoric at its most intense and self-aware converges with female into the human. Caius Gracchus' lament at the outset of the Civil Wars distracting Rome even before Virgil's birth was famous (apud Cic., *De Oratore* III. §214):[26]

> 'Quo me miser conferam? Quo vertam? In Capitoliumne? At fratris sanguine madet. An domum? Matremne ut miseram lamentantem videam et abiectam.'
>
> 'Poor wretch, where shall I take myself? Where shall I turn? To the Capitol? It is still soaked with my brother's blood. To my home? To see my poor mother, mourning and downcast?'

With the paeonic run of short syllables after a longum in *sanguine madet* here may be compared αὐτός ἐστιν ὁ κτανὼν / τὸν παῖδα τὸν ἐμόν in Thetis' lament over the body of Achilles in Aeschylus (apud Plato, *Rep.* III. 383b), which also shows marked use of anaphora and homoeoteleuton.

Nec te tua funera mater ... (*Aen.* IX. 486). The resort by Gracchus to his mother is absolutely in Virgil's manner.[27] And, harking back, the listener to Gracchus' voice knew what had happened to him.

In this version of the *subiectio*, considering and rejecting a number of

---

[25] This point is developed below, pp. 323–24, where Aristotle, *Politics* VIII. 1342a 4–16, is quoted.

[26] It is adduced by R. Heinze, *Virgils epische Technik*, p. 136, n. 1, who remarks on its kinship with the lament of Ennius' Medea (Warmington, *ROL* I, 284–85 = p. 118, 217–18, Jocelyn). All this fits perfectly into the structure of Virgil's poem and aesthetic.

[27] See above, pp. 46 ff., below, pp. 223–24, and more generally Susan Ford Wiltshire, *Public and Private in Vergil's* Aeneid (Amherst 1989).

false alternatives, we seem to hear something of Euripides' stricken Heracles (1283–86):

> ἐς ποῖον ἱερὸν ἢ πανήγυριν φίλων
> εἶμ'; οὐ γὰρ ἄτας εὐπροσηγόρους ἔχω.
> ἀλλ' "Αργος ἔλθω; πῶς, ἐπεὶ φεύγω πάτραν;
> φέρ' ἀλλ' ἐς ἄλλην δή τιν' ὁρμήσω πόλιν; ...

'To what temple, what solemn gathering of friends shall I go? The dooms I carry with me are not conversation pieces! Shall I go to Argos? How so, since I am an exile from my own land? Come then, shall I set out for some other city?'

This is adapted by Seneca in his *Hercules Furens* (1321).[28]

But if, unexpectedly on the lips of a Roman statesman, we also hear something of Euripides' Medea (502–04), imitated by Ennius (cf. also Apollonius IV. 378), we are bound to catch the tones of what would be Dido. *Nomadum* in her outcry again signals the presence of the hollow pastoral:

> en, quid ago? rursusne procos inrisa priores
> experiar, Nomadumque petam conubia supplex,...
> Iliacas igitur classis atque ultima Teucrum
> iussa sequar ...?
> quid tum? sola fuga nautas comitabor ovantis? ... (IV. 534 ff. excerpted)

But what do I mean to do? Shall I, already laughed to scorn, make trial again of my old suitors, and humbly seek a match with wandering shepherds? ... Shall I then chase after Ilium's ships, ready to discharge the Trojans' most menial commands? ... What next? Shall I fly off on my own, to keep company with their triumphant crews?

Like Tiberius Gracchus, Dido's husband had been brutally murdered. It is our foreknowledge (by vertical time) of what was in store for her which fills her words with the pathos felt in those of Caius Gracchus, and which alone makes the evocation of such a model appropriate and decorous.

"Rhetorical" is not a satisfactory term for these questions, which are in fact, as we shall see, a defining mark of the way Virgil's women talk. If man is a social animal and speech our most human characteristic, as Isocrates argued,[29] a "question not expecting any answer" is not a "lively way of making a statement," but an implicit denial of the whole dialogic basis of society (*veras audire et reddere voces*): not a trick, but a desolating acceptance of isolation and dissolution.

Parallels to Dido's rhetoric here indicate that she was treading the topical

---

[28] On the Hercules theme in the *Aeneid*, Appendix, below, pp. 329 ff. It encompasses *Dido furens*.

[29] *Antidosis* §293–94; cf. Aristotle, *Pol.* I. 1253a 10 *al*.; Dante, *Vulg. Eloq.* I. ii; *Convivio* III. 7.

path of the abandoned heroine.[30] But Virgil is doing more than follow the familiar round. It is a *historical* reality (a reality he knew) which is the genesis of his larger, cross-gendered recasting of the heroic experience. Into what mould? Cicero's Crassus adds a comment on Gracchus' outburst:

> quae sic ab illo esse acta constabat oculis, voce, gestu, inimici ut lacrimas tenere non possent. haec ideo dico pluribus, quod genus hoc totum oratores, qui sunt veritatis ipsius actores, reliquerunt; imitatores autem veritatis, histriones, occupaverunt.
>
> It was reported that all this was delivered by him with such looks, tone of voice and gesture that his very enemies could not restrain their tears. My reason for expanding on this point is that our modern speakers, for all their commitment to representing the truth, have entirely abandoned this style, leaving stage-actors, who only play at truth, to usurp it.

This suggests that Gracchus' emotional style was essentially that of the tragic actor. "Hypocritical" Virgil (*hypocrisis*, *Vita Don.* §29) would not have had any difficulty in borrowing it.

But, in doing that, he would have been acknowledging what Gracchus had already sensed at the very opening of Rome's troubled century of Civil War, that only tragedy could do justice to its horrors, and produce the κάθαρσις (Aristotle, *Politics* VIII. 1342a 11) which the citizen *vates* desired. In an apocalyptic age, what might have seemed escapism ultimately becomes realism (*veritas*). The children's bodies on this Roman stage, including those of Cornelia's children, are not leaking cranberry juice,[31] but real blood. Just as the Attic stage had held up to the Athenians in their imperial century a mirror of their history and morals; just as Shakespeare would perform that same role for the English confronting a New World; so in its new era Virgil's tragedy would interpret to Romans their sanguinary past and their future calling.

Cornelia, mother of the Gracchi, was not always "mourning and downcast." She presided over her sons' education (Tac., *Dialogus* 28; cf. Plutarch, *C. Gracchus* 19), and is praised by Cicero (*Brutus* §211) for her own style. How did women then react to these calamities, what rhetoric framed their utterance? Can tragedy employ comic methods without denaturing itself? Most importantly perhaps of all, what is the use of rhetoric to a poetic discourse for which words are too often both inadequate and misleading?

---

[30] Sophocles, *Ajax* 514 ff. (Tecmessa); Catullus 64. 177 (Ariadne): *Roman Catullus*, pp. 407 ff. Further parallels in G. Mooney's note to Apollonius, *Arg.* IV. 355; below, p. 129.

[31] To borrow a phrase from Alexander Blok's Балаганчик (1906), itself the product of a revolutionary and bloody time.

A Rhetoric of Silences

For, if "rhetoric" suggests ῥῆσις, "talking," Virgil's rhetoric of omission and silence (*inceptus clamor frustratur hiantis*, VI. 493) is not like that.

In Attic tragedy, Aeschylus had made pointed use of the pregnant silence (Aristophanes, *Frogs* 911–13): of what the pantomime matured into αὐδήεσσα or φωνήεσσα σιωπή (Nonnus, *Dion*. XIX. 156; *Anth. Pal.* IX. 505. 18). Simonides had already called painting "silent poetry" (Plutarch, *de Glor. Ath.* 3. 346f), and Greek vases illustrate both the interaction of painting with poetry, and the technique of not saying all.[32] Familiar on the stage (and even more familiar if the pantomime, as Weinreich argues, was already known in classical Athens), the sophisticated art of narration by silence had also been made famous in the classical period (late 5th c.) by the painter Timanthes of Sicyon. Cicero relates how, in depicting the sacrifice of Iphigenia, Timanthes indicated varying degrees of sorrow among the spectators waiting at the altar.[33] It is permissible to interpret his remarks. The priest Calchas stood there, sorry, of course, though for him perhaps this was the almost routine fulfilment of a religious duty. Next was Odysseus, calculating, shrewd, even so less impervious to human feeling than his clerical colleague. Then Menelaus: with what eyes could he watch his virginal niece being cut down in the flower of her youthful beauty, for the sake of his honour and desire to recover his adulterous wife? Finally, the girl's father stood by the altar—Agamemnon. What were his feelings? His daughter, his own flesh and blood, was to die in order to preserve his position and prestige as commander-in-chief. Did he weep? Did he try to seem resolute? How would he look? The painter showed him turned away, and (in a sublime version of normal Greek behaviour) muffled in his robe. Silence spoke louder than words. It was for the spectator to supply the father's feelings from his own heart and to his own satisfaction.

---

[32] K. Schefold, *Gotter- und Heldensagen der Griechen in der spätarchaischen Kunst*, notes, for example (p. 272), *komplettierendes Erzählen* (a version of vertical time) and *Gegenüberstellung* (the viewer to supply the link between discrete episodes, already a version of Callimachus' αὐτὸς ἐπιφράσσαιτο).

[33] *Orator* 22. §74: "The painter saw, when, at the sacrifice of Iphigenia, Calchas was sad, Ulysses more sad, Menelaus in mourning, that Agamemnon's head had to be muffled, since he could not depict with the brush that supreme degree of grief"; cf. Pliny, *N. H.* XXXV. 73: "He veiled the face of her actual father, unable to depict it satisfactorily." A version of Timanthes' painting from the House of the Tragic Poet at Pompeii is preserved in Naples. See also the relief on the circular marble altar signed by Cleomenes (the sculptor of Marcellus' funeral statue), now in the Uffizi Gallery, Florence.

Chapter Five

This leap into another dimension, from showing to not-showing, made Timanthes' picture celebrated. And, as Aristotle's oxymoronic ὁμαλῶς ἀνώμαλον suggests (*Poetics* 1454a 27-28), these techniques of antithesis more generally were familiar to dramatists. The hypothesis to Euripides' *Medea* records that some evidently unsophisticated critics blamed the author for inconsistencies in his heroine's character. Ὑπόκρισις recurs:

μέμφονται δὲ αὐτῷ τὸ μὴ πεφυλαχέναι τὴν ὑπόκρισιν τῇ Μηδείᾳ, ἀλλὰ προσπεσεῖν εἰς δάκρυα, ὅτε ἐπεβούλευσεν Ἰάσονι καὶ τῇ γυναικί.

He is faulted for not sustaining Medea's role, and for her resort to tears when plotting against Jason and his wife.[34]

Dido is Medea's heiress. This gives some small indication of the ears we must lend to the interpretation of her polyphonic role in the epic.

Philodemus emphasised the importance of music. "Heard melodies are sweet, but those unheard are sweeter" is Keats' anticipation of the adage that the music begins where the orchestra stops. Dido, whose melodies are certainly heard,[35] is more notable for such silences:

tacitum vivit sub pectore vulnus. (IV. 67; cf. 689)

incipit effari mediaque in voce resistit. (IV. 76)

totumque pererrat
luminibus tacitis et sic accensa profatur. (IV. 363-64)

haec effata silet, pallor simul occupat ora. (IV. 499)

What does *sic* (οὕτως εἰκῇ) imply in the third example here? *Tacitum vulnus, tacita lumina* are extraordinary (Gallan?) extensions of the meaning of simple words. The "silent moon" of the Greeks' treacherous return (*tacita luna*, II. 255) will become the silent Dido of Book VI.

In a last example from Book IV, *sermonem*, whose etymology the poet supplies elsewhere (VI. 160), is particularly cruel. Its aftermath, a climax and culmination carefully integrated within the fabric of the poem, is heard later in Book VI:

his medium dictis s e r m o n e m abrumpit et auras
aegra fugit ... (IV. 388-89)

illa solo fixos oculos aversa tenebat,

---

[34] In a similar vein Eisenstein remarks: "In ancient tragedy one is frequently struck, not so much by a double, divided nature, but at times and above all by the sometimes unmotivated breakdown of a character into another extreme, incommensurate and irreconcilable with the first, into another contradiction" (Избранные Произведения III, p. 137). The difference is that he approves of this method of composition.

[35] Cf. Jan Novák, *Dido. Cantata on the fourth book of Vergil's* Aeneid (1967).

nec magis incepto vultum sermone movetur
quam si dura silex aut stet Marpesia cautes. (VI. 469-71)

471. The proper name is suggestively ambiguous. Marpesia was an Amazon queen and leader of an expedition which in Priam's boyhood sacked Troy. Still in Asia Minor, she was killed by barbarians (Justin II. 4. 12; Orosius I. 15). Marpessa, wife of the headstrong Idas, rejected the love of Apollo (Apollodorus, I. 7. 9).[36] She committed suicide on learning of her husband's death (Pausanias, IV. 2. 7). Her daughter was Cleopatra (*Iliad* IX. 556).

We already noted the parallel of VI. 469 here with I. 482. Dido has never in fact been good at *sermo* with Aeneas. One senses the artificiality at her banquet (I. 748).

After IV. 387, there is no further direct exchange between the two former lovers. Aeneas, though he would like to soothe her pain with words, goes instead to his ships (393-96). We are asked to find our own way into Dido's heart. As was noted earlier, a woman sees differently (IV. 408-10):

quis tibi tum, Dido, cernenti talia sensus,
quosve dabas gemitus, cum litora fervere late
prospiceres arce ex summa ... !

What were your feelings, Dido at that sight? What sighs came from you when you saw from your high tower the feverish bustle along the shore?

The pantomime is not far away. Virgil turns us into choreographers, matching his lyrical outburst with his character's silent, interpretative dance. Turnus' last confusions are an extreme example of this (*tum pectore sensus / vertuntur varii*, XII. 914-15). Once again we find *verto*. In his case, *videt* (918) opens onto emptiness.

Both Dido and Turnus were favourite pantomime roles. It is this kinship with musical or operatic performance which justifies us in making allowance in the *Aeneid* generally for more silences than theirs. Formal oratory certainly knew of the *intervallum* (Cicero, *Orator* §53; auctor ad Herennium, III. §21). But this is more. The characters' ceaseless whirl of thought is not stilled when they are seen in action; rather it is their actions which, by a kind of μετάληψις αἰσθήσεως, we must hear and interpret. "To hear with eyes belongs to love's fine wit." Callimachus' already cited αὐτὸς ἐπιφράσσαιτο, τάμοι δ' ἄπο μῆκος ἀοιδῇ had heralded this hypersensitivity.[37] It is the Marsyan (Dante, *Par.* 1. 19-21) poetic which

---

[36] A relief showing Marpessa spurning the advances of Apollo is found in the centre of a Calene bowl (BM GR 1873.8-20.429 [Vase G 132], 300-100 B.C.).

[37] On which also see Demetrius, *De Eloc.* 222, who adduces Theophrastus. See further μὴ λαλέοντος τοῦ ὀρχηστοῦ ἀκούειν, Lucian, *Salt.* 62; *quae solet in lepido Polyhymnia docta theatro / Muta loqui*, Dracontius, *Medea* 17-18; O. Weinreich, *Epigramm und Pantomimus* (Heidelberg 1948), pp. 115 ff. Shakespeare, *Sonnets* 23, end, quoted above, is adduced by Thomas Mann,

later induced Michelangelo to put his own face on his depiction of St. Bartholomew's flayed skin in the Sistine Chapel.

The abrupt ending of a speech before the end of a line is part of this suggestivity.[38] The technique, not Homeric, looks like a version of the dramatic ἀντιλαβή, the division of a line between speakers; in Virgil, between character and narrator / chorus. But music more generally imposes its own structures. When the poet listened to his characters speak and fall silent, how could he avoid noting what their teachers had taught them?[39]

Character and Aspiration

Some rhetorical rules, it was suggested, came to be devised by too rational teachers, who forgot that the original impulse of their discipline was musical, transrational. But not everyone forgot. Caius Gracchus (to mention him yet again) famously employed a flute-player to give his voice its pitch (Cic., *de Or.* III. §225 *al.*). His contemporary Lucilius' jests at the Isocratean manner (181–88, M.) were not "academic." They show that the Isocratean ideal of musical (balanced, assonant) speech was still alive.

In poetry, that is, as Dante defined it, musical rhetoric, two kinds of utterance are at work: one reveals character, and the other aspiration. One tells us something about the person speaking, and the other sets narrative in an ever-varying scale of revelation.

These two types may be illustrated. Opening her interview with her sister Ismene, Sophocles' Antigone begins grandiloquently. Αὐτάδελφον, later borrowed by Lycophron (*Alex.* 432), is Aeschylean, Ἰσμήνης κάρα is quasi-epic. But then she falls into a curious incoherence (1–3):

Ὦ κοινὸν αὐτάδελφον Ἰσμήνης κάρα,
ἆρ' οἶσθ' ὅτι Ζεὺς τῶν ἀπ' Οἰδίπου κακῶν—
ὁποῖον οὐχὶ νῷν ἔτι ζώσαιν τελεῖ;

Doktor Faustus (Frankfurt 1956), p. 84 ("Die Musik und das Auge"). Edith Wharton makes a lady from New York society refer with bitterness to the "*speaking* silence" (her italics) of English debutantes: "Their eyes and smiles were eloquent. She hoped it would teach their own girls that they need not chatter like magpies." *The Buccaneers* (Penguin edition 1994), p. 68. Add Meleager, *A.P.* XII. 63. 1; 122.3; 159. 3 (these homoerotic).

[38] Cf. J. Kvičala, cited by Norden ad VI. 45 ff.; see also his notes at 155, 885f. Austin collects some examples on IV. 276.

[39] The discussion in *The Classical Epic Tradition*, c. VI (pp. 245 ff.) may also be compared. Again, it insists on the *Aeneid* as *performed* art, rather than as a static γυμνάσιον εἰς ἐξήγησιν γραμματικήν (Clem. Alex., *Stromateis* V. 676 P. = G. Dindorf III [Oxford 1869], p. 40). Since Clement lists Euphorion, Callimachus and Lycophron as examples of his thesis, how much had been forgotten!

> My own dearest sister, Ismene! Do you know that of the ills we inherit from Oedipus—which of them Zeus does not fulfil for us twain while we still live?

'Οποῖον clumsily re-interprets the ὅτι in the familiar οἶσθ' ὅτι, "you know that."[40] She is already thinking beyond life. Her mood is fraught, and her whole speech reveals it. The effect is enlarged by the estranging duals.

Dido (whose speeches will be examined at more length in the next chapter) stands in this tradition. In conversation with her sister, she too begins with an exclamatory question (IV. 10). Like Antigone, she feels that she is to die (*sepulcro*, 29). In his proem, the poet himself had hammered on this point (*vulnus, saucia, infixi*). Her tragic exaggerations in this speech (she sees herself like some Capaneus blasted into hell) blend oddly with her yearning for life.

This is Dido playing a part. Elsewhere, drawn from a different script, the studied casualness of her understated remarks speaks volumes:

> quae mihi reddat eum vel eo me solvat amantem. (IV. 479)[41]
> quam mihi cum dederit cumulatam morte remittam. (IV. 436)
> non licuit thalami expertem sine crimine vitam
> degere more ferae ... (IV. 550–51).

This kind of transrational language, sometimes for commentators bordering on incoherence, exploits a "natural" eloquence whose enhancement by the skilled artist is not a betrayal of immediacy, but a revelation of latent possibilities. Comic Menander was a master of this sort of rhetoric, and he was thought to have been a close imitator of life itself.

There is also the revelatory, visionary mode, appropriate to the *vates*. In the first example here, Dido uses another of her characteristic apostrophes to blast the future's hopes:[42]

> ... 'Nullus amor populis nec foedera sunto.
> exoriare aliquis nostris ex ossibus ultor ...
> ...pugnent ipsique nepotesque.'   (IV. 624–25, 629)

In Book VI, the Sibyl lays down terms for an entrance ticket to hell:

> 'Duc nigras pecudes; ea prima piacula sunto.
> sic demum lucos Stygis et regna invia vivis
> aspicies.' dixit, pressoque obmutuit ore.   (VI. 153–55)

---

[40] Only then do we know what exactly it means. "O, τι—quod vix credas ita distinxisse poetam—maturius auditori tradit quod melius exspectatur.

[41] "This is a curious line, of deliberate near-prose," R. G. Austin *ad loc*. His comments on all three examples adduced may be perused.

[42] Cf. *exuviae*, IV. 651. The form is found elsewhere only as a nominative (XI. 577, Camilla). *Pudor* at IV. 27 is another vocatival hapax. Dido lives in an apostrophaic but often unresponsive world ("disobliging other").

These are the only two uses of *sunto* in the poem. Dido's hypermetric ending (IV. 629) crowns her rhetoric of silence. The Sibyl's ἀντιλαβή also speaks on.

As part of Virgilian cross-gendering, this manner is also used by or of males. In the examples offered, Jupiter speaks more triumphantly than men:

> 'His ego nec rerum metas nec tempora pono:
> imperium s i n e f i n e dedi ...'   (I. 278–79)

> 'Heu, miserande puer, si qua fata aspera rumpas,
> tu Marcellus eris! manibus date lilia plenis,
> purpureos spargam flores animamque nepotis
> his saltem accumulem donis, et fungar inani
> munere.' sic fatus ...   (VI. 882–86)

> Vitaque cum gemitu fugit indignata sub umbras.   (XII. 952)

What does Anchises' *inani / munere* say here (cf. IV. 217–18), what does *indignata* say in the last example? The poet, in two cases talking about generations yet to be born, in the other about one to be lost, is not so much noting the character of the speaker as marking the limits of Roman and human experience. Un discours sans bornes se prolonge dans l'infini.

It will be seen that these modes, the ethopoeic and the apocalyptic, do not wholly coincide with the Apolline and "furious" styles already noted.[43] There is too much suffering for one of those categories to contain it neatly.

Words

Choice of words (ἐκλογὴ ὀνομάτων, *dilectus verborum*) was one of the rhetorician's chief tasks. This is where the concordance comes into its own, revealing associations and echoes present to the τορὸν οὖας of the composing poet, but too faint to tweak the critic's fuzzy organ. Some occurrences in the *Aeneid* of words such as *infelix* and *thalamus* have previously been noted.[44] Every student will embroider (καταποικίλλειν, an Isocratean term) these patterns.[45]

Words only make sense as *paroles*, as part of a language. Virgil's religious language both employs words of a certain type, and casts them into inherited, pre-rational moulds. His prayers and hymns are an obvious instance.[46] The study of these ancient frames of discourse often carries the

---

[43] Above, p. 9. Apollo inspires his own fury (VI. 100–01).

[44] Above, pp. 49 ff.

[45] R.O.A.M. Lyne, *Words and the Poet* (Oxford 1989).

[46] Frances V. Hixon, *Roman Prayer Language. Livy and the* Aeneid *of Vergil* (Beiträge zur Altertumskunde 30, Stuttgart 1993).

enquirer into anthropology. It is not the exegete's task here either to impose or to dispose, but rather to observe.

Other frames were learned consciously, in the school. Naevius, it was noted, linked *blande* with *docte* (19. 1); and Ennius, who joined *doctus* with *fidelis* in a (self-?) eulogy (*Ann*. 279, Sk.), also praised *docta dicta* (*Ann*. 250). This was hardly a fault. If speech is indeed our most human characteristic, rhetoric, the linguistic version of good manners, is quite literally civilising—and the *vates* was a *civis*.[47]

The choice of words to fill these epic frames then is not any merely mechanical eschewal of "low" expressions, but the effort, by avoiding the mundane, to leave room for the Muse. But not in search of a monotonous sublime! Art determines utterance.

Virgil of course used, like Homer, an inherited treasure of lofty language. But an increasing use has been detected in the second half of the *Aeneid* of "unpoetic" ὀνόματα κύρια: words such as *gladius*, *necare*, (transitive) *occidere*—to which one may add ugly words such as *mussare*—suited perhaps to its despairingly bloody message.[48] Yet that half was introduced by an appeal to Erato. Is this yet more influence of feminine, comic realism? Is this ugliness of war what women "see"? Juturna's legalistic *virginitas* and *reponit* may be added here, part of a marriage contract which went wrong.[49] In earlier books, medical and physiological language was perverted: *uterus, fetus*. Metaphors were realised unexpectedly: *vulnus alit venis* (the fetus Dido feeds is her maturing deathstroke). Even Juno, goddess

---

[47] Hor., *Odes* I. 32. 5. See below (p. 313) on the quite un-Homeric use of the vocatival *cives* in the *Aeneid*.

[48] B. Axelson, *Unpoetische Wörter* (Lund 1945), p. 144, a book which E. Fraenkel described as "stets erregend." —In view of a recent assertion that the concept of "prosaic" words was unknown to antiquity, clarification is needed. Aristotle certainly knew that there were "low" words: λέξεως δὲ ἀρετὴ σαφῆ καὶ μὴ ταπεινὴν εἶναι, *Poetics* 1458a 18; cf. *Rhetoric* III. 1404b 24–25, quoted above at note 17. In Aristotle's train, Theophrastus had rejected ὀνόματα μικρὰ καὶ ταπεινά (Dion. Hal., *de Isocr.* c. 16, p. 101 R.). So did the later rhetorical tradition, encapsulated, for example, in "Virgil's Wheel" (illustrated in *The Classical Epic Tradition*, p. 250). Romans certainly understood what was meant by Horace's *Musa pedestris* (*Sat*. II. 6. 17 = Callimachus' Μουσέων πεζὸς νομός, *Aet*. fr. 112. 9; cf. *LSJ*⁹ s.v. πεζός II. 1. See also *Ars Poetica* 95, *Epp*. II. 1. 250–51). Admittedly, for them not all prose was prosaic in our sense. Some prose could display artistic (and therefore "poetic") qualities: ποιητικόν, Isocrates, *In Soph*. §12; cf. Tacitus, *Dial*. 20. 4–7, and the extended German use of "Dichter" (the medieval *dictator*).

[49] *Virginitas* in epic here is extraordinary, though it is matched by the lawyer's *repono*. It is a religious / legal term (cf. the context of Catullus 62. 62), and comes close to this when used of Camilla, XI. 583. Ovid picks it up (*Met*. III. 255).

of marriage, can say *conceptumque excute foedus* ("abort the treaty [of peace] conceived," XII. 158).

In the right circumstances, Virgil, like the Italian epicists, like Milton, may resort even to the colloquial, as when Hecuba bids Priam join her with a phrase from comedy (II. 523). What does Dido conceal in such simple words as *fuit aut tibi quicquam dulce meum* (IV. 317–18)?[50] Clearly her unique *parvulus* (IV. 328) is meant to reveal a depth of frustrated maternal feeling, just as Andromache's *avunculus Hector* (III. 343; cf. XII. 440) drew us into the family circle. This is comedy set in the service of Melpomene.

But—also like Milton, and like Racine and Pindar—the poet habitually deploys large words that trail into penumbral vagueness.[51] The meaning of all his vocabulary, elaborate or simple, is enlarged by an ever-varying music of alliteration and assonance. Certain words he joins with others by quite irrational associations.[52] Some and perhaps most of the process governing these procedures was no doubt unconscious. In an accomplished virtuoso, much would have been deployed by apparent instinct, "second nature."

Quintilian's advice was *pectus est ... quod disertos facit, et vis mentis* (X. 7. 15), and with the latter phrase, which is not to be interpreted in any coldly intellectual sense, may be compared one of Varro's etymologies in the *De Poematis* for *vates: a vi mentis*. *Donne, ch'avete intelletto d'amore, ...* sang Dante ("Ladies, who have intelligence of love," *Vita Nuova*, canzone prima). Virgil's prescient women, who are less inclined to have trouble feeling their emotions, and who certainly do not lack the mind's power, would be Quintilian's ideal students, were it not that, like Hamlet, they have bad dreams. They cannot always maintain the academic balance. Though comedy is their genre, they cannot always be comic. Comedy, after all, promises rebirth. There are times however when their eloquence soars from love through sorrow into stillness, and from stillness into a hate dissatisfied with words.

---

[50] *Dulcis* is used 23 times, but the form *dulce* is found elsewhere only at IV. 493 (Dido again) and XII. 882 (Juturna).

[51] "Die grossen Pathetiker wie Pindar haben die Gabe, inexakt zu sein," F. Dornseiff, *Pindars Stil* (Berlin 1921), p. 23. On Virgil, J. Worstbrock, *Elemente einer Poetik der* Aeneis (Münster 1963). V. Shklovsky can still criticise Tolstoy for the same vagueness: Материал и Стиль в Романе Льва Толстого ‚Война и Мир' (Moscow 1928). In fact Tolstoy, overtly no friend of the Classics, had recovered, thanks to the remembering genre, the Classical tradition.

[52] F. X. Roiron, *Étude sur l'imagination auditive de Virgile* (Paris 1908).

VI

THE RHETORIC OF VIRGIL'S WOMEN—II

Dido

Paene comicus stilus est, nec mirum, ubi de amore tractatur (Servius ad *Aen.* IV, init.). Comedy, like the iambic in general, is the genre of laughter and survival, rebirth and resurrection. How does Dido survive? How, before that, does she play out her part?

Menander was to be one of Cynthia's models (Prop. IV. 5. 43; cf. III. 21. 28). There is certainly Menandrean theatre in *Aeneid* IV; for example, in Dido's appeal to her sister to act as intermediary (424). The comic device of the amatory go-between[1] fits in with the bias Servius remarks. Dido's eventual suicide, using Aeneas' phallic sword, on her *notum ... cubile* (648) inverts the comic device of the concluding wedding, found, for example, in the *Dyscolus*, as earlier in Aristophanes. And the only overt allusion to theatrical performances as such in the *Aeneid* (since the theatre of Book V is circensian) also occurs in IV (471), where Dido, who is building a theatre at Carthage (I. 427), dreams as if she were acting parts in or elaborated from Euripides, ancestor of New Comedy, such as those of Orestes or Pentheus —significantly, mad, liminal parts, flirting with laughter, of the kind that attracted the pantomimists. She has clearly attended too many shows already, which may explain why her book is so organised into dramatic set pieces: the queen in conversation with her sister, in passionate exchange with Aeneas, in soliloquy. This (again!) is the art of Racine, of the *Comédie française*.

Book IV is divided by its triple *at regina* (1, 296, 504) into three acts: the fire and wound of love; the treachery; the wound and fire of death. Just as much as in Ovid, celebrated for his *Medea*, everything becomes a matter of intellect undermined by emotion, here (by contrast with the black comedy of the Medea in *Metamorphoses* VII) with tragic implications, both for her

---

[1] E.g. *Perikeiromene* 508-10. Shakespeare's *Twelfth Night* uses the same trick. — In general, the studies of F. H. Sandbach and J. S. Feneron on Menander's ethopoeic language are again relevant (above, p. 103, n. 8). See also *Roman Catullus*, pp. 299-302.

and the city she represents. Her visits to the deserted banqueting hall by moonlight,[2] with the echo of Aeneas' own words (IV. 81b = II. 9b), are clearly the haunting of a now empty stage. In brief, hinted, quasi-pantomimic episodes she goes to Juno's temple, or ranges distraught about her city. Indeed we may adapt to the queen what Lord Spencer said of his sister, that she who was matched with the goddess of hunting (I. 499) by an ironic reversal becomes the supremely hunted (IV. 69; cf. *more ferae*, 551). The symbolic hunt is the chief occasion when Dido seems to step outside the palace into the open air before her death. She is the quarry (*capta*, IV. 330).[3] Trapped in the fateful cave she makes no speech, not even an "I do." Her pantomimic dance of love with Aeneas is left to our imaginations. Was it replicated in Aeneas' round-dance of death (XII. 763–64) with Turnus?

When she does speak, of course her words cannot be fitted into mere schemes. Does a symphonist write mere scales? Such schemes are valuable for the deviations they indicate as much as the conformities. If Dido, for example, appears to echo (IV. 308) not only Thrasonides' (*Misoumenos* 263) and Catullus' use of the third person for the first, but also Caesar's; or if she recalls, in her first persons, the spirit of Scipionic epitaphs (see below), this is not because she is Scipio or Caesar, even though she may (*dux femina facti*) have marshalled her people to its new home. Her wounds will be inflicted by Amor. There remains a felt counterpoint between the pattern and the pathos.[4]

Alliteration and rhythm are endemic to Latin. Even prose rhetoric uses them, and Dido's speeches, since Virgil wrote them, are continuously reinforced by the transrational devices of musical sound. There is repeated contrast between what she does not know and the reader does. Heightened by such half-heard ironies, her words rise into recitative and aria.

---

[2] Again the sensibility of Debussy. "La Terrasse des Audiences du Clair de Lune," one of the *Préludes*, echoes a Japanese painting of the late Heian period by Fujiwara Takaoshi ("The Imperial Palace by Moonlight"), noted by S. M. Eisenstein (Теоретические Исследования III, p. 279), who speaks of "ocular music" ("to hear with eyes ... "). Cf. from Debussy's *Images*: "Et la lune descend sur le temple qui fut," itself a verse quotation.

[3] Eisenstein's "Aristophanes effect" (above, p. 23). Love as huntsman / soldier was an old topos. Virgil asks us to understand it as more than a cliché. The sarcophagus from Grottarossa now in the Palazzo Massimo, with a hunting scene perhaps from *Aeneid* IV, is described below, p. 139.

[4] The pattern Semitic Dido fills with such pathos extends to include that of Semitic Christ, reflecting on His mission in the Gospels, conscious of the Cross (cf. Mark 10:45), and also at such times speaking of Himself in the third person. Matthew 26:24 (echoed at Mark 14:21 and Luke 22:22) records a third person, a curse and an allusion to treachery.

From what is supremely her book, some characteristic frames may be noted. She likes, for example, symmetrical blocks of twenty or so lines.[5] In them, she habitually uses language pointing to doom and death, even when on the surface she still has cause to hope. Her first verb in IV is *terrent* (9), and her dreams seem to be of the "black" kind.[6] This reinforces the tone set as early as line 1 by Virgil himself (*saucia*). As the book progresses, she and Aeneas combine to make the amatory metaphor real.

She alone in this book uses *fuisset* (18), with its sighing might-have-been, a tense from which she extracts unforgettable pathos at 327, and then raises to passionate intensity in her curse at 603, developed with a clear reminiscence of Medea (Apollonius, *Arg.* IV. 391–93). Ultimately she converts her sister to this idiom (*eadem me ad fata vocasses*, 678; *tulissem*, 604, *tulisses*, 679). Mezentius will later pick up this mannerism (X. 854, *dedissem*; cf. XI. 162, Pallas' mother; *dedissem*, IV. 606).

This first, theatrical outburst (9–29) is meant to define her characteristic stance. An emotional infatuation is seeking logical cover. The speech is divided by the repeated *Anna* (9, 20) into segments of 11 and 10 lines. The initial vocative is a sign of earnest engagement, here even of agitation. Her question (10) mingling with exclamations (*quae, quem, quam, quibus*) and repenting repetitions (*si mihi ... si non*, 15, 18), rises to the epanalepsis of *umbras / umbras* (25–26), a trick not used in this way in any other speech in the poem, and to the exaltation of the (unique) apostrophe to *Pudor* (27),[7] to fall back to yet more alliterative repetition in her anaphoric reference to the dead Sychaeus (*ille ... ille*, 28–29). Her last word confirms the dark, minor tone of her remarks. No wonder so highly charged a confession ends in tears (30). She feels that no good can come of it.

The poet enhances his effects by making her use a tissue of (for the *Aeneid*) ill-omened words: *iugali* (16: cf. IV. 496); *pertaesum* (18: cf. *taedet*, IV. 451); *thalami* (18: see above, p. 11); *agnosco veteris vestigia flammae*[8] (23: cf. *flammae*, IV. 670; *Elissae ... flammis*, V. 3–4). *Agnosco* also described the futile mimicry of dead Troy in Sicily (III. 351). *Vestigia* was

---

[5] Noted by Nelis, *op. cit.*, p. 141. For this kind of thing in Plautus, Fraenkel, *Elementi plautini in Plauto* (Florence 1960), p. 219, adduced in *Roman Catullus*, p. 312. Belling carries his analyses of IV into great detail: *Studien über die Compositionskunst*, pp. 205 ff.

[6] This term is explained below, p. 167.

[7] *Pudor* shows nine instances, of which only IV. 27 is vocatival, and is presumably a tragic apostrophe of the Ὦ τλῆμον Ἀρετή sort (Nauck, *TGF*, p. 910, no. 374): cf. ὦ Πλοῦτε καὶ Τυραννί κτλ, Soph., *Oed. Rex* 380.

[8] The line (23) attracted the attention of Dante (*Purg.* 30. 48). Once again Dante's comedy easily reverses Virgil's congeneric tragedy.

last heard in reference to the Cyclops (III. 659, 669). Three words especially anticipate the culmination of the epic: *dehiscat* (24: cf. X. 675, Turnus; XII. 883, Juturna); *umbras* (25, 26: cf. XII. 952); *violo* (27: XII. 797 *al.*: see the discussion of this line on p. 60, above). The listener to this speech will add his own examples (e.g. *Erebo*, 26 [ערב]: cf. IV. 510, *al.*).

The suppressed sexuality of the queen's remarks also attracts attention. She protests too much, as Anna sees. Whatever *armis* means (11), *culpae* (19) is especially used of sexual offences, and *succumbere* in the same line, only here in Virgil, is a word used by Catullus (111. 3) and Ovid (*Fasti* II. 810) of the female yielding to the male. Dido hardly realises any of this. Less engaged, we do.[9]

She admires the soldier's bravery and fearlessness (11), because these are qualities she herself possesses. She will ultimately commit suicide by the soldier's method of the sword rather than, like queen Amata, by the woman's noose. Yet she is for all that a woman, looking for a commitment she never finds. *Nec vana fides* (12) strikes a recurring, here for the moment determinedly and deceivingly optimistic, yet ultimately despairing, note (*nusquam tuta fides*, 373; *non servata fides cineri promissa Sychaeo*, 552). Over the whole hangs the shade of the murdered husband and that cheated first love (*fefellit*, 17, another leitmotif).[10]

Her sister's reply (31–53), with its more carefully argued logic, may serve as a partial foil. The reader knows how gross is the counterpoint between its hopes of fruitful happiness and their eventual upshot. It equally opens with a vocative, this one emotional, tragic, periphrastic (*o luce magis dilecta sorori*), the hint of and contrast with lunar Dido's shadows establishing a typical chiaroscuro (see also IV. 692). A question follows, and another. Then *esto*, typical also of Juno (VII. 313, X. 67, XII. 821).[11]

---

[9] It might however be fruitful if all the speeches by women in the *Aeneid* were combed for their sexual vocabulary and *double-entendre*.

[10] II. 744 (Creusa). The repetition links her with bereaved Aeneas (and cf. *falsi ... genitoris*, I. 716). The seven examples in the poem end badly, in declining mode (XII. 246). Cf. "Dicemo bello il canto, quando le voci di quello, secondo il debito dell' arte, sono intra sè rispondenti" (Dante, *Convivio* I. 5). The poet goes on to argue that this occurs more in Latin [than in Italian], because Latin uses art.

[11] And perhaps of the idea that women in the *Aeneid* ultimately do not so much bring about events as simply put up with and try to steer around them. The escape from Tyre to Carthage was a glorious exception. Dido characteristically sees that as an act of vengeance (*ulta virum*, IV. 656). Yet, in spite of VI. 840, *ulciscor* (4 exx.) / *ultor* / *ultrix* (6 exx. each) are not on the whole good words in the *Aeneid*. Brutus was an *ultor* (VI. 818), and later executed his own sons. Hence perhaps the hesitancy with the Helena-episode in II. 567 ff. (*ulcisci*, 576).

The statement of the facts as the speaker sees them leads into yet a third question, and then a fourth. A fifth is to come. Especially the latter part of Anna's speech, loyally and naively forecasting a splendid outcome from the match Dido has in mind, is loaded with tragic irony. The patent falsity of its up-beat contradiction of the sombre tones of Dido's last words suggests how much in fact those last words must be true.

We spoke of Dido's "rhetoric of silences." She never speaks to Aeneas in the part of Book IV describing what must have been her moment of brief and illusory happiness. During the hunt and whatever went on in the cave there is silence. This (matching the silences between Aeneas and Ascanius, Aeneas and Lavinia) is already authorial editing of the most biased kind. We are challenged to act as choreographers, to add the rhythm of our own heartbeats.

And later, unlike Calypso, who receives a divine message telling her to let Odysseus go, when Aeneas goes, Dido receives no message. She is not central enough to history's purposes. Unlike even Circe, she is left guessing, and when her frustration at last finds an outlet, her first words to him since Book I (753–56) are filled with hissing sigmatism suited to serpentine Medea: *dissimulare etiam sperasti, perfide, tantum / posse nefas tacitusque mea decedere terra*? (IV. 305–06). Aeneas, if we may believe what he had said to his captains (293–94), did not in fact mean to leave in silence. Dido projects her own world on to him.

She shares, we noted, Medea's thirst for revenge. Medea had notoriously killed her own children. The huge difference is that she escaped in her dragon chariot (Ovid, *Met*. VII. 398), while Dido keeps sounding the note of her own death. But is she closer to Medea than this? Medea escaped to threaten Prince Theseus' life, as the *Hecale* related. Dido will certainly follow Aeneas: *sequar atris ignibus absens* ... (384). Must she however die before she can begin her Medean work of threatening Aeneas' future, Troy's children in whatever sense?

The powerful emotion of these lines (305–30) is generated at one level by their contrasts and repetitions. The deserted heroine was a favourite Hellenistic character (above, p. 112), as Ovid's *Heroides* also prove. *Hospes* (323) is compared with a phrase from Callimachus himself (Δημοφόων, ἄδικε ξένε, fr. 556 Pf.). By the principle of external reference, allied to the Alexandrian demand for novelty, Virgil has both to pay homage to these topoi and to avoid merely echoing them.

But there is also the principle of internal reference, already remarked in Dido's opening speech (IV. 9–29). In this speech, words such as *dulce*

(318), *pudor* (322), *fama* (323) must be mirrored in the contexts which the poet has established for them.[12]

Les mots se font les paroles. Words are organized. Once again, the preferred device here is that of the rhetorical question, of which her speech contains eight instances. She attempts to use logic, which we know she is borrowing from her sister (cf. 52–53), to dissuade him from setting out: the winter storms, his unknown destination. Her reference to herself in the third person (308), here clearly not Caesarean, bares the unhinging centre of her disintegrating personality (cf. 595), and prepares for the later use noted at 383. Although the poet elsewhere in this book certainly relishes the few-word, mouth-filling verse characteristic of Euphorion (*aut Agamemnonius scaenis agitatus Orestes*), here there are scattered concessions to a more intimate style. Dido is allowed to use rather colloquial, Menandrean rhythms (314–15, 317).

Her allusion to her failed longing for a child,[13] celebrated though it is, hardly chimes with epic dignity. *Suboles* (IV. 328; only here in the *Aeneid*), originally at least, seems to have been a Roman farmer's or shepherd's word,[14] and this would be further "hollow pastoral." *Capta ac deserta* at the end (330) is certainly more than the emphatic repetition of synonyms beloved of early Latin. The Callimachean lover / huntsman boasted of his indifference to a stricken prey (*Epigr.* 33). Aeneas, ἄδικος ξένος, in her eyes is this lover. But there is more. With its ambiguous inclusion of the city in its range of reference (cf. 669–71), the phrase embraces the identification of leader and people[15] familiar from Livy's *Poenus, Romanus*. Dido is after all a queen. But its pathos picks up and enlarges into the feminine a comparison exploited by Plautus.[16]

Again, a contrast is immediately supplied. Aeneas' dignified answer (333–61), though three lines longer than her accusation, shows only one question. Stating and refuting the charge, falsely contrasting his (manly) brevity with her (feminine) verbosity (*pauca ... plurima*), explaining the

---

[12] For *dulcis*, see above, p. 120. *Pudor* was mentioned above, n. 7. *Fama* occurs 63 times. The examples at IV. 173 and 666; VII. 104; XII. 608 (*per urbes / per urbem*) establish a formulaic pattern.

[13] Quoted below, p. 141.

[14] Cf. Horace's *lascivi suboles gregis*, *Odes* III. 13. 8; *Ecl.* 4. 49; *Geo.* III. 71, 308; IV. 100.

[15] Cf. Macdonell, *Sanskrit Grammar*, p. 180, 3 c; Shakespeare's "Denmark" for "Denmark's king."

[16] *Most.* 91 ff., house = man. Cf. Dido's own *miserere domus labentis*, IV. 318; NT Matt. 7:24–27: more largely *ecce relinquetur vobis domus vestra deserta*, NT Matt. 23:38; cf. פ׳ב in *TWAT* I, cols. 636–37 (Hoffner).

grounds for his own behaviour, accusing his adversary of inconsistency, appealing for calm, he sets out his case with far more measured eloquence. For him, *dulcis* (342) applies, not to any private satisfactions, but to the remnants of his people (שְׁאָר יְשׁוּב).

Dido's rejoinder (365-87) borrows from familiar, unworthy topoi. Part (365-67) may be compared with Catullus 60. She starts with negatives, *nec ... nec*, giving the lie to the claims she had herself made earlier (12). At 369-70, she alludes to Aeneas in the third person, almost as if she were addressing another audience, a jury, posterity; and yet again, this is not so much the Ciceronian manner as perhaps a symptom of mental dissociation, of which, in a fleeting moment of clarity, she later becomes aware (*heu Furiis incensa feror*, 376; cf. XII. 946).

Facit indignatio versum, inspiring in her a (second-)natural rhetoric. She fires off five questions in a row (368-71). With emphatic first persons, noted in Roman *elogia*, as in Augustus' own account of his stewardship,[17] she lists her *res gestae*: *excepi, locavi, reduxi*. This is the language of the tombstone. With *nunc ... nunc ... nunc* she pours contempt on his religious claims. Then comes her dismissal and curse (381-87), with the clear premise and hint of her sacrificial death for the sake of revenge.

Her later, comic appeal to her sister to act as intermediary (416-36), already noted, contains even so a quasi-liturgical repetition (*requiem spatiumque*). It is reinforced by the inherited device of alliteration. All that is traditional. Her words remain a supreme example of the exploitation of ordinary language (*ex communibus verbis*) for extraordinary purposes (433-34):

> tempus inane peto, requiem spatiumque furori,
> dum mea me victam doceat fortuna dolere.

Inanis and *furor* are favourite words in the poem, here appearing with a misleading air of casualness. *Mea ... fortuna* points up the humility of the loser. Not for her the bold conquest of fortune to which Aeneas is called by the Sibyl (VI. 95-96). Disarmingly, she admits her offence and (like Turnus) her defeat (cf. *victum*, XII. 936). This, "the poetry of defeat from the point of view of the defeated" (Bowra), is quite new in Roman epic.

Her first lines in this speech to Anna are couched in terms of studied nonchalance (*properari* impersonal, 416). Her sorrow was half-expected anyway, and accordingly she will be able to endure it to the end (419-20). What an effort she is making to seem reasonable and resigned! Yet the

---

[17] *Comparavi ... vindicavi*, R.G. 1; *accumulavi ... genui ... petiei ... optenui* in Warmington, *ROL*, vol. IV, p. 8, no. 10 (Scipio Hispanus).

repeated vocatives *Anna ... soror ... Anna ... soror* (416, 420; 421, 424) lend urgency. This nonchalance overlies a painful emotion (*miserae*, 420, 429), with which the picture offered by *puppibus et laeti nautae imposuere coronas* (418) contrasts so strongly. Halfway through, as she imagines the message which Anna is to take (425-27), she lapses into the familiar frame of the *remotio criminis* (*ad Her.* I. 15. §25) with its concluding *enthymema* (428). The only questions occur towards the end (428-29), and are quickly dropped. The mysterious, alliterative assonance of *cumulatam morte remittam* (436) hints at what cost this apparent tranquillity is purchased. "Heaped high with death": but whose death (or deaths) does she mean? The queen speaks more pregnantly than we guess at the time. Is there some satiric allusion in this language of payment and interest to indemnities historically inflicted on Carthage by Rome, to what has been called Roman "mercantilism," criticised even by Horace?

It is this tone of feigned optimism which prevails in her later explanation to Anna that (here unlike Turnus, XII. 913) she has "found a way" (478-98). Her speech of 21 lines here precisely balances the 21 lines of her earlier remarks to her sister at 416-36. In an admission of the impossibility of real communication, her real feelings too deep for words, she has again taken this tone from Anna's proem. There is an air of deliberate disengagement, although the language in fact shows that she is anticipating suicide. And now, as she comes closer to her death, Dido draws closer to Medea, *spargens umida mella soporiferumque papaver* (486)—with its nominative present participle, its weak caesura, its alliteration and its self-indulgent adjective, another Euphorionic and neoteric line. This is the metamorphosis which awaits her.

Unable to sleep, once more Medea, Dido ponders her desperate situation (534-52). In this unwitnessed monologue there are eight questions, since now there is no need to pretend any calm. Wildly, she accuses her sister of being at the root of her troubles. The speech ends on a note of fantasy of a kind possible only with the greatest of poets, when the queen of Carthage (קְרָת הֲדָשְׁת, "New City"), so generously proud of her achievement (*urbem quam statuo vestra est*, I. 573), imagines herself as some sort of woodland creature free of the constraints of all civilised living (550-52: it is noteworthy that *thalamus* here is viewed as such a constraint). But she *is* that creature, fatally wounded by the hunter! This element of unreality, dissociation, surfacing again later in the figure of woodland Camilla, is typical of the poem. Here its hollow pastoral serves to distance the dying (*moritura*, 308, 415, 519, 604) heroine from the conventional epic world.

Seeing the Trojan fleet under sail, knowing (like Ariadne on Naxos) that all is now lost, Dido bursts into a second monologue of despair, disintegration and hatred—and hatred of the child (590–629). Medea again looms. The implied allusions culminate in a series of self-condemnatory might-have-beens. She could have scattered his limbs over the sea as Medea scattered those of Apsyrtus. But, in the development, there is more, and it is here that we again feel the proximity of the pantomine with its dazzling, polyprosopic sequences.[18] She could have treated his allies and even Ascanius as Tantalus treated Pelops. Varius and Seneca are not far.

Her frustration passes over into a series of her favourite pluperfect, "unfulfilled" subjunctives (603–06), which in their turn introduce a solemn prayer to the all-seeing, all-avenging Sun. Later, Aeneas will pray to the Sun as he seeks to make his (short-lived) peace with Latinus (XII. 176). That perhaps was Augustan. But what dark sun is Dido's? The Sun was Medea's and Circe's ancestor, and we may find in the allusions to Circe in the proem to the second half of the poem (VII. 19–20) yet another token of a haunting, Medean presence there. Dido's Cyclopean (*Od.* IX. 530–35) curses are to be literally fulfilled in the "Iliadic" books, and then, with their covert allusion to Hannibal (625), spill over, by a fine example of Virgil's vertical time, into history, and into more than the fight with Carthage. It was already suggested that the ruthless bloodiness of these later books prefigures and in turn is coloured by the Social and Civil Wars.

Her dying words are broken into longer (651–58) and shorter (659–662) symmetrical fractions, eight and four lines. Again there is something of the laconic, lapidary style already noted: *vixi ... peregi ... statui ... vidi ... recepi.* This is offset by an initial vocative, and by pathetic self-address. No longer do we hear the wish that Aeneas had left a son. Dido imagines that she would have been *felix, heu nimium felix* (657) if his fleet had never landed in Africa. But earlier (36–37), she had listened while Anna recalled just how impossible any other husband was. Now she has disconnected *felicitas* from children. At the end, the leitmotif of *mori, mors* echoes again.

Here too there is latent myth. Dido is behaving (*os impressa toro*) like Sophocles' Deianeira (*Trach.* 917–19), like Euripides' Alcestis (*Alc.* 183–84).[19] And again, roles blend. Alcestis had died for love—and then been brought back by Hercules. Deianeira, in her mistaken eagerness to re-kindle his love, had caused her Hercules' fiery death. Perhaps this gives another dimension to *Furiis accensus* in Book XII (946; cf. *Furiis incensa,* IV. 376;

---

[18] For this in Roman comedy, Fraenkel, *Elementi plautini*, pp. 21 ff.

[19] See Heinze, *Virgils epische Technik*, p. 137, n. 2. Below, pp. 143–44.

subitoque accensa furore, 697), and to the parallel found there with the Hercules of Book VIII (*Furiis exarserat*, 219).

Her earliest words already attracted attention. There, her noble *non ignara mali miseris succurrere disco* (I. 630) sounds like a New Comic aphorism, adapting the old cliché πάθει μάθος in a way bearing tribute to φιλανθρωπία. Its present tense is noteworthy (cf. ἄνδρα οὐ γινώσκω on Mary's lips, Luke 1:34). Dido's reactive psychology is overwrought from the first. She has lived in a world of treachery and murder since she first lost Sychaeus. In Libya, she is surrounded at the best by the unwanted attentions of Iarbas and his ilk, at the worst by threats (I. 563–64, IV. 39).

The result is that (*more ferae*) she is moved by instinct rather than by discursive thought. When she puts too much weight on faltering reason, she tends to overbalance into a world of fantasy, conforming to mythical archetypes such as mad Pentheus in a more and more uncontrolled way. Yet the contrast between her *parvulus Aeneas* and Catullus' *Torquatus parvulus* (61. 209) is deliberately imposed by her creator. In the end, for all her yearning, for all her comedic posturing, Virgil allows no place among her masks for the role of loving mother with loving child.

Venus and Juno

Venus appeals successfully to Jupiter (I. 229–53), humbly assuming the role of the *Iliad*'s Thetis. Her speech opens with an emotionally positioned vocative, and contains five questions. Jupiter's answering affirmation (257–96), though so much longer (40 ~ 25 lines), both postpones its vocative and shows no questions at all.

Elsewhere however Virgil's goddesses are not so fortunate.[20] A characteristic speech-pattern, familiar to Cicero (who plays variations on it at the start of the *Second Philippic*), emerges. An opening question or exclamation confronts a surprising or unwelcome turn of affairs. The speaker then contrasts this unhappy state with past *exempla* illustrating the opposite. A resolve may be made or an appeal directed to another for a change to what the speaker considers better. Such change, objectively (rationally) viewed, may be of the most implausible, even outlandish kind.

Juno's first speech (I. 37–49) already shows this pattern: exclamation, *exemplum* and then self-reproach, concluding in a final bitter question. The

---

[20] Martina Steinkühler, *Macht und Ohnmacht der Götter im Spiegel ihrer Reden* (Ammersbek bei Hamburg, 1989).

repeated rhythms of lines 46–49 (all showing *dsssds*) build into a hysterical monotony of self-laceration. Her appeal to another will follow.[21]

This way of talking means however that Virgil's women are too often heard as brooding (*manet alta mente repostum*, I. 26), caught at some stage off guard by reverses of fortune, unfairnesses, of which they are only now resentfully aware; and hence the emotionality and defeatism of their declarations. The solution (illusory, as it often transpires) to their troubles can usually be provided only by another; and this other may disoblige. The growing conviction of this likelihood may result in a final solemn curse. The *Second Philippic* attenuates its concluding wish, but the end of the *De Corona* already sets the tone.

A later speech by Juno (VII. 293–322) is evidently a model for that given by Ovid to the same goddess in the second book of the *Metamorphoses* (512 ff.; cf. Statius, *Theb.* I. 250–82). It is a rich rhetorical construct. It echoes its opening *contraria* (VII. 293) from IV. 628 (cf. *invenere viam*, 297; *inveni … viam*, IV. 478). It traces the outline already described. An initial exclamation is followed by two rhetorical questions. Against the backdrop of mythological allusion there is repetition (of the imprecise *medius*), sarcastic admission, self-reproach, use of contrasting *exempla* with final negating question, hysterical resolve, a concluding apocalyptic curse. *Hac gener atque socer* (317) evokes memories of the Civil War (*Aen.* VI. 830–31), itself a clash between families. *Pronuba* recalls Dido's ill-starred match (IV. 166: these are the only two Virgilian instances of the noun). There has already been medical innuendo (*excussos*, 299; *alveo* suggesting *alvo*, 303), and there is a flood of contraceptive vitriol (320–21, *praegnas, enixa, partus*) to follow. How curious all this sounds on the lips of the goddess of marriage!

Just as with Dido's hesitancies, so with Juno's. Virgil experiments with the satiric hexameter inside epic, as Juvenal will later experiment with the epic hexameter inside satire. At 310–11—

> … quod si mea numina non sunt
> magna satis, dubitem haud equidem implorare quod usquam est.

And if my own powers lack force, I would not shrink from appealing to anything anywhere.

— the heroic line, with its implied hint of the "disobliging other," seems to fall to pieces under the pressure of emotion. This (helped by the religious *implorare*) is in Catullan vein.

---

[21] Compare the speech of love-sick Iarbas, IV. 206–19.

Again *esto* (313). Women delay destiny and the inevitable (315), rather than help to create and shape them. But in doing this, they frustrate the very essence of their natures.

The debate between Venus and Juno at the start of Book X (18–62 ~ 63–95) pits the two protagonists against each other in a version of Sophistic ἀντιλογία, found also, for example, in Euripides' *Medea*. There is a ratio of about 4:3. The first speaker takes 44.5 lines (a kind of ἀντιλαβή at the end) and the second 32.5 (Juno *begins* in mid-line).

Venus, so careful to observe it earlier (I. 342), now breaks the Alexandrian rule of brevity (*paucis, non ... pauca*, 16–17), so great is her emotion. She uses (according to Mynors) seven questions. Juno's briefer remarks are punctuated by fifteen question marks.

Like Dido and Juno, Venus is allowed to use colloquial-sounding, almost halting rhythms, recalling certain Catullan epigrams (*namque aliud quid sit quod iam implorare queamus? Aen.* X. 19). They do not exclude grander effects: the triple indirect questions of 20–22; the triple statement of the threat to the Trojans at 26–29; the double conditionals of 31–33 and 33–35; the aposiopesis of 36 and 37.

She makes great use of absurd irony (of the sort liked by Cicero) to hammer home her point: let the destined empire go, let Aeneas suffer the storm and whatever fortune is his, so long as Ascanius survives. What was the point anyway of all these wanderings? The Trojans should be put back in Troy, to endure its doom.[22] Driven to such extremes, this becomes a school-room rhetoric of the type also relished by Seneca and Lucan.

Juno's indignant, pseudo-dialogic answer shows the old Roman pattern of theme and variation (divided in the examples cited by //), characteristic also of the Psalms, yet with just enough antithesis in the variations here to escape the charge of simple repetition of moribund tricks:

> quid me alta silentia cogis
> rumpere // et obductum verbis vulgare dolorem? (63–64)

Obductus dolor, another instance of the *callida iunctura*, contains a hint of the scarring of a painful wound (cf. I. 25).

With this liturgical structure may be compared *bella sequi // aut hostem regi se inferre Latino* (66); *linquere castra // vitam committere ventis* (68–69); *summam belli // muros* (70), *Tyrrhenamque fidem // aut gentis agitare quietas* (71) and so on throughout. This lends a certain stateliness to her discourse, without ever letting it degenerate into mere πολυλογία.

---

[22] In a sense, that is what they are enduring already (cf. *iterum*, X. 61), but even a goddess does not realise this.

With the repeated *nos* (84, 88–89) she seeks to switch the guilt of inconsistency entirely back onto her opponent, as Cicero switches it back to Verres.[23] Her *tum decuit* (94) is shared with Dido (IV. 597).

The impotent *esto* recurs (67). Yet eventually, as warlike Italy is contrasted with shifty, lubricious Troy, the goddess sees in play the whole struggle between Europe and Asia (87–91). Here she more than Venus speaks for Rome. What other *gravidam bellis Urbem* (87) did Virgil's listeners best know? Even so, the metaphor contradicts the goddess's own values.

Venus, meeting her son for the first time in the reader's apprehension of the poem (I. 314), is in playful, even flirtatious mood, though her first words challenging knowledge of the whereabouts of her huntress sisters are both a continuation of a recurrent imagery in the poem and an anticipation of the hunt of IV (*spumantis apri*, I. 324 / *spumantem ... aprum*, IV. 158–59).[24] Her subsequent tale (335–70) of Dido's foundation of Carthage—with its ghost, a typical piece of popular narrative—is long on heightened emotion. It makes musical use of alliteration to evoke the queen's vulnerability: *et aegram / multa malus simulans vana spe lusit amantem* (351–52). *Aegra* here especially looks ahead to Book IV (35, 389). *Simulans* is Helen (VI. 517). Dido's ill-starred love match with Sychaeus sets the stage for the future. There will be the reshuffling ("mixing") of motifs which was noted earlier: for her, a love cheated by Aeneas (*nostris inluserit advena regnis*, IV. 591); for him, a maimed spectre who tells all (Hector [II. 270] / Anchises [cf. *fulminis adflavit ventis et contigit igni*, II. 649; IV. 351]); later, a sudden flight by sea. Here, there are no questions, except at the very end (369–70) where they occur naturally within a long established epic convention.

In Book XII, in not so much calmer as more determined and calculating mood, though one in which Jupiter still senses her waves of anger (831), Juno wrings from her spouse his final concessions (808–28). The comic counterpart of her role would be that of some offended wife putting one over on her uncomprehending husband. It was not fated that Troy should vanish from history, as we are told here it must (819); and there have been many occasions in the second half of the poem where it looked as if a new Troy would be founded, wherever that might be (*Troiam ... nascentem* on Juno's own lips, X. 74–75). But now the Trojans are to lose everything that made

---

[23] *Simul ac tute coeperis ... mihi suscensere desinito*, *Verrine* V. §19.

[24] Cleverly taken up by Vegio: *ceu spumantis apri*, *Supplementum* 134; cf. *spumabat ferus ore vomens* (Turnus), 351.

them what they were: name, language, dress.²⁵ As Juno gains her point, once again, her typical *esto* is cunningly in evidence (821). She appears to be resigned, but this is her moment. There is great use of emphatic anaphora at the end (*pro ... pro ... cum ... cum ... ne ... neu ... aut ... aut ... sit ... sint ... sit ... occidit ... occiderit*). Is this some legal document? It is impossible to argue that we are not to take her seriously. Imperial authors such as Lucan and Juvenal would note that even so her carefully laid plans failed.

Juturna

The last speech by a woman in the *Aeneid* is Juturna's, who realises that her brother is to die (XII. 872–84). She cannot follow him, and her immortality, ostensibly a recompense from Jupiter for her rape, turns out to be a curse. She has suffered a cruel deviation from the time-honoured pattern (IV. 198; VII. 657; X. 551) by which such affairs normally lead to the birth of a heroic son. As a water nymph, she finds a Homeric parallel in Thetis. Her appeal on behalf of her warrior, unlike that of Venus / Thetis for Aeneas in Book I, goes unheard.

The truncated end of the poem, lacking the closure offered by the *Iliad*, means that the doomed hero's lamentation by a surviving female has to occur ahead of time. The 13–line speech here contains ten questions and one exclamation. The initial statement of the reverse of fortune is followed by the acknowledgment of incapacity, and a fleeting allusion to the past (*haec pro virginitate reponit*, 878²⁶). This is what survives of the *exemplum*. The possibility of an appeal for help has already been exhausted by the nature of the gift of immortality received (again the "disobliging other"). This last indignity is left to echo in our minds as the disappointed goddess, *multa gemens* (886), reluctantly plunges back into her stream: *se fluvio dea condidit alto*. There is a pathetic contrast with the optimism about Juno shown by Father Tiber.²⁷

A parallel has been drawn²⁸ with Bion's Aphrodite, and this whiff of Hellenistic / Semitic romance (אדון) hints that Dido cannot be too far away (*Adonis* 52–53):

---

²⁵ Servius' apt comment on IV. 618 (*pacis iniquae*) is quoted below, p. 251.

²⁶ Below, p. 205.

²⁷ VIII. 60; cf. *deinde lacu Fluvius se condidit alto / ima petens*, 66–67. More on *multa gemens*, below, p. 154.

²⁸ By J. D. Reed, ed., *Bion of Smyrna. The Fragments and the* Adonis (Cambridge 1997), p. 227. But Aphrodite is hardly a virgin! This is more of Virgil's "hollow pastoral." Once again, the Roman poet transforms and refines

>   ἁ δὲ τάλαινα
> ζώω καὶ θεὸς ἐμμί, καὶ οὐ δύναμαί σε διώκειν ...
> And I, poor wretch, live, and am a goddess, and cannot follow you.

In Juturna's cry to her brother, the desolating *dulce* is heard again (XII. 880–83; cf. IV. 318):

> 'possem tantos finire dolores
> nunc certe, et misero fratri comes ire per umbras!
> immortalis ego, aut quicquam mihi dulce meorum
> te sine, frater, erit?'
>
> 'I might put an end to my great sufferings here and now, and go with my unhappy brother on his journey to the shades. Am I immortal? Or will anything of mine be sweet to me without you, my brother?'

Te sine is perhaps an ironic echo of the sacral idiom.[29] In some ways, Juturna's fraternal anguish recalls Catullus', or the maternal sorrow of Homer's Thetis. But at least Thetis was able to transport her dead Achilles to the Isles of the Blest. For Turnus, no such happiness is in store.

Unguibus ora soror foedans et pectora pugnis (871) is repeated from IV. 673 (cf. XI. 86), where Anna wishes she had died with her sister. This is Juturna's predicament (*comitemne sororem / sprevisti moriens*, IV. 677–78: *misero fratri comes ire*, XII. 881), and the full pathos of her words is not to be understood without reference to Dido, whose *tellus optem prius ima dehiscat* (IV. 24) finds here its last fulfilment (*o quae satis ima dehiscat / terra mihi?* XII. 883–84). A link is also provided by the characteristic *umbras* (IV. 25; XII. 881). This paves the way for Turnus' own fate (XII. 952).

Scholars have found in Virgil Jungian "shadows," but Juturna / Turnus clearly also illustrate a feature of primitive religion, already seen in Hebrew, in which the divine is both feminine and masculine. Rome's patron, Pales, illustrates this ambivalence, and so do Etruscan Vertumnus / Voltumna.[30] Within the *Aeneid*, Juturna carries with her the sympathies the poem's conclusion fails to lavish on Turnus. Both are ill-treated by the gods, both

---

the lush eroticism of his Alexandrian models. There is also an echo of Calypso's protest (*Od.* V. 116 ff.). Dido was Calypso.

[29] E. Norden, *Agnostos Theos* (Leipzig–Berlin 1913), p. 157, note 3; p. 175, note 1. Cf. *Roman Catullus*, pp. 208–09. *Te sine* to his dead father, Statius, *Silvae* V. 3. 5.

[30] So also Cacus / Caca, Servius on *Aen.* VIII. 190. The Museo Palatino preserves an altar from the Velabrum, restored in the time of Sulla, inscribed *sei deo sei deivae sac[rum]* (inv. 379604). O. Weinreich even notes from the diary of a disturbed mental patient *Jesus / Jesin* (*Menekrates Zeus und Salmoneus* [Stuttgart 1933], pp. 113 ff.).

robbed of any hopes of normal marriage, both childless. There are other doubles (twins) of this kind in the poem: Camilla / Pallas (linked by their virginal deaths), Camilla / Turnus (XI. 831 = XII. 952). Certainly one of the functions of the *Aeneid*'s women is to open in the epic construct a channel for feelings which the military, propagandist, "Homerising" pastiche, of the type sidestepped by Horace (*Odes* I. 6), rather than practised by Homer himself, had excluded. But, when Virgil gives them this role, what part of their essential nature, their *felicitas*, does he force them to surrender?

Lavinia

Eisenstein's "leap into another dimension," noted earlier, was typical of what he calls the "pathetic" style. In Virgil's pantomimic rhetoric, therefore, the ultimate case is that of silent Lavinia, already prefigured in Dido's rhetoric of silences. Virginal Lavinia, absurdly made, like some second Helen, *causa mali tanti* (XI. 480), says nothing at all anywhere (here anticipating her namesake in Vegio). She is the instrument of destiny, marked out by the oracles for a foreign groom without any regard to personal inclination.

She is a character in a tragedy, and therefore her aura of innocence has a darker tinge. Her mother Amata's madness and ultimate suicide are strongly reminiscent of Dido (Mackail). In Book XII, even her maidenly blushes on hearing her future discussed, which in some ways seem the most natural thing in the world, are turned into a token of the future disastrous course of events.[31] At this point, the individual face vanishes into history.

Such silences on the part of elegiac women in the so-called poetry of sexual liberation are noted elsewhere.[32] The elegists use addresses to their women to unburden themselves, often satirically, sometimes in praise, rarely for any genuine exchange of thoughts. Rather than that, the iambic stereotype established by Archilochus and reinforced by Lucilius, as later by Juvenal, takes over. Cynthia is allowed to unburden herself only when she is dead, and in that elegy, reversing his poetic routine, Propertius says nothing to her.

There had been an iambic element in the epic tradition right from the days of Homer's Thersites, and it would have been easy for Virgil to extend its censorious scope to women. There was precedent. Tragic Prometheus would not resort to "woman-imitating upturnings of his hands" (*P. V.*

---

[31] *Augustus and the New Poetry*, pp. 241–42. Above, p. 60.
[32] *Augustan Propertius*, pp. 285 ff.

1005), clearly to be accompanied by prayerful entreaties. Plato, prose-poet *par excellence*, both disapproved of Homeric heroes manifesting their emotions too grossly, and dismissed the womenfolk from Socrates' death-cell. In official Rome, *matronas publico arceant* was Fabius Maximus' advice after Cannae (Livy XXII. 55. 6). Before an audience so naturally receptive to Stoic precepts as the Roman, could Virgil have deployed his shrieking females and expected complete sympathy?

The poet certainly exploited an iambic element in drawing celestial anti-heroines such as Juno, and even, in certain moods, Venus. Allecto is from hell itself. Even Dido becomes an avenging spirit, the Clytaemnestra of whom she had dreamed. But he was not content with that. Women are in his epic because they are necessary, so that, within his dark framework, their fearful questions may cast unwelcome, indecorous shadows on the refulgent arms (VIII. 592–93; cf. 623). Perhaps he sensed that it is the nature of women to defy categories and blend the contradictory—and to suffer for it. So often, because they are shifted to the margins of the world of war and empire, they must peep from shadows,[33] cast in the role of lunatics (Dido), oddities (Camilla, Juturna), crazies (Amata), ciphers (the *matres*). To the straight men of the day, who stood in the spotlight of history, no doubt they seemed awkward clowns whose place was in the wings. Shakespeare's *Antony and Cleopatra* plays on and enhances this distinction: calculating Octavian; his impetuous, posturing, queenly adversary, with her immortal longings, paradoxically thrust into centre-stage. Queen Dido has much of this. Virgil, for whom Cleopatra was fresh in memory, took Shakespeare's risk.

He had begun his poem with a question of his own: *tantaene animis caelestibus irae?* (I. 11). After that, he allows his women to carry the burden of his anguished curiosity. That is proper in his high tragedy. How strange however that, as his creation unfolds, human mothers rarely even talk *of* their own children—though desolate Creusa (II. 789) and doomed Amata (VII. 359) are probative exceptions. No human mother ever talks *to* her own child unless he is dead.

---

[33] See below, p. 168, on women as dreamers.

VII

DIDO

The Queen of Carthage

The conflict with Carthage was regarded by Sallust (*Cat.* 10. 1) as the last moment of Rome's greatness, before decline set in. Augustus' poets, anxious to promote moral reform, accordingly pay homage to this apogee: Propertius (III. 11. 59), Horace (*Odes* IV. 4. 49, *al.*). Since it was also Ennius' theme, it conditions the *Aeneid* right from the outset (I. 13), and Silius Italicus saw this link (*Pun.* I. 81–82). The struggle was fearful, as Lucretius still attests (III. 833–37). Dido, Carthage's sovereign representative, threatens Troy's children with the avenger to be unleashed (*Aen.* IV. 625). She cannot then have been viewed by Augustans with too much moral or intellectual sympathy. Moderns, who have not suffered her curse, should avoid an unhistorical approach, determined by emotional sympathy, to her role in the *Aeneid*. But Virgil would not be Virgil if he had not seen her with both eyes.

Anna soror...; *di morientis Elissae....* The Bible has made "Eliza" and "Anne" the names of English queens, obscuring the exotic frisson they must have inspired in pagan Romans. In their Punic context no doubt those were ordinary enough names. "Dido" is more difficult. It may perhaps best be regarded, like "Je*didi*ah," "the darling of the Lord" (= the future King Solomon, II Sam. 12:25), as a claim to legitimacy more than a proper name, linked with the Semitic and even cross-linguistic roots also found in דוד / דויד "David," a king "after God's own heart."[1] As the feminine of

---

[1] דד (τιτθός, "'breast,' better 'teat, nipple'"); דוד ("swing," "rock," "dandle," "fondle," "love" [cf. ἀτιτάλλειν]); דוד, "love": *Hebrew and English Lexicon of the Old Testament*, edd. F. Brown *et al.* (repr. Oxford 1979), pp. 186–87, *s. vv.*; *TWAT* II, cols. 152–67 *s.v.* דוד (Sanmartin-Ascaso); 167–75 *s.v.* דוד (Carlson); N. Wyatt, "'Jedidiah' and Cognate Forms as a Title of Royal Legitimation," *Biblica* 66 (1985), 112–25. Further bibliography in *TWAT* X, pp. 493–94. 'Dido' is a title. The queen's actual name is 'Eliza' ('ss' in *Elissa* representing foreign 'z,' as, for example, in *comissor* / κωμάζω). Virgil knows this. It is only after him that 'Dido' occurs in the oblique cases, since, *pace* OLD, 'Dido' at IV. 383 is not the accusative. The Ethiopian 'Candace' may be

"David" (cf. "Jedidah," II Kings 22:1), it offers a token and guarantee of status. In general, there is a strong sexual connotation, but no suppression of the natural outcome of such passion. On the male side, ἱερέα κτίλον Ἀφροδίτας ("sacred ram of Aphrodite,") of Sicilian Hiero (Pindar, *Py.* 2. 17) may also be compared.[2] Sicily was where Greek and Semite met. Was this Aphrodite then also Astarte, whose sacred (and virile!) consort the king thus becomes, whose royal status Pindar thus legitimises?

If this is so, how pathetically what is Dido's title more than name contrasts with her fate. This was already clear in antiquity. A white Luna marble sarcophagus from the second half of the second century A.D., found in 1964 at Grottarossa along the Via Cassia, and now in the Palazzo Massimo alle Terme in Rome (inv. 168186), unexpectedly contained the mummy of a sickly eight-year-old girl, obviously, to judge by the style of burial and the ornaments left with her, of good (and foreign?) family. She had a doll, naturally enough. But curiously the front of her tomb shows a stag hunt reminiscent of the royal hunt in Book IV of the *Aeneid* (130–59). Aeneas is seen on foot. Dido herself—if indeed this is Dido—is visible only in the left background, and in profile, turned away from Aeneas and the spectator, perhaps because she was riding side-saddle. More prominently, there is Ascanius with beaters. An Eros in the foreground holds his torch down in funerary style.[3] The shorter side on the right shows a youthful horseman (again Ascanius?) attacking a wild boar (*optat aprum*, IV. 159). *Si quis mihi parvulus aula* ... came later in Book IV. How telling—and how subtle a reading of the poem—to find the hunt itself suitable in this way for the commemoration of a dead child, its Dido already eclipsed, its Eros already in mourning!

Dido indeed lurks at the centre of the apocalyptic and central Book VI, the crescent moon hidden by a bank of clouds (VI. 453). There, we think of the brutal fate meted out by Apollonius' Heracles to the daughters of Hesperus (*Arg.* IV. 1479–80; cf. *Hesperidum, Aen.* IV. 484). But other symmetries are possible. If the *Aeneid* is divided into thirds, *il libro di*

---

compared (NT Acts 8:27), also a title ('Queen'), but then mistaken by non-native speakers for a proper name.

[2] Literally "priest-ram." "Ram" is also important here as the totem of the ruler's virility (*virtus*). It is why Aeetes, for example, had to retain the Golden Fleece. Accius' *Brutus* (vv. 17–28, Warmington) is relevant. Further discussion in "The Golden Fleece, Imperial Dream," *A Companion to Apollonius Rhodius*, pp. 313–15.

[3] *Ecce puer Veneris fert eversamque pharetram / et ... sine luce facem*, Ovid, *Am.* III. 9. 7–8. — In general, J. Huskinson, *Roman Children's Sarcophagi. Their Decoration and its Social Significance* (Oxford 1996).

Didone, culminating in her death, ends one of the sections thus created. The other two conclude with the description of the Shield of Aeneas, on which the defeat of her avatar Cleopatra figures so prominently;[4] and the death of Turnus, which itself does not lack echoes of Dido's suicide. This configuration suggests that our response to her cannot be confined to sentimentality. She is more serious both as a political opponent (which in this context means also a religious opponent), and as a force for destruction. The Medusa / music theme of Pindar's twelfth *Pythian* may be compared. There, to metamorphose the monster's shriek of pain, Athene devised the flute. For Virgil, only an Apolline, vatic poet can draw harmony out of such discord.[5]

But it suggests too transformation, blending, of the Empedoclean kinds Apollonius finds in Circe's entourage (IV. 672–73), half one thing and half another. This trick had been familiar to the poet since Silenus' song in the sixth eclogue. Yet, amid this lubricity, Dido remains a queen, *regina*. The title, perhaps Virgil's translation of "Dido," is reiterated (29 times!) purposely, and not simply as a pejorative. There is sentiment, and this is the greatness of the Augustans and Romans, that they do not deny their adversaries dignity, as Horace did not in the end deny it to Queen Cleopatra, or Livy to Sophoniba.[6] Dido pays a price for her cross-grained encounter with fate (*fata obstant*, IV. 440). Virgil understands this. She encapsulates the poem's theme of childlessness.

Those poignant words that she had uttered when she realised Aeneas was preparing to leave her were already mentioned (above, p. 120) as a supreme experiment in epic form. The anaphora is commonplace, but much else is

---

[4] Cleopatra is never referred to by name in extant Augustan literature, always as *regina* (cf. *Aen*. VIII. 696). This provides at least a verbal link with Dido *regina*.

[5] Dido / Medea / Medusa: D. L. Page notes (ed. *Medea*, Oxford 1938, p. xxvii) the portrayal on an Attic black-figured lecythos (BM 1926.4.17.1) of a Medea with snakes on either side of her head. The snake-haired Medusa repeated in the decorations of the Temple of the Palatine Apollo (Antiquario Palatino, Room V) was perhaps intended to represent Cleopatra. The "Farnese Cup" (an Alexandrian agate-sardonyx cameo), now in Naples (inv. 27611, 2nd–1st cc. B.C.), already has an image of Medusa on the outside and inside an allegorical scene set in Egypt. Servius Danielis however reports that four lines relating to Medusa, which were to be introduced after VI. 289 (entrance to hell), were *removed* by the *Aeneid's* editors (see Mynors, *praef*. p. xii).

[6] בעל יֿנפס (Sfni-Bal), "Baal has covered me." Cf. Livy XXX. 12–15 = Petrarch, *Africa* V. The physical beauty, ready intelligence, unswerving devotion to her father and country and resolute courage in the face of death attributed by the Roman historian to this daughter of a Carthaginian general are more than Hellenistic embroidery. Editors note Cleopatra (a Greek), but what of Dido?

extraordinary here, more than the diminutive[7] (327–30):

> 'saltem si qua mihi de te suscepta fuisset
> ante fugam suboles, si quis mihi parvulus aula
> luderet Aeneas, qui te tamen ore referret,
> non equidem omnino capta ac deserta viderer.'

'At least if I had bred some child of yours before your flight, if some baby Aeneas were playing in my palace, whose looks at least might recall yours, I would not now seem all taken and abandoned.'

Dido, we saw, specialises in "unfulfilled" pluperfect subjunctives of this sort (*fuisset* again, IV. 603). *Suscepta* is not far from *concepta*, and in some ways more frank (*susceptus semine*, Plautus, *Amph.* 1139). *Suboles* is a shepherd's or farmer's term. The queen speaks plainly about a delicate subject. Women are not afraid of biological realities. They have too much at risk.

Moving enough—but how in fact did Carthaginian nobles treat their children? Already Ennius knew what the urns of Salammbo have confirmed.[8] No Roman schoolboy therefore could be unaware. Virgil says nothing openly of this barbarism to mar his picture of the brilliant Hellenistic court kept at Carthage—though, as the story of Crassus' head produced during a performance of songs from the *Bacchae* at the court of the Arsacidae (Plutarch, *Crassus* 33) attests, or John the Baptist's during a birthday celebration at the court of Herod (NT Mt. 14:11), there was plenty of such ugliness beneath the glittering surface of philhellene φαντασία.[9]

Phoenician Dido's barbarism is discovered by degrees. Carthage was "expunged" in 146 B.C., but as late as 61 Julius Caesar had "expunged a deeply ingrained barbarity" from the ancestral practices of Gades, a Phoenician colony.[10] In Virgil's depiction, Dido is a bitterly frustrated

---

[7] *Saltem*, for example, occurring three times elsewhere in the *Aeneid* (I. 557; VI. 371, 885), and always in emotional contexts, is a wonderful example of the poet's ability to load a colloquialism with epic pathos.

[8] *Poeni soliti suos sacrificare puellos* (*Ann.* 214, Sk.): cf. Silius, *Pun.* IV. 765–67; Tertullian, *Apol.* 9. "Their sons and their daughters they sacrificed to foreign demons; they shed innocent blood, the blood of sons and daughters offered to the gods of Canaan, and the land was polluted with blood" (Psalm 106:37–38, NEB). See *TWAT* IV, cols. 950 ff., 957–68 (חלל: Seybold, Fabry).

[9] Μετὰ πολλῆς φαντασίας, NT Acts 25:23 (procession of Agrippa and Berenice); εἰς φαντασίαν μοναρχίας, Origen, *Dialogus cum Heraclide* 4. *The Grand Procession of Ptolemy Philadelphus* (ed. E. E. Rice, Oxford 1983) offers an illuminating sidelight on its age. Calculating Cleopatra posing at Tarsus (Plutarch, *Antony* 26) is familiar.

[10] *Inveteratam quandam barbariam ex Gaditanorum moribus disciplinaque delerit*, Cicero, *Balb.* 19. §40. *Disciplina* sounds very much like "religious observance" (*Etruscorum, Druidum disciplina*). Was this child-sacrifice?

mother, determined to have a child at any cost, who in the event, defying the fates (I. 22), conceives the Furies (*ergo ubi concepit Furias*, IV. 474) and so turns into dehumanising Circe and murderous Medea, much worse than anything in Apollonius; into what Roman folklore and satire knew as a child-devouring *lamia*.[11] *Non potui ... ipsum absumere ferro / Ascanium patriisque epulandum ponere mensis?* (IV. 600–02): as the poem advances, she becomes what earlier she had regretted she could not become. But this is the overthrow of a noble mind, the perversion of the most natural instinct.

Dido's Roles

In the course of these transformations, she blends many parts (*turbam reddet in uno*, Manilius V. 484). As a refugee, she is Danae, foundress of Turnus' Ardea, expelled from home and sent to wander over the waters (VII. 410). As Diana, goddess of the moon, she is also Isis / Io (the device on Turnus' shield, VII. 789), and this aids her association with Egypt. She is abandoned Ariadne (*reginae* catachrestically, VI. 28). She meets us as Arctinus' Amazon Queen Penthesilea (I. 490–93; cf. *ducit*, 490, *dux femina facti*, 364).[12] The assimilation ultimately links her with Camilla / Penthesilea (XI. 600–63), catachrestically also a *regina* (XI. 703, 801), herself linked with Turnus (XI. 831 = XII. 952). Doomed Camilla was a *virgo* (XI. 664). So was doomed Penthesilea (I. 493), who made a disfiguring forfeit (ἀ-μάζων, "lacking a breast") to secure her status as a warrior queen. Dido's breast, *recens a vulnere*, is equally disfigured.[13]

As usual with Virgil, the web of allusion is even more closely woven. Another Amazon queen mentioned with Camilla, Hippolyte (XI. 661), robbed of her girdle by labouring Hercules (the scene was visible to Augustans on the Temple of Apollo Sosianus), may provide a parallel with Pallas' loss of his belt to Turnus. He too has associations with Dido.[14] Amazon Marpesia, who may be hinted at when we meet Dido in Hades (VI. 471), had already come to grief after sacking Troy. It was there that

---

[11] Lucilius, frr. 484, 1065, M.; Horace, *A.P.* 340; cf. Ovid, *Fasti* VI. 131 ff.; Statius, *Theb.* I. 596 ff.

[12] She is also a queen bee (cf. I. 430), but *Georgics* IV shows that the ideal and sexless community there purchased its tranquillity by banishing the males, an insight Dido acquires too late (cf. *Aen*, IV. 657–58).

[13] *Infixi pectore vultus* ~ *infixum ... pectore vulnus*, IV. 4 and 689. "Dost thou not see my baby at my breast / That sucks the nurse asleep?" asks Shakespeare's Cleopatra with her asp (V. ii. 304–05). This is more gentle.

[14] Below, pp. 227 ff.

Penthesilea's encounter with Achilles, if it engendered eros,[15] also ended in death.

Aeneas is Penthesilea / Dido's Achilles. His breast is martial: *quam forti pectore et armis* (IV. 11). Venus, goddess of love, will sheathe it in blood-red steel (*sanguineam*, VIII. 622). Remorselessly, ineluctably, from the first book on, the poet's imagination sets in motion this scenario. If to recall attention to the heroic days of the Punic Wars was the standby of Romans (including Cicero) seeking to restore past glories, with what qualifications Augustan Virgil performs his task!

Penthesilea is already *furens* (I. 491), and Dido too quickly loses control (712–14). But her turmoil takes a characteristic form (*infelix*, 712, 749). In Book I it is her cruel deception by the false boy Ascanius who is not Ascanius that robs her of reason and balance. Deludedly fondling one royal son, how could she help but long for another? At the start of IV, we may think of her as already in fancy pregnant, but, in an oxymoronic reversal of the expected joy of normal pregnancy, she is nursing with her veins, not a baby, but a *vulnus*. The fire and the wound here are those of her eventual death, when she will stab herself on the pyre and its bed with Aeneas' phallic sword, *non hos quaesitum munus in usus* (647). Her union with Aeneas in the cave has negated all that marriage promises (*leti ... malorum*, 169). The last *cubile* she mounts (648, cf. *toro*, 650) is that of suicide.

Here she is like Sophocles' Deianeira and Euripides' Alcestis (Heinze). But she shares her fiery death with Heracles himself. That hero too combines the pyre (πυράν, *Trachiniae* 1254) and the steel (χάλυβος, *ibid*. 1260).

Deianeira's speaking name ("man-ravager") made her function clear and, by Dido's identification with her, Aeneas is turned into a suicidal Hercules.[16] Like Dido, Deianeira chooses a sword (*Trach*. 912–13, 915–21, 930–31):

> ἐπεὶ δὲ τῶνδ' ἔληξεν, ἐξαίφνης σφ' ὁρῶ
> τὸν Ἡράκλειον θάλαμον εἰσορμωμένην....
> ... ὁρῶ δὲ τὴν γυναῖκα δεμνίοις
> τοῖς Ἡρακλείοις στρωτὰ βάλλουσαν φάρη.
> ὅπως δ' ἐτέλεσε τοῦτ', ἐπενθοροῦσ' ἄνω
> καθέζετ' ἐν μέσοισιν εὐνατηρίοις,

---

[15] The cup in Munich has been interpreted in this sense: P. E. Arias and M. Hirmer, *A History of Greek Vase Painting*, nos. 168, 169, with their commentary on pp. 351–52. See also the volute crater from Ruvo by the Niobides Painter, now in Naples (inv. 81673). — For Marpesia / Marpessa, above, p. 115. Hercules / Hippolyte figured on the pediment of the Temple of Apollo Sosianus, restored by Octavian: below, p. 329.

[16] On Hercules / Aeneas in the poem, already implied by the storm in Book I, cf. Appendix, below, p. 331.

Chapter Seven

καὶ δακρύων ῥήξασα θερμὰ νάματα
ἔλεξεν, 'ὦ λέχη τε καὶ νυμφεῖ' ἐμά,
τὸ λοιπὸν ἤδη χαίρεθ', ... '
ὁρῶμεν αὐτὴν ἀμφιπλῆγι φασγάνῳ
πλευρὰν ὑφ' ἧπαρ καὶ φρένας πεπληγμένην.

That ended her laments, and suddenly I saw her rushing into the chamber she shared with Heracles.... I saw his wife strewing cloths on Heracles' couch. That over, she leaped on top and sat there on the bed. Hot tears suddenly coursed down her face as she cried; 'O bed and bridal chamber of mine, now and forever farewell! ... ' And then we saw the queen, her side beneath her heart and breast pierced by a two-edged sword.

Conlapsam aspiciunt comites....

Alcestis was later a favourite pantomime role.[17] The similarity between Dido and Euripides' heroine is particularly clear. Both are in the prime of youth and beauty; both kiss the nuptial couch before they are to die; and both reflect on the man with whom they shared it, now seen as the cause of their deaths (*Alcestis*, 175–79, 183):

κἄπειτα θάλαμον ἐσπεσοῦσα καὶ λέχος,
ἐνταῦθα δὴ 'δάκρυσε καὶ λέγει τάδε·
'῏Ω λέκτρον, ἔνθα παρθένει' ἔλυσ' ἐγὼ
κορεύματ' ἐκ τοῦδ' ἀνδρός, οὗ θνῄσκω πέρι,
χαῖρ' ... '
κυνεῖ δὲ προσπίτνουσα....

And then, bursting into her bedchamber and falling on the bed, she dissolved in tears with these words: 'O bed, where I surrendered my maidenhood to the man for whose sake I am now dying, farewell'... and falling on the bed, she kissed it.

Apollonius had made Medea kiss her couch before she fled with Jason (*Arg.* IV. 26), but Virgil's treatment of these scenes in his high tragedy is denser and—to use an Aristotelian (*Rhet.* III. 1411b 27 ff.) and Callimachean (*Aet.* I, fr. 1. 40) term—more "energetic" (*Aen.* IV. 648–50, 659):

hic, postquam Iliacas vestis notumque cubile
conspexit, paulum lacrimis et mente morata,
incubuitque toro dixitque novissima verba ...
dixit, et os impressa toro ...

Here, seeing the Trojan robes and the bed she knew too well, for a little she hesitated while she fought her tears and tried to come to terms with her plight. Then she fell on the couch and spoke for the last time.... Afterwards, kissing the couch ...

650. *Incubuit* here looks back to *incubat* at 83.

---

[17] As perhaps the *Alcestis Barcinonensis*, if that is a stage libretto, reminds us. Euripides' *Alcestis* has undeniably comic (komic) features. Laughter and the κῶμος triumph over Death.

Like Alcestis in the play (*Alc.* 170), Dido too has visited the altars (*Aen.* IV. 62). But there are important differences. Chaste Alcestis' surrender of her maidenhood to her first husband is hardly parallel with Dido's guilty surrender to Aeneas of her pledge to Sychaeus (IV. 552; cf. Dante, *Inf.* 5. 62; *Par.* 9. 97–98). Dido may be trying to make up for her offence by an act of suttee for which she supplies her own eulogy (655–56; cf. ἐγκωμιασθεῖσα ... σφάζεται, Herodotus V. 5). Perhaps it is this belated atonement which guarantees her reunion with her husband in Book VI (474).

Alcestis at least is able to bid children farewell, and here she offers a closer resemblance to Propertius' Cornelia (IV. 11). Dido presents a pathetic contrast. *Nec dulcis natos Veneris nec praemia noris?* her sister had asked (IV. 33), in a scene combining Menandrean insight with epic dignity. The pathetic *dulcis* now recurs (*dulces exuviae*, 651). This vocatival *exuviae*, an instance of Dido's fondness for apostrophe, is hapax in the poem,[18] and the answer to Anna's hopeful question, with its proper Roman priorities, is in the end "No."

In these early books, pantomimic, polyprosopic Dido inevitably plays a number of parts drawn from Homeric and Apollonian originals.[19] Her magic and threats make her Medea. Graciously welcoming her version of Odysseus / Jason to her royal home, she is Arete / Alcinous / Hypsipyle. She receives as a gift Helen's old finery (I. 650). Trying to keep the reluctant hero on her Ogygia, she is pathetic Calypso, though not yet so aware of the gods' cruelty, as her indignant, naive assertion about Juno and Jupiter shows (IV. 371–72).

Aeneas' landing in Libya is actually modelled after Odysseus' landing on Circe's island of Aeaea (*Aen.* I. 180–82 ~ *Od.* X. 146–47).[20] His slaying of stags to feed his men follows the action of Odysseus there. Dido welcomes him and his Aeneadae with Circe's lines (*Aen.* I. 613–18, 623–24, 627–30 ~ *Od.* X. 323–335). A wonderful irony underlies these first words, which echo Circe's surprised rejoinder when she finds that she cannot metamorphose Odysseus, thanks to his possession of a special herb given to him by Hermes. In a frank enough fashion, she accordingly proposes that she and he should retire to bed (X. 333–35). A myth attributed sons (Agrius and Latinus) or a son (Telegonus) to her as a result of this union (Hesiod, *Theog.* 1013–14). In Dido's more dignified speech, this proposal is replaced by the invitation to all Aeneas' men to enter her palace (I. 627). Here she is

---

[18] Above, pp. 17, 123.

[19] For these parallels, see Knauer, pp. 138, 178–79: Nelis, pp. 165, 334.

[20] Knauer, pp. 174 ff.

like Hypsipyle (*Arg.* I. 832-33)—who is pregnant when Jason leaves (I. 898). The reader of Homer and Apollonius guessed what was hardly yet in her mind. When eventually it happened, for her, there would be no son (Juturna motif).

Circe and Hypsipyle are unlike Dido in letting their lovers depart without the slightest fuss. That aspect of Virgil's heroine is shared with Calypso, though there are striking differences in the courtesy with which she is handled by the gods. In Homer, Hermes travels to remote Ogygia carrying Zeus' orders only to Calypso, and listens patiently to her tirade against the divine jealousy of the little piece of happiness she has tried to create for herself (*Od.* V. 118 ff.). This outburst is reserved by Virgil for Juturna (XII. 872-84)—though who is listening to her?—and helps to strengthen our sense of Dido's presence towards the end of the poem's last book. In Book IV, Dido is not afforded any divine explanation. Mercury visits only Aeneas. Homer provides a subtext. His Calypso is a daughter of Atlas (*Od.* I. 52), and Atlas is where Virgil's Mercury first halts (*Aen.* IV. 247 ~ *Od.* I. 51-54). But Atlas exemplifies the punishment inflicted on rebels against the divine order. His stony, grotesque form, anticipating Dante's Satan (cf. *mento*, IV. 250; *menti, Inf.* 34. 53), also looks ahead to Dido / Niobe (*quam si dura silex aut stet Marpesia cautes*, VI. 471)—though this is a Niobe without tears.[21]

Yet, at the site of Rome, Evander recalls that Atlas is the common ancestor both of the Arcadians and Trojans (VIII. 142). This is ominous enough, but the most ominous of all these Homeric precedents is that of Circe. It is Circe whose magic and debasing influences, which would have utterly frustrated Odysseus' return home, most correspond to the spells which Dido seeks to work.

And Circe persists. How could she not, if she is the mother of Latinus?[22] The scene in Book VII (10-24), where the Aeneadae ostensibly sail past her island, is imitated from Homer's description (*Od.* X. 210-33; V. 55-64) both of Circe's palace and Calypso's cave, and here the admixture of Calypso is the extra proof of the lurking presence of Dido, λιλαιομένη πόσιν εἶναι.

Virgil pays careful attention to the Homeric sequence. In Homer, the

---

[21] *Lacrimasque ciebat* (VI. 468) may then allude to his effort to soften her heart. The death of the Niobids was represented on the doors of the temple of the Palatine Apollo (*Tantalidos*, Prop. II. 31. 14).

[22] M. West (ed. *Theogony*, p. 434) notes a contradiction between *Aeneid* VII. 47 and XII. 164 (*Solis avi*). Myth is manipulable, since its atemporal, "aoristic," and transrational (prelogical or alogical) universe can never meet anachronistic demands for consistency. Like Callimachus and many other poets, Virgil adapts it as it suits him.

death of Odysseus' companion Elpenor precedes the final departure from Aeaea and follows the visit to the underworld. Opening Book VII, Virgil retains the death in its Homeric place, but makes it instead the death of Aeneas' old nurse, Caieta. (Aeneas had had a nurse therefore, when Dido [IV. 633] had lost hers!) Now her demise marks the disappearance of the hero's last contact with family normality. Circe's island however is heard only in the distance, and it looks as if it will be bypassed. But, as it turns out, in Virgil's *inextricabilis error* the Aeneadae will after all not avoid it. Their transforming Aeaea will be Italy, and since, unlike Odysseus, he is destined never to go back home, eventually Aeneas will formally marry into Circe's family (into the line of altered Picus, VII. 189), and before that be presented by his future father-in-law Latinus with a horse foaled as a result of one of thieving (*furata*) Circe's tricks. *Nothos* (VII. 283) here is contemptuous enough.[23]

Virgil's description both of the island and of what Circe did to her victims merits then a fresh look.[24] It begins by raising hell (VII. 15–20):

> hinc exaudiri gemitus iraeque leonum
> vincla recusantum et s a e v a sub nocte rudentum,
> saetigerique sues atque in praesepibus ursi
> s a e v i r e ac formae magnorum ululare luporum,
> quos hominum ex facie dea s a e v a potentibus herbis
> induerat Circe in vultus ac terga ferarum.

> From there came sounds, the groans of angry lions, chafing at their chains and roaring under cover of the wild night. Bristly boars and bears in their dens went wild, what seemed like great wolves howled. They had been men, but the wild goddess with her drastic herbs had clothed them with the looks and bodies of savage beasts.

15a. Cf. VI. 557–58, *hinc exaudiri gemitus et saeva sonare / verbera, tum stridor ferri tractaeque catenae.*

16. The Leonine rhyme is noteworthy. Cf. *bellantum iuvenum et duro sub Marte cadentum* (XII. 410), the dull ache of war. Readers will recall Rilke's caged tiger: *Ihm ist als ob es tausend Stäbe gäbe, / Und hinter tausend Stäben, keine Welt.*

16. *Saeva* (P) is right (cf. *saeva* at VI. 557, quoted above) against the vapid *sera* (derived from an intermediate *seva*) of other manuscripts. *Sera* weakens the threefold repetition of that root in the passage. In general, see Mackail's note on *Aeneid* X. 813.

18. *formae* anticipates Ovid's *formas*, *Met.* I. 1.

---

[23] There is also a parallel with Anchises' trickery in *Iliad* V. 265–72. Without Laomedon's knowledge, he bred his mares to the horses given by Zeus to Tros as a recompense for the loss of Ganymede. Of the six resulting foals, he kept four and gave two to Aeneas, who in this sense became what Virgil calls *Laomedontius heros*. How many connections focus in this story!

[24] See also above, p. 72.

18. *ululare*, normally of women, is also a word of Book IV (168, 609; *ululatu*, 667).

The goddess turns men into beasts not merely physically, but morally. The allegorists had already interpreted her enchantments in this sense, as Horace, among others, shows (*Epp.* I. 2. 23). But the scene is slanted by Virgil towards the infernal and demonic. This is because it is to acquire "economic" significance throughout the rest of the poem. It explains those comparisons of the champions in Italy with wild beasts to which commentators call attention,[25] and adds resonance to *saevus*, which eventually comes to characterise both *pius Aeneas* himself (XII. 107), and the *saevus dolor* (XII. 945) which inspires him to kill Turnus.

Circe the magician is allied to Medea the magician. They were after all aunt and niece. The aunt may sink general humanity in brutish beasts. It is the niece who provides the cruel malice of the vengeful witch and murderous mother. After her death, Dido wears both these masks.

Carthage / Crete

She is also both King Minos' erring wife Pasiphae (and this is where she fits into the bull imagery of the poem[26]) and his erring daughter Ariadne, abandoned by her lover to Dionysus (cf. IV. 300–03). The reality behind all this is conveyed by the poet in chilling retrospect. Carthage has been a kind of Crete. A Homeric allusion corroborates this identification. As the Aeneadae leave Libya, a storm threatens (V. 8–11):

> Ut pelagus tenuere rates, nec iam amplius ulla
> occurrit tellus, maria undique et undique caelum,
> olli caeruleus supra caput astitit imber
> noctem hiememque ferens, et inhorruit unda tenebris.

> The ships were on the open main, no land in sight, only sea and sky on every side. A dark cloud gathered overhead, pregnant with night and storm, and the wave shuddered in its shadow.

But earlier, when the Aeneadae were leaving Crete, we heard (III. 192–95):

> Postquam altum tenuere rates, nec iam amplius ullae
> apparent terrae, caelum undique et undique pontus,
> tum mihi caeruleus supra caput astitit imber
> noctem hiememque ferens, et inhorruit unda tenebris.

This is partly modelled on a passage in *Odyssey* XIV (301–04), where the

---

[25] V. Pöschl, *The Art of Vergil* (Eng. tr. Ann Arbor 1962), pp. 97–100.
[26] M[ᾶσσον ἢ ταῦρος] βοᾷ of Pasiphae, Euripides, *Cretes* 44 (Page, Loeb *Select Papyri* III, p. 76): cf. *Ecl.* 6. 45–60.

reference to Crete is quite specific:[27]

ἀλλ' ὅτε δὴ Κρήτην μὲν ἐλείπομεν, οὐδέ τις ἄλλη
φαίνετο γαιάων, ἀλλ' οὐρανὸς ἠδὲ θάλασσα,
δὴ τότε κυανέην νεφέλην ἔστησε Κρονίων
νηὸς ὕπερ γλαφυρῆς, ἤχλυσε δὲ πόντος ὑπ' αὐτῆς ...

Now as we left Crete, with no other land in sight, only sky and sea, then Cronus' son gathered a dark cloud above our hollow ship, and the way grew black beneath it.

Odysseus is telling a lying tale to Eumaeus. What sort of tale did Aeneas tell (as she came to perceive it) to his Carthaginian listener (IV. 597–99)? What Libya / Crete is left at the beginning of Book V, and interpreted at prophetic Cumae at the beginning of Book VI?

It seems clear that Virgil's Homer-*imitatio* is meant to do more than display his careful reading. In Dido's Aeneas, there is more than a touch of Odysseus (and of Jason!). But of course, as we seek to assimilate them, we tend to remake those we imagine we like in our own image and likeness.

When therefore in Book VI Aeneas first sets foot on Italian soil, at Cumae, he is certainly looking to hear news of his future. But his recent past at least is already staring him in the face. *Magnum reginae sed enim miseratus amorem*.... On the doors of Apollo's temple, the tale of flying Daedalus' Cretan misadventures and mistaken sympathy for Pasiphae's crazy, bestial passion reflects Aeneas' own experiences in the Crete which was Carthage (*nemora inter Cresia*, IV. 70). The story of the labyrinth built for the Minotaur concerns a monstrous birth (*Veneris monimenta nefandae*, 26), fed on human sacrifice (again מלך) and rightly put down by Theseus —who is one of the precedents for his own case cited by him to the Sibyl (*quid Thesea magnum*, VI. 122). Alas, that Theseus ended in hell (VI. 617–18)!

Catullus' savage Minotaur (*saevum monstrum*, 64. 101) is felled like an oak or cone-laden pine (105–06). In Apollonius, Talos, Crete's guardian, collapses under Medea's spell (IV. 1682–86) like some mighty pine-tree left half-hewn by the foresters to topple overnight. Editors compare the ash-tree which in Virgil symbolises Troy's own fall (*Aen*. II. 626). Reversing the picture, Aeneas has resisted the blasts of Dido's passion (IV. 441). But will he resist to the end? His mother, for Horace *mater saeva Cupidinum*, supplies him with a *Cretan* herb (XII. 412) for his last fight *saevo ... pectore* (XII. 888). Odysseus took the μῶλυ (*Od*. X. 305), but does Aeneas

---

[27] It also recalls *Od*. XII. 403–06, where the Companions are about to commit the offence which dooms them by eating the cattle of the Sun. See *The Classical Epic Tradition*, p. 163. The Sun is Circe's and Medea's ancestor.

receive a variant of the herb given by Medea to Jason (*Arg.* III. 1042), later the murderer of Apsyrtus? Will it overthrow his moral resolve so that, instead of heeding his father's summons to clemency (VI. 853), he sends Turnus down to darkness (XII. 952)?

Medea has already guessed at the treacheries of her man (IV. 383–86):

> μνήσαιο δὲ καί ποτ' ἐμεῖο
> στρευγόμενος καμάτοισι, δέρος δέ τοι ἶσον ὀνείρῳ
> οἴχοιτ' εἰς ἔρεβος μεταμώνιον· ἐκ δέ σε πάτρης
> αὐτίκ' ἐμαὶ ἐλάσειαν Ἐρινύες....

'May you remember even me one day, tormented by your troubles, and may your Fleece vanish to no purpose like a dream into darkness, and forthwith may my Furies drive you from your native land.'

Lines from this speech (378–81), which Virgil evidently studied with great care, were quoted earlier as a model for Dido's use of the *subiectio*. Jason will have ample leisure to discover more of this side of his wife's talents. Dido's threats (IV. 382–86; 604–06; cf. *finibus extorris*, 616) recall Medea's (*Arg.* IV. 392–93). And, given her vow to pursue him in her absence (*Aen.* IV. 384), her ghostly presence lurking everywhere (386), can Aeneas in *Aeneid* VI have extricated either himself, or Ascanius? The labyrinth, paraphrased here as *inextricabilis error* (27), was specifically evoked in the previous book (*Labyrinthus*, V. 588) to describe the manoeuvres of the young riders in the *lusus Troiae*, their pledge to the past (Anchises) and the future (Augustus), made in Sicily.[28] Iulus cavorts in that display on a horse provided by Dido as a memorial of her misdirected love (V. 571–72)—and *error* may mean just that (*ut me malus abstulit error! Ecl.* 8. 41).

Dido, keeping strange company in hell, may still be in her own labyrinth (*errabat silva in magna*, VI. 451), caught in what is the first perhaps of all those forests of Arden which the Classical / pastoral tradition, epic and dramatic, has planted. If Aeneas has not extricated himself from it, it is a love (cf. *dulcique adfatus amore est*, 455) which will prove deadly.[29]

---

[28] Above, p. 4. Cf. Robert W. Cruttwell, *Virgil's Mind at Work: An Analysis of the Symbolism of the* Aeneid (1947, repr. Westport 1971). More generally, Penelope R. Doob, *The Idea of the Labyrinth from Classical Antiquity to the Middle Ages* (Ithaca 1990); Håkan Lövgren, *Eisenstein's Labyrinth: Aspects of a Cinematic Synthesis of the Arts* (Stockholm 1996). Norden's remarks are always worth recalling: *Aus altrömischen Priesterbüchern* (Lund 1939), pp. 185 ff.

[29] Below, p. 154. The sentimentality of the scene must not be over-interpreted. T. S. Eliot pointed out that the sentimentality of the Paolo and Francesca episode in Dante does not mean that the lovers were wrongly punished, only that the sentimentality which had come to define their world was now all they had. Virgil's *inde datum molitur iter* (477) must be given due weight. *Molitur* is a loaded term (I. 33). Cf. IV. 233, Jupiter's message of rebuke.

Again, in Virgil's imagination, this takes a characteristic form. In the course of his efforts to escape, Daedalus lost his own son. But earlier there had been another death, that of Minos' son Androgeos (20). To atone for it, the Athenians were condemned to sacrifice their children, *septena quotannis corpora natorum* (21–22). Not all this deadly series is logically necessary to a poetic paraphrase of Carthage and its menace. Its presence betrays the poet's imaginative bias, what the Pindarist would call his *Keimentschluß*.

Omnibus umbra locis

Κρῆτες ἀεὶ ψευσταί.... Epimenides' tag is immortalised by Callimachus and St. Paul. *Creta mendax* (cf. Ovid, *A.A.* I. 298), the home of illicit loves, was also the alleged burial place of Zeus, and therefore the denial of the *Aeneid*'s (and *Iliad*'s, I. 5) basic premise. The central human female character in Virgil's poem, Dido, living in her substitute Crete,[30] explicitly denies that premise (IV. 379–80). She plays in fact the most negative human role, and this continues through the use of repeated language and imagery long after she has committed suicide.

The *Odyssey* had already attributed its hero's persistent troubles to the unrelenting wrath of Poseidon over the blinding of Polyphemus (I. 68–75). In the *Aeneid*, Juno is the heiress of Poseidon, and Dido of the Cyclops, whose curses, as well as Medea's, she echoes (IV. 612b–20 = *Od.* IX. 532–35). But in their fulfilment she takes a more active role than he.

The pathetic *infelix Dido* is a recurring formula, but any child of Dido and Aeneas would have been a denial of destiny. The epithet means more than "unhappy." Dido, barren, frustrated, "furious" and therefore set in Juno's pattern,[31] is turned by her experience of its unyielding laws (*desine fata deum* ...) into a vengeful monster, unfruitful and making unfruitful. Her pregnancy is with Furies (*concepit*, IV. 474). Anna, more innocent, cannot "conceive" the extent of her sister's madness (501–02):

> nec tantos mente furores
> concipit aut graviora timet quam morte Sychaei.

Her mind cannot take in such frenzies. She fears nothing worse than at Sychaeus' death.

A repeated verb makes her point. But what happened at Sychaeus' death was a hasty flight, and that is also to be repeated, only not by Dido, whose cold life instead will withdraw into the winds.

---

[30] Which is as it were to the Trojans what Egypt was for the Israelites, another pilgrim people: *TWAT* IV, cols. 1099–1111 s.v. מצרים (Ringgren, Fabry).

[31] Cf. her appeal at IV. 608; *contraria* is a leitmotif she adopts at 628.

A recurring line (IV. 126 = I. 73) already alerted us to all this. Dido's hope of marriage (IV. 103–04) will be as empty as the marriage promised by Juno to stormy Aeolus; and of course, just as pointlessly as Juno (VII. 299), she too storms (IV. 532, 564). At the end, she wishes that she might have been left as a wild creature (550–51):

> 'non licuit thalami expertem sine crimine vitam
> degere more ferae.'

'It was not my lot to live a life with no part of the marriage chamber, innocent, like some wild creature.'

The audience knows how ill-omened is the resonance of *thalamus* in the poem. This is again out of Virgil's "hollow pastoral." The wilderness is really no refuge when a careless shepherd is seeking his prey (IV. 71). In Book VII, in killing Silvia's stag while it swims in some woodland stream, Ascanius will repeat this inherited pattern—and trigger the bloody wars, *plus quam civilia*, marking the Trojans' debut in Italy.

These wars match old adversaries. *Quis novus hic nostris successit sedibus hospes?* asks Dido (IV. 10), using the adjective which describes Ovid's metamorphoses (I. 1), and the noun which she will later throw back in Aeneas' face (*Aen.* IV. 323). The queen thinks that she has welcomed to her palace a single hero, Aeneas. Uncharacteristically for a woman, and for a Semitic Phoenician, she is working with horizontal rather than vertical time.[32] Her mistake is not to realise that Aeneas is still carrying with him old Anchises (II. 804, IV. 599). For Aeneas, Anchises is both past and future, as is made explicit at the end of Book VIII, where the gesture which concludes Book II (*sublato genitore*) is repeated: *attollens umero famamque et fata nepotum* (731). It is Anchises' ghost which haunts him, Anchises who is to spoil her happiness (IV. 351, 427; VI. 694–96).

But, if Anchises continues to exercise influence from beyond the grave, Dido will not decline the challenge. Structurally, the most important point about her is that she does not disappear from the action at the end of Book IV, one third of the way through the poem. What a waste of a character that would have been!

Among Augustan poets, iambic Horace had established the theme of vengeful survival at the level of the mime (*Epodes* 5. 83 ff.). Epic Virgil signals it quite clearly when, in Juno's temple at Carthage, he allows Aeneas to witness once more, as it were to "iterate," the great events of the Trojan War (I. 466–93). The locale is significant, given what we know already of Juno. Just like the carved figures on the temple doors at Cumae,

---

[32] Cf. Glossary of Critical Terms, below, *s. v.* "vertical time."

Dido 153

the painted stories Aeneas sees here are more than ornament. They anticipate the future of the Trojans in Italy: the raid on Rhesus' camp parallels the raid of Nisus and Euryalus (IX. 176 ff.); the death of Troilus will recur in the death of Pallas (X. 439 ff.), and even in that of Turnus;[33] the procession to the temple of Athena is repeated by Amata leading the women of Latium, with Lavinia (= Helen) at her side (XI. 477 ff.). Its phrasing, as we saw, anticipates the final parting of Dido and Aeneas in Hades (I. 482 ~ VI. 469)—even before they have met. The death of Hector will also be that of Turnus, through whose words, however, an old father will appeal for mercy in vain (XII. 930 ff.). Aeneas himself is linked by the allusion to "arms" with doomed Memnon, immortalised in Greek painting[34]—and by Ovid in his lament for Tibullus (*Am.* III. 9. 1)—as the counterpart of dead Achilles. Venus herself later makes the comparison explicit (VIII. 383–84).[35] Priam will be Latinus (VII. 246). Finally, Penthesilea *furens* is both Camilla (XI. 660–63; cf. *bellatrix*, I. 493; VII. 805, only in these two places) and the model of Dido, who now sweeps imperiously into view, to hear the explanations and decide the fate of the Trojan newcomers.

But the poet has also told us in famous lines what to think of these iterated scenes. Anticipating *quaeque ipse miserrima vidi* (II. 5), the Gygean *videt* here is characteristically internalised (I. 456–65):

> videt Iliacas ex ordine pugnas
> bellaque iam fama totum vulgata per orbem,
> Atridas Priamumque et saevum ambobus Achillem.
> constitit et lacrimans 'quis iam locus,' inquit, 'Achate,
> quae regio in terris nostri non plena laboris?   460
> en Priamus. sunt hic etiam sua praemia laudi,
> sunt lacrimae rerum et mentem mortalia tangunt.
> solve metus; feret haec aliquam tibi fama salutem.'
> sic ait atque animum pictura pascit inani
> multa gemens, largoque umectat flumine vultum.   465

He saw Troy's battles in sequence, the wars celebrated now throughout the world: the sons of Atreus, and Priam, and Achilles who raged against both sides. He halted and with tears cried, 'What place by now, Achates, what land in all the earth is not overflowing with our suffering? See, here is Priam. Here too then prowess reaps its rewards, here are tears for human fortune and the fates of men move hearts. Lay aside your fears. This story will bring you

---

[33] *Impar*, I. 475, XII. 216. Troilus dragged behind his chariot is a sort of Hector, one of Turnus' originals.

[34] The cup by Douris (Louvre G 115), dated about 490, is familiar. Scholars rightly refer to its interior scene (Eos with the dead body of her son) as a "pietà." See also below, p. 224.

[35] Memnon was also the slayer of Antilochus (*Od.* IV. 187–88), who saved his father Nestor (Pindar, *Py.* 6. 30, after Arctinus). This is parallel to Aeneas' killing of Lausus, who had saved his father Mezentius, in Book X.

deliverance in some guise.' With these words, he fed his heart on the insubstantial painting, with many a sigh, tears coursing down his cheeks.

458. *saevum*: see above on VII. 16–19. *Saevum ambobus* = Cicero's *senseram quam idem essent.*

463. *solvite corde metum, Teucri*, in Dido's first address (562). These gracious exchanges of *humanitas* may occur before the divine imperative gets to work.

463. *aliquam* may be compared with Pindar's verecund (religious, Hellenic) use of τις: see *Pindar's Art*, p. 48; Slater's *Lexicon, s.v.*, p. 505, col. 2, B.

465. *multa gemens*: *multa gemens magnoque animum labefactus amore* (leaving Dido), IV. 395; *multa gemens casuque animum concussus amici* (death of Palinurus), V. 869; *multa gemens, et se fluvio dea condidit alto* (Juturna leaving Turnus), XII. 886. All this looks back ultimately to *Geo.* III. 226, the defeated bull—who will be Turnus in Book XII (715 ff.): see below, p. 228.

Feret haec aliquam tibi fama salutem. This is exactly what we are to think of the story told in the *Aeneid*. The "Iliadic" later events of the *Aeneid* are not determined merely by a poetic of imitation ("allusion"). This poet both understands the essential claim of all myth, that only one thing has ever happened,[36] and signals how that one thing is to be apprehended—with tears (δι' ἐλέου καὶ φόβου), and the hope of something better, *salus*, σωτηρία. This is the vatic lesson which he wants his poem to instil. But, by the same token, since these prophetic pictures are in Dido's Carthage, and since she herself is identified with one at least of their heroines, we cannot banish her vengeful presence from the tragic series yet to be unfolded.

In the centre of Book VI, Dido unexpectedly crosses Aeneas' path. The scene, as was already noted, is interpreted as a reversal of their parting in IV. There she wept, and he remained obdurate. Now he weeps, and she turns away. How sad. The commentators enjoy elaborating the contrasts and echoes. But Virgil knew that empires are not run on sentiment. He asks Erato to inspire precisely the most bloody part of his poem (VII. 37). The *dulcis amor* of VI. 455 is a destructive force (*improbe Amor*, IV. 412; *Furiis agitatus amor*, XII. 668; cf. XII. 70 and 282). She had already turned away (IV. 362)! Her silence here is a climax, not a novelty.[37] Neither the Homeric nor Apollonian parallels are to be dismissed. Silent, suicidal Dido is silent, suicidal Ajax, and this has resonance in the rest of the story. If she is like Heracles' victims in Apollonius, the Hesperides, the simile of the half-glimpsed moon here (VI. 453–54) makes her also into Apollonius' Heracles (*Arg.* IV. 1479–80). This has even more relevance. As Virgil develops them, both parallels turn out to be dangerous.

---

[36] "Vorlogisches Denken," below, pp. 158–59.

[37] Above, pp. 113 ff.

Even greater danger lurks. Dido is *recens a vulnere* (VI. 450). There is a tragic parallel. So was Clytaemnestra in Aeschylus' *Eumenides*. Her ghost appears there early in the play (100–05) both to rouse the sleeping Furies to action and to disturb Orestes. Her syntax is fractured (παθοῦσα ... μου, 100-01), a token of her emotional state. At 104 she turns to address her son, who, before taking his leave in company with Hermes, has evidently sunk into an exhausted slumber. She is like Virgil's Eriphyle, *crudelis nati monstrantem vulnera* (VI. 446)—and this is the poet's way of signalling to the discerning listener what is in his mind. Dido too, *gravi ... saucia cura* (IV. 1), still carries the marks of the blows dealt by a beloved child since, for her, the love kindled by Cupid / Ascanius has played this part. Here is Clytaemnestra:

>παθοῦσα δ' οὕτω δεινὰ πρὸς τῶν φιλτάτων— 100
>οὐδεὶς ὑπέρ μου δαιμόνων μηνίεται
>κατασφαγείσης πρὸς χερῶν μητροκτόνων.
>ὅρα δὲ πληγὰς τάσδε καρδίᾳ σέθεν·
>εὕδουσα γὰρ φρὴν ὄμμασιν λαμπρύνεται,
>ἐν ἡμέρᾳ δὲ μοῖρ' ἀπρόσκοπος βροτῶν. 105

Having endured such monstrous sufferings inflicted by my dearest kin—no spirit is angry in my defence, cut down as I was by the hands of one that slew his own mother. Yes, look at these wounds in my heart—dealt by you! In sleep the mind is gifted with eyes clear enough for that. It is by day that the fate of men is blind.

But Clytaemnestra had already made an appearance in Dido's imagination (IV. 471–73, tr. below, p. 170):

>aut Agamemnonius scaenis agitatus Orestes,
>armatam facibus matrem et serpentibus atris
>cum fugit, ultricesque sedent in limine Dirae.

In hell, this piece of theatre is realised. Wounded Dido too will raise the Furies to haunt, sometimes directly, sometimes through their agents, the one she considers responsible for her bloody death.[38]

The same general lesson is given at the start of Book VII, where Virgil, it was noted, evokes Erato (37) from the very opening of Apollonius III. The borrowing is extraordinary. It looks as if Erato is to be made the incongruous Muse of a historical epic (VII. 37–44):

>Nunc age, qui reges, Erato, quae tempora rerum,
>quis Latio antiquo fuerit status, advena classem

---

[38] The poet seems in fact to point to a performance of Aeschylus' play in which Orestes awoke still seeing his threatening mother, and then ran terrified off stage (and how much more dramatic this *coup de théâtre* than Orestes' supposed tame departure *before* his mother's ghost so unexpectedly arises).

> cum primum Ausoniis exercitus appulit oris,
> expediam, et primae revocabo exordia pugnae.   40
> tu vatem, tu, diva, mone. dicam horrida bella,
> dicam acies actosque animis in funera reges,
> Tyrrhenamque manum totamque sub arma coactam
> Hesperiam.
>
> Come, Erato, what kings, what moment of history, what the state of ancient Latium when the intruding host first brought its fleet to Western shores —this will now be my theme, recalling the beginnings of their first clash. You, goddess, you must remind the bard. Dread wars will be my tale, battle lines and princes herded by passion towards death, Etruria's band and all Italy gathered under arms.
>
> 37. *tempora rerum*, preferred by E. Fraenkel, is defended both by *rerum ... tempora* at I. 278 and by Maphaeus Vegius' *in tempore rerum* (*Supplementum* 460). To punctuate after *tempora* (Mynors) both obscures the anaphora and ignores the *callida iunctura*.
>
> 41. *bella, horrida bella* on the lips of the Sibyl-*vates*, VI. 86. Vatic Virgil claims to follow where she led. *Eadem horrida belli fata* summon Aeneas to tears after Pallas' death (XI. 96–97).

The language provocatively skirts the historian's prose.[39] But Virgil is playing a literary game with the style of military epic, the opposite of Ennius' when he used a Callimachean dream to open his un-Callimachean *Annales*—just as *vates* here is the opposite of anything Ennius could have countenanced.[40] Ennius meant after all—in spite of the bravura passages in *Annales* I—in the end to write history poetry. Virgil means to be *mythistoricus*, to rewrite history in terms of myth, to write, in Aristotle's language, τὰ καθόλου rather than τὰ καθ' ἕκαστον (*Poetics* 1451b 7).

There is no doubt about the allusion to the *Argonautica*. In both cases, the appeal occurs halfway through the epic action, after a dangerous sea voyage and before even more testing land adventures. And those final books of the *Argonautica* are dominated by the person of Medea. Yet, to explain Virgil's Erato, commentators refer to Lavinia, which is absurdly to overplay her role. In what Apollonian sense are Lavinia and Aeneas ever in love? Rabid Turnus may be in love (*illum turbat amor*, XII. 70). But what kind of parallel with Jason does he make? The analogy demands an *arriving* hero, *advena*, exactly what Aeneas is. The second part of the *Aeneid* is not a love story by any normal standard. Yet, as in Apollonius, there is a driving female force in this half of the epic, in this case supplied in the first place

---

[39] Fraenkel adduces Polybius, VI. 11. 2, ὁποῖόν τι κατ' ἐκείνους ὑπῆρχε τοὺς καιρούς κτλ. and Tacitus, *Hist*. I. 4, *qualis status Urbis* etc. (*Kleine Beiträge*, II, p. 149, n. 2).

[40] See the chapter on the *vates*, pp. 306 ff., below. The word signals the satirical / salvific aspects of *Aeneid* VII–XII.

by Juno. How can Lavinia, dumb blonde (*flavos ... crinis*, XII. 605) that she is, never speaking at all in the poem, be any human counterpart to her?

The reason why Lavinia is made quite literally a κωφὸν πρόσωπον is that her character then cries out for supplementation, for a further voice,[41] for *odi et amo*. Dido had evoked Juno and the vengeful denizens of hell (IV. 608–10), and in answer the second half of the poem, by contrast with the first, develops a much greater *basso profondo* of malice. What the actors do at the level of simple narrative is continually doubled by hints and suggestions—and downright interventions—of the demonic (*flectere si nequeo superos, Acheronta movebo*, VII. 312; cf. *nunc etiam manis ... movet*, X. 39–40). It is now that Dido's *concepit Furias* (IV. 474) comes to term. The spirits of wickedness in high places brood over the action on earth, remorselessly, mercilessly pressing now this champion and now that into the fray, and toward death (X. 439, 689; XI. 727). Whatever the *lacrimae rerum* welling in the eyes of mortals, there is no sense at all that they move these gods. All this is especially visible in the treatment afforded Turnus (XII. 101; cf. *furere ante furorem*, 680), and in his experience at the end, of which Allecto has been the horrible precursor (VII. 435–66; cf. XII. 914). But Amata and Juturna are other instances. Aeneas himself was ultimately marked as *Furiis accensus* (XII. 946).

Given the need to balance this equation, to find a human character who both carries the weight of erotic Medea and is on a par with malicious Juno within the economy of Books VII–XII of the poem, we must then turn back to Dido, whose uncontrolled passions and magic arts are certainly modelled on her predecessor. This is already felt in IV, where Aeneas is an intruding Jason who will however leave the plundering of Carthage / Colchis to his descendants. Dido, like Medea, is abandoned for a dynastically suitable marriage.

Dido herself dimly senses all this when she evokes and diverts Medea's treatment of Apsyrtus, meant after all to *save* her lover (IV. 600–01):

> 'non potui abreptum divellere corpus et undis
> spargere?'

'Could I not have seized his body, torn it to pieces and scattered it over the waves?'

She means, not to save Aeneas, but to destroy him.

Medea, so charming in many senses, was a murderess: of her brother, of Pelias, of Creon and his daughter, eventually of her own children; the would-be poisoner of her stepson Theseus, as every reader of the *Hecale*,

---

[41] Again Virgil's rhetoric of silences: above, p. 112.

including Ovid (*Met.* VII. 406), remembered. In the passage just noted, Dido goes on to wish she had played Atreus with Ascanius (601–02)—here a Lamia indeed! For Aeneas she wishes a wrenching separation from his son (616), and a miserable end like that of Priam (620), after he has seen the unworthy deaths of his own people. How could all these dire predictions be left as mere words, any more than the Cyclops' curses in the *Odyssey*? How could Aeneas' sufferings in the second half of the poem be divorced from the woman whose imprecations they fulfil? It is now that Mercury's earlier warnings begin to acquire their appropriate resonance (IV. 560–70):

> 'nate dea, potes hoc sub casu ducere somnos,   560
> nec quae te circum stent deinde pericula cernis,
> demens, nec Zephyros audis spirare secundos?
> illa dolos dirumque nefas in pectore versat
> certa mori, variosque irarum concitat aestus.
> non fugis hinc praeceps, dum praecipitare potestas?   565
> iam mare turbari trabibus saevasque videbis
> conlucere faces, iam fervere litora flammis,
> si te his attigerit terris Aurora morantem.
> heia age, rumpe moras. varium et mutabile semper
> femina.'

'Goddess-born, can you prolong your slumbers while fortune threatens, unaware what coming dangers surround you, mad fool, not hearing the breath of favourable winds? She plots guile and dread horror in her heart, resolved to die, and stirs shifting tides of seething anger. Are you not off from here in headlong flight, while headlong flight is yours? Soon your eyes will witness the sea churning with ships, the light of frenzied torches, the shoreline hot with flames, if dawn catches you lingering in this land. Up with you, no more delay! Woman was ever fickle and changeable.'

562. vocatival *demens* is the language of the diatribe (*demens*, Prop. II. 18b. 23, *al.*; *o demens*, Martial VII. 25. 4; ἄφρων, NT Lk. 12:20), but it also recalls Appius Caecus' *mentes ... dementes* in Ennius (*Ann.* 199–200, Sk.). Dido herself is *demens* at IV. 78, but no god intervenes to help her.

564. *Allecto in Teucros Stygiis se concitat alis*, VII. 476. Cf. XI. 742, 784.

566. *saevas* is again noteworthy. See above on the proem to Book VII.

How many of the *Aeneid*'s dawns serve to shed light on disaster! The Trojan fleet will burn in the very next book. *Varium et mutabile* may look like the satirical topos, repeated in Figaro's "la donna è mobile." But it also alludes to Dido's versatility (*versat*, 563; cf. *scaena ... versis ... frontibus*, *Geo.* III. 24) in shifting identities, and that will come to full fruition with her death.

Dido in Italy

Myth universalises. It is attempting "pre-logically" to establish what are now called "scientific" (universally valid and replicable) laws, and this is why Aristotle regards poetry, which uses the universals of myth, as "more philosophical and serious than history" (*Poetics* 1451b 5–6), concerned with incidental particulars. But if, as the culmination of its attempt at universality, myth asserts that in the end only one thing ever happened, the Augustans felt this even about what they knew from Ennius as their history in a tragic, even despairing sense (Hor., *Epodes* 7. 17–20):

> sic est. acerba fata Romanos agunt,
>   scelusque fraternae necis,
> ut inmerentis fluxit in terram Remi
>   sacer nepotibus cruor.
>
> So it is. Harsh fates hound the Romans, the guilt of a brother's murder, ever since innocent Remus' blood flowed on the ground, to bring a curse on his descendants.

17. *cum Romana suos egit Discordia civis*, Prop. I. 22. 5.

If the ancient link of blood and earth here recalls Genesis,[42] the careful symmetry which parallels *Aeneid* VII with *Aeneid* I illustrates Horace's point in Roman pre-history. In Italy, for the Aeneadae, the old story of the *Iliad* begins to unravel a second time (*iterum*, VI. 94, VII. 322).[43] Yet not all changes. If Lavinia is Helen (VI. 93, XI. 479–80), so also was Dido (I. 650; cf. VII. 364). And if, in this *Iliad*, the *Odyssey* and its Circe (the mother of Latinus) continue, Dido / Circe must survive in some way. Aeneas, who has landed at the mouth of the Tiber like Odysseus on Ithaca, or Jason on Lemnos,[44] recognises that Italy is his destined home with words he had used to her (*hic domus, haec patria est*, VII. 122; cf. *hic amor, haec patria est*, IV. 347).

Dido had threatened to haunt Aeneas, and this she does. In the event, her *inveni, germana, viam ... quae mihi reddat eum ...* (IV. 478–79) is to be understood literally.[45] So is her *omnibus umbra locis adero* (IV. 386). Yet, in Apollonius, it is not so much Medea as her sister Chalciope who makes

---

[42] "The voice of thy brother's blood crieth unto Me from the ground" (4:10).

[43] Cf. also *Iliacosque i t e r u m demens audire labores / exposcit* [sc. Dido], IV. 78–79. The lesson of the poem is that she will not learn from the past (she is *demens*). Here she offers the paradigm of all its characters, and even of any malcontents in the poet's Roman audience. Lucan picks up this iteration: *consurgunt partes iterum*, I. 692. The only hope is to break out of the maze under a new sort of leader.

[44] Ithaca: Knauer, p. 241, following a hint given by Heyne. Lemnos: ἀνέμοιο λιπόντος, *Arg.* I. 607 = *Aen.* VII. 27, *cum venti posuere*: H. Fränkel, *Noten zu den* Argonautika *des Apollonios* (Munich 1968), p. 89. See also Lycophron, *Alex.* 1273–74.

[45] Interesting in another perspective: J. Watkins, *The Specter of Dido: Spenser and Virgilian Epic* (New Haven 1995).

this threat (*Arg.* III. 703-04):

> ... ἢ σοίγε, φίλοις σὺν παισὶ θανοῦσα,
> εἴην ἐξ Ἀίδεω στυγερὴ μετόπισθεν Ἐρινύς.

'Or, dead with my dear sons, may I be to you in after days a Fury from hell.'

Heard over this contrasting echo, *infelix* Dido's similar threat betrays the hidden, barren ground of her own vow.

Dido / Deianeira earlier invited a comparison with Aeneas / Hercules. With Hercules, Bacchus was another model for Hellenistic princes (*Aen.* VI. 801-05; Horace, *Odes* IV. 8. 29-34). Cavafy's confusion of the two in his Ἀπολείπειν ὁ Θεὸς Ἀντώνιον is telling.[46] Bacchic themes provide a powerful link between the two halves of Virgil's poem. Helen had behaved like a sort of bacchant celebrating Troy's fall (VI. 517). At the banquet in her palace Dido, who had received Helen's gew-gaws (I. 650), drank in the flames of her infatuation with Aeneas and his possibility of a future (*laticemque Lyaeum*, I. 686; compare Cupid / Ascanius' saffron robe at 711 with ἐπὶ κροκωτῷ, Aristophanes, *Frogs* 46). *Adsit laetitiae Bacchus dator et bona Iuno* (I. 734) is her deluded cry.

In Book IV the queen's bacchic fury bursts out unrestrained (300-03):

> saevit inops animi totamque incensa per urbem
> bacchatur, qualis commotis excita sacris
> Thyias, ubi audito stimulant trieterica Baccho
> orgia nocturnusque vocat clamore Cithaeron.

Distraught she rages, hurtling on fire through all the city, like a bacchant, a worshipper of the god, goaded by the epiphany she senses at the mystic celebration, to whom the sacred mountain calls at night.

Later, she dreams that she is Pentheus, of double vision (469-70). From now on, the association of Bacchus and Dido is constant. But bacchants famously handled and even wore serpents (Horace, *Odes* II. 19. 19; Naevius, *Lycurgus* 25 W.). In Book V, as the Trojans take their ease in Sicily (*Baccho*, 77), the iridescent serpent appears to bode well for their fortunes. But even here, there is already a reminiscence of Dido's death (V. 89 ~ IV. 701), and before the book is out, with the burning of Trojan ships, the might-have-been of IV is almost a reality.

In Italy, as the Senatorial decree of 186 B.C. attests, Bacchus had a political aspect.[47] There, he and the serpent mean something rather different.

---

[46] A convenient text in *Medieval and Modern Greek Poetry*, ed. C. A. Trypanis (Oxford 1968), no. 201, p. 223. See also West, *East Face of Helicon*, p. 487.

[47] Bacchus had appeared on the coinage of the rebellious allies during the Social War (reverse of denarius with Oscan legend *mutil embratur* [= C. PAPIUS MUTILUS IMPERATOR] now in the Staatliches Münzkabinett, Berlin, reproduced in

Events in Book VII take a fury-filled turn. Juno / Aeolus of Book I are now transformed into Juno / Allecto. Fury has hardly been missing before, but this further ratcheting of the screw expresses the malevolent and nightmarish dimensions of the second half of the poem. Allecto, herself a bacchant (X. 41), tosses one of the serpents from her own snaky locks into the heart of Lavinia's mother, Amata, and the queen's assumed[48] Bacchic *furor* spreads to the other women, and ends in the call for war (VII. 346, 385, 580). At its climax, in the bull-similes of Book XII, Bacchus as bull (φάνηθι ταῦρος, Euripides, *Bacchae* 1017) lives on.[49]

Wherever the forces opposed to Aeneas appear, they bring with them death. But Aeneas himself seems to broadcast death. In Book XII, Amata, sooner than face him as son-in-law, commits suicide (593 ff.). *At regina* (54) echoes the triple *at regina* of IV (1, 296, 504). *Nova pugnae conterrita sorte* (54) and *moritura* (55, 602) echo *fatis exterrita* (IV. 450) and *moritura* (IV. 415, 519, 604). It seems a strange misjudgment of Virgilian art to suppose that these and other parallels are proof of redundancy. As early as *Poenorum ... in arvis* (XII. 4; cf. 37b = IV. 595b) the poet signals that Dido is not to be absent from this book.[50]

But she is also at work in the deaths of Nisus and Euryalus, and of Pallas. Ascanius promises the former extravagant gifts if they succeed in their mission. They include:

cratera antiquum, quem dat Sidonia Dido. (IX. 266)

His words are wild and, since they are borrowed from Agamemnon's vain effort to appease sullen Achilles (*Il.* IX. 121 ff.), the discerning listeners at this point know that the whole enterprise is doomed. What they know from Dido's presence is that the failure will be accompanied by a slaughter fit to glut hell's vengeful demons. *Dat* here, so often interpreted as a historical present, is a fine example of vertical time. The queen continues to give. *Cnosius* (305) fulfils a similar signposting function (cf. VI. 23).

At the start of Book VIII, in a metamorphosis anticipating that of the very end of the poem, Aeneas himself appears as a sort of Medea / Dido,

---

J. Vogt, *Römische Geschichte* [Freiburg 1955], p. 272). His importance to the Etruscans as "παχε" is attested by many inscriptions.

[48] Quamquam pro *simulato* (385) *stimulato* mallemus (cf. IV. 302, *audito stimulant trieterica Baccho*). Regina ultro deum invitat atque lacessit.

[49] See also above, p. 68, on the material dealing with the combat of two bulls from *Georgics* III broken by the *Aeneid* into two segments for Books VII and XII.

[50] *Poenorum* only here and at IV. 134, the eager wait for the queen at the start of the hunt.

tossing sleeplessly on his anxious couch. It is particularly the simile which betrays this astonishing transformation. There is no allusion in Apollonius' original to the moon. The moon is Dido (I. 499, VI. 454). Certain characteristic words recur: the Gygean *videns*; *versat*; *imagine* (VIII. 18–27):

> Talia per Latium, quae Laomedontius heros
> cuncta videns magno curarum fluctuat aestu,
> atque animum nunc huc celerem nunc dividit illuc   20
> in partisque rapit varias perque omnia versat:
> sicut aquae tremulum labris ubi lumen aënis
> sole repercussum aut radiantis imagine lunae
> omnia pervolitat late loca, iamque sub auras
> erigitur summique ferit laquearia tecti.   25
>   Nox erat et terras animalia fessa per omnis
> alituum pecudumque genus sopor altus habebat ...

Such Latium's state. All this the hero saw, Laomedon's heir, tossing on a mighty tide of troubles. He was in two minds, swiftly turning his thoughts, now this way, now that, exploring every changing side, and all chances —just as when from water in bronze vessels a quivering light is thrown by the sun or the reflection of the shining moon, and darts ranging through every place, even rising into the air and striking the fretted ceiling of some lofty room.

It was night, and through all the earth deep sleep held weary creatures fast, bird and beast ...

18. *Laomedontius heros*: IV. 542; cf. *Geo.* I. 502. See also p. 147, n. 23, above on Anchises' trickery.

19. *magnoque irarum fluctuat aestu* of Dido, IV. 532.

20–21. cf. IV. 285–86, where, in response to Mercury's warning, Aeneas starts his preparations for leaving.

25. *laquearibus*, I. 726, Dido's palace (the *Aeneid*'s only other use of the noun).

In Apollonius, Medea, who is already in love, is debating whether she may help Jason or not (III. 744, 751, 755–59):

> Νὺξ μὲν ἔπειτ' ἐπὶ γαῖαν ἄγεν κνέφας ...
> ἀλλὰ μάλ' οὐ Μήδειαν ἐπὶ γλυκερὸς λάβεν ὕπνος....
> πυκνὰ δέ οἱ κραδίη στηθέων ἔντοσθεν ἔθυιεν,
> ἠελίου ὥς τίς τε δόμοις ἔνι πάλλεται αἴγλη
> ὕδατος ἐξανιοῦσα, τὸ δὴ νέον ἠὲ λέβητι
> ἠέ που ἐν γαυλῷ κέχυται· ἡ δ' ἔνθα καὶ ἔνθα
> ὠκείῃ στροφάλιγγι τινάσσεται ἀίσσουσα.

Night then drew darkness over the earth ... but sweet sleep did not seize Medea ... and often her heart raged within her breast, as a ray of sunlight in the house comes dancing from water just poured into a bowl or even into some pail. This way and that it quivers and darts with swift shivering.

She decides that she may, and this is where the whole fateful story of their relationship, of her trust and his ultimate betrayal, begins to unfold.

Can this theme of broken trust have fresh relevance to Aeneas? His troubles are relieved by the apparition of Father Tiber, who advises him to seek help from the Arcadian settlers at the site of what will be Rome. It is here that we learn for the first time the name of Pallas, ancestor of the Arcadians. But the reminiscence of Juno's miscalculated cleverness (VIII. 49 = IV. 115), and of Juturna's despair (VIII. 66b ~ XII. 886b), does not augur well. Old Pallas is the sire of young Pallas, whom his father Evander will send to be Aeneas' ally—and to his end. It will be he who will receive Dido's robe as his shroud (XI. 74). Aeneas mediates this death too.

Quite marked repetitions make the connection. Book XI begins with an echo of IV (XI. 1 = IV. 129, from the royal hunt at Carthage). Aeneas has just killed Lausus (described at X. 829 as *infelix*) and his father Mezentius, and lost Pallas. The Trojans are victorious, but at terrible cost (= *videatque indigna suorum funera*, IV. 617–18). There are many pyres to be lit (XI. 182–202). When the body of Pallas arrives home, the streets are lined with funeral torches. The mothers "fire the grieving city" with their lament (147). We could be in burning Carthage (IV. 670).

Aeneas brings out one of two robes that Dido had made for him, to be put on Pallas' corpse. *Laeta / maestus* here are in tragic antithesis (XI. 72–77):

> Tum geminas vestis auroque ostroque rigentis
> extulit Aeneas, quas illi laeta laborum
> ipsa suis quondam manibus Sidonia Dido
> fecerat, et tenui telas discreverat auro.
> harum unam iuveni supremum maestus honorem
> induit arsurasque comas obnubit amictu.

Then Aeneas brought out twin robes, stiff with gold and purple, which Sidonian Dido had once made for him with her own hands, happy in her toil, parting the weft with threads of gold. One of these, a last mark of respect, he sadly put upon the young soldier, and with that covering veiled the locks so soon to burn.

Obnubit (unique in the poem) at the end is suggestive. It was perhaps a term originally associated with the bride at the Roman marriage rite, *nuptiae*.

One of these robes he had been wearing when he was assailed (*invadit*, IV. 265; cf. XII. 497) by Mercury with Jupiter's message (IV. 263–64):

> dives quae munera Dido
> fecerat, et tenui telas discreverat auro.

Royal Dido had fashioned these gifts, parting the weft with threads of gold.

Is this her return assault?

Old Acoetes, sent in vain by Pallas' father to act as armour-bearer and guardian, has to be guided behind the bier, so worn out is he by grief and age. *Infelix* again attracts attention (XI. 85–86):

> ducitur infelix aevo confectus Acoetes,
> pectora nunc foedans pugnis, nunc unguibus ora.

Withered Acoetes, worn out with age, was escorted in the procession, now beating his breast with his fists, now with his nails scratching his face.

It is the behaviour of Anna, when she hears of Dido's suicide (IV. 673):

> unguibus ora soror foedans et pectora pugnis ...

A sister, her nails scratching her face, her fists beating her breasts ...

When Aeneas had asked Evander for help, it was generously given:

> auxilio laetos dimittam opibusque iuvabo. (VIII. 171)

But Dido had already made that same offer:

> auxilio tutos dimittam opibusque iuvabo. (I. 571)

But, when they were "sent off," were they really either *tuti* or *laeti*?

The attentive listener already knew that Pallas was doomed, even as his father bade him a last farewell (VIII. 583–84):

> haec genitor digressu dicta supremo
> fundebat; famuli conlapsum in tecta ferebant.

These prayers a father poured out at his last parting. His servants carried him fainting to his room.

583. *digressu* only here and at III. 482, childless Andromache (= childless Dido) *digressu maesta supremo*. Cf. *discessu*, VI. 464 (= Hercules / Cacus, VIII. 215).

How else did Dido's last interview with Aeneas end (IV. 391–92)?

> ... suscipiunt famulae conlapsaque membra
> marmoreo referunt thalamo stratisque reponunt.

Her maids caught her and carried her fainting limbs back to her marble chamber, and set her on the bed.

Once again a *thalamus* is deadly. *Conlapsa* prepares for *conlapsam* (664).

Dido's sister, witnessing her death, is replicated not only in Acoetes but in Juturna. Again *infelix* is heard (XII. 869–71; 871 = IV. 673):

> At procul ut Dirae stridorem agnovit et alas,
> infelix crinis scindit Iuturna solutos
> unguibus ora soror foedans et pectora pugnis:...

But when close by she recognised the Fury's hissing wings, barren Juturna, his sister, tore her loose-hanging hair, her nails scratching her face, her fists beating her breasts.

Both Dido (VI. 469 ff.) and Turnus (IX. 806 ff.) are Ajax. Like Ajax, Dido commits suicide. Virgil recalls this motif at the moment when Aeneas speaks to his son for the only time in the poem (XII. 435–36 ~ Sophocles, *Ajax* 550–51, Accius *trag.* 123 W.; Macrobius VI. 1. 58).

Infelix Balteus

With erotic mischief in mind, Hera borrowed Aphrodite's belt (*Il.* XIV. 214 ff.). In an act of symbolic rape, Hippolyte's belt was taken by Hercules, as the Temple of Apollo Sosianus advertised. Reversing (and confirming) this motif, Turnus' belt, taken from Pallas,[51] showed the murder of the sons of Aegyptus by the Danaids, a theme from the decorations of the Temple of Apollo Palatinus, linked, via Io / Isis, with Egypt and Cleopatra. One of the ancestors of the Danaids was Belus (בעל), and this is the name Virgil chooses for Dido's father (I. 621), who in other sources is Mutto or Mettes.

At the end of the poem, when Aeneas sees this belt, echoes of Dido multiply (XII. 945–49):

> Ille, oculis postquam saevi monimenta doloris
> exuviasque hausit, Furiis accensus et ira
> terribilis: 'tune hinc spoliis indute meorum
> eripiare mihi? Pallas te hoc vulnere, Pallas
> immolat et poenam scelerato ex sanguine sumit.'

> He drank in the reminders of his wild grief offered by the belt stripped from the dead. Kindled by the Furies and fearful in his wrath, 'Clad in the spoils of my own kin, are you to be snatched from my grasp? It is Pallas with this wound, Pallas, who sacrifices you and takes satisfaction from your guilty blood.'

946. *heu Furiis incensa feror*, IV. 376; *subitoque accensa furore*, 697.

947. *terribilis* in association with *irae* was used of Aeneas in this book at 498–99: *terribilis saevam nullo discrimine caedem / suscitat, irarumque omnis effundit habenas* (contrast the calming gesture of Jupiter, V. 818). The epithet may be used of royalty at times in compliment, a sense going back to Egyptian notions of the monarch as divine (*TWAT* III, s.v. ירא, col. 877 *infra*; cf. Ammianus Marcellinus XVII. 4. 11, *aculeos quoque innasci debere*). This is seen in the Psalms (*confiteor tibi quia terribiliter magnificatus es*, Vulg. Ps. cxxxviii:14; cf. cxlv:6) and in Virgil at XII. 852 (*meritas aut bello territat urbes*, *sc.* Iuppiter; cf. XII. 262, Aeneas). It is noted in the Roman idea of kingship (*Masinissam recenti ... victoria terribilem*, Livy XXX. 8. 7; [Mithridates] *terribilis*, Vell. II. 18. 3). Cicero says of Pompey: *cuius virtute terribilior erat populus Romanus exteris gentibus* (*Phil.* II. §65), though Horace shows that this fear may also be inspired in subjects at home (*Odes* III. 1. 5). Pindar, who sketches much of the theory of later kingship, had already said that Hiero will run up on his (domestic) enemies like a wolf (*Py.* 2. 84). Иван Грозный equally suggests the dangers of this, and *ira* was not normally recommended anyway.[52]

---

[51] He evidently viewed him as a traitor to the Italian cause. See below, p. 230, on the feudal symbolism of "belt," living on, for example, in the phrase "a belted earl."

[52] Polybius notes that Philip V, who claimed irate Achilles as his ancestor (Silius, XV. 292; cf. Perseus, Prop. IV. 11. 39), habitually indulged in anger and hot temper (τὸ πλεῖον ὀργῇ καὶ θυμῷ χρώμενος, XVI. 28, cited by Shipley,

Saevi here (945) is telling. Whatever the precepts of Hellenistic or philhellene courtiers (cf. *facere omnia saeve / non impune licet, nisi cum facis*, Lucan VIII. 492–93), whatever the δεινότης of a Tigellinus (Dio Cass., *Hist. Rom.* LXII. 27. 3), Augustus himself practised *civilitas* (Suet., *Aug.* 51). The reader recognises *monimenta* (IV. 498), *dolor* (IV. 419, 474, 547, 679, 693), *exuviae* (IV. 651), *haurire* (IV. 661). *Ira, vulnus, poena, sanguis* may be added.

Pallas ... immolat (948–49). *Immolat*, though not one of Dido's words in Book IV, deserves special note (cf. X. 519, 541, the only other instances). Pallas, young and innocent, in death seeking retaliation like the *puer* in *Epode* 5, is made to take over from Aeneas as acting subject. But, in allowing himself to be metamorphosed in this way into one so like dead Dido, the Pallas who wore in death her robe (XI. 77), Aeneas has assumed her vengeful identity (IV. 625, 656, 659). The scene with Helen in Book II (577 ff.) where he earlier contemplated revenge had been excised. But the temptation had evidently persisted. Now he yields to it.

In the end therefore, Dido got her man. Meanwhile, if Lavinia has overtly been made into the whole object of the war between Turnus and the Trojans, the theme of the posterity which she will bear to Aeneas (VI. 764) inevitably has as its reverse the posterity which Turnus is to lose. The last thought with which the *Aeneid* leaves the reader therefore is of a complete denial for those outside a certain charmed circle of normal married fruitfulness and happiness. Pallas and Lausus and Camilla have died unmarried, and Pallas has even been demonised. Turnus dies unmarried. Juturna had no child. The Danaids slew their husbands before children could be born. *Ac velut in somnis ...* (XII. 908). How well this last simile catches the helplessness paralysing the victim of these dark forces. *Infelix* Dido had shared it (*in somnis*, IV. 466) before she plunged into her hell and, from there, rose to share the Furies who were her children (IV. 474).

The Greek World after Alexander, p. 62). This served him well once, but obviously was not to his advantage in the long run.

VIII

DIDO AND VIRGILIAN NIGHTMARES

> O God, I could be bounded in a nutshell and
> count myself a king of infinite space, were it not that
> I have bad dreams.
>
> Shakespeare, *Hamlet* II. ii. 255–57

Factual and Emotive Elements

Quae me suspensam insomnia terrent! (IV. 9). The *Aeneid*'s world is nightmarish even if we judge it by so recent an example as Catullus, whose central poems certainly describe sleeping characters, but no sleeping horrors. Attis and Ariadne both awake to reflect on their predicaments.

Dreams have a long history, and a traditional etiquette.[1] Their perception by the primitive mentality is often not easily defined in modern terms. They imply strange states of consciousness, waking within sleep; sometimes they might perhaps be better described as a vision of the half-awake, what Macrobius (*Comm.* I. 3. 2), following Cicero, calls a φάντασμα or *visum*. Dreamers, though they may be the vessels of divine revelation, perhaps because of that, are ambiguous figures. Joseph, wearing what was

---

[1] חלם, *TWAT* II, cols. 986–98; (Bergman *et al.*); ὄναρ, *Theolog. Wörterbuch zum Neuen Testament* (ed. G. Kittel), V. 220–38 (Oepke); cf. A. L. Oppenheim, "The Interpretation of Dreams in the Ancient Near East with a Translation of an Assyrian Dream Book," *Trans. Am. Philosoph. Society*, N.S. 46/3 (Philadelphia 1956), 179–374. Following F. Leo (*Geschichte der röm. Lit.* I [Berlin 1913], p. 179, n. 2), Oppenheim distinguishes (p. 230) dreams as divine revelations from those reflecting the psychology of the dreamer, which may be either good or bad, confusing, abnormal, "dark," "black." Virgil certainly echoes (like Shakespeare's Clarence [*Richard III*, I. iv. 1–63]) some of the ancient conventions of these apparitions.— H. R. Steiner, *Der Traum in der Aeneis* (Bern 1952), is standard. Two older dissertations are noted: W. S. Messer, *The Dream in Homer and Greek Tragedy* (New York 1918); J. B. Stearns, *Studies of the Dream as a Technical Device in Latin Epic and Drama*, vii (Lancaster, Pennsylvania 1927). A more historical study: G. Weber, *Kaiser, Träume und Visionen in Prinzipat und Spätantike* (Stuttgart 2000).

at one time perceived as his jester's coat of many colours, offers a good example: a "master of dreams" (בַּעַל הַחֲלֹמוֹת, Gen. 37:19), sold into exile and slavery, imprisoned, eventually the saviour of his people.

Epic dreams are usually informative. A god appears to a sleeping hero and gives instructions. This is a religious pattern. We still find it, for example, in St. Matthew (1:20, Joseph), and certainly in the *Aeneid*.

Yet fantastic, "psychological" dreams are also old, as *Gilgamesh* shows. Homer himself narrates a waking vision which seems like a nightmarish trance, and is in effect the "death-dream" of the Suitors.[2] Greek tragedy makes great use of psychological dreams, and it is here, in reaction to a male-oriented, male-logical *polis*, that there seems much greater interest in women as dreamers, what above (p. 137) we have called "peepers," recoverers from the shadows of the hidden and rejected. Atossa in Aeschylus' *Persae* (176 ff.) is an instance. Euripides' Iphigenia is another (*IT* 44 ff.). Later, as real life caught up with art, Caesar's Calpurnia received a dream foreboding her supremely logical husband's death (Suet., *Jul.* 81). Pilate's wife is yet another in this line, speaking words Dido might have used: πολλὰ γὰρ ἔπαθον σήμερον κατ' ὄναρ δι' αὐτόν (Matt. 27:19). She confirms a general distinction between the factual (admonitory / instructional) dreams sent to men and the emotive dreams of women.[3]

Dreams sprang from and contributed to the restless atmosphere of the Hellenistic world, too big for its own good. Apollonius' allusions to them provide a fine illustration of thematic harmony in the structure of his epic.[4] There, they play a notable part in the poet's effort to put Medea's tormented mind before his readers.

The *Aeneid*'s dreams, created for another civilisation that seemed to have grown too big for its own good (*nec se Roma ferens*, Lucan I. 72), form the culmination of this Apollonian tradition. They are either given to Dido, or conditioned, in this poetic of hypersensitivity, by her hinted presence. Because she is forever looking for a child, this is one of the ways in which, however faintly, this theme is carried throughout the epic.

---

[2] *Od.* XX. 345 ff. Compare Circe's dream in Apollonius (*Arg.* IV. 664). For the term, "death dream," Oppenheim, p. 213. Lucan gives one to Pompey (VII. 7 ff.), significantly of a theatre and therefore portending resurrection. This is the motif Virgil exploits for Dido (*scaenis*, IV. 471).

[3] Still valid for Corneille: *Quoi, vous vous arrêtez aux songes d'une femme* etc. at the start of *Polyeucte* (1643). Turnus' agitation (XII. 908) is made more apparent.

[4] *The Classical Epic Tradition*, p. 86.

Dreams Given to Dido

There is only one dream in Homer in which a dead hero appears to a sleeper, and that is towards the finale of the *Iliad*.[5] Virgil *starts* the sequence of dreams in his epic with a report of such a dream (I. 353 ff.). The fact that our introduction to Dido, a childless widow, begins like this sets the tone for our whole acquaintance with her. She too, like Aeneas, is a refugee from her home and city. Venus tells how the ghost of her murdered husband Sychaeus, still bearing about him the imprint of his wounds, had appeared to warn her against her brother. This is parallel to mutilated Hector's appearance to Aeneas in Troy (II. 268 ff.), with a similar warning of impending doom. Yet it also contains prophetic (vatic?) elements anticipating Aeneas' own hasty flight from Carthage after Mercury's warning. The "mixing" in this way of motifs in due course separately applicable is characteristic. For both protagonists in this shifting counterpoint—we learn it yet again—there is no freedom of choice, only the fulfilment of prefigured destiny. His destiny is to find a future and found a city. Hers is to lose both.[6]

Later, talking to Anna, Dido alludes briefly, as we saw, to repeated dreams. Here, Virgil is establishing her kinship with Medea, shortly to be in conversation with her sister (*insomnia terrent*, IV. 9 ~ ἐφόβησαν ὄνειροι, *Arg*. III. 636). More then than the Homeric enters Dido's mix. She is Apollonius' Medea certainly—but, from that story, also Lemnian Hypsipyle, and Cretan Ariadne. Ariadne, for Catullus the supreme instance of the used and abandoned helpmate, had in Apollonius again been used by Jason to lend colour to his half-true salesman's pitch to Medea (*Arg*. III. 998). It is this Alexandrian epic which provides both the example of a loving, queenly heroine, in need of a king, yet left by an eligible, voyaging hero; and of a dangerous, rescuing princess who will be dropped at his peril by an anti-hero who finds that he has to make a dynastically advantageous marriage. This in Virgil is his trick (and tic) of the "disobliging other."

---

[5] Patroclus appearing to Achilles (*Il*. XXIII. 75 ff.): Steiner, p. 96. The appearance of a ghost with the marks of violence still upon it (Steiner, p. 26; H. D. Jocelyn, *Ennius*, no. xxv) is a folk-motif, picked up by Virgil at the beginning and end (*recens a vulnere*, VI. 450: above, p. 155, Clytaemnestra) of our formal acquaintance with Dido, but it finds some parallel in the NT account of Christ's apparition to Thomas (John 20:24–27, although Christ specifically denies that he is a πνεῦμα). There are also parallels in Lucian (τραυματίαι, *Menippus* 10 [ed. Macleod II, p. 268]).

[6] Burning Troy is patterned after burning Carthage: above, p. 14. See *The Classical Epic Tradition*, pp. 176–77, for more on this.

The Homeric / Cyclic scenes in Juno's temple at Carthage show that Dido has had an appropriate Hellenistic education, enough to satisfy Alexandrian Ptolemy.[7] But she is like Alexandrian Propertius in not always keeping her myths under control. The jumbled sequences of IV. 469–71 (Pentheus, Orestes, both with Furies) and 600–02 (Medea, Atreus) are the proof of that. This technique of polyprosopic blending hints that the mention of her theatre (I. 427) is not an idle detail. Lists of favourite tragic pantomimic themes would eventually include mad scenes from the *Aeneid*. It was suggested above (pp. 82 ff.) that this kinship explains Melpomene's (or Clio's) place at Virgil's side in the Sousse mosaic.

The theatrical / pantomimic nightmare occurring at IV. 465–73 is again therefore relevant. At 469 here the Gygean *videt* recurs:

>   agit ipse furentem   465
> in somnis ferus Aeneas, semperque relinqui
> sola sibi, semper longam incomitata videtur
> ire viam, et Tyrios deserta quaerere terra,
> Eumenidum veluti demens videt agmina Pentheus
> et solem geminum et duplices se ostendere Thebas,   470
> aut Agamemnonius scaenis agitatus Orestes,
> armatam facibus matrem et serpentibus atris
> cum fugit ultricesque sedent in limine Dirae.

Wild Aeneas hunts her in her mad dreams, and always there she is being left to herself, always following some long path, her courtiers lost, looking for her Tyrians in the desert waste—just like mad Pentheus seeing a vision of the troops of Furies, a twin sun, a double Thebes; or Agamemnon's Orestes hounded over the stage, running from his mother while she wields her torches and dark serpents, and the vengeful spirits of hell sit at the threshold.

Dido is evidently an actress. In her sick fantasy, horror is piled on horror. *Ferus / furentem*: a madman chases a mad woman, isolated, abandoned, demented and degraded by Bacchus, hunted by a murdered mother, the Furies lying in wait at the door. We are already in a dream, but this dream somehow contains a stage, another sort of dream. Virgil's imagination weaves seamlessly between these worlds.[8] His *scaenis* (471) emphasises that absence of footlights between stagy realities which Bakhtin notes as

---

[7] "Homer crowned by the World and Time" is mentioned above (p. 80). Cf. T.B.L. Webster, *Hellenistic Poetry and Art* (London 1964), p. 145, n. 1. On Homer-worship in later antiquity, C. O. Brink, "Ennius and the Hellenistic Worship of Homer," *American Journal of Philology* XCIII (1972), 547–67.

[8] This metamorphosing, Shakespearean sensibility is already Pindaric: ἐπάμεροι· τί δέ τις, τί δ' οὔ τις; σκιᾶς ὄναρ ἄνθρωπος ... (*Py.* 8. 95–96): cf. "Life's but a walking shadow, a poor player etc.," *Macbeth* V. v. 23. Cf. *scaena* in the proem to *Georgics* III (24), a passage from which Pindaric imagery is not absent either.

typical of the carnival style. The twinning (470) recalled from Euripides' *Bacchae* (918–19) is another telling clue. Part of this scene is liminal (473). Nothing is superfluous. Bacchus and Clytaemnestra will recur.[9]

This dream has been linked[10] with that astonishing piece surviving from the first book of Ennius' *Annales* in which Ilia relates her encounter with Mars (fr. 34–50, Sk.). The *brevitas* of this passage more generally shows how great was the loss imposed by Augustan formal refinement of earlier Roman taste. Ilia's isolation and feeling of terror are sympathetically and sensitively conveyed. Moschus' Europē (150 B.C.?) shows a similar reaction after another prophetic and symbolic dream.[11] What Hellenistic model inspired such imitations? Did it derive from some tragedy?

Yet, in his imitation, Virgil has reversed the fruitful promise of the *Annales*. Whatever Ilia's terrors, they were after all to issue in the birth of the twins who would strive to be the first founders of the City. There is no such promise for *infelix* Dido—nor here for Pentheus and Orestes, haunting her stage. Dido is alone (we hear it repeatedly). Her persecutor Aeneas is cast in the role of some sort of Fury (*Eumenidum ... Dirae*). In these last lines we also perhaps hear an anticipation of Turnus, himself to suffer persecution from the Dirae (XII. 845) in his confrontation with Aeneas. He too eventually seems to be in a nightmarish dream (908). But, as Virgil's first persons there suggest, this nightmare now encompasses us all.[12]

Turnus is marked for death and, coming so soon before her suicide, this passage of *Aeneid* IV is also Dido's "death dream." *Agit ipse furentem* picks up motifs from the earlier part of the book (*furentem*, 65; *pastor agens telis*, 71). How far does her prophetic vision correspond to what her experience of death will be? *Aeneid* VI certainly gives us the picture of some sort of romantic reunion with Sychaeus (474). But is that all? Was Dido also active in the upper world, as her *sequar atris ignibus absens* (IV. 384), noted earlier, threatens? Like Alcestis, she dies for love, and Eros had been defined by Plato (who refers to Alcestis) as the constant striving to become one with the beloved, even in death.[13] Perhaps Dido's fearful vision of isolation

---

[9] Above, pp. 160–61 (Bacchus); 155 (Clytaemnestra).

[10] Leo, *loc. cit.*; Steiner, pp. 20–22, 50. Above, p. 87.

[11] "Ἡ δ' ἀπὸ μὲν στρωτῶν λεχέων θόρε δειμαίνουσα, / παλλομένη κραδίην ... / ὀψὲ δὲ δειμαλέην ἀνενείκατο παρθένος αὐδήν (16–17, 20). If Europē's reaction seems a little overdone, presumably these were the sentiments demanded by the topos (cf. *Argonautica* III. 633–35). Ennius had died in 169, but Moschus can hardly be borrowing.

[12] Cf. OT Isaiah 25:7, quoted below, p. 264, n. 42.

[13] Καὶ ἐπειδὰν ἀποθάνητε, ἐκεῖ αὖ ἐν Ἅιδου ἀντὶ δυοῖν ἕνα εἶναι κοινῇ τεθνεῶτε, *Symp*. 192e 3–4. It depends of course on whether we take the

172   *Chapter Eight*

(*semperque relinqui / sola sibi*) may explain her continual chase after a living soul into which she can pour herself, until at the end, with the help of dead Pallas (XII. 948), she pours herself into, and transforms, *pius* Aeneas into another victim of the Furies (*Furiis incensa*, IV. 376; *Furiis accensus*, XII. 946). In this last metamorphosis he thus becomes what he has already personified for her. Perhaps we may finally say of her epic career what Aristotle said of tragedy (*Poetics* 1449a 14–15): πολλὰς μεταβολὰς μεταβαλοῦσα ... ἐπαύσατο, ἐπεὶ ἔσχε τὴν αὐτῆς φύσιν.[14]

Dreams Conditioned by her Hinted Presence

Exoriare aliquis nostris ex ossibus ultor (IV. 625). Interpreters refer this prayer of Dido for an avenging son to Hannibal, though she herself makes it clear that she intends no such temporal restrictions: *nunc, olim, quocumque dabunt se tempore vires* (627). The phrase obviously applies also to Turnus who, like Dido, becomes Juno's disposable instrument in the effort to thwart the divine purpose: crazed, degraded, and abandoned when no useful purpose is any longer served.

In Book VII, Turnus is asleep. The scene which begins at v. 413 ends with his awakening (v. 458). The intervening lines therefore describe a dream. The net aspiring to snare its full implications must be cast widely.

Dido had difficulty in sleeping even when the rest of the world was at peace (*carpebant ... soporem*, IV. 522). At one with his universe, Aeneas was asleep when he was visited by warning Mercury (*carpebat somnos*, IV. 555). Turnus may be sleeping like that when he is visited by the disguised Allecto, but this is the last for him of any peaceful slumbers (VII. 413–16):

> tectis hic Turnus in altis
> iam mediam nigra carpebat nocte quietem.
> Allecto torvam faciem et furialia membra
> exuit ...

It was black midnight, and Turnus in the lofty palace was reaping his rest. Allecto put off her savage features and Fury's limbs ...

This is the last of the three instances in the poem of the imperfect of *carpo*.

Allecto, Juno's handmaid, is (of course) a *virgo* (VII. 331), and, in the

---

re-union with Sychaeus as the full story. *Nocturnosque movet Manis* (IV. 490) is said of Dido. It became true of Juno: *nunc etiam Manis ... movet* (X. 39–40). Perhaps Dido was one of those moved. — For Dido / Alcestis, above, p. 144.

[14] The art of Aristotle's period here is not always understood. After some initial gyrations, it eventually settles down with ἔσχε τὴν αὐτῆς φύσιν into the final dimeter of an iambic, tragic trimeter. Sound matches sense, an old rhetorician's ploy.

light of this, her mistress' *fecundum concute pectus* addressed to her in the same context is ironic mockery (VII. 338; cf. Turnus' *effeta* at VII. 440). There is no charity in hell.

Allecto bears a divine Word (428). Unless Latinus agrees to give him Lavinia as his wife (*coniugium*, 433; cf. IV. 172), Turnus is to burn the Trojans with their fleet.

He laughs at the officious advice. The goddess, always irascible, is nettled beyond endurance (445, 456–60). She appears in all her deadly ugliness:

> Talibus Allecto dictis exarsit in iras....
> sic effata facem iuveni coniecit et atro
> lumine fumantis fixit sub pectore taedas.
> olli somnum ingens rumpit pavor, ossaque et artus
> perfundit toto proruptus corpore sudor.
> arma amens fremit ...

At these words, Allecto blazed into anger ... with this riposte, she hurled her torch at the young prince and planted her smoking brand with its dark light deep in his breast. A vast panic burst through his sleep, a sweat broke out all over his body and drenched his bones and limbs. Mad, he roared for arms.

456–457: *atro lumine*, like *atris ignibus*, is characteristic. Below, p. 218.

This scene with Allecto is surreal. Nero planned to dance the role of Turnus (Suet., *Nero* 54), and the metamorphosis and operatic exaltation here is close to the spirit of Ovid or Seneca; among Greek playwrights, of Euripides.[15] Its immediate epic inspiration is said to be the deceptive dream sent by Zeus to Agamemnon at the start of Book II of the *Iliad* (16–52; cf. *Il.* X. 1, the obvious outcome). In that case, once again, the effect of a Homeric original is reversed. Zeus wants to honour Achilles. Whom does Juno want to honour?

This kind of confrontation between the human and the demonic resonates so much with the reader because it is filled with old discords, some of them Semitic. A passage from the Old Testament *Wisdom of Solomon* may be compared. The Egyptians have been tossing in tormented slumbers. After their rejection of God's warnings, the first-born of Egypt are slain (18:14–19):[16]

> All things were lying in peace and silence, and night in her swift course was half spent, when Thy almighty Word [O God] leapt from heaven from Thy

---

[15] The Phrygian slave in the *Orestes* (1369 ff.) suggests an Asiatic origin for this style. For the *Heracles* of Euripides, below, p. 228.

[16] The background of the book is said to be Alexandrian. Chapter 17, an amazing piece of Hellenistic bravura writing, is also worth the attention of the student of dreams.

royal throne into the midst of that doomed land like a relentless warrior, bearing the sharp sword of Thy inflexible decree, and stood and filled it all with death, his head touching the heavens, his feet on earth. At once nightmare phantoms appalled them, and unlooked-for fears set upon them.... (New English Bible, *Apocrypha*, p. 115, adapted)

And after the encounter with Allecto?

This towering Word is itself reminiscent of Homer's Eris (*Il.* IV. 439–43):

ὦρσε δὲ τοὺς μὲν Ἄρης, τοὺς δὲ γλαυκῶπις Ἀθήνη,
Δεῖμός τ' ἠδὲ Φόβος καὶ Ἔρις ἄμοτον μεμαυῖα,
Ἄρεος ἀνδροφόνοιο κασιγνήτη ἑτάρη τε,
ἥ τ' ὀλίγη μὲν πρῶτα κορύσσεται, αὐτὰρ ἔπειτα
οὐρανῷ ἐστήριξε κάρη καὶ ἐπὶ χθονὶ βαίνει.

The Greeks were urged on by flashing-eyed Athene, the Trojans by Ares, and by Terror and Rout, and Discord in her ceaseless rage, murderous Ares' sister and comrade. Small she is when she first rears her crest, but then she plants her head in heaven, while her feet still tread the earth.

439. The δέ clause introducing Athene is intruded (Wilamowitz on Euripides, *Heracles* 222). Athene is then dropped, and the sense continues with reference to Ares. The best recourse for the translator is perhaps to present the sense more straightforwardly.

This in turn was something echoed by the *Aeneid* (IV. 176–77, Fama about to traduce Dido and Aeneas; cf. XII. 331–36, Turnus / Mars).

Sinister enough, but more is needed to justify such emotional, deadly intensity. At one level, that of black, macabre comedy, Turnus / Erysichthon,[17] eventually transformed into a howling wolf (*fremit*, IX. 60; cf. VII. 460), will now hunger for human flesh (IX. 63–64):

collecta fatigat edendi
ex longo rabies et siccae sanguine fauces.

A long-gathering, raging appetite wears him down, and a maw athirst for blood.

—and the old analogy between battles and banquets still recurs, for example, in Plautus and Cicero.[18]

But, among all these legacies, Dido still lurks, as she must wherever we hear of Furies (*ergo ubi concepit Furias*). At the centre of Book VI, she had

---

[17]Above, p. 96, for the parallel of economy throughout this scene to Callimachus, *hy. Dem.* 42 ff. (Erysichthon / Demeter).

[18] Battles / meals: *Verrine* V. §28. More generally, Athenaeus X. 421 c-d, citing Mnesimachus (II. 441 K.) and Phoenix of Colophon, cf. 438a. Meals / battles: Heliodorus, *Aethiop.* I. 4; III. 10; V. 32. See also Nisus and Mezentius, IX. 340a = X. 724a, *suadet enim vesana fames*. Rosa Ehrenreich notes the continuance of the tradition in modern Oxford: *A Garden of Paper Flowers* (London 1994), p. 147.

rejected Aeneas' apologies, silent like Ajax in the *Odyssey* (XI. 563). But she shares this identification with Turnus.[19] Both she and he, like Ajax, were stricken with a madness which would end in death.

Like Ajax, Turnus had hoped to avenge himself on a slippery adversary for the loss of a prize he claimed as his by right (the arms of Achilles stolen by Odysseus ~ Lavinia stolen by Aeneas). Sophocles describes how Ajax's plot had begun at dead of night, to be frustrated when Athene drove him instead to make a demented attack on sheep and cattle (cf. *Aen.* IX. 59–64). Tecmessa had tried to stay his hand, only to be brusquely dismissed (*Ajax* 285–88, 292–93):

> κεῖνος γὰρ ἄκρας νυκτός, ἡνίχ' ἕσπεροι
> λαμπτῆρες οὐκέτ' ᾖθον, ἄμφηκες λαβὼν
> ἐμαίετ' ἔγχος ἐξόδους ἕρπειν κενάς.
> κἀγὼ 'πιπλήσσω ...
> ὃ δ' εἶπε πρός με βαί', ἀεὶ δ' ὑμνούμενα·
> 'γύναι, γυναιξὶ κόσμον ἡ σιγὴ φέρει ... '

> For at dead of night, when the lamps of evening were no longer blazing, he seized his two-edged sword, eager to take vain paths abroad. I chided him, ... but his answer was the old curt tale: 'Woman, women find honour in silence.'

So Turnus dismisses Calybe. But, on an even crueller note, if indeed we may think of Dido as childless Andromache's childless sister,[20] the admonition to a woman not to interfere owes some sort of debt to the language found in the parting of Hector and Andromache in *Iliad* VI. Earlier in the scene, when Turnus was still able to speak for himself, he had refused to be provoked by Calybe / Allecto. She was told to busy herself with her temple duties. War and peace were matters for soldiers (VII. 443–44):

> 'cura tibi divum effigies et templa tueri;
> bella viri p a c e m que gerent quis bella gerenda.'

> 'Your task is to look after the images and temples of the gods. War and peace will be the work of men, whose work war is.'

Here, however faintly, he was echoing doomed Hector, gently but heroically reproving his wife for her loving reproaches to him (VI. 490–93):

> ἀλλ' εἰς οἶκον ἰοῦσα τὰ σ' αὐτῆς ἔργα κόμιζε,
> ἱστόν τ' ἠλακάτην τε, καὶ ἀμφιπόλοισι κέλευε
> ἔργον ἐποίχεσθαι· πόλεμος δ' ἄνδρεσσι μελήσει
> πᾶσι, μάλιστα δ' ἐμοί, τοὶ 'Ιλίῳ ἐγγεγάασιν.

> 'Go back into the house and look after your own work, the loom and the

---

[19] IX. 806 ff. ~ *Il.* XVI. 102 ff. Above, p. 164. Aeneas is also Ajax when he speaks to Ascanius for the only time in the poem (XII. 435–36).

[20] Above, p. 50.

distaff, and bid the servants get on with their tasks. War will be a matter for men—for all, but most of all for me—Troy's native sons.'

Πόλεμος δ' ἄνδρεσσι μελήσει: neither these words nor any other of the Homeric parallels adduced to this formulaic passage refer to peace. Yet Turnus does just that. He appears as a sober (Roman) statesman,[21] even like Ascanius (IX. 279). His phrase is ultimately religious: "Understand that this day I offer you the choice of a blessing and a curse" (Moses, Dt. 11:26; cf. 30:15).

But this is the last time Turnus will use the word *pax* in any positive way. The Homeric reminiscence once again lends profound pathos. Turnus will lose Lavinia and any son he might have had, as much as Hector will lose Andromache and Astyanax. And, like Hector, he will lose horribly and humiliatingly, while Aeneas / Achilles will show that he has after all learned nothing from his study of the past in Juno's temple at Carthage. But the peer of *infelix*, widowed Andromache is *infelix*, widowed Dido. Both she and Turnus are cheated of normality by Furies.

Turnus' final nightmare occurs in Book XII (908–14):

> ac velut in somnis, oculos ubi languida pressit
> nocte quies, nequiquam avidos extendere cursus
> velle videmur, et in mediis conatibus aegri   910
> succidimus; non lingua valet, non corpore notae
> sufficiunt vires, nec vox aut verba sequuntur;
> sic Turno, quacumque viam virtute petivit,
> successum dea dira negat.

It was like a dream, when the drowsy sleep of night-time overwhelms our eyes. In fancy we are desperately trying to run away, but collapse fainting in the middle of our exertions. Our tongue does not respond—our usual physical strength is of no avail—no voice or words ensue. So with Turnus. Wherever he used his courage to seek a path, the dread goddess denied him any outcome.

908. *In somnis* in this position only at I. 353 (Sychaeus appearing to Dido); IV. 353 (Anchises' appearances to Aeneas reported by him to Dido); IV. 557 (Mercury warns Aeneas to leave so as to avoid the danger posed by Dido, the recapitulation of I. 353).

911–12. *Non lingua valet* is picked up and amplified by *nec vox aut verba sequuntur*. The *non ... vires* clause intrudes. See above, pp. 174, 182.

The use of the first person plural here, involving narrator and listener in a common bond of sympathy as *aegri*, is extraordinary. Dido too is *aegra* (IV. 35, 389). The futile running is like her fruitless searching already noted in Book IV (468). But, if we are prepared to find in her *odi et amo*, there is

---

[21] See Livy XXI. 18. 13 (*vobis bellum et pacem portamus: utrum placet sumite*) and Silius, *Pun.* II. 384 (*bellum se gestare sinu pacemque*). Contrast *bella manu letumque gero* (Allecto), *letum* instead of *pacem*, below at VII. 455.

more. The paralysis of Turnus' voice, given such emphasis, is not really in point (and shortly he will in fact speak).[22] If it recalls Lucretius' description of the symptoms of fear (III. 154–57; cf. *succidere*, 156), it also recalls Sappho's ode—and Catullus' translation—describing the symptoms of love.[23] At this point, *illum turbat amor* (XII. 70; cf. *Furiis agitatus amor*, 668, *turbidus*, 671) finds its crowning illustration. But here is also where once loving Dido's poetic of silences comes to rest.

Dido had cast a shadow over the beginning of Aeneas' whole Italian campaign. The scene in which he is unable to sleep (VIII. 18–27) was already remarked (above, pp. 161–62). It contains a number of reminiscences of Book IV.[24] *Laomedontius* (18) is especially noteworthy. With *heros* there is a note almost of parody.[25] Laomedon's chief claim to fame was that he cheated Poseidon and Apollo of their promised reward for building the walls of Troy, and then Hercules over the deliverance of his daughter. This first destruction of Troy by Hercules is mentioned in the prayer sung in his honour by Evander's priests at the site of Rome (VIII. 290–91)—a curious exploit for Trojan visitors to concelebrate. Virgil saw Rome's troubles in his day as a recurrence of this old curse (*Geo.* I. 501–02).

In Apollonius, the beautiful simile of the reflected light (perhaps borrowed from Stoic psychology) was applied to Medea, and one expects any transference of it to relate to Dido. It reads strangely here. But the *Argonautica* in any case refers only to sunbeams, and Virgil's intruded allusion to moonlight could only remind the attentive among his audience of Dido / Diana. Blended with Iuno Lucina, Diana was also the goddess of childbirth (Catullus 34. 13–14; Horace, *Carm. Saec.* 15; cf. *Ecl.* 4. 10), an extra dimension of poignancy.

Further Dreams of this Kind

Some other dreams may be briefly passed in review:

---

[22] Steiner, *op. cit.*, p. 74.

[23] Virgil's *non lingua valet* = *lingua sed torpet* in Catullus: cf. φώναισ' οὐδ' ἓν ἔτ' εἴκει = *nihil est super mi* [vocis?]. More in West, *East Face of Helicon*, pp. 527–28.

[24] VIII.18 ~ *necdum / Laomedonteae sentis periuria gentis*, IV. 541–42 (cf. VII. 105); VIII. 19 ~ *fluctuat aestu*, IV. 532; VIII. 20–21 = IV. 285–86; VIII. 22–25 ~ Apollonius III. 756 ff. (see above, p. 162); VIII. 25: cf. *laquearibus*, I. 726; VIII. 26–27: cf. IV. 522, 525.

[25] Cf. Ovid's *Cythereius heros* of Aeneas (below, p. 196). Midas is *Berecyntius heros* at *Met.* XI. 106, just after making his fateful choice. See above, p. 147, n. 23, for Anchises' trickery in the *Iliad*.

Hector appears to the sleeping Aeneas (*Aeneid* II. 268–97), the unexpected repetition, as was noted, of a unique and climactic Iliadic motif found already in *Aeneid* I. The links with Dido's dream about Sychaeus (I. 353) are: the warning of imminent danger (*celerare fugam*, I. 357; *fuge*, II. 289; cf. φεῦγε, NT Matt. 2:13); the handing over of a sacred / treasured item, the *veteres thesauri* or the Penates (in Matthew παρέλαβεν τὸ παιδίον καὶ τὴν μητέρα αὐτοῦ, *loc. cit.* 14). Both these features are traditional,[26] but they acquire significance within the poem by the device of internal reference. Later, in Book IV, Mercury appears and asks *non fugis hinc praeceps?* (565). The welfare of Aeneas' son is, as the hero knows already, paramount (IV. 234, 274). His mother, even a substitute mother, unlike the mother in St. Matthew's story, has "unhappily" (II. 772) ceased to count.

Aeneas is told by the Penates that Crete is not to be his home (III. 147 ff.). He is to seek Italy, birthplace of Dardanus (167)—exactly what Dido denies (IV. 365; cf. the bitter sarcasm of 381). The abortive settlement in Crete prefigures the abortive settlement in Carthage, and Crete is eventually linked explicitly with Carthage (*nemora inter Cresia*, IV. 70; *reginae*, VI. 28).[27] There is a need to escape from both. The storm which follows this episode in Book III anticipates the storm of Book V, where the Trojans are leaving Carthage, and is modelled on storms in the *Odyssey* where Odysseus is escaping from Thrinacria (though now bearing the Sun's curse too; cf. IV. 607) or hypocritically claiming to be a shipwrecked Cretan merchant.[28]

A minor point may be added. The night is quite unnecessarily moonlit, and this is emphasised by a bold inversion of the Gallan type.[29] In

---

[26] Dreaming Hesiod's receipt of the ὄζος from the Muses is familiar (*Theog.* 30. See M. L. West's commentary, p. 160). Oppenheim (p. 190) refers to Pindar, *Ol.* 13. 65 ff. (Pallas hands to dreaming Bellerophon the bridle for Pegasus). See also Oppenheim, p. 212 where, in the discussion of the use of signs to confirm a dream, there is a reference to *Aen.* VIII. 42 ff.

[27] *Regina* is applied *abusive* (see Norden's note) to Cretan Ariadne (who is thereby blended with her mother, Pasiphae, enamoured of a bull). Supremely Dido's title, it must also recall her. Both rescuing heroines were abandoned by voyaging lovers. Later, found at the centre of the book describing Aeneas' visit to the Lower World (VI. 450), Dido herself is a sort of Minotaur at the centre of the Cretan Labyrinth (cf. VI. 27, V. 588). Cf. *miseratus amorem* (VI. 28), *miseratur euntem* (VI. 476).

[28] See above, p. 148, for the storms of III. 192 ff. and V. 9 ff.; *The Classical Epic Tradition*, p. 170.

[29] *Qua se / plena per insertas fundebat luna fenestras*, 151–52 (= "inserta per plenas [*sc.* lunae lumine] fenestras"; cf. *inserti* ... *radii*, Lucretius II. 115). Compare Gallus' *templa* ... *fixa* ... *spolieis* for "spolia (ad)fixa templis."

combination with *nox erat* (III. 147; cf. *nox erat* IV. 522, VIII. 26, the only other instances of this phrase in the poem), the scenery of this inevitably recalls lunar Dido.

Just as dead Sychaeus reportedly appeared to Dido (I. 353), dead Anchises is reported as appearing to Aeneas (IV. 351–53):

> 'me patris Anchisae, quotiens umentibus umbris
> nox operit terras, quotiens astra ignea surgunt,
> admonet in somnis et turbida terret imago.'

'My father Anchises, each time the night covers the earth with her dank shades, at each rising of the fiery stars, admonishes me in dreams, troubling and scaring me with his ghost.'

The *Iliad* is close (XXIII. 105–07):

> παννυχίη γάρ μοι Πατροκλῆος δειλοῖο
> ψυχὴ ἐφεστήκει γοόωσά τε μυρομένη τε,
> καί μοι ἕκαστ' ἐπέτελλεν, ἔϊκτο δὲ θέσκελον αὐτῷ.

'All night the spirit of my poor Patroclus stood over me, wailing and lamenting, laying on me each of his behests, and wonderful was the semblance to the man.'

The adaptation furnishes a good instance of Virgil's dramatic and painterly reworking of his original, while preserving his debt. "Night" and "fire" offer a typical chiaroscuro. *Imago* is emphasised by hyperbaton.

The motif, uniquely applied in Homer to Achilles and Patroclus, is in fact overworked in the *Aeneid* to form a skein of implicit allusions to their parting and his death which seems to encapsulate for Virgil the most heart-rending aspect of the Trojan conflict.[30] We may be meant to think ahead to Book V and the celebration due there of Anchises' obsequies, where Dido is implicitly evoked (V. 89 ~ IV. 701). But the mosaic of these references also takes in Camilla / Patroclus, and she in turn is paired with Dido through Penthesilea. It is against this Homeric example of comradeship and fidelity that the quarrel of Dido and Aeneas resonates so discordantly.

The epiphany of *Aeneid* IV. 554–72, again linked to other contexts by *in somnis*, was noted above. Aeneas is enjoying sleep after making all preparations for departure when he is advised by Mercury to set sail immediately. Dido's angry tide is in full flood (532). He is in imminent danger. There is a similarity to the scene in *Iliad* X (148 ff.) where the Greeks are in imminent danger from Hector. Nestor rouses Diomedes among

Scholars adduce *intenditque locum sertis* (= intendit serta loco), IV. 506. Above, p. 107.

[30] The details are provided by Knauer, pp. 298, 305–8. Below, p. 185.

other leaders—not of course to depart, but for the council of war leading on to the *Doloneia*.

But, although the *Doloneia* has a closer parallel later in *Aeneid* IX, the relevance of this episode here is that the Trojans in turn, as once their Thracian allies, might be the object of indiscriminate slaughter, and this is exactly what Dido threatens as she sees them going (600 ff.). Virgil evokes a fleeting memory of the Homeric scene to enhance the immediacy of the threat to Aeneas. Later, the Trojans will replicate the *Doloneia* more precisely, and there an antique mixing bowl presented by Dido (*dat*, in the present tense, IX. 266) will be among the prizes offered to Nisus and Euryalus, tempting them into their unworthy escapade.

In Book V (636) Iris disguises herself as Beroe and entices the Trojan women to attempt the burning of the fleet. She asserts that vatic Cassandra has appeared to her in a dream (*imago*, 636) to urge this course. This is a lie, but the scheme obviously suits Dido's plans (*implessemque foros flammis*, IV. 605). Iris provides the link, in both cases sent by Juno: cf. *mille trahens varios adverso sole colores*, IV. 701 ~ *per mille coloribus arcum*, V. 609. Four ships are lost (V. 699). Again, this thwarted plan plays a role in the economy of the poem. In Book IX, another fire threatens but does not actually touch Aeneas' ships. Before that can happen, they are metamorphosed by Cybele (115–22). But this is not quite faithful to Homer, where in fact the Trojans do half-burn one of the ships (*Il.* XVI. 122–23, 294). As with the hint of the *Doloneia* in Book IV, this scene in V, hinting at dead Dido and her last imprecations, complements a differently slanted episode in IX.

Later in *Aeneid* V (722–40) Anchises appears in a dream to Aeneas and advises him to accept the counsel of Nautes. This is adapted from *Odyssey* X. 488 ff., where Circe gives instructions to Odysseus. In both cases the hero is told that he must visit the Lower World, at whose numerical centre, for Aeneas, Dido will lurk. But Dido is Circe—an equivalence which has already attracted attention.[31] Here opposites blend.

Aeneid VII (92–101) describes the incubation dream of Latinus.[32] By divine command, the king, rejecting home-bred suitors, is bidden to await a foreign bridegroom for his daughter, and a union promising a glorious future. The Sibyl (VI. 93–94) and Juno (VII. 319–22) draw parallels between this situation and that of Paris' foreign match. They see or suggest a repetition. Here we learn that the Trojans are to enjoy some sort of

---

[31] Above, pp. 146–47. Circe recurs on the way to and in Italy.

[32] Quite archaic in form: Oppenheim, p. 188.

reversal (*verti*, VII. 101) of that earlier doom-laden experience.

Latinus is Priam (VII. 246), but literary antecedents for this episode are to be sought, not so much in Homer (where they are of the most distant kind), as in later tragedy. Hecuba's dream of the son she would bear troubled her husband the king. Cicero's quotation (*Div*. I. §42) suggests that Ennius' handling of the Euripidean theme was well known at Rome (*Alexander*, Vol. 1, p. 234, 38–49 Warmington = Jocelyn, pp. 77–78, 50–61):

> Mater gravida parere se ardentem facem   50
> visa est in somnis Hecuba, quo facto pater
> rex ipse Priamus somnio mentis metu
> perculsus, curis sumptus suspirantibus,
> exsacrificabat hostiis balantibus.
> Tum coniecturam postulat pacem petens,   55
> ut se edoceret obsecrans Apollinem
> quo sese vertant tantae sortes somnium.
> Ibi ex oraclo voce divina edidit
> Apollo puerum primus Priamo qui foret
> postilla natus temperaret tollere;   60
> eum esse exitium Troiae, pestem Pergamo.

His mother Hecuba, heavy with child, dreamed she gave birth to a blazing brand. At that his father, King Priam himself, his heart stricken with fear over the dream, seized with sighs and cares, offered many a sacrifice of bleating sheep. Then he asked for an interpretation, seeking to be reconciled with the gods, imploring Apollo for an explanation of the turn of meaning of such fearful lots in the dream. Thereupon, from his oracle, in prophetic tones Apollo declared that Priam should forbear to raise the first son to be born to him after that, for he was Troy's doom, Pergamum's ruin.

54. *centum lanigeras mactabat rite bidentis*, Aen. VII. 93.
58. *subita ex alto vox reddita luco est*, VII. 95.

But the child *was* saved, and later re-appeared as victor at his own funeral games. It was Cassandra who greeted her long-lost brother Paris' arrival at court in inspired words (p. 242, 67–72 W. = Jocelyn, p. 76, 41–46 adapted):

> adest, adest fax obvoluta sanguine atque incendio;
> multos annos latuit. Cives, ferte opem et restinguite! ...
> Iamque mari magno classis cita!
> texitur; exitium examen rapit;
> adveniet fera velivolantibus
> navibus, complevit manus litora.

Here, here comes the torch wrapped about in blood and fire! For many years it has lain hidden. Citizens, help, quench it!

And now on the main a swift fleet! It is being crafted—a swarm is hastening destruction. It will come—a wild company with sail-flying ships—and has filled all our shores.

Texitur is intruded between the first clause and the third.[33] By vertical time, in her trance Cassandra sees the Greek fleet both under construction and already standing out to sea.

Virgil, following his usual practice, is blending a number of figures and scenes. Latinus may be well disposed, but Aeneas' arrival will be greeted by Latinus' wife Amata with despair and madness. She is an amalgam of Cassandra and Euripides' Hecuba. According to Hyginus (*Fab.* 91), the dream of Hecuba on which Priam had sought enlightenment from Apollo was that she had given birth to a fiery brand out of which came many snakes. Fire and snakes characterise Amata's frenzy (*coluber*, VII. 352; *ignem*, 355). Aeneas then, in this context, is Paris. Turnus was already Achilles (VI. 89)—and it was after all Paris who had eventually brought Achilles low (VI. 57–58).

This was not the first time that Aeneas, *improbus advena* (XII. 261), had thrust himself into foreign parts and interfered with marriage plans. The principle of iteration is again at work. The covert allusion to Paris retroactively links all this with Dido / Helen, and the bitter prayer of her rejected suitor Iarbas (IV. 215):

'et nunc ille Paris, cum semiviro comitatu ...'

Some connection to Book IV is also provided by Fama at the end of this scene (VII. 104–06):

sed circum late volitans iam Fama per urbes
Ausonias tulerat, cum Laomedontia pubes
gramineo ripae religavit ab aggere classem.

But now Fame, everywhere aflutter around the cities of Italy, had carried the news, when the host of Laomedon's heirs moored its fleet to the grassy knoll of the shore.

104. *it Fama per urbes*, IV. 173; cf. *volitans pennata per urbem / nuntia Fama ruit*, IX. 473–74, death of Euryalus; *et iam Fama volans, tanti praenuntia luctus*, XI. 139, death of Pallas.

105. *necdum / Laomedonteae sentis periuria gentis*, IV. 541–42.

Fama has not been mentioned since that book. There, her appearance was partly modelled on Homer's Strife (*Il.* IV. 442–43, quoted above). Since this book of the *Iliad* influences so clearly the action of Book XII of the *Aeneid*, once again the tightly meshed economy of Virgil's poem is visible. Whatever the talk of peace, Book VII heralds war.

But the most striking feature here in VII is the unexpected reference to Laomedon, already remarked when it recurs at the start of book VIII (18).

---

[33] Cf. Lachmann on Propertius IV. 3. 15 ff. (pp. 242–43 of the 1816 edition). For similar syntax in Greek, above, p. 174.

Heracles had led the Greek heroes to Troy to exact vengeance Λαομεδοντιᾶν ὑπὲρ ἀμπλακιᾶν (Pindar, *Isth.* 6. 29; *ut bello egregias idem disiecerit urbes / Troiamque Oechaliamque, Aen.* VIII. 290–91: Virgil's addition of Oechalia supplies a covert allusion to Deianeira). Laomedon was slain, but his persisting ἀμπλακία / ἁμαρτία ensured that, if the struggles in Italy were to be the repetition of the battles before Troy, there must be an element of tragedy—for both sides. Not even the Greeks regarded the Trojan War as a story of success, and Diomedes has reason to point this out to Venulus (XI. 252 ff.). As the Trojans arrive at Latinus' court, Virgil mutes any expected fanfare with foreboding, with a dream alluding to Paris and Helen, and ultimately therefore to Aeneas and Dido.

Aeneid VII. 319–22 and X. 704–05, overt allusions to Hecuba's dream at the birth of Paris, fit easily into this framework. They represent the dark side of the Italian adventure. When, by this equation, Virgil thrusts on Aeneas a false lineage for the sake of making him, like Paris, Priam's heir, Lavinia / Helen (XI. 477 ff.) must inevitably recall the previous pairing of Dido / Helen (*ornatus Argivae Helenae*, I. 650). Lavinia is dumb throughout this tragedy, although her role in easing the Aeneadae into their needed network of Italian kinships was obviously crucial. If ultimately Troy as such disappears, and if there was some feuding over the succession at Alba Longa, downplayed in Virgil's tale,[34] perhaps these subliminal hints about her mythical doublet are meant to prepare us for such a chequered history. A poetic of silences must in its culmination encompass even one who never speaks.

At *Aeneid* X. 219–45, Aeneas' ships, now metamorphosed into seanymphs to save them from being burned (IX. 77 ff.), appear to him and give him news of his men under siege by the Rutulians. The speech of Cymodocea, introduced by *vigilasne, deum gens, Aenea? vigila* (228–29), suggests that this is the sort of half-drowsing apparition (φάντασμα / *visum*) to which Macrobius refers.

The episode, recalling the elemental clash of fire with water, is a good illustration of Virgil's "binocular vision." In spite of Aeneas' own professed readiness to tell it as it happened (II. 12–13), in some important ways his creator's fancy darts away, in what has been called declining mode, from sober confrontation with the realities of death: *horresco referens* (II. 204), for example, leads into the quite unrealistic appearance of the serpents, the horror being more important than the relation. It even perhaps darts away from the calm contemplation of the human condition. Here, Hellenistic

---

[34] Yet not wholly. See p. 302 below.

metamorphosis of the most Romantic sort completely shatters any claim the epic might make to factuality.[35]

But Virgil is never simply a Hellenistic poet (no Roman poet is). In Book IX (69 ff.), it was Turnus who, at his moment of greatest apparent success, had threatened to hurl fire onto the Trojan ships. In its way, this is another "inept" Homeric borrowing of a type noted elsewhere in the *Aeneid*. The Iliadic pattern is reiterated quite pointlessly. The loss of the fleet would in reality have been of little consequence, since where were the Aeneadae now proposing to sail? But it is saved (and lost) by a miraculous intervention, a privilege already secured by Cybele, the Great Mother, from Jupiter, and its ships turned instead into creatures of the water. Cybele had already detained Creusa back in Asia Minor (II. 788). We know her as Rome's peculiar model and patroness (VI. 784).

The Homeric parallel is clearly with the moment of Hector's greatest success in the *Iliad*, where he too threatens to burn the Greek fleet, inspiring the poet to a solemn address to the Muses (*Il*. XVI. 112–13: cf. *Aen*. IX. 525–28):

> Ἔσπετε νῦν μοι, Μοῦσαι, Ὀλύμπια δώματ' ἔχουσαι,
> ὅππως δὴ πρῶτον πῦρ ἔμπεσε νηυσὶν Ἀχαιῶν.

Follow now for me with the tale, Muses, dwellers in Olympus, of how fire first fell on the Achaeans' ships.

Fire will *not* however fall on the Trojan ships. Virgil, ostensibly echoing the *Iliad*, presents us with another instance of reversal (*Aen*. IX. 77–79):

> Quis deus, o Musae, tam saeva incendia Teucris
> a v e r t i t ? tantos ratibus quis d e p u l i t ignis?
> dicite: prisca fides facto, sed fama perennis.

What god, ye Muses, turned away such raging flames from the Trojans? Who drove such great fires from their ships? You tell the tale. Ancient is the story's warranty, but its fame outlives the years.

And it is obvious how much bigger and more real a threat was posed by the Trojan assault in the *Iliad*, since the Greeks were planning after all one day to sail back home, as Achilles remarks (XVI. 82). It is this imminent danger which provokes Patroclus' ill-starred return to the fray, which then in turn brings about Achilles' own return and ultimately Hector's death.

Homer uses his scene to give a sympathetic portrayal of the deep affection between the two Greek heroes: Patroclus, understanding Achilles' anger, but feeling for his countrymen; Achilles, for ever nursing his grudge. Patroclus chides his friend (XVI. 33–35):

---

[35] Τὴν δ' ἀλήθειαν διὰ τί προσέθηκεν ὅμως ἀπορῶ was already noted from Philodemus (above, p. 91, note 41).

νηλεές, οὐκ ἄρα σοί γε πατὴρ ἦν ἱππότα Πηλεύς,
οὐδὲ Θέτις μήτηρ· γλαυκὴ δέ σε τίκτε θάλασσα
πέτραι τ' ἠλίβατοι, ὅτι τοι νόος ἐστὶν ἀπηνής.

'Ruthless! Your father is not after all knightly Peleus, nor Thetis your mother. It was the grey sea that bore you, and the steep crags, so cruel is your heart.'

But there is another reversal. The same or similar language may be used to express the *odi* of *amo*, the hatred of love. This Iliadic rejoinder has long been noted as the ultimate literary ancestor of Dido's despairing outburst to Aeneas (IV. 365–67), though clearly the topos had passed since Homer through many mutations, including those found in Catullus (60; 64. 154 ff., Ariadne, where Homer's allusion to the sea recurs).

The echoes of *Iliad* XVI in *Aeneid* X are quite strong. Virgil's imitation presents its usual *verzerrtes Bild*. At one level, with the arrival of Aeneas, a reversal of fortune similar to that overtaking Hector awaits Turnus. But Achilles / Aeneas is not Patroclus! That identification is reserved for Pallas, Camilla and Turnus.[36] It is in losing Pallas that Aeneas loses his Patroclus. But, by taking Pallas' belt, it is Turnus among these heroes who will meet death wearing borrowed armour. There is dizzying metamorphosis. But, among it all, the voice of burning Dido, who had herself wanted to cast fire on the Trojan ships (IV. 605), is heard again.

The Sensibility of the Aeneid

Dido's dreams allow space for reflection on the general sensibility evinced by the *Aeneid*, and its already suggested unsuitability as a medium for the child. So great an artist and "Classic" (in Eliot's sense) as Virgil allows our thoughts broad scope.

A study of later Russian painting[37] calls attention to *Joseph in Prison Interpreting the Dreams of Pharaoh's Butler and Baker*, painted by Alexander Ivanov in 1827, and now in St. Petersburg. The author notes:

> Ivanov used the story — Joseph, while in prison with the servants of the Pharaoh, foretells deliverance and good fortune for the butler and execution for the baker — to explore various artistic possibilities. By using one model for both dreamers (thus depicting them as twins, equal in every sense) he abandons them, as it were, to the hand of fate, which then ordains death for the one and reprieve for the other. Some kind of external power begins to rule

---

[36] See Knauer, pp. 300–01, 310. The echo of XI. 831 at XII. 952 links Turnus with Camilla, as a similar echo links Homer's Hector with Patroclus (*Il.* XXII. 362–63 = XVI. 856–57).

[37] Dmitri V. Sarabianov, *Russian Art. From Neoclassicism to the Avant-Garde. 1800–1917* (New York 1990). The quotation is adapted from p. 69.

their lives. It seems to lurk in the dark shadow in which their separate figures are picked out by the light. This deadly game of fate, which paralyses their will and ability to act, went well beyond the classical approach to the interpretation of real events. Ivanov here stretched to the limit the traditional classical technique of forming figures by means of chiaroscuro.

Senseram quam idem essent. Whether Ivanov "went well beyond the classical approach to ... real events" in his picture is no doubt for experts to decide. "Chiaroscuro" offers a clue. Typical of the *Aeneid*, this *dédoublement* is part of what we have already called Virgil's "binocular vision." Who is the poet's Achilles? Who his Hector?

The *Aeneid* is not therefore a poem of ultimate certainties, and its continual sallies into fantasy and ambiguity have always been found attractive.[38] But this *sfumatura* was a deeply layered feature of the poet's psyche right from the first (*fumant ... umbrae*, *Ecl.* 1. 82–83). In an earlier chapter, the undersea and underground worlds of the Aristaeus episode closing the *Georgics* seemed characteristic of a poetic imagination always aware of a shadowy fourth dimension lending both depth and instability to normality. The Gygean perception is rather like that in certain Etruscan tomb-paintings, where the red of vigorous life in the here and now is so often twinned with the blue of a remoter, deadlier vision. The beings inhabiting that other dimension are indifferent to larger human values. Cyrene is certainly concerned for her son. What does she—or the deities of Hell—care about the feelings and fate of Orpheus and Eurydice?

If for the ancient listener the *Aeneid* was continually shadowed at every turn by its evocations of the *Iliad* and *Odyssey* in both its halves, that is not then some display of "learning," in an academic sense, but rather the awareness of a second world, an echo-chamber in which the iterations of a new story which is not new reverberate to infinity.

This second sight is also the world of dreams which has been noted here. It is part of an even larger dimension to the poet's imagination which has been variously described. At one level, it belongs to the poet's musicality, since music most readily escapes from the careful calculations of rationality, defiantly using those same calculations to soar off into the spheres; and on this basis even the *numeros memini, si verba tenerem* of the *Eclogues* (9. 45) becomes evidence of an already profoundly felt poetic. The Orpheus of

---

[38] As by Eduard Fraenkel, *Kleine Beiträge*, II, pp. 224–25, "Carattere della poesia augustea": "... l'uomo educato alla scuola di Platone deve sapere che per lui l' ὄντως ὄν è celato per sempre e che deve contentarsi di una riproduzione, un εἶδος, un' idea." He then cites *rerumque ignarus imagine gaudet* from *Aen.* VIII. 730. The first poem of Rilke's *Sonette an Orpheus* is profoundly relevant (see below, p. 306: a full text in *Latin Compositions*, p. 94).

the *Georgics* tuned such music to even sadder notes (IV. 464–66):

> ipse cava solans aegrum testudine amorem
> te, dulcis coniunx, te solo in litore secum,
> te veniente die, te decedente canebat.

Her husband, comforting his love-sick heart on his hollow lyre, alone on the empty shore, sang of nothing but his sweet wife from dawn to dusk.

465. *Litore* reminds one of so many littoral scenes in Propertius (*Augustan Propertius*, index, *s. vv.* "water / shore / sea"). Is there some borrowing in both him and Virgil from a lost Gallan scenario?

The whole tale is full of these unearthly harmonies. They are small defence against what Dr. Johnson calls the arrows of pain.

At another level, there is poetic irony. In Callimachus and Ovid, deployed to comic effect, such irony goes unchallenged, and Virgil simply subverts (better, ἀποσεμνύνει) Callimachus' comic Erysichthon, to take this example, in his handling of Turnus' confrontation with Calybe / Allecto. But even in those poets' comedy there is an edge at times more wounding. Virgil's tragic, mournful irony ranges from the lightest touch of felt convention to the exquisitely and deliberately sad. His universe is bound by iron laws, suited to an Age of Iron (*ferrea ... gens*, *Ecl.* 4. 8–9). *Ferrum* indeed for "sword," showing well over one hundred examples in the *Aeneid*, is typical of his words. Yet human beings are not iron, but flesh and blood, as Tibullus, himself a soldier, points out.

At the end, Turnus' spirit flies off to join the shades. *Omnia abeunt in mysterium*. Within the economy of the poem the listener knows something after all about these shades. *Aeneid* VI has acted as an introduction. But from it Aeneas departed, as if over some Lethe, through the Gate of False Dreams. This, the supreme illustration of the poet's technique of half-assertion, is certainly not to be devalued by reductive interpretation. Nor does it mean on the other side that the revelations Aeneas has enjoyed are in some way false, since resolutions of this sort belong to the *esprit de géométrie* rather than the requisite *esprit de finesse*. These gods are not always doing geometry.

There are no precise answers. Perhaps one should say that all this betrays the sensibility of the looking-glass. The poet draws us through the mirrored surface of his watery universe into the humanly impossible. Ultimately Cyrene and her ladies in the *Georgics* are like *belles dames* in some mediaeval, moated castle, rehearsing and embroidering the *amours* of the gods in their withdrawing room, their barons meanwhile presiding over the dungeons of the damned. Cyrene hears her child, but only to gloss over his offence against Eurydice (and give him privileged advice on how to deal with metamorphosis). In the *Aeneid*, this veil is pulled aside to reveal something more terrifying: *apparent dirae facies inimicaque Troiae / numina magna deum*.... If Orpheus, lingering on his shore, the poetic champion and recorder of a human love, is destroyed by Bacchic forces which should inspire, so are Dido and Amata. Yet, at the human level, it is Dido who presides over the *Aeneid*'s dark and dream-filled world.

This kind of sensibility has been discovered in Statius—who was after all Virgil's admirer and imitator. In him, it has been ranged with tokens denoting the end of civilisations.[39] But, if Domitian marked a turning point in the history of the emperors, Augustus marked an even greater turning point in the history of the Roman state. This is why Tacitus ultimately felt obliged to trace his story further back, from the end of the Julio-Claudians in the *Histories* to their beginning in the *Annales*. In fact, these grand dimensions had already engaged the spirit of a vatic poet who is also in his way the historian of Rome's soul.

Cato had enquired after *Origines*. Virgil followed him: *Musa, mihi causas memora* .... But, in studying this familiar statement of the *Aeneid*'s scope, the reader must not neglect its religious aspect,[40] visible even in Callimachus' *Aetia*. Unlike his predecessors, in his story, Virgil discovered dimensions too large for comfort. And, in so dark a world, with its dreams and nightmares, what place for the innocent ordinariness of children? Frenzied Dido's children by Aeneas or thrust at Aeneas are the fruits of her avenging hatred. They are summoned into existence—Pallas, Lausus, Camilla, Juturna / Turnus—only to be sucked dry. Another chapter must ask whether this dismal imbroglio also sweeps into its web Ascanius / Iulus.

---

[39] H. Cancik, *Untersuchungen zur lyrischen Kunst des P. Papinius Statius* (Hildesheim 1965); idem, in *Aufstieg und Niedergang der röm. Welt*, 32.5 (1986), 2702–04. — A recent volume by Christopher Wood (*Victorian Painting* [London 1999]) notes (p. 182) that the story of Orpheus and Eurydice was a favourite with English artists of the second half of the century, as the Empire of Victoria's reign began its decline towards the debacle of 1914–18.

[40] Δι' ἣν ἔθνησκεν αἰτίαν (an iambic dimeter), OT Wisdom of Solomon, 18:18. Cf. ἵνα μὴ ἀγνοοῦντες δι' ὃ κακῶς πάσχουσιν ἀπόλωνται in the sequel (19). The *esse videatur* rhythm at the end in the second quotation here is noteworthy. See "*Esse Videatur* Rhythm in the Greek New Testament *Gospels* and *Acts of the Apostles*," *ICS* X (1985), 53–66.

IX

WOMEN AND CHILDREN: THE SUPPORTING CAST

Epic Women and Children

Women in epic are at least as old as *Gilgamesh*. Their revelatory function, aimed at bringing man to terms with his mortality, was remarked. More tragic than the *Odyssey*, the *Iliad* gives this task to Thetis, a mother, one among a Homeric galaxy of women characters.

Aeneas' mother, starring in a more confusing sky, shares this role with Juno, whose doomed Achilles is Turnus. But between Homer and Virgil there are characteristic differences. Virgil's habit of conflating Homeric originals inevitably concentrates his range (Nausicaa altered into Venus and Dido). He prefers depth to light. At the same time, he masculinises. None of Homer's mortal women (not even the *Odyssey*'s Arete) is an "executive" like single Dido, or fights—and dies—on the field of battle like single Camilla. None of Virgil's goddesses is quite as feminine as the Athene who brushes away an arrow from a favourite as if she were sweeping away a fly from a sleeping infant (*Il.* IV. 130–31), or the Aphrodite who ventures into the fray and then complains loudly to her mummy that she has received a scratch (*Il.* V. 370). None of Virgil's gods is compared to a child kicking over a sand castle (*Il.* XV. 362).[1] Homer shows us baby Achilles, spluttering wine on Phoenix' breast (*Il.* IX. 491), and weeping Patroclus like a toddler asking to be picked up (*Il.* XVI. 7–10). Aphrodite's spoiled brat in Apollonius (III. 91 ff.), lounging with Ganymede, his impertinence carefully registered by her supercilious guests, is a modern pre-teen. The *Aeneid*'s children, whipping a top, turn into a symbol of Amata's mad

---

[1] Apollo's crushing might is well illustrated in the Homeric passage, but there is also something in the Greek poet which corresponds to Alexandrian rococo. The remark of A. Severyns has a lot of truth in it: "Dans ces tableaux olympiens, la note humoristique se fait parfois presque tendre et le raffinement d' Homère annonce étonnament celui d'un Callimaque" (*Homère l'artiste* [Brussels 1948], p. 101). See below, Appendix, for Homeric divine comedy turning to human tragedy as the scene at the end of *Iliad* I is developed in XIV and XV.

frenzy (VII. 378). The domestic scene before the decision to leave Troy is resolved by an epiphany (II. 680). Ascanius on Queen Dido's lap is really scheming Cupid (I. 717–22). Our museums illustrate the contrasting figures, occurring as early as Byzantine art, of the Mother and Child, even of the divine Child at the breast![2] It is as if the Roman poet, in dignifying and mythologising his world, shuts out of it the casual indecorum of family life. The women who do gain entrance are altered, sentimentalised (Camilla), demonised (Dido, Amata); some are neutered (Andromache, Creusa, even Lavinia). The children too often have no future.

This mentality was long established in the poet. The baby of *Eclogue* 4 becomes unreal, part of a Golden Age fantasy. For all their highly organised polity, the bees of *Georgics* IV, though they have offspring, live without sex (197–99). To their utopia, the males make small contribution: *ignavum fucos pecus a praesepibus arcent* (168), just as Amazonian queen Dido (I. 490), whose bee subjects were earlier seen at work (I. 430), thinks she would have been *felix* if Aeneas' ships had never intruded into her realm (IV. 657–58). In *Georgics* III, where the sexual impulse is felt, the animal kingdom, again just like Dido (cf. *Aen.* IV. 516 and *Geo.* III. 280; *Geo.* III. 263 and *Aen.* IV. 308), is dragged down by it to madness and destruction. It is from this book of the *Georgics*, as was repeatedly noted, that Virgil draws unifying imagery for the second half of the *Aeneid*.

Women in the Aeneid

Ἡ δ' ἀέκουσ' ἅμα τοῖσι γυνὴ κίεν writes Homer of Briseis in an immortal line (*Il.* I. 348). Γυνή is etymologically ambiguous (the "undifferentiated primitive"), as Byron's "queen of queans" attests. It might even mean "wife." But in the *Aeneid* the dominant generic term for a woman is *virgo*, which shows 47 examples (*virgineus* five, *virginitas* three). *Femina* by contrast occurs nine times, *mulier* once (VII. 661, *mixta deo mulier*); *femineus* 11 times, *muliebris* once (XI. 687).

Wives (and still less mothers!) do not come off well, curious in an epic which of its very nature has to comprehend a distant future. This is true in spite of the 84 examples of *mater* (in various senses) and 13 of *genetrix* which are listed.[3]

---

[2] Cf. the Madonna del Latte: Franciscan sanctuary, Greccio, Italy (14th c.); Beccafumi, Palazzo Barberini inv. 2410. Contrast *ab ubere raptos* (VI. 428).

[3] Above, pp. 46–49. One example of *matrona* and seven of *maternus* may be added. Virgil's mothers are never happy figures. *Uxor* is never found. Mercury uses *uxorius* contemptuously of Aeneas at Carthage (IV. 266). For *felix* and *thalamus* see above, pp. 11, 49 ff., 62, 164.

Mulier too could mean "wife" but, in Virgil's heroic world, a *mulier* is evidently woman in her weakness. *Feminae* by contrast are important, though usually for mischief. Turnus' speech in Book IX offers a good perspective. His (unique) *peccare* here, with its sexual connotation, is extraordinary in epic.[4] He shares Dido's *fuisset* (140–42):

> '"sed periisse semel satis est": peccare fuisset
> ante satis, penitus modo non genus omne perosos
> femineum ... '

'"One destruction is enough"—yes, and one preceding sin of lust should have been enough. Deep should have been their hatred for almost the whole tribe of women.'

Their experience with Helen should have warned the Trojans off once and for all. This is quite unlike the recovered status accorded her by the *Odyssey*. Turnus strikes the tone of some puritanical preacher denouncing Eve.

In the *Iliad*, Helen may be accepted, even admired. The *Aeneid*'s Helen is unforgiven, and unforgiving. Dido is her Protean heiress: *varium et mutabile semper / femina* (IV. 569–70). Her subtle perfume must often be sensitively sampled. Some of this was already noted. Turnus illustrates the point further. In the book where he will come closest to victory, he disparages the Trojans' paltry defences, *leti discrimina parva* (IX. 143), "tiny barriers against death" (cf. X. 511). But his phrase echoes that used of the Trojans' passage between Scylla and Charybdis in Book III, just before they land in Africa (*leti discrimine parvo*, 685). In Horace, Charybdis could be a perhaps now flaccid metonymy for love's dangers (*Odes* I. 27. 19). But here in Book IX is she another proof of Virgil's tendency to realise his metaphors? Dido's Charybdean love had not devoured the Trojans in Carthage. There, it was left at the level of impotent wish (600–06). But, in Book IX, in the person of Turnus, and with Juno's encouragement (VII. 302), will she now, as a similar phrase recurs, have a second try, while Aeneas' absence makes Ascanius vulnerable? Is this her monstrous ("Lamian") side on display?[5]

After Dido, it is unsurprising that so many of the *Aeneid*'s other women are either wholly or in part inhuman: nymphs, Furies, personifications such as Fama or Nox or Turnus' retinue (XII. 335–36), or those others that bivouac at inferno's gate (VI. 275–77, 280–81):

---

[4] There are six instances in the *Metamorphoses*, only one clearly sexual (IX. 458, Byblis). In Ovid's elegies, R. Pichon lists 20 examples, though only four in Tibullus and four in Propertius: *De Sermone Amatorio apud Latinos Elegiarum Scriptores* (Paris 1902), p. 227. Venus uses *peccata* as a noun, *Aen.* X. 32.

[5] Compare *nullo discrimine*, I. 574 (the generous offer) and its reversal at X. 108; XII. 498 and 770 (the deadliness and sacrilege of war).

>   tristisque Senectus
> ... et malesuada Fames ac turpis Egestas,
> terribiles visu formae ...
> ferreique Eumenidum thalami et Discordia demens,
> vipereum crinem vittis innexa cruentis ...

> Gloomy Age ... and evil-counselling Appetite and ugly Want, shapes of fearful aspect ... the iron dens of the Furies, and mad Discord, her snaky locks entwined with bloody bands ...

Thalami adds its usual sour note. This grotesquerie, in which we find Ovid's *formae*, may be explained in part by the pull on the Roman psyche of the satiric / iambic, a force affecting lyrical Horace and even elegiac Propertius.[6] But there is some evidence of the bias (*Keimentschluß*) of Virgil's own imagination (cf. *Geo.* III. 552).

Many women turn out to have found room in Hell, though only Lavinia and Ilia, ciphers at best, have a place there among Rome's heroes yet to be. We meet some more celebrated on other grounds just after the dead infants and their caterwauling, both the prelude to Aeneas' vision and the overture to yet more innocent suffering. In this liminal passage (427), verse 429 shows a liturgical redundancy of an old-fashioned sort (VI. 426–29):

> Continuo auditae voces vagitus et ingens
> infantumque animae flentes, in limine primo
> quos dulcis vitae exsortis et ab ubere raptos
> abstulit atra dies et funere mersit acerbo.

> At once voices were heard, vast wailing, the spirits of children weeping. On the very threshold they had lost their part in life's sweetness and been snatched from the breast. A dark day had carried them off and plunged them in doom's unripe bitterness.

Women in love follow. Their home is in the Fields of Mourning, which offer a sort of quarantine, since evidently in the poet's mind for such women love is a chronic, bloody disease. Cretan Phaedra and Pasiphae are here. Metamorphosing, transsexual Caeneus (his return to womanhood apparently an invention of the poet) makes an unexpected lead-in to Dido. *Cernit* (446) here is Gygean (VI. 442–50):

>   hic quos durus amor crudeli tabe peredit
>   secreti celant calles et myrtea circum
>   silva tegit; curae non ipsa in morte relinquunt.
>   his Phaedram Procrimque locis maestamque Eriphylen   445
>   crudelis nati monstrantem vulnera cernit,
>   Euadnenque et Pasiphaen; his Laodamia
>   it comes, et iuvenis quondam, nunc femina, Caeneus
>   rursus et in veterem fato revoluta figuram.
>   inter quas Phoenissa recens a vulnere Dido ...   450

---

[6] *Augustan Propertius*, pp. 137–38, 485–91.

Here are those whom harsh love has devoured with cruel wasting, hidden by secret paths, concealed by a wood of myrtles. Even in death, their troubles persist. Here he saw Phaedra and grieving Eriphyle, still pointing to the wounds inflicted by her cruel son, and Euadne and Pasiphae. At their side went Laodamia, and Caeneus, once a youth, now a woman, turned back by fate into her old shape. With them was Phoenician Dido, her wound still fresh....[7]

Sentiment is an uncertain guide to the interpretation of the passage. Do all Dido's companions in fact reflect facets of her own unstable identity? She shares her wound at least with Eriphyle, and Clytaemnestra.

* * *

Among the poem's more human women, Anna, Dido's sister, at first hardly exists in her own right. Where is she before Book IV? In New Comedy, the young hero so often discusses his problems with some sort of male companion. Now, in Book IV, in a rediscovery of comedy's iambic roots[8] (and to preserve the parallel with Hypsipyle), the heroine becomes protagonist. Modelled in part on Apollonius' Polyxo and Chalciope, Anna is accordingly introduced, as it seems innocuously enough, to combine the roles of sister and nurse (slave) / confidante. But later she acquires some of her sister's mutable longevity, recurring at least twice in the guise of Acoetes and Juturna.[9] All these echoes are drumbeats of death.

It is she who dwells on the naturalness of Dido's feelings (IV. 33):

'nec dulcis natos Veneris nec praemia noris?'

'Shall you not know the bliss of children, or the delights of love?'

The answer to the first part of this question at least was no. But what of her own prospects? Dido ascribes to her a particular friendship with Aeneas (IV. 421–22). Is this fantasy? Or did Aeneas, needing someone to talk to, perhaps find it easier to talk to a woman with no designs on him? But had she no designs on him? Ovid's Lavinia certainly thought she had (*Fasti* III.

---

[7] Austin comments (ad v. 449, pp. 161–62 of his edition): "An incestuous woman, a notorious traitress, a woman of unnatural lust, a bizarre man-woman; Procris, a jealous and suspicious wife (and, in Apollodorus' version, immoral); the devoted Euadne, the loving Laodamia—such, we find, are Dido's companions." Euadne flung herself on her husband's funeral pyre (Eur., *Supp.* 1016–20). With VI. 447b (Laodamia) may be paralleled *Il.* VI. 197b, which would go on to give a link with Sarpedon (a key background figure in the *Aeneid*: Knauer, pp. 298–301). In any case, the title of Laevius' *Protesilaudamia* suggests the degree to which husband and wife coalesced in untimely death. It is clear how much Virgil has concentrated and tragedified the leisurely tale of *Od.* XI. 235 ff.

[8] Cf. "Iambe / Iambos and the Rape of a Genre," above, p. 86. This is what Servius' *paene comicus stilus est* implies. Euripides' Phaedra and Medea had done this, but evidently the New Comic example had come to set the tone.

[9] IV. 673, XI. 86, XII. 871: above, pp. 135, 163.

633). Varro indeed made Anna rather than Dido perish for love of Aeneas.[10] Such things happen. Tolstoy nearly married his eventual wife's sister. Was there some sort of latent tension to the relationship between Anna and Dido (certainly worthy of Menander) to which we are insensitive?[11]

In the end, Dido accuses her sister of being too sympathetic, and pushing her into her predicament (548–49). This is one of those profound insights into the delusional mind for which the poet is admired. It is noteworthy that the final escape, as it was for Gallus (*Ecl.* 10. 51), is back into the (hollow) pastoral (*degere more ferae*, 551). But Anna herself is not to fulfil any of what she regards as her sister's natural ambitions.

The vignette of Andromache early in the poem called for all Virgil's delicacy and sympathy.[12] Hector, her husband, in the *Iliad* Aeneas' rival, has already been shown generously commissioning his cousin to assume his responsibilities as Troy's and Priam's (and Laomedon's!) heir (II. 291–97). He poses no threat now because he is dead. Andromache, still surviving, must be treated with dignity, yet as irrelevant. Accordingly, she and Helenus at Buthrotum (III. 294 ff.), barren, she half out of this world (311), are found engaged in the vain reconstruction of a past which cannot be reconstructed. The lesson of this episode must surely modify ahead of time in the poem all the hero's own stammered hopes for a second Troy (III. 504–05; IV. 344).

Andromache did in fact have a surviving heir, but it was not her son. Whether however Ascanius, *Astyanactis imago*, could wholly replace him, whether his fall undermined the standing of Ascanius, must be asked later. *Imago* does not promise well.

Cassandra, Hecuba's prophetic daughter, futilely foretells the threat posed by the Horse (II. 246). She too will bear no children. In a scene clearly mirroring Greek iconography, we see her dragged off into captivity, and her betrothed Coroebus slain (II. 407–08). Yet, if not for her, her future will live. Anchises, slowly realising the truth of her revelation that the Trojans are to make for Italy, posthumously accords her the title *vates* (III. 187). Iris, primed by Juno, cynically confers on her the same title (V. 636; cf. X. 68). In dying with Agamemnon, she will in this sense win new life and a new voice, though the private cost is what most attracts the poet's art.

---

[10] Servius ad IV. 682: cf. ad V. 4.

[11] "I believe it often happens, that a man, before he has quite made up his own mind, will distinguish the sister or intimate friend of the woman he is really thinking of, more than the woman herself" (Jane Austen, *Mansfield Park*, c. 12).

[12] See above, p. 50, for the parallel with Homer (Helen / Telemachus). The episode is discussed in *The Classical Epic Tradition*, pp. 174–75.

Hecuba herself, in the *Iliad* a tragic queen and mother, had passed into tradition as a vengeful (*ulcisci*, Ovid, *Met*. XIII. 546) bitch (κυνός, Euripides, *Hec*. 1273). In the *Aeneid*, her more dignified role is to fade away, and in doing that to encapsulate the end of her line (II. 501, 515). Her decrepit husband Priam and her hundred *nurus* die before her. The poet daringly sketches the affection between the old couple,[13] so soon to watch the death of their citizen son Polites, so soon to be parted.

Amata, married to old Latinus / Priam (VII. 246), might from her name have offered a similar picture of wifely devotion, some sort of model perhaps of those simple conjugal virtues bachelor Horace loves to celebrate. Instead she is made a version of the post-Homeric Hecuba,[14] picking up the sinister features which Virgil's Hecuba loses, and encouraging our identification of Latinus with Priam. Resentful of the proposed match with Aeneas, heedless of its promise of children, fired by Allecto, even sexually roused (VII. 353), like some parody of Agave she leads the Latin women in feigned (or aggravated?) Bacchic rebellion against the glib dispositions of the men. Eventually, still vainly allied with Turnus, like Sophocles' Jocasta, she hangs herself, leaving her daughter, the new Helen, to face whatever future is in store for her with the Trojan stranger, *improbus advena*, the new Paris, quite alone.

At least she is allowed to speak. Lavinia, on whom the future depends, says nothing. Whatever hints we have even of her appearance (XII. 67–68) are, as it turns out, impersonal, and their very presence suggests that she is taken out of the epic flow, into a different, unreal realm.

The minor women characters of the poem include Circe, whose Italy and family line Aeneas makes his own. She was Medea's aunt, and hence the Erato borrowed from Apollonius at VII. 37, as Aeneas lands in Italy / Aeaea (Knauer). But she is far less moral than in Apollonius (*Arg*. IV. 747–48: contrast *furata*, *Aen*. VII. 283). Was it to her brutalising transformations of the human that the Protean poet felt a particular sensitivity? Mother of Latinus, magician-wife of Picus, she affords a gliding transition into the suprahuman.

Astarte Divided[15]

Virgil's unquiet spirit finds no rest on earth, and certainly none in heaven. Part of the explanation for this may lie in his awareness of old

---

[13] *Huc tandem concede*, 523. Paene comicus stilus est.

[14] *Cisseis*, VII. 320, X. 705.

[15] On Astarte, cf. *TWAT* VI, cols. 453–63 (H.-P. Müller).

traditions. The basic polarity of the *Aeneid*'s goddesses lies between Juno and Venus. But Semitic Ishtar / Astarte *combines* their separated powers. She is goddess of both war and love, mistress of lions, personifying the feral power of brute creation. In Hebrew at least, scholars note the paradox that a female deity has a proper name of masculine form. The analytical, geometrical Greeks were compelled by the bias of their genius to break up this unity into what they considered its "logical" elements. Impelled by convention, Vigil follows them, of course. But he is too great a poet not to find this compromise uneasy.

It is therefore for us one of the poem's more paradoxical metamorphoses that it turns Juno into the enemy of marriage and children, and the skittish wife of Vulcan into their patroness. Even so, love and marriage and their divinities are set as far apart as in any of the elegists. This is particularly visible in the spectator sport they make of the bloody battles of X (760). Tisiphone ranges among the opposing lines like Etruscan Vanth (761). The goddesses' catty confrontation at the council of the gods earlier (X. 16 ff., 62 ff.), where irrational half-truths nauseate, issues in this human havoc.

Aeneadum genetrix ... per te quoniam genus omne animantum concipitur. Lucretius may celebrate the conceptive life-force, but the *Aeneid* hardly ever uses *concipio* in this straightforward way. And what kind of figure does Virgil's Venus cut? She is a goddess of sex more than babies. Transformed into the protagonist of empire (I. 229), she does not fit well into the role of either Thetis or Eos (VIII. 383–84).[16] Is she closer to Pindar's political Persephone (*Nem.* 1. 13–18[17]), another goddess without children of her own?

It perhaps seems natural that as a mother Venus should continue to foster an immortal interest in Aeneas' welfare. If he was a soldier, was he then already what Ovid calls *Cythereius heros*?[18] Love's warfare was an old topos (cf. *Aen.* IV. 93, *spolia ampla*). But how often here that warfare turns deadly! We find her buying him invincible arms, for example, by granting a night of (barren) passion to Vulcan (VIII. 387)—unless the "arms" are somehow the reflection and memento of this encounter. She is seen using a

[16] Both of these parts imply ill-starred deaths for the sons (Achilles or Memnon) concerned. Cf. *nigri Memnonis arma*, I. 489: above, pp. 36, 153.

[17] The promise of rule over Sicily made by Zeus to Persephone here obviously suits Aetnean Hiero's political ambitions, and is a far closer parallel to Jupiter / Venus in *Aeneid* I than any supplied by Homer's Zeus / Thetis.

[18] *Met.* XIII. 625, XIV. 584; *Fasti* III. 611: above, p. 177. The lover / hero eventually became a commonplace, producing the *heros* / *eros* topos of the Middle Ages and Renaissance. Cf. Chaucer's "The loveres maladye of Hereos" (*Knight's Tale* 1373–74).

Cretan (!) herb to restore him for his last struggle with Turnus (XII. 412); inspiring him to hurl fire onto Latinus' city, as once he had brought it to Dido's (*flammae*, IV. 23, 670; *flammis*, V. 4; XII. 573). This goddess has no part with Εἰρήνη κουροτρόφος.[19] And her coquettish behaviour has also been remarked. She appears for the first time in the narrative sequence to her son, the new Paris, disguised as a Spartan (I. 314–16), and therefore like Helen. *Nuda genu*, she flirts with him (I. 320), and leaves him as in the *Odyssey* she leaves adulterous Ares (I. 415 ~ *Od.* VIII. 362). Here she certainly recalls *Gilgamesh*'s picture of Ishtar and her many lovers.

In her efforts to secure the succession for her child, she seems as ruthlessly determined as any imperial mother, in some ways looking ahead to the younger Agrippina, cozening Vulcan / Claudius into making arms for stepson Aeneas / Nero. Turnus is eliminated like Britannicus. She is shocked by her son's suffering and by Juturna's daring (XII. 411, 786, *indigno, indignata*), but how much that feral instinct contrasts with Turnus' moral and intellectual shock (*indignata*, 952) at his own fate. He is a loser. Her distinction is to be identified with history's winning side, and, in its service, all is pious.

The Ennian *Saturnia Juno*, occurring seven times (with seven variants), becomes a stock phrase, contradicting the Greek tradition in which Κρονίδης is on the whole reserved for Zeus.[20] In so primitive a figure as Saturn, there is necessarily a strange ambiguity, which Juno inherits. On the one side, he is the god of the Golden Age, as Virgil knew (VI. 794, VII. 201–04). Then, justice was practised spontaneously. But, if he was (like Aeneas) an exile in Latium,[21] he had in fact been persecuted by his son Jupiter for his

---

[19] Illumined by Hutton, *Themes of Peace*, e.g. pp. 169 ff. on Stobaeus (*Florilegium* 55) and Vida ("Paci" in *Poemata*, 1550). Cf. Hesiod, *Erga* 228; Eur., *Bacchae* 420. Cephisodotus' statue of the goddess is dated to 375 B.C.

[20] In 207 B.C., towards the end of the Second Punic War, Juno received extraordinary honours on the Aventine, with a procession, and a hymn written by Livius Andronicus. A surviving fragment (12 Buechner = W. 16, p. 30) is sometimes attributed to this hymn: *sancta puer Saturni filia regina*. This has the same "Saturnian" ring as Ennius' *Iuno Saturnia*. *Regina* as a divine title is sinister (cf. "Regina" at Tarquinia, Livy VII. 18. 3). Virgil picks up this old tradition. It is not a question of mechanical translation on his part from Greek.

[21] Cf. *Latiumque vocari / maluit, his quoniam latuisset tutus in oris, Aen.* VIII. 322-23; and *vix in Italia locum in quo lateret invenit*, Ennius apud Lactant., *Div. Inst.* I. 14 = Warmington, *ROL* I, p. 422. The emphasis in A. O. Lovejoy and G. Boas (*Primitivism and Related Ideas in Antiquity* [Baltimore 1935, repr. 1997]) on the "hard" and "soft" views taken by the ancients of early man is another facet of the undifferentiated primitive, reflected in the ambiguous aspects of Saturn's character.

198   Chapter Nine

cannibalistic cruelty, and *frigida Saturni ... stella* (*Geo.* I. 336) hints at this aspect of his character. And, in matters sexual, like father, like son (*Geo.* III. 93; cf. *Aen.* XII. 142–45).

In her father's mould, Homer's Hera already seemed prepared to eat Priam, his children and his subjects raw (*Il.* IV. 35–36; cf. XXII. 347, Achilles; XXIV. 212–13, Priam). Epics, now lost, no doubt painted a picture of the unrelenting persecution by the goddess of laborious Heracles, which Pindar's first *Nemean* shows as beginning even in the cradle. Following this model, and perhaps also under some Etruscan influence,[22] the *Aeneid* shifts the darker side of Saturn, attested in the *Georgics* (and in Roman Africa[23]), to Juno. Conscious of her fading charms (X. 613), burning with resentment, right from the first she is presented as a dissatisfied wife, *Iuno aeternum servans sub pectore vulnus* (I. 36).[24] There is an obvious parallel with Lucretius (II. 639):

aeternumque daret matri sub pectore volnus.

And set an everlasting wound deep in a mother's heart.

This was the experience of Juno's own mother, and now it is inherited by her daughter.

Callimachus had painted the picture of an angry Hera, hindering Leto's delivery (*Hy.* IV. 55 ff.). This analogy perhaps makes *rapti Ganymedis honores* and *spretaeque iniuria formae* more than mere pique. Frustrated sexuality is at the root of Virgil's *causae* (I. 8; cf. Callimachus' τὸν αἴτιον, *loc. cit.* 221). Ganymede in fact recurs on the cloak which Cloanthus wins for his victory in the boat race (V. 252). But, though Callimachus' Hera is

---

[22] Uni / Astarte at Pyrgi, where Temple A showed a relief (470–60 B.C.) of Tydeus at Thebes gnawing the head of his adversary, now restored and exhibited at the Villa Giulia. Stesichorus is suggested as a possible source. A parallel is certainly provided by Livy's description of the aftermath of Cannae (XXII. 51. 9). The Etruscan fondness for the macabre may have played some role in generating a new iconography. Tuscan Dante however takes it (*Inf.* 32. 130) from Neapolitan Statius (*Theb.* VIII. 736 ff.)—who took it from where?

[23] His name is found on Algerian inscriptions of the Roman period: J. and P. Alquier: "Stèles votives à Saturne decouvertes près de N'gaous [Algérie]," *Comptes Rendus de l' Académie des Inscriptions et Belles-Lettres* (1931), 21–26; J. Carcopino, "Survivances par substitution des sacrifices d'enfants dans l'Afrique romaine," *Revue de l'Histoire des Religions* 106 (1932), 592–99. Further bibliography in *TWAT* IV, cols. 957–58. In general, R. Klibansky *et al.*, *Saturn and Melancholy* (New York 1964), pp. 193–94; C. O. Brink, *Horace on Poetry, the 'Ars Poetica'* (Cambridge 1971), p. 334.

[24] The reading of her character by Ovid in his story of Callisto may be compared: *Met.* II. 508 ff. Cf. S. J. Harrison's edition of *Aeneid* X (Oxford 1991), pp. 221–22.

quickly appeased (244), Juno is not, and this is a defiant challenge which she will not fail to answer. Shortly she sends Iris / Beroe to burn all the Trojan craft (*Saturnia Iuno*, V. 606 = IX. 2, where Juno eggs on Turnus). After Book V Cloanthus never reappears.

Though Juno is the goddess of marriage, curiously the only son of her own marriage appears to be the grim god of fire. In the *Iliad*, the limping Hephaestus notoriously cuts a comic figure. The *Aeneid* makes Vulcan much more terrible, fit master of the one-eyed Etnaean Cyclopes. Outside the episode of the Shield, he is never active in the poem, except (like fire) as a destructive force; and, for women and children, even the Shield is not uniformly good. This aspect of his power is particularly evident when we find that he is the father (VIII. 198: but by what mother?) of monstrous, cannibal (again the Saturnian echo) Cacus—in the very book where he forges arms for Aeneas!

Dam of such a demonic son, Juno engenders a series of disappointed hopes. She persuades Aeolus (αἴολος, "shifting"), for example, to unleash a violent storm on the Trojans after they have left Sicily and dead Anchises, and offers him her choice from no less than fourteen beautiful nymphs, one of whom will be his wife and proud mother of his children (I. 71). In the parallel passage in the *Iliad* (XIV. 268–69), Hera leaves children unmentioned. Juno's domesticity intrudes oddly into the mythic world. But we hear no indication that her overdone offer is ever realised. The unsanctioned scheme is ended by Juno's brother Neptune. Aeolus is reminded of his limitations, and with that he vanishes from the story.

He is however associated with one already realised pregnancy, that of his prison and its frenzied southerlies (I. 50–52):

> Talia flammato secum dea corde volutans
> nimborum in patriam, loca **feta** furentibus Austris,
> Aeoliam venit.

> With such thoughts whirling in her fiery breast the goddess comes to the home of the storm clouds, haunts pregnant with raging storm-winds, Aeolus' land.

"Pregnant with raging storm-winds": are we to think of the mares of the *Georgics* (III. 273–79)?

> ore omnes versae in Zephyrum stant rupibus altis,
> exceptantque levis auras, et saepe sine ullis
> coniugiis vento gravidae (mirabile dictu)
> saxa per et scopulos et depressas convallis
> diffugiunt, non, Eure, tuos, neque solis ad ortus,
> in Borean Caurumque, aut unde nigerrimus Auster
> nascitur et pluvio contristat frigore caelum.

All turn their faces towards the west wind, standing on the high crags, trying to catch the fickle breezes. Often, unmated, made pregnant by the wind in miraculous fashion, they flee away over rocks and cliffs and deep-sunk valleys. But not to the east, not to the sun's rising, but to the north and northwest, or to that quarter whence the threatening storm-wind of the south rises, that overcasts the sky with rain and cold.

This wild, romantic scene, quite different in ethos, for example, from Homer's picture of the horses of doomed Patroclus (*Il.* XVI. 150–51), is from the book of love as nature's scourge, too much perhaps in the poet's mind as he organised his *Aeneid*. The mountain prison of the winds there, without parallel in the *Odyssey*, is an anticipation of Enceladus' imprisoning Etna.

Virgins

Often both Venus and Juno, sexually initiated though they may be, prefer to work through or as youthfully innocent, even celibate agents. Shimmering Iris is one example (*virgo*, V. 610). The same noun implausibly describes Venus / Nausicaa the first time we meet her on earth (I. 327), to begin that extraordinary series of metamorphoses already noted. Mutton dressed as lamb! How much Homer's Nausicaa is devalued.

But elsewhere virginity is demonised. The virgin Sibyl holds the key to hell, and its personnel are largely *virgines*. Among them, Allecto, a version of Ennius' Discordia, is the most infamous (VII. 331). At her side squat perverted creatures such as the Dirae. There are the hook-handed Harpies, whose spokeswoman is Celaeno. Scylla and Charybdis are among those of uncertain status.[25]

Iris, in Homer usually the messenger of Zeus, becomes in Virgil largely the messenger of his ominous wife: *Irim de caelo misit Saturnia Iuno* (V. 606 = IX. 2). Euripides (*Heracles* 831) and Callimachus (*Hy.* IV. 232) had set the precedent. The beautiful rainbow goddess is turned into the harbinger of death and destruction, as Anchises has his way (IV. 701 ~ V. 89).

Virginitas unites Camilla (XI. 583) and Juturna (XII. 141, 878). To keep company with unwed Turnus and his twin, barren Juturna, Camilla must be a *virgo*, in her case dedicated to Diana by her father at the very outset of her life.

She was already anticipated in the "Thracian" Harpalyce of I. 316–17 (cf. *Threissa*, XI. 858, the only two examples of this adjective in the poem), and

---

[25] III. 420, 684; VII. 302. Juno resents the safe haven represented by *alveo*, VII. 303. At 309 she calls herself *infelix*.

perhaps was owed in some degree to Callimachus.[26] She shares her quickness with the foals of Erichthonius (*Il.* XX. 225-29)—and with Apollonius' Euphemus (*Arg.* I. 182-84), though he is destined to found a city (*Arg.* IV. 1731 ff.) and she not. In the end, she is another of Virgil's "hollow" pastoral fantasies, a woodland sprite who somehow is pressed (like her rustic creator) into national, fatal service. Her women's lib is achieved at the cost of assimilation to the most brutal of male epic warriors (cf. XI. 698, 724). At the end, in becoming a woman (*femineo ... amore*, 782), she loses concentration and meets her death.

Like Dido, she is a queen (XI. 703, 801). She has a sister, to whom she looks as she is dying:

'hactenus, Acca soror, potui ... ' (XI. 823)

Her death may recall those of Sarpedon and Patroclus (Knauer). But Homer knows no sisters on the field.

Camilla serves as a node in a skein of references. First of all, she dies exactly like her ally Turnus,[27] and this, by the principle of polyphony, must modify our reaction to his end. The repetition cannot now underscore, like its Iliadic parallel, a mere gesture of revenge.[28]

The repeated line means then that her Homeric original is in one sense Patroclus. But Patroclus also acts as a double to Virgil's Pallas, so close to Aeneas / Achilles (XI. 438), who also receives new armour (VIII. 383). Later speculation had suggested that Patroclus' relationship with Achilles was sexual (Plato, *Symp.* 179e), and there is some element of unrealised sexuality in Pallas (cf. the Sapphic comparison at XI. 68–71) as in Camilla (XI. 581–82). What a tangled web is woven by this network of half-erotic allusions. None of this dust however would be fruitful. And, if Aeneas' Patroclus is Pallas, who brought such a youth to do a man's work?

What kind of Patroclus is Camilla? In the *Iliad*, Patroclus joins the fray as a substitute for Achilles, wearing his armour. He is a hero with some claims on the mythic reality he shares with his peers. Fantastic Camilla is out of folklore. And Patroclus would be avenged, unlike Camilla. There is this resemblance in difference, that in playing Patroclus she evidently acts as an understudy for Turnus, "economically" postponing his death. It is he who, taking Pallas' belt, will wear borrowed, fatal armour. Yet his words to her (*ducis et tu concipe curam*, XI. 519; cf. *ducis Euandri*, X. 370) have a

---

[26] See Austin's note *ad loc.*

[27] XI. 831 = XII. 952; cf. *hactenus*, X. 625, XI. 823, only here without tmesis in the *Aeneid*.

[28] *Il.* XVI. 856-57, Patroclus = XXII. 362-63, Hector: Knauer, pp. 310 ff.

pathetic ring quite alien here to the Homeric. *Concipe* echoes falsely (*ergo ubi concepit Furias* of Dido, IV. 474). *Cura* too is from Dido's ambience. *Ducis* recalls *dux femina facti*, used of Dido by Venus (I. 364).

And, if Camilla is the handmaid of Diana, it was with Diana / Luna that Dido had been notably compared (I. 499; VI. 454). She is also linked with Dido via Penthesilea (XI. 662–63; I. 490–91), and to appreciate the full richness of Virgil's invention, it would be necessary to know more about the *Aethiopis* of Arctinus. Greek painting may have suggested that Penthesilea, slain by Achilles, inspired in her conqueror a mutual attraction.[29] The listener already guessed then how the relationship of Dido / Penthesilea with Aeneas / Achilles was likely to end. Camilla / Penthesilea dies by the hand of skulking Arruns, but it is in becoming a woman (XI. 782) that she is doomed.

She may certainly be faulted for her naive delight in killing. It is as if her strange upbringing had failed to develop in her any human sense, and perhaps here she is the example of what Dido's suggestive *more ferae* (IV. 551) really implied. Both she and Dido are Amazons (*Aen.* I. 490, immediately followed by Dido's entry; XI. 648, 660). Both (like Quintus' Penthesilea, *Posthom.* I. 664–65) are compared to Diana / Artemis. Perhaps this is their final flaw: they cannot live in civil, "Urban" society.

Such resorts to fantasy (declensions) are not of course the mark of any kind of moral cowardice on Virgil's part, but the fastidiousness of the artist, disbelieving, with Aristotle and Philodemus, in the claim to totality of abrasive and intrusive "facts." It is the aloofness noted in the language of Racine. But both Racine and Virgil (and Seneca *tragicus* as third?) are their own torturers, themselves magnifying the moral ugliness from which they then shrink in revulsion.

Lost Children

If on the other side a woman's instinct has traditionally been to create a safe home and bring up children, how little that natural ambition finds fulfilment in the *Aeneid*! One of the most pathetic topoi of Book II shows the Trojan *matres* kissing the doors they now must leave.[30] Later, the women are collected as prisoners (766). Sinon's allusion to his *dulcis natos* (II. 138) is part of his hypocrisy. He attacks his Trojan audience at their

---

[29] Above, p. 143. This perhaps was what the *Aethiopis* had said or implied. It is certainly the development of the theme we find in Quintus (*Posthom.* I. 659 ff.).

[30] 489–90, a scene with touches paralleled in Livy, I. 29, the destruction of Alba Longa. — For the desolation on Troy's last night, above, p. 13.

most vulnerable point, as Juno and Venus are attacking listening Dido. Laocoon's young sons are devoured by Neptune's strangling serpents (213–15). Such Trojans as survive are *profugi*.

No doubt the myths Virgil and his audience knew were filled with these vicissitudes, though often the point of such tales, as Pindar's odes illustrate, was that somehow the line persisted. Virgil's Troy, and even its Trojans, qua Trojans, would not persist: *occidit, occideritque sinas cum nomine Troia* (XII. 828; cf. Hor., *Odes* III. 3. 18 ff.). This was quite a contradiction even of Ennius.[31] But Virgil's perceptions were sharpened by historical realities: *suis et ipsa Roma viribus ruit*. Rome's wars with Hannibal and others, the struggles for the loot of empire, the civil wars and their proscriptions, had all but wiped out the famous families. Such nobles as had survived were producing few children. After the Battle of Actium in 31 B.C., Augustus took immediate steps to increase the power and prestige of the old Italian houses by revising the roll of the senate (Suet., *Aug.* 35), a move designed to eliminate non-Italian members. He encouraged the birth of children by enacting in 18 and again in 9 B.C. laws intended to curb adultery and promote marriage. To the aristocracy, at least to those willing to listen, he preached a similar message: produce progeny, and limit lust (Horace, *Carmen saeculare*; *Odes* IV. 15).

Children need fathers. Yet, to this natural duty, Horace's own Torquatus ode (IV. 7) was a complete contradiction, as to Catullus 61. Similarly, Propertius had already echoed official policy in urging blue-blooded Tullus, his old patron, who seems to have become another confirmed bachelor, to return home (III. 22. 41–42):

> hic tibi ad eloquium cives, hic ampla nepotum
> spes et venturae coniugis aptus amor.

> Here are citizens awaiting your eloquence, here there is generous hope of descendants and the fitting affection of a wife to be.

But Propertius had also hinted at difficulties, perhaps more than his own (II. 7). And it was already seen that *spes nepotum* was used by Virgil, in bitter irony, of Priam's doomed line (II. 503). Augustan Rome's major poet presents the vatic example of what had happened and could happen again.

Juturna

The minor women characters climax in Book XII with Juturna. She cannot be demonised. She betrayed no Roman cause. Her *lacus* (Ovid, *Fasti*

---

[31] *Ann.* 344–45, Sk. ~ *Aen.* VII. 295–96, *num capti potuere capi? num incensa cremavit / Troia viros*? The equation had been too easily made.

I. 708) is still pointed out in the Forum. It is she who supplies the missing half of her brother's character, distorted ever since his encounter with Allecto in Book VII. It is she who joins her brother in pronouncing his elogium ahead of time (XII. 646–49 + 872–84).

Perhaps she was to be introduced as early as Book X, where it is difficult to believe the suggestion that *soror alma* (439) refers to Juno. Yet even the confusion Juturna / Juno would reveal how much the identity of the one is lost in that of the overwhelming ("disobliging") other. In Book XII, where we now meet her for the first time, Juno addresses her and encourages her to assist her brother. The language starts from patent flattery (XII. 142–45):

> 'nympha, decus fluviorum, animo gratissima nostro,
> scis ut te cunctis unam, quaecumque Latinae
> magnanimi Iovis ingratum ascendere cubile,
> praetulerim caelique libens in parte locarim ... '

> 'Nymph, river-beauty, most pleasing to my heart, you know well what favour I have shown you beyond all other reluctant Latin bedmates of great-souled Jove, and my gracious assent to setting you in some part of heaven.'

An Apollonian echo here (*Arg.* IV. 790–92) suggests that Juturna is half-identified with Thetis. This reconfirms the identification of Turnus with Achilles. But eventually there follows the crude and violent *aut tu bella cie conceptumque excute foedus* (158), a line whose second part means "abort the treaty which has been conceived."[32] Is this the goddess of marriage and childbirth speaking here? Juno has used the same verb at VII. 299–300:

> 'quin etiam patria e x c u s s o s infesta per undas
> ausa sequi ...'

> 'To crown all, I pried them from their country and resolutely chased them in my anger over the waves.'

She has as it were shaken them loose from the womb of their fathers' land.

Virgil reports that, as a consolation prize for the loss of her virginity—which still leaves her childless—Jupiter tosses Juturna immortality (XII. 140–41). But it was *goddesses* who usually secured, or tried to secure, immortality for a consort (Tithonus), even for a child (Achilles, Meleager), often with dire consequences. When gods indulged themselves with mortal women, in both Greek and Roman mythology, there were offspring, ἐπεὶ οὐκ ἀποφώλιοι εὐναὶ / ἀθανάτων (*Od.* XI. 249–50). The resigned approach on the part of Greek aristocrats to such licence accepted that an ounce of divinity in a genealogy was better than a pound of humdrum

---

[32] *Neve daret partus, ictu temeraria caeco / visceribus crescens excutiebat onus*, Ovid, *Fasti* I. 623–24; cf. *TLL s.v.* col. 1309, 48–50. W. R. Inge, *Classical Review* 8 (1894), 26, pro suo pudore adds "perhaps."

legitimacy, and noble families were proud to trace their ancestry back to this type of encounter, and to patronise obliging poets: *Musa dedit fidibus divos puerosque deorum ... referre* (Horace, A.P. 83, 85). After all, to say nothing of Ilia and Mars and their twins, Caesar himself was a descendant of Venus and Anchises. Virgil's Iarbas (IV. 198), Aventinus (VII. 656–61) and Tarquitus (X. 550–51) illustrate the normal paradigm, indulged in these cases because the outcome has no importance for the poet.

But Juturna, deviating from the mythical norm, and unlike other mortal women who had attracted a heavenly lover, did not bear a child.[33] Instead, she receives the *masculine* award of "immortality with dire consequences." She is bitterly conscious of this fate (XII. 878–80, 882–83):

> 'haec pro virginitate reponit?
> quo vitam dedit aeternam? cur mortis adempta est
> condicio? ...
> immortalis ego? aut quicquam mihi dulce meorum
> te sine, frater, erit?'

'Is this my recompense from him for my maidenhood? Why did he give me eternal life? Why am I robbed of the possibility of death? Am I an immortal? Or will anything of mine hold attraction for me without my brother?'

878. *Numquamne reponam*, Juvenal 1. 1, with L. Friedlaender's note. He translates it there by 'vergelten.' The word is certainly ambiguous: *idem reponere*, 'to pay back in the same coin.'

If *reponit* and *condicio* are legal language in her words here, *te sine*, picked up by Statius in his *Lament for his Dead Father* (*Silvae*. V. 3. 238), may be a delirious inversion of the familiar sacral idiom.[34] *Virginitas* has previously been met at XI. 583 (Camilla) and XII. 141. Now it echoes for the last time.

Her six questions in her final remarks (Mynors) are part of Virgil's notion of "feminine syntax." She is pleading a case. Immortality, normally such a coveted prize in the heroic / poetic world, has paradoxically become a curse. The full malice of Juno's *caelique libens in parte locarim* (XII. 145) is only now apparent.[35] The hollow reflections of sages on the value of

---

[33] Above, p. 166. This is the principle of foiled expectation (παρὰ προσδοκίαν), noted in Alexandrian narrative technique. Virgil's "disobliging other" is a variant of it. Apollonius' Sinope, who tricks both Zeus and Apollo into sparing her virginity (*Arg.* II. 946 ff.), shows a lighter side to this motif which, as so often with things Alexandrian, Virgil slants towards the tragic.

[34] E. Norden, *Agnostos Theos*, p. 157, note 3; *Roman Catullus*, pp. 208–09. For other aspects of Juturna's last speech, including its debt to Moschus, see above, pp. 119, 134.

[35] Contrast Petrarch's *In qual parte del ciel* etc. praising Laura's beauty (*Rime in Vita di Madonna Laura*, clix). This is Italian normality.

death, still persuasive, for example, to Dean Swift, in defining the dignity of the human lot, echo emptily in Juturna's words. Her short-lived brother is her only solace, and him she is to lose. Her *dulce* here is shared (in that form) only with Dido (IV. 318, 493).

Nessun maggior dolore (*Inf.* 5. 121). Juturna poses the dilemma of the "straight" (univocal) reading of the *Aeneid* with particular acuteness. For her, the traditional, mythical mould of divine rape and its inevitable, heroic issue has been broken, not to spare her, but so that she may reap a reward of everlasting pain. She recapitulates for ever the poem's theme of childlessness.

X

THE MEN CHARACTERS—I: THE SUPPORTING CAST

> Wandering between two worlds,
> One dead, the other powerless to be born.
> M. Arnold, *Stanzas from La Grande Chartreuse* 85–86

Lists

The *Aeneid* is about Aeneas, the ancestor of Rome. An epic warrior of this sort, engaged in so mighty an enterprise, needs comrades, twins, peers, as Gilgamesh needed Enkidu. But there was a lost generation. Many who might have qualified to make the voyage lay dead at windy Troy, as many of Rome's great nobles lay dead at Philippi or Pharsalia or elsewhere (*Geo.* I. 489–97; cf. Cicero, *Philippic* II. §37; Tacitus, *Ann.* I. 2). For the Aeneadae in Italy there were iterated, and more than civil, wars. The *Aeneid*'s twins are too often therefore ghostly presences (*O terque quaterque beati*, I. 94), spirits from the Homeric, sometimes Cyclic / Pindaric or Apollonian, past, whose shadowy forms envelop and blur the silhouette of the present. Nowhere is this more obvious than in the *Lusus Troiae* (*veterumque agnoscunt ora parentum*, V. 576). The male supporting cast of the epic is often there—or not there—to enhance themes quite contradictory of any militaristic eulogy, and of the hope for the future to which the story is committed whether by its exordium, or by its occasional enigmatic hints.

We hear this note also in the poet's roll-calls of the missing, fleeting, ambiguous.[1] Such lists may be capricious.[2] Virgil uses a large number of

---

[1] The religious list of the mighty dead is familiar from the litanies of the saints, the Canon of the Roman Mass ("Lini, Cleti, Clementis, Xysti," etc.). No doubt its origin lay in genealogy, as the proems to Matthew and Luke suggest. Already the poets adapt it to their own purposes.

[2] We hear, for example, of the trouble taken to appoint Matthias (NT Acts 1:23–26), and then nothing more of him. Paul by contrast is never listed. Epic Ovid lists Actaeon's hounds (*Met.* III. 206 ff.), as Cato had named the bravest of

masculine proper names. But, in the majority of minor instances, the name is divorced from identity. Abas, for example, does duty as a Greek (III. 286), a Trojan (I. 121) and an Etruscan (X. 170, 427). Sthenelus is a Greek (II. 261) and a Trojan (XII. 341). Corynaeus is killed at IX. 571 and able to singe Ebysus' beard at XII. 298. Idaeus, Numa, Phegeus, Remulus and Thymoetes are similar resurgents. Ucalegon / Οὐκ ἀλέγων (II. 312; cf. Juvenal III. 199) borders on the comic.[3] Nautes / ναύτης (V. 704, 728), pupil of Tritonian Pallas, is another casually named bit-player. There are many such momentary occurrences: Alcanor, Amycus, Asilas, Clonius, Clytius, Crethus, Ebysus, Eurytion, Fadus.... Two heroes, Hydaspes (X. 747) and Hypanis (II. 340, 428), borrow the names of famous rivers (as it were, "Thames" and "Hudson"). Liris (XI. 670) is tributary to their company. *Hypanisque Dymasque* indeed, joining Aeneas' Trojan band together and perishing together—and doing little in the meantime—seem greater ciphers than Rosencrantz and Guildenstern. Who are these people? Did they have families? Who knows? The poet does not care about the person so long as he can create the impression of particularity.

Tasso imitates this in the *Gerusalemme Liberata* (Araspe, Muleasse, Tigrane), but the reader should recognise how peculiar it is. Odysseus' willingness to endanger his life and enterprise so that the Cyclops would know the identity of his assailant (IX. 504; ironically parodied at *Aen*. I. 378) shows how much store the Greek hero set by his name.[4] And, in this tradition, Greek vases of the classical period often carefully label the participants in the heroic action. Even in the first century B.C., the *Tabula Iliaca*, preserved on the Capitoline, accompanies its scenes with what the most recent catalogue calls "explicit inscriptions." Byzantine iconography would follow this convention. But, in other instances, this concern wanes. The Alexander mosaic now in Naples, omitting names, allows us to

---

the Carthaginian elephants (Pliny, *N.H.* VIII. 11). Ovid's use of the list in general (e.g. *Met.* II. 217–226; III. 171–72; VIII. 299 ff.), as of the recurring proper name, calls for further study.

[3] Cf. James J. O'Hara, *True Names: Vergil and the Alexandrian Tradition of Etymological Wordplay* (Ann Arbor 1996), and the earlier study of Catherine Saunders, "Sources of the Names of Trojans and Latins in Vergil's *Aeneid*," *Trans. Am. Phil. Assoc.* 71 (1940), 537–55. Michael Paschalis' *Virgil's* Aeneid. *Semantic Relations and Proper Names* (Oxford 1997) is a bold experiment in developing the whole significance of the poem from its plays on speaking names. Punning of this sort, as Hebrew shows, is certainly an old device, in Greek with comic, tragic and religious antecedents: ἐνδυστυχῆσαι τοὖνομ' ἐπιτήδειος εἶ.

[4] See also *TWAT* VIII, *s.v.* שׁם, cols. 122 ff. (Reiterer, Fabry).

distinguish the main protagonists and no more.[5] Frenzied scenes of battle on Hellenistic and Etruscan or Roman sarcophagi certainly convey a vivid sense of hotly contested warfare. The exploit may have been famous. Who the individual contestants were is largely guesswork. A different poetic was in play, with different imperatives. Lyrical Pindar, in an ode concerned with brevity (βραχύν, *Py.* 4. 248), had shortened the list of Jason's crew to 12 (*ibid.* 171–82). Telling the same story, epic Apollonius had dutifully catalogued 54 Argonauts, but in the event, in his musical handling of his theme, let only a minority (21) recur. The others are film extras, hired for the day, fixed in the medium, and then sent off to their irrelevant lives.

For all Odysseus' preoccupation with his own name, elsewhere even Homer is forgetful, as Horace remembers (*A.P.* 359). Pylaemenes is often cited, dying at *Il.* V. 576, accompanying his son's corpse at XIII. 643 ff. —though that was a natural enough tribute from the dead to the dead and is perhaps meant as an example of non-sequential (vertical) narrative. The poet has unique names. He has lists, though one at least illustrates the closeness of his name to the hero of which we have spoken (*Il.* XI. 299–305):

> Ἔνθα τίνα πρῶτον, τίνα δ' ὕστατον ἐξενάριξεν
> Ἕκτωρ Πριαμίδης, ὅτε οἱ Ζεὺς κῦδος ἔδωκεν;
> Ἀσαῖον μὲν πρῶτα καὶ Αὐτόνοον καὶ Ὀπίτην,
> καὶ Δόλοπα Κλυτίδην καὶ Ὀφέλτιον ἠδ' Ἀγέλαον,
> Αἴσυμνόν τ' Ὦρόν τε καὶ Ἱππόνοον μενεχάρμην.
> τοὺς ἄρ' ὅ γ' ἡγεμόνας Δαναῶν ἕλεν, αὐτὰρ ἔπειτα
> πληθύν....

Here, whom first and whom last did Hector, son of Priam, despoil, when Zeus granted him glory? First Asaeus, and Autonous and Opites, and Dolops, son of Clytius, and Opheltius and Agelaus, and Aesymnus and Orus and Hipponous, steadfast in the fray. These were the leaders of the Greeks whom he took, but only then the common crowd.

The leaders at least are named. It is the herd (πληθύς) which is left anonymous (cf. *Il.* XVII. 260–61). Virgil imitates this (*plebem*, IX. 343).

All this may be permissible enough in Homer. He was writing universally. His story, told about and outside the past, claimed validity for all time; and, in that sense, the names are not what matters (Aristotle, *Poetics* 1451b 10 ff.). Yet Virgil adds to whatever claim he implicitly

---

[5] To take this further, in Paolo Veronese's painting of *The Family of Darius Before Alexander the Great* (London, NG 294: mid-16th century), art historians have displayed an inability to tell which figure is Alexander and which Hephaestion. But perhaps the painter himself, who in 1573 insouciantly changed the title of his *Last Supper* into *The Feast in the House of Levi* as the easiest way of placating the Inquisition, did not care for that degree of particularity.

makes of that sort an extra claim of pressing relevance to the history of his own time and city (Iulus / Julius: cf. Clausus / Claudia, VII. 707–08). For him, by his chosen premise, the (Roman) future does matter. The catalogue of heroes in Book VI makes that clear. But elsewhere does he always discharge his responsibility so plausibly? In his catalogue of the Italians in Book VII, he replaces individual heroes largely with allusions to peoples and tribes. The πληθύς has taken over. There is something of the spirit of Cato's *Origines* about this. Among those who survive this levelling, Virbius (VII. 762), for example, is never mentioned again. A similar analysis may be applied to the shorter catalogue of Aeneas' allies in Book X (166–212).

As the son of Hippolytus, Virbius offers the poet (like Cupavo in Book X) the chance to narrate a picturesque αἴτιον. What is its relevance to rational history? Was indeed rational history (even rationalistic history, of the kind he might have found in Cato) overlaid in him by transrational music, theatricality? He was the intimate of Gallus, the admirer of the Euphorion who wrote the languorous, Tennysonian χθιζόν μοι κνώσσοντι παρ' Ἀργανθώνιον αἶπος (Powell, no. 75); and one suspects at times in Virgil's epic that same influence of what has been called *la poésie verbale grecque*. Quintilian remarks (XII. 10. 33): *tanto est sermo Graecus Latino iucundior, ut nostri poetae, quotiens dulce carmen esse voluerunt, illorum id nominibus exornent.* Virgil practised this. The Aristaeus-episode in the last book of the *Georgics*, for example, had listed Cyrene's nymphs: *Drymoque Xanthoque Ligeaque Phyllodoceque* (336: the whole passage may be studied). Scholars refer us to Hesiod, and Hellenistic virtuosity had refined the example of that master. But who cares who these nymphs or their descendants were?

In fact, a list of this Hesiodic sort had been *excised* from the *Iliad* (XVIII. 39–49) by Zenodotus and Aristarchus. Yet in the *Aeneid*, a similar list recurs (V. 823–26). Virgil ignores academic purism when it hampers his *imagination auditive*. It was noted earlier that he likes to take half-comic devices of this sort from his Hellenistic forebears and lend them tragic resonance. This is the atmosphere conveyed by his epic battle scenes (XI. 673–75):

> his addit Amastrum
> Hippotaden, sequiturque incumbens eminus hasta
> Tereaque Harpalycumque et Demophoonta Chromimque.

Amastrus, Hippotas' son, was her next victim, then with a mighty throw of her spear she went after Tereus and Harpalycus, and Demophoon and Chromis.

Amastrus (for all his patronymic), Tereus, Harpalycus, Demophoon and

Chromis occur nowhere else in the poem. Nor do we ever hear of Amastrus' father except here.

A similar case is found in the next book (XII. 362–64):

> huic comitem Asbyten coniecta cuspide mittit
> Chloreaque Sybarimque Daretaque Thersilochumque
> et sternacis equi lapsum cervice Thymoeten.

With a cast of his spear, he despatched Asbytes along with him, and Chloreus and Sybaris and Dares and Thersilochus, and one who slid from the neck of his rearing horse, Thymoetes.

Of this group, Asbytes is mentioned only here. Vatic Chloreus had appeared in Book XI (768 ff.), where he attracted Camilla's attention not so much by any heroic deed as by his extraordinary get-up. Dares is the stalwart boxer of Book V, the only man to challenge Paris, and killer of Butes in Hector's funeral games (370–74)—though a Butes still plays some part in the story (IX. 647, XI. 690). How extraordinary that we have heard nothing of Dares since Sicily, and now all we hear is that he was killed! Without a fight?[6] Thersilochus here is another resurgent. At VI. 483, he was dead. Now he (or who?) dies again. Thymoetes at the end has a certain history (II. 32, X. 123)—provided he is the same person (which Mynors disputes) on each of the three occasions where he is mentioned.

There are thumb-nail sketches of some of the dying. Sometimes the contrivance is palpable. Antores is killed by a weapon which Mezentius has aimed at Aeneas. There is emotional epanadiplosis, hypermetre. The ominous *infelix*, the sentimental *dulcis* recur (X. 778–82):

> egregium Antoren latus inter et ilia figit,
> Herculis Antoren comitem, qui missus ab Argis
> haeserat Euandro atque Itala consederat urbe.
> sternitur infelix alieno vulnere, caelumque
> aspicit et dulcis moriens reminiscitur Argos.

It pierced the noble Antores between his side and flanks—Antores, who had been Hercules' comrade. Sent from Argos, he had joined Evander and settled in his Italian city. Unfruitful, he was laid low by a wound meant for another, and now he looked up at the sky, and in death remembered the sweetness of Argos.

Of course such things happen (cf. *Il.* XIII. 518; XIV. 462–63; XVII. 609), but it is the kind of oddity which delights Ovid and Lucan. In any case, this is the only time Antores makes an appearance in the poem.

---

[6] Even so, he is luckier than his pugilistic rival, Entellus, who never makes it outside the confines of Book V. Similarly, Sergestus, ancestor of the gens Sergia though he may be (V. 121), is heard of later only in a formulaic line meant to remind us of the flight from Dido's Libya (IV. 288 = XII. 561). Similar instances are noted below.

Such affective repetition recurs (XII. 546–47):

> hic tibi [sc. *Aeole*] mortis erant metae, domus alta sub Ida,
> Lyrnesi domus alta, solo Laurente sepulcrum.
>
> Here for you were set death's bounds. Your high home was at Ida's foot, at Lyrnessus your high home, in Laurentine soil your grave.

Aeolus is found only here, though there has been an Aeolides in Book IX (774). Yet, since he was among Turnus' victims, that son can have been of no solace to his father. Perhaps indeed the silence about him at this point implies that there was no intended relationship, and Aeolides was just as much a saccharine and momentary fiction as Aeolus.

Another epanadiplosis relates to another Aeolides (VI. 162–65):

> atque illi Misenum in litore sicco
> ut venere vident, indigna morte peremptum,
> Misenum Aeoliden, quo non praestantior alter
> aere ciere viros, Martemque accendere cantu.
>
> Unexpectedly, on arriving they saw Misenus on the drying shore, carried off by an undeserved death—Misenus, son of Aeolus, than whom none better at summoning the warriors with his trumpet and kindling their martial spirit by his notes.

Repetitio of this sort certainly occurs from time to time in Homer, as when Nireus is praised as the fairest youth to come to Troy, or Andromache protests her isolation to Hector.[7] These are high points. In Hellenistic poetry, the device became more widespread. It begins life for Virgil as a pastoral ornament (*Ecl.* 6. 20–21, 55–56; 4. 58–59).

As with the euphonious lists, so with the lingering recall. In these Virgilian passages, whatever their formal differences, the reader is very close to the spirit breathed by the funerary epigrams of the *Anthology*: there is the same wry lachrymosity, the perfection of the file imposed on imperfect experience, forcing art to compensate for nature's fault. Something may be deduced about what we have called Virgil's "declining mode,"[8] little about how real families encounter the miseries of war. Rhetoric or, to be fairer, music is sublimating feeling.

De la musique avant toute chose. Here we retread ground already trodden, notably in our Chapters III and IV. Even Aristotle acknowledged the power of music (*Poetics* 1450b 16); and Crates of Mallos, who lectured at Rome

---

[7] Cf. Norden on *Aen.* VI. 164, p. 183 of his commentary. The example at *Iliad* VI. 395–96 is remarkable, greatly adding to the ethos of this wrenching scene. *Iliad* VII. 137–38 is perhaps less fraught.

[8] Above, c. II. One thinks of Wilfrid Owen's "bugles calling for them from sad shires" (*Anthem for Doomed Youth*). What is the influence of this Virgilian mode on the English poets inspired by the events of 1914–18, on Housman?

in the second century, is reported by Philodemus to have urged the supreme importance for serious poetry of its sound.[9] Quintilian's nominal *dulcedo* seems close. Is there another influence? Virgil's poem, like the contemporary stage, is crowded with many extras, but is not individuality drowned out by the flutes and pipes of supra-personal (histrionic) "business," even magnificence?[10] And it was pantomimic Pylades who had arrogated the Homeric αὐλῶν συρίγγων τ' ἐνοπήν, ὅμαδόν τ' ἀνθρώπων (*Il*. X. 13).

Character

Yet both the pantomimist (as Friedlaender documents) and the epic poet had also to pay attention to character. Aristotle had praised Homer for precisely that (*Poetics* 1460a 9–11):

ὁ δὲ ὀλίγα φροιμιασάμενος εὐθὺς εἰσάγει ἄνδρα ἢ γυναῖκα ἢ ἄλλο τι ἦθος, καὶ οὐδέν' ἀήθη ἀλλ' ἔχοντα ἦθος.

After a brief prologue he loses no time in introducing a man or a woman or some other character, and no one without character, always with.

What student even of the opening pages of the *Iliad* does not sense the justice of his remarks?

And Virgil does paint character. Drances, for example—a more dignified, Roman version of unruly Thersites—is worthy of a (minor!) place in one of Dostoevsky's novels; that is, in the satirical / religious records of a society fissured and even mortally wounded by the fateful hand of a military and administrative genius, but still powerfully aware of old traditions, of family hierarchy. For Russia, this genius was Napoleon. For the poet, it was Julius Caesar, and this society was that of the dying Roman Republic, mirrored also in Cicero, Sallust and Lucan (Livy).

In Book XI, he builds up his portrait with a number of touches. Finally, as Drances confronts Turnus in an outburst of pent-up hostility, we hear that his social footing was insecure (XI. 340–41):

... genus huic materna superbum
nobilitas dabat, incertum de patre ferebat.

It was his mother's blue blood that gave him his proud lineage. No one quite knew who his father was.

---

[9] Περὶ Ποιημάτων V, col. 25; ed. Mangoni, p. 152.

[10] In the Hellenistic theatre, Cicero and Horace alike complained that spectacle was taking over from reasoned discourse: *Ad Fam.* VII. 1. 2; cf. Horace, *Epp.* II. 1. 187 ff., and contrast Aristotle, *Poetics* 1450b 16–20. See also Callimachus, fr. 282, Pf.; *Roman Catullus*, p. 278, n. 5.

This explains his generosity (his attempt to buy standing); his talkativeness (the mark of his social uncertainty); his lack of self-confidence in battle (he could not be sure of the survival of his line). With great astuteness, Vegio (*Supplementum* 329) shows him, his arch-enemy (and his better) Turnus now dead, eventually leading the peace delegation to Aeneas, still discoursing volubly and venomously, still establishing his role.

Mezentius, another of these figures, again has more to tell us about the Republican world Virgil knew than about the heroic age. He is an exile, guilty of macabre cruelty, *contemptor divum*, like some Giant, like Capaneus in Aeschylus' *Seven Against Thebes* (v. 424), yet with a soft spot for his son and his animal. This is a character out of Byron or one of his imitators, perhaps better a sort of Stavrogin from *The Possessed*. Is this Catiline? Will it be Caligula? Or Heliogabalus? In Russia, such types portended the deadly revolution of 1917. What further twist of the Roman revolution do they evince in Augustan Virgil? This is a future interacting with the fictional past which offers less promise than official eulogy.[11]

Like Hector and Achilles, Mezentius speaks to his horse: *Rhaebe, diu, res si qua diu mortalibus ulla est, / viximus* (X. 861–62; cf. *Il*. VIII. 185; XIX. 400). This too is a folk-motif, famously mirrored in Alexander's devotion to his Bucephalus, though how much more desolating its associations in Virgil's poem. With Mezentius' words we may compare Dido's *vixi* (IV. 653); and the poet's *si qua est ea gloria*, at Caieta's death (VII. 4). Are the gods he despises newcomers (a Promethean theme[12])? But what fire has he brought to men? Is he then a romantic creating his own values (cf. Nisus' question, IX. 185), a Nietzschean, one of the numerous monsters Nietzsche spawned, and notably in Russia? When public structures weaken and collapse, persistent motifs surface from the stratum they once overlaid, as Catherine the Great's St. Petersburg yielded in 1917 to the Moscow of a new Ivan the Terrible. But, even in post-Renaissance Italy, the "fantastic" epics of Ariosto, Tasso and Marino blossomed from the detritus of a century of questioning, self-conscious and therefore corrosive religious reform. And the sensibility of the fantastic *Aeneid*, written under the patronage of another self-conscious religious reformer? It is one of the

---

[11] And in the same way some of the stories Livy tells towards the end of Book I about the ruthlessness of the royal feuds prosecuted by the Tarquins and their womenfolk seem to anticipate the pages of Tacitus. See above, p. 197 (Venus / Vulcan / Aeneas ~ Agrippina / Claudius / Nero).

[12] Aeneas certainly echoes the *Prometheus Vinctus*: *Aen*. VI. 103–04 = οὐδέ μοι ποταίνιον / πῆμ' οὐδὲν ἥξει (102–03). Maecenas wrote a *Prometheus*: Seneca, *Epp*. 19. 9. The unique fragment finds a parallel in Horace's *Odes* (II. 10. 11–12).

proofs of the *Aeneid's* vatic status that it contains within itself in this way the seeds, both historical and literary, of past and future ages: *quae sint, quae fuerint, quae mox ventura trahantur.* Will Mezentius one day be emperor? A throwback to the last of Rome's kings? Julian the Apostate?

The death of Lausus, Mezentius' son, is developed from the similar self-sacrificial death, portrayed in Arctinus' *Aethiopis*, of Antilochus.[13] Again Virgil's bias is manifest. Though Antilochus had in the event saved his father Nestor, Lausus' attempt to save his father Mezentius (X. 800 ff.) ends in death for both. It is in killing Lausus / Antilochus that Aeneas confirms his own identification with short-lived Memnon (*Aen.* I. 489; cf. VIII. 384).

But how can sinister Mezentius be well-meaning Nestor? How can such an oddity sire a son such as Lausus? Could the father be wholly bad, if his son showed such nobility?[14] This is certainly a *coincidentia oppositorum*. The topos is that sons *betray* their fathers' standards. Pindar alludes to this (*Py.* 6. 44–45) and Horace spells it out (*aetas parentum* ...). Its contradiction, in an author so modern as Virgil, again suggests the reflectivity of the philosophical lecture room (here πότερον διδακτὸν ἡ ἀρετή).

Mezentius, an exile, himself doomed, loses his son Lausus, and Mezentius' son is in some sense a second son for Aeneas (and in that case one murdered by his father): a son showing qualities dear to Aeneas himself. *Imago* recurs in a context also using the Gygean *vidit* (X. 821–24):

> At vero ut vultum vidit morientis et ora—
> ora modis Anchisiades pallentia miris,
> ingemuit miserans graviter dextramque tetendit,
> et mentem patriae subiit pietatis imago.

> But when he saw the face and countenance of the dying youth—son of Anchises looking at a countenance wondrously pale—he sighed in profound pity, stretching out his right hand, while a vision of devotion to a father pierced his heart.

As the body is lifted from the ground, its hair matted with blood, we see Greek pictures, certainly of Patroclus, but also of Memnon, Sarpedon.[15]

---

[13] Fraenkel, *Kleine Beiträge*, II, pp. 173 ff.: above, p. 153, n. 35.

[14] Epic reminiscences even link Mezentius both with Jason and with the Greeks' resistance to Hector: *Aen.* X. 693 = *Arg.* III. 1294 = *Il.* XV. 618.

[15] Thanatos Painter, P. E. Arias and M. Hirmer, *A History of Greek Vase Painting*, pp. 361–62. See also below, p. 224, n. 32. Sarpedon, to whom the *Aeneid* makes repeated allusion (I. 100; IX. 697; X. 125, 471), illustrated the powerlessness even of the greatest of the gods to rescue a son from fate (*Il.* XVI. 431 ff.). He falls victim to Patroclus, who is himself to fall victim to Hector. This deadly sequence seems to have captured Virgil's attention, especially in his

Mezentius himself, hearing the news, pouring dust upon his hair, is like Catullus' Aegeus (64. 224), or like Latinus later (XII. 611). His last request is to be buried with his son (X. 906). Lausus' mother is no doubt dead (*parentum manibus*, X. 827–28), and in any case is mentioned only as her son dies, and in a line reminiscent of Dido (*et tunicam molli mater quam neverat auro*, X. 818 ~ *et tenui telas discreverat auro*, IV. 264 = XI. 75, dead Pallas). Is Dido then her double? She even peeps through the grim features of the wounded father as he asks after his slain rescuer: *multa super Lauso rogitat* (X. 839). This is Dido at her banquet: *multa super Priamo rogitans, super Hectore multa* (I. 750).[16] The ghastly series continues.

Lesser Heroes

The lesser heroes of the poem who play some part in the action are not normally guaranteed children of any sort. Aeneas' entourage offers the first example of this. What children, for example, may *fidus Achates* expect? What *gens* did he found at Rome? Among Greeks, bearing arms for a warrior, as Achates does for Aeneas (I. 188), was a task for slaves, σκευοφόροι. What armour does Pylades carry for Orestes? Is Achates then a slave-confidant from New Comedy? If he is more, he is not a Homeric θεράπων. Rather, he shares something of the un-Homeric ὑπασπιστής, the Hebrew נשא הצנה.[17] Misenus, already noted as a dead Aeolides, is in this category (VI. 164). Homer's Hector had no personal trumpeter, for reasons well known to the ancient commentators.[18] Virgil, often so careful to heed them, here again breaks completely with their exegeses. By acquiring aides of this sort, Aeneas is made more oriental, Asian, "barbaric."

---

treatment of Pallas (Knauer, pp. 298–301, noted above, p. 31). But what it implies here is that Lausus too is caught up in the paradigm.

[16] These are the only two occurrences of the verb in the epic, and the only uses of *super* with the ablative of a proper name.

[17] I Sam. 17:41. Cf. נשא כלים, though that is a young man (נער, Judges 9:54; I Sam. 14:1 *al.*). In all these places, the LXX uses a participial phrase, rather than a noun because it is closely following the Hebrew, where there are no *nomina agentis* of the IE sort. So in Pindar (ὑπασπίζων, *Nem.* 9. 34, for Chromius), obviously not used of a slave, nor understood by Euripides in that way (ὑπασπίζων, *Heracleidae* 216). Both Sicily and Cyprus were islands where Greeks encountered Semitic civilisations. Perhaps that led to an enhancement of the armour-bearer's status. Cyprian Onesilus had a Carian ὑπασπιστής who is treated as a sort of trusty NCO by his royal master (Herod. V. 111). Is this the model for Achates? Cf. W. S. Anderson, "Chalinus *armiger* in Plautus' *Casina*," *ICS* VIII (1983), 11 with n. 1.

[18] Ad *Il.* XVIII. 219. The war trumpet is Etruscan (Lydian?). See also OT Numbers c. 10; שופר, תקע in the lexica.

Misenus, foolish enough to challenge the gods, died before he could get beyond the Italian shore (VI. 174). Polites, murdered as old Priam watched, is the father of a second Priamus (V. 564–65), but what *progenies* of this name did in fact enhance Italian stock? What children may Pallas expect, when he has finished aiding Aeneas? Nisus and Euryalus are specifically described each as *infelix*.

Virgil's lost generation had its survivors. With what an operatic gesture (Berlioz!) Aeneas greets his followers in Dido's temple (I. 610–12):

> sic fatus amicum
> Ilionea petit dextra laevaque Serestum,
> post alios, fortemque Gyan fortemque Cloanthum.

With these words he clasps his loyal Ilioneus with his right hand, with his left Serestus, then the others, stalwart Gyas and stalwart Cloanthus.

Of these, perhaps Ilioneus plays the biggest part, but even he disappears after Book IX. Cloanthus, it was noted, vanishes after Book V. Gyas is a *Latin* at X. 318. There are indeed whole books in which such companions go unmentioned. How different all this from the *Iliad*.

If we except characters of this sort, there are few mature heroes, apart perhaps from Aeneas himself. The others tend either to be young and pathetic, or dodderingly old, good only for tears or fainting fits. Vatic Helenus in his museum at Buthrotum proves this rule more than contradicts it. What interests the poet is evidently not vivacious ("dramatic") interaction among sturdy peers but, as with his *matres*, a chorus, a frieze. This is why there are so many blank or generic faces. And, set against this often ill-defined backdrop, the poem must approximate to classical French drama, in which the solitary protagonists are engaged in dialogue not so much with each other, as with themselves, or with an ideal audience to which they explain in resonant and musical language their often ill-grounded determinations to pursue at whatever cost whatever courses myth or self-will or both dictate. Turnus illustrates the point.

In so far as this is true, Virgil's narrative set-up, in debt to the pantomime and even the mime (of the *Fragmentum Grenfellianum* sort), does not aim to accommodate families or children, except where they may serve as temporary props to heighten emotion (*pueri innuptaeque puellae*), since they could only be distractions from the adult monologue. What characteristic differences, to return to that example, between the immortal liveliness of Homer's parting of Hector and Andromache, which includes baby Astyanax (*Il.* VI. 400), and the wan deathliness of the encounter after Astyanax's murder (*Aen*. III. 301 ff.). What a difference even from Horace (*Odes* IV. 15. 25–32). This discrepancy defines what sort of poem Virgil wrote.

An associated motif deserves attention. Hard pressed by Aeolus' storm, Aeneas paradoxically congratulates those sons who fell at Troy before the eyes of their fathers (*ante ora patrum*, I. 94–95). Andromache, it was noted, adapts the motif to Polyxena (III. 321). One such death was that of Polites, killed in the presence of Hecuba and Priam by Neoptolemus (*natum ante ora patris*, II. 663).

The theme recurs. Earlier in Book II, Coroebus, Cassandra's ill-starred suitor, has had the clever notion of borrowing Greek arms. But the Trojans then think he and his company are Greeks, and shower javelins down on them from the shrine of the virgin goddess Minerva (II. 411–12):

> oriturque miserrima caedes
> armorum facie et Graiarum errore iubarum.

An unhappy slaughter ensued, caused by the look of their arms and the confusion over their Greek crests.

These two motifs are later combined, as the horror continues in Latium (XI. 885–89):

> oriturque miserrima caedes
> defendentum armis aditus inque arma ruentum.
> exclusi ante oculos lacrimantumque ora parentum
> pars in praecipitis fossas urgente ruina
> volvitur ...

An unhappy slaughter ensued, some defending with arms the approaches and others rushing upon those arms. Shut out, before the very eyes and faces of their weeping parents, some were toppled into the steep ditches beneath a rain of missiles.

In both cases, it is a question of "friendly fire." In both cases, fathers and mothers watch. These iterations seem built into the very fabric of the poem.

Lux Maligna: Palinurus

Chiaroscuro appealed to the imaginations of both Propertius and Racine.[19] Virgil's poetic imagination is indeed more at home with such half light than with light unblemished. In the first half of the poem, we see this in the nocturnal fires of burning Troy, but also in those of Dido's banquet (*noctem flammis funalia vincunt*, I. 727), her funeral pyre (V. 2, *atros*; 4, *flammis*), and again in her whole lunar existence: compared to armed Diana when we first meet her (I. 499), haunting the deserted banqueting hall at

---

[19] Both of course Virgil's admirers. Lunar Cynthia inevitably has *lumina nigra* (II. 12. 23; cf. IV. 3. 14). *Flamme noire* is noted by L. Spitzer as a leitmotif in *Phèdre*: "Die klassische Dämpfung in Racines Stil," *Archivum Romanicum* XII (1928), p. 455.

moonset in her palace at Carthage (IV. 81), in Hades like some half-glimpsed crescent in the clouds (VI. 453–54).

The *circulus lunaris* was already known to the ancients as the sphere of giddy uncertainty (cf. Cicero, *Nat. Deorum* II. §56), and its ambience matches Dido's erotic *furor* with Propertius'. This Debussyesque elusiveness may envelop then more than women. In Virgil, it conditions the account of Aeneas' experience in Hades (*per incertam lunam sub luce maligna*, VI. 270). Among the poem's lesser men, perhaps it reaches a climax in the fate of Palinurus (V. 833 ff.), who in an unearthly encounter with Somnus under a clear night sky (851; cf. VI. 338, *dum sidera servat*) loses control of Aeneas' craft exactly when his guidance is most needed. Aeneas senses the danger and takes over just in time (V. 867). As he ponders his helmsman's fate, we hear again *multa gemens* (869).[20]

This adventure, whether moonlit or not, is in stark contrast with the happy rescue by Aphrodite of Apollonius' Butes (*Arg.* IV. 912–19). It is mainly modelled on the (post-Homeric) fate of Odysseus' helmsman Baios, whose tomb gave his name to Baiae (Lycophron, *Alexandra* 694; Silius Italicus VIII. 539). For Virgil, Palinurus' fate prefigures the fatal course and dead end of the Trojans' coming Italian ordeal, and once again betrays the poet's typical declension in the face of the negative. Confronted by the primitive and horrible, his imagination responds, not with clinical ("Parnassian") objectivity, but by taking refuge in the fanciful and unreal. There was an old folk tradition that, in the handselling of any great enterprise, the gods had to be placated by the offering of a precious life, as Iphigenia was sacrificed at Aulis, as later Turnus died, and Remus' life was offered at the building of Rome's walls; and this practice is in Virgil's mind here (*unum pro multis dabitur caput*, 815).[21] But in what a twilight of melancholy enchantment the poet has wrapped whatever tribal memory he had of this barbarous rite!

Virgil's imagination normally operates on several levels. At the level of literary imitation, he may also have modelled his story on Homer's account of Menelaus' loss of his pilot Phrontis (*Od.* III. 278–85). On the surface at least, that meant more retardation than here. In the subsequent storm,[22]

---

[20] Above, p. 154. It was the phrase with which Aeneas had reflected on the scenes at Troy (I. 465), or turned away from Dido (IV. 395)—and with which Juturna would contemplate an eternity of sterile suffering (XII. 886).

[21] Cf. NT John 11:50; Τοῦ Γιοφυριοῦ τῆς Ἄρτας, *Medieval and Modern Greek Poetry*, ed. C. A. Trypanis (Oxford 1951), no. 92, with the note on p. 262.

[22] Cf. *Aen.* VI. 355–56 for the survival of the Homeric storm motif in Virgil. There is no storm at the end of Book V.

some Greeks were driven to Crete; others, including Menelaus himself, to Egypt, where according to one version, he would find Helen. This was the adventure in Virgil's mind when he framed the story of Aristaeus' encounter with vatic Proteus at the end of *Georgics* IV.

But Menelaus subsequently made his way back home, laden with treasure, his wife recovered. Aeneas is not therefore Menelaus. Are we then to think of him as driven to Crete? He will have occasion as soon as he lands in his new home to review his history in term of the Cretan scenes on Apollo's doors. Their deadly nature and hint of continuing malice was already noted. In Book XII, Aeneas will be restored for combat with a Cretan herb (412), perhaps a last perversion of the pastoral motif. The poet does not wish to say any of this outright, content to load his minor character with a weight of latent meaning.

Nisus and Euryalus

The episode of Nisus and Euryalus in Book IX (224 ff.) is another instance of this evasive fantasy as it afflicts men—but men who had mothers. It begins with speculative (Euripidean? Dostoevskian?) psychology (184–85), to which the hearer must supply his own answer. *Dira cupido* here is an apocalyptic leitmotif (VI. 373, 721).

The action proper opens with a "typical scene." The world is asleep, except for the anxious hero(es). Again there is chiaroscuro. The Rutulian camp shows *interrupti ignes aterque ad sidera fumus* (239). There are several similar moments in the *Iliad*,[23] some accompanied by stars and fires. In the *Aeneid*, Dido (IV. 522) and Aeneas (VIII. 18) both share these insomniac discomforts.

Messengers are needed to alert Aeneas to the plight of the besieged Trojans. Young though they are, Nisus and Euryalus will seek him out. Weeping for joy, first old Aletes (ἀλήτης, evidently the Greek for a Trojan refugee[24]) and then Iulus promise large rewards, among them a mixing bowl that is the gift of Sidonian Dido (*dat*, 266), a reminiscence of the *Iliad* (XXIII. 741) taken from Achilles' prizes for his footrace, the background to our first meeting with the pair in Book V. If Turnus is beaten, they will receive his horse, shield and red crest (cf. VII. 785). There will be prizes of

---

[23] The reader is referred to Knauer for the details of Homeric imitation throughout.

[24] Ἀλητής ("vagabond," "social outcast") is used of the disguised Odysseus by the contemptuous Suitors, *Od.* XX. 377. Cf. Pindar, *Ol.* 1. 58, εὐφροσύνας ἀλᾶται of outcast Tantalus, unable now to share the bonhomie of the symposium.

slaves, women *and* men, and all the land Latinus owns. Euryalus will be particularly close to Prince Iulus in his enterprises to come.

Aged Aletes and youthful Iulus negatively illustrate the *Aeneid*'s missing generation. Their promises in any case are too lavish. Aeneas himself will not rob Latinus of anything—except his daughter. Dido's present tense strikes an ominous note, and her mixing bowl recalls the Bacchic imagery which envelops her (IV. 301). Turnus' crest was Etnaean (VII. 786). The odd mixture of emotion and extravagance in all this, set against its glimmering backdrop, again feels and sounds operatic, and is echoed in Statius' account of Hopleus and Dymas in *Thebaid* X. By Virgil's technique of blending, the episode in fact is conflated from incidents on the *Greek* side in Books IX and X of the *Iliad*: the futile embassy to the tent of Achilles to secure his return by the promise, understandable enough in that context, of abundant gifts; and the successful sally into Rhesus' camp, accompanied by much slaughter, with the eventual capture of his horses, by Odysseus and Diomedes. Among these two stories of success and failure, characteristically Virgil has emphasised failure. And, also characteristically, this failure lies among the young, Nisus, Euryalus, Iulus. Like Nisus (430), Euryalus is *infelix* (390).

The tale easily divides into the familiar, unsatisfying pattern: on the one hand, the sheer brutality of the senseless slaughter, which in the case of these adversaries is a more than civil bloodshed; and on the other the sentimentality of Euryalus' last wishes for his mother, and in general of the relationship between the two comrades, ending with the needless (and therefore unsoldierly) death of them both, and the consequent frustration of the mission to Aeneas which was the whole object of the exercise. Real armies cannot afford such self-indulgence. No effort is made to reconcile these two extremes of love and murder. It is as if two irresponsible children are let loose into killing fields of adult sufferings beyond their comprehension and, as realisation begins to dawn (354), try to make up by their own insubordinate deaths.

The pair are to set off on their fruitless errand (312–13). Iulus gives a sword made in Crete (*Cnosius*, 305). "Loyal" Aletes gives his own helmet. Crete, the land of liars, is a dangerous provenance, and a similar gesture of exchanging helmets will betray Euryalus (373). It had already betrayed Coroebus in the fight to save Troy (II. 392: "friendly fire" motif).

Too soon, Nisus is distracted. While Euryalus acts as lookout, he slays first Rhamnes *augur*, and then Remus with his attendants: a priest and the homonym of Romulus' twin. A simile compares the two murderous

Trojans to a marauding lion (339), conventionally enough,[25] though lion similes will also describe Mezentius (X. 723) and Turnus (XII. 4; cf. IV. 159)—both enemies. Virgil also chooses to anticipate a phrase he will later use of Mezentius (*suadet enim vesana fames*, IX. 340a = X. 724a). *Molle pecus mutumque metu* (341) of their victims does not enhance their killers' heroism. Once again, the pastoral is perverted, "hollow." Those who ought to be shepherds (if these are their kinsfolk) have become predators.

They continue their bloody work. But a band of Rutulians is abroad, and suddenly, as his stolen helmet catches the treacherous half-light, *sublustri noctis in umbra* (373), Euryalus is taken. Nisus' futile prayer to the moon for aid (404 ff.) supplies a discordant key to all this romance (cf. Statius, *Theb.* X. 365; I. 337). The reader is bound to think of Diana / Dido (I. 499)—it was her mixing bowl which was on offer. Perhaps we are to suppose that, under her baneful, "lunatic," influence, the whole Trojan military effort at this point is rendered completely futile, as purposed effort yields to pointless slaughter.

Stiffnesses of rhythm and phraseology here and there in the passage (*stant longis adnixi hastis et scuta tenentes*, 229) alert the reader to possible Ennian borrowings. Eventually there is a definite allusion to Romulus' murder of Remus (422 = *Ann.* 95, Sk.). Volcens, adapting Romulus' language, will kill Euryalus / Remus as representative of Nisus too. These wars are indeed *plus quam civilia*.... Romulus survived, but Virgil makes both these twins die. Observing the threat, Nisus betrays himself, but in vain. Euryalus in death is like a wild flower shorn by the plough, or poppies weighed down by rain. Nisus succeeds in killing his killer, in the moment of his own death. The most famous example of this was Polynices' last-minute killing of the apparently triumphant Eteocles (Eur., *Phoen.* 1419–25: cf. Statius, *Theb.* XI. 565–73). The visitor to the museums of Etruria will recall how frequent this motif is on Etruscan sarcophagi, even on those of women.

The flower similes here anticipate that used for Pallas (XI. 68–71). Their principal Homeric parallel is with Gorgythion, slain by Teucer (*Il.* VIII. 306 ff.). Gorgythion was a son of Priam,[26] and Euryalus' mother was Priam's descendant (IX. 284). Apollonius (*Arg.* III. 1399) adapts the imagery for the earth-born warriors, half-formed creatures fighting among themselves and rightly slain by Jason at the end of his ordeal. But a more recent association in Roman poetry of such similes was with lyric. In his

---

[25] There may be a reminiscence of Heracles: Theocritus 13. 61–63. Cf. below, p. 233 (Turnus).

[26] See also Euphorbus, *Il.* XVII. 53–60.

sapphic poem 11 (22–24), Catullus had spoken of his love for his *puella* as like a flower at the edge of a meadow, touched by the passing plough. In his poem 62 (39 ff.), his chorus of maidens had sung of virginity, whose loss is like the plucking of a flower. Both images may be traceable to a fragment of Sappho (105c, Lobel–Page), describing the hyacinth trampled underfoot on the mountainside by shepherds. Her metre and dialect in these two brief lines are epic.

Evidently what interests Virgil in Euryalus' death is the loss of virginity. As in Maecenas' Esquiline garden, Thanatos and Eros meet.[27] From some strange arsenogenesis the Roman race is to spring forth, and this is why, as was remarked, the poet echoed from Ennius in this self-sacrificial scene the archaic brutality of Romulus' killing of Remus. That would be consonant with Augustan practice,[28] if not propaganda, but what a twist has been given to the old Ennian story!

Virgil interrupts his tale to promise immortality to Nisus and Euryalus, "so long as the house of Aeneas shall dwell by the steadfast rock of the Capitol" (IX. 445–49). Horace's *dum Capitolium / scandet cum tacita virgine pontifex* (*Odes* III. 30. 8–9) seems to suggest that this allusion to the unbudging Capitol was an official theme, since it was the Capitol that Cleopatra had threatened (*Odes* I. 37. 6; Prop. III. 11. 45; Ovid, *Met.* XV. 828). Yet *immobile* is oxymoronic when juxtaposed with the young, and perhaps reminds us of Dido's marble paralysis in the centre of Book VI (Niobe theme)—or Cleomenes' commemorative statue of Marcellus. In any case, it is bombast. Nisus and Euryalus turn out to be "superfluous men." Aeneas finds out by other means what they should have told him directly, and neither Trojan resistance nor Rutulian aggression is affected by their murderous escapade.

The Rutulians decapitate their victims and display their heads on pikes (465–67). This gruesome episode, worthy of Thracian or Sullan manners,[29] is introduced by an indication of time last met in Book IV (584–85), as Dido watched Aeneas sail away. Perhaps this is a supreme touch of her maleficence.

The crowning sentimentality comes when Euryalus' old mother is told of

[27] A statue from there in the Museo dei Conservatori is identified as either.

[28] As Caesarion, for example, had experienced it: above, p. 11; cf. later Agrippa Postumus. *Dede neci* (*Geo.* IV. 90) gives pause for thought. For Augustan propaganda, see the intaglio now in Florence mentioned below (pp. 273–74).

[29] Marazov, ed., *Ancient Gold. The Wealth of the Thracians*, catalogue nos. 96, 97, 98. Such beheading was also Celtic: Davies, *The Isles*, p. 76. For Sulla, above, p. 18. West notes Semitic parallels: *East Face of Helicon*, p. 388.

her son's death. Her 17-line outburst contains six questions.[30] She is (of course) *infelix* (477). Her speech at one point incongruously echoes that of Catullus' abandoned Ariadne (*alitibusque*, 486; cf. Cat. 64. 152). Aeneas will himself pick up this dative in robbing another *mater* of her son (X. 559). There are sallies which remind one of Lucan's black humour (*hoc sum terraque marique secuta*, said as she contemplates the mangled corpse, 490–92). *Abrumpere* at the end recalls Dido.[31]

Again our effort to grasp the sentiment of all this is frustrated without more Greek epic, more indeed of the *Aethiopis*. In *Olympian* 2, Pindar notes that what unites so many of the great heroes is their shared fate (79–83):

'Αχιλλέα τ' ἔνεικ', ἐπεὶ Ζηνὸς ἦτορ
λιταῖς ἔπεισε, μάτηρ·
ὃς Ἕκτορα σφᾶλε, Τροίας
ἄμαχον ἀστραβῆ κίονα, Κύκνον τε θανάτῳ πόρεν,
'Αοῦς τε παῖδ' Αἰθίοπα.

And there Achilles was carried, after the heart of Zeus yielded to her persuasive prayers, by his mother—the hero who brought down Hector, invincible, steadfast pillar of Troy, and gave Cycnus over to death, and Dawn's son, the Ethiopian [Memnon].

The scene with Thetis / Achilles at vv. 79–80 of this passage, not from the *Iliad*, is modelled by Pindar after Eos / Memnon, part of his use, eagerly exploited by Virgil later, of the device of carnival twinning. It was in the *Aethiopis* that Eos gathered up the body of Memnon and then obtained for him immortality from Zeus.[32] It will be obvious how prominent in the Greek poet's structured verse is the allusion to the mother. Here is another convergence of the epic imagination with lyric, a feature of the musical dimension which has always been noticed in Virgil. It is indeed characteristic of the Roman genius as a whole, and at times powerfully expressed already in both Plautus and Ennius.

[30] See above, p. 126, on this device.

[31] *Abrumpere vitam*, IX. 497 ~ *abrumpere lucem*, IV. 631; cf. *abrumpere vitam* as Evander says goodbye to Pallas, VIII. 579.

[32] Originally Thetis hardly needed to beg in this way for dead Achilles. The gods admired his valour so much that they rewarded him with the Isles of the Blest (Plato, *Symp.* 180b). Later taste, conflating *Il.* I. 495 ff. with the scene from Arctinus, paralleled the two heroes and their mothers, Thetis and Eos: e.g. Aeschylus, *Psychostasia* (fr. 205, Mette); cf. Ovid, *Amores* III. 9. 1. The iconography became well established in art: K. Schefold, *Götter- und Heldensagen der Griechen in der spätarchaischen Kunst*, pp. 241 ff. See the inner medallion of the cup by Douris from about 490, reproduced by Arias and Hirmer, *History of Greek Vase Painting*, plate 145, with the commentary on p. 341. For the equivalence Aeneas / Memnon, aided by Lausus / Antilochus, above, pp. 9, 196.

Inferno

The first half of the poem had culminated with a vatic vision of the last things. In the later books, unlike Dante's *Comedy*, Virgil's tragedy proceeds backwards, from whatever *Paradiso* its author drew to his *Inferno*; and the manner of his subtle declension hardens into something less supple, more angular, mirrored in awkward language, in keeping with a marked increase in the sense of hell and its perditions. Juno in Book VII repeats and worsens Juno in Book I. Allecto worsens Aeolus. This uncreative twinning, aided by the constant allusions to Homer and other poets, in the second half of the poem persists as far as the final duel (XII. 845 ff.), where Achilles and Hector (or is it Hector and Achilles?) needlessly re-enact their deadly struggle before the offended sensibilities of a morally more sophisticated age. *Genitor* is especially cruel and even cynical at the opening of this scene (843).

In Book X, Aeneas kills Lausus, who has saved his father's life, in a spasm of wild anger (*saevae ... irae*, 813). Earlier, *furit* has been used of him (802). We have a rehearsal for the killing of Turnus at the end (*saevi*, XII. 945, *Furiis ... ira*, 946). He regards Lausus' *pietas* (X. 812) as an error. Too late, he is reminded of his own *pietas* (824). The scene is strongly reminiscent of Greek art.[33] There can be no question here of anything but tragedy (Dante, *Inf.* 20. 113). But the appropriate reaction to its ἁμαρτία is ἔλεος καὶ φόβος.

When the poem is heard as a whole, there is a steadily more audible rattle in these later books of sterility and death. It becomes a charnel-house of the imagination: *caedis acervos*, X. 245; *ingentis Rutulorum linquis acervos*, X. 509; *tot stragis acervos*, XI. 384. This is iteration gone wild (cf. I. 100–01). Slaughter is made a spectator sport.[34] This was already noted in Books X and XI, where at times the contending protagonists seem to be sent onto the stage to kill or die as if by some divine *lanista* (an Etruscan word) setting on his pairs from the sidelines. Often our sense of disillusion is enhanced by a literary dissociation and even disjuncture of sensibility, in which fantasy sits uneasily with bloody reality. This is particularly marked in the case of Nisus and Euryalus, as we just saw, but the effect also works by omission. Would Aeneas have accepted ransom for Turnus' corpse? If he had, would he have been behaving any better than

---

[33] *Sanguine turpantem comptos de more capillos* (832); the motif is familiar from depictions of Hector, but compare also Ajax carrying the body of Achilles on the outer side of the handle of the François vase in Florence.

[34] *Spectabit*, X. 245; *cuperem ipse parens spectator adesset*, X. 443; *hic Venus, hinc contra spectat Saturnia Iuno*, X. 760; *observans oculis*, XI. 726.

Turnus with Pallas (X. 492)? Suddenly, the reading of the *Aeneid* as *comédie noire* by Boccaccio, Chaucer and Ariosto, as sentimental tragedy by Tasso, no longer seems the bizarre outcome of some biased or naive historical period, but quite firmly founded on close attention to the master's text. Three of these at least invite the relieving grace of laughter. Virgil leaves off with irony.

Pallas and Turnus

Pallas, matched (but not quite) with the noble Lausus (X. 433-34), has already demanded attention.[35] The really extraordinary feature noted is that the entire episode in Book VIII between Aeneas and Pallas' father Evander is filled with reminiscences of Dido. It was she who had promised help (I. 571), and this is echoed by Evander (VIII. 171). Pallas leaves for war, and his fainting father guesses what will happen (VIII. 584 ~ IV. 391). When Pallas' body is brought back home, old Acoetes accompanies the bier. He behaves exactly like dead Dido's sister Anna (XI. 86 ~ IV. 673). There were other similarities.

One of the grounds for Aeneas' appeal to Evander is kinship. He is sure that the ancestor of Troy, Dardanus, was the son of Atlas' daughter, Electra. And the Arcadians for their part are the children of Mercury the son of Maia, and she in her turn was Atlas' daughter (VIII. 134-41). Arcadians and Trojans are (almost!) cousins. But Titanic Atlas has already occurred. Ominously, he is lodged in Africa. Arriving in Book IV to warn Aeneas that he must leave Carthage, Mercury, *Maia genitus* (I. 297), first halts on Mount Atlas, anthropomorphised to exhibit all the oozing salivations of old age (IV. 246-51), proof of the irresistibility of the divine will, avatar of Dante's frozen Satan (*Inf.* 34. 53). At Dido's banquet, Iopas, pupil of great Atlas, was Dido's court bard (I. 740). The queen could not know that his bookish Aratean lore had in fact already been exciting reality for the Trojan voyagers as they were about to glimpse Italy (I. 744 = III. 516), and that therefore any hopes she had of detaining them in Carthage were already doomed. Does all this talk of common ancestry portend well? At the site of Rome, Hercules had fought with Cacus. Aeneas will become Aegaeon (X. 565). Are Anchises and Dido, shadowy rivals behind and beyond the actors on stage, impatient for another conflict between men and monsters? Is old Evander their unwitting mouthpiece and medium?

At the beginning and end of his part Pallas is in fact linked with Hercules (VIII. 102 ff.; X. 460 ff.), whose heroic ambivalences have also

---

[35] Above, pp. 163 ff.

been noted. His Iliadic analogues are Sarpedon and then Patroclus, though, if Patroclus, a mature warrior, incurs guilt in going beyond Achilles' injunction not to attack the Trojans, it is hardly possible to think of Pallas as guilty of anything except youthful bravado. Through Patroclus, his character blends into that of Camilla.

Pallas and Camilla also cross over into Turnus. Pallas tackles the Latin Achilles (VI. 89), even though he has unequal powers (*viribus imparibus*, X. 459). He is like Troilus, *infelix puer atque impar congressus Achilli* (I. 475), for Callimachus and Cicero a sad icon of youthful tears (fr. 491, Pf.; *Tusc. Disp.* I. §93). But is not Turnus himself *impar* (XII. 216), when he challenges, *non viribus aequis* (218), the Trojan Achilles (XI. 438)? *Fugiens amissis ... armis*, said of Troilus (I. 474), is exactly what happens to him (XII. 742-43). Does that diminish his responsibility? In the debate over the morality of his death, Virgil's ever-turning, "versatile" *sceneggiamento* (cf. *Geo.* III. 24) prevents us from fixing labels.

Turnus is blamed for picking on a mere boy (*Pallantis pueri*, XII. 943), though he does that by the divine ordinance which withholds Lausus and Pallas from what would be a more even duel (X. 436-40). It is true that ancient morality does not excuse human transgression on the simple ground that it was commanded by a god. But is Turnus an unusual case? If he is the Latin Achilles, Homer had already made his Achilles draw a parallel between his short life and that of Heracles (*Il.* XVIII. 117). Heracles went mad. Turnus' fate is to be possessed and feminised by an evil which does more than enlarge temptations already at work within. His *caput quassans* (XII. 894) is that of Juno (*quassans caput*, VII. 292). He ingests the hell let loose against him (*intus*, VII. 464) by Allecto. But at the end he is allowed to pronounce his own noble elogium, showing himself fully aware of his doom. *Sancta* here (cf. *sanctissima* of Evander's departed wife, XI. 158) is particularly appropriate to the dead, the "Holy Souls in Purgatory" of Catholic piety[36] (XII. 646-49):

> 'vos o mihi, Manes,
> este boni, quoniam superis aversa voluntas.
> sancta ad vos anima atque istius inscia culpae
> descendam magnorum haud umquam indignus avorum.'

'Ye spirits of the world below, be gracious to me, since the goodwill of the gods above is turned away. A holy spirit will I come down to you, innocent of that guilt of theirs, never unworthy of my mighty ancestors.'

---

[36] Even so, in *anima* the feminine lingers. The apotheosis of this is found in the use by St. John of the Cross of the feminine gender of *alma* to enable his vision of Christ as the Divine Lover in pursuit of His beloved, *Amada en el Amado transformada* (*Canción de la subida del Monte Carmelo*, after 1563).

Culpae has occurred in this form only in *Aeneid* IV (19, dative). Here, on Turnus' lips, the genitive describes Dido's and Aeneas' sexual guilt, one betraying a husband (IV. 19; 172), the other, a second Paris (cf. *culpatusve Paris*, II. 602), stealing a wife.[37] To compound his offence, as *Laomedontius heros*, Aeneas is in no position to boast of his ancestors! To the charge of such moral lubricity, earlier found on Iarbas' lips (*et nunc ille Paris*, IV. 215), Turnus pleads innocent. Would not Augustus himself have approved? Turnus' encounter with the Fury (XII. 865-66) and defiantly heroic *non me tua fervida terrent / dicta, ferox. di me terrent et Iuppiter hostis* (894-95) are paradoxically part of his final rehabilitation in his listeners' minds. Can anyone overcome such adversaries?

Earlier, when he was still able to speak for himself, he refused to be provoked by Calybe / Allecto.[38] She was told to busy herself with her temple duties. Appearing in all her hellish power, she hurled a burning brand and planted smouldering torches deep in the young hero's breast. Panic-stricken, drenched with sweat, Turnus is beside himself (VII. 458–62). That does not excuse him in ancient theology, but moderns should not use that ancient, tragic point of view to justify easy verdicts on his deserts.

Turnus / Hercules

Behind Turnus looms the mad Heracles of Euripides' play. There, Iris is sent by jealous Hera to command Lyssa to add a sinister climax to the hero's labours for Eurystheus—the murder of his own children. The poet dwells twice on his altered appearance, the first time in excited trochees. Heracles becomes a sort of Minotaur (867–70, Wilamowitz):

> ἦν ἰδοὺ καὶ δὴ τινάσσει κρᾶτα βαλβίδων ἄπο
> καὶ διαστρόφους ἑλίσσει σῖγα γοργωποὺς κόρας,
> ἀμπνοὰς δ' οὐ σωφρονίζει, ταῦρος ὣς ἐς ἐμβολήν,
> δεινὰ μυκᾶται δὲ Κῆρας ἀνακαλῶν τὰς Ταρτάρου.

> Look, he shakes his head from its very socket, and silently rolls his savage eyes. His breathing labours, out of control, like that of a bull about to charge. Horribly he bellows, summoning the Fates of hell.

867. *caput quassans*, XII. 894. Cf. *Od.* V. 285, κινήσας δὲ κάρη (Poseidon).
868. *huc illuc volvens oculos*, IV. 363; *huc ora ferebat et illuc*, VIII. 229; *oculis micat acribus ignis*, XII. 102.

---

[37] *Culpare* is found uniquely in *Aeneid* II. It occurs in the *Metamorphoses* four times. The *Aeneid* has four instances of *culpa*, the *Metamorphoses* 18. For the elegists see Pichon, *s.vv.*, pp. 118-19. *Culpare* is relatively rare there, but cf. Prop. II. 1. 49. Turnus' degree of moral revulsion is evident.

[38] Above, p. 175.

869. *Martis anheli*, XII. 790; *taurus*, XII. 103.
870. *fremit*, VII. 460; IX. 60.

Later, there is a grotesque: bloodshot eyes, a foaming mouth and maniacal laughter (931–35):

οὐκέθ' αὐτὸς ἦν,
ἀλλ' ἐν στροφαῖσιν ὀμμάτων ἐφθαρμένος,
ῥίζας τ' ἐν ὄσσοις αἱματῶπας ἐκβαλὼν
ἀφρὸν κατέσταζ' εὔτριχος γενειάδος.
ἔλεξε δ' ἅμα γέλωτι παραπεπληγμένῳ ...

He was no longer the same, but corrupted, his eyes rolling and sprouting a bloodshot network, foam dripping from his full beard, twisted laughter accompanying his words.

935. *inridens*, VII. 435.

This is the situation parallel with jealous Juno's sending of Allecto against Turnus.[39] Virgil, once again in "declining" mode, is vaguer than Euripides about physical detail, and more interested in the emotions. In his extraordinary analysis of an abnormal psychological state, *pavor* catches the attention. The Fury's victim is "scared," intimidated, overwhelmed by the superior power of evil, no longer a whole person responsible for his own decisions. His sweat, shared with Sophocles' tormented Heracles (*Trach.* 767), is the symptom of his overwrought condition.[40] It is in this context that some words are heard or iterated which will become characteristic of the poem's later unfolding: *arma, amens, saevit, scelerata, insania*.

Scelerata is immediately interesting. In the *Aeneid, scelerare* itself is used in its infinitival form only once, of Aeneas' unwitting violation of the cornel clump which has grown from Polydorus' corpse (III. 42). The past participle, repeated in the same context (*scelerata ... terra*, III. 60), is used to mean "displeasing to the gods," "sinful." In the undifferentiated primitive, these "objective" and "subjective" senses are not always rigidly distinguished as already the name "Via Scelerata" attests. Their range may indeed be extended. Sibyl speaks of the "sinful threshold" (VI. 563) in Hades beyond

---

[39] See p. 96 for an allusion to Aeschylus' *Xantriae* (Heinze). A red-figure calyx-crater made in Apulia c. 350–340 B.C., the eponymous vase of the Lycurgus Painter (BM GR 1849.6.23.48 [Vase F217]), shows the Thracian king driven mad by Dionysus. He has killed his son Dryas and now proceeds to attack his wife. Above hovers Lyssa, while an old retainer at the bottom, "a stock figure in drama," suggests that the scene was perhaps inspired by Aeschylus' *Edonoi*. Here the hinted themes of Dido / Amata / Bacchus, and of childlessness, again attract attention.

[40] *Et coepit p a v e r e et taedere*, Mark 14:33. Cf. *factus in agonia prolixius orabat. Et factus est s u d o r eius sicut guttae sanguinis decurrentis in terram*, Luke 22:43–44.

which the guilty are imprisoned and tortured. The threshold had committed no sin. This catachresis would explain, even for those unwilling to accept its authenticity, *sceleratas ... poenas* in the Helen episode (II. 576), "criminal penalties." And sometimes, in a larger perspective, these verdicts simply show incomprehension of the divine will. The Trojans explain Laocoon's death by his "sinful" hurling of his spear at the Horse (II. 231). Turnus, aware enough as we saw of their *culpa*, condemns the Trojans as a *gens scelerata* for stealing his bride (IX. 137).

When it recurs at the end of the poem (*poenam scelerato ex sanguine sumit*, XII. 949), Aeneas, as is the way with conquerors, is deflecting the blame onto the conquered. Can we simply decide the matter without reflection in his favour? Commentators are inclined to take the word as describing Turnus' subjective guilt. He has slain Pallas, and he must now pay the price. But can it mean that already at VII. 461? There, it seems to be a general condemnation of any kind of blood lust. And, at the end, if Turnus has been consumed and subsumed by devouring, demonic force, metamorphosed into a Cacus, can we merely treat his death as a matter of epic necessity? The pathos of his character derives from the tension between his irresistible inspiration and his youthful unsuitability for the hellish role he is summoned by it to play. He is a confidant of queen Amata and seems not unacceptable to Lavinia. If he deserves to die like Penelope's suitors, must it not first be shown that he has behaved like Penelope's suitors? Even to say that is to put oneself in Drances' company. Not even his most ardent critic will argue that he deserves to die like Hector. Does he die like Dido / Heracles? But that is Μοῖρα, Ἀνάγκη, tragedy!

The Belt

The proximate cause of Turnus' death is Pallas' belt, taken as spoil.[41] It

---

[41] See W. R. Barnes, "Seeing Things: Ancient Commentary on the *Iliad* at the end of the *Aeneid*" in *Amor: Roma* (Cambridge 1999), pp. 60–70. — On the importance of the belt to the Indo–European warrior, cf. *Ancient Gold*, p. 62. G. Widengren, "Le symbolisme de la ceinture" (*Archaeologica Iranica = Iranica Antiqua* 8 [Leiden 1968], 133–55), notes it as a sign of quasi-feudal loyalty. He cites (143) Xenophon (*Anabasis* I. 6. 10) where, on Cyrus' order, the disloyal Orontas is seized by the belt in token of the withdrawal of his lord's protection and sentence of death, just as when the rebellious Jean de Baliol surrendered to Edward I in 1296, "his tabard, hood, and girdle were stripped from him in the ceremony reserved for treasonable knights" (Davies, *The Isles*, p. 374). In seizing Pallas' belt, Turnus, commander of the Italian forces, affirms a similar sentence, since Arcadian Pallas, wearing an image that exalts Argive Danaus, in alliance with foreign intruders, is a traitor to the Italian cause. But, in putting it on himself, he assumes the same fate. In any case, Cyrus had held a trial by jury

already wound its way even into our chapter on Dido (above, p. 165). Its evil impress has already been noted.

Its Homeric parallel is not so much the armour of Achilles taken by Hector from Patroclus as the golden belt of Heracles, glimpsed by Odysseus in Hades (*Od.* XI. 609–14):

> σμερδαλέος δέ οἱ ἀμφὶ περὶ στήθεσσιν ἀορτὴρ
> χρύσεος ἦν τελαμών, ἵνα θέσκελα ἔργα τέτυκτο,
> ἄρκτοι τ' ἀγρότεροί τε σύες χαροποί τε λέοντες,
> ὑσμῖναί τε μάχαι τε φόνοι τ' ἀνδροκτασίαι τε.
> μὴ τεχνησάμενος μηδ' ἄλλο τι τεχνήσαιτο,
> ὃς κεῖνον τελαμῶνα ἑῇ ἐγκάτθετο τέχνῃ.

A fearful band circled his breast, a golden belt, whereon were wrought deeds to amaze: bears, and wild boars and glaring lions, and affrays and battles and murders and slayings of men. May he who crafted it never craft again—the one who added to his store of cunning that belt.

Virgil's adaptation chooses a theme of murderous wives.

Its tragic parallel is the shirt of Nessus. The sword and the pyre of suicidal Dido made her already Deianeira / Heracles, and there is some further indirect reminiscence of her here. In Sicily, Aeneas had offered as second prize in the footrace—in which we first hear of Nisus and Euryalus (V. 294) —an "Amazonian" quiver and golden belt (V. 311–13):

> 'alter Amazoniam pharetram plenamque sagittis
> Threiciis, lato quam circum amplectitur auro
> balteus ...'

> 'The second [shall take] a quiver used by the Amazons, full of Thracian arrows, surrounded by a broad belt of gold.'

This prize replaces the "Sidonian" silver bowl which Achilles had offered to his contestants in the footrace (*Il.* XXIII. 743), reserved by Virgil for a pathetic reminder, at the start of their fatal adventure (IX. 266), of our first acquaintance with Nisus and Euryalus.

Amazoniam here is not casual. As Dido makes her first entrance, Aeneas has just been gazing at Amazonian Penthesilea (I. 490–91). Later, Camilla is actually compared to Penthesilea, a passage also referring to Hippolyte (XI. 661–62), whose loss of her belt to Heracles was visible in Augustan Rome on the pediment of the Temple of Apollo Sosianus.[42] That was a kind of rape. Evidently, there was the same element of latent sexuality in the encounter of Pallas with Turnus as that already noted in the deaths of

---

first, just as King Edward held a formal ceremony: cf. *iudiciis legitimis ultus*, Augustus, *R.G.* 2. There spoke the Roman. This is what both Turnus and Aeneas failed to learn.

[42] Below, p. 329.

some of Virgil's other young men (cf. *intactum*, X. 504; *intactam* of Dido, I. 345). As with Penthesilea and Achilles, as with the Danaids and their bridegrooms, Eros and Thanatos keep easy company.

Hercules' Odyssean belt, if its pictorial lessons were applied to the *Aeneid*, might look ahead to Circe's transformations of the warriors of Troy and Italy. If it furnishes a model for Pallas' belt, this would again hint that, in taking it up, Turnus makes himself into a mad Hercules. In Apollonius, when Hylas is lost, Polyphemus searches for him like some frustrated beast of prey (I. 1243–47). Theocritus had adapted the simile to Heracles himself (13. 61 ff.). Virgil in turn elaborated these passages to describe Turnus' frustrated attack on the Trojan encampment (IX. 59). But Aeneas too will become this Hercules, and hence the parallels remarked above between the adventure with Cacus in Book VIII and the end of Book XII.

Yet Heracles was presented by Euripides as a hero who in the end repents, and is nobly saved by his friend and comrade Theseus. The comradeship of the pair is still visible on the temple pediment just mentioned. Neither Aeneas nor Turnus can find such help. The *Aeneid*'s Theseus is himself in hell (VI. 618). What Virgil has done with Hercules is to take a powerful symbol of imperial propaganda, much manipulated, for example, by Horace, one which elsewhere he is quite willing to use in its official register (VI. 801–03; VIII. 285–305), and show us its reverse. Hercules' madness twins its heirs with other selves. More visible in Turnus, it lurks behind the many masks assumed by Aeneas. Such *dédoublement* always attracts the poet's imagination. Now it makes the duel with which the *Aeneid* concludes into a fratricidal strife of identities, "one dead, the other powerless to be born." The dead identity is that of the hopeless dream on the part of the Italian tribes, as recent as the Social War, of an autonomous Italy, independent of Rome. The other, for Aeneas powerless to be born, is that of Augustan Rome. But that ideal only Augustus can realise (cf. VIII. 678). *Tuque prior, tu parce....* In Aeneas' case, these words of his father fell on deaf ears. Augustus heard them: *victorque omnibus veniam petentibus civibus peperci* (R. G. 3).

The Death of Turnus

In Book XII, whatever Turnus' excesses earlier in the poem, he is consistently presented with sympathy.[43] His language contributes to this effect. It acts as a touchstone by which the changes in his character may be assessed.

---

[43] The reader is referred to the fuller analysis in *Augustus and the New Poetry*, pp. 239–59, and to Knauer's parallels.

Virgil's women, as earlier noted, asked lots of questions. In the debate between Venus and Juno at Jupiter's council at the start of Book X, for example (18–95), Venus' seven questions provoke Juno's 14. Yet in Drances' already mentioned speech at the council of war in Latinus' palace (XI. 343–75), only one question is found (361), though so tense a confrontation between old enemies might have been expected to generate a similar excitement. Turnus' answer however, twice as long (378–444; 67 lines to Drances' 33), though, on the surface, studiedly rational, even restrained, in the event contains eight questions. The poet notes at its start its heated undertone: *talibus exarsit dictis violentia Turni* (376; cf. *violentia*, 354; XII. 9 and 45, the only instances in the poem, all of Turnus). The questions betray its presence.[44]

The hero, whose volcanic (*Aetnaeos*, VII. 786) emotions are so clearly signalled in this way, has been carefully constructed. In Book X, when he is reduced to the depths of soldierly humiliation by the trick Juno plays on him with her empty image of Aeneas, he upbraids Jupiter (668–79). His prayer here displays nine questions in its twelve lines. A telling phrase both looks back to Dido and ahead to his sister's final despairs: *o quae satis ima dehiscat / terra mihi* (X. 675–76; cf. XII. 883–84, Juturna, and IV. 24, Dido). One of his problems is evidently to be feminised (Hercules / Omphale motif: cf. IV. 261–64), and his already cited description of himself in Book XII as *sancta ... anima* (648) was remarked as the culmination of this. These eighteen lines of his elogium (XII. 632–49) contain seven questions.

Yet he ends his last words to his sister heroically, with an allusion to his mighty ancestors; and part of his heroism is that, in Book XII, as he assumes his fate, and realises that women have been making a fool out of him, he uses questions less and less. After the instances just noted, though more than 300 lines remain, there are no more. The only previous questions in that entire book have been at 620–21 (informatory). The grand acceptance of death which comes at 646–49 is a prayer and defiant statement. Turnus hurls no questions at Aeneas.

Much of the melancholy portrait the poet paints of Turnus in Book XII has to do with the hope—or lack of hope—of posterity: what the securing of Troy's children will cost someone else. Internal reference provides a context. At the very beginning, he is a wounded lion, whose hunter is a contemptible *latro* (7). *Poenorum qualis in arvis* (4): the scene is set in Africa. The listener senses the presence of Dido and her hunt (*Poenorum*, IV. 134, only in these

---

[44] *Exardesco* here is also telling: cf. VII. 445 (Allecto); VIII. 219 (Hercules in combat with Cacus).

two places).⁴⁵ More directly, the comparison takes us back to IX. 761–62, at that stage of the battle between the Latins and Trojans where only the *furor* shown by Turnus robbed his side of victory. Turnus in retreat there was compared to a lion balked by huntsmen (Ajax!). At X. 454, when he was about to slay Pallas, he was also compared to a lion—and of course it was by taking spoils from Pallas that he eventually ensured his own death (X. 501).

External reference points above all to a magnificent simile in *Iliad* XX. Only here do we find the lion wounded, and the resolve to kill or die come what may. Only here is Aineias the opponent (XX. 164–73):

> Πηλεΐδης δ' ἑτέρωθεν ἐναντίον ὦρτο λέων ὥς,
> σίντης, ὅν τε καὶ ἄνδρες ἀποκτάμεναι μεμάασιν
> ἀγρόμενοι, πᾶς δῆμος· ὁ δὲ πρῶτον μὲν ἀτίζων
> ἔρχεται, ἀλλ' ὅτε κέν τις ἀρηϊθόων αἰζηῶν
> δουρὶ βάλῃ, ἑάλη τε χανών, περί τ' ἀφρὸς ὀδόντας
> γίγνεται, ἐν δέ τέ οἱ κραδίῃ στένει ἄλκιμον ἦτορ,
> οὐρῇ δὲ πλευράς τε καὶ ἰσχία ἀμφοτέρωθεν
> μαστίεται, ἓ δ' αὐτὸν ἐποτρύνει μαχέσασθαι,
> γλαυκιόων δ' ἰθὺς φέρεται μένει, ἤν τινα πέφνῃ
> ἀνδρῶν, ἢ αὐτὸς φθίεται πρώτῳ ἐν ὁμίλῳ.

On the other side the son of Peleus rose up like a lion, a ravager, whom the warriors longed to slay, with the whole tribe hunting: at first he stalks in contempt of them, but when one of the stalwart youths strikes him with his spear, he gathers himself, maw open, while foam collects around his teeth, his brave heart growling in his breast. With his tail he lashes his sides and flanks both right and left, urging himself to the fight. Then, glowering in his might, he charges straight forward against the warriors, to see whom he may kill, or himself die in the front of the battle.

The foaming mouth (168) is that of Euripides' Heracles (*Heracles* 934).

And the continuance (174–75):

> ὣς 'Αχιλῆ' ὄτρυνε μένος καὶ θυμὸς ἀγήνωρ
> ἀντίον ἐλθέμεναι μεγαλήτορος Αἰνείαο.

So his might and noble spirit urged on Achilles to face great-hearted Aineias.

Alius Latio iam partus Achilles (VI. 89). It seems clear that the Sibyl's words have come true enough.

For Virgil, this was one of the most telling moments in the entire *Iliad*. Aineias, confronted by lion-hearted Achilles, has time to rehearse his lineage, as it were to plead a case. He is not the direct descendant of lying Laomedon, and it is here that he will be proclaimed by Poseidon ἀναίτιος, guiltless of whatever offence Priam and his line have committed, and

---

⁴⁵ Compare also *bina manu lato crispans hastilia ferro*, I. 313 and XII. 165 (only here): Aeneas meeting Venus on the outskirts of Carthage and about to hear Dido's story / Turnus arriving for the abortive celebration of peace.

guaranteed the right to be one day king over the Trojans (XX. 307–08).[46]

Yet how oddly the Roman has developed his borrowing. Once again, there is a strange counterpoint. In the *Iliad*, Aineias' clash with this adversary might have proved risky, but Poseidon intervenes to cast a mist over Achilles' eyes. He removes from Aineias' shield the spear which Achilles has thrown, and spirits him away to the outskirts of the field (cf. *Aeneid* X. 636 ff.). Achilles recognises the facts (XX. 347–48):

ἦ ῥα καὶ Αἰνείας φίλος ἀθανάτοισι θεοῖσιν
ἦεν· ἀτάρ μιν ἔφην μὰψ αὔτως εὐχετάασθαι.

Truly Aineias is dear to the immortal gods. I had thought that his boasting was all to no purpose.

In Virgil's adaptation, who is who? Turnus' Homeric counterpart is the greater warrior, Achilles, but he will in the end be the lesser warrior, like Aineias. There will however be no intervening deity to spirit him to safety, and how paltry in that direction the later meanderings of charioteering Juturna! Yet Turnus / Achilles is not to lose this battle because he is in some way αἴτιος, *causa mali tanti*—a phrase that is not applied to him —but because both he and Aeneas are pawns in a divine plan. The decision between the two has little to do with any immediate question of juridical guilt or innocence. How wrong and false it is to import such notions into this tragic (and vatic) world. In real life (since the *Aeneid* is also about history), how little the *Rechtsfrage* has to do with the quarrel between Caesar and Pompey, and its Augustan resolution!

The ambiguities of some of Turnus' subsequent statements maintain an awareness of his imminent death and of his brave readiness. Like Dido, he speaks of himself in the third person (*neque enim Turno mora libera mortis*, XII. 74), a sign perhaps of a disintegrating or regressing personality.[47] He wins sympathy from Amata and Juturna, and from his own followers. His sister above all is able to draw our attention to the cruelty of the gods of which she herself has already borne the brunt.

Like Aeneas, Turnus is also Paris and Hector (cf. especially *Aen*. XI. 493–97 ~ *Il*. VI. 506; XV. 263). At the end (*Aen*. XII. 896), he looks around for a great stone to hurl at his adversary. Several Iliadic passages are blended. In one (XII. 445 ff.), Hector leads an attack on the Greek wall, smashing open its gate with a massive stone. It is one of his supreme moments of glory, and an occasion which had a parallel in Turnus' own victorious career (*Aen*. IX. 756 ff.), now ironically recalled when he is about

---

[46] See below, p. 244.

[47] "Je est un autre," A. Rimbaud, *Lettre du Voyant* (Charlesville 1871).

to suffer the last extreme of defeat. A second Jason (cf. *Arg*. III. 1367), Hector carries the stone as easily as a shepherd carries a fleece (*Il*. XII. 451).[48]

In a later passage (*Il*. XXI. 403 ff.), Athene, who is evidently enjoying herself (γέλασσε, 408), strikes down Ares with a great stone. But Turnus has earlier been compared to Mars (XII. 332). Now the Roman Ares is just such a figure of ridicule and pathos as his Greek counterpart.

But there is also a reminiscence of an earlier contest. In *Iliad* V, Diomedes and Aineias confront each other. Diomedes seizes a stone, and hurls it at Aineias. Aineias is hit (305-10):

> τῷ βάλεν Αἰνείαο κατ' ἰσχίον, ἔνθα τε μηρὸς
> ἰσχίῳ ἐνστρέφεται, κοτύλην δέ τέ μιν καλέουσι·
> θλάσσε δέ οἱ κοτύλην, πρὸς δ' ἄμφω ῥῆξε τένοντε·
> ὦσε δ' ἀπὸ ῥινὸν τρηχὺς λίθος· αὐτὰρ ὅ γ' ἥρως
> ἔστη γνὺξ ἐριπὼν καὶ ἐρείσατο χειρὶ παχείῃ
> γαίης· ἀμφὶ δὲ ὄσσε κελαινὴ νὺξ ἐκάλυψε.

With it he struck Aineias in the hip where the thigh turns in the joint, the cup as it is called. He smashed that cup, and broke both tendons as well. The rough stone tore away the skin, and the hero came to a stop, falling on his knees, and with his mighty hand steadied himself on the ground. Dark night began to shroud both his eyes.

This is a dangerous moment, but there is a rescuer on hand (311-16):

> καί νύ κεν ἔνθ' ἀπόλοιτο ἄναξ ἀνδρῶν Αἰνείας,
> εἰ μὴ ἄρ' ὀξὺ νόησε Διὸς θυγάτηρ Ἀφροδίτη,
> μήτηρ, ἥ μιν ὑπ' Ἀγχίσῃ τέκε βουκολέοντι·
> ἀμφὶ δ' ἑὸν φίλον υἱὸν ἐχεύατο πήχεε λευκώ,
> πρόσθε δέ οἱ πέπλοιο φαεινοῦ πτύγμ' ἐκάλυψεν,
> ἕρκος ἔμεν βελέων ...

And now Aineias, lord of men, would have perished on the spot, had Aphrodite, Zeus' daughter, not been quick to keep open a mother's sharp eye—she who had borne him to shepherding Anchises. Around her own dear son she spread her two white arms and covered him in a fold of her shining robe, to guard against these missiles.

Βουκολέοντι—but this pastoral is not "hollow," like Virgil's. For Aineias, it offers refuge.

As we read and re-read the incidents of *Aeneid* XII, Virgil's artistry is found to have combined and blended these reminiscences into a storied radiance shedding more colour than light. Yet how much their confusions reflect the dazzle of human experience, which blinds the eye looking for

---

[48] A simile in this passage is recalled when Vulcan rises early to fashion Aeneas' Shield: *Il*. XII. 433: cf. Apollonius, *Arg*. III. 291, *Aen*. VIII. 407. See above, p. 59.

simple perspectives of guilt or innocence. How much Turnus needed the mother whom Virgil never mentions!

And this is the lesson we are meant to hear in the poem, since it was not told about then only, but about then and now. Virgil could not be relevant to the hundred years' war following the assassinations of Tiberius and Caius Gracchus if he had simply proclaimed a tale of success.

Evidently his principal hearer, *Hectoreis ... maior avis*, accepted all this with good grace. But, even if Virgil finally meant to contrast bad (*sceleratus*) Turnus with good (*pius*) Aeneas, and even if he has convinced some sophisticated moderns, polyprosopic and polyphonic art speaks with its own voices. The *Iliad* demanded a short-lived hero. How long has the Aeneas who is also Achilles / Memnon / Hercules to live? Later legend in any case found him less congenial than any of these heroes. In the first half of the twelfth century, Conrad of Hirsau, for example, suggested that, by his cruelty, he made himself unpopular with his subjects, and that the gods eventually struck him with lightning.[49] On the other side, Dante at least saw orphaned, childless, twinned Turnus and Camilla (XI. 831 = XII. 952) for the brave champions they were.

The Morality of Turnus' Death[50]

For failing to heed monstrous Humbaba's plea for mercy, either Gilgamesh or Enkidu had to die. This was felt right in the second millennium B.C. In any discussion therefore of Aeneas' failure to heed Turnus' plea, the humane reader who finds the incident immoral hardly needs to be warned against Christian prejudice.[51] Indeed, when Christian Ariosto, living in an age which sometimes afforded few courtesies to religious

---

[49] E. R. Curtius, *Europäische Literatur und lateinisches Mittelalter*, p. 462. See further Alanus de Insulis and Bernardus Silvestris, *ibid.*, pp. 126, 128. V. Pöschl (*The Art of Vergil*, p. 94) notes Dante's verdict (*Inf.* 1. 107–08).

[50] West, *East Face of Helicon*, p. 216, notes traditional elements at work when a second warrior (in Virgil's case, dead Pallas) intervenes to prevent mercy to one defeated. The question raised by the *Aeneid* is: was tradition enough to satisfy the claims of Hellenistic / Roman morality? Excellent ἐποχή on this point in Nelis, *op. cit.*, p. 373.

[51] Although, if we want such "prejudice," Bishop Synesius (*Epp.* 41, p. 124, Garzya) supplies a fine example: cf. ὁ τιμωρός ... τῇ μοχθηρίᾳ τῆς φύσεως χαριζόμενος ταῖς κοιναῖς συμφοραῖς ἐπεξέρχεται ("procura pubbliche calamità compiacendo alla sua natura malvagia"). Obviously in fact a writer of Synesius' stamp reflects a long, composite tradition, part of which may easily have been accessible to Virgil and his contemporaries. To divide Christianity and the Classics is to negate what the European achievement, and *literae humaniores*, have been about.

opponents, adapts the last line of the *Aeneid* to the end of his *Orlando Furioso*, he alters it significantly to make his point:

> bestemmiando fuggí l'alma sdegnosa,
> che fu sí altiera al mondo, e sí orgogliosa. (*O.F.* XLVI. 140)

> Blaspheming fled the disdainful soul [of Rodomonte the Saracen], so haughty in the world, so filled with pride.

But of what blasphemy is Turnus guilty? His soul, passing to another world, becomes "consecrated to the divine," even "righteous" (XII. 648).[52]

Juvenal, who cites the example of Hercules' hardiness, bids us pray for a mind untouched by anger (*nesciat irasci*, X. 360). Aeneas is not merely angry with Turnus, but *Furiis accensus*. There are indeed *Furiae iustae* (VIII. 494, Mezentius), and in Cicero Furius had prophesied[53] that such avenging spirits, haunting the guilty, would be present at murderous Verres' trial (cf. Horace, *Epodes* 5. 87 ff.). Yet the same speech contrasts Pompey's generous forgiveness of the Sertorian rebels (§153). Christianity itself is ambivalent. Following St. Paul (Romans 13:4), Synesius *may* permit judges to be angry.[54] But, in view of all the damage which the Furies' fires have wrought since Book VII, how can Aeneas' act at the end here possibly be lauded as the quasi-judicial infliction of a well-deserved penalty? *Ira furor brevis est*, wrote Horace (*Epp.* I. 2. 62), echoing Stoic tradition, and paralleling Virgil's own *Furiis ... et ira*. In his *De Ira*, Seneca argued that it has no part among the accoutrements of a good prince, as Augustus understood: *clementiae civilitatisque eius multa et magna documenta sunt* (Suet., *Aug.* 51). In Virgil's age, the Romans had come to value different qualities from those of Ennius' *horridus miles*. Brutus, who as consul executed his own sons for treachery, is *infelix, utcumque ferent ea facta minores* (VI. 822). *Saevas* is noteworthy in this passage (819).

And at this point we again touch on the *Aeneid*'s relationship to historical experience. The Civil Wars intrude as early as the *Eclogues*, and

---

[52] In general, the combat of Rinaldo and Soliman at the end of Tasso's *Gerusalemme Liberata*, itself modelled on that of Aeneas and Turnus, may also be compared (XX. 105–08).

[53] *Ab dis manibus innocentium Poenas sceleratorumque Furias in tuum iudicium esse venturas* (*Verrine* V. §113). But has Virgil presented Turnus in such a way that he is properly associated with Verres or Mezentius? Both these monsters were in any case to be dealt with *iudiciis legitimis* (Aug., *R. G.* 2; cf. *Aen.* VIII. 495, *supplicium*), not by a summary killing on the field. Aeneas is carrying out Evander's request (XI. 178–81), but as commander should he?

[54] If ὀργίζονται is correct at *Epp.* 2, p. 158B (so Hercher, *Epistolographi Graeci*). Garzya (p. 68) reads μάχονται. Cf. νεμεσᾷς, supposed to be addressed to the emperor, *Epp.* 73, Garzya, p. 219.

The Men Characters—I: The Supporting Cast 239

certainly colour the *Georgics*. With the Social Wars, they profoundly affect the *Aeneid*, in which it is quite wrong to see merely eulogy of the present in the past. There are negatives already in the *Eclogues*. At the end of the *Aeneid* stands *fugit indignata sub umbras*. The participle, a Gygean window into Turnus' mind, is also meant for the listener to the line. *En quo Discordia civis / produxit miseros!*[55]

Is Turnus a *civis*? He certainly uses that term of address (XI. 459). Yet "Turnus" / *turan* is an Etruscan name (Lydian τύραννος), and Livy (I. 2) links him closely with Etruscan Mezentius, also a "tyrant" (*Aen*. VIII. 483). But Asian Aeneas himself is a tyrant (VII. 266, XII. 75). This enhances the horror of the poem's conclusion.

But, just as Aeneas is (via Dardanus and Rome) Italian, Turnus is also Italian (*Latinis*, VII. 96). How had Italians fared at the hands of Romans? Aeneas' Shield seems to revel in the details of the bizarre execution by Tullus of the treacherous Alban king Mettius Fufetius (VIII. 642–45), but Livy comments on that same atrocity (I. 28. 11):

> avertere omnes ab tanta foeditate spectaculi oculos. primum ultimumque illud supplicium apud Romanos exempli parum memoris legum humanarum fuit: in aliis gloriari licet nulli gentium mitiores placuisse poenas.
>
> All the spectators averted their gaze from so revolting a sight. That was the first and last punishment among Romans showing forgetfulness of the claims of humanity. In other instances no people may boast of imposing its penalties in a greater spirit of forgiveness.

This view of the Roman exercise of *imperium* was older than Livy (Sallust, *Cat*. 9. 5, modelled on Isocrates, *Or*. IV [*Pan*.] §80); but here also speaks the voice of the Augustan Age, doubly loud if the Albans were kinsmen of the Romans. Again Aeneas could not hear.[56]

There is a general sense however in which even so Turnus might hope to survive, and in which Aeneas' Troy does not (XII. 827–28):

---

[55] "I am sick and tired of war. Its glory is all moonshine. It is only those who have neither fired a shot nor heard the shrieks and groans of the wounded who cry aloud for blood, more vengeance, more desolation. War is hell": from remarks attributed to General W. Sherman in an address to the Michigan Military Academy, quoted by R. Hughes, *American Visions* (New York 1997), p. 207. Hughes comments: "It was a Greek moment." But, since the general was referring to a Civil War, was it not also a Virgilian moment?—There is an extraordinary contrast between the views of a veteran soldier on vengeance, and those of study-bound professors of humanities (literae humaniores?) pointing out sagely that it is right and good so to do.

[56] A mural inscription in the lower basilica of San Lorenzo fuori le Mura (Rome) records the martyrdom of St. Hippolytus *collis religatus equorum*. But that was under a different emperor and in another age.

> 'sit Romana potens Itala virtute propago:
> occidit, occideritque sinas cum nomine Troia.'

'Let Rome's stock draw strength from Italy's manhood. Troy has fallen. Let it and its name lie!'

But, to come to particulars, what Roman gens did trace its ancestry to Turnus? His last nightmare (XII. 908 ff.) well expresses that bewildering kaleidoscope (kakeidoscope?) of experience which war entails for all.

How great the Romans were that they adopted this poem as their national epic! Unflinchingly, while their great families petered out around them to leave the barren residues drily sifted by modern prosopographers, they traced the pattern and paradigm which Virgil, preceded by vatic Horace, had not so much imposed on their history as deciphered within it. Here at last poet and historian could unite in the discovery of the universal.

As he bade farewell to Pallas' corpse, Aeneas had turned back to *eadem horrida belli fata* (XI. 96–97). That was pointless iteration. The hope of the future lay with Augustus Caesar. But he had broken out of the Homeric prison. He was not the invader and killer but the leader and uniter of Italians and their now *Romana ... oppida* (*Geo.* II. 176) against barbarian foes, *Italos Augustus agens in proelia Caesar*.

XI

THE MEN CHARACTERS—II: AENEAS

> Jede dumpfe Umkehr der Welt hat solche Enterbte,
> denen das Frühere nicht, und noch nicht das Nächste gehört.
>
> R. M. Rilke

The Aeneid *as Tragedy*

If the program of the *Aeneid* was developed in the *Georgics*, it was already embryonic in the hollow pastoral of the *Eclogues*. Some of this was remarked earlier. But the *Eclogues* also proclaim an infant saviour, a Golden Age. For that, a new Argo will be needed—and a new assault on Troy (*Eclogues* 4. 34–36):

> alter erit tum Tiphys, et altera quae vehat Argo
> delectos heroas; erunt etiam altera bella
> atque iterum ad Troiam magnus mittetur Achilles.

The renewal of the cycle which joins the Argonautic expedition with the sack of Troy will be a preliminary to paradise.[1] Perhaps it was this topos which Catullus 64, in which baby Achilles will enjoy such a bloody future (338 ff.), was meant to negate, by among other things its double mention of Pharsalia (37). The *Aeneid* (*alius Latio iam partus Achilles*, VI. 89) plays on it more positively. Trojan Aeneas' Italian wars are to lead in some fashion to Augustus' *aureum saeculum* (VI. 792–93). Lucan's *Pharsalia* takes this up (I. 33 ff.).

Iterum therefore of *Eclogue* 4 becomes a leitmotif in the *Aeneid*, part of the process and gestation of greater things. In the *Eclogue*, the heir of this New Age will be the child whose birth is saluted. For the *Aeneid*, the corollary is that, like Achilles, when that time comes, Aeneas will be superannuated. For transients whose day is past, there can be no personal

---

[1] Marie Tanner, *The Last Descendant of Aeneas* (New Haven 1993), pp. 5 ff. Some background to an often unjustly neglected thematic already visible in Pindar's fourth *Pythian* is developed in "The Golden Fleece. Imperial Dream": *A Companion to Apollonius*, pp. 309–40.

success stories. This development was implicit in the Classical tradition, and evident in its way since *Gilgamesh*.

The Greeks perceived this in their characteristic fashion. Aristotle, the admirer of Homer, had laid down that epic must be "dramatic" (*Poetics* c. 23). For so exalted a genre, that meant "tragic." Is the *Aeneid* a tragedy? Though Dante thought so (*Inf.* 20. 113), Virgil, replacing the *Iliad*, the story of a city, not with a *Romaid*, but with an *Aeneid*, the story of one man, appeared to be going back on Aristotle's plural (μιμοῦνται... πράττοντας, *Poetics* 1448a 1). His protagonist was no longer one among several peers, not even *primus inter pares*, but the very centre of the tale. And he claimed some contact with history, something which in poetry Aristotle abominated (*Poetics* c. 9). Was unity then to be sacrificed to the casual detail of events, tragedy to eulogy?

There is some incidental eulogy in the *Iliad*, even of Aeneas (see below). Eulogy on a larger scale, with its often spurious claim to historical truth, presented a real threat, as Horace repeatedly suggests (*Sat.* II. 1. 10-12; *Odes* I. 6; *Epp.* II. 1. 250). Already Pindar knew an interpretation of Homer which saw the *Odyssey* at least as contemporary propaganda, enabling its hero unfairly to defeat Ajax in the contest for the arms of Achilles (*Nem.* 7. 20-30); and this view of epic, notably exemplified in Choerilus of Iasos, would increasingly come to furbish Hellenistic antitheses: ἅλις πάντεσσιν Ὅμηρος says the disappointed Theocritus (16. 20). Callimachus rejected this kind of poetry, which persisted, to take only these examples, in Latin with Claudian and Corippus, in Byzantine literature with the iambics of Georgius Pisides. Apollonius had implicitly protested against it. And, in spite of the countervailing example of Ennius, in spite of his chosen title, with Virgil too, Aristotle would prevail. In the event, Aeneas' uniqueness would lie in his pious unfaithfulness to guilty origins from which however ultimately he could not free himself. It was to be this failing struggle with more than human powers which would bestow on the *Aeneid* the structural tautness, polyphony and tragic ἁμαρτία demanded in an Aristotelian epic. Eulogy in it would be, not so much of the hero, as of ones and one still to come. History would be a vision and no more.

This was certainly to break loose from "das hellenistische Epos," in the sense in which such public relations pieces have been lauded or fantasised by moderns. No doubt, both *Gilgamesh* and the *Odyssey* centre around the adventures of a single hero. But, in these explorations, in spite of Pindar, the protagonist is not looking to win votes. Rather, he comes to an understanding of his own identity and mortality through his encounters with the workings of the divine, and the vehicle of that divine is woman. This is what Callimachus and Apollonius in their different ways had understood (Hecale, Medea). We again sense the presence of this paradigm—and the telling divergence from it—when we consider the *Aeneid*'s last scene. What sort of divine, what sort of woman does Aeneas, *Furiis accensus*, ultimately encounter? What Roman identity has he discovered—or, if discovered, abandoned—there (*Romane ... parcere*, VI. 851, 853)? How does he obey dead Anchises' injunction (*proice tela manu*, VI. 835)? What sense has he of his mortality—a mystery whose awful secret he hands off to Turnus?

Structure and Modifications: Greece and Etruria

Aristotle had spurned epics whose only focus was a random string of individual adventures (*Poetics* 1451a 19–30):

διὸ πάντες ἐοίκασιν ἁμαρτάνειν ὅσοι τῶν ποιητῶν Ἡρακληίδα Θησηίδα καὶ τὰ τοιαῦτα ποιήματα πεποιήκασιν· οἴονται γάρ, ἐπεὶ εἷς ἦν ὁ Ἡρακλῆς, ἕνα καὶ τὸν μῦθον εἶναι προσήκειν. ὁ δ' Ὅμηρος ὥσπερ καὶ τὰ ἄλλα διαφέρει καὶ τοῦτ' ἔοικεν καλῶς ἰδεῖν, ἤτοι διὰ τέχνην ἢ διὰ φύσιν· Ὀδύσσειαν γὰρ ποιῶν οὐκ ἐποίησεν ἅπαντα ὅσα αὐτῷ συνέβη, οἷον πληγῆναι μὲν ἐν τῷ Παρνάσσῳ, μανῆναι δὲ προσποιήσασθαι ἐν τῷ ἀγερμῷ, ὧν οὐδὲν θατέρου γενομένου ἀναγκαῖον ἦν ἢ εἰκὸς θάτερον γενέσθαι, ἀλλὰ περὶ μίαν πρᾶξιν οἵαν λέγομεν τὴν Ὀδύσσειαν συνέστησεν, ὁμοίως δὲ καὶ τὴν Ἰλιάδα.

That explains the mistake of all those poets who have composed a *Heracleid* or *Theseid* or something of the sort, under the impression that the uniqueness of a Heracles guarantees a unified plot. Homer's general superiority is again illustrated in this particular instance, whether owed to art or nature. His *Odyssey* does not recount all Odysseus' adventures, such as his wounding on Mount Parnassus, or his feigned madness at the gathering of the Greek forces, neither of which events necessarily entailed or implied the other. He organized the *Odyssey* around the sort of unified action we are describing, and similarly the *Iliad*.

Elsewhere in the *Poetics* he describes the unity of an impressive work of literary art as like that of a living creature (1451a 3). This is already Platonic (*Phaedrus* 264c 2–5).

But the genius of Homer was more than to see that organic unity was necessary. At what a later critic regarded (*De Subl.* 9. 13) as the height of his inspiration, the poet had not written an *Achilleid*, but an *Iliad*, not the story of a single hero, but of many. The characters all had their own parts to play. To Aristotle, it seemed that the essence of Homer's poetic was interaction (*Poetics* 1450b 3–4). In his πρᾶξις, there is more than one πράττων, and therefore more than one voice. This is why Homer could so easily be viewed by Aristotle's own teacher as the founding father of modern (Attic) tragedy with its two or three agonists (τούτων τῶν τραγικῶν πρῶτος διδάσκαλός τε καὶ ἡγεμών, *Rep.* X. 595c 1), what the Romans would have called its *inventor*.[2] Even when such poetry makes use of *Monolog und Selbstgespräch* (Schadewaldt), its essence is dialogic, here a debate conducted with a divided self. It was this connatural dialogue which, with the aid of iambic Archilochus, tragedy had recovered from epic.

Yet, if we accept with Dante that Virgil too was a tragedian, he evidently earns this title in a more than Iliadic sense. The tragic model, so often emphasising the fate of one major protagonist (Orestes, Heracles), has interfered in a particular way. Following that pattern, Virgil largely reduces the Aeneadae to foil, though not even the *Odyssey's* ἑταῖροι are quite like that.

Conversely, Homer did not write an *Aeneid*, though his Aeneas occupies a peculiar place, depicted as brave enough, second only in prowess to Hector (*Il.* V. 467), but even so an ambivalent figure, who reflects resentfully on Priam's failure to show him proper respect (*Il.* XIII. 460). In some way he apparently represented a dynastic threat. Later, as was noted in the previous discussion of Turnus,[3] Poseidon remarks that Zeus has lost patience with Priam, and that it is Aeneas' line which will secure the survival of Dardanus' race (XX. 307–08):

νῦν δὲ δὴ Αἰνείαο βίη Τρώεσσιν ἀνάξει,
καὶ παίδων παῖδες, τοί κεν μετόπισθε γένωνται.

But, as it is, mighty Aeneas will be king over the Trojans, and his children's children to be born in after days.

Aeneas himself is ἀναίτιος, "guiltless" (297). This is the tradition refracted in Xenophon (*Cyn.* I. 15) and Lycophron (*Alexandra* 1268–70), and still visible in Livy (I. 1), who carefully distinguishes Aeneas and Antenor from the rest of the defeated Trojans. These heroes had not only enjoyed long-standing ties of friendship with the conquering Greeks, but had also steadfastly supported peace and Helen's restoration. Their freedom to go their way was justified by their comparative innocence.

Even so, traditional Troy was doomed. Where then would the Troy to be ruled by Aeneas' descendants be? In Italy? So Aeneas believes: *illic fas regna resurgere Troiae* (I. 206; cf. *Troiam ... nascentem* on Juno's lips, X. 74–75). The hero had played a part in Rome's story long before Virgil came

---

[2] Cf. Livy II. 56. 6, where Volero is *inventor legis*, while Laetorius is its *auctor recentior*, evidently its supporter and furtherer. This terminology was transferred to literary history, naturally enough, since literature had its own laws (Horace, *A.P.* 135; *Epp.* II. 2. 109; cf. *A.P.* 274). In *Sat.* I. 10. 48 and 66, Lucilius is said to be the founder of satire (*inventor*) and not some mere practitioner and furtherer (*auctor*) of a native genre (*Graecis intacti carminis*) already established.

[3] Above, pp. 234–35. In general, M. L. West ad Hesiod, *Theogony* 1008.

to write, in Greek prose narratives, but even in Greek poetry. In Lycophron's riddling version (1226-80), once again, Aeneas' descendants are to the fore: Romulus and Remus (1232-33); the blessed fatherland he will build, even "restore to life": πάτραν / ἐν ὀψιτέκνοις ὀλβίαν δωμήσεται (1271-72; cf. δωμήσατο of resurrected Scylla, 48). Virgil's Aeneas echoes Lycophron's πάτραν: *hic amor, haec patria est* (IV. 347). By the time of Naevius' Latin epic, Aeneas was too firmly entrenched among the founding fathers for Roman listeners so much as to contemplate his omission.

Greek influence on Roman κτίσις-legend is one thing. Much odder is the rescue from Etruscan Veii of a figurine showing Aeneas bearing Anchises on his shoulders.[4] The same theme is seen on an Etruscan gem (first half of fifth century).[5] Who were the borrowers here? Tarchon and Tursenos already figure in Cassandra's prophecy in Lycophron (*Alex.* 1248), sons of Mysian Telephus and allies of Aeneas. Tursenos is clear enough. Tarchon (ancestor of the Tarquins) is Hittite.[6] With these links, the Etruscans are appropriately said by Herodotus to have come from Asia Minor. Did they bring their story of ship-borne, migrating ancestors with them and, at a time when their cultural influence was dominant, impose it on Rome, whose Latin inhabitants could obviously make no such claim? Certainly, in Virgil, "Asian" Aeneas (XII. 15) both receives the Lydian / Etruscan title of *tyrannus* (VII. 266, XII. 75), and counts Etruria as his chief ally. He traces Dardanus' origins back to Etruscan Corythus (*Corythi Tyrrhena ab sede*, VII. 209). Arcadian though he may be, King Evander at the site of Rome puts on "Etruscan sandals" (VIII. 458), some forerunner perhaps of the senator's *calcei*.

But why is all this appropriate? Historically, Etruria was known as the *enemy* of Rome; and, on the other side, if the Roman state was tempted to forget that it was constituted from Latins, the revival of such memories was a feature of Augustus' propaganda (cf. *Aen.* VI. 773-75; VII. 641 ff.,

---

[4] Now in the Villa Giulia. Sybille Haynes says there are several examples, which however she attributes to "Roman settlers" (*Etruscan Civilization*, p. 205). A black-figure amphora in the Vatican (no. 34532, end of 6th c.), made for the Etruscan market, shows on side A Aeneas with the grey-haired Anchises on his back, but otherwise unaccompanied. Side B has a leave-taking. The Etruscan mirror now in the Capitoline Museums (inv. MAI 49: 4th c.), showing a wolf suckling twins, probably from the Lago di Bolsena, is unfortunately still in dispute.

[5] G.M.A. Richter, *The Engraved Gems of the Greeks, Romans and Etruscans* I (London 1968), p. 211, no. 861.

[6] O. R. Gurney, *The Hittites* (rev. ed. London 1990), p. 114. In general, Marta Sordi, *Il mito troiano e l'eredità etrusca di Roma* (Milan 1989).

catalogue of Turnus' allies). Was there perhaps a political motive at work in Virgil's day to explain why Turnus / τύραννος (X. 448), even in Livy closely associated with Etruscan Mezentius, is transformed by the poet into an *Italian* leader (VII. 96)? In exactly this vein, Dionysius of Halicarnassus labours to prove (contradicting Herodotus) that the Etruscans were themselves autochthonous. Virgil's story of Dardanus' origin was meant to suggest the same Italian autochthony for the Trojans. For them, Asia Minor had evidently been a diversion from the mainstream of history.[7] Cruel and blasphemous Mezentius for his part is an exile, dissociated from his people in a sort of *regifugium* occurring *avant la lettre*. Etruscan history is as it were sanitised.

In all this, reasons of state may be suspected. Julius' experiments with Hellenistic paradigms of monarchy had proved fatal. Another model was needed. The Chiusi statue of the emperor, in something of the Etruscan manner,[8] hints that, with Maecenas to advise, he was looking to Etruscan models—now found by the compliant Dionysius to be after all native to Italy—for the trappings and rationale of his new, Apolline sun-kingship, to culminate in the celebration of the (Etruscan) Ludi Saeculares.[9]

In the poet's own lifetime, Lucretius had re-emphasised the notion that the Romans were *Aeneadae*, and in that sense Venus' own children—strange in an epic expounding the theory that the gods are unconcerned about human affairs, unless there was an ulterior motive, overlaying Epicureanism with Roman politics. Was he reviving memories of the sexual power of an Asian Aphrodite[10] to please the learned and libidinous—and ambitious—ex-praetor of Bithynia to whom he offered his work? Perhaps Memmius, "Memmiades" in Lucretius' proem, already claimed descent from Trojan Mnestheus (*Aen.* V. 117: cf. XII. 127). Such ideas were in the air. It was a time when Varro wrote *De Familiis Troianis*, setting out the names of those Roman families who could trace their ancestry back as if to some "Mayflower."

---

[7] The "Lydian" Tiber (II. 781–82) is there to welcome Aeneas home to his "ancient mother" (III. 96).

[8] Noted by C. Picard, "Chronique de la Sculpture Étrusco-latine (1935)," *Revue des Études latines* 14 (1936), 162.

[9] A *saeculum* of 100 or 110 years is obviously longer than a human lifespan, which is what *saeculum* ought to describe if it were purely Latin in this context (*multaque vivendo mortalia vincere saecla*). Such longer "ages" in the history of peoples are Etruscan (cf. Plutarch, *Sulla* VII. 4). Etruscan influence is also suggested by the fact that it was Claudius, married first to Urgulanilla, and the author of 20 books of Τυρσηνικά, who celebrated the Games again.

[10] A "voluptuous" ivory figurine of the goddess, recovered from Zeugma (built by Seleucus I opposite Apamea, the birthplace of Posidonius), is in the museum at Gazantiep (Turkey). Aphrodisias, Octavian's staunch ally, is well known.

Julius Caesar, to whom Varro dedicated in 47 B.C. a section of his *Antiquitates*, took this speculation up.[11] His family had in any case begun as early as 125 to revive for political purposes memories of its link with Venus Genetrix. Characteristically, Caesar was willing to push the thesis to its logical conclusion. We are told that, had he lived, he might even have gone so far as to refound old Troy—something Aeneas knows is against the fates (IV. 340 ff.). Horace, anticipating Virgil, makes Juno specifically forbid it.[12]

Already the outline is visible of Virgil's modification of his inherited historical materials. With Dionysius, we are not to think of Aeneas' Etruscan allies, "Lydian" though they may be called (VIII. 479; IX. 11; X. 155), who include Etruscan Mantuans (X. 203), as alien intruders on Italian soil, any more than Aeneas himself (III. 167). With the Caesars, the poet also accepted *Aeneadae* for the Romans (VIII. 648) but, schooled by the lessons of past history, censored Homer's hint of dynastic feuding between Aeneas and Priam's house (*Il.* XX. 179–86). His Aeneas, the servant of the fates, is Priam's rightful heir, receiving in trust from dead Hector the sacred emblems and fires of Troy (II. 296–97, 320). There will, however, be no return to Asia Minor.

Yet these simple changes had unfortunate implications. Not only must "Dardan" Aeneas now be conducting a civil war in Italy but, if he is Priam's heir, he acquires the baggage of Priam's line (*Priami gestamen*, VII. 246). This makes him, perhaps unfairly—certainly most unfortunately—"Laomedontian" (*Aen.* VIII. 18; cf. *Geo.* I. 502). Whether then he remains ἀναίτιος, as Homer's Poseidon had called him, and as Livy still suggests—whether that could even be possible for a tragic hero—and what exactly his promised children would be, are questions to be asked later.

What does "Aeneid" *Imply?*

The title *Aeneis* is so much a part of literary culture that its oddity in its Roman and Augustan context escapes attention. Republican Naevius and Ennius, for all that they were "history poets," had avoided anything of the sort. The best-known Greek epics to be named after a (quasi-)historical hero in this way (now that Choerilus of Samos has been shown not to have

---

[11] See R. M. Ogilvie's *Commentary* on Livy I. 3. 2 (pp. 42–43). Meyer (*Caesars Monarchie*, p. 510) notes Caesar's interest in Venus genetrix, to whom he built a temple in 46; and concomitantly in the eponymous Iulus, child of Aeneas, once "Ilus" (I. 267–68: cf. VI. 650).

[12] See below, p. 252.

written a *Lysandreia*) perhaps dealt with Alexander the Great.[13] He had certainly founded numerous Alexandrias. In Rome, he was a powerful model, for Pompey, for Caesar, for Augustus. He had appealed to the Etruscans. As שמש / Helios indeed he is found in one of the cities conquered by Camillus soon after Veii (Livy V. 26).[14]

In what sense is the *Aeneid* an *Alexandriad*? Naturally enough, a poem called after a hero raises the expectation that it will deal with his prowess. No doubt, in spite of modern scepticism, many epics of that sort were undertaken, promising to trace auspicious beginnings to a successful end. Pindar's first *Nemean*, written for Chromius, viceroy of the newly founded city of Aetna, already sketches their outline.[15] But even so, the more worthwhile they were, the more they must have cheated complacent expectation. Alexander, who employed as his court poet Choerilus of Iasos,

---

[13] Cf. the *Alexandrias* of Arrian: Lloyd-Jones / Parsons, *Supplementum Hellenisticum*, p. 81–82, nos. 207–09. If Alexander was Choerilus of Iasos' Achilles (Lloyd-Jones / Parsons, no. 333: see below), that epic, whatever its exact title, must have said something about the man as well as his accomplishments.

[14] At least if the bust of Apollo from the temple at Lo Scasato (Falerii veteres), now in the Villa Giulia, has the features of Alexander Helios: see M. Bieber, *The Sculpture of the Hellenistic Age* (repr. New York 1961), fig. 713; much handsomer photographs in *Art of the Etruscans* (M. Moretti *et al.*, London 1970), p. 231, and in *Villa Giulia Museum. The Antiquities of the Faliscans* (Carlucci — De Lucia [Rome 1998]), cover and p. 53. See also *Latinitas* XXXXIX (2001), 339 (V. Bracco). On שמש / Helios see *Augustan Propertius*, p. 83, n. 64. Augustus and Nero would later erect statues of Apollo with their own features, to be followed by the emperor Constantine. Similarly, on the second-century A.D. altar of Mithras beneath San Clemente in Rome, Mithras has the features of Lysippus' Alexander. — On Camillus as a pre-princeps, below, p. 252, n. 21.

[15] Heracles' strangling of the snakes in his cradle is made to prefigure his fight on the side of the gods against the snake-limbed Giants and eventual apotheosis, a topos implicit in the song of the Salii in *Aeneid* VIII (288–89, 298–300), applied by Ovid to Caius Caesar (*A.A.* I. 181 ff.), and suggested for a marble infant in the Palazzo Nuovo which may be intended as the youthful Annius Verus or Caracalla (Albertoni, *Capitoline Museums*, p. 52). It is indicated on a Romanesque ivory gaming counter of the 12th century now in London (BM M&LA 1929,6–4,1), and familiar to moderns from Sir Joshua Reynolds' picture of the scene painted for Catherine the Great, now in the Hermitage. See also a twelfth-century bronze Hansa bowl (BM M&LA 1921,325,1) where it is included with the labours of Hercules, and said to be owed to "current moralistic and school literature." This interpretation is given, both in Pindar and on the ivory, by Teiresias, spokesman (προφάτης, *Nem.* 1. 60) of Zeus most High—surely then a *vates* if the poet had had that term. What a contradiction of the topos therefore when Virgil makes Aeneas a Giant (X. 565–68; below, p. 257). But then his opponent Turnus, wearing his deadly belt, must become a Hercules, appropriately mad but paradoxically—for the time being—losing.

is reported to have said that he would sooner be Homer's Thersites than Choerilus' Achilles. He wept at Achilles' tomb, because Achilles (unlike himself!) had found someone worthy to celebrate his achievement. In the Hellenic mentality, the reason for such dissatisfaction lies deeper than mere disdain for incompetence. For that imagination, impatient with humdrum history, epic, as Plato and Aristotle both saw, was closely allied with tragedy; and the crescendo of a heroic ἀριστεία demanded also the *basso profondo* of the hero's subsequent, compensatory fall. Part of Achilles' heroism is his awareness of his own ever-imminent death, which he actually compares with that of Heracles (*Il.* XVIII. 117). Did Alexander / Heracles / Achilles, impatient with Choerilus' unalloyed praises, already then sense the bounds to which his own death at the age of 32 would so closely conform? Almost 2000 years later, the *Alexandreis* of Walter of Châtillon still follows this persistent pattern. If Virgil not so much perhaps diverges from it as abbreviates it, perhaps he expected an audience of sufficient maturity to understand what he was doing (αὐτὸς ἐπιφράσσαιτο...). There cannot be a triumphant Aeneas without denial of the generic obligation. This is particularly evident in Aeneas' identification (via his killing of Lausus) with Memnon, the slayer of Antilochus, paralleled with Achilles in Greek art (and in Ovid) for his short life and his grief-stricken mother.

The argument which the hero makes to the Sibyl justifying his claim to descend into the world below confirms this presage. His first precedent is Orpheus: *si potuit manis accersere coniugis Orpheus* ... (VI. 119–20). With an editorialising glibness rivalling that of Apollonius' Jason on Ariadne (*Arg.* III. 997 ff.), he refrains from mentioning what the poet of *Georgics* IV knew too well about the outcome of that adventure. As *vates*, Orpheus was certainly a model for Augustus,[16] and for later rulers (Tacitus, *Dial.* 12. 4), and therefore for Augustus' putative ancestor from Troy. But what kind of a model could he be in Virgil's universe? His loss of Eurydice had already set the pattern of Aeneas' loss of his Creusa / Eurydice at Troy. Were the *manes coniugis* which Aeneas would now summon up those of lurking Dido? His appeals here to damned Theseus and mad Hercules are even more ominous.

The Aeneid *as* Ktisis

We spoke already of "κτίσις-legend." The *Aeneid* advertises itself as a Κτίσις at its very outset (*dum conderet urbem*, I. 5). But what could be the

---

[16] As implied by Horace, whose Solon / Augustus (*A.P.* 399) climaxes a list opening with Orpheus and culminating in Apollo *citharoedus* (*A.P.* 392, 407) —the Palatine Apollo. Cf. Fraenkel, *Horace*, pp. 276 ff. Below, pp. 283, 310.

epic model for that? Neither Homer's *Iliad* nor Apollonius' *Argonautica* (nor indeed Walter's *Alexandreis*) is the story of the founding of a city. Odysseus boasts of being, like Ares, πτολιπόρθιος (*Od.* IX. 504: cf. *Il.* II. 278, 728). For Κτίσεις in verse, Apollonius had elaborated a separate sub-genre,[17] and again its paradigm is already felt in the choral lyric: for example, in Pindar's allusions to Hiero's Aetna (*Py.* 3. 69, *al.*), or, in his fourth *Pythian*, to Cyrene; in Bacchylides' eleventh ode.

Sometimes such foundations had a chequered history, as the Metapontion of Bacchylides 11 shows. Ennius' story of Rome's foundation was deadly. The *Aeneid* itself does not speak with one voice about the city that its hero is to build. Chronology, dealing with events *ante Urbem conditam condendamve*, made any direct foundation of Rome by Aeneas, for Virgil's more critical spirit, impossible, even though Boeotian Plutarch still notes (*Romulus* 2. 1) Romanus, the son of Aeneas by Circe, as Rome's coloniser. But Virgil's Aeneas will found only an interim Italian city, and even that we never see him doing.[18] Was it to be a resurgent Troy? On the one hand, in Book IV, Aeneas acknowledges that in seeking Italy he is obeying the will of the gods, rather than his own inclination to set up a Pergamum restored (*recidiva ... Pergama*, 344; cf. VII. 322); and in Book III Buthrotum already signals to him and us the deadness of any effort to re-establish such a new Troy *falsi Simoentis ad undam* (302). But later in the poem this seems to be forgotten, even by the gods (*dum Latium Teucri recidivaque Pergama quaerunt*, X. 58). So astute a critic as Vegio (wrongly) read the poem as heralding the foundation in Italy of a second Trojan settlement: *dehinc pace tenebis / Sub placida gentem Iliacam* (*Suppl.* 577–78: see also below, p. 279).

The *Aeneid* exhibits then another variation from the traditional, since its κτίσις requires the hero to represent a distant future foundation, and a people yet to come. In one way, Virgil appears to satisfy this requirement. There is the suggestion of a clear transition. Supremely, the gens Iulia was Trojan,

---

[17] J. U. Powell, *Collectanea Alexandrina*, pp. 5–8. Cf. no. 4, 'Αλεξανδρείας Κτίσις. E. Norden, who sees Κτίσεις as essentially a prose genre, refers to Timaeus and Polemon of Ilion (*Römische Literatur* [Leipzig 1954], p. 25). As models for Ennius, he cites Demosthenes of Bithynia and Theodotus of Samaria (p. 16). These are interesting provenances.

[18] There is a city / camp in Book VII (157–59, 290), serving as a woolly and ambiguous expedient. Contrast *iactaque Lavinis moenia litoribus*, Prop. II. 34. 64, what obviously was expected. A handsome Quattrocento manuscript of Virgil's works in Florence (Laurentian Library, Med. Pal. 69, A.D. 1403), with its illustration (fol. 64v) showing by vertical time Aeneas' landing in Italy and the building of a city already in progress, also indicates the normality from which the *Aeneid* so strikingly deviates.

The Men Characters—II: Aeneas

descended from Aeneas' own son (I. 288). The poet explains that certain other members of Rome's great families had Trojan ancestors: the already mentioned Memmii (V. 117), the Sergii (V. 121), the Cluentii (V. 123), the Atii (V. 568), the Claudii (VII. 708). A Capys (II. 35) rules at Alba Longa (VI. 768).

Yet the *gens Troiana* is not to be "transferred" (Vegio's term, *Suppl.* 94) so easily. All these children of theirs would at best be mongrels, hybrids (*genus Ausonio mixtum ... sanguine*, XII. 838). It was noted above how little role some of these Trojan ciphers actually play in the epic action; and we certainly never see any of the Aeneadae in the process of settling down in Italy, though we have been shown false starts in Crete and Carthage. How easy it would have been to make even some fleeting allusion to the first birth on Italian soil from Trojan stock.[19]

More generally, it is hard to reconcile any larger survival of culture or ideas or even dress with the repudiation of Troy conceded to Juno at the end (XII. 824–28, 834–37).[20] But this repudiation, recurring, for example, in Horace, is an Augustan topos. More than half a Roman ode is dedicated to it. Juno speaks (*Odes* III. 3. 18–28):

> '... Ilion, Ilion
> fatalis incestusque iudex
>   et mulier peregrina vertit
> in pulverem, ex quo destituit deos
> mercede pacta Laomedon, mihi
>   castaeque damnatum Minervae
>   cum populo et duce fraudulento.
> iam nec Lacaenae splendet adulterae
> famosus hospes nec Priami domus
>   periura pugnaces Achivos
>   Hectoreis opibus refringit.'

'That deadly, unclean judge and his foreign woman have turned Ilion into dust —Ilion, damned by me and chaste Minerva from the time when Laomedon cheated the gods of their promised fee, damned along with its people and its swindler-boss. Now the Spartan adulteress's ill-famed guest has lost his shine, nor does Priam's perjured house now break, with any Hector's aid, the battle-lines of the Greeks.'

---

[19] *Consilium Troes magnis de rebus habebant. / Ecce autem ducibus fertur vagitus ad aures / Nascentis pueri, Troiae qui primus ab oris / Finibus Italiae datus est de sanguine Teucri* etc. The passage writes itself. But who would have been the mother? In fact, the only *vagitus* in the *Aeneid* is heard in hell (VI. 426).

[20] Cf. Servius on *Aen.* IV. 618: PACIS INIQUAE *ut supra diximus* [ad I. 6] *propter perditam linguam, habitum, nomen, quae solet victor imponere, sicut in duodecimo postulat Iuno.* What would the early American colonists, for example, have said if told that the price of their securing a safe foothold would be their complete assimilation in language, morals and costume to the indigenous tribes?

The pejorative terms multiply. Troy is morally doomed in the eyes of the gods. Vatic Horace had already made a god of the sea condemn the elopement of Paris with Helen and predict its disastrous outcome in an ode following one said by Quintilian to be an allegory of the dangers facing the ship of state (*navis, Odes* I. 14. 1 ~ *navibus* I. 15. 1).

Virgil also fosters this impression by his allusions to Troy's perjuries, its Eastern opulence, its immoral couple, and especially by his emphasis at the start on the root cause of Juno's resentments (I. 26–28):

> ... manet alta mente repostum
> iudicium Paridis spretaeque iniuria formae
> et genus invisum et rapti Ganymedis honores.

In the depths of her heart there lingers the fostered memory of Paris' Judgment and the resented slight to her beauty, and that hated tribe and the privileges showered on raped Ganymede.

All these episodes attest uncontrolled appetites. The detested Trojans, in the person of Paris, had preferred pleasure to family virtue—and the Aeneadae were their sin-laden heirs, for how otherwise would the patroness of the marriage bond have so unrelentingly persecuted them? *Pius* though he may be, Aeneas himself is blended at times by his creator into lubricious Paris (I. 650; cf. IV. 215; VI. 93; VII. 321, 362; XI. 484), seducing Dido / Helen from her allegiance to Sychaeus, Lavinia / Helen from her betrothed Turnus.

For Horace, there can even be too much *pietas* (*Odes* III. 3. 57–60):

> 'sed bellicosis fata Quiritibus
> haec lege dico, ne nimium pii
> rebusque fidentes avitae
> tecta velint reparare Troiae.'

'But for the warlike children of Quirinus I proclaim their destinies on this condition: they are not to be over-dutiful nor, full of confidence in their fortunes, to decide to rebuild the homes of their ancestral Troy.'

There is need to break with old ways. At what quite inexplicable length does Livy's Camillus, himself a pre-Julius,[21] eloquently reject on religious grounds the idea that Rome could ever change its imperial seat (V. 51–54)! How can this not emphasise an official Augustan theme (*Capitoli immobile saxum*, IX. 448)?

Equally, following Augustus' own injunction to Tiberius against filling

---

[21] J. Hellegouarc'h, "Le principat de Camille," *Revue des Études latines* 48 (1970), 112–32. Even under Nero, the notion that Veii might be an alternative to Rome was still familiar enough to form the basis of a joke (Suet., *Nero* 39). Livy's Camillus / Julius is made to reject for Augustan reasons a scheme for a change of locale which in fact the real Julius was suspected of harbouring in a more radical way (Suet., *Jul.* 79).

up the City with a motley throng (Dio LVI. 33. 3), Lucan (VII. 405) and Juvenal (III. 61–62) hammer on the theme of the Roman bloodline, and its dilution by an Oriental tide. Could then an Augustan poet depict it as corrupted at its very source? Virgil had to perform the apparently impossible feat of showing a Trojan hero, carrying the promise of the future, who completed his mission with stubborn determination and then lost his own and his children's Oriental identity—dress, language, culture, religion—but not his credibility.

Rome as Troy: The Legacy of Laomedon

He could do this plausibly in the context of his time because he looked, not at myth, but at the Romans of his own distracted age, for his models. Satire of a sort was never far away from the Roman mind, and certainly not from the vatic writer of epic. *Motus doceri gaudet Ionicos* ... (*Odes* III. 6. 21): Horace was repeating the denunciations already on the lips of Africanus Minor. Ultimately, the corrupted "Troy" from which his and Virgil's listeners were to escape was the Urbs as they had known it before Augustus, which had culminated in the betrayals inspired by Antony and Cleopatra (Horace, *Epodes* 9; *Aen.* VIII. 685–88)—though earlier Cleopatra had ties to Julius himself. That was the real decadence with which there had to be a break, and this is why Augustus, the victor of Actium, undertook *morum ... regimen* (Suet., *Aug.* 27). There had been too much compromise with the East. This theme, so prominent on the Shield, or in the Temple of the Palatine Apollo, the lesson of the clash with Dido / Medea, is already sensed in Catullus' central poems.

Certainly Republican Rome, for all its offences and long civil wars, had traditions which could be rescued (*veteres ... artis*, Horace, *Odes* IV. 15. 12). Troy could be made respectable after the fact by being loosely and at intervals associated with them. Etruria could be re-interpreted to show that many such legacies were not after all imports from Asia, but domestic products. None of this however could alter the basic need for reform.

Lot emerged from the fires of sinful Sodom because he was an innocent man, though like Aeneas he lost his wife in the process. This was evidently an established pattern, yet it highlights another peculiarity about Virgil's picture of his hero. Unlike Lot, unlike Livy's Aeneas, Virgil's Aeneas *shares* his city's guilt.[22] This was quite contradictory of Homer's ἀναίτιος. It was Priam (*Priami domus periura*, Horace, III. 3. 26–27) rather than

---

[22] *Immeritam* (III. 2), on Aeneas' lips, is therefore a quite partisan flourish.

Anchises who was the son of Laomedon.[23] Through his father, Aeneas was descended from Capys and Assaracus (*Il.* XX. 239), and elsewhere Virgil seems sensitive to this distinction, using Assaracus' name in contexts prophetic of triumph and victory (*Aen.* I. 284; VI. 650, 778; IX. 643; XII. 127). To be made Priam's heir (VII. 246) meant to be lumped in with a cheat, and this in turn had significance even for Rome. The poet saw it as the ultimate cause of the Civil Wars (*Geo.* I. 501–02):

> ... satis iam pridem sanguine nostro
> Laomedonteae luimus periuria Troiae.

> For too long now with our own blood we have been atoning for the perjuries of Laomedon's Troy.

In self-reproach, thinking of her betrayer, Dido bitterly echoes her creator's words (IV. 541–42): *necdum / Laomedonteae sentis periuria gentis?* Her perfidious (IV. 366) Aeneas is even a kind of Sinon (*periurique arte Sinonis*, II. 195), doing to her city (IV. 669) what Sinon had done to Troy.

But, if his link with Laomedon was unfair at the start, Aeneas / Paris, who is also Odysseus and Jason, seems to grow into his mixed inheritance. He will marry into Circe's line, and she was a counterfeiter and thief (VII. 283). The record shows that in the event he is guilty of a series of questionable actions. He arrives at the Tiber as Jason arrives at Lemnos, still therefore pursued by memories of Dido / Hypsipyle.[24] Was he right to leave Dido? Will he be right now to take Lavinia away from her betrothed? To enlist callow, doomed Pallas on his side, to kill Lausus and Turnus? Could he ever have debated earlier, in burning Troy, whether to take revenge by slaying Helen? The answer depends on our notion of morality, *Staatsrecht*. Aeneas is not his own man. The only domestic scene in which he is involved occurs against the backdrop of fire and slaughter in Book II, where, after witnessing Priam's murder, he suddenly thinks of his father, wife and son (560–63), forgotten after Hector's apparition (314), and goes home to rescue them. The old man's exasperating obstinacy, Creusa's despairing cry as her husband makes again for the fray, the miracle which

---

[23] Unlike the tale in Dionysius of Mytilene (Scytobrachion), now dated to the 3rd c. B.C., whose Priam was *opposed* to his father Laomedon's wicked schemes: J. S. Rusten, *Dionysius Scytobrachion* (Opladen 1982), p. 41. Maffeo Vegio ingeniously got around the difficulty by making the death of Astyanax atone for Laomedon's guilt: cf. *De morte Astyanactis opus iocundum et miserabile* (Callii impressum 1475), p. 10: *sed dura luisti* [sc. Astyanax] / *Supplicia et poenas quae Laomedonta manebant / Nil veritum in divos peccare, et culpa nepotes / Criminis insontes tetigit*. Virgil does not seem to develop this argument at all.

[24] Ἀνέμοιο λιπόντος, *Arg.* I. 607 = *Aen.* VII. 27, *cum venti posuere*: above, p. 159, n. 44.

intervenes to change everything, are wonderfully conveyed. But private faces fit ill into public places. The miracle is a sign of something larger than a family destiny. Soon after, as Troy collapses, Creusa disappears.[25] At the end, the fatherly figure who once, in Sicily, had restrained the anger of Entellus (*pater Aeneas procedere longius iras ... saevire animis ... haud passus*, V. 461–62) will ignore *Anchises genitor* (XII. 934), and himself, when he confronts Turnus, give way to the feelings he had once controlled (*saevi ... ira*, 945–46). This family is to be ruthlessly divided, its values twisted to fit a framework of Herculean frenzy, if that is the price of empire. Domitian / Hercules, Commodus / Hercules show what lay in store.

Hercules, Cacus, Aeneas, Turnus

Already in his effort to secure that empire, Aeneas must walk at the margins of conventional virtue[26]—one reason perhaps why he visits marginal lands (Crete, Carthage), or encounters ghosts (Thrace). A metaphorical Crete indeed seems to travel with him. There is the danger and even probability of overstepping bounds. Horace, as was seen, had already sketched the concept of *nimia pietas*. If a flaw (ἁμαρτία) must inevitably attend the hero of a tragic epic, the story of Hercules and Cacus (the aetion of the founding of the Ara Maxima) in Book VIII is peculiarly adapted to reveal its working.

As Aeneas arrives at Pallanteum, mighty shadows of imperial Rome and its mission to civilise mankind fall across the rustic idyll. Already Evander is aware that there was a fight to be engaged. The inhuman *semihomo / monstrum / semifer* Cacus[27] had to be done down, so that the Urbs and its

---

[25] Contrary to Naevius' story: Warmington, *ROL*, fr. 5–7, II, p. 48. Caesar's denarius was noted (above, p. 7). As early as the 5th century, a black-figure amphora perhaps from Vulci, now in the British Museum (GR 1836.224.138, 490–480 B.C.), shows "Aineias escaping from Troy with Creusa at his side." Oddly, Ascanius is not immediately identifiable (cf. Lycophron, *Alex.* 1263, quoted below, p. 265). See also the amphora mentioned in note 4, above.

[26] G. B. Conte (*Virgilio. Il genere e i suoi confini* [Milan 1984²], p. 79), in fact, divides his personality into "subjective" and "objective" functions. This risks disintegration, but there is certainly some sense of moral schizophrenia. Cf. Godo Lieberg, "Aeneas und der sterbende Lausus," *Res Publica Litterarum* XVII (1994), 61–79.

[27] *Monstrum* was used of cannibal, Etnaean Polyphemus (III. 658). Virgil uses *semifer* here with much more pejorative implications than other authors (and than his other instance at X. 212?) in order to make his point. Lucretius applies the word to piping Pan (IV. 587). The poet invents *semihomo* only for this spot. Ovid's use of the word for the antisocial, antisympotic Centaurs (*Met.* XII. 536) is relevant, since Evander invites Aeneas to join him in a symposium (VIII.

Apollo (VIII. 336), even its Jupiter (353) might come about.

Here Virgil's epic plumbs ancient depths. Etruscan Cacu was a handsome prince.[28] This rustler Cacus, haunting the minds of peasants, is a version of Humbaba in *Gilgamesh*, the "perennial Monster Herdsman," who, in Sumerian poetry, has a fiery aspect as well, "perhaps connected with the volcano." Rome is built on volcanic terrain.[29] What old tales persisted? Had Cacu(s) been recast by Latin folk-memory in a primitive mould? He is not a cannibal in Propertius and Livy. Does Virgil intend a sort of Cylops? That would certainly revive thoughts of Dido (IV. 612b–20 ~ *Od.* IX. 528–35).

Such stories had already been rationalised, allegorised. Philosophers spoke of the need to conquer the savage within (Lucretius III. 978 ff.). The imperial Hercules and his conquests are familiar.[30] But was Cacus, with his *mens effera* (VIII. 205), the only monster here?[31] Hercules himself had two sides. Sophocles and Euripides had painted a hero driven insane. Which side does Virgil depict? His hero, engaging in a frenzied struggle with a demonic adversary, is himself fired by the Furies and rages like a wild animal. Vivid nominative present participles, and a hypermetric line, set the scene (219–20, 228–31), in which *Alcides* and *Tirynthius* both describe the hero:

> hic vero Alcidae Furiis exarserat atro
> felle dolor:...
> ecce furens animis aderat Tirynthius omnemque
> accessum lustrans huc ora ferebat et illuc,
> dentibus infrendens. ter totum fervidus ira
> lustrat Aventini montem ...

175–78). None of these words is applied to Turnus. Aeneas is *semivir* twice (IV. 215; XII. 99), in what looks like another Virgilian neologism.

[28] As is seen on a mirror from Bolsena in the British Museum (BM Cat. Bronzes 633): cf. J. Penny Small, *Cacus and Marsyas in Etrusco-Roman Legend* (Princeton 1982). — The quotations following here are from N. K. Sandars, *The Epic of Gilgamesh* (Penguin Classics rev. ed. 1972), p. 34.

[29] The city has a chequered geological history. H.-B. de Saussure reports in his university lectures of 1775 that the *ossa balaenarum* have been unearthed from volcanic *pozzolane* there (Geneva Public Library, BPU Ms. lat. 288, p. 64): cf. *solum cui Roma insistit totum materiis vulcanicis constat.... In Etruria, quam plurima illorum montium vestigia deprehenduntur,* p. 106.

[30] E.g. *Pan. Lat.* II. 2. 1 (X, Mynors, p. 245). Theocritus 17 with its choral lyric predecessors is relevant. The Renaissance and Baroque greatly exploited the analogy (e.g. in Zurbarán's paintings for the Habsburg Philip IV in the Buen Retiro). For a survival of this even in papal eulogy, see *Lelio Guidiccioni, Latin Poems*, edd. Newmans, pp. 52–53, 256. More in the Appendix, below, pp. 337–38.

[31] *Effera* occurs five other times in the *Aeneid*, always in this form: IV. 642 (suicidal Dido); VII. 787 (Turnus' crest); VIII. 6 (the young Latin warriors; cf. *saevit*, 5); VIII. 484 and X. 898 (Mezentius).

At this the Furies kindled in Hercules indignation, the dark gall rising....
See, the hero of Argos was on hand, his anger raging, looking this way and that for every approach, gnashing his teeth. Hot with anger, thrice he surveyed the whole Aventine Hill.

219. *Furiis exarserat* ~ *Furiis accensus*, XII. 946. Cf. *Furiis incensa*, IV. 376; *furens animis* at 228.

220. *felle* in reference to the Fury, XII. 857 (only these two places in the poem). *Dolor* is not a good guide to action. In Book II, for example, Venus asks Aeneas to dismiss it (594–95), as Jupiter asks Juno (XII. 801). Cf. IX. 66, Turnus.

230. *infrendens*, III. 664 (Polyphemus); X. 718 (Mezentius simile).

230. *fervidus ira* ~ *fervidus*, XII. 951 (cf. 894–95, *tua fervida ... dicta, ferox*), Aeneas; *Messapus ... avidus confundere foedus ... fervidus*, XII. 289–90, 293; *Turnus ... fervidus ardet*, XII. 324–25. Cf. *fervidus* IX. 72 (Turnus); IX. 350 (Euryalus: cf. *incensus ... perfurit*, 342–43); 736 (Pandarus); X. 788 (Aeneas assailing Mezentius, and soon to kill Lausus).

What kind of imperial example is this? Is this grotesque duel between two wild opponents framed to fit the pattern Rome forces both on its champions and its enemies?[32]

From narrating Evander, Aeneas will recruit Pallas to his cause. Pallas regards Hercules as his patron (X. 461), and his eventual death seems to produce in Aeneas a moral breakdown of Herculean proportions. Straying beyond bounds, he embarks on a train of slaughter, eventually to be compared with the rebellious Giant Aegaeon.[33] He has been metamorphosed, from Hercules to one of Hercules' adversaries. The element of grotesquerie is marked (X. 565–70):

> Aegaeon qualis, centum cui bracchia dicunt
> centenasque manus, quinquaginta oribus ignem
> pectoribusque arsisse, Iovis cum fulmina contra
> tot paribus streperet clipeis, tot stringeret ensis:
> sic toto Aeneas desaevit in aequore victor,
> ut semel intepuit mucro.

Just like Aegaeon, who story tells had a hundred arms, a hundred hands, while from fifty mouths and breasts fire blazed when, fending off Jove's thunderbolts, he hissed and wielded shields to match, and drew as many swords. So Aeneas vented his victorious rage over the field, once his blade grew warm.

Desaevit, used elsewhere in the poem only by Anna (talking to Dido) of the storms of winter (IV. 52), so incongruous when applied to the *pius* hero, initiates a whole pattern of allusion which culminates at the end of XII.

---

[32] *Senseram quam idem essent.* Compare the general role assigned to the Dirae in Jupiter's plans, XII. 849–52. On Hercules' dual nature in the poem, below, pp. 261, 336.

[33] Contrast Aegaeon as Zeus' *champion* in Homer, *Iliad* I. 404.

When Aeneas kills Turnus there, he has caught sight of the *infelix balteus* taken from Pallas, depicting the murder of their husbands by the Danaids (X. 495–505; XII. 941–42). This triggers in him a *saevus dolor* (945). But the celebrated point of the story was that one Danaid spared her husband's life.[34] This is ignored by Virgil. Aeneas "drank in" the reminder of his savage grief (*hausit*, 946). A shame he could not drink in its moral lesson.

For the Romans, these moral debates were not about abstractions. In an earlier appreciation of the values Romans had absorbed from their Greek teachers, Cicero, himself murdered to glut the resentment of Antony / Hercules, had seen things quite differently (*Tusc. Disp.* IV. 50):

> De Africano quidem ... vel iurare possum non illum iracundia tum inflammatum fuisse, cum in acie M. Allienum Pelignum scuto protexerit gladiumque hosti in pectus infixerit.... Quid igitur huc adhibetis iram? an fortitudo nisi insanire coepit impetus suos non habet? Quid? Herculem, quem in caelum ista ipsa, quam vos iracundiam esse vultis, sustulit fortitudo, iratumne censes conflixisse cum Erymanthio apro aut leone Nemeaeo? ... vide ne fortitudo minime sit rabiosa sitque iracundia tota levitatis; neque enim est ulla fortitudo, quae rationis est expers.

> In Scipio's case ... I will go so far as to swear that he was not on fire with ill temper when on the battlefield he put his shield over his countryman and planted his sword in the assailant's breast.... What then is the relevance of anger here? Does courage have no energy of its own without drawing on madness? Hercules was raised to heaven, not by what you define as his ill temper, but by his courage. Was he angry when he challenged the Erymanthian boar or the Nemean lion? True bravery is far from crazy, and ill temper is a sign of an irresponsible disposition. There is in fact no courage without a basis in reason.

Virgil himself accepts this. His words echo the Stoic source on which Cicero too was dependent (*rationis expers* ~ *non te rationis egentem*, VIII. 299). But there is a contradiction between two aspects of Hercules, as between two aspects of Aeneas. Moderns are familiar with such duality.

The divided world of the *Eclogues* was noted earlier. Here, in the early Rome of Book VIII, the hollow pastoral again intrudes into epic. Like Meliboeus (*Ecl.* 1. 64), Evander the Arcadian is an exile. Like some Roman veteran (*Ecl.* 9. 2), Hercules is an *advena* (*Aen.* X. 460). This is the token of recurring concerns, even contradictions, in the poet's own imagination.

In the *Aeneid*, once again, innocence is to be violated by interloping war. Later, the reception of Pallas' body at Pallanteum in Book XI is like some re-enactment of dead Hector's return to Troy. The price of glory is paid by the death of children, as the spectator of Cumae's temple gates with their Cretan theme had already learned.

---

[34] Horace, *Odes* III. 11. 33–34, *una de multis face nuptiali / digna*; Propertius IV. 7. 63, *sine fraude*.

Te minor laetum reget aequus orbem (Jupiter / Augustus: Hor., *Odes* I. 12. 57). Impatient with such restraint, a poet of the *Anthology* ultimately lauds his emperor as Ζῆνα τὸν Αἰνεάδην (IX. 307. 4); and a bronze statue (from Herculaneum!) of Augustus himself as Jupiter, holding the thunderbolt, is now in Naples. But, if that is an ominous evolution Virgil's Aeneas can hardly understand, even at their most favourable, the subtexts of the poem insist that, still locked in the Trojan past, endlessly repeating outdated paradigms, he draws a Pallas who is also Troilus and Sarpedon away from his father's tutelage, away from bucolic simplicities, into his first—and last—battles. How much as this story is played out there will be of Dido and her suicide! And Pallas is matched by the poet (X. 433-34) with his coeval Lausus, who behaves like Arctinus' Antilochus, dying to save his father in an act of self-sacrifice no Roman could condemn. What is the point then of all this killing? That is a question Aeneas is rarely allowed to ask.[35]

Can this simply be a heroic misadventure? Is not the poet rather commenting on the Rome he knew, the pastoral he knew? Into his own bucolic world had dropped the usurping legionary / *advena*. In Book VIII, for the first time, at what will be Rome, Aeneas / Hercules accepts and imposes the thrusting power of *imperium* (509; cf. 381). Was its influence wholly for the good? Did not the affirmation of that, of the *dulce et decorum*, need an act of vatic faith?

And what had been the outcome of Heracles' madness? In Euripides, he had returned triumphantly from Hades to fall victim himself to the virgin daughter of Night, Lyssa (Frenzy); and, under that baneful influence, to murder his wife and children. In Virgil, the two heroes at first divide ("twin") this inheritance. Aeneas returns from Hades, where Palinurus had hailed him by a Herculean epithet as *invicte* (VI. 365: cf. MAXENTII INVICT on the inscription still seen in his Circus). Yet it is Turnus who is then driven mad by Allecto / Lyssa, and who comes to wear, like Homer's Heracles, a deadly belt. Another Fury will assail him as he dies. But the linguistic parallels linking frenzied Hercules in Book VIII with Aeneas at the end of XII are hardly propitious. Do they suggest that Aeneas becomes Turnus as Heracles became a Cacus? That he too, a second Heracles, in fulfilling his relentless labours, will deaden his own children's consciences by bequeathing to them the example of ruthless civil war? If he is not his children's killer, will he be that of his brother (*fuit et tibi talis Anchises genitor*)?

---

[35] He does ask it in Book XII (*quo ruitis?* 313 = Horace's *quo, quo scelesti ruitis? Epodes* 7. 1), but to no purpose.

260   *Chapter Eleven*

The greatness of the ancients, as was noted, is that they did not excuse the personal trespasses which even divine commissions enjoined.[36] Aeschylus' Agamemnon and Orestes found this out (*Agamemnonius scaenis agitatus Orestes*, IV. 471). In spite of Homer's Poseidon and his ἀναίτιος, for this classical sensibility, only god is ἀναίτιος (αἰτία ἑλομένου· θεὸς ἀναίτιος, Plato, *Rep*. X. 617e). In Aeneas' case, his unwavering perseverance in the service of *fatum* is crossed with repeated reminiscences of Apollonius' portrait of Jason,[37] a comparison reinforced by Dido's increasingly marked identification with Medea and Hypsipyle. But eventually, in Euripides, Jason's heroism was engulfed by the banality of self-interest, while the lesson of Apollonius' epic was that ultimately the hero was inadequate to his task. Aeneas is grander. His pushing beyond expected morality makes him into a Faustian figure. But such figures raise hell (and hence Allecto and the other Furies of the poem's second half). There is a price to be paid. In Hades, Catiline hung from a beetling crag and trembled before the jaws of the Furies (*pendentem scopulo Furiarumque ora trementem*, VIII. 669). Here is where Aeneas' own *Furiis accensus* bears progeny. It is after this on the Shield that the Augustan, Apolline victory at Actium over the monsters of the past is described.

To trivialise Aeneas' misbehaviour, or (still worse) to suggest that it is not misbehaviour at all, falls short then of the poem's concept of the heroic. Fully to understand that, as was suggested, we must look outside the mythical world to the Rome of Virgil's day. There, underground forces had sapped old social structures, moral cataclysm washed away traditional markers. This is the morbid, topsy-turvy universe (*everso ... saeclo*, *Geo*. I. 500, cf. 505) whose ailments Lucretius and Sallust diagnosed, both reacting to Thucydides' picture of plague-stricken Periclean Athens (cf. *Geo*. III. 440 ff.). Aeneas' legacy was tainted. Only under Augustus / Solon could Rome become an Athens cleansed of factional plague by healing Apollo.

Perhaps we may again draw an analogy with the Third Rome. All this

---

[36] This tragic problem particularly exercised Aeschylus, for example. See A. Lesky, *Die tragische Dichtung der Hellenen* (Göttingen 1956), pp. 93–98. Cf. θεὸς μὲν α ἰ τ ί α ν φύει βροτοῖς / ὅταν κακῶσαι δῶμα παμπήδην θέλῃ, Aesch. fr. 154a. 16, Radt (= Mette, p. 96 = Plato, *Rep*. II. 380a *al*.) with Virgil's *Musa mihi c a u s a s memora, quo numine laeso* etc. Virgil particularises the θεός.

[37] "In the more trivial, no less than in the more important, features of his character, Aeneas is drawn after Jason: not only is he the daring adventurer, the intrepid navigator, the faithless seducer, but he leaves home weeping": J. Henry, *Aeneidea* II, p. 359. G. Mooney actually compares the Golden Fleece with the Golden Bough (ad *Arg*. IV. 124, p. 309 of his commentary). This might explain the Gate of False Dreams (cf. *Arg*. IV. 384–85). See D. Nelis, *op. cit., passim*.

also plumbs in its way the demonic slough through which in 1917 the empire of a last Caesar / Tsar slid into ruin. Dostoevsky has seemed relevant before. Sallust's picture of Catiline has indeed something of that grotesque sort about it (*Bell. Cat.* 5. 3–4). Shall we grant the historian more insight into his age than the poet? Of course Aeneas is too honourable for any of this! But suppose one asked Dido? Suppose one listened again to those glib *adynata* which formed his first words to her? In any case, we noted the ancestor of the gens Sergia in his entourage (V. 121). His creator lived in what had been the Rome of Iuppiter Iulius, the author of a youthful *Laudes Herculis* (Suet., *Jul.* 56), where such moral deviations were no longer the lunatic forays of a Salmoneus (VI. 585), but calculating rationalism. With Varius he rebukes (VI. 621–22) the Caesarian Antony who had also been Hercules. His hero presented to Romans a double, Herculean possibility, the germ of supreme greatness and of tragic madness, and vatically offered them the choice and warning. This was the service the poet rendered to Augustus. But if even Augustus appeared in Hercules' city as Jupiter, how long before Caligula and Nero would illustrate more vividly the urgency of Virgil's admonition?

The Way into the Future

For the bearer of future greatness, as Ascanius' father *magnae spes altera Romae* (XII. 168), Aeneas is curiously fixated on his questionable past. To return to Troy, we saw, would have been his dearest wish (IV. 342). He continues to think of his mission as the founding of a new Troy (cf. Aletes' present tense at IX. 247). The Augustan reader knew that he would not do this. One of the poem's greatest silences is the concealment of this knowledge from its hero (the "principle of foiled expectation").

Yet, in a sense, he does return to Troy—but to its battlefield, since on arriving in Italy to found his new Troy he is greeted by the Sibyl with the news that everything is to begin again (VI. 88–89). *Iterum* here is characteristic (cf. *Ecl.* 4. 36). But Horace's Juno, in that Roman ode which reads like a commentary on the διάνοια of the whole *Aeneid*, had warned against such iterations (*Odes* III. 3. 61–64):

> 'Troiae renascens alite lugubri
> fortuna tristi clade i t e r a b i t u r,
> ducente victrices catervas
> coniuge me Iovis et sorore.'

'Troy's fortune will be reborn with gloomy omen and will be repeated amid miserable defeat, while I, Jove's wife and sister, captain the conquering hordes.'

61. *Troiam ... nascentem, Aen.* X. 74–75, here flagrantly contradicted.

64. *Iovisque / et soror et coniunx, Aen.* I. 46–47.

Yet Virgil's Juno—so deep is the insult she has suffered—insists on rather than forbids this pattern. Again we hear *iterum* (VII. 319–22):

> 'nec face tantum
> Cisseis praegnas ignis enixa iugalis;
> quin idem Veneri partus suus et Paris alter,
> funestaeque i t e r u m recidiva in Pergama taedae.'

'Nor was it only Hecuba whose child was a firebrand and who gave birth to fire. Her child remains the same for Venus, a second Paris, and these marriage torches again bring doom on a restored Troy.'

And, in the event, the new Hector (cf. *Il.* XIII. 754 ~ *Aen.* XII. 701–03), killing the new Achilles, cannot roll back the past, as Venus' own withering irony (X. 59–62) proves. Doggedly (*canis*, XII. 751) playing out a superannuated script, her son perseveres to the end as destiny's dupe.

But there was hope. It was through Apolline Augustus, Sun-King and champion of peace (all themes recurring in Horace), that a light shone (*Aen.* XII. 161–64):

> Interea reges ingenti mole Latinus
> quadriiugo vehitur curru (cui tempora circum
> aurati bis sex radii fulgentia cingunt,
> Solis avi specimen) ...

Meanwhile forth come the kings of mighty frame. Latinus rides out in a chariot drawn by four horses, round his gleaming temples twelve golden rays, the emblem of the Sun his grandfather.

How curiously here the old and feeble king suddenly acquires *ingens moles*, the divine גדב![38] His radiate diadem is that which Augustus' father dreamed he saw his infant son wearing (Suet., *Aug.* 94). Earlier (VI. 69), Aeneas transcends anything he will do himself in vowing to found the Temple of the Palatine Apollo, which Augustus built. On the Shield, again quite unlike Aeneas, Augustus leads the peoples of Italy (VIII. 678) against all the Oriental excesses with which Egypt and even Troy itself could be associated. At the end, it is Augustus who sits at the snow-white threshold of shining Phoebus to count the tribute of the conquered nations. Perhaps there is some allusion to a statue of the god in the precinct of Apollo Palatinus with the emperor's features, and certainly an Apollo citharoedus stood by his tomb.[39]

Augustus may be a transfigured Latinus, but he is not Aeneas. In a

---

[38] This is the *maiorque videri* of VI. 49, topical in supernatural apparitions.

[39] Erika Simon, *Augustus. Kunst und Leben in Rom* (Munich 1986), p. 21.

passage close to the spirit of Virgil's depiction of Aeneas' Shield, and also glorifying the victory at Actium, Propertius, who elsewhere does not spare some criticisms of Hercules (IV. 9), encapsulates the major difference: *Auguste, Hectoreis cognite m a i o r avis* (IV. 6. 38; cf. *nec te Troia capit* of Ascanius, *Aen.* IX. 644). Augustus is greater than his warring (and Civil-warring) Trojan forebears. Jupiter indeed had foretold a different destiny to come (I. 261–96)—but to Venus. Rising beyond himself, Anchises had seen that such a commission would demand new values (VI. 851–53):

> 'tu regere imperio populos, Romane, memento
> (hae tibi erunt artes), pacique imponere morem,
> parcere subiectis et debellare superbos.'

> 'You, Roman, must remember to rule the peoples with authority—these shall be your skills—and to set a moral stamp on peace, to spare the conquered and war down the stiff-necked.'

His apostrophe is no longer to Aeneas. *Romane* shows that these are imperial doctrines. Cicero's *Pro Marcello* had already provided a commentary on the role in them of mercy.[40] Augustus picks up *parcere* with *peperci* in the *Res Gestae* (3).

At the end, Aeneas urged Ascanius to learn *fortunam ex aliis* (XII. 436). Was he confessing a failure? Earlier, he had been instructed by the Sibyl to go *beyond* fortune: *tu ne cede malis, sed contra audentior ito / quam tua te Fortuna sinet* (VI. 95–96),[41] and Augustus saw Fortune as a cruel enemy (*atrox*, Suet., *Tib.* 23; cf. *R. G.* 14). *Ecce par deo dignum, vir fortis cum fortuna mala conpositus, utique si et provocavit* wrote Seneca (*Prov.* 2. 9). Whatever his intermittent and increasingly frenzied efforts, unlike Augustus, and quite unlike the Cato whose image he carries on his Shield, Aeneas never finally broke out of the Homeric stereotype by challenging Fortune.

But Rome too had been snared in his apparently *inextricabilis error* (*Geo.* I. 489–92):

> ergo inter sese paribus concurrere telis
> Romanas acies i t e r u m videre Philippi;
> nec fuit indignum superis b i s sanguine nostro
> Emathiam et latos Haemi pinguescere campos.

---

[40] *Adversarium ... extollere i a c e n t e m* , §8. In 54, he had declared in the *Pro Rabirio Postumo* (§2): *Satis est homines imprudentia lapsos non erigere, urgere vero iacentis ... certe est in h u m an u m*. Cf. Horace's *i a c e n t e m lenis in hostem*, *Carmen Saeculare* 51–52: E. Fraenkel, *Horace*, p. 376, n. 3.

[41] The echo of the line by Venus at X. 49 offers the tame *et quacumque viam dederit Fortuna sequatur*. This is when she has already surrendered the thought of empire (42), and thinks merely of a re-established Troy (58): cf. however Seneca, *De Const. Sap.* 1, *supra Fortunam*. F. Cumont may be usefully consulted: *Lux Perpetua* (Paris 1949), p. 113, n. 4.

So Philippi again witnessed the clash of Roman battle lines, their weapons matched. The gods above were not shocked that twice with our blood Thessaly and the broad fields of Haemus should grow fat.

The parallelism, a supremely tragic *dédoublement*, profoundly impressed Lucan (*iterum*, *Phars.* I. 692). Perhaps it was this similarity (later re-emphasised by Livy?) which set Virgil's mind working about the structure of an epic in which the imposed imitation of a famous model would also be a devastating commentary on human inability to learn from the past.

If then Propertius had proudly declared that something greater was in gestation than the *Iliad* (II. 34. 66), for Virgil this was more than the typical Roman desire to outdo (*Überbietung*), or any sort of Alexandrian ζῆλος. He was a Roman; for him the purpose of literature was to be useful. Those who do not study the lessons of history are condemned to repeat its mistakes. Aeneas is caught in the pattern he discovers already in Book I in Juno's temple at Carthage, and this unhappy cycle is forced on him by the gods. He is too small a hero to challenge it.

At the end, Turnus finds himself in a nightmarish web[42] from which there is no escape (XII. 910-11). But both heroes have circled in their dance of death like the children in the *Lusus Troiae* (*orbis*, XII. 763; V. 584). Perhaps here we may understand the ineptness of some of the poem's Homeric parallels noted by commentators—the Nisus and Euryalus escapade again comes to mind—as a deliberate clue to the falsity and lack of conviction inherent in this sort of mindless iteration. *Nascetur ridiculus mus* (*A.P.* 139) was Horace's reaction to a poet promising a retelling of "Priam's fortune and the glorious war."[43] With unerring surefootedness, Virgil trod this treacherous ground. He used his foray into *crambe repetita* certainly to prove his mastery of the poetics of allusion, but also to generate from his tragedy of recurrences and "imitations" a vatic lesson.

Can such pregnant imitation be fruitful with any new and different future? What words and promises, in the poem at least, do Lavinia and Aeneas ever exchange? And yet from their union hangs the destiny of an empire! In their own dialogue with destiny, will the poem's perhaps too literate listeners fare any better? A poetic of silences (αὐτὸς ἐπιφράσσαιτο ...) is no longer to be appreciated as mere τέχνη. It demands our cutting (ברא, τάμοι), creative, responsive, civil human word.

---

[42] פְּנֵי־הַלּוֹט הַלּוֹט, Isaiah 25:7; cf. *Il.* XIII. 359; West, *East Face*, p. 568.

[43] *A.P.* 137, *fortunam Priami cantabo et nobile bellum*; cf. *Forsitan et Priami fuerint quae fata requiras*, *Aen.* II. 506.

XII

THE MEN CHARACTERS—III: ANCHISES AND IULUS / ASCANIUS

Anchises

In the *Iliad*, though the poem is not especially concerned with him, Anchises' lineage and family are well sketched. Son of Capys (XX. 239), he is Priam's cousin and, unlike Priam, not directly descended from guilty Laomedon—though, as we saw, he does have a blemish on his record. It was he who, without Laomedon's knowledge, cheating a cheat, had bred his mares to the horses given by Zeus to Tros as a recompense for the loss of Ganymede (*Iliad* V. 265–72). Of the six resulting foals, he kept four and gave two to his son Aeneas, who in this sense became the heir of a trickster. In Italy, Latinus will unwittingly revive for him a memory of this episode (*Aen.* VII. 280–83).

This Homeric Anchises is the father of a number of daughters, the eldest married to the brave Alcathous (*Il.* XIII. 427 ff.). He apparently has a second son, Echepolus, king of Sicyon (XXIII. 296 ff.), and vassal of Agamemnon. Was he perhaps the fruit of his father's visit to Greece in Priam's entourage (*Aen.* VIII. 157)? In Lycophron, Anchises certainly has a bastard son, Elymus, ancestor of the Sicilian Elymi (*Alex.* 965). But Echepolus, along with his siblings, must be eliminated from Virgil's story. We hear there of no daughters. His Anchises has one son, who famously bore out of Troy this part of his past.

Whatever the sources of Naevius' tale, in which Anchises and Aeneas both left Troy with their wives,[1] Lycophron already knew that Aeneas would thrust aside not only his wife but also his children at Troy for the sake of his father and household gods (παρώσας καὶ δάμαρτα καὶ τέκνα, 1263). Yet Lycophron's Anchises is merely γεραιός. In Virgil, he is not without some more mysterious imperfection (II. 647–49):

> 'iam pridem invisus divis et inutilis annos
> demoror, ex quo me divum pater atque hominum rex

---

[1] Above, p. 14.

> fulminis adflavit ventis et contigit igni.'

'For too long now hateful to the gods, serving no purpose, I have been only stemming the tide of my years, ever since the father of gods and lord of men blasted me with his rushing thunderbolt and touched me with his fire.'

This is a tradition drawn from outside the *Iliad* (cf. *Hymn. Hom.* 5. 286–88). According to it, his encounter with Aphrodite, from which Aeneas was born, offers another instance of the dire consequences attending mortal men paired with goddesses.[2] It has left him withered, weakened: χαλεποὶ δὲ θεοὶ φαίνεσθαι ἐναργεῖς. Somehow it too aroused the jealousy of the gods. Elsewhere in the poem, he is *invalidus* (VI. 114). This aspect of his character may well be obscured at times (VIII. 162–63), but it must not be forgotten, or treated as a mere artistic device. Certainly, one may recall blind Teiresias (and there was a version of the story maintaining that Anchises himself was blind). Certainly it is true that the physical weakness of old age is traditionally allowed to justify its claim to spiritual insight. But like son, like father: there is also the suggestion that what survives from Troy is imperfect, *Troia gaza per undas*, damaged goods. Aeneas' adversaries are quick to note resemblances with the unscrupulous past.

Like Dido, mortal Anchises too survives long after he is ostensibly dead. At the very end, we hear him in a better key. Turnus appeals to Anchises' memory in the hope of finding mercy (XII. 932–34):

> 'miseri te si qua parentis
> tangere cura potest, oro (fuit et tibi talis
> Anchises genitor) Dauni miserere senectae ... '

'If some thought for my unhappy father may touch you (just such a one to you was your father Anchises), I beg, take pity on Daunus' old age.'

Insinuatio though it was, Aeneas might have been expected to hear this plea, which would have been no more than the fulfilment of the imperial programme of Book VI, dictated after all by Anchises. But Anchises spoke, as we heard, to the Roman (VI. 851), and this is an insight Aeneas does not enjoy (*ignarus*, VIII. 730). He reiterates the example of Achilles after the death of Patroclus (*Il.* XXI. 99 ff.)—but not the example of Achilles listening to Priam's μνῆσαι πατρὸς σοῖο (*Il.* XXIV. 486; cf. 507) and softening his heart. At the critical moment, the sight of Pallas' Herculean belt and its bloody *thalami* unhinges him—he had seen all that at Troy—and he gives way to the Furies and their fires. Here at the end, in the long struggle between her ghost and Anchises', burning, furious Dido wins.

In Book V, Anchises wins. Aeneas arrives in Sicily unaware, as he later

---

[2] The motif is as old as Gilgamesh's reproaches to Ishtar: ed. George, pp. 49–50.

claims (VI. 463), of Dido's suicide. He then celebrates his father's funeral rites in a *theatri circus* (288–89; cf. 109, 551). This locale is not casually chosen. The circus was a place of resurrection (above, p. 5). The dead could live again. This was the whole long Etruscan tradition incorporated in the rite of gladiators (Entellus / Dares) at Roman funerals. Aeneas is making a Roman choice to lend his father fresh life. This implies for him a choice against Dido. It also implies, notably in the labyrinthine *Lusus Troiae*, a choice for a Julian / Ilian future (Suet., *Jul*. 39). But Anchises will tell him what Julius must do: *proice tela manu, sanguis meus* (VI. 835). Aeneas cannot hear this. For all his devotion to his father, in the final analysis, he does not choose the right things. *Fallit te incautum pietas tua* ....[3]

Anchises' games are borrowed both from the *Iliad* (Patroclus) and the *Odyssey* (Odysseus on Scheria).[4] They are linked with events of the later books. Time is reversed. The funerals are celebrated before the deaths occur. The most obvious illustration of this is supplied by Nisus and Euryalus, not returning until IX, re-enacting there the self-sacrificial gestures of Book V, their heads then paraded. No obsequies now for them! In the later half of the poem, for all its Iliadic parallels, the principle of foiled expectation accordingly ensures there are no funeral games. When Camilla / Patroclus or Turnus / Patroclus die, we will not hear again what we have already heard. The absence of such rites of closure enhances the gloomy atmosphere pervading this second part of the story, of which the homecoming of Pallas in Book XI provides a supreme illustration. No resurrections are portended here. Setting his funeral games for Archemorus (ἀρχὴ μόρου) in Book VI *before* the civil war at Thebes has begun, Statius showed that he had learned from this, and from its Greek models.[5]

In Book V Virgil is also, within the economy of the poem as the listener apprehends it, substituting Anchises for Dido. Dido's court formed after all some parallel to welcoming Scheria, with its rescuing Nausicaa / Arete. On

---

[3] *Aen*. X. 812: cf. *Geo*. IV. 488 (Orpheus). Juno's *nimium pii* in Horace is noted above, p. 252.

[4] For the Homeric parallels, see Knauer's indexes, pp. 389 ff.

[5] Conversely, in using the "If I had many tongues" topos *after* the carnage of battle (*Theb*. XII. 797–99), while Homer uses it in Book II of the *Iliad* (489–90) *before* his account of the fighting has begun, he is recalling for us (like General Sherman later) what the pomp and panoply of war come down to in the end. Virgil even more radically uses it for the punishments of the damned (VI. 625–27). See "De Statio epico animadversiones," *Latomus* XXXIV (1975), 80–89. — With his imitation in *Aen*. V of the *Iliad*'s funeral games of Patroclus, Virgil is anticipating the death of Camilla / Patroclus in *Aen*. XI and, in so far as Amazonian Dido and Camilla share an identity, the games of V will ultimately make do for both. But this becomes clear only in retrospect.

Scheria, there were games. With Dido's suicide, what funeral games does emotional logic, reinforced by the requirement of *imitatio*, now demand? But whose instead do we get? The foiling of expectation is emphasised by a verbal repetition. As Aeneas stands by his father's tomb, a serpent glides out, glistening in the light, just like a rainbow (V. 88–89):

> ceu nubibus arcus
> mille iacit varios adverso sole colores.

As a rainbow in the clouds casts a thousand motley hues, reflecting the sun.

But the last time we heard about the rainbow was when Juno sent Iris down to cut a lock of Dido's hair so that she might be released from her death agony (IV. 700–02):

> ergo Iris croceis per caelum roscida pennis
> mille trahens varios adverso sole colores
> devolat et supra caput astitit.

So dewy Iris through the sky on saffron wings, trailing a thousand hues as she caught the sun, flew down and alighted above her head.

Cheated even out of her obsequies, Dido knew all along that her battle was with Anchises. Aeneas had told her as much (IV. 351–53), and Anchises says the same (VI. 694).

Aeneas' memory is guilty of some telling lapses. It was of course Mercury who had appeared at Jupiter's behest and told him that he should leave Carthage (IV. 271). Soon afterwards, in trying to explain his behaviour to Dido, he thinks rather of his father (IV. 351). Later, when the Trojans find themselves unwittingly fulfilling in Italy Celaeno's threat that one day they would hungrily eat their very tables (III. 256–57), he again thinks of his father (VII. 122–23):

> genitor mihi talia namque
> (nunc repeto) Anchises fatorum arcana reliquit:
> 'cum te, nate, fames ignota ad litora vectum
> accisis coget dapibus consumere mensas ... '

For my father Anchises, as I now recall, left me such secret revelations of destiny: 'When, my son, you have been carried to unknown shores, and hunger shall force you at your scanty meal to eat the tables ...'

Aeneas remembers in the detail of direct speech an incident for which the poet has used quite a different mouthpiece. This may be a proof that the *Aeneid* lacked the finishing touch.[6] But how telling in another aspect these

---

[6] This is the reverse of the pattern in Book II, where the warning apparition of Hector (270) is ignored under the influence of *furor iraque* (316), and eventually Venus herself must intervene (589). — On the prophecy of the tables, see

confusions of Anchises with Mercury / Jupiter in Book IV; with a "dark" (κελαινή) Fury (*Furiarum ego maxima*, III. 252) in Book VII. People do indeed "remember" incidents which never happened, and they certainly distort their memories of what did happen. Something more important cuts across reality. For Aeneas, that something more important, even when the reality in question is divine, is Anchises. He assimilates the cruellest things—even a Fury—into his ancestry. This has consequences. At the end, as he kills Turnus, his father's memory is displaced by the Furies' (dark?) fires. His *pietas* towards Pallas and Evander (cf. XI. 178-79) becomes, to adapt Horace's language, *nimia*, and this is the excess which constitutes his tragic ἁμαρτία.

When Aeneas first meets Evander, the old king revives for him the unexpected memory of his father in all his youthful vigour (VIII. 162-63). Priam had been on a visit to his sister at Salamis, and had first stopped in Arcadia. He was accompanied by a retinue of Trojan nobles, tallest of whom was Anchises. He and Evander had exchanged gifts, including two bridles,[7] now presented in turn to Pallas.

There are a number of similar encounters with old family friends in Homer, but a parallel with Apollonius is more direct. After various adventures, but in particular after Pollux's defeat of pugilist Amycus, the Argonauts are warmly welcomed by Lycus, king of the Mariandyni, who eventually decides to send his son Dascylus to join the heroes on the rest of their adventure (II. 803). Dascylus, unmentioned at Colchis, is dropped off on the Argonauts' return, to find his own way home (IV. 298).

In the course of recounting his story to the king, Jason has to explain that Heracles (anticipating Dascylus?) was already abandoned, at Cius. Lycus sympathises with the deprivation this implies. In his own younger days, he has met the hero in his father's palace, and remembers his prowess as a boxer (II. 774 ff.). This both offers some similarity to Evander's youthful memories of Anchises and would be another illustration of Heracles' tendency to appear in Virgil's poem obliquely.[8]

Dascylus is a more fortunate Pallas. Lycus is Evander. But the shadow of Heracles, cast on this scene in *Aeneid* VIII by its reminiscence of the *Argonautica*, throws a chill on the very beginning of Pallas' heroic exploit

---

Lycophron, *Alex.* 1250-52. Shortly Lycophron speaks of the sow, white in the *Aeneid* (III. 392), as κελαινή (1256).

[7] *Frenatis lucent in equis*, in the *Lusus Troiae*, V. 554; *frena* in the funeral offerings, XI. 195.

[8] Maecenas had a pugilist Hercules in his *horti* (M. C. inv. 1088): Albertoni, *Capitoline Museums*, p. 198.

(cf. X. 461, 464). There is even another elusive hint of Dido. Earlier, Virgil had borrowed from Apollonius on his Heracles (*Arg.* IV. 1477–78 = *Aen.* VI. 453–54) to recall the unheroic aftermath of another invasion of the pastoral, the ghastly consequences of the stealing of the golden apples from the Hesperides, the image of Dido's fate at the hands of Aeneas (*Hesperidum*, IV. 484). Dido will contribute a robe to Pallas' bier (XI. 72–75).

Anchises inevitably becomes part of Virgil's poetic of silences, most nobly perhaps when he alerts his son to what the slaying of Lausus really means (X. 822). But, when he speaks, it is he who carries the imperial and Augustan message, nowhere more gloriously than in the injunctions concluding Book VI. They would have sounded hollow on the lips of Aeneas, emerging with the false dreams by the Ivory Gate. *Hic vir, hic est....* A new beginning more consciously made offered better hope.

Iulus / Ascanius

And finally there is Ascanius, confounded for dynastic reasons with Iulus.[9] If Lycophron, and the evidence of Greek vases, had said that Aeneas "thrust aside" both wife and children in order to rescue his father, Virgil thrusts aside the wife. He thrusts aside whatever other children there were. One child he had to keep.

The analysis of the *Aeneid*'s epic technique presented earlier already suggested that so intemperate a poem, pathetically ranging between opposite, "adult" extremes, was not well adapted for the normality of children. It is not until the last book of the *Aeneid* that we are given any indication of affection between the hero and his son. He solaces the fearful Iulus at XII. 110 (cf. 399), a scene illustrated on a Pompeian painting preserved in Naples (inv. 9009). Even there, though he has his arm around the weeping boy, he has turned away.

The only occasion when Aeneas is shown actually speaking to him is in this same book (435–40), as he faces what might be (and indeed in the poem is) his last battle. The solemnity of his words needs a Homeric analogue to make its full impact. The lines resonate so deeply because they are also Virgil's adaptation of the parting of Hector and Andromache, a scene which establishes the tragic tonality of the *Iliad* (VI. 391–502), and was already evoked to illumine Turnus' interview with Allecto.[10] The link is made by a quotation from Andromache's speech in *Aeneid* III, thus complementing the only two occasions when such an odd word as *avunculus* appears in the epic:

---

[9] On him, M. Petrini, *The Child and the Hero*, pp. 87 ff.

[10] Above, p. 175.

et pater Aeneas et avunculus excitat Hector. (III. 343)
et pater Aeneas et avunculus excitet Hector. (XII. 440)

Δαιμόνιε, φθίσει σε τὸ σὸν μένος (VI. 407). The *Iliad* was shadowed by the premonition that the champion of Troy, in spite of all his victories, might one day meet his match, bringing doom upon his wife and son. In that instance, the listener knows that the premonition was true enough. But if Ascanius is the *imago* of Astyanax (III. 489)? Does that twinning inspire no reflections? Such *dédoublement* cannot be given a univocal interpretation. The ambiguity about whether a Trojan Ascanius made it to Italy, reflected in the tradition, is built by the poet into the structure of his identity.

And what broad humanity Homer has displayed! How reduced all this is in the hands of the Roman poet! There are no women now, no baby, simply a father and adolescent son. And here, if the son makes no rejoinder, how different he is even from baby Astyanax, whose alarm at his father's martial panoply elicits such smiling sympathy. What does Ascanius' silence say?[11]

But the first book of the *Aeneid* had deployed an equal silence. Venus puts Ascanius to sleep so that, in the cruel deception played on Dido, changeling Cupid can take his place (cf. *oscula*, I. 687; XII. 434, another incongruous word in epic). If a parallel is rightly traced between Juno's demeanour in the first and seventh books, Cupid, who drives Dido mad with burning passion, so soon to turn to burning hatred, corresponds in the economy of the action to Allecto. Her effect on Turnus is similar, and equally has something disordered and sexual about it (*Erato*, VII. 37; *illum turbat amor*, XII. 70). Cupid loses the spoiled and all too human airs Eros irritatingly but plausibly displays in Apollonius, and becomes, in retrospect at least, demonic. Meanwhile, the child is treated no differently from the adult characters: not valued for his own sake, but as it were chloroformed and exploited, used to further historical and extra-historical ends.

As the only surviving heir of royal Priam's line, as Aeneas' son, Ascanius carries a huge burden of destiny in the poem. His double name itself is not without ill-starred Homeric or Apollonian precedent (Astyanax / Scamandrius, *Il.* VI. 402–03; Apsyrtus / Phaethon, *Arg.* III. 245). But among Romans that duplicity must have struck a different chord. Its most obvious parallel was the change of names assumed by the Octavius who became Octavian / Augustus, the former denoting his adoption, the second —which might at one time actually have been "Romulus"—recalling the foundation of the City *augusto imperio*. The whole ancient (religious)

---

[11] This is the technique of Timanthes' veiled Agamemnon (above, p. 113). But, in Virgil's rhetoric of silences, it is dangerous to give the silence here one interpretation and no more.

tradition,[12] renewed in the assumption by popes and potentates of new names upon accession, received here a fresh fillip: and, if religious, ambivalent, mysterious.

Ascanius / Iulus at times is a kind of pre-Augustus, notably when he is withdrawn from the battlefield by Apollo, and called to a destiny more than Trojan (*nec te Troia capit*, IX. 644). Even so, the story outside Virgil (in the Elder Cato, for example) concerning Ascanius / Iulus was tangled.[13] Whose son was he, Creusa's or Lavinia's? Livy himself, who advertises his admiration for the emperor (IV. 20. 7), was not sure (I. 3. 2). If he was Lavinia's, his maternal bond with Troy was snapped, and all the careful pathos of Virgil's *Bildungsroman* goes for nothing. But there was also some memory of this Ascanius as quarrelsome and even ruthless. How soon the pattern of civil strife began!

As names, both Ascanius (*Il*. II. 862; XIII. 792) and Iulus / Ilus (*Aen*. I. 268) aroused Trojan echoes. Yet an Ilus is also a Rutulian (X. 401–02). What such a doublet really means for Aeneas' son—only once, in contravention of the whole epic manner, *Aenides* (IX. 653)—is that he carries two possibilities, Italian and Trojan. Yet an Italian link makes him part of a civil war. A Trojan link renews the threat from Juno. What had in fact happened to his descendant Julius? Was Augustus his heir, or rather Pompey's?

Within his poem, evidently Virgil took pains to sketch Ascanius' slow maturity, from the child gripping his father's hand on the way out of collapsing Troy (but why not his mother's?) to the excited boy who careers around at Dido's hunt, and then the youngster who in Sicily shows his paces on Dido's horse in the Labyrinth of the *Lusus Troiae*, and is first to bring aid to the burning fleet. Later comes the impetuous slayer of Silvia's pet stag; the impulsive youth generally in charge of the defence of the camp while his father is away seeking help; the novice warrior claiming his first victim—and protectively warned off by Apollo (IX. 653 ff.; the Homeric parallel makes him Patroclus); the downcast witness of his father's wound (XII. 399).

But this developing career raises questions. Ascanius' slaying of the pet

---

[12] It has Semitic parallels: Abram / Abraham; Simon / Peter; James and John / Boanerges, and so on.

[13] Austin on *Aen*. II. 563. If the sceptical tale that his mother was Lavinia was simply Marian propaganda (Ogilvie, *Commentary on Livy Books 1–5*, p. 43), it is surprising that it persisted so long. Plutarch (*Jul*. 1) and Suetonius (*Jul*. 1) alike record Sulla's remark that the recalcitrant Julius Caesar had in him many Mariuses. Why would the Marians choose to go on piquing a Marian on a sensitive point of family pride? Was Livy a Marian?

deer at the beginning of the Trojans' adventure in Italy was fraught with dire associations and results. It recalled, for example, Agamemnon's ill-omened hunt at Aulis, at the beginning of the Greek adventure against Troy. His most noteworthy act as *praefectus castris* is to despatch Nisus and Euryalus on a mission which degenerates into mayhem.[14] His wild promises to them of reward are quite misplaced, and in any case suggest that Latinus is to be treated as a conquered foe. What Achilles has to be placated here? Distracted by toys, the pair are apparently just as immature as the young prince who sends them on their last enterprise. An Ascanius / Patroclus raises even more questions.

The Abnormality of Description

Yet Ascanius / Iulus enjoys an extraordinary privilege. Already in Book II (683) he receives a variant of what would become the imperial halo (*nimbus*,נזר), the token of the divine presence.[15] Later, unlike Dido, unlike the Helen of Book II, he is described (X. 132-38):

> ipse inter medios, Veneris iustissima cura,
> Dardanius caput, ecce, puer detectus honestum,
> qualis gemma micat fulvum quae dividit aurum,
> aut collo decus aut capiti, vel quale per artem   135
> inclusum buxo aut Oricia terebintho
> lucet ebur; fusos cervix cui lactea crinis
> accipit et molli subnectens circulus auro.

Himself in the midst, Venus' most worthy charge, see! the young prince of Troy has uncovered his noble head, as a jewel sparkles that parts tawny gold, ornament for neck or head; as ivory gleams with skilful marquetry, enclosed in boxwood or Illyrian terebinth. A milky neck caught his flowing locks that wore a circlet made of malleable gold.

The poet is hinting at the court art of the Augustan cameo (cf. I. 590-93): even more obviously if the *fulvum aurum* of line 134 here alludes, not so much to the metal, as to a vein of brown in the stone, cunningly exploited by the skilled craftsman to form part of his portrait. A sardonyx in the British Museum, for example, showing a bust of Augustus wearing the aegis, uses exactly this technique.[16] A carnelian in Florence (NMA inv.

---

[14] Q. Cicero's indiscretion in Gaul may be distantly compared: *Bell. Gall.* VI. 36-40.

[15] On the nimbus as the sign of royal destiny, Marazov, *Ancient Gold*, p. 67. Alexander's ἀναστολή is perhaps a version of it: cf. Plutarch, *Pompey* 2.

[16] The so-called 'Blacas cameo' (Gems 3577). "Such professions of divinity were apparently thought beyond the pale for public consumption, but quite suitable for private adulation" (Lucilla Burn, *The British Museum Book of Greek and Roman Art* [1991], p. 183). Her fig. 179 (p. 210) depicts a sard intaglio

14914) shows, within a *circulus aureus*, busts of Caius and Lucius Caesar on one side, and on the other the *lupus Martius* feeding Romulus and Remus while Faustulus looks on. Is Virgil's picture of Ascanius in this line? Is it the image of a son Augustus either never had, or lost?

Such cameos were meant at first as tokens of divinity. In time, their use became more commonplace. A gold medallion with a sardonyx cameo in Rome, perhaps from the third century A.D., once thought to show an imperial couple, is now interpreted as that of an ordinary husband and wife.[17] But in the epic, public poet we should realise how odd a cameo is. Propertius offers a hint of Cynthia's appearance (II. 2)—in elegiacs. In hexameters, description is not normal. Homer's *Iliad* describes the grotesque Λιταί (IX. 502). He says something of the beauty of dead Hector (XXIV. 418–21). His Helen, like a host of others, is left to our imaginations. Apollonius half-describes divine Apollo (II. 674 ff.), or the serpent (IV. 127 ff.). Jason and Medea we must guess at.

As the picture of the serpent hints, description seems to aid the demonic vision in particular. Euphorion has left a magnificent picture of Cerberus (Powell fr. 51, p. 40). Sallust, interested in the demented psyche, also described doomed Catiline's matching physical appearance (15. 5). Tellingly, it is often easier for man to recognise hell than paradise, for which "apophatic" negatives are typically called into play.

Eurybates, the herald, is described in the *Odyssey* (XIX. 246). Heralds were sacred, and in this case there is some hint of the grotesque. Yet, even in the *Odyssey*, theorising Horace notes description's abnormal and secondary place: *ut speciosa dehinc miracula promat / Antiphaten Scyllamque et cum Cyclope Charybdin* (A.P. 144–45). He is notoriously

---

dated between 30 and 10 B.C. showing a head which may be that of the emperor's sister, Octavia, and, with other illustrations there from later imperial art, exemplifies the poet's *molli ... circulus auro*. For similar *circuli* see also pp. 51–55 of *Ancient Rome*, ed. G. Bartoloni, (Florence 2002): head of Augustus dated 20 B.C. now in Florence (NMA inv. 14913) on p. 51. Cameos of this sort had Alexandrian precedents: *A Handbook of Roman Art*, ed. M. Henig (Phaidon, Oxford 1983), p. 155: see his section there on "Augustan Gems," beginning on p. 153. There are wonderful examples in the Farnese Collection in Naples, among them a sardonyx-onyx cameo from Herculaneum of the youthful Octavian (inv. 25876). A sardonyx cameo (post 217 A.D.), meant for private viewing, said to show Caracalla's apotheosis, is preserved in the Bibliothèque Municipale at Nancy (*Aurea Roma*, edd. Ensoli / La Rocca, p. 551, no. 205). A striking onyx fragment from even later antiquity, in shades of colour from white to black, found at Kusatak in Serbia, is in the National Museum, Belgrade ("Cameo of a Victorious Emperor," 325–60 A.D.), and may confirm that these originally private portraits eventually enjoyed more general dissemination.

[17] *The Capitoline Museums*, p. 132.

hostile even to the otiose *ekphrasis topou* (14 ff.). Certainly, Ovid's descriptions in the *Metamorphoses* are celebrated. That is his proof that we are in a world of fantasy.

If, as an Augustan (Horace, *A.P.* 1 ff.; Vitruvius VII. 5), Virgil cherishes an interest in the physically grotesque, he is regularly compelled by generic decorum, just like Ovid, to displace it to monsters and metamorphoses. For him, they help to establish the atmosphere—in the tradition of Dante, it was called above an inferno—in which his heroic action habitually unfolds. Any human being thrust into this different realm must also be abnormal.

Sometimes, that means comic. In this tradition, lyric (komic) Pindar's Heracles verged on the laughable, while his victorious Melissus was "contemptible to look at."[18] But, just as komic Pindar had more flatteringly described heroic Jason (*Py.* 4. 78 ff.), Virgil can exceptionally describe his young prince, since he too is the vehicle of an as yet unrealised future; and for the same reason hint, with the aid of Greek lyric, at Lavinia's conventional milk and roses (XII. 67–69).

Yet, as in the case of Lavinia, the description of Iulus is not realistic. The reader feels himself already transported to the Greek novel,[19] even to the theory of descriptions dictating that they should begin *a capite*.[20] Aristotle's *Poetics* shows that Simonides' parallel between the painter's and the poet's art had become routine.[21] But equally, if pushed too far, if it became merely an excuse for ὄψις, description contradicted Aristotle's theory that epic was essentially dramatic, a matter of characters shown in action. No time there for any static admiration of the picturesque. *Semper ad eventum festinat*: Virgil, author of a supremely dramatic poem, certainly felt this. Why the deviation here towards romance?

The answer has to do with the remembering genre. Epic is a composite,

---

[18] Μορφὰν βραχύς of Heracles, *Isth.* 4. 53. Melissus is ὀνοτὸς ἰδέσθαι, *ibid.*, 50.

[19] Though it has been argued that the novel's descriptions are meant as contributions to the narrative: S. Bartsch, *Decoding the Ancient Novel. The Reader and the Role of Description in Heliodorus and Achilles Tatius* (Princeton 1989). Description was an element of the ancient poetic variously handled by different authors: see *The Classical Epic Tradition*, pp. 288–89.

[20] Cf. E. Faral, *Les Arts Poétiques du XIIe et du XIIIe Siècles* (Paris 1924), pp. 80–81, though he does not mention the Προγυμνάσματα of Aphthonius or Hermogenes. It is noted in medical texts such as those by Celsus, Scribonius Largus, parts of Pliny the Elder, by von Albrecht, *Gesch. Röm. Lit.*, I, p. 452.

[21] Simonides: apud Plutarch, *De Glor. Athen.* 3; Aristotle and painting: e.g. παραπλήσιον γάρ ἐστιν καὶ ἐπὶ τῆς γραφικῆς κτλ, 1450a 39–50b 3; and ὄψις, 1450b 16–20. Cf. ὡς ἐν γραφαῖς already in Aeschylus (*Aga.* 242).

and even subsumes the comic / iambic: bustling Hephaestus (ἄσβεστος ... γέλως, *Il.* I. 599), ugly Thersites (γελοῖιον, II. 215), disguised Odysseus (γελόωντες, *Od.* XVIII. 40). Archilochus, the supreme iambist, had offered descriptions: of a hetaera, of a bandy-legged general (25, 60, Diehl). The second of this pair is still in the mould of Thersites, though the paradox is that here there is acceptance rather than rejection. The first is that of someone outside the social calculus, to that extent קדש, uncanny.[22] But קדש also means "holy." Archilochus was also the inventor of the primal epinician (Pindar, *Ol.* 9. 1), and in some way, as ἐξάρχων, at the root of tragedy (fr. 77 + Aristotle, *Poetics* 1449a 11). Was he no longer an iambist in those genres?

Description then is in its first inspiration comic / iambic, but also apocalyptic, revelatory, as the final book of the New Testament still shows.[23] How could the Romans, with their native weakness for the iambic / satiric, not be alert to this complexity? *Describere*, which one expects to mean neutrally "describe," varies in sense between "pillory" and "caricature,"[24] and is used by Horace (*Sat.* II. 1. 33) of satiric Lucilius' no doubt slanted musings on his own life. Elsewhere, *Orazio satiro* (*Inf.* 4. 89) could daringly, comically hint at his own (semi-grotesque) physical appearance (*Epp.* I. 20. 24). But he was also a *vates*.

We suggested above the presence of vatic satire in the *Aeneid*. Yet the *Aeneid*, though certainly not a rule-bound epic in some artificial, academic sense, is straight-laced enough to avoid as a rule the detailed personal description which an iambic presence might have encouraged. That becomes possible and normal only later, when epic is comedified, sometimes with the aid of the principle of suppressed laughter,[25] and its rhetoric runs away with Horace's maxim *ut pictura poesis*.

But, if Virgil's sensibility is serio-comic, his vision is binocular. He sees his reality through two quite different prisms. There is the hellish revelation of monstrous horrors: Atlas, Fama, the Cyclopes, Allecto, Laocoon and the serpents, even in its way the overtowering, leaping, pregnant Horse; and, above all, the demons / gods assailing Troy (*apparent dirae facies*, II. 622). Yet, with his other eye, he finds an inscape of magical fantasy. Palinurus is an instance of this. Dido's lunar face is another. Virginal, sylvan Camilla's bloody career combines both perspectives. They

---

[22] *TWAT* VI, cols. 1179 ff. *s.v.* (Kornfeld, Ringgren).

[23] Nothing is normally described in the Gospels. There is a hint of the splendour of the Herodean Temple (Lk. 21:5, *al.*), in a prophecy of its doom.

[24] See the article in *TLL* V. 1, cols. 659–60 (lines 65 left—25 right).

[25] Glossary of Critical Terms, below, p. 344.

are not described. But the epic is waiting to flower and climax into that luxuriance.

The description of Ascanius, matching and offsetting the apocalyptic visions witnessed elsewhere in the poem, is therefore an important clue to the poet's level of intent. Ascanius is caught up into the other prism, the other, Ovidian half of Virgil's world. It is wrong to apply to him therefore any too realistic criteria. In the event, for all the picture on offer here, Augustan Livy showed no disloyalty in preferring not to dogmatise about what exactly his origins were. The Ara Pacis still leaves us guessing. How weak a peg such an *imago* was on which to hang the future! Augustus found that out.

XIII

THE FUTURE

> 'Vissi a Roma sotto 'l buono Augusto ...'
> Dante, *Inf.* 1. 71

Troy's Children in Vegio's Aeneidos Supplementum

The future is children, and there is no reason why children should not play some positive role in epic, however marginal. Homer and Tolstoy illustrate the point; and certainly Virgil shows us toddler Astyanax being "dragged" by his mother to visit his grandparents (II. 457). But that charming memory enhances a scene of death and destruction. Its child is doomed. Invaluable criticism of the *Aeneid* more generally in this regard is implied in the *Supplementum* ("Thirteenth Book") appended to the edition of Virgil published at Venice in 1471 and written by "Maphaeus Vegius" (Maffeo Vegio).

Some incidental allusions to this virtuoso piece have already been made. Detailed comparison with Virgil's genuine work is a separate study.[1] But the first and most obvious point is that it was written at all. How many loose ends may be neatly tied up in this way, what celebrations of the future at least suggested!

Vegio, with typical acumen, confronts directly an ambiguity left by the *Aeneid*. How can the line of inheritance realistically depend on Ascanius, when there is to be a new wife, Lavinia (for Creusa's son a stepmother), and new children, with all the native clan support they will naturally enjoy as Latinus' direct heirs? He does not solve the difficulty. His Aeneas hails

---

[1] Cf. *Maphaeus Vegius and his Thirteenth Book of the* Aeneid. *A Chapter on Virgil in the Renaissance*, Anna Cox Brinton (Stanford 1930); B. Schneider, *Das Aeneissupplement des Maffeo Vegio* (Heidelberg 1985). See also W. S. Maguiness, *The Thirteenth Book of the Aeneid* (Virgil Society, London 1957). Towards the end of Vegio's piece (479–89), when Lavinia, receiving a necklace once worn by Andromache, reverses the *ornatus Argivae Helenae* bestowed by Virgil's Aeneas on Dido (I. 650), this will evidently make her (adopted?) son the new Astyanax. Vegio's *De Morte Astyanactis* (1475), in spite of its relative brevity, is therefore worth consulting (above, p. 254, n. 23). There Venus quite specifically tells Andromache that the compensation for the death of her son will be the future reserved for Aeneas (*tuus Aeneas servabitur*, etc., pp. 4–5).

Iulus as the repository of *spes una patris* (75), but within less than twenty lines we find that even so the role of Lavinia is indispensable:

> 'Dabit inde mihi Lavinia coniux,
> Bello acri defensa, Italo cum sanguine mixtam
> Troianam transferre aeterna in saecula gentem.' (92–94)

> 'Lavinia will be my wife, fought for so hard in battle. She it is who will grant to me to shift the race of Troy, now mingled with Italian blood, towards endless centuries of life.'

This is reiterated later (*generique nepotes / Troianos Italo admixtos in saecula mittat*, 370–71). The repeated *Troianam / Troianos* and *in saecula* seem to portend centuries of fruitful intercourse between Trojan and Italian. But how can the Trojan line, with less and less Trojan blood in it as each generation passes, hope to live on in any recognisable sense? This inherited dilemma is never resolved.

In this vein, a striking scene towards the conclusion of Vegio's brief poem depicts the wedding feast, which may be viewed as the "normal" counterpart to the false, counterfeit hopes of Dido's banquet at the end of *Aeneid* I. Latinus expresses admiration for (the real) Iulus, and his wisdom older than his years (501–04).[2] By an extraordinarily bold leap of imagination, Aeneas is saluted as *felix* (507). The epithet recurs when, after a prophecy of Lavinia's future children, Venus exclaims to Aeneas: *o felix quem tanta manent!* (577).

In Vegio, a double *felicitas*—of a sort. Imposing her humiliating terms, Virgil's Juno certainly talks of *conubia felicia* (XII. 821). But the poet never calls Aeneas himself *felix*. On the contrary, clouding Ascanius' prospects even further, his Troy is dead (XII. 828). Young Trojan princes do not have a good survival rate. Is this one perhaps a Polydorus?[3] At the end of the *Aeneid* there is no reconciling banquet. Instead, the epic hangs a gigantic and umbraceous question mark over its story. The poet was quite as capable of understanding what he had omitted as Vegio. If he chose not to write a thirteenth book, that choice with all its puzzles must condition our response to what we have.

Fictional Times

In any talk about the future, time is of the essence. Narrative fiction presupposes two times: the first is the aorist (ἀ-όριστος χρόνος, "indefinite

---

[2] The *puer / senex* topos, already used by Pindar to flatter Hiero I (*Py.* 2. 65): Curtius, *Europäische Literatur*, p. 106, §8: cf. *sapientia / fortitudo*, ibid., p. 179.

[3] Cf. XII. 772 ff. and III. 24 ff.

tense") of the events described—past in some sense, but embracing the gnomic, the universal, and therefore the future, whenever (ποτέ, *olim*); the second is the "specious present" of the narrator / listener. These times (in German criticism *erzählte Zeit* and *Erzählzeit*) may intersect in differing ways. Years may be passed over in a sentence. A moment of suspense may fill several pages.

There is also the question of what Philodemus calls ἀλήθεια ("the facts"). At one extreme, the story may be offered as mythical, without specific historical reference, united with us perhaps only by a shared bond of humanity. Apollonius' *Argonautica* would on the whole be an example of this universality. At another, there may be some sort of claim to historical veracity. Here, the aorist's value tends to be reduced, clogged by particulars. In a version of this, what is ostensibly about a different time and place may be simply a disguise for, a method of estranging, the present. The allegory would be an instance. The *roman à clef* forms a tiresome twig on this great tree. The un-Apollonian handling of the myth of the Argonauts by Valerius Flaccus and even perhaps by Varro Atacinus, though not wholly of this kind, would illustrate the Roman bias towards literature which is also relevant, useful, in that sense "historical."

Roman poetry indeed relished the "historic present" (of which Greek epic, like Pindar later, makes no use) right from the first. Virgil is especially fond of it, and the *Aeneid* has sometimes been assimilated to the second model here. *Tantae molis erat Romanam condere gentem*. The mythical narrative is interpreted as a disguise for the triumphant struggles of the Romans to realise their imperial destiny. Aeneas is or becomes a version of Augustus. Is he closest to him when celebrating the *Lusus Troiae* at his father's funeral games? Yet even there, in that Cretan Labyrinth (V. 588), Dido intrudes (571). And in it too the crack of a whip drowns the music of the spheres.

The glorious promise of the exordium to the *Aeneid* itself conceals a *suggestio falsi* (I. 5–7):

>... dum conderet urbem,
>inferretque deos Latio, genus unde Latinum
>Albanique patres, atque altae moenia Romae.

> Till he could found a city, and bring his gods to Latium. Thence springs the Latin race, and the fathers of Alba, and the walls of lofty Rome.

The "city" in line 5 here sounds like, but disappointingly is not, Rome. The gods which Aeneas brought to Latium were no doubt the *magni di* of III. 12 and VIII. 679, the Penates, important at Lavinium (Servius on *Aen.* II. 296). But were they Trojan? Their name is Latin enough (*penus*), and Jupiter appears to promise a fresh start in Italy for the Trojans even in religious observances (XII. 836). And to what does *unde* refer? If it means that the *genus Latinum* came from Latium, the statement is true, but vacuous. It can hardly refer to Aeneas. He found the Latini, ruled by Latinus, Circe's Λατῖνος, already *in situ*, Remulus and Camilla already paragons of the kind of Italian hardiness praised by Horace. But, even if it were plausible, how is any claim by Aeneas to be their founding father compatible with the concessions made to Juno at the end of Book XII? There, Jupiter allows the Trojans to "subside." The *Albani patres* themselves (in spite of Capys) were joined to Troy only by the most tenuous thread of Hellenistic speculation.

Patriotic and poetic licence must of course have its place. But we suggested above that the *Aeneid*'s links with Italian history are normally the mirror, not of any peaceful settlement, and hardly of the victorious confrontation with Carthage which largely formed Ennius' theme, but of the Social and Civil Wars which coloured (*decoloravere*, Horace, *Odes* II. 1. 35) the poet's youth. From this maze of turmoil, what Greek idiom would call an Ἰλιὰς κακῶν, Augustus' merit was to have found an escape. He offered peace.[4] Aeneas in the end cannot offer peace, as Livy confirms (I. 2. 5), though the gods may plan peace of a sort above his head. The *Aeneid* is not then a eulogy even if, in lauding the emperor and Rome, it intermittently plays those trumpets.

Huius in adventum iam nunc et Caspia regna / responsis horrent divum et Maeotia tellus ... (VI. 798–99). "Advent" continues to be celebrated by Christians. Such a messianic emperor (שַׂר־שָׁלוֹם, Isaiah 9:5; "pax et princeps"[5]), "coming" (בָּא) "on that day" (בְּיוֹם הַהוּא), cannot form part of a closed or complete system bounded by the poem's surface narrative. An age of gold, breaking through into "end time," bursts such boundaries. On principle then, there cannot be any simple correlation between Augustus' *aurea saecula* (VI. 792–93) and the experience of the Trojans whose wanderings and wars Virgil describes. Though the poet's language on occasion may tantalisingly seem to lend that interpretation plausibility, his poem's times are more subtly intertwined. On the one side, there is the re-enactment ("iteration") of the Homeric paradigm, and this is where Aeneas is most deeply engaged. In the course of these reiterations, the most striking example he sets is that of Rome's maltreatment of the Italians, culminating

---

[4] The implications of this are explored by Hutton, *Themes of Peace*, pp. 28 ff.

[5] The phrase derived by R. Syme in *The Roman Revolution* (Oxford 1939) from Velleius (II. 131. 1) will serve, though *principem* there is a conjecture of Justus Lipsius, and Velleius in any case is speaking of Tiberius.

in the killing of Turnus.[6] Octavian, by contrast, exacting an oath of allegiance from Italians to himself in 32 B.C., was trying to create Italy as a political unit.[7] There is then the promise of a better future, and this is where Augustus will be found. The reader lives in that future. Jupiter and Anchises prophesy it from beyond. Apollo and his Sibyl are its mediators. Aeneas, who had emerged from Hades by the Ivory Gate, is only dimly and fleetingly aware of it: *ignarus imagine gaudet.*

This means that in the poem the two times of which we spoke (mythical and Augustan) are in conflict more often than they are reconciled. The inhabitants of its myth, locked like Aeolus' winds within the cave of their suffering (*indignantes,* I. 55; *indignata,* XII. 952), largely experience the historical promise as both *imago* and *umbra*. More precise revelations are often half-understood signposts towards destinations they themselves will never reach. Sometimes they lose their way (III. 381–83).[8]

What Virgil has really done is to switch the paradigms of history and myth. Mythical Aeneas is made to live in brutal history. Historical Augustus is a mythical, mystical vision yet to be realised.

The Eclogues, *the* Georgics, *the* Aeneid

The child is father of the man. The youthful Leonardo's angels in his master Verrocchio's *Baptism of Christ* are the token of that. Virgil himself is an example of such vertical time. Already in the *Eclogues* certain themes characteristic of the epic poet and his "hollow pastoral" were found: themes of exile, of lost love, of shadows, on which the duskings of Theocritus' pines cast only a broken light.[9] *Advena* ambivalently links the Roman veteran in Moeris's anguish (*Ecl.* 9. 2) and Aeneas in that of Dido (IV.

---

[6] But also in the war with Turnus' allies: cf. *Aen.* XII. 500–04: *obitum* here is echoed from IV. 694 (Dido), the only other occurrence of the word in the *Aeneid.*

[7] Hence the listing of the *castelli Romani* at VI. 773–75; the *laudes Italiae* both in *Georgics* II (136 ff.) and in Propertius (III. 22). *Romana per oppida* at *Geo.* II. 176 is an extraordinary oxymoron intended to make Augustus' point. On the Shield, Augustus leads the Italians (VIII. 678) and afterwards gives thanks *dis Italis* (715) for his victory. *Italiam fato profugus* (I. 2) opens a persistent drumbeat. Even so, Metternich could still say in 1849 that Italy was not a country but a geographical concept. Forse è ancora vero.

[8] Aeneas, for example, receives a promise from Apollo (III. 94 ff.) which seems in retrospect to refer to Italy, but which Anchises, himself destined never to reach Italy, interprets as referring to Crete. In the light of the doors at Cumae, which interpretation is correct?

[9] Above, p. 93. See further J. S. Macdonald, *Studies in Allusion in the* Eclogues *of Vergil* (diss. Urbana 1997).

591); the Aeneadae (VII. 38) and, in the prayer of doomed Pallas, Hercules (X. 460). Even for Tolumnius *augur*, Aeneas is *improbus advena* (XII. 261; compare Aeneas' own thoughts at X. 516). There is the *vates* (*Ecl.* 7. 28; 9. 34; *Aen.* VII. 41). And there is also the theme of the baby whose birth will herald the wars preceding the restoration of a Golden Age (*nascitur ordo, Ecl.* 4. 5; *Aen.* VII. 44). But who or whose is this baby? And who could succeed him by natural piety? Where is he in the *Aeneid*, except in Dido's pathetic, unreal *parvulus*? In the comic, Utopian world which greets his birth in the *Eclogues*, what we have called the poet's typical declension in the face of too much reality prevails. Fantasy obscures fact, sentiment certainty. This too is characteristic. Tuned to a tragic key by the *Aeneid*, it engenders Troilus, Astyanax, Polydorus. Do the promises about *Troianus ... Caesar* (I. 286) and Augustus (VI. 792), about Ascanius / Iulus (VI. 789–90), obliterate their memory?

The *Georgics* were also a preparation and propaedeutic for the *Aeneid*. Like the *Eclogues* (1. 42, *iuvenem*), they also promise a messiah (I. 500, *iuvenem*). Here too, the listener finds the polyphony of irresolution, the contradicted assertion: about the value of the peasant's labour, for example, or of the city. There are the "pessimistic odd" books, the "optimistic even" —except that the even books end with the episode of Aristaeus, and the loss of his wife by doomed Orpheus, surely one of the most desolate of limitations set upon the power of the poet. For all his love, no children are mentioned here. And, though Horace makes Orpheus the supreme example of the *vates* (*A.P.* 392, 400), and Tacitus, like later iconography,[10] of the saviour / ruler (*Dial.* 12), in this passage at the end of the *Georgics*, Proteus is the *vates* (IV. 387), and he vanishes into the sea (528–29). Later, Aeneas, who has also lost his Creusa / Eurydice, will naively appeal to Orpheus as proof that one may descend to hell (VI. 119).

The *Georgics* also attest to Virgil's persistent inability to find a human place for the erotic. The Hellenistic, romantic adventure of Hero and Leander (*Geo.* III. 244, 258–63), losing its identifying names, becomes part of the crude urge and appetite sweeping over the farmer's animals—and it is from this book that Virgil chooses the similes which frame *Aeneid* VII–XII,

---

[10] Below, p. 310. King David as Orpheus is a suggestive conjunction (*Oxf. Dict. Byz.* III, p. 1538, *s.v.* "Orpheus"; p. 1588, *s.v.* "Paris Psalter"). The unusually large number of Orpheus mosaics in Britain is evidence of "religious and philosophical currents of the late Roman world," according to P. Johnson, *Romano-British Mosaics* (Shire Publications, Princes Risborough, 2nd ed. 1987), p. 61. The so-called "Orphic Hall" at Littlecote is one of approximately fourteen examples. Was all this nostalgia for a now impossible dream? See also above, p. 67.

lending a more sardonic tone to his *Erato* (VII. 37). In their ideal commonwealth, the bees of *Georgics* IV know nothing of sex (198–99). Bee-keeping Aristaeus cannot unite appetite and love. This disconnectedness too would carry over into the epic concept. *Nec ... haec in foedera veni ... Italiam ... hic amor ... est* (*Aen*. IV. 338–39, 346–47). Sex for their queen disables Dido's bees (I. 430 ~ IV. 86).

The proem to *Georgics* III, already typical, was noted earlier. Virgil sketches a festive scene, which includes a temple, whose presiding deity will be Caesar: *in medio mihi Caesar erit templumque tenebit* (16). The encroachment upon the future is overt. There will be games, and an imaginary theatre, whose curtain and *scaenae frons* will also glorify Caesar's house.[11] In the poet-charioteer of this passage, some debt to Pindar's metaphors may be found.[12] Like the Pindaric ode, this flight of fancy also touches historical reality, in this case the *ludi* honouring the victory of Actium, and no doubt in some aspect the promised temple of the Palatine Apollo, or the statues eventually set up in the exedra of Augustus' Forum (cf. *Aen*. VII. 177).

The themes depicted in Virgil's *impresa* include victories: over the Britons, the East, the Parthians—the essential prerequisites for the establishment of a Golden Age. Among famous ancestors will be found the Trojans (*Geo*. III. 34–36):

> stabunt et Parii lapides, spirantia signa,
> Assaraci proles demissaeque ab Iove gentis
> nomina, Trosque parens et Troiae Cynthius auctor.

There too will stand statues of Parian marble, breathing life, the children of Assaracus, the names of a race descended from Jove, with father Tros and Cynthian Apollo, Troy's founder.

35–36. *Ilusque Assaracusque et Troiae Dardanus auctor*, *Aen*. VI. 650. Apollo was the *auctor* of the city by the part he played in the building of its wall. He was also peculiarly the patron of the sun-king, Augustus.[13]

---

[11] One is reminded of those splendid but temporary structures with which great cities of the Renaissance greeted the arrival of their lords. Dürer designed one for Maximilian I. Louvain's Blijde Inkomststraat ("Via felicis adventus") preserves the memory of the practice.

[12] See Slater's *Lexicon s.vv.* ἅρμα, δίφρος. Cf. Propertius III. 1. 11–12.

[13] See P. Zanker, *The Power of Images* (Eng. tr., Ann Arbor 1988), p. 144, on Augustus' *solarium*, which included his beehive (Etruscan) tomb, where on the emperor's birthday, officially celebrated at the summer solstice, the shadow cast by the obelisk (now in front of the Palazzo Montecitorio) pointed to the Ara Pacis. Fragments of a colossal statue of Apollo citharoedus in his long robe were recovered nearby (Erika Simon, *Augustus*, p. 30). Latinus' *radiata corona* (XII. 162–64; above, p. 262) is part of this ancient ideology. Cf. *utero Atiae* (Augustus' mother) *iubar solis exortum*, Suet., *Aug*. 94.

Proles here however refers, not forward to the future, but back. In the epic to be written one day, Caesar's *nomen* will survive throughout the years (47). But there is no room made in all this for children yet to come. Perhaps we assume their presence. But our passage begins with *stabunt*. A risk for this kind of eulogy, already visible in *Eclogue* 4, is that, in stopping time, it may stop the natural processes of birth and regeneration.

In the *Aeneid*, the poet seems to use children to exemplify all that contradicts their innocence. Cupid / Ascanius in Book I were remarked. In Book VII, a simile describes the wild coursing of Queen Amata through the city streets which will lead on to war. *Immensam* here, more suitable to Jonah's Nineveh, is a token of Virgil's surreal poetic (*Aen.* VII. 377–83):

> immensam sine more furit lymphata per urbem.
> ceu quondam torto volitans sub verbere turbo,
> quem pueri magno in gyro vacua atria circum
> intenti ludo exercent—ille actus habena   380
> curvatis fertur spatiis; stupet inscia supra
> impubesque manus mirata volubile buxum;
> dant animos plagae ...

Crazy, unchecked, she rages through the endless city, like a top turning beneath the twisted lash, whipped and sent spinning around the empty courtyard by children busy with their sport: driven by the thong it races along its circling course, with the ignorant, immature troop gaping in amazement at the rolling wood. The very blows they rain down feed their frenzy.

Naturally such boys cannot understand the headlong destinies in which they are caught up. This top seems to become a sort of chariot in a frenzied race.[14] Such violence inspires bloodlust. *Vacua atria* were where Pyrrhus chased Polites to his death (II. 528). Other phrasing is repeated when Aeneas reacts to the ship / sea-nymph's grisly prophecy of his coming victory: *crastina lux ... ingentis Rutulae spectabit caedis acervos ... stupet inscius ipse Tros Anchisiades* (X. 244–45, 249–50). The patronymic is noteworthy. Virgil echoes part of this in his own person when bidding farewell to Pallas / Sarpedon: *cum tamen ingentis Rutulorum linquis acervos* (X. 509; cf. *Sarpedon*, 471). The Rutuli were Latins. Silius even uses the term to mean "Roman." What a ugly epitaph for one so young!

Tyrrhus in Book VII is the royal herdsman. Tyrrhus' young sons (*pueri*, VII. 484), with their sister Silvia, have taken a fawn from its dam, and made a pet of it. Ascanius kills it. His arrow passes—inevitably—*perque uterum*

---

[14] *Spatium* (381) being the *t. t.* for a "lap": *addunt in spatia, ... fertur equis auriga neque audit currus habenas* of the chariot of state out of control, *Geo.* I. 513–14. Tacitus ironically makes charioteering Phaethon / Nero use the word in his riposte to Seneca: *prima imperii spatia ingredimur, Ann.* XIV. 56.

...*perque ilia* (499). It is almost as if the mention of children triggers the impulse to contradict the principle of birth. The next time we hear of Tyrrhus' sons, one of them is killed (531–34).

But all this is part of a pattern. When Aeneas' name is first mentioned (I. 92), in a wild reversal of normality, he is congratulating those who died at Troy under their parents' gaze (I. 94–96).[15] In Book XI we count the deadly cost—but the deadly cost of a marriage! (215–17):

> hic matres miseraeque nurus, hic cara sororum
> pectora maerentum puerique parentibus orbi
> dirum exsecrantur bellum Turnique hymenaeos.
>
> Here the mothers and unhappy wives, here the loving hearts of grieving sisters and children robbed of their fathers, all curse the dread war and Turnus' marriage plans.

Acron, *Graius homo, infectos linquens profugus hymenaeos* (X. 720), slain by Mezentius, seemed by these topsy-turvy standards a more normal case. Is there any context in the poem where *hymenaei* refers to happy fruitfulness?[16] Already Orpheus had set the precedent (*Geo.* IV. 516). The contrast with Catullus' epithalamium (poem 61) is startling.

The Victor: Eulogy and Prophecy

The *Aeneid*'s victor, the hero who is blessed with issue, had even so been greeted on his first entry to the Lower World by *vagitus et ingens / infantumque animae flentes in limine primo* (VI. 426–27; contrast *Od.* XI. 38–41, where no dead infants greet Odysseus). Dido prayed (IV. 618–20) that Aeneas, after yielding to the terms of an unfair peace, might not enjoy his kingdom or the relief for which he had longed, but rather fall before his time, and lie unburied on the shore. Her speech is modelled on the Cyclops' imprecations (*Od.* IX. 528–35), and for Odysseus all came true. Must not Dido's words be equally fulfilled? The moment of her curse, uttered as the light of dawn reveals to her the cold finalities of day, is linked by two repeated lines with the ghastly disfigurement by Turnus of Nisus and Euryalus (IV. 584–85 = IX. 459–60). In the event most of its details here

---

[15] The usual topos is seen in the pitiable *impositique rogis iuvenes ante ora parentum*, VI. 308. For its ramifications in the poem, above, p. 218.

[16] The best example is XI. 355: *quin natam egregio genero dignisque hymenaeis / des pater, et pacem hanc aeterno foedere iungas*. But even this is from Drances' speech assailing Turnus, and therefore tinged with his malice—and what is the outcome? The other examples in the *Aeneid* are: I. 651 (Paris); III. 328 (Paris); IV. 99, 127, 316 (all deluded Dido); VI. 623 (incest); VII. 344, 358, 398, 555 (Amata / Juno: marriage as bone of contention); XII. 805: *deformare domum et luctu miscere hymenaeos* (Jupiter to Juno).

are realised in the poem. Aeneas *is* harassed by the warfare of a bold people; he *is* an exile (especially if Troy is never to be refounded in any shape or form); he *is* torn away from Iulus' embrace, when he has to go off to beg for Evander's aid; and he *does* witness the undeserved deaths of his own friends and followers, notably Pallas, to whose corpse the queen contributes a coverlet (XI. 74: its twin is held in reserve). Is it only the last part of all this—*mediaque inhumatus harena*—which remains unrealised? Such a fate would have made him the counterpart of Priam (II. 557)—and he certainly carried some of Priam's regalia with him (VII. 246). In accepting it from him, Latinus takes on Priam's role, to see his Hector (Turnus) dead. But Aeneas himself claims kinship with Hector (XII. 440), quite apart from those occasions when the economy of the epic forces him into this role. How did this Hector end? Or Memnon, or Achilles, with whom elsewhere Aeneas is identified? Is he perhaps to be Pompey's paradigm? That would make him truly Augustus' spiritual ancestor.

Yet a court poem such as the *Aeneid* demanded some sort of eulogy —Pindar, the Alexandrians, and Augustan, epic Varius offer the proof—and the eulogy liked a happy presage for the future, a complimentary reference to posterity. The poet appears to discharge his duty. Lucretius had used *Aeneadae* for the Romans, and Virgil uses the same patronymic for his Trojans. On the Shield, we see the *Aeneadae* defending, like Augustus later, Roman liberty (VIII. 648). Aeneas receives the respectful title of *pater*.[17] The *Aeneadae* are his children in a special sense, the political future. This is certainly how Vegio saw the poem.[18]

Sometimes, recalling for us messianic prophecies in Isaiah, eulogy is more overt (III. 97–99):

> 'hic domus Aeneae cunctis dominabitur oris
> et nati natorum et qui nascentur ab illis.'
> haec Phoebus ...

> 'Here the house of Aeneas shall have dominion over every shore—and their children's children, and those to be born from them.' These were Phoebus' words.

Domus and *dominabitur* were already found in Jupiter's prophecy in Book I (279, 281–88):

> 'quin aspera Iuno ...
> consilia in melius referet, mecumque fovebit

---

[17] It is found most often in Book V. Elsewhere, it rings his story to childless Dido (II. 2, III. 716). It prepares for Turnus' death (XII. 697).

[18] *Supplementum*, 507–08, 558 ff. More generally, Andrew Fichter, *Poets Historical: Dynastic Epic in the Renaissance* (New Haven 1982).

> Romanos, rerum do mi n o s gentemque togatam.
> sic placitum. veniet lustris labentibus aetas
> cum domus Assaraci Phthiam clarasque Mycenas
> servitio premet ac victis do min a bi t ur Argis.   285
> nascetur pulchra Troianus origine Caesar,
> imperium Oceano, famam qui terminet astris,
> Iulius, a magno demissum nomen Iulo.'

'Even harsh Juno ... will change her plans for the better, and at my side will cherish the Romans, the lords of the world, the people of the toga. Such is my pleasure. The time will come as the years glide past when the house of Assaracus will hold down in slavery Phthia and bright Mycenae, and lord in conquered Argos. A Trojan Caesar shall be born from fair beginnings, Julius, a name bequeathed by mighty Iulus.'

And, when we are told that Silvius will reign in Alba Longa, *dominabitur* recurs (VI. 766).

But other examples of the verb are less promising: *incensa Danai dominantur in urbe* (II. 327); *urbs antiqua ruit multos dominata per annos* (II. 363); *summa dominarier arce* of Aeneas' ambiguous relationship with Laurentum (VII. 70). *Dominus* is usually invidious in some way.[19] *Servitium* (265) recurs only of the Trojan women enslaved after Troy's fall (III. 327). All this perhaps emphasises the iterated tit-for-tat of history, the pendulum swing. But, in a Golden Age, by definition time has stopped. The pendulum will not now swing. However excusable poetically, this paresis is wrong politically, and in any case quite inconsistent with the Roman sense of a continually growing body of law responding to evolution and change —a response celebrated in the concept *Urbs / orbis* by Rutilius Namatianus and still distinguishing for Dante the Emperor Justinian (*Par.* 6. 12).

The promise of immortality to Nisus and Euryalus, with its portentous allusion to the immobile Capitol, was noted above (p. 223). Its placement after their bloody adventure gives pause for thought. The best known illustration however of the effort to fulfil the eulogistic need is seen in Book VI (756–59):

> 'Nunc age, Dardaniam prolem quae deinde sequatur
> gloria, qui maneant Itala de gente nepotes,
> inlustris animas nostrumque in nomen ituras,
> expediam dictis, et te tua fata docebo.'

'Come now, my words will explain what later fame is to attend the children of Dardanus, what descendants await them from Italian stock, glorious spirits fated to enter on our name; and I will teach you your destiny.'

No effort on the part of exegetes to undercut the patriotic dignity and

---

[19] Varius' allusion to Mark Antony (*do m i n um que potentem*), borrowed from the *De Morte* for *Aen.* VI. 621, is noted below, p. 317.

majesty of passages such as this can ever convince, of course. But, equally obviously, here too there will be blood. In the Roman ideology, children are welcome because there is an army to restock and an empire to be administered. This is visible again in a later book (VII. 257–58):

> huic progeniem virtute futuram
> egregiam et totum quae viribus occupet orbem.

His children should be distinguished for their valour, and destined to seize with their might the whole world.

And earlier we heard of Lavinia (VII. 79–80):

> namque fore inlustrem fama fatisque canebant
> ipsam, sed populo magnum portendere bellum.

For their prophecies told that she would be glorious in fame and destiny—as queen, but that to the people she heralded great war.

80. *Ipsam* here refers to "the mistress of the house." *Suamque norat / ipsam*, Catullus 3. 6–7.

Defiant Propertius, acting perhaps as a tolerated safety valve for the pressure of public opinion at Rome, rejected this fertility with a difference: *nullus de nostro sanguine miles erit* (II. 7. 14). Among those of that mentality, children cannot be adored simply for their own sake. For a Roman, there is a *moles*, a task: *super et Garamantas et Indos / proferet imperium* (VI. 794–95).

Within this propaganda world, resonant in childless Horace, at one level, it was certainly possible for the poet to emphasise the theme of fruitfulness. So in the praises of Augustus, where a recast Asia looms particularly close. Rome, so important to Augustan ideology, receives the *felix* denied to Aeneas (VI. 781–87):

> 'en huius, nate, auspiciis illa incluta Roma
> imperium terris, animos aequabit Olympo,
> septemque una sibi muro circumdabit arces,
> felix prole virum: qualis Berecyntia mater
> invehitur curru Phrygias turrita per urbes   785
> laeta deum partu, centum complexa nepotes,
> omnis caelicolas, omnis supera alta tenentis.'

'See, under his auspices, my son, glorious Rome shall match her empire with the world, her courage with high heaven. She is but one city, yet her wall shall surround seven citadels, and blessed is she in her manly sons. Just so the Great Mother rides tower-crowned on her chariot through the cities of Phrygia, rejoicing in the gods her offspring, embracing her countless children, all dwellers in the sky, all tenants of the vaults above.'

787. Cf. Δὸς δέ μοι ἑξήκοντα χορίτιδας Ὠκεανίνας, / πάσας εἰνέτεας, πάσας ἔτι παῖδας ἀμίτρους, baby Artemis' precocious request to her father in Callimachus, *Hy*. III. 13–14.

But, though Alexandrian poetry might enjoy dancing girls, these sons are to be warriors, fighters. It was the Great Mother who, perhaps for dynastic reasons, had detained Creusa in Asia Minor (II. 788), in a kind of repetition and re-evaluation of the fate of Catullus' Attis;[20] and, as was noted, it was she who, in one of those declensions from reality typical of the Virgilian fantasy, would later transform Aeneas' ships. Here in Book VI, again we have a characteristic adaptation of Callimachean comedy[21] (and here specifically comedy affecting children) to the epic and, as the context veers towards the contemporary, tragic. The more than Civil War (826 ff.; *socer ... gener*, 830, 831) and Marcellus (860 ff.) will follow.

Peace and Children

Among the topoi of the Golden Age, Εἰρήνη κουροτρόφος played a traditional role (Horace, *Odes* IV. 5. 23). Thematically, the most important part of Anchises' eulogy ought then to be taken up with Augustus and his descendants: *hic Caesar et omnis Iuli / progenies* (VI. 789–90). But, in the event, the *progenies* stops at this point. Virgil had always been fascinated by the Golden Age, which recurs in all three of his poems. To herald the fourth eclogue's child of fancy, there would be new Argonauts, a new Achilles at Troy. In the *Aeneid*'s *praeparatio evangelica*, there is certainly a new Jason and a new Achilles. But once that is over, once a saviour takes the throne, the essence of such an Age for Virgil is unchangeability. In this paradise, there is no need of a future, and this becomes clear in the concluding comparisons with Hercules and Bacchus. What worthy children succeed such demigods? There may have been mighty effort before (I. 33) but, with the advent (VI. 798) of Augustus (cf. VIII. 201, Hercules), things have reached a point of equilibrium.

Yet, even in this balancing harmony, there are discordant notes; not those of the social critic wilfully out of tune, but of any poet wanting to

---

[20] Atys takes part in the *Lusus Troiae* (V. 568–69: only here). In a charming terracotta statuette of Aeneas with Anchises and Ascanius from Pompeii, now in Naples (inv. 110338), of uncertain (Augustan, post-Augustan?) date, little Ascanius wears a Phrygian hat and carries a shepherd's *pedum*, the same iconography as Attis.

[21] See pp. 95–96 above on Erysichthon / Turnus from the sixth hymn. It is in this spirit that we are to understand *invitus, regina, tuo de litore cessi* (VI. 460 ~ Catullus 66. 39, the translation of the Βερενίκης Πλόκαμος). It is not parody, any more than Dante's borrowings and transpositions from Ovid are parody. Perhaps Dido had hoped to be, like Berenice, the loyal partner in bedroom and council chamber of a Hellenistic prince. After the experience of Cleopatra, the *vates* no longer has room for these courtesies.

give an honest assessment of Roman history as in the event it had unfolded. Virgil makes this clear by a simple structural device. Dido is the centre of the whole book. The centre of the prophetic passage which starts at VI. 756 and concludes with the end of the book (146 lines) is occupied, not by eulogy of the Trojan line and its Roman descendants, but by solemn warning. Pompey and Caesar may be *concordes animae* now, in the night, but what of the future? In *Monoecus* here (μόνοικος), there is yet another allusion to Hercules (828–31):

> 'heu quantum inter se bellum, si lumina vitae
> attigerint, quantas acies stragemque ciebunt,
> aggeribus socer Alpinis atque arce Monoeci   830
> descendens, gener adversis instructus Eois.'

'Alas, what mutual war, if they shall ever have reached the light of life, what battles and slaughter will they stir! — the father-in-law coming down from the ramparts of the Alps and the lonely citadel of Hercules, the son-in-law with the armies of the East at his back.'

Both Pompey and Caesar had links with Hercules. Caesar, whose youthful *Laudes Herculis* (Suet., *Jul.* 56) were noted earlier, claimed the Herculean title *invictus*.[22] Pompey erected a statue of Hercules by Myron in the *aedes* he built probably in 61 on his return from Asia (Pliny, *N.H.* XXXIV. §57), perhaps near the Ara Maxima.[23] Yet Hercules, too successful, driven mad, had murdered his own children. What Julius and Pompey had done, Catullus knew: *socer generque, perdidistis omnia*: "father-in-law, son-in-law, you have ruined everything" (29. 24). He puts his point in familial terms, and Virgil repeats them here. The phrase becomes stereotyped in this context.[24]

When therefore, in her great curse, Juno also uses *gener atque socer*, we can only think again of Pompey and Caesar (VII. 317–22):

> 'hac gener atque socer coeant mercede suorum:
> sanguine Troiano et Rutulo dotabere, virgo,

---

[22] *Aen.* VIII. 293, Hercules; Dio XLIII. 45, Julius; cf. Hor., *Sat.* II. 1. 11, *Caesaris invicti*, Augustus; *Aen.* VI. 365, *invicte* of Aeneas as potential σωτήρ.

[23] An over life-size gilt-bronze statue of the hero now in the Sala degli Orazi e Curiazi of the Palazzo dei Conservatori, a first-century B.C. copy of a fourth-century Lysippan original, was found near the Ara Maxima in the 15th century, and is said to be from a temple in the area. (For Lysippus and Alexander, cf. Hor., *Epp.* II. 1. 240). Pompey's emulation of Alexander is attested e.g. by Plutarch, *Pomp.* 46. The imposing gilt-bronze statue of Hercules recovered from the vicinity of Pompey's Theatre in 1864 and now in the Vatican (Sala Rotonda, inv. 252) is dated to the late 2nd century A.D. Did it replace a similar earlier statue?

[24] *Roman Catullus*, p. 181. Add *socerum gener sepultura prohibuit*, Livy I. 49. 1 (Servius / Tarquin the Proud), anticipating the *bella plus quam civilia* of a later epoch. Lucan purports to be afraid that Caesar might deny Pompey a tomb (VIII. 714a).

> et Bellona manet te pronuba. nec face tantum
> Cisseis praegnas ignis enixa iugalis;
> quin idem Veneri partus suus et Paris alter,
> funestaeque iterum recidiva in Pergama taedae.'

'Let father-in-law and son-in-law come together with this reward for their kin. Your dowry, maiden, will be Trojan and Rutulian blood, the goddess of war awaits you as matron of honour. It was not Hecuba alone who was with child and gave birth to a firebrand. No, for Venus her own child plays the same part, a second Paris; and a restored Troy will find once again deadly marriage torches confronting it.'

The goddess of marriage gloats maliciously, demonically, over the deaths she is to cause. *Iterum* catches the attention. If it is to be a recapitulation of the Trojan cycle on Italian soil, the *Aeneid* looks ahead to a future of the most violent and horrible kind. In Ennius' adaptation of Euripides' *Alexander*, Cassandra had made that clear to Roman audiences for generations (Warmington, *ROL*, I, p. 242, 73–75 = Jocelyn, p. 77, 47–49, re-arranged):

> Eheu videte! iudicavit inclutum
> iudicium inter deas tres aliquis,
> quo iudicio Lacedaemonia
> mulier Furiarum una adveniet.

Ah, see, a famous judgment delivered by some stranger among three goddesses, by which judgment a Spartan women shall come, one of the Furies.

The metre is a senarius followed by three anapaestic dimeters. *Deas* is treated as a monosyllable. *Lacedaemonia* has a Greek *longum* at the end. Synapheia is observed (*Roman Catullus*, p. 208, n. 13).

48. *Aliquis* (= Paris) is the pregnant use of the indefinite in a threatening context (*exoriare aliquis nostris ex ossibus ultor, Aen.* IV. 625; more comically, κακὸν ἥκει τινί, Aristophanes, *Frogs* 552).

49. *adveniet* anticipates (and inspires?) Virgil's *advena*, above, p. 18.

In the play, Paris was as it were restored from the dead to destroy his city. And if Aeneas, in Italy to burn Laurentum, is Paris? But we also are invited to see the *Aeneid's* new Helen (VI. 93–94) in a different light, as *Furiarum una*. Even if the old Helen was an Erinys (II. 573), that is too strong for Lavinia. Evidently Dido, whose representative one day will be invading Hannibal, acts as stand-in (cf. I. 650): *ergo ubi concepit Furias....*

The exalted cry of Ennius' Andromacha after the debacle is extraordinary (Warmington, p. 252, 106–08 = Jocelyn, p. 86, 92–94):

> haec omnia vidi inflammari,
> Priamo vi vitam evitari,
> Iovis aram sanguine turpari....

All these I saw go up inflamed, Priam's life by violence maimed, the altar of Jove by blood defamed.

But these are the theatrical, tragic memories already flooding into the hearts of Virgil's Roman listeners to his Book II. How could they later greet the Sibyl's *iterum* (VI. 94) with anything but alarm? It has been observed that some of these passages seem to be in the poet's mind elsewhere.[25]

The vision of Rome's heroes ends with that of young Marcellus (VI. 860 ff.), in whose name, as we saw, the emperor dedicated a resurrecting theatre. It plays some part in Propertius' own laudation pronounced over the dead youth (III. 18. 13). Is the *Aeneid* itself a resurrecting—and admonitory—theatre? A picture-show (I. 466–93)?

Anchises' *si qua fata aspera rumpas* here (VI. 882) echoes and interprets his earlier *te tua fata docebo* (759). The promise of Augustus rests on the power to force a way through and beyond the harshness of the fates (*audentior ... quam ... Fortuna*, VI. 95–96). But there is a subjunctive. Is that hope of breakthrough—had it been—could it ever be—possible? It would hardly be plausible then to claim that the poet, dangling such a pathetic conundrum before his audience, offered panegyric unalloyed. *Sunt lacrimae rerum*. It is one of the reasons why he is so admired, and why his art will never be explained from the rhetorician's handbook. And, if he *ends* with this scene, to be followed by the concluding dismissal through the Gate of False Dreams, how can we claim that the eulogistic demand is not gravely qualified? Where does this future lead? Towards transforming Circe?[26]

Elsewhere, the theme of Εἰρήνη κουροτρόφος is grudgingly (*esto*) but perhaps less ambiguously developed (*Aen.* XII. 821–22):

'cum iam conubiis pacem felicibus (esto)
component, cum iam leges et foedera iungent ... '

'When soon now they arrange peace, with fruitful marriages—so be it—when soon they agree their terms and treaties of union ... '

This is the spirit of the Ara Pacis. *Felicibus* here takes back all the examples of *infelix* which have characterised the poem's—and history's—losers. And, on this reading, the *Aeneid* heralds a new generation, new fulfilment. But the terms the Trojans must accept, as Servius notes,[27] are those of the defeated. This is still a "Saturnian" Juno (XII. 807; cf. I. 23).

---

[25] Already cited in illustration of Latinus' incubation dream. See above, p. 181. In general, Stanislaw Stabryla, *Latin Tragedy in Virgil's Poetry* (Eng. tr. Wroclaw 1970); Michael Wigodsky, *Vergil and Early Latin Poetry*, Hermes Einzelschriften 24 (Wiesbaden 1972).

[26] Who lurks by Odyssean logic at the start of Book VII: above, p. 147. But she was already perhaps associated with the circus (so at least Tertullian: above, p. 4), which is found in Book V (109, 289, 551; cf. VIII. 636).

[27] Above, p. 251.

Apollo and Mars

Instances were already cited where Virgil is eager to trace back, in Varro's footsteps, the Roman *gentes* to their Trojan roots (V. 121 *al.*). In this line, Aeneas, according to his father, will enjoy a long and fruitful life (VI. 760–65):

> 'ille, vides, pura iuvenis qui nititur hasta,
> proxima sorte tenet lucis loca, primus ad auras
> aetherias Italo commixtus sanguine surget,
> Silvius, Albanum nomen, tua postuma proles,
> quem tibi l o n g a e v o serum Lavinia coniunx
> educet silvis regem regumque parentem.'

'Over there, the young prince you see leaning on a headless spear—he is allotted the next place in the light, the first to arise to breathe heaven's air sprung from mingled Italian blood, Silvius, a name he takes from Alba, your last child, whom in your old age late shall your wife Lavinia bear you in the woods, a king and the father of kings.'

But this Italian *iuvenis* leans on a weapon of war. And the drawback to such eulogy for any Roman student of the past was that its conflict with reality quickly became apparent. For all Juno's sly haggling, as Troy vanished into Rome, *pax* would not immediately ensue. There was to be an intrusion into the bloodline to make Laomedon's offence look pale. It is now that Mars and his grim quarrels come into focus, and the poet is well aware of his ambiguous gifts. Rome is "the great city of Mavors" even as she honours Marcellus' death (VI. 872).

The "Mars of Todi" in the Vatican Museo Etrusco (inv. 13886) wears on his armour a Latin inscription written in Etruscan characters. Though Mars is a Latin god, and often denoted as such (*horrentis Marte Latinos*, X. 237), and though Turnus is like Mars (XII. 332; cf. X. 22), Trojan / Etruscan Aeneas also comes under his influence, not always for good. *Saevit toto Mars impius orbe* had been the poet's despairing cry in an earlier time (*Geo.* I. 511). And, even if Mars is especially and naturally a god of the second half of the *Aeneid*, he is already found in the first. An instance occurs in the macabre scene with metamorphosed Polydorus (III. 35).

Tendimus in Latium, sedes ubi fata quietas / ostendunt; illic fas regna resurgere Troiae ("Latium is our journey's end, for there Troy's kingdom is allowed to rise again": I. 205–06). Beautiful lines, but by the principle of foiled expectation, such a resolution does not and cannot occur in the *Aeneid*. As they stand, are these words anything more than a καλὸν ψεῦδος? Troy in fact is finished. Certainly Augustus celebrated peace, as the last of Horace's odes reiterates (IV. 15. 9). But Italy and Rome, in the eyes of the Aeneadae, even of Jupiter, are quite unpeaceful. This point is paradoxically rammed home by repeated images of birth: *Marte gravis geminam partu dabit Ilia prolem*, I. 274 ("pregnant by Mars" or "pregnant with war"?); *gravidam imperiis belloque frementem / Italiam*, IV. 229–30 (cf. *bellum, o terra hospita, portas*, III. 539); *gravidam bellis urbem*, X. 87. In Book VII, Juno uses the example of Mars' treatment of the Lapiths to pour scorn on her own weakness (304–05). Snaky Allecto (VII. 450, 561, 658) rouses the god's might (540, 550; cf. 582). *Martius anguis* is Ovidian (*Met*. III. 32), but here Statius' reading of the role of the *Martius anguis* in the history of his feuding brothers may be relevant.[28]

These frenzied impulses would in the end be channelled, and, for all his devotion to Mars Ultor, it would be Augustus who would channel them. This is the lesson of Aeneas' Shield, where the god rages (*saevit* once more) until Actian Apollo bends his bow to secure the emperor victory against Antony and Cleopatra (VIII. 700–05):

> saevit medio in certamine Mavors   700
> caelatus ferro, tristesque ex aethere Dirae,
> et scissa gaudens vadit Discordia palla,
> quam cum sanguineo sequitur Bellona flagello.
> Actius haec cernens arcum intendebat Apollo
> desuper ...   705

Mars rages in the midst of the fray, carved in iron, and gloomy Furies from the sky; and full of glee Discord strides, her robe torn, while the battle-goddess comes behind wielding her blood-stained scourge. At this sight, Actian Apollo was bending his bow from on high.

701. *ex aethere Dirae*: cf. XII. 845 ff.

702. *Discordia* became a code-word for the Civil War: *civilis discordiae vel potius belli*, Cic., *Fam*. XVI. 11. 2; *en quo Discordia civis / produxit miseros*, *Ecl*. 1. 71–72; *exoritur trepidos inter Discordia civis*, *Aen*. XII. 583; *cum Romana suos egit Discordia civis*, Prop. I. 22. 5. Ennius' Discordia (*Ann*. 225–26, Sk.), by contrast, had signalled the outbreak of war against a *foreign* foe.

703. *flagello* at the *Lusus Troiae*: above, p. 5.

704. Cf. Propertius' description of Apollo's landing on Augustus' ship at Actium (IV. 6. 27 ff.). The Winged Victory of the Louvre still excites. One senses from her agitated draperies the Aegean etesians, signs of the divine רוח, πνεῦμα.

Here, the deadly spirit of incessant warfare is brought to some sort of resolution by Augustus' own patron, the god of light.

---

[28] *The Classical Epic Tradition*, pp. 235 ff. The fratricidal struggle of Eteocles and Polynices was a favourite in Etruscan art (above, p. 222). It is found, for example, in the François Tomb, where it may be intended as a parallel to the fratricidal combat of Cneve Tarchunies and Marce Camitlnas, also depicted there: *Gli Etruschi*, ed. M. Cristofani, pp. 70–71.

296   *Chapter Thirteen*

Mars,[29] associated, for example, with Pallas' death (VIII. 516; cf. VIII. 557; XI. 153), is evidently dangerous without controlling Apollo. And, as the *Aeneid* moves towards its end, we hear Apollo's name less and less. In Book X, Aeneas outrageously slays the son of Haemon, priest of Phoebus and Diana, and will dedicate his spoils to Mars (537–42):

> nec procul Haemonides, Phoebi Triviaeque sacerdos,
> infula cui sacra redimibat tempora vitta,
> totus conlucens veste atque insignibus albis,
> quem congressus agit campo, lapsumque superstans   540
> immolat ingentique umbra tegit. arma Serestus
> lecta refert umeris tibi, rex Gradive, tropaeum.

Close by, Haemon's son, priest of Apollo and Diana, his temples bound by his holy fillet, shone from head to foot in the white robe and tokens of his office. Aeneas challenged him and drove him over the field. Standing over his prostrate body he sacrificed him, covering him with his mighty shade. It was Serestus who picked up and shouldered his arms, to be carried away as an offering to Mars.

541. See Norden on ἐπισκιάζω, *Die Geburt des Kindes* (repr. Stuttgart 1958), pp. 92 ff. Here however the shade is that of some destroying angel: cf. צלמות.

In this passage, *immolat* and *umbra* certainly anticipate the vocabulary of Turnus' death.

Book XII is marked as the book of Mars by *adverso Marte* in its first line. *Certamina Martis* define (73, 790) this last struggle, in which the poet finds a kind of anticipation of the civil wars of his day (503–04). In them, already Lucretius had seen Mars as "master of the savage works of war" (I. 32–33). Horace's seventh epode[30] had noted the legacy of the Romans' original sin. His bitter comments help us to see that, in Turnus (compared to *Martius lupus* at IX. 566, to Mars at XII. 332) and martial Aeneas (XII. 108), Romulus and Remus, both Mars' sons, are proleptically at grips in their fratricidal confrontation (cf. XII. 430b = XI. 488b).

Augustus himself allowed his adopted sons Caius and Lucius to be paired with the *Martius lupus*, here no doubt in the spirit of reconciliation prophesied by Jupiter (*Aen*. I. 292).[31] Rome before Augustus would characteristically be Martial in a less benign sense. The concept of vertical

---

[29] If those scholars are correct who draw parallels between Mars and Hercules (cf. Macrobius III. 12. 5–6), fresh vistas are added to Hercules' refracted presence in the poem, and notably perhaps to its finale.

[30] Quoted above, p. 159. If Allecto is Ennius' Discordia, this identification aids the interpretation of the "Iliadic" action of Books VII–XII as a version of the "discord" of the Civil Wars. But it also adds to our sense of a Punic presence.

[31] Above, p. 23. See also a marble altar from the Augustan period in Florence (NMA inv. 13725), showing on its front an eagle with spreading wings, with the wolf nursing Romulus and Remus below.

time entails that, in the vatic poem, this Martial future is here now. Once again *saevus* attracts attention (XII. 107–08):

> Nec minus interea maternis saevus in armis
> Aeneas acuit Martem et se suscitat ira.

And with just such fury, wearing the arms his mother gave, Aeneas sharpens his warlike spirit and provokes himself with anger.

108. *Se suscitat ira* makes the hero like a lion contemplating the fray: cf. *Il.* XX. 170, Achilles about to assail Aeneas (above, p. 234).

This description, with its hint of the angry lion, recalls the conventional picture painted by Horace in his *dulce et decorum* ode, which appears as if modelled ahead of time on scenes from the last book of the *Aeneid*. The epic / tragic τειχοσκοπία is traditional,[32] but did Horace see these women standing perhaps on the walls of Laurentum? Are they Amata and her daughter Lavinia? Is this *tyrannus* Turnus (X. 448), *non viribus aequis* (XII. 218)?

> illum ex moenibus hosticis
> matrona bellantis tyranni
> prospiciens et adulta virgo
> suspiret eheu ne rudis agminum
> sponsus lacessat regius asperum
> tactu leonem, quem cruenta
> per medias rapit ira caedis. (*Odes* III. 2. 6–12)

Let the wife of the warring satrap and his grown daughter see [the Roman champion] from their defiant walls and sigh alas, lest a royal bridegroom unschooled in battle challenge the lion savage to the touch, driven by bloody anger through the carnage.

The Virgilian passage cited also looks ahead to Aeneas' return to the fray. *Nullo discrimine* here, though in one aspect the fulfilment of the divine will (X. 108), is feral (XII. 496–99):

> multa Iovem et laesi testatus foederis aras,
> iam tandem invadit medios et Marte secundo
> terribilis s a e v a m n u l l o d i s c r i m i n e caedem
> s u s c i t a t, i r a r u m que omnis effundit habenas.

With many a protest to Jove and to the altars of the now broken truce, at long last he strides into the fray. Mars' blessing makes him terrible. He provokes savage slaughter at random, giving free rein to all his pent-up anger.

497. cf. *invadunt Martem*, 712, of Turnus and Aeneas in their last combat.

498. *terribilis*, XII. 947; above, p. 165.

Saev-, *suscitat* and *ira* recur here from the earlier passage in Book XII (107–08). *Habenas* makes Aeneas a charioteer careering out of control (*Geo.* I. 512–14).

---

[32] Cf. West, *East Face of Helicon*, pp. 389, 553.

In this civil slaughter, tellingly, the god of healing refuses to heal Aeneas' wound (XII. 402–03, 405–07, 409–10):

>   Phoebique potentibus herbis
> nequiquam trepidat ...
>   ... nihil auctor Apollo
> subvenit, et saevus campis magis et magis horror
> crebrescit propiusque malum est ...
>   ... it tristis ad aethera clamor
> bellantum iuvenum et duro sub Marte cadentum.

And with Phoebus' drastic herbs [Iapyx] fusses to no purpose ... Apollo's patronage proves unavailable, and on the field the savage turmoil grows worse, as the mischief comes ever nearer ... a desolating din rises to the sky of young men warring and falling victim to ruthless Mars.

This may be contrasted with a scene in the *Iliad* where Apollo does heal Hector (XV. 262; cf. XVI. 528–29, Glaucus). Here, it is left to Aeneas' tricky (*laeta dolis*, VIII. 393) mother, like Medea aiding her Jason, to produce a herb from Cretan Mount Ida (412) which will enable her son to return to his Homeric combat with Turnus. Κρῆτες ἀεὶ ψεῦσται: the symbolism of Crete in the poem is by now familiar. Another Mount Ida had been the scene of Ganymede's Rape (V. 252, 254) and Paris' Judgment, precisely the provocations felt most bitterly by Juno (I. 27–28). And now, as Aeneas re-arms, he is Turnus' twin (*suras incluserat auro*, XII. 430b = XI. 488b): Romulus and Remus indeed.

In his prayer, before the truce was violated, Aeneas had appealed to *inclute Mavors* as *pater* (XII. 179–80). Later in the prayer we hear that Mars is to be "ours." Victoria here, granting prizes, is the goddess (187–88):

> 'sin nostrum adnuerit nobis Victoria Martem,
>   (ut potius reor, et potius di numine firment) ...'

'But if Victory grants Mars to us (as I incline to think—and may the gods incline to ratify that by their power) ...'

What peace however is she equipped to bestow as Victory's ornament?

A dramatic evocation of Mars' power in Book XII is found in the simile accompanying Turnus' wild assaults, at the point where, with Aeneas' withdrawal from the field, he briefly fancies that he has a chance of winning. *Thraca* is barbarous, ominous (XII. 331–36):

>   qualis apud gelidi cum flumina concitus Hebri
>   sanguineus Mavors clipeo crepat atque furentis
>   bella movens immittit equos; illi aequore aperto
>   ante Notos Zephyrumque volant, gemit ultima pulsu
>   Thraca pedum circumque atrae Formidinis ora
>   Iraeque Insidiaeque, dei comitatus, aguntur.

... just as bloody Mars speeds by Hebrus' cold stream, clashing his shield, coursing his wild horses, rousing war. Over the open field they fly, outstripping the winds, while furthest Thrace groans to the beat of their hooves, and around race in the god's train dark Fear's looming faces, and Wrath, and Ambush.

Among Homeric parallels noted is a scene from the *Iliad* where however the *Trojans* are urged on by Ares, and the Greeks by Athene (IV. 439–43).[33] The "inept" borrowing produces a confusion worse confounded.

The wolf nourishing Romulus and Remus *Mavortis in antro* is naturally shown on Aeneas' Shield (VIII. 630). Nothing could be more germane to the Roman state. But what then of Turnus, enemy of what would be the Roman state, as in an earlier book he presses home his attack (IX. 563, 565–66)?

> qualis ...
> ... matri multis balatibus agnum
> Martius a stabulis rapuit lupus ...

Just ... as a wolf of Mars snatches a lamb from the byres, for all its ewe's bleatings ...

Senseram enim quam idem essent: Cicero's despairing comment (*ad Att.* X. 8. 5) on the participants in the Civil Wars of his day has seemed relevant too often.

The *Iliad*'s Strife (IV. 440–43) had already provided the model for Fama in *Aeneid* IV (176–77), the canker in the rosebud of Dido's brief honeymoon. Is Dido still lurking? She is a kind of Penthesilea, and martial Camilla's retinue in Book XI resembles the Amazons surrounding Hippolyte or Penthesilea. Thrace recurs (XI. 659–63):

> quales Threiciae cum flumina Thermodontis
> pulsant et pictis bellantur Amazones armis,
> seu circum Hippolyten seu cum se Martia curru
> Penthesilea refert, magnoque ululante tumultu
> feminea exsultant lunatis agmina peltis.

As the Thracian Amazons trample the streams of Thermodon, warring with their painted weapons, sometimes gathering around Hippolyte; or when her chariot brings back martial Penthesilea, and in their battle lines with wild hullabaloo the women leap and brandish their crescent shields.

659–60. *flumina ... pulsant* quia interdum Amazones flumen agmine infesto vel ingrediuntur vel etiam traiciunt, equorum simul ungulis aquam respergentibus.

663. Cf. *ducit Amazonidum lunatis agmina peltis / Penthesilea furens*, 1. 490–91, just before Dido, so soon to be *furens* herself, makes her appearance in Juno's temple at Carthage. *Lunatis* makes the connection with Diana / *luna*.

Is Camilla the link between Dido and Turnus? *Amazones* (ἀμάζονες, "the breastless ones") peculiarly suits the *Aeneid*'s theme of childlessness.

---

[33] Cited and translated above, p. 174.

In another parallel from the *Iliad* to the Mars-simile in *Aeneid* XII (331 ff.), Idomeneus and his squire Meriones re-arm for the defence against the Trojan advance (XIII. 295-305):

> Ὣς φάτο, Μηριόνης δὲ θοῷ ἀτάλαντος Ἄρηϊ   295
> καρπαλίμως κλισίηθεν ἀνείλετο χάλκεον ἔγχος,
> βῆ δὲ μετ' Ἰδομενῆα μέγα πτολέμοιο μεμηλώς.
> οἷος δὲ βροτολοιγὸς Ἄρης πόλεμόνδε μέτεισι,
> τῷ δὲ Φόβος φίλος υἱὸς ἅμα κρατερὸς καὶ ἀταρβὴς
> ἕσπετο, ὅς τ' ἐφόβησε ταλάφρονά περ πολεμιστήν·   300
> τὼ μὲν ἄρ' ἐκ Θρῄκης Ἐφύρους μέτα θωρήσσεσθον,
> ἠὲ μετὰ Φλεγύας μεγαλήτορας· οὐδ' ἄρα τώ γε
> ἔκλυον ἀμφοτέρων, ἑτέροισι δὲ κῦδος ἔδωκαν·
> τοῖοι Μηριόνης τε καὶ Ἰδομενεύς, ἀγοὶ ἀνδρῶν,
> ἤϊσαν ἐς πόλεμον κεκορυθμένοι αἴθοπι χαλκῷ.   305

At that, Meriones, like swift Ares, quickly took his bronze spear from his tent, and followed Idomeneus, with great eagerness for the fight. And just as Ares, destroyer of men, goes to the battle, and in his train his dear son Panic mighty and fearless, scaring even the sturdiest warrior—the two of them from Thrace arm to join the Ephyri or perhaps the stouthearted Phlegyans: it is not to both sides that they give ear, but to one that they lend glory—such were Meriones and Idomeneus, princes of men, as they made their way to the battle, armed in blazing bronze.

The story of Idomeneus of Crete (!), whose ἀριστεία this book of the *Iliad* contains, is narrated by Servius (ad *Aen*. III. 121). On his voyage home from Troy, a storm befell his ships, and he vowed if he were saved to sacrifice to Poseidon the first thing to meet him on his return. Jephtha had met his daughter (OT Judges 11:29–40); and, by the folk-tale logic of such narratives, Idomeneus was met by his son.[34] A life was forfeit. But, while fulfilling or trying to fulfill his vow, he was forced to leave Crete for Italy because a pestilence broke out. Servius tells this tale because Aeneas had already encountered a similar pestilence in Book III when he tried to establish his own abortive settlement on that ambiguous island. Diomedes refers to the story obliquely (*Aen*. XI. 264–65) in his litany of woes besetting the Greeks as punishment for their treatment of Troy.

Cretan rulers had disasters with their sons (and with their wives and daughters!). The deaths Aeneas viewed on the temple doors at Cumae included the fate of Androgeos (VI. 20). These are not happy associations. The poet did not of course intend his listeners to compare his narrative and Homer's in minute detail as he recited. But in the background of his Martial imagery lurks the suggestion of childlessness, of brutal strife induced by a Mars who was not one among many divine characters influencing the destiny of the Romans, but their direct ancestor and "father." What kind of

---

[34] More parallels in West, *East Face of Helicon*, p. 442, note 10.

The Price of Peace

Martial Romulus' murder of Remus could somehow perhaps be palliated: *Remo cum fratre Quirinus*, I. 292. But his example persisted. Only recently, murdered Julius had claimed the title Quirinus without perhaps studying its still latent implications. Octavian himself almost became Romulus, and there are still perhaps regretful echoes of this in Propertius' last book, in a poem where the emperor receives his adoptive father's stamp of approval (IV. 6. 59).[35] In the event, however, he decided the Civil Wars in favour of Remus (cf. Prop. IV. 1. 9).

Given then that these Civil Wars—which had included a Social War—were only too painful a reality and memory, in what sense may it be argued that Juno's threats in Book VII were abated or unfulfilled in the harsh outcome? What is happening in these final books of the poem is that the historical experiences of Rome in Italy, and the sufferings of the Italians at Rome's hands, are being raised to mythical status, since the assertion of any myth, underpinning its claim to universality, is that only one thing ever happened. Virgil's epic talks about reconciliation on the surface, but its deep structure proclaims something quite the opposite. This point-counterpoint between the possibility of peace and the experience of war is evoked (what more appropriate?) in terms of families (*socer generque*) in need of a rescuer. Lucan, Nero's Virgil, understood this quite clearly (*cognatasque acies*, I. 4; *venturo fata Neroni*, 33). Virgil too has a rescuer in mind. Yet, whatever the *Aeneid* says more positively in this vein, it always comes with the proviso that, when this golden *otium* is realised, it may make children otiose.[36]

On the surface, everything was done for Ascanius.[37] But who was Ascanius? Aeneas' last and only Italian child, according to Anchises, was to be Silvius: *longaevo serum Lavinia coniunx*.... In this passage from Book VI (764, quoted above, p. 294), the late-born child is as much folk motif as history. But there was some ambiguity. Elsewhere in the *Aeneid*, Jupiter seems to prophesy only three years of rule for Aeneas in Latium (*tertia*,

---

[35] *Altera classis erat Teucro damnata Quirino*, IV. 6. 21. Octavian is "the Trojan Quirinus."

[36] Above, p. 26. Hence so much silliness among Rome's gilded youth, for example, under Nero. Turgenev's лишние люди ("superfluous people") come to mind, his term for the disaffected, rootless intellectuals who eventually in 1917 would bring down the Eastern Empire.

[37] See also the earlier discussion, pp. 270 ff., above.

ternaque, I. 265–66). The hinted identification elsewhere of Aeneas with Memnon and other short-lived heroes would confirm this brief span. What can *longaevus* mean here? In the poem Priam, Anchises, the Sibyl, Latinus, Turnus' father Daunus understandably merit *longaevus*. But how can Silvius' father be *longaevus*, unless the convention of the *Aeneid*, by which children are always vulnerable and defenceless, and their parents feeble or doomed, is again at work, remodelling even Aeneas?

And why was Silvius born in a wood? One legend, recounted by Cato, reported that the child was posthumous, and that his mother Lavinia, maltreated by Iulus, had fled to the forest to avoid his caprice. A more decorous tale urged that Aeneas was still alive (even if *longaevus*!), to defend the boy, and that, if he was born in the forest, it was for unknown reasons.

Yet Augustan Livy is not so sure. In his account (I. 2), Aeneas dies soon after defeating Turnus and his Etruscan ally Mezentius. Ascanius / Iulus is still too young to succeed, and his mother Lavinia has to act for him. Aeneas Silvius is Ascanius' grandson (I. 3. 6). Creusa's son has uncertain status.

The ruling house of Alba did not lack problems (Numitor / Amulius). According to Servius, a later Aeneas Silvius mentioned by Virgil (VI. 769–70) had trouble claiming his royal inheritance from his guardian. The poet's *si unquam* (770) may actually hint at the otherwise unattested tale. He does not necessarily share then any impulse to gloss over this internal feud.

The reconciliation between Juno and Jupiter preliminary to all this bickering, and concluding Book XII, hangs loosely and falsely in the air, partly perhaps because its Iliadic parallel is the agreement between Zeus and Hera that nothing can save Troy in the long term. In the first line here, τοι must be given its full force (XV. 69–71):

> Ἐκ τοῦ δ' ἄν τοι ἔπειτα παλίωξιν παρὰ νηῶν
> αἰὲν ἐγὼ τεύχοιμι διαμπερές, εἰς ὅ κ' Ἀχαιοὶ
> Ἴλιον αἰπὺ ἕλοιεν....

'But from that moment [the death of Hector], I will bring about to please you a pursuit in turn from the ships, incessant, unending, until the Achaeans take steep Ilion.'

It is in the preceding passage (vv. 24–30) that Zeus remembers his wife's maltreatment of Heracles. Once again that ambiguous figure looms.

The terms of the "unfair peace" (*pacis iniquae*, IV. 618) are spelled out at XII. 823–28. Under them, the Latins are not to be absorbed, but rather absorb. *Delenda est Carthago* becomes *delenda est Troia*. They culminate in Troy's final expunging from history (828):

> 'ne vetus indigenas nomen mutare Latinos
> neu Troias fieri iubeas Teucrosque vocari

The Future

aut vocem mutare viros aut vertere vestem.   825
sit Latium, sint Albani per saecula reges,
sit Romana potens Itala virtute propago:
occidit, occideritque sinas cum nomine Troia.'

'Do not bid the native Latins change their old name, or become Trojans and be called Teucrians; do not bid those warriors alter their tongue and adopt strange garb. Let Latium be, let there be kings of Alba through the ages, let Roman stock be made mighty by Italian valour. Troy has fallen, and let it lie along with its name.'

This is compared[38] with a conversation in the *Odyssey* between Zeus and Athene. Zeus speaks (XXIV. 482–86):

ἐπεὶ δὴ μνηστῆρας ἐτίσατο δῖος Ὀδυσσεύς,
ὅρκια πιστὰ ταμόντες ὁ μὲν βασιλευέτω αἰεί,
ἡμεῖς δ' αὖ παίδων τε κασιγνήτων τε φόνοιο
ἔκλησιν θέωμεν· τοὶ δ' ἀλλήλους φιλεόντων
ὡς τὸ πάρος, πλοῦτος δὲ καὶ εἰρήνη ἅλις ἔστω.

'Godlike Oysseus has finished his vengeance on the suitors, and now let all pledge loyalty. Let him rule for ever, and let us bring about [among the Suitors' families] forgetfulness of the murder of their children and brothers. Let them be friends as before, and let there be wealth and peace in abundance.'

Here too, an element of convention is marked (483 = "O king, live for ever!"). And it is precisely here that we can note how unlike the *Odyssey* the *Aeneid* is. The discrepancies are evident. Juno has to be cajoled, whereas Athene makes an overture to secure peace among the male relatives of the Suitors who are looking for revenge for their dead. She bids Odysseus end his quarrel in response to an omen from Zeus: ἴσχεο, παῦε δὲ νεῖκος ὁμοιίου πολέμοιο (543). Then the *Odyssey* can end on a note of reconciliation.

But what ἔκλησις, what reconciliation, in the *Aeneid*? *Tuque prior, tu parce, genus qui ducis Olympo, / proice tela manu, sanguis meus* (VI. 834–35). Anchises had certainly laid down the premise for such reconciliation, and it is to Anchises that Turnus appeals (XII. 934). But his words fall on deaf ears. And, when peace does come, what surrender does Odysseus make of his very identity as a Greek, to match the surrender by Aeneas of his identity as a Trojan?[39]

---

[38] By Knauer, pp. 322 ff.

[39] Cf. "They did not destroy the peoples round about, as the Lord had commanded them to do, but they mingled (cf. Virgil's *commixtus*, VI. 762; *commixti*, XII. 835) with the nations (בגוים ויתערבו), learning their ways; they worshipped their idols, and were ensnared by them. Their sons and daughters they sacrificed to foreign demons; they shed innocent blood, the blood of sons and daughters offered to the gods of Canaan, and the land was polluted with blood" (Psalm 106:34–38, NEB). Here any thought of colonisers

If Juno then has been "cajoled," it is into a reluctant acceptance of everything she wants. In his subsequent duel with Turnus / Patroclus,[40] Aeneas / Hector is tempted to stop, but perseveres under the influence of the wildest emotions. He is again the *Iliad*'s angry Achilles (cf. *Aen*. XI. 438), but, if Achilles is now to kill Patroclus, there will be no scene here of restoration and recognition of shared humanity.

And the Homeric paradigms are to switch once more. Achilles took a ransom in gold. In taking Lavinia as his prize, Aeneas makes himself —within the poem's alternatives—into a Paris. This is what Juno had prophesied (*Cisseis*, VII. 320, X. 705), and Amata sarcastically condemned (VII. 363–64). But if Aeneas is Achilles' slayer Paris (*Il.* XXII. 359), with that transformation, Turnus is again Achilles (cf. VI. 89, IX. 742), and the Homeric parallels, as so often in this poet, become giddily unstable.

The child is father of the man. Ascanius began the Italian wars with his ill-aimed arrow (*derexit spicula*, VII. 497). Paris, thanks to Apollo's help, had killed Achilles with an arrow (*derexti tela*, VI. 57; cf. Ovid, *Met*. XII. 606, *derexit spicula*). At the end here, Aeneas / Paris hurls a spear, but Virgil, like Ovid (*tela ... spicula, Met*. XII. 601), makes *telum* do for both (*Aen*. VI. 57, XII. 919) and the darker note intrudes dully into the reader's consciousness. Paris would himself eventually fall victim to an arrow shot by Philoctetes, who had inherited the bow of burning Heracles. It is this burning Hercules who finally engulfs both Turnus and Aeneas.

Fugit indignata sub umbras. Among such shades, what place will Rutulian Turnus fill? Does *indignata* signal that he will be silent, resentful Ajax / Dido? Achilles ended, after the sacrifice of Polyxena, in the Isles of the Blest. He had Thetis. Memnon had Eos. Aeneas is "owed to heaven" (XII. 795). So is Romulus (Ennius, *Ann*. xxxiii, Sk.). As with Juturna, so with her brother, once again, unfairness. Turnus has no mother, no goddess, to plead for him.

Does Aeneas ever send back his body? Maphaeus Vegius says so, but the *Aeneid* does not. Is closure to be denied? Will there rather in Italy be endless blood feud? Is Turnus the first of many Italian chiefs to die?[41] Given these vast differences from the *Odyssey*, what kind of future, when all is said and done, will Aeneas / Sulla have? *Ingentis Rutulorum linquis acervos / totam*

---

disappearing into the colonised population is anathema. This is surely far more normal than the fate in store for the Aeneadae. See also Daniel on the dangers of intermarriage: "iron does not mix with clay," OT Daniel 2:43–44.

[40] *Il*. XVI. 792, στρεφεδίνηθεν ~ *vertuntur, Aen*. XII. 915; cf. στῆ δὲ ταφών, 806 ~ *cunctatur*, 916.

[41] Cf. Turnus Herdonius, Livy I. 50. 3 ff.

Italiam caedibus replevit (*Aen.* X. 509 ~ Livy, *Epit.* lxxxviii).

The answer is patent. For the Romans, simple, "pious" imitation of a famous ancestor was too much: to adapt Horace, *nimia pietas*. Someone greater was needed, to break out of the vicious circle of Homeric and historical paradigm. That someone was the poet's most loyal patron: *Auguste, Hectoreis cognite maior avis* (Propertius IV. 6. 38), for whom he composed *nescio quid maius ... Iliade* (*id.* II. 34. 66). Augustus is the saviour prophesied both in Book I (257–96) and in Book VI (789–805). But, as prophecies, these declarations are necessarily enigmatic, perceived through a glass darkly (VIII. 730: cf. *porta ... eburna*, VI. 898). The poem heralds a future which Aeneas, trapped in the orbs of his Cretan labyrinth, will never enter.

XIV

THE *VATES*

> Nur wer die Leier schon hob,
> auch unter Schatten ...
>
> R.M. Rilke, *Sonneten an Orpheus* I. 9

The Vates *as Preacher and Satirist*

Horace—*Orazio satiro* in Dante's phrase—opens his Roman cycle of *Odes* by defining his audience as *virgines puerique* (III. 1. 4). The last of them ends with a devastating vision of the series of sins engrossing Rome's past, present and future (6. 45–48). With his moralising, he was rehearsing and enlarging for the new generation the training he had received himself as a boy: *insuevit pater optimus hoc me, / ut fugerem exemplis vitiorum quaeque notando* (*Sat.* I. 4. 105–06). This was intensification rather than novelty. Roman literature in general had to be useful in this way (*tanto tamque utili labori*, Sallust, *Jug.* 4. 3), character-building for the young (*iuventuti utilitatis*, Cicero, *Phil.* II. §20). As often as not it had to preach. Ennius himself had felt both these pressures.

Our "late and distracted age" (E. Fraenkel) has perhaps grown unfamiliar with the moral criticisms integral to the technique of the sermon; and this ignorance has fostered the notion that the negative elements undoubtedly present in the *Aeneid* (as in Horace) reveal a poet out of sympathy with the regime of Augustus, even though Augustus himself was so profoundly concerned with the reform of contemporary morals. The theory of the *vates* aids in dispelling this illusion.[1]

In the first place, such moralising is not meant to drive the congregation out of church, or to be the whole story. Some of its most famous examples

---

[1] See *Augustus and the New Poetry* and *The Concept of* Vates *in Augustan Poetry* (Coll. Latomus vols. 88 and 89, Brussels 1967). More recently, Elisabeth Henry, *The Vigour of Prophecy* (Bristol 1989); J. J. O'Hara, *Death and the Optimistic Prophecy in Vergil's* Aeneid. P. R. Hardie's *Virgil's* Aeneid: *Cosmos and Imperium* (Oxford 1986) illustrates the role in the *Aeneid* of Posidonius' *vates* / φυσιολόγος.

urge, not despair, but μετάνοια, a change of heart, inspired by a contemplation and admission of past mistakes. This is Horace's goal. At a more exalted level, that is the goal of Dante's *Comedy*, and of its begetter, the *Aeneid*: *feret haec aliquam tibi fama salutem*.

Virgil and Horace were both *vates*. The vatic ideal grew at Rome in fruitful, volcanic soil. If Virgil was also in the first place a Roman poet, Rome was not Greece. Nothing shows this more clearly than Hellenistic Philodemus' hot denial that poetry serves any sort of social purpose.[2] At Rome, the concept of *utilitas* just noted in Cicero takes priority. Horace may advocate its combination with the *dulce* (*A.P.* 343). But the *vates* himself is uncompromisingly *utilis Urbi* (*Epp.* II. 1. 124). His predecessor Alcaeus was *Lesbius civis* (*Odes* I. 32. 5), just as vatic Lucan (I. 63; IX. 980) makes Cato call Pompey a *civis ... utilis* (IX. 190–91). Augustan Propertius tells us that Cassandra's *furor* was *patriae ... utilis* (III. 13. 65). For both him (IV. 1. 51) and Virgil (*Aen*. III. 187) Cassandra was a *vates*.

Even Roman poets who had no time for *vates* were concerned with preaching and evangelising, none more than Epicurean Lucretius.[3] There was a shared national bent. Whatever then may have been the theoretical influence of Stoic Posidonius in rehabilitating among cultivated Romans what he called οὐάτεις,[4] the *vates* in Augustan poetry is an outgrowth of a feature native to the Roman mentality and its tinge of *Italum acetum*—the satirical. Satire is typical, even in ostensibly non-satirical genres. Ennius himself, for all his dislike of the *vates*, certainly preached at his Romans— and also "contaminated" his Homeric epic with satirical touches, here perhaps a better disciple of Homer than orthodoxy allowed. The *Iliad* had already pilloried Thersites for impudently assailing the heroic values of his society. In Homer's distorting mirror, he was made to look as crooked as his opinions. On the other side, iambic Archilochus showed his independent spirit precisely by praising a bandy-legged general (60 D.). Yet our museums quickly prove that the Greeks in general tended to dwell on the

---

[2] This is the argument developed with great energy at the opening of Book V of the Περὶ Ποιημάτων. See Anastasia Summers, *Philodemus' Περὶ ποιημάτων and Horace's Ars Poetica: Adapting Alexandrian Aesthetics to Epicurean and Roman Traditions* (diss. Urbana 1995). Philodemus had both a Lucretius at Herculaneum (above, p. 95, n. 50) and an Ennius. There was evidently lively literary exchange.

[3] Kirk M. Summers, *The Debate over Contemporary Religion in Cicero and Lucretius* (diss. Urbana 1993).

[4] He found them in Gaul (Strabo IV. 4. 4), and the word is said to be Indo-European, but see also the Etruscan *vatieχe*, "verbo probabilmente indicante un atto di consacrazione," according to M. Pallottino, *Etruscologia*[7] (Milan 1992), p. 508.

ideal, τὰ καλὰ τρέψαντες ἔξω (Pindar, *Py*. 3. 83).[5] The contrasting Roman interest in the ugly (attested by names such as "Varus," "Naso," "Strabo") inevitably implied for them the fascinated acknowledgment of deviations from the standard among their own kind ("Scaevola," "Sedigitus").[6] When Rome's most famous orator is found to be called after the chickpea, Thersites is no longer on the margins, but at the centre.

Certainly, Augustan art displayed classicising, Atticising aspirations. But, in spite of the straight-laced literary theory reflected in the opening of Horace's *Ars Poetica*, it also continued to be interested in the grotesque. This taste was particularly characteristic of the imperial circle. Vitruvius provides the evidence (*De Arch.* VII. 5). Horace's own strictures end, as has been remarked, with the unusual composite of a bear rattling the bars of its cage suddenly identified with a blood-sucking leech (*A.P.* 472–76). The dog-headed Aeneas carrying a dog-headed Anchises, with a dog-headed Ascanius at his side, found at Stabiae (Naples inv. 9089) shows that such assaults on Greek convention could encompass even the loftiest ideals of the age.[7]

Religious Inspiration

Visioni ed Estasi was the title of a recent (2003–04) exhibition in Rome of baroque pictures of sanctity. Such things have a long tradition behind them. The Sibyl herself alters before she can utter her prophecy (*non vultus,*

---

[5] Archilochus is dismissed in *Py*. 2. 55, even though he had in fact written the primal epinician (*Ol*. 9. 1). See also Quintilian XII. 10. 9: *ad veritatem Lysippum ac Praxitelen accessisse optime adfirmant: nam Demetrius tamquam nimius in ea re reprenditur et fuit similitudinis quam pulchritudinis amantior*. In illustration of Demetrius ἀνθρωποποιός at work, editors note the description of what may be his statue of the Corinthian general Pellichus (Lucian, *Philops*. 18). Yet Fürtwängler was suspicious of this, and it looks as if what Lucian says may be influenced by the exaggerations of Roman satire. The epigrams of "Loukillios" / Lucilius in the *Anthology*, for example, composed in the time of Nero, are obviously written under a pseudonym borrowed from a famous Roman predecessor, and this Hellenisation of a Roman bias is their gimmick.

[6] Their native propensity was stimulated by Hellenistic interest in the marginal grotesque, but no more. Hence Republican Oliver Cromwell's "warts and all": cf. the reproduction of Samuel Cooper's painting in S. Schama, *A History of Britain* (New York 2001), II, p. 223. This was a conscious choice in favour of Roman brusquerie, an amusing contrast with so much late-18th / early-19th century French neo-classical flirtation with Rome (Houdin, David, Ingres), which preserved nevertheless the Greek hankering for formal perfection.

[7] And hence the caricature on a woodcut by Niccolò Boldrini (early 1540's) of Laocoon and his sons as writhing monkeys is perfectly Roman in taste: see John Hale, *The Civilization of Europe in the Renaissance* (New York 1994), illustration on p. 201.

non color unus, VI. 47). The metamorphosing grotesque inevitably touches another world. Given its transrational bias, Roman moralising is bound ultimately to invoke the gods—and demons—who are that world's denizens. Critics are sometimes tempted to view the divine machinery in epic as a tiresome convention,[8] and allusions to the divine in general are similarly dismissed. This is self-projection, and quite wrong. It is particularly wrong in the age of Augustus, where the revival of religion and the concomitant exaltation of the princeps cannot be understood as mere lip service without devaluing the achievement of Augustan public art.[9] Over the Palatine and over the residence of the emperor himself presided charioteering Apollo, god of the sun. As *citharoedus* in his temple, Apollo was flanked by his mother Latona and his sister Diana. Collected and safeguarded there were the Sibylline oracles and other prophecies. It was the fulfilment of a promise made by Aeneas (*Aen.* VI. 69–74). On earth, Augustus was the supreme *vates*, since the implied comparison by Horace in the *Ars Poetica* of the *vates* with the social reconciler Solon of Athens (*leges incidere ligno*, 399) can only apply to the emperor. Apollo too was a *vates* (*Aen.* VI. 12). If Augustus' own features were displayed on a statue of Apollo in the temple precinct, this parallelism would have been overwhelming.[10] How seriously he took all this is becoming more apparent in recent study of the iconography of the period.[11] The fragments of a colossal statue of Apollo citharoedus in his long robe have been recovered near his tomb. Whose features did it have? The sundial / *horologium* also set up there in A.D. 9 implied, for example,

---

[8] See on all this D. C. Feeny, *The Gods in Epic: Poets and Critics of the Classical Tradition* (Oxford 1991).

[9] R. M. Ogilvie, *The Romans and their Gods in the Time of Augustus* (London 1969). For the Alexandrian background, see L. Koenen, "The Ptolemaic King as a Religious Figure," in *Images and Ideologies: Self-Definition in the Hellenistic World*, edd. A. Bulloch *et al.* (Berkeley 1993).

[10] Cf. *ipse sedens niveo candentis limine Phoebi*, *Aen.* VIII. 720, where both *sedens* and *limine* are sacral. If there was another colossal statue of the god outside the temple, different from the one by Scopas inside, again Nero with his colossus and Domus Aurea would be seen as the heir, even if on an exaggerated scale, of Augustan ideology. Nero's statue was eventually modified by Constantine to suit himself. Its fragments may still be viewed on the Capitol. The Museo Palatino preserves a wall painting of a seated Apollo contemplating his lyre which perhaps came from Augustus' house (inv. 379982). "Ὅστις ἐμῷ βασιλῆι, καὶ Ἀπόλλωνι μάχοιτο, Callimachus, *Hy.* II. 27. But how much more this becomes in imperial Rome.

[11] An aureus from Lyons, dated as late as 15 B.C., has a portrait of Augustus and Apollo with his lyre: BMC Augustus 468(5) and 459(6). The legend at the bottom is ACT. Cf. P. Zanker, *The Power of Images*; E. Simon, *Augustus*, above, p. 284, n. 13.

that Augustus himself was a sun-king (like Latinus, *Aen.* XII. 162–64). This is to say nothing of the Pantheon and its luminous *oculus*.

Truth and Time

The supreme *vates* was Orpheus, the first precedent cited by Aeneas to the Sibyl in justification of his plea to be allowed to visit the Lower World (VI. 119). Later we find applied to him an unmistakable allusion to the statue of Apollo citharoedus (*longa cum veste sacerdos*, VI. 645: cf. *Pythius in longa ... veste*, Prop. II. 31. 16). Orpheus was a poet-king, the civiliser of mankind, close to Apollo, as Horace emphasises in a passage which begins with the poet and ends with the god (*A.P.* 391–407). Tacitus concurs (*Dial.* 12. 4). Early believers made him into an icon of Christ. Even in seventeenth-century India we find him as a model for the Mogul emperors.[12]

Virgil's Orphic / Apolline epic could not then have been Augustan in any narrower, Maecenatian[13] sense without claiming religious inspiration. Like St. John's Gospel, it offers the λόγος of an ἀρχή, the account of the new creation which is Augustan Rome. Like Genesis, it is interested in aetiologies (*Musa, mihi c a u s a s memora*). It is couched in the religious language of *pietas* and *fatum*, and all this makes it ultimately unamenable to rationalist (intellectualising) criticism. Two of the greatest difficulties it presents for such criticism affect its notion of truth and its concept of time. These difficulties may be addressed here in reverse order.

Novit namque omnia vates, / quae sint, quae fuerint, quae mox ventura trahantur; / quippe ita Neptuno visum est ... (*Geo.* IV. 392–94). There is about *traho* here something Stoic,[14] perhaps ultimately Posidonian. Ovid

---

[12] See Lawrence James, *Raj* (New York 1998), p. 4, for Shahjahan holding court in the Red Fort in Delhi with a panel over his head "which portrays Orpheus playing his lute before wild beasts who, bewitched by his music, are calmly seated around him. The scene was a reminder to the emperor and his successors that they were Solomonic kings. Like the Thracian musician, they were bringers of harmony, spreading peace among their subjects who, if left to their own devices, would live according to the laws of the jungle." The representation of Christ as Orpheus is familiar: *Oxf. Dict. Byzantium*, III, p. 1538. He was of course also Helios: above, p. 5. See further Elisabeth Henry, *Orpheus with his Lute: Poetry and the Renewal of Life* (Carbondale 1992).

[13] This nomenclature is explained below, p. 325. Maecenas may have shared something of the Etruscan religious outlook; its concept of ages, for example, or of the all-pervasive power of the gods (A. J. Pfiffig, *Religio Etrusca*, Graz 1975). His poetry, so obtusely criticised by Spanish Seneca, is Etruscan in spirit (cf. *Aen.* XI. 736–40).

[14] *Ducunt volentem fata, nolentem t r a h u n t*, Seneca, *Epp.* 107. 11. Lucan inherits this idiom: II. 287, 567; VII. 346, 415; cf. X. 384–85: *attrahit illos / in*

adapts for Apollo the same Homeric line:[15] *per me quod eritque fuitque / estque patet* (*Met.* I. 517–18). The prophet, like his god, knows of things that are, that were, and that are ineluctably to come. Yet Virgil and Ovid, both Romans, have both changed the tense of the Homeric passage they are imitating. Virgil's *novit*, replacing ἤδη, a perfect / present for a pluperfect, means that for his *vates* time is *here*, vertical, hanging over his head and falling away from beneath his feet like a ladder to which for the moment, in descending, he clings—precariously, since "moment" means "movement." There are not three well-defined times: present, past and future. There is the present and what is not the present: Cronus / Saturn for ever devouring his children. Of all that who knows what, or how? Overlaid though they may be by more "rational" concepts, traces of this primitive dichotomy persist in the Greco–Roman mentality.[16] In this poet they loom large.

The truth discovered in this way is not Euclidean, as the relevance of musical and cinematographic analogies to Virgil's art already hints. The *vates* at the end of the *Georgics* is a god of the sea. His Protean truth will not then be anything cut and dried. The *Aeneid*'s habit of hovering on various temporal planes was already remarked. The temple-paintings of Carthage, seen now, ostensibly illustrating the past, emblazon the iterations yet to come in Italy. At Dido's banquet, while describing the fate of Troy, Aeneas is already speaking to the unsuspecting queen about a fiery destruction which will one day overwhelm her own city (IV. 669–71; cf. *fuit / ruit* I. 12, II. 363), and which in turn might overwhelm Rome—as, under the last of the Julio-Claudians, it did. She in turn curses him both with a Hannibal of whom rationally she can know nothing; and, more nearly, with the fates which will befall him as the Italian half of the poem unrolls (IV. 615–29). It was proposed above that the bloody sequence of events leading to victory over Turnus was some sort of pre- (and post-) figuring of the Italian horrors of the last agony of the Republic. In this sense, Virgil wrote a historical epic in which myth was employed to seize the universal in the now, a mythical epic for which history became a tool cutting the now from the womb of the universal: Caesarean section.

---

nostras Fortuna manus. Perhaps it is influenced by ἕλκω in the sense "drag into court" (LSJ[9] *s.v.* A. II. 3; Bauer–Arndt–Gingrich, *s.v.* 1. a, p. 251).

[15] *Iliad* I. 70; cf. Hesiod, *Theog.* 38.

[16] And elsewhere. The mysteries of the Etruscan verb, with its "injunctive" (which may refer to either the past or the present), are discussed by Helmut Rix in *Gli Etruschi*, ed. M. Cristofani, pp. 220–24. Cf. the Latin *praesens historicum*. Students of *literae humaniores* will also take in the syntax of the Hebrew verb and its perfective / imperfective aspects. See also above, pp. 27, 91.

What the vatic seine dredges from the vast flux will demand shifting, dissociable expression. The poet's estranging language (*nova cacozelia*), aided for his first audiences by his *vox et os et hypocrisis*, has been analysed by scholars: his jarring oddities; his large, penumbral words; his plain simplicities in blurring conjunction (*callida iunctura*); his irrational combinations (Roiron); his insistent euphony defying reductive paraphrase; his repetitiousness ("theme and variation") reminiscent of the Hebrew Psalms (and of Hebrew narrative more generally); his internal, polyphonic cross-references; his skewed Homeric allegiance and yet marked avoidance, by comparison with Homer, of the chattering detail; his tragification of the comic; his poetic of silences.[17] What he says or does not say about his world is more than a matter of leaving his listener to do his work for him. It is Delphic in this way because he feels the inadequacy of our construct of time.

In other poets, tension, danger, may provoke moments of imminent clarity. Aeschylus' Cassandra knew this (*Aga.* 1178–79, 1183):

καὶ μὴν ὁ χρησμὸς οὐκέτ' ἐκ καλυμμάτων
ἔσται δεδορκώς, νεογάμου νύμφης δίκην ...
... φρενώσω δ' οὐκέτ' ἐξ αἰνιγμάτων.

And see, my oracle shall no longer peep out from behind veils, like some newly-wed bride.... My precepts shall no longer spring from riddles.

Shakespeare's John of Gaunt seems close. But these are not typical, as Pindar's and Lycophron's kennings attest. And if Greek rhetorical theory lauded σαφήνεια and ἐνάργεια, Roman *evidentia* (as Quintilian admits) was sometimes more honoured in the breach. Livy, Virgil's contemporary, immortalised a teacher who urged on his students with σκότισον.[18] Here is where the Virgilian *umbrae* find their place.

In a nation so addicted to religion, what Polybius defines as δεισιδαιμονία, Hebrew as יְהוָה יִרְאַת, the "fear of the Lord,"[19] this was not a fault. Least of all can such language be brought to account by a

---

[17] "Und alles schwieg. Doch selbst in der Verschweigung / ging neuer Anfang, Wink und Wandel vor" (Rilke). The end of Wittgenstein's *Tractatus* is also in point: "wovon man nicht sprechen kann, darüber muß man schweigen" (6. 74. 7). Helenus' silence about Dido may perhaps be categorised here. This religious silence (cf. הַסְכֵּת: *favete linguis*) is more than Callimachus' literary αὐτὸς ἐπιφράσσαιτο (above, p. 81). The difference makes the Roman genius Roman.

[18] Quintilian VIII. 2. 18. Even Greek critics such as Dionysius of Halicarnassus had to accommodate Thucydides, estranging recorder of Athens' slow agony.

[19] See יָרֵא in *TWAT* III, cols. 869–93, especially col. 876, *infra*, adducing from Latin authors Lucretius V. 1161–1240; Statius, *Theb.* III. 661 (H. F. Fuhs).

Cartesianism calling for *idées claires et distinctes*. To argue that a poem must either display the commitment of a party pamphlet or be "subversive" is to misunderstand the nature of religious—and artistic—language. And how grossly unfair to the genius of Rome!

There is as much unfairness in the demand that the *Aeneid* should show logical ("philosophical") consistency of viewpoint. The poem has of course general themes which help its unity: the idea, for example, of the ultimate founding of a new order in Italy: a Golden Age restored by a messianic king. But there is a price to be paid for redemption. Sometimes ugly particularities cloak and clog this whole, and the work of synthesis is always contributed freshly by the listener / performer, as in the interpretation of a symphonic score. Even as late as Book XII, what do we make, for example, of an all-wise Jupiter who has treated Juturna so heartlessly? Or who uses a hellish Fury to demoralise her brother?

The poem's truth is not one of correspondence, but coherence, verging on incoherence. The *vates* himself enjoys ambiguous status. Certainly the *vates* who embodied the Augustan poetic ideal was also a *civis*. But he was not a hired hack, a mouthpiece, a purveyor of the kind of historical "cyclic" epic offered for sale by Choerilus of Iasos (Hor., *Epp*. II. 1. 233)! Using an un-Homeric turn of phrase, iambic Archilochus had upbraided the Lemnians: ὦ λιπερνῆτες πολῖται... (52 D.). In his sixteenth epode, iambic Horace had tried to imitate him, though there admittedly without any use by the freedman's son of "citizens!" Yet the *o plebs* of the *Odes* (III. 14. 1) still astonishes. The unexpected use of the vocatival *cives* in the *Aeneid* proves that Virgil was as aware of the public demand as Horace.[20]

For such vatic, visionary sensibilities, everything is approximation. Yet Plato's *aporia*, Dante's failure of the lofty imagination,[21] are not defects. They are to be expected. *Vitaque cum gemitu fugit indignata sub umbras* (*Aen*. XI. 831 = XII. 952): what a desolating contrast with the funeral banquet which concludes the *Iliad*, the wedding feast ending Vegio's *Supplementum*! It is precisely *not* at the end that Homer uses the repeated

[20] Πολίτης occurs at *Iliad* XV. 558, XXII. 429; *Odyssey* VII. 131, XVII. 206. Πολιῆτας is found at *Il*. II. 806. None of these instances is vocatival. Virgil's ninefold use of *cives* in that way (II. 42; V. 196, 671; IX. 36, 783; XI. 243, 305, 459; XII. 572) is therefore quite un-Homeric. It is Pindaric (*Py*. 4. 117; *Nem*. 2. 24) and Ennian (*Ann*. 385, Sk.). To whom indeed were *Ann*. 494–95 addressed?

[21] *A l'alta fantasia qui mancò possa, Paradiso* 33. 142. But *aporiare* is also one of Dante's Latin words (*Vulg. El*. II. iv. 1). Ἀπορία is not an intellectual bafflement in the face of a mental brick wall, but the sudden apprehension of new, unfathomed, heart-stopping possibilities (cf. ἠπόρει ... ἡδέως of Herod, NT Mark 6:20). Le roi échappait avec plaisir aux problèmes du moment pour goûter les mystères éternels.

lines (XVI. 856 = XXII. 362) which Virgil is imitating. The greatness of Augustus lay in his willingness to tolerate such shadows, such exits from the Gate of False Dreams, provided he was convinced that they were conjured in defence of the common cause.

Laughter and the Transrational

In any case, when Virgil's darkness is found too visible, the closeness of prophet and satirist / jester, evident enough in both Archilochus and vatic Horace, must be borne in mind. The seer returning to the cave is both mocker (*ridentem dicere verum / quid vetat? Sat.* I. 1. 24–25), and (self-) mocked (*vivit siliquis et pane secundo, Epp.* II. 1. 123). In literature more generally, this finds its supreme illustration not only in Plato's own amplification of his master's ironies, but also in Dante's *Comedy*, in which eventually didactic Beatrice shines on dim Dante the light shed on Socrates in the *Symposium* by scolding Diotima. What self-deprecation! Yet what talents more dedicated to the welfare of their cities and nations?

Such a poetry, concerned with *mystères* rather than *problèmes* (Gabriel Marcel), finds its best expression in the medium of the *spoudogeloion*, the serio-comic, the ambiguous-ironic (*seria ludo, Ecl.* 7. 17; Hor., *A.P.* 226). What we moderns seem to hear in the lecturer's monotone as we scan impatiently down our pages is in fact sung antistrophically, echoed by more than one voice. Sometimes these other voices introduce an element verging on parody, as when sensual Venus appears to her son as if she were girlish Nausicaa, or when Allecto / Turnus is modelled after Callimachus' Demeter / Erysichthon, or Aeneas uses the plaintive words of the *Coma Berenices* to apologise to Dido for his reluctant departure. Cybele's *nepotes* had been Callimachus' dancing-girls. Dido herself appears to be confounded with Odysseus' mother Anticleia.[22]

It can never be assumed therefore that laughter is not consonant with the sermon. It is the prelude to the resurrection of whatever is mocked. Turnus' *vatem inridens* is a special case of this (VII. 435). His misplaced merriment calls into fresh life the very powers of hell he thought he could disdain. But there is "reduced" laughter, Bakhtin's редуцированный смех. Virgil's vatic ironies are in this mood, ending in the tears which are the specialty of the sentimental poet. Of course, within the decorum of so lofty a genre as epic, laughter must be diminished, and hence the absence noted by critics in the *Aeneid* of a sense of humour. But perhaps they are looking for a humour too crudely defined. Virgil's laughter may be the smile greeting the advent

---

[22] See Knauer, p. 113.

of a new age of peace (I. 254, XII. 829; *Ecl.* 4. 60, 62).

Aut videt aut vidisse putat. The *Aeneid*'s elusive poetic was already made our quarry. Hellenistic theory, as we see from Cicero, had sharply separated tragedy from comedy.[23] But, if the poet was inevitably constrained by his schooling, we must ask to what kind of schooling he owed most. Was it to the dull doctrines of the dominie, or to the complex subtleties of which Philodemus supplies evidence?[24] What was the influence on him (or later on Tiberius) of Parthenius of Nicaea, author of a *Metamorphoses*, his adviser *in Graecis*? Both these teachers had the ineffable advantage of practising what they preached. It is too easy to amass titbits of rhetorical orthodoxy, sometimes picked up from quite disparate periods and sources and solidified into textbook rigidities; and then to assume unthinkingly that unthinking Virgil was their mechanical exponent. But were his closest known Greek poet-friends like that? And, on the Roman side, what about the frustrating inconsequentialities of his friend Horace's epic / didactic *Ars Poetica*, so vexatiously unhelpful to the dogmatic mind? Or the implied poetic of Propertius' elegies, the work of another profound admirer? What indeed about the poetry of his mentor Gallus? It is *this* Augustan aesthetic which must condition the questions we put to the *Aeneid*.

Ποιητικοῦ πράγματος τεταγμένην τέχνην παράδειγμα φέροντες λελήθασι σφᾶς αὐτούς says Isocrates of certain teachers of his day (XIII. 12): "they have unwittingly tried to make creativity a matter of rules." The Classical artist surely needs τάξις. But he also needs space, distance, multi-dimensional room, all the more necessary if his world is crowded with the spirits of wickedness in high places. He needs, in other words, a transrational, religious freedom. Virgil felt this. It explains why strangely, at the end of the *Georgics*, it is not Orpheus but Proteus who is called (three times) a *vates*. Orpheus / Gallus was too close to suffering. The Protean artist had to move back, to resort to different ploys in the face of the tormenting, destructive questions, to be allowed to metamorphose. At the end of the *Aeneid*, old Latinus the sun-king is in a stupor (XII. 707), what Pindar calls a δύσφορον θάμβος (*Nem.* 1. 55), withdrawn from the fray even as some sort of Herculean revelation is about to occur.

Virgil's shifting subterfuges ("declensions") may annoy. But our criticism of him cannot be too straightforward if we are to mirror his Lobachevskian geometry, in which parallel lines after all meet; in which

---

[23] Above, p. 97, n. 55.

[24] *Philodemus and Poetry. Poetic Theory and Practice in Lucretius, Philodemus, and Horace*, ed. Dirk Obbink (Oxford 1995); A. Summers, above, p. 307, note 2.

Hector, for example, turns out to be Achilles, Achilles, Hector, and both of them mad Ajax.

Prophetic Ambivalence

Delius inspirat vates (VI. 12). Himself a *vates*, Apollo makes *vates* his instruments, a truth which the Sibyl, who receives that title 13 times, supremely illustrates.[25] Apollo was Augustus' god. When the poem luxuriates in his sunshine, the "second time" of the *Aeneid* is most evident.[26] Yet revelation of the divine is often bathed in half-light. In Book II, amid the nocturnal glare of Troy's smoking fires, Venus must pull away the cloud which "blunts" (*hebetat*, 605) Aeneas' perceptions. The neologism, recurring only in the Apolline Book VI (732),[27] makes a characteristic blur. In Book III, when the Penates appear as Apollo's go-betweens, if there is *multum lumen*, closer inspection shows it to be that of the moon (152). Most of all, this is true of the revelations of the Underworld, approached *quale per incertam lunam, sub luce maligna*. It is not surprising then that the greatest revelations are found on wide and misty plains (*aëris in campis latis*, VI. 887) on the other side of the Ivory Gate—or on Aeneas' Shield. There the emperor, sitting at shining Phoebus' threshold, counts the spoils of the conquered world, and fixes them to the temple's proud doors (Gallus!). Yet the Shield is a sort of mirror-image, something therefore inherently uncertain, *non enarrabile textum* (VIII. 625), hardly understood by its bearer.

For all its revelations, even Book III contained no direct warning of the danger posed by Dido, whose stand-in is the Etnaean Cyclops. Aeneas' relationship with Apollo is accordingly ambiguous, and diminishes as the epic proceeds. It is ambiguous when in Book IV, in the guise of Apollo (144; *Cretes*, 146), he is both found in company with Dido / Diana and yet will receive from Apollo the order to move on (345–46, 376–78).[28] Was his Apolline appearance then merely an illusion, a mirage of her distorted

---

[25] Cf. also *pii vates et Phoebo digna locuti*, VI. 662; Helenus, III. 358.

[26] For the terms "first" and "second" time, above, p. 280.

[27] Cf. ἀμβλυώττει, Plato, *Rep.* VII. 516e 9, 517d 6.

[28] *Augur Apollo* at 376 echoes Horace's *augur Apollo*, *Odes* I. 2. 32, picked up at *Carm. Saec.* 61–62, *augur ... Phoebus*. But *augur* is related to *augustus*! *Augusto augurio postquam incluta condita Roma est*, Ennius, *Ann.* 155, Sk. The queen shows her ineligibility for survival in using the sacred title so sarcastically. But it is a mark of Aeneas' own blindness that she has to use it, while he, still locked in Asia Minor, had referred merely to (Euphorion's and Gallus') Apollo Gryneus (cf. *Ecl.* 6. 72–73).

perception? It diminishes when in Book X he "sacrifices" (*immolat*, 541; *immolet* of human sacrifice, X. 519, *immolat*, XII. 949) Haemonides, *Phoebi Triviaeque sacerdos* (537; cf. VI. 35), to Mars. In XII, already noted as Mars' book, Apollo seemed unwilling to lend the hero his healing aid (405). It is as if Aeneas is caught in oracular *ambages* he cannot fathom (VI. 99–100), degraded to the status of baffled bull (XII. 716). Is he too a Minotaur? In earlier chapters we have suggested that he remains trapped in the Cretan labyrinth he studied on the door of Apollo's temple at Cumae. He could not finally learn the object lesson offered by the prophetic god, which for Daedalus had meant the loss of his son: *non haec tibi litora suasit / Delius aut Cretae iussit considere Apollo* (III. 161–62). This is why Venus is left to prime him, not wholly successfully (XII. 746–47), for the circling *orbes* of his last, merciless combat: and she, *laeta dolis*, uses a Cretan herb.

Discite iustitiam moniti.... Virgil signals indeed (VI. 620) that there was a hero who had escaped from the Cretan labyrinth, only to prove that his experience had taught him nothing. This contradiction of the usual and less damnatory story, apparently still regarded as paradigmatic by Aeneas himself (VI. 122), was more than mythical parade or Callimachean inconsistency. Here, the *Aeneid*'s first time plays into its second. Theseus and Phlegyas in Hades are directly followed by Mark Antony, and a quotation from a famous (though now lost) propaganda piece of the day (VI. 621–22):

> vendidit hic auro patriam dominumque potentem
> imposuit; fixit leges pretio atque refixit.

Here is one who sold his country for gold and set over it a mighty despot. For a price he made and unmade laws.

This piece was Varius' *De Morte*.

Antony lost self-control. Theseus was a great king led astray by the call of friendship. Phlegyas offended Apollo. Virgil warns us off such behaviour. Perhaps just as the allegorisers went to work, but certainly before the term "didactic epic" annexed its own sub-genre, Euripides and Aeschylus agree that the duty of the poet is to make men better in their cities (Aristophanes, *Frogs* 1009–10; cf. χρήστ' ἐδίδαξεν of Homer, 1035). Even within the economy of the *Iliad*, angry Achilles slowly and painfully learned the drawbacks of indulging his sense of personal honour at the cost of the common good. Within the more pessimistic economy of the *Aeneid*, angry (XII. 946) Aeneas needed to learn the drawbacks of reliving the bloody patterns of the past, and perhaps never did.

His descendants could. In writing his epic, the poet had exactly the same public purpose as Augustan Livy (*Praef.* 10):

> Hoc illud est praecipue in cognitione rerum salubre ac frugiferum, omnis te exempli documenta in inlustri posita monumento intueri; inde tibi tuaeque reipublicae quod imitere capias, inde foedum inceptu foedum exitu quod vites.
>
> The particular salutary return from studying history is to view evidence of every sort of behaviour set out clearly in the record. From there, you may select for yourself and your country precedent for imitation, and precedent for avoidance, dreadful at its outset and dreadful in its outcome.

Livy, who does not claim the title for himself, describes Q. Fabius, reputed to have been augur for 62 years, as a *vates* (XXX. 28. 2). Earlier he has cited Ennius in praise of the Cunctator (*ibid.* 26. 9), and Ennius detested *vates*. In the historian, the Augustan paradox is apparent. In defining his view of himself, poetic Virgil is less confused (VII. 41):

> tu vatem, tu, diva, mone. dicam horrida bella ...

The echo of the vatic Sibyl's words at VI. 86–87 is clear:

> 'bella, horrida bella,
> et Thybrim multo spumantem sanguine cerno.'

The second half of his poem will unfold her vision of the horrid repetitions (*iterum*, VI. 94) to come in Italy.[29] There, *eadem horrida belli fata* still summon Aeneas to tears (XI. 96–97).

The Moral Universe of the Aeneid

Though the physical oddity of Virgil's nightmarish world, its kinship with Ovid's *Metamorphoses*, has received scrutiny here,[30] in a *vates* his moral universe must also pass under review. Democritus had remarked the role of "melancholy" in the poetic temperament. Aristotle and his pupil Theophrastus had studied character. Horace alludes to both themes (*A.P.* 295, 156). But at Rome such quirks were more than matter for the philosopher / rhetorician's or even the doctor's Hippocratean textbooks. They might serve as public provocations of satirical and comic laughter. When the undifferentiated sensibility acquired refinement, to "note" them was often to further a social aim.[31] As emperors increasingly fell victim to the μανία Plato had diagnosed in the tyrant, an epic illustrating mania's outcome became more and more a national hymn.

Its poet lived, after all, in a reflective age. Cicero had perhaps coined

---

[29] On these iterations, see Index Rerum et Nominum, below.

[30] Above, pp. 65 ff. — The remarks on the "moral universe" of the poem supplement what was already said above, e.g. pp. 237, 306.

[31] *Notare*, "to brand with shame" (cf. Hor., *Sat.* I. 4. 106 quoted above, p. 306), comes from the censors' quinquennial scrutiny.

―and certainly circulated―the term *humanitas*. Horace had meditated among the woods of Academus, Virgil had frequented the groups around Philodemus and Siro. No educated Roman was unfamiliar with the moral doctrines of the Hellenistic philosophers, or their reflections on the duties of the good king, a topic on which, in the train of Theophrastus, Philodemus too had written. At the court of the new Augustus, Seneca reiterated these precepts: *De Clementia, De Ira*. Horace supplies the evidence of Augustan concerns: about anger, greed and pride; about the causes of war and the downfall of civilisations (*Odes* I. 16); about the brevity of human life, personal responsibility, self-restraint and―supremely for Augustus―mercy to the conquered.[32] He echoes Stoic views of the dangers of any action inspired by *ira*, and *a fortiori* by the Furies. In lines anticipating (recalling?) Virgil's *Furor ... centum vinctus aënis post tergum nodis* (*Aen.* I. 294–95) he urges that the *animus* ("spirit") of *furor* must be chained (*Epp.* I. 2. 59–63, 20 B.C.?):

> qui non moderabitur irae,
> infectum volet esse dolor quod suaserit et mens,
> dum poenas odio per vim festinat inulto.
> ira furor brevis est: animum rege, qui nisi paret,
> imperat: hunc frenis, hunc tu compesce catena.

The man unable to control his anger will wish undone what indignation and impulse may have convinced him to do, in his violent eagerness to glut his hatred unavenged. Anger is a fit of madness. Take hold of your feelings, for if you do not master them, they will master you. To quieten them you need a bridle and even a chain.

Dolor, poenas, odio ... inulto: this reads like a commentary on parts of the *Aeneid*―which of course Horace may well have known―written ahead of its final publication, and on Dido's moral universe. Perhaps Hellenistic queens and kings had such self-gratifying prerogatives. Perhaps Trojan Aeneas, acting out the role of Homeric hero, could be allowed to behave like that. The Roman *imperator* could not. Augustan interest in the history of the *spolia opima* (Livy IV. 20; cf. *Aen.* VI. 859; Prop. IV. 10), won for slaughtering an enemy leader and taking his armour, was antiquarian and perhaps political, but not inspired by personal ambition or bellicosity felt for any Turnus.

Cicero, λόγιος ἀνὴρ καὶ φιλόπατρις, had nobly striven to Romanise

---

[32] *Clarus Anchisae Venerisque sanguis / ... bellante prior, iacentem / lenis in hostem, Carm. Saec.* 50–52. E. Fraenkel contrasts the treatment of the conquered kings in Joshua 10:24 (*Horace*, pp. 160–61, where he also adduces his note at *Agamemnon* 907). See *TWAT* II. 347 ff. (הדה, Fabry), VII. 330 ff. (רגלים, Stendebach). ― Cicero's views on anger are also noted above, p. 258.

discussion of these ideas at the very outset of his public career. He contrasts Verres with Pompey and notes their different treatment of Sertorius' followers (*Verr.* V. §§152–53):

> Forum plenum et basilicas istorum hominum videmus, et animo aequo videmus; civilis enim dissensionis et seu amentiae seu fati seu calamitatis non est iste molestus exitus, in quo reliquos saltem civis incolumis licet conservare.
> ... Quem non ille [Cn. Pompeius] summo cum studio salvum incolumemque servavit? cui civi supplicanti non illa dextera invicta fidem porrexit et spem salutis ostendit?... tua defensio furoris cuiusdam [te coarguit] et immanitatis et inauditae crudelitatis et paene novae proscriptionis.

> We see our forum and its public halls crowded with men of that sort, and see it without alarm. Such an outcome of that falling-out among citizens—whether we call it madness or destiny or misfortune—is not unwelcome, if it allows us at least to preserve the lives of the citizens we have left.
> ... Which of them did not Pompey display the greatest zeal for keeping safe and sound? When any citizen sought pardon, to whom did that victorious right hand not extend a pledge of trust or show a promise of deliverance?... Your line of defence proves you guilty of a kind of madness and monstrosity, of unparalleled cruelty—almost indeed of a fresh proscription.

Furor is significant here. *Dextera invicta* is the application to Pompey of an old oriental formula, found both in the Psalms and Herodotus.[33] But the main point is that this is a right hand, not of despotic cruelty, but of mercy. Aeneas ultimately rejected a right hand stretched out in entreaty (XII. 930). Those who justify Aeneas by Verres should ask themselves what they are doing. Cicero says of Pompey what Augustus says of himself more modestly: *victorque omnibus veniam petentibus civibus peperci* (*R.G.* 3). Turnus, it was noted, had been allowed to call the Italians *cives* (XI. 459).

Cicero is still talking this way at the end of his life (*Pro Deiotaro* §8):

> Quam ob rem hoc nos primum metu, Caesar, per fidem et constantiam et clementiam tuam libera, ne residere in te ullam partem iracundiae suspicemur. Per dexteram istam te oro quam regi Deiotaro hospes hospiti porrexisti....

> Let me then first and foremost, Caesar, appeal to your sense of loyalty, steadfast purpose and spirit of forgiveness. Rid us of our fear and apprehension that some trace of resentment still lingers in your heart. I beg this of you by that right hand of yours, which once you extended to king Deiotarus in pledge of mutual friendship.

Caesar himself, who both planned a temple to *Clementia Caesaris* and put that legend on his coins, had written to Oppius (*ad Att.* IX. 7. C):

> Haec nova sit ratio vincendi, ut misericordia et liberalitate nos muniamus.

---

[33] *TWAT* III, cols. 422 ff. *s.v.* ͳ᾽ (Bergman, von Soden, Ackroyd); καὶ γὰρ δύναμις ὑπὲρ ἄνθρωπον ἡ βασιλέος ἐστὶ καὶ χεὶρ ὑπερμήκης, Herodotus VIII. 140. β 2. Δύναμις here is also sacral (Pindar, *Nem.* 1. 57; Bauer—Arndt—Gingrich, *s.v.*, p. 207, 4 and 7).

Our novel experiment in conquest must be to build around ourselves a protective wall of mercy and generosity.

It is true that those he had spared eventually murdered him, and were rightly punished, after resort to *iudicia legitima*, by Mars Ultor. But they were spared first. Yet Anchises is so eager for reconciliation that, assuming a father's privilege, he actually reminds Julius (perhaps rather unfairly) of his duty (VI. 834–35):

> 'tuque prior, tu parce, genus qui ducis Olympo!
> proice tela manu, sanguis meus....'

'You take the lead in forgiving, you who trace your descent from heaven! Cast down those weapons from your hand, my own blood....'

Augustus, whatever his record may have been as Octavian, rescued this poem and published it.

Although then we certainly may not import specifically "modern" notions[34] into the understanding of the end of the *Aeneid*, we have every right to bring to it whatever is gleaned now from the rich harvest of Greco-Roman moral reflection (including that of New Comedy), and whatever common sense judgments we may claim, because of our shared humanity, to share with Classical antiquity.[35] It dehumanises the *Aeneid* when we diminish its moral boundaries in order to gloss over the tragic ἁμαρτία at its end. This is not consonant with the aim of *literae humaniores*.

Sallust had already traced the accelerating decline of Rome, culminating in the Civil War, to the murder of the Gracchi and subsequent bloodthirsty vengeance of the *nobiles* (*Jug.* 42. 4):

> Quae res plerumque magnas civitates pessum dedit, dum alteri alteros vincere quovis modo et victos acerbius ulcisci volunt.
>
> This behaviour has more than proved the downfall of mighty states. One side uses any method to best the other, and to exact bitter revenge on the losers.

And this no doubt Hellenistic moral (Horace, *Odes* I. 16. 17–21) is the moral sensibility of the *Aeneid* in general. Julius had mastered his anger and pardoned Marcellus, and his clemency was celebrated by Cicero in a noble speech setting forth the human grandeur of such behaviour. Augustus had no intention nor indeed the possibility (if he hoped to survive) of upsetting these standards and the expectations they generated. Virgil offered him the picture of a world in which war spawned as often as not the death of

---

[34] Scholars speak as if "we moderns" were uniquely compassionate. But is not "our age" the age of genocide? Leave *nec nostri saeculi est* to Trajan!

[35] The meaning of *sensus communis* may be pondered: cf. Seneca, *Epp.* 5. 4.

innocence and its bearers, leaving pain and grief to the survivors. Could the conqueror of Philippi, Actium, Perusia, possibly have denied the truth of such a picture? Did he want his contemporaries to pretend that black was white? But, as Augustus, did he not equally want to stress his own desire for reconciliation, for *pax Augusta* (*Aen.* XII. 504)?

The task of the Augustan *vates* was not to ignore the moral failings of his age, whichever party they disfigured, but to present them in a larger perspective. There had been grievous faults in the heroic past, repeated ("iterated") in Rome's Civil Wars down to the blood-stained present. They had to be unflinchingly confronted, and part of Augustus' greatness is that he did not shrink from such moral honesty. But they had not stood in the path of providence, in Dante's language *la provvedenza, che governa il mondo* (*Par.* 11. 28), what Stoic and New Roman (Byzantine) statecraft called πρόνοια.[36] Could they stand in the path of providence now? In using that term, however, we again touch the delicate matter of the *Aeneid* as a Roman religious epic.

The Aeneid *as Carmen Sacrum. Catharsis*

Some of the poets around Maecenas (Varius' is the most intriguing case) had been influenced as young men by the doctrines of Epicurus in Philodemus' modern interpretations.[37] Yet, whatever they may have owed to neo-Epicurean literary theory, the Augustans broke completely with the Garden's teachings on religion as they had been promulgated by so recent a poet as Lucretius. Cicero had seen what a great danger to the *constitutio rei publicae* such teaching presented. Octavian, transmuted into Augustus, came eventually to understand what his political enemy had seen long before. How could the general who owed Actium to Apollo ever have been satisfied with Dido's pre-Epicurean notion (IV. 379–80) that the gods take no interest in human affairs?

In promoting a different view, the word was essential. Ἐν ἀρχῇ ἦν ὁ λόγος, already adduced, may be understood quite literally. The very first simile of the *Aeneid*, as has been often remarked, describes the calming effect of what may be termed *auctoritas*,[38] enhanced by reason and eloquence, on the violence of the mob. *Furor arma ministrat* (I. 150). But *pietas* and

---

[36] Διὰ τῆς σῆς προνοίας is used flatteringly to a Roman governor at NT Acts 24:2. Cf. Themistius, *Or.* 64b (Downey I, p. 94). Virgil's *fatum* and *fortuna* are crueller terms however than "Providence."

[37] He had of course dedicated a treatise Οὐεργιλίῳ καὶ Οὐαρίῳ.

[38] The word is impossible in dactyls, but may perhaps be used with caution in exegesis. It was claimed as the basis of his power by Augustus (*R.G.* 34. 3).

gravitas can resist its impulse. On Aeneas' shield, Catiline and Cato will represent a similar contrast: Catiline the victim now of the Furies he evoked, Cato arbitrating law among the pious (VIII. 668–70).

The Roman administrator and statesman of this initial simile might also have been, like Cicero, a *sacerdos publicus*. But in this prominent place it is a simile also meant to define the task of the *Aeneid*. The poem's hero may indeed illustrate Aristotle's theory of tragic ἁμαρτία (above, pp. 227 ff.). But the poem as a whole illustrates his theory of catharsis, a doctrine still persisting in ancient commentaries on the *Iliad*.[39] Perhaps we may remind ourselves of the parts of the definition which are relevant here (*Poetics* 1449b 24–25, 27–28).

> ἔστιν οὖν τραγῳδία μίμησις πράξεως σπουδαίας καὶ τελείας μέγεθος ἐχούσης ... δι' ἐλέου καὶ φόβου περαίνουσα τὴν τῶν τοιούτων παθημάτων κάθαρσιν.
>
> Tragedy then is the imitation of a serious and complete action of some magnitude ... which with the aid of pity and terror brings about the purging of that kind of feeling.

How then could it be the office of a tragedian to crown everything with a happy ending? The worst offence any moralist can commit is to disguise the unpleasant consequences of immorality. But, for the *Aeneid* to be "complete," it must look beyond its own day to a distant future, to some *deus ex machina* who will explain the divine purpose and reveal a better promise. This *deus* will be Jupiter, and his promised vicar on earth will be Augustus.[40]

Catharsis is however not simply a matter for the theatre-goer. It is commended also in the *Politics*, and we have seen the importance of such "civics" to the *vates*. A special place there is allotted to ἱερὰ μέλη, "religious melodies," which have the paradoxical effect of exciting and yet calming their listeners (VIII. 1342a 4 ff.):

> ὃ γὰρ περὶ ἐνίας συμβαίνει πάθος ψυχὰς ἰσχυρῶς, τοῦτο ἐν πάσαις ὑπάρχει, τῷ δ' ἧττον διαφέρει καὶ τῷ μᾶλλον, οἷον ἔλεος καὶ φόβος, ἔτι δ' ἐνθουσιασμός· καὶ γὰρ ὑπὸ ταύτης τῆς κινήσεως κατακώχιμοί τινές εἰσιν, ἐκ τῶν δ' ἱερῶν μελῶν ὁρῶμεν τούτους ὅταν χρήσωνται τοῖς ἐξοργιάζουσι τὴν ψυχὴν μέλεσι καθισταμένους ὥσπερ ἰατρείας τυχόντας καὶ καθάρσεως· ταὐτὸ δὴ τοῦτο ἀναγκαῖον πάσχειν καὶ τοὺς ἐλεήμονας καὶ τοὺς φοβητικοὺς καὶ τοὺς ὅλως παθητικούς, τοὺς

---

[39] L. Adam, *Die aristotelische Theorie vom Epos nach ihrer Entwicklung bei Griechen und Römern* (Wiesbaden 1889), p. 40 (from the scholia on the opening of the *Iliad*).

[40] Again Horace makes the point explicit: *tu* [Jupiter] *secundo / Caesare regnes*, *Odes* I. 12. 51–52. The statue from Herculaneum, now in Naples, showing Augustus with Jupiter's thunderbolts, was noted above, p. 259.

δ' ἄλλους καθ' ὅσον ἐπιβάλλει τῶν τοιούτων ἑκάστῳ, καὶ πᾶσι γίγνεσθαί τινα κάθαρσιν καὶ κουφίζεσθαι μεθ' ἡδονῆς· ὁμοίως δὲ καὶ τὰ μέλη τὰ καθαρτικὰ παρέχει χαρὰν ἀβλαβῆ τοῖς ἀνθρώποις.

Any emotion which strongly affects several individual souls is found in the souls of all, though in varying degrees. Pity, fear and inspiration are such emotions. The feeling of being possessed by some sort of inspiration is one to which certain individuals are particularly liable. These persons are affected by religious melodies; and, after coming under the influence of melodies which fill the soul with religious excitement, they calm down, as if they had undergone a healing and cleansing. The same sort of effect will also be produced on those who are especially subject to feelings of fear and pity, or in general to their emotions; indeed it will be produced on the rest of us, in proportion to the intensity of our feelings. The result will be that all alike will experience some sort of cleansing and some relief accompanied by pleasure. We may add that melodies especially designed to purge the emotions are likewise also a source of innocent delight to humankind. (tr. E. Barker, adapted)

This might well be thought to describe the religious intention of that vatic ἱερὸν μέλος, *carmen sacrum*, which is the *Aeneid*. Octavia notably experienced it.[41] A late manuscript here adds, surely not inappropriately, that she subsequently rewarded the poet with great munificence.

Aristotle had also insisted that the epic poet should not intervene in his own person (*Poetics* 1460a 5–8):

"Ὅμηρος δὲ ἄλλα τε πολλὰ ἄξιος ἐπαινεῖσθαι καὶ δὴ καὶ ὅτι μόνος τῶν ποιητῶν οὐκ ἀγνοεῖ ὃ δεῖ ποιεῖν αὐτόν. αὐτὸν γὰρ δεῖ τὸν ποιητὴν ἐλάχιστα λέγειν· οὐ γάρ ἐστι κατὰ ταῦτα μιμητής.

Homer deserves admiration particularly for knowing, uniquely among poets, what he should write in his own person. In fact, the poet should speak in his own person as little as possible, for in those passages he is not acting as imitator.

Virgil, as we saw in the case of Nisus and Euryalus, does not always observe this convention, and in any case his first book already makes a huge exception to it. If the second part of his poem is a repetition of the *Iliad*, in effect he has also told us what to think of these scenes before we re-encounter them (I. 462–65, translated above, p. 153):

'...sunt lacrimae rerum et mentem mortalia tangunt.
solve metus; feret haec aliquam tibi fama salutem.'
sic ait atque animum pictura pascit inani
multa gemens, largoque umectat flumine vultum.

The second line here encapsulates the vatic purpose of the *Aeneid*. At the

---

[41] *Quae cum recitationi interesset, ad illos de filio suo versus ... defecisse fertur et aegre focilata*, Vit. Don. §32. — With ἱερὸν μέλος may also be compared Dante's *lo sacrato poema*, *Par.* 23. 62; *poema sacro*, 25. 1.

end, *multa gemens* (= IV. 395, XII. 886, *al.*) appears to contradict the possibility of rational explanation. This was already noted.[42] If Virgil has seemed to dwell on these tears at the expense of his larger purpose as a poet of the Augustan regime, is there an explanation, an excuse, in Aristotle's δι' ἐλέου καὶ φόβου? Alexander wanted to be the *Iliad*'s Achilles. Does anyone wish to be the *Aeneid*'s Aeneas? The listener wakes up from Virgil's spell trembling, shocked, glad that all is over—and determined not to let its horrors happen again.

Marriage and Children

For the Roman, the good behaviour promoted by the *vates* includes marriage and children. The Maecenatians, if we may call them this,[43] are never tired of making this point. Propertius, who has urged Tullus to come home and marry (III. 22. 41–42), ends by presenting to us the example of polyphiloprogenitive Cornelia (IV. 11. 69–70):

> et serie fulcite genus. mihi cumba volenti
> solvitur, aucturis tot mea fata meis.

And sustain our house by bearing children. I can tranquilly slip my moorings with so many about to enhance my destiny.

Horace elevates himself to the ranks of the married (*Odes* IV. 15. 25 ff.; cf. *cum prole matronisque nostris*, 27). The last lines of this celebrates *almae progeniem Veneris*.

Virgil, as was seen, can use this sort of language (VI. 781–87, translated above, p. 36):

> 'en huius, nate, auspiciis illa incluta Roma
> imperium terris, animos aequabit Olympo,
> septemque una sibi muro circumdabit arces,
> felix prole virum! qualis Berecyntia mater
> invehitur curru Phrygias turrita per urbes,   785
> laeta deum partu, centum complexa nepotes,
> omnis caelicolas, omnis supera alta tenentis.'

---

[42] Above, pp. 154, 219.

[43] The term emphasises the importance of the exclusive literary circle around Maecenas, whom Horace describes both as *paucorum hominum* (*Sat.* I. 9. 44) and as "difficult at first of access" (*difficilis aditus primos habet, ibid.* 56). Given the importance of patronage at Rome, and its obligations, to speak of all poets of this period as "Augustans" in the usual loose way substitutes a temporal / historical term for one descriptive of the Roman essence. The Maecenatians had a different programme from say Tibullus (see "Saturno Rege," *Candide Iudex*, pp. 225 ff.) or Ovid, or indeed perhaps many of the others whom Ovid lists (*Tr.* IV. 10. 41 ff.). Cf. M. Gigante, ed., *Virgilio e gli Augustei* (Naples 1990).

Yet oddly, though Propertius is so often heard as a discordant liberal, it is the conservative Virgil and Horace who speak with more ambiguous voices. Once again, Republican poetry provides a touchstone. Catullus encouraged the possibility of a *Torquatus parvulus* (61. 216). Horace by contrast advises his Torquatus to indulge himself in order to cheat his heir (*Odes* IV. 7. 19–20). For him, the *Aeneid*'s virtues are of no avail against the last enemy (IV. 7. 14–16, 21–28):

>   nos ubi decidimus
> quo pater Aeneas, quo Tullus dives et Ancus,   15
>   pulvis et umbra sumus....
> cum semel occideris et de te splendida Minos
>   fecerit arbitria,
> non, Torquate, genus, non te facundia, non te
>   restituet pietas;
> infernis neque enim tenebris Diana pudicum   25
>   liberat Hippolytum,
> nec Lethaea valet Theseus abrumpere caro
>   vincula Perithoo.

But when we have once fallen to the place of father Aeneas, of royal Tullus and Ancus, we are dust and shadow.... When once you are laid low and Minos has rendered his majestic verdict on your case, Torquatus, not your lineage, not your eloquence, not your devotion will ever bring you back; for Diana cannot free chaste Hippolytus from the shades below, nor Theseus find the power to release the chains of Lethe from his dear Perithous.

In the passage adduced, Virgil's characteristic *umbra* (16) and *pietas* (24) are brought into context. What can *pater Aeneas* (15) mean here?

This is one reading of the *Aeneid*, perhaps correct, perhaps too austere. Even so, how much poor Dido's hopes of a *parvulus Aeneas* were blasted forms a leading motif of the poem. And Aeneas' mistaken optimism about Theseus was already remarked.

The Aeneid *as* ἀτελής

There is an inconcinnity therefore between Aristotle's demand that tragedy should be the imitation of a "complete action" (πράξεως ... τελείας) and the *Aeneid*. The action of Virgil's modern, Roman epic is notoriously incomplete, as Maffeo Vegio sensed in two poems on behalf of every "normal" reader. If its rhetoric of silences leaves the work of completion to posterity in this way, this implies that his poem is both a moral challenge and a vatic warning. The *Aeneid* can only be fulfilled in history, and that depends on a script which not the poet but his listeners must write.

Tusci vates were habitually summoned in a public crisis (Lucan I.

584–85; cf. Livy I. 55. 6). Was Virgil one of them? His Mantua is described by the Elder Pliny (III. 19. §130) as a last Etruscan holdout north of the Po, and his cognomen "Maro" echoes the Etruscan *maru*, the name of a magistracy,[44] its plural passing into Latin via Umbrian as *marones*. Virgil himself—who seems to know the Etruscan mentality well enough (XI. 736–40)—describes Mantua's founder as the son of *fatidica Manto* (μαντεύ-ομαι) and "the Tuscan stream" (X. 198–200). Vatic Proteus emerged from and went back to the sea. A poet conscious of this fluid heritage would stand between two worlds, as much as catabatic Orpheus or his own Aeneas. For him too, as for Propertius, the *litus* would be a *limen*.

Etruscan tombs make play with red and blue, the colours of warmth and cold, of life and death. Virgil, always conscious of their proximity, is too aware of the darkness, *umbrae*, to write convincingly about marriage and children. But by the same token he was perhaps uniquely fitted to be the poet of his age. Whatever Augustus' propaganda *de maritandis ordinibus*, there came to hang about his regime something of that *fin de siècle* sentimentality we sense in the culture, literature and music of Vienna, as the Habsburgs drew to the end of their long Caesardom.[45] The sad realities were that neither the nobles of his day nor his own efforts to secure the succession were particularly fruitful. For him, Fortuna was *atrox*, "ruthless" (Suet., *Tib.* 23).

But the Etruscan world too, with its Lydian origins, now hung on the brink of dissolution. The bronze, toga-clad "arringatore," on view in Florence, is familiar, his upraised arm, his weary expression. The Prima Porta statue shows armed, prophetic Augustus, barefoot like Moses, making a similar gesture of *adlocutio*, attended by an admiring Cupid. The difference of power and energy is palpable.

Yet the emperor of the Prima Porta statue came to acquire the "sickly" features seen in that of the Via Labicana. Perhaps then Etruscan Maecenas recruited to his literary circle too successfully. The poets clustered around him, loyal supporters of the regime though they were, were too great to be taken in by catchwords. Virgil was no sociologist. But as a *vates* he knew

---

[44] See, for example, *marunuχ* ("the office of *maru*") on a sarcophagus from the Tomba Lattanzi (Norchia: 300–275 B.C.) now in the Staatliche Museen, Berlin; *maronatei* ("during their tenure as *marones*") on an Umbrian inscription now in the Museo Archeologico in Perugia (*CIL* XI. 5389: cf. *marones*, *CIL* XI. 5390). The *cursus honorum* is said to have been *maru*, *zilaθ*, *purθ*: i.e. aedile, praetor, and perhaps something equivalent to the Greek πρύτανις, used by Pindar of Hiero.

[45] The characteristic waltz is the noisier Austrian version of the *Lusus Troiae*: cf. *wälzen*, "turn," *Umwälzung*, "revolution."

things by other than discursive reasoning. Hence the epic which celebrates the promise of a new beginning ends with a threatened intermingling and ultimate dissolution of the Trojan stock just as final as that plotted by the Greeks.

Were the dissolving Trojans, the dissolving Etruscans, the doomed Arcadians at Pallanteum, the paradigm of what Lucan later sees as the vanishing Romans (VII. 385 ff.)? Was any new beginning possible? Whatever the glorious promise of the marble city, the *Lusus Troiae*, with its carnival carousel of silent, disposable children circling to Time's whip, its labyrinthine orbs, always threatened a different paradigm. *Occidit, occideritque sinas....* So the Julio-Claudian line would end with circensian, childless Nero, murderer of Britannicus, of Octavia, of Poppaea's unborn child, and, at some point in this ghastly sequence, of his own mother. Even as Rome burned, the artist-emperor, sun-king and second Augustus in his ideology and aims, admirer of the *Aeneid*, would-be pantomime dancer of the role of Turnus, driver of Augustus' chariot (Suet., *Nero* 25), performed some verses celebrating the fall of Troy.

Ennius already had described the agonising wait to know if Romulus or Remus would be king in terms of the tense emotions of the crowd at some chariot race in the Circus Maximus (*Ann.* xlvii, Sk.). But if the chariot of state then runs out of control, as it did when Remus was murdered so soon afterwards, as it did under Nero? The real Thirteenth Book of the *Aeneid* did not need the genius of Vegio. It turned out to have been lurking all the time in the *Georgics (fertur equis auriga....* I. 514), and in the genes.

For his Augustus, Lucan wrote a carnival epic. The *Aeneid* too, though its laughter is reduced, has carnival features: its twinned, polyprosopic characters; its cyclical time, denoted by the characteristic *iterum*; supremely for our enquiries here, the circling, labyrinthine orbs of its *Lusus Troiae*. Yet already the programme of the fourth *Eclogue* had both sketched these repetitions (*atque iterum ad Troiam magnus mittetur Achilles*, 36 ~ *alius Latio iam partus Achilles*, *Aen.* VI. 89), and seen them as preparatory to a Golden Age, symbolised in a new birth. Was that promise fulfilled? What of the "hollow" pastoral we have so often encountered? The varying responses generated by the *Aeneid* itself to the questions it poses suggest that, as with all carnival experiences, there is never any dogmatic resolution to the conundrums (ἀπορίαι) it raises.

Appendix

THE *AENEID* AS *HERACLEID*[1]

> Wer nie sein Brot mit Tränen aß, ...
> Der kennt euch nicht, ihr himmlichen Mächte.
>
> Goethe

Early in Octavian's rule at Rome, the temple of Apollo Medicus, near what became the Theatre of Marcellus, was enhanced by a wooden image of the god, the Apollo Sosianus, so called because Antony's former lieutenant C. Sosius was associated with the project of renewal (cf. Pliny *N. H.* XXXVI. 28; XIII. 53). It was also refurbished with a pediment, perhaps taken from the temple of Apollo Daphnephorus in Eretria.[2] On it Hercules is seen attacking the queen of the Amazons, Hippolyte, whose death (whatever the alternative story which made her Theseus' wife) is found among the Labours on a metope at Olympia. An interior frieze of the same temple (Montemartini inv. II. 53), installed somewhat later, depicts Octavian's triple triumph of 29 B.C., also illustrated, according to Virgil, on Aeneas' Shield (*Aen.* VIII. 714). One of these triumphs was over Egypt. Queen Hippolyte may then have been interpreted as the mythical version of doomed Queen Cleopatra; and, if so, the emperor would clearly be identified with her conqueror. In any case, the deliberate policy which, in the first years of his reign, set out to assimilate Octavian to "the great Hellenistic kings" is manifested by his portraits.[3] The emperor's admiration for their predecessor

---

[1] A somewhat differently stated version of the argument here is to be found as "Hercules in the *Aeneid*. The *dementia* of Power" in *Hommages à Carl Deroux*, I–Poésie, ed. Pol Defosse (Brussels 2002), pp. 398–411. — To avoid the multiplication of cross- references to previous pages, the reader is asked to make use of the *Index Rerum et Nominum* below, *s.v.* "Hercules."

[2] Museo Montemartini, Via Ostiense, Rome, inv. II. 5. The relics of the Temple are on display in the same room: cf. *The Sculptures of Ancient Rome. The Collections of the Capitoline Museums at the Montemartini Power Plant* (Rome 1999), pp. 28, 31 and 71–77; and *The Capitoline Museums*, edd. M. Albertoni *et al.* (Rome 2000), pp. 190–92.

[3] Susan Walker and Andrew Burnett, *The Image of Augustus* (British Museum Publications 1981), p. 19; *Augustus, B. M. Occasional Paper* 16 (1981), p. 3.

and model, Alexander, is well known (Suet., *Aug.* §§18, 50); and Alexander inevitably brought Hercules in his train. Such parallelism would have made it impossible for the poets of the regime to avoid confronting the well-established ideology surrounding the hero's life and toils.

Yet Hercules and Apollo, Octavian's more particular patron, could clash. Side A of a red-figure Attic pelike, for example, now in the Villa Giulia, ascribed to the Berlin painter (inv. 50755: 500–490 B.C.), shows a quarrel between the two over the Delphic tripod in which the hero is already making off with his prize, raising his club menacingly in response to a warning gesture from Apollo.[4] In marked contrast, the Temple of the Palatine Apollo displayed a much more decorous contest for that same tripod,[5] one which left the two contestants in perfect balance. Could such a compromise satisfy Virgil?

The Iliadic Background

Nescio quid maius nascitur Iliade. Virgil came to his task by learning from his model. We have spoken of the *Aeneid* as iteration. This concept is already familiar to Homer, as we learn from an exchange between Tlepolemus, son of Heracles, and Sarpedon (*Iliad* V. 638–51), in which the second siege of Troy is paralleled with an earlier sacking at the hands of Heracles. And Heracles is important elsewhere in the *Iliad*, even lurking at the end of its first book (517 ff.). There, Zeus promises Thetis to favour the Trojans and so lend glory to Achilles. Hera, who has noted Thetis' private audience with her husband, reacts angrily in front of the assembled gods to her suspicions about its content; and in exasperation Zeus reminds her of the punishment she had to endure on a previous occasion when she wanted to thwart his will. Her son Hephaestus, who tried to help his mother at that time, in fact still bears the marks of the toss he took from Olympus to Lemnos. It is his sage advice to Hera to knuckle under which now lightens the atmosphere. By then serving wine, and making his lameness the butt of the party, he rouses the unquenchable laughter of the immortals, and thus brings matters to some sort of close. Hera and Zeus retire peacefully to their nuptial couch.

---

[4] The Etruscans apparently liked this motif, which is also found on side A of an Attic red-figure amphora from Cerveteri now in the Vatican (inv. 16513: early 5th c. B.C.). The Portonaccio Temple at Veii showed god and hero in dramatic conflict for the Cerynean Hind. The fragments are in the Villa Giulia: see Otto J. Brendel, *Etruscan Art*[2] (New Haven 1995), pp. 238–44.

[5] Museo Palatino, inv. 379639: cf. Maria Antonietta Tomei, *Museo Palatino* (Rome 1997), p. 50.

The "previous occasion" is left for the moment as an enigma. But Hera has not learned her lesson. This scene prepares the way for her activities in Books XIV and XV, towards the end of the poem's second third, where she decides to use her womanly wiles to distract Zeus, so that in his absence Poseidon may give the hard-pressed Achaeans some sort of respite. While Zeus is overcome by love and sleep, with Poseidon's aid the Greeks regain the advantage, and Hector himself receives a grievous wound (XIV. 409 ff.). But then Zeus awakes (XV. 4), is angrily apprised of the situation, bullies his brother into withdrawing, and sends Apollo to rally the Trojans. The Greeks are so threatened that Achilles allows Patroclus to join the fray, dressed in borrowed armour. Patroclus slays Sarpedon, but is himself killed by Hector; and now Achilles himself will return to the field and eventually kill Hector in return, signalling Troy's inevitable doom. Hera's scheme has worked after all. The son of Thetis for his part has not won much, even though the clownish Hephaestus of Book I, who then supplied wine to the immortals, will now supply him with splendid armour to replace that lost by Patroclus. He comes back to set in motion the events which will lead to his own death, still without his girl, and now without his closest comrade.

To further her plot in Book XIV, Hera appeals to Hypnos, god of sleep and brother of Death (231 ff.), who recalls to her that earlier occasion, in Book I a mere hint, which went awry. He consents this second time when she sweetens her request with the offer of Pasithea in marriage. In Book XV, when Zeus awakes, he also reminds his wife of the same occasion, which is at last explained. Her offence then was that, lulling her husband to rest, she had approached Boreas, the North Wind, and persuaded him to blow her enemy Heracles' ship far off course (XV. 24–28).

Finally, in Book XVIII, talking to his mother, knowing that honour demands his return to the battle, Achilles compares his own short life with that of Heracles (117). The action at the end of Book I of the *Iliad* becomes in this way a structural prop, signposting the decisive turn against Troy which ultimately events must take. At first its link with Heracles is a riddle in the background; then in Books XIV and XV it develops its allusions more clearly; and at the end the theme comes to the very fore with an explicit reference by the "best of the Acheans" (cf. XVIII. 105–06) to his Heraclean, tragic destiny.

Virgil, an ardent student of Homer's poem, has used an implicit Heracles theme in his epic in an equally loaded fashion.

Hercules in the Aeneid

The poet has been thought to have waited to discharge his full duty to

Hercules until Book VIII, but in fact, in imitation of the economy of the *Iliad*, the hero is introduced covertly (from a normal perspective needlessly) quite early, in a way which suggests how little the distinction already made by Macrobius (V. 2. 6) between an "Odyssean" first half of the poem and an "Iliadic" second half is to be forced. It is he who lurks at the onset of the storm which befalls Aeneas' ships (I. 65 ff.). With its accent on Aeolus, the scene looks Odyssean, but in reality the Aiolos of *Odyssey* X (1 ff.) has not much in common with the Aeolus of *Aeneid* I. Aiolos is not inspired by a malicious goddess, there is no promise to him of a nubile nymph, and the storm which befalls Odysseus is entirely the fault of his jealous and prying crew. Least of all is Aiolos the warden of some symbolic mountain prison, which in Virgil anticipates the burden of oppressive Etna laid upon Enceladus, and of Atlas' sufferings, both these pointers to what Aeneas' encounter with Dido will cost.[6] After Pallas' loss, he is explicitly compared to a rebellious Giant (X. 565). In Book XII (701–03), he is Athos, Eryx and *pater Appenninus*. Eryx was the home of the worship of Carthaginian Astarte, already known to Romans in the third century as Venus. These are his imprisoning mountains.

The Roman poet, conscious of his need for unity, mindful of the *Iliad*'s artistry, has remodelled the Odyssean episode of *Aeneid* I on the lines of the Hera / Boreas of *Iliad* XV, with touches of Hera / Hypnos from *Iliad* XIV. It is the *Iliad* which supplies the key elements missing in the *Odyssey*, even, in its whiff of the erotic (Zeus / Hera), and the volcanic (Lemnos), the aroma of Dido. It is here that we find a malicious Hera defying the will of Zeus, the promise of a nymph as bribe, a storm unleashed by an obsequious wind-god, amatory intrigue, an angry discovery of a plot by a superior divinity.

Heracles, the hero beset in this way by Hera's conjured storm, is returning home from his sack of Troy (*Il.* XIV. 251), where, after rescuing Hesione, he had been cheated of his reward by her father Laomedon (*Il.* V. 640, 649; XX. 144–48); and perhaps also from the defeat of the Amazons, and the vanquishing of their queen (cf. schol. Pindar, Drachmann III, p. 52, ad v. 64a = 38 Boeckh). In one respect then, the parallel he offers with Aeneas is more of circumstance than precision: Troy destroyed for a moral failure—although in fact Troy *is* destroyed for its moral failings in the *Aeneid*, and Aeneas must at least tacitly assent in Book XII to this arrangement made over his head between Jupiter and Juno. But Dido is well aware of the Trojans' Laomedontian ancestry, and in the hint of a voyaging

---

[6] And see also above, p. 282, for the link between *indignantes* (I. 55) and Turnus' *indignata* at the very end (XII. 952).

hero who in one account slays an Amazon queen, her doom is already sensed. This refraction more than reflection indicates that Virgil —typically—will use a famous model, not to establish some naive equivalence, but to shed a broken light on the pretensions of his character.

Ambivalence of Hercules

All this is quite surprising, in many respects. In an earlier programmatic passage, Virgil had explicitly disparaged the tedium of such hackneyed stuff: *quis aut Eurysthea durum / aut inlaudati nescit Busiridis aras? (Geo.* III. 4–5). The tone there is Callimachean. Aristotle had already spoken disdainfully of such picaresque poetry (*Poetics* 1451a 19–30), whose difficulties may perhaps be assessed by studying the list of the Labours, with its fifteenfold repetition of τε, found in the first stasimon of Euripides' *Heracles* (364–426). There could not then be any literary or narratological motive impelling Virgil to take up a theme so potentially diffuse. Certainly, Heracles is an important if ambivalent character in Apollonius' *Argonautica*. He was after all a member of the original crew, and at the departure stood a good chance of displacing Jason as captain. In the *Aeneid*, he must be an intruder.[7] His destruction of Troy (*Aen.* VIII. 291) predates Homer's by a generation. He can play no direct role in the action Aeneas knew and saw.

Yet even in the *Iliad* so primitive a character maintains a presence; and later, as was noted, talking to his mother, Achilles drew a parallel between his own short life and that of Heracles (XVIII. 117). At Rome, Hercules' importance in general, and to Augustus / Alexander in particular, made it impossible for the poet of the national epic to ignore him. But, with binocular vision in play, Virgil's reaction to him was complex. We can see this by glancing forward to the court of the new Augustus, Nero, and the ideology fostered there. In *Epistle* 90, Seneca traces Posidonius' picture of the Golden Age and its wise rulers, identified by him with *sapientes*; later by Tacitus (*Dial.* §12), writing in a time which was to spawn Hercules / Domitian, with *vates*.[8] Earlier (*Epp.* 18. §12), quoting *Aeneid* VIII (364–65), Seneca alludes to the Stoic ideal of Hercules the saint, the friend of poverty and simplicity. Yet, in his dramas, he twice paints a portrait of a Hercules which is hardly that of the uncomplaining Stoic *sapiens*, and it has

---

[7] Which indeed is what he is: *advena*, X. 460: cf. 516 (Aeneas).

[8] For a statue of Domitian as Hercules, see Martial IX. 64 and 65. A colossal Hercules in basalt, now in Parma, has been interpreted as an idealised Domitian: see Tomei, p. 151. She associates it with a torso of Hercules with lion-skin from the Domus Augustana.

been acutely suggested that this is because he wanted his audience to learn the power even over so great a hero of the negative influence of *furor*.[9] Elsewhere (*Epp.* 94. §62), repeating the same noun, he speaks scornfully of Alexander, urged on in his conquests by a *furor aliena vastandi*. This time, the king is contrasted unfavourably with his mythical ancestor. The condemnation is extended both to Pompey and Julius Caesar (*ibid.*, §§64–65).

Under his new, Apolline emperor,[10] Seneca is reacting to the *Problematik* of the *Aeneid*, with its double-sided picture of Hercules as both furious killer and paragon of rationality. If the only worthwhile criticism of poetry is made by poets, as a tag from Goethe suggests,[11] we should take a lesson from him.

Aeneas as Hercules

In the *Aeneid*, what principally makes pious Aeneas, bringing his gods to Latium, into an avatar of Hercules is the unrelenting persecution the labouring hero suffers from Juno / Hera. The theme is announced right at the start (I. 9–11):

> quidve dolens r e g i n a d e u m tot volvere casus
> insignem pietate virum, t o t a d i r e l a b o r e s
> impulerit....

Or with what resentment the queen of the gods drove a hero noted for his devotion to wade through so many mischances, to come to so much suffering.

Some form of the noun *labor* occurs in the *Aeneid* over 70 times. But Aeneas' *labores* and persecution by Juno are shared with Hercules, as the song of the Salii at the site of Rome proclaims (VIII. 290–93):

> ut bello egregias idem disiecerit urbes,
> Troiamque Oechaliamque, ut duros mille l a b o r e s
> rege sub Eurystheo f a t i s I u n o n i s i n i q u a e
> pertulerit....

How that same hero scattered famous cities in war, Troy and Oechalia, how he bore to the end, in subjection to King Eurystheus, a thousand harsh sufferings, through the destiny imposed on him by unfair Juno.

---

[9] M. W. MacKenzie, *Hercules in the Early Roman Empire with Particular Reference to Literature* (diss. Cornell 1967), pp. 150–55.

[10] *Facundo comitatus Apolline Caesar*, Calpurnius Siculus, *Ecl.* 4. 87; cf. 7. 84. This was more than a poetic flight. A terracotta lamp, for example, from Campania, now in the British Museum (GR 1980.10–8.3; about A.D. 60), shows Victory crowning Nero as the Sun-God, Sol.

[11] *Wer den Dichter will verstehen / Muß in Dichters Lande gehen.*

Later, the mention of Melampus, Hercules' old comrade, calls forth another reference to the *labores* (X. 320–21).

In a masterpiece of narrative, Pindar had depicted a persecution of Heracles by Hera which began as early as the cradle (*Nem* 1. 33 ff.). There, Teiresias associates the present defeat of the serpents with the ultimate, victorious stand against the (serpent-limbed[12]) Giants who one day would assail the gods. The persecution and toils are similarly linked at the start of Euripides' *Heracles*. Heracles has made a pact with Eurystheus to pacify the land. Here too we find a dedicated hero bent on a civilising mission, a cruel Hera and the labours she inflicts (20–22):

> ... ἐξημερῶσαι γαῖαν, εἴθ' "Ηρας ὕπο
> κέντροις δαμασθείς, εἴτε του χρεὼν μέτα.
> καὶ τοὺς μὲν ἄλλους ἐξεμόχθησεν πόνους ...
>
> ... to bring calm order to the land, whether [in agreeing to this] he was tamed by the goads Hera wields, or was haunted by some destiny. His other labours he has now concluded....

All this language was obviously conventional. Transfer it to epic and we could be reading a *Heracleis*. In the light of Euripides' του χρεὼν[13] and his own *fatis* used of Hercules in Book VIII, it is hardly surprising if Virgil speaks, in the context of Aeneas' *labores*, also of Aeneas' *fatum* (I. 2). Apollonius had already spoken of Heracles' μοῖρα (I. 1317).

The toils however were not to be the whole story. At the end, the hero would be promoted to heaven, as the first *Nemean* already emphasises. This provides another bond with the fate of Aeneas (XII. 794–95):

> indigetem Aenean scis ipsa (et scire fateris)
> deberi caelo fatisque ad sidera tolli.
>
> Aeneas is claimed as its own by heaven: you know it yourself and admit you do. The fates will raise him to the stars.

Once again, by the idiom noted in a previous chapter, the second clause is intruded into the syntactical structure. In the background here looms the deification of Romulus / Quirinus, itself based on a Herculean model.[14]

---

[12] Κεῖνο ... ἑρπετόν of Typhon, *Py.* 1. 25. Yet Aeneas becomes a Giant (above, p. 257).

[13] Editors apparently prefer here the definite article τοῦ, but the indefinite enclitic adds a touch of Pindaric, religious reticence. — There is something of the Semitic model of Astarte and consort in Hera's relationship with Hercules. Κέντροις refers to her sexual aggressiveness, too often frustrated, her ambivalent *odi et amo* with her husband's lusty bastard, whom an Etruscan mirror now in Florence (inv. 72740) shows her actually suckling. Cf. "La Madonna allatta San Bernardo," Galleria Colonna (inv. 114), Rome.

[14] *Augustus and the New Poetry*, p. 68.

The *Aeneid*'s exordium makes allusion to Hera's persecution twice. The second instance is that already cited (I. 9–11). The first appears, if we substitute for Juno Poseidon, to assimilate Aeneas to Odysseus (I. 3–4):

> multum ille et terris iactatus et alto,
> vi superum, saevae memorem Iunonis ob iram.

Storm-tossed Odysseus was another laborious hero (cf. Horace, *Epodes* 16. 60), and that identification there is no reason to deny. But here too, as the passages adduced above from the *Iliad* indicate, there is a latent reference to Homer's storm-tossed Heracles. Seneca brackets the pair in the Stoic pantheon (*Const. Sap.* 2. 1).

Certain shadows of this sort were noted in previous discussion:[15] Dido / Heracles—with suggestions of Aeneas / Heracles—in the Apollonian simile of VI. 453; Anchises / Heracles (via *Argon.* II. 803) in VIII. 154 ff. The most striking parallels however were those of Heracles / Lyssa (from Euripides' play) with Turnus / Allecto in Book VII. There, Turnus divided an inheritance with Aeneas. Euripides' Heracles both returned from Hades and was driven mad. Aeneas, who had cited the precedent of Hercules for his own catabasis (VI. 123), like Hercules, returned from Hades. Madness for the moment he handed off to his rival.

But did Aeneas slowly come to assume the whole legacy? The ambivalent impression created by frenzied Hercules at the site of Rome was discussed already. Pallas, recruited from there to Aeneas' cause, and his particular protégé, stands also under the special patronage of Hercules. He wears a belt which appears to recall that worn by Heracles when Odysseus sees him in Hades. In both cases its impress is gruesome. It is Hercules to whom he prays as he seeks to slay Turnus (X. 460–63), only for Jupiter to say that he can no more be saved against the will of the fates than Sarpedon (cf. *Il.* XV. 67). Homer's doomed Sarpedon is a key figure in the symbolic structure of the *Aeneid*.[16] This is why *ingens Sarpedon* encapsulates its deadly sequences right from the "Herculean" storm of Book I (99–100).

If Turnus erred in taking spoils from Pallas, this is exactly what Pallas planned to do to him (X. 462). Pallas will in fact turn the tables on Turnus at the very end of the poem, when he seems to take over as the agent of its last act of vengeance (*Pallas ... Pallas*, XII. 948). *Victoremque ferant morientia lumina Turni* (X. 463) in his prayer to Hercules is an anticipation of what happens there (*vicisti ... victum*, XII. 936).

Pallas' posthumous champion and even re-incarnation (since it is Pallas

---

[15] Especially in chapter XIII, pp. 278 ff., *passim*.

[16] Knauer, *Die* Aeneis *und Homer*, pp. 298 ff.

who gives the death blow at the end) is Aeneas. Aeneas stands in (vainly) for the Hercules who earlier could do nothing to save the son of his old host. How can he not then, like some new Patroclus dressed in a borrowed identity, take on himself the full legacy of which the poets speak? A dead representative of a lost generation mediates this transformation.

Boldness of Virgil's Critique: Hercules and Urban VIII

The boldness of Virgil's epic imagination attracts attention. Pompey, whose "Magnus" made him Alexander's heir, built a temple of Hercules. In the reign of the new Pompey, Augustus, it becomes clear that the hero was to be adapted by imperial propaganda as a model for the enlightened despot, selflessly surrendering his life in the struggle to rid his people of their monsters, and rewarded after his death with the status of godhead. Horace (cf. *Odes* III. 14. 1; IV. 8. 30) and Virgil (*Aen.* VI. 801) both refer to these Stoic ideas, which eventually became part of official panegyric (*Pan. Lat.* ed. Mynors, p. 245).

It is all the more striking therefore that Virgil was not content to repeat unquestioningly the official line. Plato had prophesied that tyrants must go mad (*Rep.* IX. 573b 4, 578a 11). Already in the days of the "tyrannical" (Thuc. II. 63. 2; III. 37. 2) Athenian Empire, a critique of Heracles had been raised, not only by Euripides, but also by Sophocles, erstwhile general and Hellenotamias. The hero, paralleled at Athens by the national hero Theseus, perhaps offered a dangerous incentive to overreaching politicians, and this may lie behind Thucydides' unique use of the Hippocratean μανιώδης to describe Cleon's promise to capture Sphacteria (IV. 39. 3). Turnus calls Aeneas *tyrannus* in the book which will end with his death (XII. 75), and imperial Aeneas' tragic destiny is, it seems, to become mad Hercules; to accept, in other words, the fate which in Book VII is temporarily diverted to his rival. Augustus, like Trajan,[17] avoided that pitfall, but the statue of Domitian as Hercules mentioned by Martial, the bust of Commodus / Hercules preserved on the Capitol, show that not all emperors would be so lucky.

In 1515 Benedictus Chelidonius, a Benedictine monk and humanist of the day, had honoured a Habsburg wedding by supplying the text for a *Voluptatis cum Virtute Disceptatio*.[18] The Habsburg Charles V, elected in

---

[17] Whose fragmentary statue with the Herculean lion-skin is still to be seen in the Palazzo Massimo alle Terme, first floor.

[18] Cf. M. Reiterer, *Die Herkulesentscheidung von Prodikos und ihre frühhumanistische Rezeption in der* Voluptatis cum Virtute Disceptatio *des B. Chelidonius* (diss. Vienna 1955).

1519, inherited this and other traditions of imperial cult from antiquity. By 1535 court artists were fostering the image of a Christian Hercules. Defying Pindaric cautions (*Ol.* 3. 43–45; *Nem.* 7. 52), the emperor's arms showed the Pillars of Hercules with the motto *plus ultra*.

A hundred years later, the Latin poems of Lelio Guidiccioni,[19] drawing their inspiration from a comparison between the Ara Maxima and Bernini's baldacchino in St. Peter's, show how attractive this temptation remained even for the Christian bishop whose Inquisitors would condemn Galileo. There the Pope is *Alcides melior*, a "better Hercules," who has reached the uttermost bound of human achievement. The phrase is modelled on Martial's flattery of Domitian as *maior Alcides* (IX. 64. 6). The parallel Urban VIII / Hercules, implied by the title *Ara Maxima*, quoted from *Aeneid* VIII, blends into a vision of the pillars of the canopy as "pillars of Hercules," the traditional name for the Straits of Gibraltar, commonly regarded by the ancients as the bound of the known world. They cannot be crossed! The immediate purpose of this is precisely to contradict the *plus ultra* of the Habsburgs, but the tone of the original also suggests an allusion to Pope Leo I's "Thus far and no farther," addressed to Attila (cf. Lucan's *huc usque licet* [I. 192], addressed by Rome to Julius Caesar). Of course the poet says or implies so much more.

Urban / Hercules inflicted such moral injury on his Church that John Paul II has felt the need over three centuries later to apologise for it publicly. *Novit namque omnia vates*. To claim that Aeneas is morally unimpaired at the end of the poem is to miss not only the subtlety of the poet's critique of a too facile political slogan, but also his vatic foresight into the shape of things to come. For if, like so many of Rome's *imperatores*, their predecessors[20] and successors, their forebear Aeneas becomes Hercules, what kind of transformation that involves is a question which will be and has been decided in history.

---

[19] The text has been edited by J.K. Newman and F.S. Newman (Hildesheim 1992).

[20] Even as early as the expelled Etruscan kings: see the group from the Sant'Omobono area identified with Hercules and Athena, plate IX in *La Grande Roma dei Tarquini*, ed. M. Cristofani (Rome 1990), with the commentary on pp. 119–20. The story is thought to be linked with Herodotus' tale (I. 60) about the expelled Athenian tyrant Pisistratus.

Glossary of Critical Terms
Booklist
Index Locorum Vergilianorum
Index Locorum Ceterorum
Index Rerum et Nominum

GLOSSARY OF CRITICAL TERMS

Literary criticism is inevitably imprecise but, if it is not to be a mere medley of musings and first impressions, it must make some claim to a methodology. A number of technical terms have therefore been applied to poetic texts in the course of our discussion, some inherited from the past, some borrowed from more recent forays, notably those of the Russian Formalists, or from the work of Sergei Eisenstein, Olga Freudenberg and Mikhail Bakhtin. In particular, Bakhtin's theory of the carnival paradigm detectable in the most diverse literatures, set out in his books on Rabelais and Dostoevsky, is an inexhaustible mine of fresh ideas.

A single paradigm can never suffice. In Rome itself, for example, at the moment of writing, exhibitions attest a renewed sympathy with the theatricality and emotionality of the baroque (Caravaggio, Guercino, Bernini, even Velázquez, patronised by Innocent X); and that has certainly been one immensely influential way in which Italy has received her Classical inheritance. Virgil has his baroque side. No doubt other insights are yet to be exploited. *Non uno itinere perveniri potest ad tam grande mysterium.*

Many of the terms set out below are already defined in appendixes to *The Classical Epic Tradition* (1986), pp. 515–33, and *Roman Catullus* (1990), pp. 457–65.

Among those occurring above are:

Aristophanes effect: the unexpected realisation of a metaphor, as when in Aristophanes the "King's Eye" turns out to be an actual official who quite literally "keeps an eye" on things. Plautus makes much use of such "on the spot" transformations: see E. Fraenkel, *Elementi plautini in Plauto*, pp. 21 ff. But sometimes this originally comic device may be exploited to tragic effect, as when Virgil turns the topos "my love burns like the fires of Etna" into both the volcanic fires of the end of Book III and the funeral pyre of IV, with its implied destruction of Carthage itself. Aristotle had said that tragedy developed out of comedy by a process of solemnisation (ὀψὲ ἀπεσεμνύνθη, *Poetics* 1449a 20–21), and this is an illustration of his point.

Binocular squint / Binocular vision: Virgil's habit of presenting surreal, twinned aspects of his reality in the same context. Hercules twins into Turnus and Aeneas. More largely, Troy twins into Carthage and Rome.

Glossary of Critical Terms

Catharsis: the physical release (e.g. by laughter, tears, both) of powerful emotions, triggering a psycho-therapeutic cleansing.

Declension, declining mode: Virgil's tendency to be in diminuendo, minor key: his awareness of shadows; his reluctance to engage in univocal triumphalism; his shrinking from the horror of what he describes (*quamquam animus meminisse horret luctuque refugit*); his habit of taking refuge in fantasy (Dido's *degere more ferae*; Camilla).

Disobliging other: the frustrated expectation of help perceived as owed (Dido, Juturna).

Drama / dramatic: a polyprosopic (*q.v.*) literary form, originally comic (meant to raise a laugh), later tragic (meant to stir pity and fear): often however combining both effects. See also *recitatio* below.

Gygean *video*: the use of the language of perception to communicate an inner rather than objective vision of events (Aeneas' *quaeque ipse miserrima vidi*; *videt* in Turnus' death scene). See also "inscape" below.

Hollow pastoral: the use of pastoral language or scenery to deny rather than enhance the expectation of refuge and tranquillity (*pastor agens telis*).

Inept borrowing: the deliberate adducing of a literary parallel to a passage which turns out not to square with the context (Aeolus in *Aen.* I / Aiolos in *Od.* X: Nisus and Euryalus in *Aen.* IX / *Doloneia* in *Iliad* X). Lavinia / Helen (*Aen.* XI. 477 ff. = *Il.* VI. 286 ff.) form another such odd couple.

Inscape: G. M. Hopkins' term for the poet's vision of the inner nature of the material world. Cf. *spiritus intus alit*, *Aen.* VI. 726.

Irony: a felt counterpoint between what is said and what is real.

Keimentschluß: a term borrowed from the aesthetic of Friedrich Schleiermacher: cf. M. Redeker, *Friedrich Schleiermachers Leben und Werk* (Berlin 1968: Eng. tr. John Wallhausser, Philadelphia 1973, pp. 174 ff.). It describes the "seminal" or "germinal decision" (not necessarily consciously or rationally taken) on the part of a creative author, his characteristic bias. For Tolstoy, his preoccupation with the process of dying: in Virgil's case, his declining mode, his unreceptiveness to boisterous life.

Leap into another dimension: Eisenstein's term for the sudden turn of narrative towards a different medium; for example, a resort to song rather than speech at a moment of great emotional crisis (Ophelia in *Hamlet*); to rhyme rather than blank verse for the plucking of the apple and its consequences in *Paradise Lost*. Virgilian instances on the small scale might be the use of an unepic diminutive such as *parvulus* by overwrought Dido, or of "unpoetic" language in general (B. Axelson) in the later part of his epic.

More broadly, his whole "iterated" narrative continually shifts (see "shift," сдвиг, below) Homeric clarity into an unresolved chiaroscuro.

Limen / litus: the carnival style likes to disorient or unbalance the familiar world of its heroes by catching them on the precarious edge of change. The shore (Polydorus) or threshold (Cumae) are particular locales where such change is felt as imminent. What if the door opens, if the sea disgorges monstrous serpents, or for long years dissolves the certainties of *terra firma* into a watery and stormy waste (*Troia gaza per undas*, I. 119)?

Maecenatian: a suggested term for "Augustan" when the reference is to the circle around Maecenas / Augustus. Certainly Tibullus and even Ovid are Augustan, if by that is meant a mere assignment of dates, but Virgil, Horace and Propertius were Augustan in a quite different and richer sense. A blanket term confounds these distinctions.

Marsyan: with Virgil's "poetic of hypersensitivity" (see below), which ultimately killed him, may be compared Dante's allusion to Marsyas as he prepares for a supreme poetic effort (*Par.* 1. 20). Similarly, Michelangelo put his own face on the flayed skin of St. Bartholomew in his "Last Judgment" as a token of his supreme effort, evidenced by his remarks in *Sonnet* V (Guasti: dated to 1509). In general then, an adjective describing the artist's willingness, at whatever cost to himself and his own rational defences, to give free rein to what Dante calls "l'alta fantasia" (*Par.* 33. 142: cf. *fantasia*, 24. 24.) *Fantasia* is picked up by Michelangelo in a late sonnet (1554) addressed to Vasari (LXV, Guasti): *l'affettuosa fantasia*, v. 5.

Musical style: not only assonance and alliteration, but the use of devices such as repetition of words and motifs, numerical balance, along with a pervasive ambiguity and emotionality.

Peralogicality (πέρα λόγου): what is "beyond" the Greek binary concept of reason (μὲν ... δέ), which impinged on the Romans only tangentially.

Poetic of hypersensitivity: the overloading by the peralogical, Marsyan poet of text (which thus becomes as it were "supertext") with suggestive subtext, characteristic of his musical style.

Polyphony: applied to literature, a narrative with many voices, none to be neglected and yet all to be eventually absorbed by the sensitive listener into a personal, unique harmony of the whole.

Polyprosopy: the assumption of many masks by the same actor, typical of the pantomime (*turbam reddet in uno*, Manilius V. 482, Housman; πολυπρόσωπος, Plutarch, *quaest. conv.* II. 711F); Virgil's habit of letting his characters switch between different Homeric or other counter-parts, in such a way that rivals share the same original.

Principle of foiled expectation: the story leads one to expect or anticipate what does not in the event happen. Aeneas expects rest in Latium and instead finds war; Dido's death is followed by Anchises' funeral rites; Juturna does not bear Jupiter a heroic son; Aeneas does not anticipate Augustus (*clarus Anchisae Venerisque sanguis ... iacentem lenis in hostem*, Horace, *Carm. Saec.* 50, 51–52) by generously sparing his Italian *civis veniam petens*, Turnus. Vegio's *Supplementum* to Book XII is a contrasting example of a normal reaction to this ploy. See also "disobliging other," "hollow pastoral" above.

Recitatio: Virgil was a master of the oral presentation of his work, famous for what Donatus (*Vita Verg.* §29) reports as his *vox et os et hypocrisis* ("his voice, his facial expression and his acting power"). Such a method of delivering his poem to his listeners (rather than readers) must have assimilated it to drama from the very outset. Each scene belongs to a play, perhaps better a tragic mime, whose different actors are brought vividly before us. *Recitatio* thus becomes the single most important concept in our reception and understanding of what he wrote.

Rhetoric of silence: the musical device of pauses and rests. Each hearer fills in the silence with his own thoughts. In poetry, the deliberate embodiment of silence within the literary structure, meant as the extreme instance of the involvement of the listener in the genesis of the creative totality. A Greek device, yet notably attested in Roman Virgil's treatment of Dido.

Scrambling of motifs: the dreamlike evocation by the narrator of the elements of a previous scene without imposing the same order or sense on them at their reappearance. A variant of the film director's "mixing."

Shift (Formalist сдвиг): the jolt given by the artist (*ecce autem ...*) to whatever stereotyped, routine response is already in ponderous gestation in his listeners' minds: the alteration of perception compelling us to see rather than recognise. See, for example, "principle of foiled expectation" above.

Suppressed (reduced) laughter: the survival of the tricks of comedy (mistaken identity, use of a go-between by lovers) even where the comic overbalances into the tragic. Shakespeare's *Othello* uses, in its first act especially, the "business" of New Comedy (elopement of a daughter, a protesting father, Iago as a cunning slave) to lay the foundation for a tragic dénouement. Virgil sets up Book IV in a similar fashion.

Transrationality: see "peralogicality" above. Virgil's avoidance of Greek clarity. His liking for monsters such as Allecto. His observance of the principle that music is systematic ambiguity ("die Zweideutigkeit als System," Thomas Mann, *Doktor Faustus* [repr. Frankfurt 1956], p. 66).

Twinning: (cf. Euripides, *Bacchae* 918–19). Characters appear in pairs (Aeneas / Turnus; Turnus / Juturna), even when the other half of the pair is supplied by a divided self (Dido). Originally comic (Plautus' *Amphitruo*, Shakespeare's *Comedy of Errors*), often however verging towards, or lapsing into, the tragic and schizophrenic. Puns are a linguistic version of this.

Undifferentiated primitive: the absence of hard and fast ("logical") distinctions in early cultures. What is later antithetically categorised, especially by the Greek binary apprehension of the world, for the Romans coalesces into an indiscriminate complex. Words may mean their opposites (*lustrum*). A god may be male / female. This ambiguity may even affect definitions of time (*olim*) and place (*procul*). Poetry's vagueness, its ambiguous music and painterly chiaroscuro, aims to restore this sort of perception.

Univocity: the antithesis of the polyphonic / dialogic style. Univocity (*una vox*) assumes a privileged access to the truth on the part of the speaker, which he then expounds, while his other characters, and eventually his audience, silently listen: a manner perhaps suited to the textbook, but not to any art claiming to be dramatic (and not even to the pulpit: cf. the etymology of "homily," "sermon."). Virgil avoids the dangers of this during Aeneas' narrative in Books II and III, for example, partly by giving Aeneas a "dramatic" tale to tell, and partly by requiring us to gauge the reactions of Aeneas' principal auditor, Dido, to the fiery destruction of Troy which is also that of Carthage, to an Etna which is also the sign of her demonic fires. This is the unresolved (and irresoluble) psychic struggle which drives her mad.

Vertical time: if Western civilisations tend to think of time as horizontal or circular, time is apprehended by other cultures as an upright line, making everything accessible in the present regardless of what we call futurity or pastness. Jacob's ladder (סלם) is the relevant paradigm: *Augustan Propertius*, pp. 184–87. Place and time measure the same present reality. Cf. "Cadmus" / קדם, "eastern" *and* "ancient."

BOOKLIST

Μὴ ζῴην μετ'ἀμουσίας. The concept of *literae humaniores* entails that the φιλόλογος / φιλόσοφος prepares to interpret a great work of art by studying other great works of art, especially those whose genial authors may be supposed to have "received" its influence. In Virgil's case this means above all the Italian masters of epic, and particularly Dante, as Norden understood. In his *De Vulgari Eloquentia*, Dante defined poetry as *fictio rethorica musicaque poita*. Since his mentor Virgil was a musical poet, these great works of art also include the masterpieces of the concert hall and opera house.

But he was also a great painter. Heinrich WÖLFFLIN's *Die klassische Kunst* (tr. P. and L. MURRAY, "Classic Art," London 1952) and Denis MAHON's *Studies in Seicento Art and Theory* (London 1947) will open the eyes even of students of the Virgilian and Roman aesthetic. Such books must be supplemented by visits to the sites, the museums, the art galleries, with appropriate perusal of their reports and catalogues. Two of these in particular deserve mention here, from opposite ends of the time-scale: *La Grande Roma dei Tarquinii*, Catalogo della Mostra a cura di Mauro CRISTOFANI (Rome 1990); and *Aurea Roma. Dalla Città Pagana alla Città Cristiana*, a cura di Serena ENSOLI ed Eugenio LA ROCCA (Rome 2000). The first of these underlines once again that the student of Roman civilisation, like the student of what Curtius calls "Europäische Kultur" more generally, cannot afford to neglect Etruria, la Toscana, la Tuscia.

We must not neglect either the aesthetic of what is conventionally and wrongly called "Byzantine," and ought to be called "Constantinopolitan," even "Eastern Roman," civilisation. Here are writ large the sometimes inchoate motifs of Augustan and imperial Rome: luminous magnificence, for example, (the Pantheon / Santa Sophia); implicit spirituality (Via Labicana statue / Rublev's *Trinity*[1]). Some aspects of these immense, intensely researched and yet for Classicists often still to be explored themes were noted in our edition of Guidiccioni (1992), listed below, and in an issue of *Illinois Classical Studies* ("Byzantium and its Legacy," XII. 2, 1987). The catalogues of exhibitions on "Byzantine" art and culture held in recent years (1997, 2004) at the Metropolitan Museum, New York, the latter published by Yale University Press, are timely and relevant.

---

[1] See the monograph by N. DEMINA, Троица Андрея Рублева (Moscow 1963), especially «Содержание и Символика Троицы,» pp. 37 ff.

Ad doctorum libros deveniamus. W. SUERBAUM's "Hundert Jahre Vergil-Forschung. Eine systematische Arbeitsbibliographie mit besonderer Berücksichtigung der *Aeneis*" in *Aufstieg und Niedergang der römischen Welt*, 2. 31. 1 (1980), occupies pp. 1–358. In early 1998 the Library of Congress Catalog recorded about 150 books on the *Aeneid* published since 1975. Both lists show that it is neither possible nor appropriate to offer even a statistically accurate sampling from the vast repertoire of Virgilian studies at the end of so unpretentious a work as this. Readers looking for the more important books since 1980 are referred to M. VON ALBRECHT, *Geschichte der römischen Literatur* (Munich 1994), pp. 559–61 (and to the English translation, *A History of Roman Literature* I, Leiden 1997, pp. 702–06). For a more lively if selective presentation, put together by D. FOWLER, see pages 290–91 of the English version of G. B. CONTE's *Letteratura latina* (= *Latin Literature: A History*, Baltimore 1994).

Primo contendis Homero.... Obviously, no study of the *Aeneid* may begin in our time without careful perusal of G. N. KNAUER, *Die Aeneis und Homer* (Göttingen 1964). But (as Knauer and others point out) Virgil also studied carefully the *Argonautica* of Apollonius Rhodius. D. NELIS, in his *Vergil's* Aeneid *and the* Argonautica *of Apollonius Rhodius* (Leeds 2001), has put every student in his debt by fulfilling this exhausting challenge to scholarship. An interpretative volume edited by T. D. PAPANGHELIS and A. RENGAKOS, *A Companion to Apollonius Rhodius* (Leiden 2001), offers a guide to recent thinking on the poem and its author.

The most formative influences, LEO, HEINZE, NORDEN, CURTIUS, the lectures of Eduard FRAENKEL, naturally tend to be taken for granted, and perhaps not to receive the warm recognition they deserve. Hic sit locus eorum merita in re publica litterarum conservanda commemorandi.

Once again, a particular debt is owed to the writings of the Russian Formalists, and of other twentieth-century Russian critics and theorists such as S. EISENSTEIN, O. FREUDENBERG and M. BAKHTIN.

The acronym *ROL* refers to E. H. WARMINGTON's *Remains of Old Latin* (Loeb Classical Library, 4 volumes). In the case of Ennius' *scaenica* cross-references are made to H. D. JOCELYN (*The Tragedies of Ennius*, Cambridge 1967). The *Annales* are cited from O. SKUTSCH's edition (Oxford 1985).

TWAT refers to BOTTERWECK–RINGGREN–FABRY, edd., *Theologisches Wörterbuch zum Alten Testament* (Stuttgart 1973–).

BAUER–ARNDT–GINGRICH refers to *A Greek-English Lexicon of the New Testament* published by The University of Chicago Press and the Syndics of the Cambridge University Press, 1957.

The text of Virgil used has generally been that of R. A. B. MYNORS (Oxford 1969).

The *Epic of Gilgamesh* has been cited from Andrew GEORGE's edition (Penguin 1999). The edition of N. K. SANDARS (Penguin Classics, rev. ed. 1972) was also consulted.

Works mentioned in the body of the text by title only are to be found below under "NEWMAN."

Reference works and editions likely to be generally familiar are not as a rule relisted.

Other books or articles noted include:

ADAM, L., *Die aristotelische Theorie vom Epos nach ihrer Entwicklung bei Griechen und Römern*, Wiesbaden 1889.

ALBERTONI, Margherita *et al.*, *The Capitoline Museums* (Eng. tr. D. A. ARYA and Silvia MARI), Rome 2000.

ALBRECHT, M. VON, *Die Parenthese in Ovids* Metamorphosen *und ihre dichterische Funktion*, Hildesheim 1964.

ALFÖLDI, A., *Die Kontorniaten*, Budapest 1943.

ALQUIER, J. and P., "Stèles votives à Saturne decouvertes près de N'gaous [Algérie]," *Comptes Rendus de l'Académie des Inscriptions et Belles-Lettres* (1931), 21–26.

ANDERSON, W. S., "Chalinus *armiger* in Plautus' *Casina*," *ICS* VIII (1983).

ARIAS, P. E. and HIRMER, M., *A History of Greek Vase Painting* (Eng. tr.), London 1962.

AXELSON, B., *Unpoetische Wörter*, Lund 1945.

BALDO, Gianluigi, *Dall'* Eneide *alle* Metamorfosi*: il codice epico di Ovidio* (Studi, testi, documenti 7), Padova 1995.

BARCHIESI, A., *La traccia del modello. Effetti omerici nella narrazione virgiliana*, Pisa 1984.

BARNES, W. R., "Seeing Things: Ancient Commentary on the *Iliad* at the end of the *Aeneid*," *Amor: Roma* (Cambridge 1999), pp. 60–70. See under BRAUND and MEYER below.

BARTOLONI, Gilda *et al.*, edd., *Ancient Rome* (catalogue of the homonymous exhibition held at the Provincial Museum, Edmonton, Alberta, October 12, 2002–April 21, 2003), Florence 2002.

BARTSCH, S., *Decoding the Ancient Novel. The Reader and the Role of Description in Heliodorus and Achilles Tatius*, Princeton 1989.

BAY, S. M., ed., *Studia Palaeophilologica*, Champaign, Illinois 2004.

BELLING, H., *Studien über die Compositionskunst in der* Aeneide, Leipzig 1899.

BERRES, Thomas, *Vergil und die Helenaszene*, Heidelberg 1992.

BIEBER, M., *The Sculpture of the Hellenistic Age*, repr. New York 1961.

BILLMAYER, K., *Rhetorische Studien zu den Reden in Vergils* Aeneis (diss. Würzburg 1932).

BLANCHARD-LEMÉE. Michèle *et al.*, *Mosaics of Roman Africa* (Eng. tr. K. D. WHITEHEAD), British Museum Press 1996.

BOARDMAN, John, ed., *The Oxford History of Classical Art*, Oxford 1993.

BOLLINGER, T., *Theatralis Licentia*, Winterthur 1969.

BRAUND, S, M. and GILL, C., edd., *The Passions in Roman Thought and Literature*, Cambridge 1997.

— and MEYER, Roland, edd., *Amor: Roma. Love and Latin Literature* (presented to E. J. Kenney), Cambridge 1999.

BRENDEL, Otto J., *Etruscan Art*, second edition, New Haven 1995.

BRINK, C. O., "Ennius and the Hellenistic Worship of Homer," *American Joural of Philology* XCIII (1972), 547–67.

— *Horace on Poetry, the 'Ars Poetica'*, Cambridge 1971.

BRINTON, Anna Cox, *Maphaeus Vegius and his Thirteenth Book of the* Aeneid. *A Chapter on Virgil in the Renaissance*, Stanford 1930.

BROWN, F. et al., edd., *Hebrew and English Lexicon of the Old Testament*, repr. Oxford 1979.

BURN, Lucilla, *The British Museum Book of Greek and Roman Art*, British Museum Press 1991.

BURTON, Joan B., *Theocritus's Urban Mimes*, Berkeley 1995.

CAFIERO, Maria Laura, *Ara Pacis Augustae*, Rome 1996.

CAIRNS, F., *Virgil's Augustan Epic*, Cambridge 1989.

CANCIK, H., *Untersuchungen zur lyrischen Kunst des P. Papinius Statius*, Hildesheim 1965.

CAPELLI, Rosanna, *Museo Nazionale Romano: Palazzo Massimo alle Terme*, Rome 1998.

CARATELLI, G. P., ed., *Megale Hellas*, Milan 1983.

CARCOPINO, J., "Survivances par substitution des sacrifices d'enfants dans l'Afrique romaine," *Revue de l'Histoire des Religions* 106 (1932), 592–99.

CAROZZI, Albert V. and NEWMAN, John K., edd., *Lectures on Physical Geography Given in 1775 by Horace-Bénédict de Saussure at the Academy of Geneva*, Geneva 2003.

CONTE, G. B., *Virgilio. Il genere e i suoi confini*, second edition, Milan 1984.

CRISTOFANI, M., ed., *Gli Etruschi. Una Nuova Immagine*, Florence 1984, repr. 1993.

CRUTTWELL, Robert W., *Virgil's Mind at Work: An Analysis of the Symbolism of the* Aeneid, Basil Blackwell, Oxford 1946, repr. Westport 1971.

CUMONT, F., *Lux Perpetua*, Paris 1949.

CURTIUS, E. R., *Europäische Literatur und lateinisches Mittelalter*, Bern 1948.

DESMOND, Marilynn, *Reading Dido: gender, textuality and the medieval* Aeneid, Minneapolis 1994.

DODDS, E. R., *The Greeks and the Irrational*, Berkeley 1951.

DOOB, Penelope R., *The Idea of the Labyrinth from Classical Antiquity to the Middle Ages*, Ithaca 1990.

DORNSEIFF, F., *Pindars Stil*, Berlin 1921.

FARAL, E., *Les Arts Poétiques du XIIe et du XIIIe Siècles*, Paris 1924.

FEENY, D. C., *The Gods in Epic: Poets and Critics of the Classical Tradition*, Oxford 1991.

FENERON, J. S., *Some Elements of Menander's Style* (diss. Stanford 1976).

FICHTER, Andrew, *Poets Historical: Dynastic Epic in the Renaissance*, New Haven 1982.

FRAENKEL, E., *Elementi plautini in Plauto* (Italian tr.), Florence 1960.
— *Horace*, Oxford 1957.
— "Some Aspects of the Structure of Aeneid VII," *Kleine Beiträge zur klassischen Philologie*, vol. II, Rome 1964, pp. 145–71.
— "Vergil und die *Aithiopis*," *Kleine Beiträge zur klassischen Philologie*, vol. II, Rome 1964, pp. 173–79.
FRÄNKEL, H., *Noten zu den* Argonautika *des Apollonios*, Munich 1968.
FREUDENBERG, O., Миф и Литература Древности, Moscow 1978.
— Поэтика сюжета и жанра, Leningrad 1936.
FRIEDLAENDER, L. *Darstellungen aus der Sittengeschichte Roms*, vol. II, tenth edition, Leipzig 1922.
GALL, Dorothea, *Ipsius umbra Creusae* (Akademie der Wissenschaften und der Literatur), Mainz 1993.
GIANCOTTI, F., *Victor tristis. Lettura dell'ultimo libro dell' 'Eneide'*, Bologna 1993.
GIGANTE, Marcello, ed., *Virgilio e gli Augustei*, Naples 1990.
GRONINGEN, B. A. VAN, *La poésie verbale grecque*, Royal Netherlands Academy of Sciences, Letterkunde, N. R. 16 (1953), pp. 169–272.
GURNEY, O. R., *The Hittites*, rev. ed., London 1990.
HAFFTER, H., *Untersuchungen zur altlateinischen Dichtersprache*, Berlin 1934.
HALE, John, *The Civilization of Europe in the Renaissance*, New York 1994.
HARDIE, P. R., ed., *Virgil. Aeneid Book IX*, Cambridge 1994.
— ed., *Virgil: Critical Assessments of Classical Authors*, London 1999.
— *Virgil's* Aeneid; *Cosmos and Imperium*, Oxford 1986.
HARRISON, S. J., ed., *Oxford Readings in Vergil's* Aeneid, Oxford 1990.
HÄUSSLER, R., *Das historische Epos der Griechen und Römer bis Vergil*, Heidelberg 1976.
— *Das historische Epos von Lucan bis Silius und seine Theorie*, Heidelberg 1978.
HAYNES, Sibylle, *Etruscan Civilization. A Cultural History*, Los Angeles 2000.
HEINZE, R., *Virgils epische Technik*, repr. Stuttgart 1957.
HELLEGOUARC'H, J., "Le principat de Camille," *Revue des Études latines* 48 (1970), 112–32.
HENIG, M., ed., *A Handbook of Roman Art*, Phaidon, Oxford 1983.
HENRY, Elisabeth, *Orpheus with his Lute: Poetry and the Renewal of Life*, Carbondale 1992.
— *The Vigour of Prophecy*, Bristol 1989.
HEURGON, J., "Un exemple peu connu de la *Retractatio* Virgilienne," *Revue des Études latines* 9 (1931), 260–63.
HEUZÉ, P., *L'image du corps dans l'œuvre de Virgile*, Rome 1985.
HIGHET, G., *The Speeches in Vergil's* Aeneid, Princeton 1972.
HIXON, Frances V., *Roman Prayer Language. Livy and the* Aeneid *of Vergil* (Beiträge zur Altertumskunde 30), Stuttgart 1993.
HORSFALL, N., *A Companion to the Study of Virgil*, Leiden 1995.
— *Virgil, Aeneid 7. A Commentary*, Leiden 2000.
— *Virgilio: l'epopea in alambicco*, Naples 1991.

HUMPHREY, John H., *Roman Circuses*, London 1986.

HUSKINSON, Janet, *Roman Children's Sarcophagi. Their Decoration and its Social Significance*, Oxford 1996.

HUTTON, James, *Themes of Peace in Renaissance Poetry*, Ithaca 1984.

INGE, W. R., "Annotations in Lewis and Short's Lexicon" [*sic*], *Classical Review* 8 (1894), 26.

JENKYNS, Richard, *Virgil's Experience: Nature and History, Times, Names and Places*, Oxford 1998.

JOHNSON, P., *Romano-British Mosaics* (Shire Publications), second edition, Princes Risborough 1987.

KATSOURIS, Andreas G., *Tragic Patterns in Menander*, Athens 1975.

KITTEL, G., *Theologisches Wörterbuch zum Neuen Testament*, Stuttgart 1932–.

KLEVE, K., "Lucretius in Herculaneum," *Cronache Ercolanesi* 19 (1989), 5–28.

KLIBANSKY, R. *et al.*, *Saturn and Melancholy*, New York 1964.

KOENEN, L., "The Ptolemaic king as a Religious Figure" in *Images and Ideologies: Self-Definition in the Hellenistic World*, edd. A. BULLOCH *et al.*, Berkeley 1993.

KOFLER, Wolfgang, *Aeneas und Vergil*, Heidelberg 2003.

LEE, M. Owen, *Fathers and Sons in Virgil's* Aeneid, Albany 1979.

LESKY, A., *Die tragische Dichtung der Hellenen*, Göttingen 1956.

LIEBERG, Godo, "Aeneas und der sterbende Lausus," *Res Publica Litterarum* XVII (1994), 61–79.

LOVEJOY, A. O. and BOAS, G., *Primitivism and Related Ideas in Antiquity*, Baltimore 1935, repr. 1997.

LÖVGREN, Håkan, *Eisenstein's Labyrinth: Aspects of a Cinematic Synthesis of the Arts*, Stockholm 1996.

LUCAS, Hans, "Recusatio," *Festschrift für Johannes Vahlen* (Berlin 1900), pp. 317–33.

LUNDSTRÖM, Sven, *Acht Reden in der* Aeneis, Uppsala 1977.

LYNE, R.O.A.M., *Further Voices*, Oxford 1987.

— *Words and the Poet*, Oxford 1989.

MACDONALD, J. S., *Studies in Allusion in the* Eclogues *of Vergil* (diss. Urbana 1997).

MACKENZIE, Margery W., *Hercules in the Early Roman Empire with Particular Reference to Literature* (diss. Cornell 1967).

MAGUINESS, W. S., *The Thirteenth Book of the Aeneid* (Virgil Society), London 1957.

MAHON, D. *et al.*, *Guercino. Poesia e Sentimento nella Poesia del '600*, Rome 2003.

MANACORDA, Daniele *et al.*, *Crypta Balbi*, Rome 2000.

MARAZOV, Ivan, ed., *Ancient Gold. The Wealth of the Thracians*, New York 1998.

MARCOVICH, M., ed., "*Alcestis Barcinonensis*," *ICS* IX (1984), 111–34.

MCAUSLAND, I. and WALCOT, P., edd., *Virgil*, Oxford 1990.

MCCLURE, Laura, *Spoken like a Woman: Speech and Gender in Athenian Drama*, Princeton 1999.

MEINEKE, A., *Analecta Alexandrina*, Berlin 1843.

MENCH, Fred, "Film Sense in the Aeneid," *Arion* 8 (1969), 380–97; repr. in *Classical Myth and Culture in the Cinema*, ed. M. M. WINKLER, Oxford 2001, pp. 219–32.

MESSER, W. S., *The Dream in Homer and Greek Tragedy*, New York 1918.

MEYER, E., *Caesars Monarchie und das Principat des Pompejus*, repr. Stuttgart 1963.

MEZHERITSKY, YA. YU., «Республиканская Монархия.» Метаморфозы Идеологии и Политики Императора Августа, Moscow 1994.

MINNEN, Peter VAN, "An official act of Cleopatra (with a subscription in her own hand)," *Ancient Society* 30 (2000), 29–34.

MONTANARI, F., and LEHNUS, L., edd., *Callimaque* (*Entretiens de la Fondation Hardt* 48), Geneva 2002.

MORETTI, M. *et al.*, *Art of the Etruscans*, London 1970.

NEWMAN, J. K. "Altae Romae," *Illinois Classical Studies* XXVI (2001), 131–32.

— "Ancient Poetics and Eisenstein's Films," *Classical Myth and Culture in the Cinema*, ed. M. M. Winkler, Oxford 2001, pp. 193–218.

— "De Statio epico animadversiones," *Latomus* XXXIV (1975), 80–89.

— "*Esse Videatur* Rhythm in the Greek New Testament *Gospels* and *Acts of the Apostles*," *ICS* X. 1 (1985), 53–66.

— "Euripides' *Medea*: Structures of Estrangement," *ICS* XXVI (2001), 53–76.

— "Hercules in the *Aeneid*. The *dementia* of Power," *Hommages à Carl Deroux*, I– Poésie, ed. Pol Defosse (Brussels 2002), pp. 398–411.

— "Iambe / Iambos and the Rape of a Genre," *ICS* XXIII (1998), 101–120.

— "Memini Me Fiere Pavum," *ICS* VIII (1983), 173–93.

— "Ovid's Epic, Picasso's Art," *Latomus* LXII (2003), 362–72.

— "Pindar through the Looking-Glass," *Eos* LXXXIX (2002), 233–53.

— "Pindarica," *Rheinisches Museum für Philologie* 130 (1987), 89–93.

— "Protagoras, Gorgias and the Dialogic Principle," *ICS* X1 (1986), 43–61.

— "*Saturno Rege*: Themes of the Golden Age in Tibullus and Other Augustan Poets," *Candide Iudex. Beiträge zur augusteischen Dichtung*, ed. Anna Elissa Radke (Stuttgart 1998), pp. 225–46.

— "The Golden Fleece. Imperial Dream," *A Companion to Apollonius Rhodius*, edd. PAPANGHELIS, T. D. and RENGAKOS, A. (Leiden 2001), pp. 309–40.

— *Augustan Propertius*, Hildesheim 1997.

— *Augustus and the New Poetry* (Coll. Latomus, vol. 88), Brussels 1967.

— *Latin Compositions* (Ex Aedibus), Urbana 1976.

— *Roman Catullus*, Hildesheim 1990.

— *The Classical Epic Tradition*, Madison 1986, repr. 2003.

— *The Concept of* Vates *in Augustan Poetry* (Coll. Latomus, vol. 89), Brussels 1967.

NEWMAN, J. K. and CAROZZI, Albert V., edd., *Lectures on Physical Geography Given in 1775 by Horace-Bénédict de Saussure at the Academy of Geneva*, Geneva 2003.

NEWMAN, J. K. and NEWMAN, Frances, "Semitic Aspects of the Greco-Roman Pastoral," *Studia Palaeophilologica*, ed. S. M. Bay (Champaign, Illinois 2004), pp. 53–69.

— edd., Lelio Guidiccioni, *Latin Poems, Rome 1633 and 1639*, Hildesheim 1992.

— *Pindar's Art*, Hildesheim 1984.

NORDEN, E., *Agnostos Theos*, Leipzig–Berlin 1913.

— *Aus altrömischen Priesterbüchern*, Lund 1939.

— *Die Geburt des Kindes*, repr. Stuttgart 1958.

OBBINK, Dirk, ed., *Philodemus and Poetry. Poetic Theory and Practice in Lucretius, Philodemus and Horace*, Oxford 1995.

OGILVIE, R. M., *The Romans and their Gods in the Time of Augustus*, London 1969.

O'HARA, James J., *Death and the Optimistic Prophecy in Vergil's* Aeneid, Princeton 1990.

— *True Names: Vergil and the Alexandrian Tradition of Etymological Wordplay*, Ann Arbor 1996.

ONIANS, J., *Art and Thought in the Hellenistic Age*, London 1979.

OPPENHEIM, A. L., "The Interpretations of Dreams in the Ancient Near East with a Translation of an Assyrian Dream Book," *Trans. Am. Philosoph. Society*, N.S. 46/3 Philadelphia (1956).

PALLOTTINO, M., *Etruscologia*, seventh edition, Milan 1992.

PARRY, A., "The Two Voices of Virgil's *Aeneid*," *Arion* 2 (1963), 66–80; repr. in *Virgil. A Collection of Critical Essays*, ed., S. COMMAGER, Englewood Cliffs, N. J. 1966, pp. 107–23.

PASCHALIS, Michael, *Virgil's* Aeneid. *Semantic Relations and Proper Names*, Oxford 1997.

PERKELL, Christine, ed., *Reading Vergil's* Aeneid. *An Interpretive Guide*, Oklahoma 1999.

PETRINI, Mark, *The Child and the Hero. Coming of Age in Catullus and Vergil*, Ann Arbor 1997.

PFIFFIG, A. J., *Religio Etrusca*, Graz 1975.

PICARD, C., "Chronique de la Sculpture Étrusco-latine (1935)," *Revue des Études latines* 14 (1936), 162.

PÖSCHL, V., *The Art of Vergil* (Eng. tr.), Ann Arbor 1962.

PUELMA PIWONKA, M. *Lucilius und Kallimachos*, Frankfurt 1949.

PUTNAM, Michael C. J., *Virgil's* Aeneid, Chapel Hill 1995.

— *Virgil's Epic Designs*, New Haven 1998.

QUINT, David, *Epic and Empire*, Princeton 1993.

REED, J. D., ed., *Bion of Smyrna. The Fragments and the* Adonis, Cambridge 1997.

REITERER, M., *Die Herkulesentscheidung von Prodikos und ihre frühhumanistische Rezeption in der* Voluptatis cum Virtute Disceptatio *des B. Chelidonius* (diss. Vienna 1955).

RENGAKOS, A., "Spannungsstrategien in den Homerischen Epen," *Euphrosyne, Studies in Ancient Epic and its Legacy in Honor of D. N. Maronitis*, edd. KAZAZIS, J. and RENGAKOS, A. (Stuttgart 1999), pp. 308–38.

RENGER, C., *Aeneas und Turnus. Analyse einer Feindschaft*, Frankfurt am Main 1985.

RICE, E. E., ed., *The Grand Procession of Ptolemy Philadelphus*, Oxford 1983.

RICHTER, G.M.A., *The Engraved Gems of the Greeks, Romans and Etruscans*, vol. I, London 1968.

ROIRON, F. X., *Étude sur l'imagination auditive de Virgile*, Paris 1908.

RUSTEN, J. S., *Dionysius Scytobrachion*, Opladen 1982.

SAFARIK, Eduard A., *Palazzo Colonna*, Rome 1999.

SANDBACH, F. H., "Menander's Manipulation of Language for Dramatic Purposes," *Ménandre* (*Entretiens de la Fondation Hardt* 16), Vandœuvres–Genève 1970, pp. 111–36.

SARABIANOV, Dmitri V., *Russian Art. From Neoclassicism to the Avant-Garde. 1800–1917*, New York 1990.

SAUNDERS, Catherine, "Sources of the Names of Trojans and Latins in Vergil's Aeneid," *Trans. Am. Phil. Assoc.* 71 (1940), 537–55.

SCHADEWALDT, W., *Monolog und Selbstgespräch. Untersuchungen zur Formgeschichte der griechischen Tragödie*, Berlin 1926.

SCHEFOLD, K., *Gotter- und Heldensagen der Griechen in der spätarchaischen Kunst*, Munich 1978.

SCHENK, P., *Die Gestalt des Turnus in Vergils* Aeneis, Königstein–Taunus 1984.

SCHMIT-NEUERBURG, Tilman, *Vergils* Aeneis *und die antike Homerexegese: Untersuchungen zum Einfluss ethischer und kritischer Homerrezeption auf* imitatio *und* aemulatio *Vergils* (*Untersuchungen zur antiken Literatur und Geschichte* 56), Berlin 1999.

SCHNEIDER, B., *Das Aeneissupplement des Maffeo Vegio*, Heidelberg 1985.

SEVERY, Beth, *Augustus and the Family at the Birth of the Roman Empire*, London 2003.

SEVERYNS, A., *Homère l'artiste*, Brussels 1948.

SHIPLEY, G., *The Greek World after Alexander*, London–New York 2000.

SIMON, Erika, *Augustus. Kunst und Leben in Rom um die Zeitenwende*, Munich 1986.

SMALL, J. Penny, *Cacus and Marsyas in Etrusco-Roman Legend*, Princeton 1982.

SORDI, Marta, *Il mito troiano e l'eredità etrusca di Roma*, Milan 1989.

SOVERI, H. F., *De ludorum memoria praecipue Tertullianea capita selecta* (diss. Helsinki 1912).

SPITZER, Leo, "Die klassische Dämpfung in Racines Stil," *Archivum Romanicum* XII (1928), 361 ff.

STABRYLA, Stanislaw, *Latin Tragedy in Virgil's Poetry* (Eng. tr.), Wroclaw 1970.

STAHL, H.-P., ed., *Vergil's* Aeneid: *Augustan Epic and Political Context*, Classical Press of Wales 1998.

STEARNS, J. B., *Studies of the Dream as a Technical Device in Latin Epic and Drama*, vii, Lancaster, Pennsylvania 1927.

STEINER, H. R., *Der Traum in der Aeneis*, Bern 1952.

STEINKÜHLER, Martina, *Macht und Ohnmacht der Götter im Spiegel ihrer Reden*, Ammersbek bei Hamburg 1989.

SUMMERS, Anastasia, *Philodemus'* Περὶ ποιημάτων *and Horace's* Ars Poetica: *Adapting Alexandrian Aesthetics to Epicurean and Roman Traditions* (diss. Urbana 1995).

SUMMERS, Kirk M., *The Debate over Contemporary Religion in Cicero and Lucretius* (diss. Urbana 1993).

SUSEMIHL, F., *Geschichte der griechischen Literatur in der Alexandrinerzeit*, repr. Hildesheim 1965.

SYME, R., *The Roman Revolution*, Oxford 1939.

TANNER, Marie, *The Last Descendant of Aeneas*, New Haven 1993.

TAYLOR, L. R., *The Divinity of the Roman Emperor*, Middletown, Conn. 1931.

TOMEI, Maria Antonietta, *Museo Palatino*, Rome 1997.

TODOROV, V. N., Эней, человек судьбы, Moscow 1993.

VEGIO, Maffeo, *De morte Astyanactis opus iocundum et miserabile*, Callii impressum 1475.

— *Libri XII Aeneidos Supplementum*, ed. Venice 1471 (British Library Cat. No. IB. 19536. a.).

WALKER, Susan, and BURNETT, Andrew, *The Image of Augustus*, British Museum Publications 1981.

— and BURNETT, Andrew, *Augustus*, B. M. Occasional Paper 16, London 1981.

— and HIGGS, Peter, edd., *Cleopatra of Egypt*, London 2001.

WALLNER, G., "Didonis iniqua sors scaenice tractata," *Latinitas* XXXXVIII (2000), 217–30.

WATKINS, John, *The Specter of Dido: Spenser and Virgilian Epic*, New Haven 1995.

WEBER, G., *Kaiser, Träume und Visionen in Prinzipat und Spätantike*, Stuttgart 2000.

WEBSTER, T. B. L., *Hellenistic Poetry and Art*, London 1964.

WEINREICH, O., *Epigramm und Pantomimus*, Heidelberg 1948.

— *Menekrates Zeus und Salmoneus*, Stuttgart 1933.

WEST, M. L., *The East Face of Helicon*, Oxford 1997.

WIDENGREN, G., "Le symbolisme de la ceinture," *Archaeologica Iranica* (*Iranica Antiqua* 8), Leiden 1968, pp. 133–55.

WIGODSKY, Michael, *Vergil and Early Latin Poetry* (*Hermes Einzelschriften* 24), Wiesbaden 1972.

WILKINSON, L. P., *The Georgics of Virgil*, Cambridge 1969.

WILLIAMS, Dyfri and OGDEN, Jack, *Greek Gold: Jewellery of the Classical World* (catalogue of the exhibition "Greek Gold," held at the British Museum, summer 1994), London 1994.

WILTSHIRE, Susan Ford, *Public and Private in Vergil's* Aeneid, Amherst 1989.

WIMMEL, W., *Kallimachos in Rom*, Wiesbaden 1960.

WINCKELMANN, J., *Geschichte der Kunst des Alterthums*, Dresden 1764.

WORSTBROCK, J., *Elemente einer Poetik der* Aeneis, Münster 1963.

WYATT, N., "'Jedidiah' and Cognate Forms as a Title of Royal Legitimation," *Biblica* 66 (1985), 112–25.

ZANKER, P., *Augustus und die Macht der Bilder*, Munich 1987 (Eng. tr., *The Power of Images in the Age of Augustus*, Ann Arbor 1988).

ZIEGLER, K., *Das hellenistische Epos*, second edition, Leipzig 1966.

INDEX LOCORUM VERGILIANORUM

Eclogues
1. 14-15, **93**.
1. 19, **94**.
1. 42, **283**.
1. 45, **102**.
1. 64, **103, 258**.
1. 71, **19, 295**.
1. 82–83, **186**.
1. 83, **93, 101**.
3. 36–43, **102**.
3. 46, **67**.
3. 90, **78**.
4. 5, **283**.
4. 5–10, **28**.
4. 7–10, **29**.
4. 8, **29**.
4. 8–9, **187**.
4. 10, **177**.
4. 25, **31**.
4. 31–36, **26**.
4. 34–36, **241**.
4. 36, **261, 328**.
4. 49, **126**.
4. 58–59, **212**.
4. 60, **315**.
4. 62, **315**.
6. 2, **80, 104**.
6. 3–5, **66**.
6. 11, **77**.
6. 20–21, **212**.
6. 41 ff., **66**.
6. 45–60, **148**.
6. 55–56, **212**.
6. 65, **94**.
6. 71, **67**.
6. 72–73, **316**.

6. 86, **102**.
7. 17, **314**.
7. 28, **94, 283**.
8. 41, **150**.
8. 90–92, **103**.
9. 2, **18, 103, 258, 282**.
9. 34, **94, 283**.
9. 45, **186**.
10. 50, **85**.
10. 50–51, **93**.
10. 51, **194**.
10. 53–54, **94**.
10. 76, **93, 102**.

Georgics
I. 84–85, **51**.
I. 237, **75**.
I. 336, **198**.
I. 342, **101**.
I. 489–92, **263**.
I. 489–97, **207**.
I. 500, **260**.
I. 500–01, **25, 177, 254**.
I. 501–04, **15**.
I. 502, **54, 162, 247**.
I. 505, **260**.
I. 507, **21**.
I. 511, **294**.
I. 512–14, **297**.
I. 513–14, **285**.
I. 514, **328**.
II. 136 ff., **282**.
II. 136–76, **39**.
II. 140, **72**.

II. 176, **21, 25, 240, 282**.
II. 314, **21**.
II. 533, **55**.
III. 4–5, **333**.
III. 16, **284**.
III. 24, **62, 77, 158, 170, 227**.
III. 24–25, **78**.
III. 34–36, **284**.
III. 35–36, **36**.
III. 47, **285**.
III. 66, **75**.
III. 71, **126**.
III. 93, **198**.
III. 209–10, **21**.
III. 219–23, **68**.
III. 226, **154**.
III. 237–41, **68**.
III. 244, **283**.
III. 258 ff., **68**.
III. 258–63, **283**.
III. 263, **190**.
III. 273–79, **199**.
III. 278–79, **29**.
III. 280, **190**.
III. 291–94, **85**.
III. 308, **126**.
III. 339, **101**.
III. 440 ff., **260**.
III. 491, **99**.
III. 552, **192**.
IV. 90, **223**.
IV. 100, **126**.
IV. 168, **190**.
IV. 197–99, **190**.

Georgics IV. 198–99, 21, **284**.
IV. 208–09, **46**.
IV. 281, **36**.
IV. 336, **210**.
IV. 387, **99, 283**.
IV. 392, **99**.
IV. 392–94, **310**.
IV. 406–11, **65**.
IV. 425, **29**.
IV. 450, **99**.
IV. 453, **99**.
IV. 464–66, **187**.
IV. 476, **14**.
IV. 488, **267**.
IV. 499–502, **47**.
IV. 516, **286**.
IV. 528–29, **283**.

Aeneid
I. 2, **282, 335**.
I. 3–4, **336**.
I. 5, **249**.
I. 5–7, **280**.
I. 6, **251**.
I. 7, **46**.
I. 8, **198**.
I. 8–9, **79**.
I. 9–11, **13, 334, 336**.
I. 11, **137**.
I. 12, **15, 311**.
I. 13, **138**.
I. 19–20, **30**.
I. 22, **142**.
I. 23, **293**.
I. 25, **132**.
I. 26, **131**.
I. 26–28, **252**.
I. 27–28, **298**.
I. 28, **57**.

I. 32–33, **296**.
I. 33, **150, 290**.
I. 36, **198**.
I. 37–49, **130–31**.
I. 46–47, **262**.
I. 50–52, **199**.
I. 55, **282, 332**.
I. 65 ff., **332**.
I. 71, **199**.
I. 73, **11, 152**.
I. 92, **64, 286**.
I. 94, **51, 207**.
I. 94–95, **218**.
I. 94–96, **286**.
I. 99, **72**.
I. 99–100, **336**.
I. 100, **31, 215**.
I. 100–01, **18, 225**.
I. 119, **16**.
I. 121, **208**.
I. 148, **10**.
I. 150, **322**.
I. 153, **109**.
I. 155, **48**.
I. 164, **78, 84**.
I. 180–82, **145**.
I. 184–93, **53**.
I. 188, **216**.
I. 205–06, **294**.
I. 206, **244**.
I. 229, **196**.
I. 229–53, **130**.
I. 237, **107**.
I. 250, **30**.
I. 254, **315**.
I. 257, **10**.
I. 257–96, **130, 305**.
I. 261–96, **263**.
I. 265, **288**.
I. 265–66, **302**.

I. 267, **43**.
I. 267–68, **247**.
I. 268, **272**.
I. 274, **36, 295**.
I. 278, **156**.
I. 278–79, **118**.
I. 279, **287**.
I. 281–88, **287–88**.
I. 283–96, **31**.
I. 284, **254**.
I. 286, **31, 283**.
I. 288, **17, 25, 251**.
I. 291–96, **30**.
I. 291–97, **10**.
I. 292, **23, 55, 296, 301**.
I. 294–95, **319**.
I. 297, **226**.
I. 313, **234**.
I. 314, **47, 133**.
I. 314–16, **197**.
I. 314–20, **62**.
I. 316–17, **200**.
I. 320, **59, 197**.
I. 324, **133**.
I. 325, **35**.
I. 327, **200**.
I. 342, **87, 132**.
I. 344, **75**.
I. 345, **232**.
I. 351, **75**.
I. 353, **176, 178, 179**.
I. 353 ff., **169**.
I. 357, **103, 178**.
I. 360, **103**.
I. 364, **142, 202**.
I. 374, **102**.
I. 378, **208**.
I. 378–79, **59**.
I. 382, **47**.

Aeneid I. 385 ff., **59**.
I. 405, **47**.
I. 407–10, **58**.
I. 415, **197**.
I. 415–17, **59**.
I. 427, **121, 170**.
I. 427–29, **84**.
I. 429, **78**.
I. 430, **103, 142, 190, 284**.
I. 444, **13**.
I. 456–65, **153**.
I. 456–93, **9, 98**.
I. 462–65, **324**.
I. 463, **74**.
I. 465, **219**.
I. 466–93, **152, 293**.
I. 474, **227**.
I. 475, **43, 50, 153, 227**.
I. 482, **61, 115, 153**.
I. 488–89, **9**.
I. 489, **35, 196, 215**.
I. 490, **190, 202**.
I. 490–91, **202, 231, 299**.
I. 490–93, **142**.
I. 491, **143**.
I. 493, **142, 153**.
I. 498–502, **62**.
I. 499, **73, 122, 162, 202, 218, 222**.
I. 500, **283**.
I. 557, **141**.
I. 562, **102, 107, 154**.
I. 563–64, **130**.
I. 571, **164, 226**.
I. 573, **14, 128**.
I. 574, **191**.
I. 585, **47**.

I. 590–93, **273**.
I. 607–08, **101**.
I. 610-12, **217**.
I. 613, **103**.
I. 613–18, **145**.
I. 617, **72**.
I. 623–24, **145**.
I. 626, **37**.
I. 627–30, **145**.
I. 630, **130**.
I. 635, **47**.
I. 641, **46**.
I. 646, **42**.
I. 650, **57, 71, 145, 159, 160, 183, 252, 278, 292**.
I. 651, **286**.
I. 652, **47**.
I. 677, **48**.
I. 678, **43**.
I. 684, **43**.
I. 686, **160**.
I. 687, **271**.
I. 711, **160**.
I. 712, **14**.
I. 712–14, **143**.
I. 716, **48, 71, 124**.
I. 717-22, **190**.
I. 718–19, **9**.
I. 720, **47**.
I. 726, **162, 177**.
I. 727, **218**.
I. 734, **160**.
I. 740, **226**.
I. 744, **226**.
I. 748, **115**.
I. 749, **143**.
I. 750, **216**.
I. 751, **35**.
I. 753, **61**.

I. 753–56, **125**.
II. 2, **45, 287**.
II. 3, **9**.
II. 5, **153**.
II. 8–9, **61**.
II. 9, **122**.
II. 12–13, **183**.
II. 13, **9**.
II. 19–20, **13**.
II. 32, **211**.
II. 35, **251**.
II. 38, **13, 53**.
II. 42, **313**.
II. 45, **52**.
II. 52, **13**.
II. 71–82, **246**.
II. 116, **52, 53**.
II. 137–38, **33**.
II. 138, **202**.
II. 195, **254**.
II. 204, **5, 183**.
II. 213–15, **53, 203**.
II. 231, **230**.
II. 238, **13, 14, 43, 53**.
II. 243, **13**.
II. 245, **52**.
II. 246, **194**.
II. 255, **114**.
II. 258, **13**.
II. 258–59, **53**.
II. 261, **208**.
II. 263, **53**.
II. 268 ff., **169**.
II. 268, **75**.
II. 268–97, **178**.
II. 270, **14, 133, 268**.
II. 291–97, **194**.
II. 296, **280**.
II. 296–97, **247**.
II. 312, **208**.

Index Locorum Vergilianorum 359

Aeneid II. 314, **254**.
II. 316, **268**.
II. 320, **13**, **247**.
II. 321, **50**.
II. 327, **288**.
II. 340, **208**.
II. 348, **208**.
II. 363, **15**, **288**, **311**.
II. 392, **221**.
II. 403, **13**.
II. 407–08, **194**.
II. 411-12, **218**.
II. 424, **13**.
II. 429, **13**.
II. 453 ff., **50**.
II. 455, **50**.
II. 455–56, **50**.
II. 455–57, **14**.
II. 457, **43**, **50**, **278**.
II. 489–90, **202**.
II. 501, **22**, **195**.
II. 503, **11**, **14**, **61**, **203**.
II. 503–05, **22**.
II. 504, **13**, **16**.
II. 506, **264**.
II. 515, **195**.
II. 523, **120**.
II. 526, **14**.
II. 527, **33**.
II. 528, **285**.
II. 531, **42**.
II. 538, **33**.
II. 549, **14**.
II. 551, **33**.
II. 557, **16**, **287**.
II. 557–58, **55**.
II. 560, **48**.
II. 560–63, **254**.
II. 563, **272**.

II. 567 ff., **124**.
II. 573, **292**.
II. 576, **230**.
II. 577 ff., **166**.
II. 589, **268**.
II. 594–95, **257**.
II. 597, **47**.
II. 598, **43**.
II. 602, **228**.
II. 605, **316**.
II. 612–13, **13**.
II. 622, **276**.
II. 626, **149**.
II. 634 ff., **46**.
II. 644, **39**.
II. 647–49, **265**.
II. 649, **133**.
II. 651, **47**.
II. 663, **33**, **42**, **218**.
II. 673, **47**.
II. 673–79, **47**.
II. 674, **45**, **47**.
II. 677, **47**.
II. 678, **47**.
II. 680, **190**.
II. 681, **43**.
II. 683, **273**.
II. 711, **47**.
II. 715, **46**.
II. 724, **45**.
II. 725, **47**.
II. 738, **14**, **47**.
II. 744, **124**.
II. 763, **16**.
II. 766, **13**, **202**.
II. 772, **50**, **178**.
II. 783, **47**, **49**.
II. 783–84, **42**.
II. 788, **184**, **290**.
II. 789, **33**, **137**.

II. 790, **47**.
II. 792–94, **14**, **47**.
II. 797, **14**, **43**.
II. 804, **152**.
III. 1, **22**.
III. 2, **13**, **253**.
III. 11, **22**.
III. 12, **280**.
III. 19, **47**.
III. 24 ff., **279**.
III. 35, **294**.
III. 42, **229**.
III. 60, **229**.
III. 74, **48**.
III. 94 ff., **282**.
III. 94–96, **39**.
III. 96, **47**, **246**.
III. 97–98, **31**, **32**.
III. 97–99, **287**.
III. 111, **47**.
III. 121, **300**.
III. 141, **29**.
III. 147, **179**.
III. 147 ff., **178**.
III. 151–52, **178**.
III. 152, **316**.
III. 161–62, **317**.
III. 167, **178**, **247**.
III. 170, **34**.
III. 180, **39**, **53**.
III. 187, **194**, **307**.
III. 192 ff., **178**.
III. 192–95, **148**.
III. 252, **269**.
III. 256–57, **268**.
III. 286, **208**.
III. 294 ff., **194**.
III. 301 ff., **217**.
III. 302, **250**.
III. 311, **194**.

Aeneid III. 321, **218**.
  III. 321–24, **51**.
  III. 326, **37**.
  III. 327, **51, 288**.
  III. 328, **286**.
  III. 339, **43**.
  III. 341, **42, 43**.
  III. 343, **120, 271**.
  III. 351, **123**.
  III. 358, **71, 316**.
  III. 381–83, **282**.
  III. 386, **71**.
  III. 392, **32**.
  III. 420, **200**.
  III. 482, **164**.
  III. 482 ff., **50**.
  III. 487, **43**.
  III. 489, **50, 271**.
  III. 493, **51**.
  III. 495, **42**.
  III. 504–05, **194**.
  III. 516, **226**.
  III. 539, **295**.
  III. 578, **24**.
  III. 584, **24, 73**.
  III. 587, **73**.
  III. 639 ff., **60**.
  III. 658, **255**.
  III. 659, **124**.
  III. 664, **257**.
  III. 669, **124**.
  III. 684, **23, 200**.
  III. 685, **191**.
  III. 716, **287**.
  IV. 1, **121, 123, 155, 161**.
  IV. 2, **73**.
  IV. 4, **142**.
  IV. 9, **123, 167, 169**.
  IV. 9–29, **125**.
IV. 9–30, **123–24**.
IV. 10, **117, 152**.
IV. 11, **59, 143**.
IV. 12, **127**.
IV. 18, **123**.
IV. 19, **228**.
IV. 23, **197**.
IV. 24, **135, 233**.
IV. 27, **117**.
IV. 29, **117**.
IV. 31–53, **124–25**.
IV. 33, **33, 145, 193**.
IV. 35, **133, 176**.
IV. 36–37, **129**.
IV. 39, **130**.
IV. 52, **257**.
IV. 52–53, **126**.
IV. 62, **145**.
IV. 64, **37**.
IV. 65, **37, 171**.
IV. 67, **114**.
IV. 68, **51**.
IV. 69, **47, 122**.
IV. 70, **149, 178**.
IV. 71, **103, 152, 171**.
IV. 71–72, **103**.
IV. 73, **53**.
IV. 76, **114**.
IV. 78, **158**.
IV. 80, **107**.
IV. 81, **122, 219**.
IV. 84, **48**.
IV. 86, **284**.
IV. 93, **196**.
IV. 99, **286**.
IV. 103–04, **152**.
IV. 115, **163**.
IV. 126, **11, 152**.
IV. 127, **286**.
IV. 129, **163**.
IV. 130–59, **139**.
IV. 133, **11**.
IV. 134, **161, 233**.
IV. 144–46, **316**.
IV. 156, **43**.
IV. 158–59, **133**.
IV. 159, **222**.
IV. 166, **52, 131**.
IV. 168, **148**.
IV. 169, **143**.
IV. 172, **49, 173, 228**.
IV. 173, **126, 182**.
IV. 173 ff., **24**.
IV. 173–88, **57**.
IV. 176–77, **174, 299**.
IV. 179, **24**.
IV. 188, **24, 27**.
IV. 198, **134, 205**.
IV. 206–19, **131**.
IV. 215, **12, 71, 182, 228, 252, 256**.
IV. 216–17, **16**.
IV. 217–18, **118**.
IV. 221, **24**.
IV. 228, **257**.
IV. 229–30, **295**.
IV. 233, **150**.
IV. 234, **50, 178**.
IV. 236, **36**.
IV. 246–51, **226**.
IV. 247, **146**.
IV. 250, **146**.
IV. 258, **37**.
IV. 261–64, **233**.
IV. 263–64, **163**.
IV. 264, **216**.
IV. 265, **163**.
IV. 266, **190**.
IV. 271, **268**.
IV. 274, **178**.

Aeneid IV. 275, **50**.
IV. 285–86, **162, 177**.
IV. 288, **211**.
IV. 293–94, **125**.
IV. 296, **121, 161**.
IV. 300–03, **148, 160**.
IV. 301, **221**.
IV. 302, **161**.
IV. 305, **103**.
IV. 305–06, **125**.
IV. 305–30, **125–26**.
IV. 308, **122, 128, 190**.
IV. 316, **286**.
IV. 317–18, **120**.
IV. 318, **126, 135, 206**.
IV. 323, **152**.
IV. 327, **123**.
IV. 327–30, **141**.
IV. 328, **23, 120**.
IV. 330, **52, 103, 122**.
IV. 333–61, **126–27**.
IV. 335–70, **133**.
IV. 338–39, **284**.
IV. 340 ff., **247**.
IV. 342, **261**.
IV. 344, **194, 250**.
IV. 345–46, **316**.
IV. 346–47, **284**.
IV. 347, **159, 245**.
IV. 351, **47, 133, 152, 268**.
IV. 351–53, **179, 268**.
IV. 353, **176**.
IV. 353–64, **114**.
IV. 354, **43**.
IV. 355, **50**.
IV. 362, **154**.
IV. 363, **228**.

IV. 365, **178**.
IV. 365–67, **185**.
IV. 365–87, **127**.
IV. 366, **103, 254**.
IV. 366–67, **24**.
IV. 371–72, **145**.
IV. 373, **124**.
IV. 376, **9, 129, 165, 172, 257, 316**.
IV. 376–78, **316**.
IV. 379–80, **151, 322**.
IV. 381, **178**.
IV. 382–86, **150**.
IV. 383, **138**.
IV. 384, **125, 150, 171**.
IV. 386, **150, 159**.
IV. 387, **115**.
IV. 388–89, **114**.
IV. 389, **133, 176**.
IV. 390, **47**.
IV. 391, **226**.
IV. 391–92, **164**.
IV. 395, **154, 219, 325**.
IV. 408, **103**.
IV. 408–10, **115**.
IV. 412, **154**.
IV. 415, **128, 161**.
IV. 416–36, **127–28**.
IV. 419, **166**.
IV. 421–22, **193**.
IV. 424, **121**.
IV. 427, **47, 152**.
IV. 436, **117**.
IV. 440, **140**.
IV. 441, **149**.
IV. 450, **161**.
IV. 450–51, **51**.
IV. 451, **123**.

IV. 463, **267**.
IV. 465–73, **170–71**.
IV. 466, **166**.
IV. 468, **176**.
IV. 469–70, **56**.
IV. 471, **78, 81, 84, 121, 168, 260**.
IV. 471–73, **155**.
IV. 472, **48**.
IV. 474, **9, 51, 52, 142, 151, 157, 166, 166, 202**.
IV. 478, **131**.
IV. 478–79, **159**.
IV. 478–98, **128**.
IV. 479, **117**.
IV. 484, **139, 270**.
IV. 486, **63**.
IV. 490, **172**.
IV. 493, **120, 206**.
IV. 496, **103, 123**.
IV. 498, **166**.
IV. 499, **114**.
IV. 501–02, **151**.
IV. 504, **121, 161**.
IV. 506, **179**.
IV. 510, **124**.
IV. 511, **73**.
IV. 515, **31**.
IV. 516, **47, 190**.
IV. 519, **128, 161**.
IV. 522, **172, 177, 179, 220**.
IV. 525, **177**.
IV. 532, **152, 162, 177, 179**.
IV. 534 ff., **111**.
IV. 534–52, **128**.
IV. 541–42, **177, 182, 254**.

Aeneid IV. 542, **13, 162**.
IV. 547, **166**.
IV. 548–49, **194**.
IV. 550–51, **117, 152**.
IV. 551, **53, 122, 194, 202**.
IV. 552, **71, 124, 145**.
IV. 554–72, **179**.
IV. 555, **172**.
IV. 557, **176**.
IV. 560–70, **158**.
IV. 564, **152**.
IV. 565, **178**.
IV. 569–70, **191**.
IV. 584–85, **223, 286**.
IV. 587, **103**.
IV. 590–629, **129**.
IV. 591, **103, 133, 283**.
IV. 595, **126, 161**.
IV. 596, **10, 49**.
IV. 597, **133**.
IV. 597–99, **149**.
IV. 599, **152**.
IV. 600 ff., **180**.
IV. 600–01, **157**.
IV. 600–02, **142, 170**.
IV. 600–06, **191**.
IV. 601–02, **158**.
IV. 603, **123, 141**.
IV. 604, **123, 128, 161**.
IV. 604–06, **52, 150**.
IV. 605, **180, 185**.
IV. 606, **123**.
IV. 607, **178**.
IV. 608, **151**.
IV. 608–10, **157**.
IV. 609, **148**.
IV. 612–20, **9, 23, 60, 151, 256**.
IV. 615–29, **311**.
IV. 616, **150, 158**.
IV. 617–18, **163**.
IV. 618, **134, 251, 302**.
IV. 618–20, **286**.
IV. 620, **158**.
IV. 622, **40**.
IV. 624–25, **117**.
IV. 625, **9, 138, 166, 172, 292**.
IV. 625–26, **60**.
IV. 627, **172**.
IV. 628, **131, 151**.
IV. 629, **117, 118**.
IV. 631, **224**.
IV. 633, **147**.
IV. 642, **256**.
IV. 647, **143**.
IV. 648, **121, 143**.
IV. 648–50, **144**.
IV. 650, **143**.
IV. 651, **117, 145, 166**.
IV. 651–62, **129**.
IV. 653, **214**.
IV. 655–56, **145**.
IV. 656, **124, 166**.
IV. 657–58, **142, 190**.
IV. 659, **144, 166**.
IV. 661, **60, 166**.
IV. 666, **126**.
IV. 667, **148**.
IV. 669, **254**.
IV. 669–71, **14, 126, 311**.
IV. 670, **52, 123, 163, 197**.
IV. 673, **135, 164, 193, 226**.
IV. 677–78, **135**.
IV. 678, **123**.
IV. 679, **123, 166**.
IV. 682, **46, 194**.
IV. 689, **114, 142**.
IV. 692, **124**.
IV. 693, **166**.
IV. 694, **282**.
IV. 697, **130, 165**.
IV. 700–02, **268**.
IV. 701, **160, 179, 180, 200**.
V. 2, **218**.
V. 3–4, **52, 123**.
V. 4, **194, 197, 218**.
V. 5, **24, 73**.
V. 8–11, **148**.
V. 9 ff., **178**.
V. 38, **48**.
V. 74, **43**.
V. 75, **20**.
V. 77, **160**.
V. 88–89, **268**.
V. 89, **160, 179, 200**.
V. 109, **267, 293**.
V. 113, **44**.
V. 117, **246, 251**.
V. 121, **211, 251, 261, 294**.
V. 121, **16**.
V. 123, **16, 251**.
V. 181, **44**.
V. 182, **44**.
V. 196, **313**.
V. 214, **33**.
V. 252, **43, 198, 298**.
V. 254, **298**.
V. 285, **32**.

Index Locorum Vergilianorum 363

Aeneid V. 288–89, **84**, **267**.
V. 289, **293**.
V. 294, **231**.
V. 296, **44**.
V. 297, **37**.
V. 311–13, **44**, **231**.
V. 349, **44**.
V. 358, **44**.
V. 363, **194**.
V. 370–74, **211**.
V. 461–62, **10**, **255**.
V. 538, **5**.
V. 545 ff., **4**.
V. 547, **5**.
V. 548, **43**.
V. 551, **4**, **267**, **293**.
V. 553, **43**.
V. 554, **269**.
V. 561, **43**.
V. 561–62, **10**.
V. 564–65, **217**.
V. 565, **30**.
V. 568, **251**.
V. 568–69, **290**.
V. 569, **43**.
V. 571, **280**.
V. 571 ff., **5**.
V. 571–72, **50**, **150**.
V. 572, **5**.
V. 576, **16**, **207**.
V. 581, **4**.
V. 584, **5**, **264**.
V. 588, **32**, **150**, **178**, **280**.
V. 591, **5**.
V. 592–93, **32**.
V. 593, **44**.
V. 599, **43**.
V. 602, **15**, **43**.
V. 605, **44**.
V. 606, **199**, **200**.
V. 609, **180**.
V. 610, **200**.
V. 621, **32**.
V. 636, **180**.
V. 645, **32**.
V. 654, **46**.
V. 664, **84**.
V. 671, **313**.
V. 674, **44**.
V. 699, **180**.
V. 704, **208**.
V. 711, **37**.
V. 715, **43**.
V. 715–18, **16**.
V. 722–40, **180**.
V. 728, **208**.
V. 750, **43**.
V. 758, **46**.
V. 811, **13**.
V. 815, **219**.
V. 817, **48**.
V. 818, **165**.
V. 823–26, **210**.
V. 833 ff., **219**.
V. 851, **219**.
V. 867, **219**.
V. 869, **154**, **219**.
VI. 12, **309**, **316**.
VI. 20, **300**.
VI. 20–22, **151**.
VI. 23, **161**.
VI. 25, **37**, **53**.
VI. 26, **149**.
VI. 27, **5**, **150**, **178**.
VI. 28, **142**, **178**.
VI. 35, **317**.
VI. 47, **309**.
VI. 49, **262**.
VI. 57, **71**, **304**.
VI. 57–58, **182**.
VI. 69, **95**, **262**.
VI. 69–74, **309**.
VI. 77–80, **9**.
VI. 86, **28**, **156**.
VI. 86–87, **318**.
VI. 89, **18**, **29**, **42**, **59**, **71**, **182**, **227**, **234**, **241**, **304**, **328**.
VI. 89–90, **33**.
VI. 93, **57**, **159**, **252**.
VI. 93–94, **11**, **180**, **292**.
VI. 94, **11**, **16**, **159**, **293**.
VI. 95–96, **127**, **263**, **293**.
VI. 99–100, **317**.
VI. 100–01, **118**.
VI. 103–04, **214**.
VI. 108, **48**.
VI. 114, **266**.
VI. 116, **32**.
VI. 119, **100**, **283**, **310**.
VI. 119–20, **249**.
VI. 122, **149**, **317**.
VI. 123, **336**.
VI. 153–55, **117**.
VI. 162–65, **212**.
VI. 164, **212**, **216**.
VI. 174, **217**.
VI. 210, **73**.
VI. 250, **48**.
VI. 270, **219**.
VI. 275–77, **191**.
VI. 280–81, **191**.
VI. 289, **140**.
VI. 307, **14**, **43**.

Aeneid VI. 308, **42**.
VI. 322, **36, 53**.
VI. 331, **200**.
VI. 338, **219**.
VI. 355–56, **219**.
VI. 365, **259, 291**.
VI. 371, **141**.
VI. 373, **220**.
VI. 426, **251**.
VI. 426 ff., **52**.
VI. 426–27, **55, 286**.
VI. 426–29, **192**.
VI. 427, **43**.
VI. 434–35, **42**.
VI. 442–50, **192**.
VI. 445, **61**.
VI. 446, **155**.
VI. 447, **193**.
VI. 449, **193**.
VI. 450, **61, 63, 155, 169, 178**.
VI. 451, **150**.
VI. 453, **139, 336**.
VI. 453–54, **56, 154, 219, 270**.
VI. 454, **162, 202**.
VI. 455, **150, 154**.
VI. 456, **52**.
VI. 456–57, **62**.
VI. 460, **62, 290**.
VI. 464, **62, 164**.
VI. 468, **146**.
VI. 469, **61, 153**.
VI. 469 ff., **164**.
VI. 469–71, **115**.
VI. 471, **9, 61, 142, 146**.
VI. 474, **145, 171**.
VI. 476, **178**.
VI. 477, **150**.

VI. 483, **211**.
VI. 493, **113**.
VI. 494–95, **63**.
VI. 495, **13**.
VI. 515, **13, 57, 133, 160**.
VI. 521, **11, 52, 62**.
VI. 557, **9, 72**.
VI. 557–58, **147**.
VI. 563, **229**.
VI. 570, **5**.
VI. 585, **261**.
VI. 609, **42**.
VI. 617–18, **149**.
VI. 618, **24, 67, 232**.
VI. 620, **317**.
VI. 621, **288**.
VI. 621–22, **261, 317**.
VI. 623, **11, 286**.
VI. 625–27, **267**.
VI. 726, **342**.
VI. 645, **310**.
VI. 648, **36**.
VI. 649, **32, 55**.
VI. 650, **247, 254, 284**.
VI. 662, **316**.
VI. 694, **268**.
VI. 694–96, **152**.
VI. 700–02, **47**.
VI. 721, **220**.
VI. 732, **316**.
VI. 756, **36, 291**.
VI. 756 ff., **25**.
VI. 756–59, **288**.
VI. 756–886, **27**.
VI. 759, **293**.
VI. 760–65, **294**.
VI. 762, **303**.
VI. 763, **36**.

VI. 764, **49, 166, 301**.
VI. 766, **288**.
VI. 768, **251**.
VI. 769–70, **302**.
VI. 773–75, **245, 282**.
VI. 778, **48, 254**.
VI. 781, **26**.
VI. 781–87, **36, 289, 325**.
VI. 784, **26, 47, 184**.
VI. 787, **25**.
VI. 789–90, **30, 283, 290**.
VI. 789–805, **305**.
VI. 792, **283**.
VI. 792–93, **241, 281**.
VI. 794, **197**.
VI. 794–95, **25, 289**.
VI. 798, **31, 290**.
VI. 798–99, **281**.
VI. 801, **337**.
VI. 801–03, **232**.
VI. 801–05, **160**.
VI. 818, **124**.
VI. 819, **238**.
VI. 822, **49, 238**.
VI. 826 ff., **290**.
VI. 827, **55**.
VI. 828–31, **291**.
VI. 830, **290**.
VI. 830–31, **19, 53, 131**.
VI. 831, **290**.
VI. 832, **43**.
VI. 834, **10**.
VI. 834–35, **303, 321**.
VI. 835, **243, 267**.
VI. 840, **124**.
VI. 851, **10, 243, 266**.
VI. 851–53, **263**.

Aeneid VI. 852, **38**.
VI. 853, **10**, **49**, **150**, **243**.
VI. 859, **319**.
VI. 860 ff., **290**, **293**.
VI. 863–66, **38**.
VI. 864, **35**.
VI. 868, **32**.
VI. 872, **294**.
VI. 875, **43**.
VI. 882, **43**, **293**.
VI. 882–86, **118**.
VI. 883, **60**.
VI. 885, **141**.
VI. 887, **316**.
VI. 898, **305**.
VII. 4, **214**.
VII. 10, **72**.
VII. 10–24, **146**.
VII. 11, **35**.
VII. 15, **9**.
VII. 15–20, **72**, **147**.
VII. 16–19, **154**.
VII. 19–20, **129**.
VII. 27, **159**, **254**.
VII. 37, **154**, **195**, **271**, **284**.
VII. 37–44, **155**.
VII. 38, **283**.
VII. 38–39, **18**.
VII. 40, **95**.
VII. 41, **283**, **318**.
VII. 41–44, **28**.
VII. 44, **29**, **31**, **283**.
VII. 47, **146**.
VII. 50–51, **21**, **35**.
VII. 52, **35**.
VII. 70, **288**.
VII. 79–80, **289**.
VII. 92–101, **180**.

VII. 93, **181**.
VII. 95, **181**.
VII. 96, **239**, **246**.
VII. 96–101, **38**.
VII. 99, **38**.
VII. 101, **181**.
VII. 104, **126**.
VII. 104–06, **182**.
VII. 105, **15**, **177**.
VII. 122, **159**.
VII. 122–23, **268**.
VII. 139, **47**.
VII. 157–59, **250**.
VII. 162, **21**.
VII. 170–91, **84**.
VII. 177, **95**, **284**.
VII. 189, **4**, **147**.
VII. 189–91, **72**.
VII. 201–04, **197**.
VII. 209, **34**, **245**.
VII. 224, **16**.
VII. 246, **153**, **181**, **195**, **247**, **254**, **287**.
VII. 253, **11**, **34**.
VII. 257–58, **30**, **289**.
VII. 262, **17**.
VII. 266, **239**, **245**.
VII. 268, **34**.
VII. 280–83, **71**, **265**.
VII. 283, **47**, **147**, **195**, **254**.
VII. 290, **250**.
VII. 292, **227**.
VII. 293, **40**.
VII. 293–322, **131–32**.
VII. 295–96, **203**.
VII. 299, **152**.
VII. 299–300, **204**.
VII. 302, **23**, **191**.

VII. 302–03, **200**.
VII. 304–05, **295**.
VII. 309, **65**, **200**.
VII. 312, **157**.
VII. 313, **124**.
VII. 314, **49**.
VII. 317, **19**, **53**.
VII. 317–22, **291–92**.
VII. 319, **52**.
VII. 319–22, **180**, **183**, **262**.
VII. 320, **53**, **195**, **304**.
VII. 321, **12**, **252**.
VII. 322, **159**, **250**.
VII. 327, **24**.
VII. 331, **48**, **172**.
VII. 338, **173**.
VII. 344, **286**.
VII. 346, **20**, **161**.
VII. 349–53, **70**.
VII. 351, **48**.
VII. 352, **182**.
VII. 353, **195**.
VII. 355, **182**.
VII. 355–56, **70**.
VII. 358, **34**, **286**.
VII. 359, **137**.
VII. 360, **34**.
VII. 362, **252**.
VII. 363–64, **304**.
VII. 364, **159**.
VII. 372, **46**.
VII. 373 ff., **96**.
VII. 377–83, **285**.
VII. 378, **190**.
VII. 385, **161**.
VII. 385 ff., **328**.
VII. 386, **34**.
VII. 387, **34**.

Aeneid VII. 390, **47**.
VII. 398, **34, 286**.
VII. 401, **49**.
VII. 410, **11, 142**.
VII. 413, **172**.
VII. 413–16, **172**.
VII. 415 ff., **95**.
VII. 428, **173**.
VII. 433, **173**.
VII. 435, **229, 314**.
VII. 435–66, **157**.
VII. 440, **173**.
VII. 441, **48**.
VII. 443–44, **175**.
VII. 445, **51, 173, 233**.
VII. 450, **295**.
VII. 455, **176**.
VII. 456–57, **10**.
VII. 456–60, **173**.
VII. 458, **172**.
VII. 458–62, **228**.
VII. 460, **34, 174, 229**.
VII. 461, **230**.
VII. 464, **227**.
VII. 476, **158**.
VII. 484, **43, 47, 285**.
VII. 496–99, **53**.
VII. 497, **304**.
VII. 499, **286**.
VII. 501–02, **47**.
VII. 518, **20**.
VII. 528–30, **68**.
VII. 531–34, **286**.
VII. 540, **295**.
VII. 550, **295**.
VII. 555, **286**.
VII. 561, **20, 295**.
VII. 575, **43**.
VII. 578–79, **39**.
VII. 580, **161**.
VII. 582, **295**.
VII. 598, **42**.
VII. 611, **46**.
VII. 635–36, **17**.
VII. 641 ff., **245**.
VII. 649, **35**.
VII. 656–61, **205**.
VII. 657, **134**.
VII. 658, **295**.
VII. 661, **190**.
VII. 691, **37**.
VII. 707–08, **210**.
VII. 708, **251**.
VII. 731, **5**.
VII. 736, **35**.
VII. 762, **48, 210**.
VII. 781, **35**.
VII. 785, **220**.
VII. 785–88, **70**.
VII. 786, **23, 60, 221, 233**.
VII. 787, **256**.
VII. 789, **142**.
VII. 789–92, **71**.
VII. 805, **153**.
VIII. 5, **256**.
VIII. 6, **256**.
VIII. 8, **17, 21**.
VIII. 18, **15, 182, 220**.
VIII. 18–27, **162, 177**.
VIII. 26, **179**.
VIII. 42 ff., **178**.
VIII. 45, **32**.
VIII. 49, **163**.
VIII. 60, **134**.
VIII. 66, **163**.
VIII. 66–67, **134**.
VIII. 72, **48**.
VIII. 84–85, **6**.
VIII. 102 ff., **226**.
VIII. 104, **35**.
VIII. 116, **20**.
VIII. 132, **46**.
VIII. 134–41, **226**.
VIII. 142, **146**.
VIII. 154 ff., **336**.
VIII. 157, **265**.
VIII. 162–63, **266, 269**.
VIII. 171, **164, 226**.
VIII. 175–78, **256**.
VIII. 197, **24**.
VIII. 198, **199**.
VIII. 201, **290**.
VIII. 205, **256**.
VIII. 215, **164**.
VIII. 219, **130, 233**.
VIII. 219–20, **256**.
VIII. 228–31, **256**.
VIII. 229, **228**.
VIII. 285–305, **232**.
VIII. 288–89, **248**.
VIII. 290–91, **177, 183**.
VIII. 290–93, **334**.
VIII. 293, **291**.
VIII. 298–300, **248**.
VIII. 299, **258**.
VIII. 301, **37**.
VIII. 322–23, **197**.
VIII. 335–36, **48**.
VIII. 336, **256**.
VIII. 353, **256**.
VIII. 364–65, **333**.
VIII. 370, **47**.
VIII. 372, **72**.
VIII. 381, **259**.
VIII. 383, **35, 201**.

Aeneid VIII. 383–84, **153, 196**.
VIII. 384, **35, 215**.
VIII. 387, **196**.
VIII. 391–93, **59**.
VIII. 393, **298**.
VIII. 407, **59, 236**.
VIII. 414, **37, 60**.
VIII. 423, **37**.
VIII. 440, **60, 73**.
VIII. 448, **5**.
VIII. 458, **245**.
VIII. 466, **35**.
VIII. 479, **247**.
VIII. 484, **256**.
VIII. 494, **238**.
VIII. 495, **238**.
VIII. 509, **259**.
VIII. 510, **48**.
VIII. 513, **19**.
VIII. 516, **296**.
VIII. 538–40, **18**.
VIII. 557, **296**.
VIII. 564, **29, 31, 48**.
VIII. 579, **224**.
VIII. 581, **43**.
VIII. 583, **49**.
VIII. 583–84, **164**.
VIII. 584, **89, 226**.
VIII. 592–93, **137**.
VIII. 622, **143**.
VIII. 623, **137**.
VIII. 625, **316**.
VIII. 626–29, **37**.
VIII. 630, **299**.
VIII. 630–34, **6**.
VIII. 632, **43, 47**.
VIII. 635, **23**.
VIII. 636, **84, 293**.
VIII. 642–45, **239**.

VIII. 648, **247, 287**.
VIII. 668–70, **323**.
VIII. 669, **260**.
VIII. 678, **25, 232, 262, 282**.
VIII. 679, **46, 280**.
VIII. 685–88, **253**.
VIII. 688, **71, 89**.
VIII. 696, **140**.
VIII. 697, **23**.
VIII. 700–05, **295**.
VIII. 703, **5**.
VIII. 710, **37**.
VIII. 714, **329**.
VIII. 715, **282**.
VIII. 720, **31, 309**.
VIII. 730, **27, 37, 59, 89, 186, 266, 305**.
VIII. 731, **152**.
VIII. 818, **247**.
VIII. 843, **239**.
IX. 2, **199, 200**.
IX. 11, **247**.
IX. 36, **313**.
IX. 59, **232**.
IX. 59–64, **175**.
IX. 60, **174, 229**.
IX. 61, **47**.
IX. 63–64, **174**.
IX. 66, **257**.
IX. 69 ff., **184**.
IX. 72, **257**.
IX. 77 ff., **183**.
IX. 77–79, **184**.
IX. 93, **35**.
IX. 108, **47**.
IX. 115–22, **180**.
IX. 137, **230**.
IX. 140–42, **191**.
IX. 143, **191**.

IX. 176 ff., **153**.
IX. 181, **44**.
IX. 185, **214**.
IX. 192, **46**.
IX. 216–17, **48**.
IX. 217, **44**.
IX. 224 ff., **220**.
IX. 229, **222**.
IX. 239, **220**.
IX. 247, **261**.
IX. 257, **48**.
IX. 261, **42**.
IX. 263, **62**.
IX. 264, **48**.
IX. 266, **5, 44, 161, 180, 220, 231**.
IX. 272, **48**.
IX. 276, **44**.
IX. 279, **176**.
IX. 284, **49, 222**.
IX. 289, **42**.
IX. 297, **49**.
IX. 302, **48**.
IX. 305, **161, 221**.
IX. 312, **45**.
IX. 312–13, **221**.
IX. 335–38, **44**.
IX. 339, **222**.
IX. 340, **174, 222**.
IX. 341, **222**.
IX. 342–43, **257**.
IX. 343, **209**.
IX. 350, **257**.
IX. 354, **221**.
IX. 373, **221, 222**.
IX. 390, **221**.
IX. 404 ff., **222**.
IX. 422, **222**.
IX. 430, **221**.
IX. 445–49, **223**.

Aeneid IX. 446–49, **98**.
IX. 448, **252**.
IX. 448–49, **26, 45**.
IX. 459–60, **286**.
IX. 465–67, **18, 223**.
IX. 473–74, **182**.
IX. 474, **48**.
IX. 477, **224**.
IX. 484, **48**.
IX. 486, **48, 110, 224**.
IX. 490–92, **224**.
IX. 495, **44**.
IX. 497, **224**.
IX. 503, **101**.
IX. 523, **37**.
IX. 525–28, **184**.
IX. 563, **299**.
IX. 565, **47**.
IX. 565–66, **299**.
IX. 566, **296**.
IX. 571, **208**.
IX. 581, **35**.
IX. 596, **47**.
IX. 602–04, **40**.
IX. 603–13, **16**.
IX. 606, **44**.
IX. 607–10, **40**.
IX. 614–20, **40**.
IX. 616, **16**.
IX. 619, **47**.
IX. 628, **47**.
IX. 641, **43**.
IX. 642, **25**.
IX. 643, **254**.
IX. 644, **25, 263, 272**.
IX. 647, **211**.
IX. 649 ff., **55**.
IX. 653 ff., **272**.
IX. 656, **43**.
IX. 697, **48, 215**.

IX. 736, **257**.
IX. 742, **18, 304**.
IX. 756 ff., **235**.
IX. 761–62, **234**.
IX. 774, **212**.
IX. 783, **313**.
IX. 806 ff., **164, 175**.
X. 8–9, **19**.
X. 16, **72**.
X. 16 ff., **196**.
X. 16–17, **132**.
X. 18–62, **132**.
X. 18–95, **233**.
X. 22, **294**.
X. 27, **17, 31**.
X. 30, **30**.
X. 32, **191**.
X. 39–40, **157, 172**.
X. 41, **161**.
X. 42, **263**.
X. 49, **263**.
X. 58, **17, 250, 263**.
X. 59–62, **262**.
X. 61, **132**.
X. 62 ff., **196**.
X. 63–95, **132–33**.
X. 67, **124**.
X. 68, **194**.
X. 70, **43**.
X. 70–71, **3**.
X. 74, **17**.
X. 74–75, **133, 244, 262**.
X. 75, **31**.
X. 76, **48**.
X. 82, **89**.
X. 87, **295**.
X. 91, **16**.
X. 92, **13**.
X. 108, **191, 297**.

X. 123, **211**.
X. 125, **215**.
X. 132–38, **57, 273**.
X. 133, **43**.
X. 155, **247**.
X. 166–212, **210**.
X. 170, **208**.
X. 172, **48**.
X. 186–93, **69**.
X. 194, **35**.
X. 198–200, **327**.
X. 199, **35**.
X. 200, **48**.
X. 203, **247**.
X. 212, **255**.
X. 219–45, **183**.
X. 236, **43**.
X. 237, **294**.
X. 244–45, **285**.
X. 245, **225**.
X. 249–50, **285**.
X. 273–75, **29**.
X. 274, **75**.
X. 275, **31**.
X. 282, **46**.
X. 315, **48**.
X. 318, **217**.
X. 320–21, **335**.
X. 328–29, **30**.
X. 353, **37**.
X. 370, **201**.
X. 389, **11**.
X. 401–02, **272**.
X. 427, **208**.
X. 433–34, **226, 259**.
X. 436–40, **227**.
X. 439, **157, 204**.
X. 439 ff., **153**.
X. 443, **42, 84, 225**.
X. 448, **246, 297**.

Aeneid X. 454, **234**.
X. 459, **227**.
X. 460, **258**, **283**, **333**.
X. 460 ff., **226**.
X. 460–63, **336**.
X. 461, **257**, **270**.
X. 462, **336**.
X. 463, **336**.
X. 464, **270**.
X. 466, **49**.
X. 469–72, **30**.
X. 470, **32**.
X. 471, **215**, **285**.
X. 492, **225**, **226**.
X. 495–505, **258**.
X. 496–98, **10**.
X. 501, **234**.
X. 504, **232**.
X. 509, **225**, **285**, **305**.
X. 511, **191**.
X. 516, **283**, **333**.
X. 519, **166**, **317**.
X. 525, **33**.
X. 532, **33**.
X. 537, **317**.
X. 537–42, **296**.
X. 541, **166**, **317**.
X. 543, **37**.
X. 550–51, **205**.
X. 551, **134**.
X. 557, **48**.
X. 559, **224**.
X. 565, **24**, **226**, **332**.
X. 565–68, **248**.
X. 565–70, **257**.
X. 597, **42**.
X. 605, **43**.
X. 613, **198**.
X. 625, **201**.
X. 636 ff., **235**.

X. 643, **89**.
X. 649, **11**.
X. 651, **47**.
X. 661, **89**.
X. 668–79, **233**.
X. 675, **124**.
X. 675–76, **89**, **233**.
X. 689, **157**.
X. 693, **215**.
X. 696, **37**.
X. 704–05, **53**, **183**.
X. 705, **12**, **195**, **304**.
X. 718, **257**.
X. 720, **286**.
X. 723, **222**.
X. 724, **174**, **222**.
X. 747, **208**.
X. 760, **225**.
X. 760–61, **196**.
X. 763, **264**.
X. 778–82, **211**.
X. 788, **257**.
X. 789, **48**.
X. 800, **33**, **48**.
X. 800 ff., **215**.
X. 802, **225**.
X. 812, **98**, **225**, **267**.
X. 813, **72**, **147**, **225**.
X. 818, **48**, **216**.
X. 821–24, **215**.
X. 822, **270**.
X. 824, **225**.
X. 825, **43**.
X. 827–28, **216**.
X. 829, **163**.
X. 832, **225**.
X. 833, **48**.
X. 839, **216**.
X. 848, **48**.
X. 854, **123**.

X. 861–62, **214**.
X. 875, **44**.
X. 898, **256**.
X. 906, **33**, **216**.
XI. 1, **163**.
XI. 25, **42**.
XI. 42, **43**.
XI. 68–71, **201**, **222**.
XI. 71, **47**.
XI. 72–75, **270**.
XI. 72–77, **163**.
XI. 74, **5**, **61**, **163**, **287**.
XI. 75, **216**.
XI. 77, **166**.
XI. 81–82, **34**.
XI. 85–86, **163**.
XI. 86, **135**, **193**, **226**.
XI. 96–97, **28**, **156**, **240**.
XI. 139, **182**.
XI. 147, **163**.
XI. 153, **296**.
XI. 158, **227**.
XI. 161, **49**.
XI. 162, **123**.
XI. 178–79, **33–34**, **269**.
XI. 178–81, **238**.
XI. 182, **75**.
XI. 186, **46**.
XI. 188–202, **163**.
XI. 195, **269**.
XI. 215–17, **44**, **286**.
XI. 243, **313**.
XI. 252 ff., **183**.
XI. 255, **60**.
XI. 264–65, **300**.
XI. 268, **16**.
XI. 271–77, **65**.

Aeneid XI. 273, **69**.
XI. 277, **60**.
XI. 305, **313**.
XI. 340–41, **213**.
XI. 343–75, **233**.
XI. 354, **233**.
XI. 355, **286**.
XI. 376, **233**.
XI. 378–444, **233**.
XI. 379, **46**.
XI. 384, **225**.
XI. 392–95, **40**.
XI. 438, **201, 227, 304**.
XI. 459, **239, 313, 320**.
XI. 477 ff., **153, 342**.
XI. 477–85, **61**.
XI. 479–80, **159**.
XI. 480, **57, 136**.
XI. 484, **252**.
XI. 488, **296, 298**.
XI. 492, **12**.
XI. 493–97, **235**.
XI. 519, **201**.
XI. 541, **43**.
XI. 542, **48**.
XI. 549, **43**.
XI. 573, **43**.
XI. 577, **117**.
XI. 578, **43**.
XI. 581–82, **201**.
XI. 583, **200, 205**.
XI. 591, **60**.
XI. 600–63, **142**.
XI. 648, **202**.
XI. 649, **59**.
XI. 659–63, **299**.
XI. 660, **202**.
XI. 660–63, **153**.
XI. 661, **142**.
XI. 661–62, **231**.
XI. 662–63, **202**.
XI. 664, **142**.
XI. 670, **208**.
XI. 673–75, **210**.
XI. 687, **190**.
XI. 690, **211**.
XI. 698, **201**.
XI. 700, **35**.
XI. 703, **142, 201**.
XI. 724, **201**.
XI. 726, **225**.
XI. 727, **157**.
XI. 736–40, **310, 327**.
XI. 742, **158**.
XI. 768 ff., **211**.
XI. 782, **201, 202**.
XI. 784, **158**.
XI. 801, **142, 201**.
XI. 823, **201**.
XI. 831, **65, 136, 142, 185, 201, 237, 313**.
XI. 848, **60**.
XI. 858, **200**.
XI. 885–89, **218**.
XI. 887, **42**.
XII. 4, **161, 222, 233**.
XII. 7, **50, 56, 233**.
XII. 9, **233**.
XII. 15, **16, 245**.
XII. 17, **49**.
XII. 27, **34**.
XII. 37, **161**.
XII. 42, **34**.
XII. 45, **233**.
XII. 52, **47**.
XII. 54, **161**.
XII. 55, **161**.
XII. 56–63, **48**.
XII. 64, **48**.
XII. 64–69, **60**.
XII. 67–68, **195**.
XII. 67–69, **22, 275**.
XII. 70, **21, 156, 177, 271**.
XII. 73, **296**.
XII. 74, **48, 235**.
XII. 75, **239, 245, 337**.
XII. 80, **49**.
XII. 95, **47**.
XII. 99, **16, 256**.
XII. 101, **157**.
XII. 102, **228**.
XII. 103, **229**.
XII. 107, **148**.
XII. 107–08, **297**.
XII. 108, **296**.
XII. 110, **270**.
XII. 127, **246, 254**.
XII. 128, **37**.
XII. 140–41, **204**.
XII. 141, **200, 205**.
XII. 142–45, **198, 204**.
XII. 142–60, **56**.
XII. 145, **205**.
XII. 158, **13, 38, 120, 204**.
XII. 161–64, **262**.
XII. 162–64, **46, 284, 310**.
XII. 164, **4, 146**.
XII. 165, **234**.
XII. 166–69, **37–38**.
XII. 168, **16**.
XII. 176, **129**.
XII. 179–80, **298**.
XII. 187–88, **298**.

Aeneid XII. 206–10, **41**.
XII. 207, **21**.
XII. 208, **73**.
XII. 209, **47**.
XII. 211, **46**.
XII. 216, **49, 153,
227**.
XII. 218, **227, 297**.
XII. 246, **124**.
XII. 258, **61**.
XII. 261, **18, 182,
283**.
XII. 262, **165**.
XII. 266, **38**.
XII. 282, **154**.
XII. 285–86, **46**.
XII. 289–90, **257**.
XII. 293, **257**.
XII. 298, **208**.
XII. 313, **259**.
XII. 318 ff., **61**.
XII. 324–25, **257**.
XII. 331 ff., **300**.
XII. 331–36, **174,
298**.
XII. 332, **236, 294,
296**.
XII. 335, **19**.
XII. 335–36, **191**.
XII. 341, **208**.
XII. 362–64, **211**.
XII. 384 ff., **61**.
XII. 394, **76**.
XII. 399, **94, 270,
272**.
XII. 402–03, **298**.
XII. 405, **317**.
XII. 405–06, **94**.
XII. 405–07, **298**.
XII. 409–10, **298**.

XII. 410, **147**.
XII. 411, **197**.
XII. 411–12, **34**.
XII. 412, **149, 197,
220, 298**.
XII. 430, **296, 298**.
XII. 434, **271**.
XII. 435, **43**.
XII. 435–36, **63, 164,
175**.
XII. 435–40, **270**.
XII. 436, **263**.
XII. 440, **45, 120,
271, 287**.
XII. 492, **12**.
XII. 496–99, **297**.
XII. 497, **163**.
XII. 498, **41, 191**.
XII. 498–99, **165**.
XII. 500–04, **282**.
XII. 503–04, **19, 296**.
XII. 504, **84, 322**.
XII. 511–12, **19**.
XII. 512, **18**.
XII. 515, **48**.
XII. 517–20, **102**.
XII. 546–47, **212**.
XII. 561, **211**.
XII. 572, **313**.
XII. 573, **197**.
XII. 583, **19, 295**.
XII. 587, **103**.
XII. 588, **21**.
XII. 593 ff., **161**.
XII. 598, **49**.
XII. 602, **161**.
XII. 605, **35, 157**.
XII. 608, **126**.
XII. 611, **216**.
XII. 620–21, **233**.

XII. 632–49, **233**.
XII. 646–49, **204,
227**.
XII. 648, **233, 238**.
XII. 668, **154, 177**.
XII. 670, **154**.
XII. 671, **177**.
XII. 680, **157**.
XII. 697, **287**.
XII. 697–98, **45**.
XII. 701–03, **262,
332**.
XII. 707, **315**.
XII. 715 ff., **154**.
XII. 715–22, **69**.
XII. 716, **317**.
XII. 742–43, **227**.
XII. 746–47, **34, 317**.
XII. 751, **96, 262**.
XII. 763, **5, 24**.
XII. 763–64, **122**.
XII. 766, **21**.
XII. 770, **191**.
XII. 770–71, **41**.
XII. 772 ff., **279**.
XII. 781, **41**.
XII. 786, **197**.
XII. 787, **73**.
XII. 790, **41, 229,
296**.
XII. 794–95, **335**.
XII. 795, **304**.
XII. 797, **124**.
XII. 801, **257**.
XII. 805, **286**.
XII. 807, **293**.
XII. 808–28, **133–34**.
XII. 821, **124, 279**.
XII. 821–22, **293**.
XII. 823–28, **302–03**.

Aeneid XII. 824–28, **251**.
XII. 827, **17**.
XII. 827–28, **39, 239–40**.
XII. 828, **22, 32, 203, 279**.
XII. 829, **315**.
XII. 834–37, **251**.
XII. 835, **303**.
XII. 835–36, **38**.
XII. 835–37, **17**.
XII. 836, **281**.
XII. 837, **100**.
XII. 838, **43, 100, 251**.
XII. 843 ff., **24**.
XII. 845, **97, 171**.
XII. 845 ff., **225, 295**.
XII. 849, **96**.
XII. 849–50, **97**.
XII. 849–52, **257**.
XII. 850, **75**.
XII. 852, **165**.
XII. 857, **257**.
XII. 865–66, **228**.
XII. 869–71, **164**.
XII. 871, **135, 193**.
XII. 872–84, **146, 204**.
XII. 872–86, **134–35**.

XII. 878, **200**.
XII. 878–80, **205**.
XII. 882, **120**.
XII. 882–83, **205**.
XII. 883, **89, 124**.
XII. 883–84, **233**.
XII. 886, **154, 163, 219, 325**.
XII. 888, **72, 149**.
XII. 891, **100**.
XII. 891–93, **65**.
XII. 894, **227, 228**.
XII. 894–95, **228, 257**.
XII. 896, **235**.
XII. 908, **166, 168, 171**.
XII. 908 ff., **240**.
XII. 908–14, **176**.
XII. 910–11, **264**.
XII. 913, **128**.
XII. 913–14, **9**.
XII. 914, **157**.
XII. 914–15, **115**.
XII. 915, **77**.
XII. 915–16, **304**.
XII. 918, **115**.
XII. 919, **304**.
XII. 930, **320**.
XII. 930 ff., **153**.
XII. 932, **42**.

XII. 932–34, **266**.
XII. 933–34, **49**.
XII. 934, **255, 303**.
XII. 936, **127, 336**.
XII. 937, **49**.
XII. 941–42, **10, 258**.
XII. 943, **43, 227**.
XII. 945, **72, 148, 166, 225, 258**.
XII. 945–46, **255**.
XII. 945–49, **165**.
XII. 946, **9, 10, 51, 127, 129, 157, 172, 225, 257, 258, 317**.
XII. 947, **297**.
XII. 948, **172, 336**.
XII. 948–49, **166**.
XII. 949, **10, 34, 230, 317**.
XII. 951, **64, 257**.
XII. 952, **65, 93, 118, 124, 135, 136, 142, 150, 185, 197, 201, 237, 282, 313, 332**.

Catalepton
5. 1, **109**.
5. 13–14, **109**.
9. 13–20, **93**.
9. 64, **77**.

INDEX LOCORUM CETERORUM

Accius, fr. 123, W., **63**.
  trag. 123 W., **164**.
Aeschylus:
  Agamemnon 242, **275**.
    1178–79, **312**.
    1183, **312**.
  Eumenides 100–05, **155**.
  Persae 176 ff., **168**.
    181–89, **17**.
  Septem 345–68, **15**.
    348–50, **4**.
    424, **214**.
  fr. 154a. 16, Radt, **260**.
  fr. 205, Mette (*Psychostasia*), **224**.
Ammianus Marcellinus XVII. 4. 11, **165**.
Anonymi Alcestis Barcinonensis 22, **47**, **144**.
Anthologia Palatina:
  IX. 505. 18 (anon.), **113**.
  IX. 647 (anon.), **88**.
  XI. 130 (Pollianus), **85**.
  XI. 218. 4 (Crates), **87**.
Appian, *Bell. Civ.* I. 94, **18**; I. 96. 6, **18**.
Apollonius Rhodius, *Argonautica* I. 1–2, **75**.
  I. 28–32, 34, **67**.
  I. 182–84, **201**.
  I. 607, **159**, **254**.
  I. 746, **27**, **58**, **89**.
  I. 832–33, **146**.
  I. 898, **146**.
  I. 1243–47, **232**.
  I. 1317, **335**.
  II. 674 ff., **274**.
  II. 774 ff., **269**.
  II. 803, **269**, **336**.
  II. 946 ff., **205**.
  III. 64, **52**.
  III. 91 ff., **189**.
  III. 245, **271**.
  III. 291, **236**.
  III. 291 ff., **59**.
  III. 633–35, **171**.
  III. 636, **169**.
  III. 703–04, **160**.
  III. 744, 751, 755–59, **162**.
  III. 850, **34**.
  III. 956–61, **29**.
  III. 997 ff., **249**.
  III. 998, **169**.
  III. 1042, **150**.
  III. 1259, **12**.
  III. 1294, **215**.
  III. 1367, **236**.
  III. 1399, **222**.
  IV. 127 ff., **274**.
  IV. 136–38, **20**.
  IV. 156 ff., **63**.
  IV. 298, **269**.
  IV. 378, **111**.
  IV. 378–81, **150**.
  IV. 383–86, **150**.
  IV. 384–85, **260**.
  IV. 391–93, **123**.
  IV. 392–93, **52**, **150**.
  IV. 596 ff., **70**.
  IV. 664, **168**.
  IV. 747–48, **195**.
  IV. 790–92, **204**.
  IV. 912–19, **219**.
  IV. 1221, **20**.
  IV. 1296–97, **20**.
  IV. 1432 ff., **63**.
  IV. 1477–78, **270**.
  IV. 1479–80, **139**, **154**.
  IV. 1521–22, **20**.
  IV. 1672, **27**, **89**.
  IV. 1682–86, **149**.
  IV. 1722–24, **20**.
  IV. 1731 ff., **201**.
Apollodorus I. 7. 9, **115**.
Archilochus 25, 60, 77, Diehl, **276**; 60, **307**; 52, **313**.
Aristophanes, *Frogs* 46, **160**; 552, **292**; 911–13, **113**; 1009–10, **317**; 1035, **317**.
Aristotle:
  Poetics c. 9, **242**.
    c. 23, **242**.
    1448b 35, **104**.
    1449a 11, **276**.
    1449a 14–15, **172**.
    1449a 20–21, **97**.
    1449b 24–25, **323**.
    1449b 27, **98**.
    1449b 27–28, **323**.
    1450a 39–1450b 3, **275**.

Poetics 1450b 3–4, **243**.
1450b 16, **212**.
1450b 16–20, **213**, **275**.
1451a 3, **243**.
1451a 19–30, **243**, **333**.
1451a 27, **87**.
1451b 5–6, **159**.
1451b 5–7, **90**.
1451b 7, **156**.
1451b 10 ff., **209**.
1453a 15–17, **98**.
1453a 29–30, **104**.
1454a 27–28, **114**.
1459b 21–22, **88**.
1460a 5–8, **324**.
1460a 7–8, **98**.
1460a 9–11, **213**.
Politics I. 1253a 10, **111**.
VIII. 1341b 1, **108**.
VIII. 1342a 4 ff., **323**.
VIII. 1342a 4–16, **110**.
VIII. 1342a 11, **112**.
Rhetoric III. 1404b 24–25, **107**.
III. 1411b 27 ff., **144**.
Athenaeus I. 20e, **76**.
X. 421 c–d, **174**.
Auctor ad Herennium
I. 15. 25, **128**.
III. 21, **115**.
Augustus Imperator, *Res Gestae* 2, **231**, **238**.
3, 3, **232**, **263**, **320**.
14, **263**.
34. 3, **322**.
Bacchylides 19 [18]. 24, **68**.
Bion, *Adonis* 52–53, **134–35**.
Boethius, *Cons. Phil.* II, m. V. 25, **23**.
Callimachus:
Aetia I, fr. 1. 40, **144**.
I, fr. 2. 2, **86**.
I, fr. 7. 19, **8**.
II, fr. 43. 56, **80**.
III, fr. 57. 1, **84**.
III, frr. 67–75, **94**.
Epigr. 6. 2, **75**.
7, **98**.
27. 1, **86**.
28, **77**, **78**.
33, **126**.
Hecale, frr. 239, 240, **86**.
frr. 239, 241, **66**.
fr. 282, **213**.
Hymns II. 27, **309**.
III. 13–14, **289**.
IV. 55 ff., **96**, **198**.
IV. 221, **198**.
IV. 228, 230, 259, **96**.
IV. 232, **200**.
VI. 40 ff., **96**.
frag. 215, **97**.
383. 1, **85**.
491, **227**.
556, **125**.
Calpurnius Siculus,
Eclogues 1. 44, **25**; 4. 64 ff., **67**; 4. 87, **334**; 7. 84, **334**.
Cassiodorus, *Var.* IV. 51. 8, **77**.
Catullus 3. 6–7, **289**.
11. 22–24, **222–23**.
29. 24, **19**, **291**.
34. 13–14, **177**.
60, **185**.
60. 2, **23**.
61, **22**.
61. 209, **130**.
61. 216, **326**.
62. 39 ff., **223**.
64. 37, 38–42, **17**.
64. 101, **149**.
64. 152, **224**.
64. 154 ff., **185**.
64. 177, **112**.
64. 224, **216**.
64. 338, **17**.
64. 397–408, **15**.
66. 39, **62**, **290**.
95. 10, **77**.
111. 3, **124**.
Cicero:
Att. I. 14. 3, **109**; IX. 7. c, **320**; X. 8. 5, **12**, **55**, **76**, **299**.
Balb. 40, **141**.
Brutus 211, **112**.
De Opt. Gen. Orat. 1, **97**.
De Oratore II. 26, **92**; II. 187, **109**; III. 45, **103**; III. 214, **110**; III. 225, **116**.
Div. I. 42, **181**.
Fam. VII. 1. 2, **213**; XVI. 11. 2, **295**.
Leg. Agr. I. 18–19, II. 86–87, **17**.

Nat. Deor. II. 56, **219**.
Orator 22. 74, **113**; 53, **115**; 70. 232–34, **107**.
Parad. VI. 2. 46, **18**.
Philippic II. 20, **306**; II. 37, **207**; II. 65, **165**.
Pro Cluentio 32, **59**.
Pro Deiotaro 8, **320**.
Pro Marc. 8, **263**.
Rab. Post. 2, **263**; 42, **82**.
Rep. VI. 18–19, **5**.
Tusc. Disp. I. 93, **227**; I. 106, **101**; III. 45, **108**; IV. 50, **258**.
Verrine V. 19, **133**; V. 28, **174**; V. 113, 153, **238**; V. 129, 47; V. 152–53, **320**.
Claudian, *De Rapt. Pros.* II. 204–05, **87**.
Demetrius, *De Eloc.* 222, **115**.
Dio Cassius, *Hist. Rom.* XLIII. 45, **291**.
LVI. 33. 3, **16**, **253**.
LXII. 27. 3, **166**.
fr. 105. 4, **18**.
Dionysius of Halicarnassus, *Comp. Verb.* 4, **107**.
Dracontius, *Medea* 17–18, **115**.
Ennius:
  Annales 34–50, Skutsch, **171**.
  36, **47**.
  38–39, **87**.
  87, **72**.
  95, **222**.
  155, **316**.
  199–200, **158**.
  207, **76**.
  209, 250, **109**.
  214, **52**, **141**.
  225–26, **19**, **295**.
  344–45, **15**, **203**.
  385, **313**.
  451, **101**.
  494–95, **313**.
  xxxiii, **304**.
  xlvii, **328**.
  Alexander 41–46, Jocelyn, **181**.
  47–49, **292**.
  50–61, **181**.
  Andromacha 89, **16**.
  92–94, **292**.
  Medea 217–18, **110**.
Euphorion Chalcidensis, Powell, no. 75, **210**; no. 51, **274**.
Euripides:
  Alcestis 170, **145**.
  175–79, 183, **144**.
  183–84, **129**.
  Bacchae 420, **197**.
  918–19, **171**.
  1017, **161**.
  Cretes 44, **148**.
  Hecuba 816, **109**.
  1273, **195**.
  Heracleidae 216, **216**.
  Heracles 20–22, **335**.
  222, **174**.
  364–426, **333**.
  823, **96**.
  831, **200**.
  867–70, **228**.
  931–35, **229**.
  934, **234**.
  1283–86, **111**.
  IT 44 ff., **168**.
  Medeae hypothesis, **114**.
  Medea 502–04, **111**.
  1041, **20**.
  Orestes 1369 ff., **173**.
  Phoen. 1419–25, **222**.
  Supp. 629, **68**.
  1016–20, **193**.
Florus, *Epit.* II. 6, **18**; II. 26, **19**.
Heliodorus, *Aethiop.* I. 4, **174**; III. 10, **174**; V. 32, **174**.
Herodotus I. 1–5, **17**.
  I. 60, **338**.
  I. 94, **44**.
  II. 171, **27**.
  V. 5, **145**.
  V. 111, **216**.
  VIII. 140. β 2, **320**.
Hesiod, *Erga* 228, **197**.
  Theog. 1, **75**.
  30, **178**.
  38, **311**.
  1008, **244**.
  1013–14, **145**.
Homer:
  Iliad I. 5, **151**.
  I. 70, **311**.
  I. 234, **21**.
  I. 234–38, **41**.
  I. 348, **190**.
  I. 404, **257**.
  I. 495 ff., **224**.
  I. 517 ff., **330**.

Iliad I. 599, **276**.
II. 16–52, **173**.
II. 215, **276**.
II. 278, **250**.
II. 489–90, **267**.
II. 728, **250**.
II. 806, **313**.
II. 862, **272**.
III. 40, **12**.
IV. 35–36, **198**.
IV. 130–31, **189**.
IV. 141 ff., **60**.
IV. 141–47, **22**.
IV. 164–65, **22**, **61**.
IV. 422, **69**.
IV. 439–43, **174**, **299**.
IV. 440–43, **299**.
IV. 442–43, **182**.
V. 265–72, **147**, **265**.
V. 305–16, **236**.
V. 330b–40, **30**.
V. 370, **189**.
V. 467, **244**.
V. 576, **209**.
V. 638–51, **330**.
V. 640, **332**.
V. 649, **332**.
VI. 57–60, **4**.
VI. 179, **23**.
VI. 197b, **193**.
VI. 244, **61**.
VI. 286 ff., **61**.
VI. 391–502, **270**.
VI. 395–96, **212**.
VI. 400, **217**.
VI. 402–03, **271**.
VI. 407, **271**.
VI. 448–49, **22**.
VI. 484, **104**.
VI. 490–93, **175**.
VI. 498, **72**.
VI. 506, **12**, **235**.
VII. 137–38, **212**.
VIII. 185, **214**.
VIII. 306 ff., **222**.
IX. 121 ff., **161**, **265**.
IX. 121–56, **62**.
IX. 491, **189**.
IX. 502, **274**.
IX. 556, **115**.
X. 1, **173**.
X. 13, **81**, **213**.
X 148 ff., **179**.
X. 304 ff., **62**.
X. 328–31, **62**.
XI. 299–305, **209**.
XII. 433, **59**, **236**.
XII. 445 ff., **235**.
XII. 451, **236**.
XIII. 295–305, **300**.
XIII. 359, **264**.
XIII. 427 ff., **265**.
XIII. 460, **244**.
XIII. 518, **211**.
XIII. 643 ff., **209**.
XIII. 754, **262**.
XIII. 792, **272**.
XIV. 214 ff., **165**.
XIV. 231 ff., **331**.
XIV. 251, **332**.
XIV. 268–69, **199**.
XIV. 292 ff., **59**.
XIV. 409 ff., **331**.
XIV. 462–63, **211**.
XV. 4, **331**.
XV. 24–28, **65**, **331**.
XV. 24–30, **302**.
XV. 67, **336**.
XV. 69–71, **302**.
XV. 262, **298**.
XV. 263, **235**.
XV. 362, **189**.
XV. 558, **313**.
XV. 618, **215**.
XV. 674 ff., **63**.
XVI. 7–10, **189**.
XVI. 33–35, **184–85**.
XVI. 82, **184**.
XVI. 102 ff., **175**.
XVI. 112–13, **184**.
XVI. 122–23, **294**, **180**.
XVI. 150–51, **200**.
XVI. 297–300, **59**.
XVI. 431 ff., **215**.
XVI. 528–29, **298**.
XVI. 792, 806, **304**.
XVI. 856, **314**.
XVI. 856–57, **185**, **201**.
XVII. 53–60, **222**.
XVII. 260–61, **209**.
XVII. 609, **211**.
XVIII. 39–49, **210**.
XVIII. 95–96, **62**.
XVIII. 105–06, **331**.
XVIII. 117, **227**, **249**, **331**, **333**.
XVIII. 176–77, **18**.
XVIII. 207–13, **29**.
XIX. 400, **214**.
XX. 144–48, **332**.
XX. 164–75, **234**.
XX. 170, **297**.
XX. 225–29, **201**.
XX. 239, **254**, **265**.

Iliad XX. 307–08, **17, 235, 244.**
XX. 347–48, **235.**
XXI. 99 ff., **266.**
XXI. 403 ff., **236.**
XXII. 26b–31, **29.**
XXII. 62–64, **4.**
XXII. 116, **57.**
XXII. 347, **198.**
XXII. 359, **304.**
XXII. 362, **314.**
XXII. 362–63, **185, 201.**
XXII. 429, **313.**
XXII. 500, **61.**
XXIII. 75 ff., **169.**
XXIII. 105–07, **179.**
XXIII. 296 ff., **265.**
XXIII. 741, **220.**
XXIII. 743, **231.**
XXIV. 212–13, **198.**
XXIV. 418–21, **274.**
XXIV. 486, 507, **266.**
Odyssey I. 51–54, **146.**
I. 68–75, **151.**
III. 278–85, **219.**
IV. 141 ff., **50.**
IV. 187–88, **153.**
V. 55–64, **146.**
V. 116 ff., **135.**
V. 118 ff., **146.**
V. 285, **228.**
VI. 102 ff., **62.**
VI. 149, **59.**
VII. 131, **313.**
VII. 241–42, **9.**
VIII. 362, **197.**
VIII. 362–66, **59.**
IX. 19–20, **59.**

IX. 504, **208, 250.**
IX. 528–35, **23, 60, 256, 286.**
IX. 530–35, **129.**
IX. 532–35, **151.**
X. 1 ff., **332.**
X. 146–47, **145.**
X. 210–33, **146.**
X. 305, **149.**
X. 323–35, **145.**
X. 330, **72.**
X. 333–35, **145.**
X. 488 ff., **180.**
XI. 38–41, **286.**
XI. 171–73, **62.**
XI. 235 ff., **193.**
XI. 249–50, **204.**
XI. 326, **61.**
XI. 330–34, **61.**
XI. 563, **62, 175.**
XI. 609–14, **231.**
XII. 70, **89.**
XII. 403–06, **149.**
XIII. 222, **58–59.**
XIV. 301–04, **148–49.**
XV. 125 ff., **50.**
XVII. 206, **313.**
XVIII. 40, **276.**
XIX. 246, **274.**
XX. 345 ff., **168.**
XX. 377, **220.**
XXIV. 482–86, 543, **303.**
Hy. 5. 286–88, **266.**
32. 19, **75.**
Horace:
 Ars Poetica 1 ff., **275.**
  14 ff., **275.**
  25, **87.**

46–48, **107.**
83, 85, **205.**
93 ff., **97, 104.**
97, **109.**
112–18, **101.**
121, **21.**
135, **244.**
137, **75, 264.**
139, **264.**
144–45, **274.**
148–50, **87.**
156, **318.**
185–88, **77.**
226, **314.**
274, **244.**
295, **318.**
335, **87.**
340, **78, 142.**
343, **307.**
357, **91.**
359, **209.**
391 ff., **77.**
391–407, **310.**
392, **99, 249, 283.**
392–400, **67.**
399, **249, 309.**
400, **283.**
407, **249.**
410–11, **106.**
472, **78.**
472–76, **308.**
476, **78.**
Carm. Saec. 15, **177.**
50–52, **319.**
51–52, **10, 263.**
61–62, **316.**
Epodes 5. 83 ff., **152.**
5. 87 ff., **238.**
7. 1, **259.**
7. 17–20, **36, 159.**

Epodes 9, **20**.
  9. 11, **89**.
  14. 9–12, **81**.
  16, **17**.
  16. 2, **15**.
  16. 60, **336**.
  17. 32–33, **23**.
  17. 33, **73**.
Epistles I. 2. 23, **71, 147**.
  I. 2. 59–63, **319**.
  I. 2. 62, **238**.
  I. 3. 14, **109**.
  I. 16. 27–29, **15**.
  I. 20. 24, **276**.
  II. 1. 123, **314**.
  II. 1. 124, **94, 307**.
  II. 1. 187 ff., **213**.
  II. 1. 189–93, **21**.
  II. 1. 213, **79**.
  II. 1. 232–34, **91**.
  II. 1. 233, **313**.
  II. 1. 240, **291**.
  II. 1. 247, **77**.
  II. 1. 250, **242**.
  II. 1. 257, **91**.
  II. 1. 258–59, **92**.
  II. 2. 109, **244**.
Odes I. 1. 34, **79**.
  I. 2. 1, **15**.
  I. 2. 32, **316**.
  I. 2. 41, **25**.
  I. 2. 41–44, **20**.
  I. 2. 45, **15**.
  I. 2. 50, **45**.
  I. 5. 9, **72**.
  I. 6, **77, 136, 242**.
  I. 12. 7–12, **67**.
  I. 12. 51–52, **323**.
  I. 12. 57, **259**.

I. 14. 1, **252**.
I. 15, **13**.
I. 15. 1, **252**.
I. 16, **319**.
I. 16. 17–21, **321**.
I. 17. 18, **81**.
I. 24. 3, **80**.
I. 24. 13, **99**.
I. 25. 19–20, **107**.
I. 27. 19, **23, 191**.
I. 32. 5, **307**.
I. 36. 16, **60**.
I. 37. 6, **223**.
II. 1. 35, **281**.
II. 3. 13–14, **60**.
II. 10. 11–12, **214**.
II. 19. 19, **160**.
II. 20. 10, **78**.
III. 1. 1, **78**.
III. 1. 4, **306**.
III. 1. 5, **165**.
III. 2. 6–12, **297**.
III. 3. 18 ff., **203**.
III. 3. 18–28, **250**.
III. 3. 18–68, **39**.
III. 3. 26–27, **253**.
III. 3. 57 ff., **17**.
III. 3. 57–60, **252**.
III. 3. 58, **16, 98**.
III. 3. 61–64, **261**.
III. 6. 21, **253**.
III. 6. 45–48, **306**.
III. 11. 33–34, **258**.
III. 13. 8, **126**.
III. 14. 1, **313, 337**.
III. 30. 8–9, **223**.
IV. 3. 23, **22**.
IV. 4. 49, **138**.
IV. 5. 23, **290**.
IV. 6. 18–20, **4**.

IV. 6. 41, **53**.
IV. 7. 14–16, **54, 326**.
IV. 7. 15–16, **23**.
IV. 7. 19, **22, 326**.
IV. 7. 21–28, **326**.
IV. 8. 29–34, **160**.
IV. 8. 30, **337**.
IV. 9. 9, **81**.
IV. 12, **93**.
IV. 15, **11**.
IV. 15. 9, **294**.
IV. 15. 12, **253**.
IV. 15. 25 ff., **325**.
IV. 15. 25–32, **217**.
Sat. I. 1. 24–25, **314**.
  I. 4. 60–62, **107**.
  I. 4. 105–06, **306**.
  I. 4. 106, **318**.
  I. 5. 48, **44**.
  I. 9. 44, **325**.
  I. 9. 56, **325**.
  I. 10. 9, **87**.
  I. 10. 43–44, **77, 92**.
  I. 10. 44–45, **93**.
  I. 10. 48, 66, **244**.
  II. 1. 10–12, **242**.
  II. 1. 11, **291**.
  II. 1. 12, **44**.
  II. 1. 33, **276**.
  II. 1. 58, **39**.
  II. 3. 60, **101**.
  II. 5. 62–63. **25**.
Hyginus, *Fab*. 91, **182**.
Isocrates:
  Antidosis 293–94, **111**.
  Pan. 80, **239**.
  In Soph. 12, **315**.
Jerome, *Epp*. 43, **77**.
Justin II. 4. 12, **115**.

Index Locorum Ceterorum 379

Juvenal:
  III. 41, 199, **15**.
  III. 61–62, **253**.
  III. 62, **17**.
  III. 199, **208**.
  VII. 1, **15**.
  VIII. 187–88, **82**.
  XI. 105, **55**.
Livius Andronicus, 12
  Buechner, **197**.
Livy:
  I. 1, **244**.
  I. 2, **239, 302**.
  I. 2. 5, **281**.
  I. 3. 2, **7, 272**.
  I. 3. 6, **302**.
  I. 28. 11, **239**.
  I. 29, **202**.
  I. 49. 1, **291**.
  I. 50. 3 ff., **304**.
  I. 55. 6, **327**.
  II. 56. 6, **244**.
  IV. 20, **319**.
  IV. 20. 7, **272**.
  IV. 37, **91**.
  VII. 18. 3, **197**.
  XXI. 18. 13, **176**.
  XXII. 2. 10–11, **74**.
  XXII. 51. 9, **198**.
  XXII. 55. 6, **137**.
  XXX. 8. 7, **165**.
  XXX. 26. 9, **318**.
  XXX. 28. 2, **318**.
  Epit. lxxxviii, **18, 305**.
  Praef. 9, **11**; 10, **317**.
Longinus, *De Subl.* 9. 13, **243**.
Lucan I. 4, **301**.
  I. 8, **94**.
  I. 33, **25, 30, 301**.
  I. 33 ff., **241**.
  I. 41, **25**.
  I. 63, **307**.
  I. 72, **15, 168**.
  I. 132–33, **76**.
  I. 158, **79**.
  I. 192, **338**.
  I. 692, **159, 264**.
  II. 287, 567, **310**.
  V. 26, **248**.
  VII. 7 ff., **168**.
  VII. 13–19, **76**.
  VII. 346, **310**.
  VII. 385 ff., **328**.
  VII. 389–408, **17**.
  VII. 405, **253**.
  VII. 415, **310**.
  VIII. 492–93, **166**.
  VIII. 714a, **291**.
  IX. 190–91, **94, 307**.
  IX. 980, **307**.
  X. 384–85, **310**.
Lucian:
  Menippus 10, **169**.
  Philops. 18, **308**.
  Salt. 62, **115**.
Lucilius, 181–88, M., **116**; 484, **142**; 621, **91**; 1065, **142**.
Lucretius:
  I. 32–33, **296**.
  II. 115, **178**.
  II. 639, **198**.
  III. 58, **83**.
  III. 154–57, **177**.
  III. 833–37, **138**.
  III. 895, **33**.
  III. 978 ff., **256**.
  IV. 587, **255**.
  V. 1161–1240, **312**.

Lycophron:
  Alexandra 102, **68**.
  132, **116**.
  184, **68**.
  320, **68**.
  602, **65**.
  694, **219**.
  965, **265**.
  1226–80, **245**.
  1232–33, **245**.
  1248, **7, 245**.
  1250–52, **269**.
  1256, **269**.
  1263, **265**.
  1268–70, **244**.
  1271–72, **245**.
  1273–74, **159**.
  1291 ff., **17**.
Macrobius:
  Sat. III. 12. 5–6, **296**.
  V. 1. 1, **109**.
  V. 2. 6, **332**.
  V. 17. 5, **81**.
  V. 17. 18, **66**.
  VI. 1. 58, **63, 164**.
  Comm. I. 3. 2, **167**.
Manilius V. 482–83, **76**.
Martial:
  II. 41. 15, **83**; **108**.
  VII. 25. 4, **158**.
  IX. 64, 65, **333**.
  IX. 64. 6, **338**.
Meleager, *A.P.* XII. 63. 1, **116**; XII. 122. 3, **116**; XII. 159. 3, **116**.
Menander:
  Misoumenos 263, **122**.
  Perikeir. 508–10, **121**.
Moschus, *Eur.* 8 ff., **17**.
  16–17, 20, **171**.

Naevius:
Bellum Pun. 2–3, W., **103**; 5–7, **255**; 19–20, **103**.
Lycurgus 25 W., **160**.
Tarentilla, 74–79, W., **103**.
Origen, *Dialogus cum Heraclide* 4, **141**.
Orosius I. 15, **115**.
Ovid:
Am. III. 9. 1, **9**, **36**, **153**, **224**.
III. 9. 7–8, **139**.
A.A. I. 181 ff., **248**.
I. 298, **151**.
Ex Ponto IV. 2. 33–36, **76**.
Fasti I. 623–24, **204**.
I. 708, **203–04**.
II. 810, **124**.
III. 611, **196**.
III. 633, **193–94**.
VI. 131 ff., **142**.
Her. 15. 12, **23**.
Met. I. 1, **147**.
I. 145, **19**.
I. 517–18, **311**.
II. 217–226, **208**.
II. 360, **73**.
II. 466 ff., **57**.
II. 508 ff., **198**.
II. 512 ff., **131**.
III. 32, **295**.
III. 171–72, **208**.
III. 206 ff., **207**.
V. 153, **47**.
VII. 398, **125**.
VII. 406, **158**.
VII. 663, **72**.

VIII. 299 ff., **208**.
IX. 458, **191**.
XI. 106, **177**.
XII. 536, **255**.
XII. 601, 606, **304**.
XIII. 546, **195**.
XIII. 625, **196**.
XIII. 868, **23**.
XIV. 320 ff., **72**.
XIV. 546 ff., **65**.
XIV. 584, **196**.
XV. 828, **223**.
Rem. Am. 491, **23**.
Tristia II. 519, **76**.
II. 533–34, **59**.
IV. 10. 41 ff., **325**.
Nonnus, *Dion.* XIX. 156, **113**.
Pacuvius, *Hermiona* 187, W., **109**.
Palladas, *A.P.* X. 72, **82–83**.
Parthenius, *Met.*, no. 636–37 (Lloyd-Jones / Parsons), **66**.
Pausanias, IV. 2., **115**.
Petrarch, *Africa* V. 399, 405, **23**.
Philodemus:
De Poematis V, ed. Mangoni, p. 137, **91**; V, col. 25; p. 152, **213**.
P. Herc. 1081a fr. 41 = 39 Hausrath, **109**.
1676, tr. C [Sbordone], **107**.
Pindar:
Isth. 4. 50, 53, **275**.
6. 29, **183**.

Nem. 1. 13–18, **196**.
1. 33 ff., **335**.
1. 55, **315**.
1. 57, **320**.
1. 60, **248**.
2. 24, **313**.
7. 14, **64**.
7. 20–30, **242**.
7. 52, **338**.
9. 34, **216**.
Ol. 1. 58, **220**.
2. 79–83, **224**.
2. 80, **9**.
2. 83, **35**.
3. 43–45, **338**.
9. 1, **276**, **308**.
13. 65 ff., **178**.
Py. 1. 25, **335**.
2. 17, **139**.
2. 36, **89**.
2. 55, **308**.
2. 65, **279**.
2. 84, **165**.
3. 83, **308**.
4. 78 ff., **275**.
4. 117, **313**.
4. 171–82, **209**.
4. 171–83, **20**.
4. 247–48, **85**.
4. 248, **87**, **209**.
5. 14, **30**.
6. 28 ff., **33**.
6. 30, **153**.
6. 44–45, **215**.
8. 95–96, **170**.
10. 31–44, **4**, **5**.
Plato:
Ion 530d, **109**.
535a, **99**.
541e 7–8, **99**.

Index Locorum Ceterorum

Phaedrus 259b–d, **79**.
  264c 2–5, **243**.
Rep. II 359d, **56**.
  III. 383b, **110**.
  VII. 516e 9, 517d 6, **316**.
  IX. 573b 4, 578a 11, **337**.
  X. 595c, **98, 243**.
  X. 617e, **260**.
Symp. 179e, **201**.
  180b, **224**.
  192e 3–4, **171**.
Plautus:
  Amph. 1139, **141**.
  M.G. I. 1. 25–30, **91**.
  Most. 91 ff., **126**.
Pliny:
  N.H. VIII. 11, **208**.
  XIII. 53, **329**.
  XXXIV. 57, **291**.
  XXXV. 73, **113**.
  XXXVI. 28, **329**.
  XXXVI. 117, **78**.
Plutarch:
  Antony 26, **141**.
  Crassus 33, **141**.
  C. Gracchus 19, **112**.
  de Glor. Ath. 3. 346f, **113**.
  Pompey 46, **291**.
  quaest. conv. II. 711F, 712E, **76**.
  Sulla VII. 4, **246**.
Polybius, VI. 11. 2, **156**.
  XVI. 28, **165**.
Prometheus Vinctus 128, **10**; 1005, **137**.
Propertius I. 21, **25**.
  I. 22. 5, **19, 159, 295**.

II. 1. 49, **228**.
II. 2, **274**.
II. 7. 14, **289**.
II. 12. 23, **218**.
II. 15. 51–52, **107**.
II. 18b. 23, **158**.
II. 31. 14, **146**.
II. 31. 15, **96**.
II. 31. 16, **310**.
II. 34. 64, **250**.
II. 34. 66, **305**.
III. 1. 29–30, **59**.
III. 3. 38, **80**.
III. 4. 19–20, **54**.
III. 11. 40, **20**.
III. 11. 45, **223**.
III. 11. 59, **138**.
III. 11. 66, **15**.
III. 13. 60, **15**.
III. 13. 65, **307**.
III. 18. 13, **293**.
III. 21. 28, **121**.
III. 22, **39**.
III. 22. 41–42, **22, 203, 325**.
IV. 1. 9, **55, 301**.
IV. 1. 51, **307**.
IV. 3. 14, **218**.
IV. 3. 15 ff., **182**.
IV. 5. 43, **121**.
IV. 6. 12, **80**.
IV. 6. 21, **26**.
IV. 6. 27 ff., **295**.
IV. 6. 38, **25, 263, 305**.
IV. 6. 62, **20**.
IV. 7. 63, **258**.
IV. 10, **319**.
IV. 11, **11, 145**.
IV. 11. 39, **165**.
IV. 11. 69–70, **325**.

Quintilian:
  I. 6. 40, **66**.
  I. 12. 18, **109**.
  II. 7. 5, **90**.
  III. 22, **282**.
  IV. 6. 21, **301**.
  VI. 2. 20, **103**.
  VIII. 2. 18, **312**.
  XII. 1. 27, **110**.
  XII. 10. 9, **308**.
  XII. 10. 33, **210**.
Quintus Smyrnaeus, *Posthom.* I. 659 ff.; I. 664–65, **202**.
Sallust:
  Cat. 5. 3–4, **261**.
  9. 5, **239**.
  10. 1, **138**.
  15. 5, **274**.
  Jug. 4. 3, **306**.
  5. 2, **18**.
  33. 3, **110**.
  42. 4, **321**.
Sappho, 105c, Lobel–Page, **223**.
Seneca:
  Clem. I. 11, **25**.
  Const. Sap. 1, **263**.
  2. 1, **336**.
  2. 2, **15**.
  Epp. 5. 4, **321**.
  18. 12, **333**.
  19. 9, **214**.
  94. 62, 64, 65, **334**.
  107. 11, **310**.
  Nat. Quaest. V. 18. 4, **7**.
  Prov. 2. 9, **263**.
  Hercules Furens 1321, **111**.

Hipp. 101–03, **23**.
Seneca Rhet., *Suas.* II.
  19, **78**.
Silius:
  Punica I. 81–82, **138**.
    II. 384, **176**.
    II. 410–11, **13**.
    IV. 765–67, **141**.
    VIII. 539, **219**.
    XV. 292, **165**.
Sophocles:
  Ajax 285–88, 292–93,
    175.
    514 ff., **112**.
    550–51, **63, 164**.
  Antigone 1–3, **116**.
  Oed. Rex 380, **123**.
  Trach. 767, **229**.
    912–13, 915–21,
    930–31, **143**.
    917–19, **129**.
    1254, 1260, **143**.
Statius:
  Silvae IV. 2. 18 ff., **84**.
    V. 3. 5, **135**.
    V. 3. 238, **205**.
  Theb. I. 250–82, **131**.
    I. 337, **222**.
    I. 596 ff., **142**.
    III. 661, **312**.
    VIII. 736 ff., **198**.
    X. 365, **222**.
    XI. 565–73, **222**.
    XII. 797–99, **267**.
Strabo IV. 4. 4, **307**.
  V. 4. 11, **18**.

Suetonius:
  Aug. 7. 2, **26**.
    18, 50, **330**.
    27, **253**.
    35, **203**.
    43, **5**.
    50, **90**.
    51, **238**.
    65, **12**.
    89, **92**.
    94, **262, 284**.
    99, **76**.
  Cal. 57. 4, **82**.
  Jul. 39, **5, 267**.
    44, **76**.
    56, **261, 291**.
    79, **252**.
    81, **168**.
  Nero 25, **328**.
    39, **252**.
    54, **81**.
  Tib. 23, **13, 263, 327**.
    70. 2, **108**.
Synesius, *Epp.* 2, p. 68,
  Garzya, **238**; 41, p.
  124, **237**; 73, p. 219,
  238.
Tacitus:
  Ann. I. 2, **207**.
    I. 6, **12**.
    I. 9, **38**.
    IV. 34, **7**.
    XIV. 2, **59**.
    XIV. 15, **39**.
    XIV. 56, **285**.
    XV. 39, **16**.

  Dial. 12, **77, 249, 283,
    333**.
    12. 4, **310**.
    13. 2, **77**.
    28, **112**.
  Hist. I. 4, **156**.
Tertullian, *De*
  Spectaculis 8, **4**.
  Apol. 9, **141**.
Themistius, *Or.* 64b
  (Downey I, p. 94),
  322.
Theocritus 16. 20, **242**.
  13. 61–63, **222, 232**.
Theophrastus, cit. Diom.
  Gramm., Keil I. p.
  484, 1–2, **3**.
Thucydides II. 63. 2,
  337.
  III. 37. 2, **337**.
  IV. 39. 3, **337**.
Varius, 5, Buechner, **15**.
Velleius Paterculus II.
  18. 3, **165**.
  II. 131. 1, **281**.
Vitruvius, *De Arch.* VII.
  5. 3–4, **77, 275, 308**.
Xenophon:
  Anabasis I. 6. 10, **230**.
  Cyn. I. 15, **244**.
  Mem. I. 3. 7, **71**.

INDEX RERUM ET NOMINUM

abigere, "abort," 59.
adynata, 101.
advent, eschatological *venturus*, 30, 31, 281.
Aeneas / Hercules, 334–35.
—ἀναίτιος, 244, 247, 253.
Aeneid as *carmen sacrum*, 322 ff.
— as ἀτελής, 326.
— as *Heracleid*, 329 ff.
— as tragedy, 98 ff., 241 ff.
—, aims of, 3.
Alexander, 248.
aliquis / τις, ominous, 292.
amatory go-between, 121.
ambiguous names, 208 ff.
ambivalence, 316.
Anchises, 265 ff.
Anna, 193 ff.
ἀντιλαβή, 118, 132.
Antilochus, 33.
Apollo and Mars, 294 ff.
— *augur*, 316.
— *citharoedus*, 309.
— Palatinus, 10, 96.
— Sosianus, 329.
Apollonius Rhodius, 20, 88–89.
ἀπορία, 313, 328.
apostrophe, 123.
Ara Pacis, 5–7, 26.
Arctinus, 215.
Aristotle, 242 ff., 323–24.
arma sexual, 59.
arte illusoria, 62–64.
Ascanius / Iulus, 16; Ascanius / Augustus, 25.
Astarte divided, 195 ff.; Astarte / Uni, 13.

Atlas, 226.
Augustan aesthetic, 315.
— cameo, 273–74.
Augustus and children, 11–13.
— and Rome, 15.
— as messianic emperor, 4, 281 (see also "advent").
— and Pompey, 4.
aurea erotic, 72.
avunculus, 270–71.

Bacchic themes, 160–61.
battles / banquets, 174.
binocular vision / squint, 21, 55 ff., 183, 186, 276.
Bion, 134.
bisexuality divine, 135.
brevitas, 87.

Caesarion, 11, 223.
calcatio colli, 38.
callida iunctura, 107, 132.
Callimachean poetic, 86 ff.
Callimachus, 66, 67, 77, 78, 80, 84, 85, 86 ff., 93, 109, 119, 125, 174, 309.
Callimachus and Virgil, 94 ff.
character, 213 ff.
— drawing, 103.
— and aspiration, 116 ff.
chiaroscuro / looking-glass, 57, 61, 100, 218, 220.
child denatured, 56.
children in Homer, 189.
Cicero, 5, 319–20.
— on anger, 258.
Circe, 4, 9, 71, 72, 145 ff., 180, 195, 293.

circus, 4, 5, 267.
— and carnival aesthetic, 82 ff., 328.
cives vocatival, 313.
Civil Wars, 17 ff., 281.
Clementia Caesaris, 320.
Cleopatra, 11.
coincidentia oppositorum, 215.
comedy, 120, 121.
— women's genre, 105.
comic / iambic, 276.
coniu(n)x, coniugium, conubium, 49.
contraceptive vitriol, 131.
creative word / waters of chaos, 109.
Cretan Labyrinth, 317.
Crete, 24, 29, 32, 34, 178, 192, 282, 298, 300, 305.
Crete / Carthage, 148 ff., 151.
culpare, 228.
Cyclops, 74.

declension, 290, 315.
declining mode, 183, 202.
demens in diatribe, 158.
dénudation du procédé, 65.
describo ("caricature"), 57; description abnormal, 273, 275, 276.
deserted heroine, 112, 125.
Dido and C. Gracchus, 110 ff.
— in Italy, 158 ff.
— roles, 142 ff.
"Dido" as title, 138–39.
dilectus verborum, 118.
Dionysius of Mytilene (Scytobrachion), 254.
Discordia, 295.
disjuncture of sensibility, 225.
disobliging other, 131, 134, 169, 204, 205.
divine both masculine and feminine, 135.
domus, dominari, 287–88.

double name, 271–72.
dramatic, δραματικός, 92, 104.
dreams, 167 ff.; death dream, 168, 170–71; incubation dream, 180.

Εἰρήνη κουροτρόφος, 293.
elogium, 127, 129.
enthymema, 128.
epic exordia, first persons in, 75.
ἐπισκιάζω sacral, 296.
Erato, 154, 155.
Eris, 174.
erotic, 283.
erzählte Zeit, Erzählzeit 280.
estranging language, 312.
Eteocles / Polynices, 222, 295.
ἠθοποιΐα, 103; ethopoeic language, 121.
Etna, 73, 74.
— love like fires of, 23, 60.
Etruria, 245 ff.; Virgil Etruscan?, 327.
eulogy, 242.
— and prophecy, 286 ff.
Euphorion, 108, 126.
external / internal reference, 125–26.

Fame, 24, 27, 57, 126.
fantasia / φαντασία, 141.
φάντασμα, 167, 183.
"fear not," sacral, 10.
felix / infelix, 49 ff., 279, 289, 293.
feminine syntax, 103.
fertility with a difference, 289.
fictional times, 279 ff.
filius, filia, 35.
foiled expectation, 205, 261, 267, 268, 294.
Fortune, 263.
friendly fire, 218.
Furor, 334.

Index Rerum et Nominum

game of war, 44.
genitor, genetrix, 48–49.
Gilgamesh, 8, 189, 237, 256.
gnatus / natus, 32.
Golden Age, 28, 190, 301, 328, 333.
Golden Bough, 41, 73.
Gorgias, 106.
Greek novel, 275.
grotesque, 73, 77, 275, 308, 309.
Grottarossa sarcophagus, 139.
Gygean *videre*, 51, 56, 84, 153, 170, 186, 192, 239.

halo, 273.
hand, sacral, 320.
hearing with eyes, 115, 122.
heifer / girl, 68.
Hellenistic epic, 85 ff.
Hercules, 37, 65, 111, 143, 177, 198, 226–27, 238, 248, 255 ff., 283, 291; Aeneas / Hercules, 334 ff.; Turnus / Hercules, 228 ff.; Domitian / Hercules, 333, 337–38; Trajan / Hercules, 337.
— and Apollo in conflict, 330.
— and Athena at Sant'Omobono, 338.
heres, 22–23.
heros / eros, 196.
historic present, 27, 91.
history 90 ff.; history poetry, 19.
hollow pastoral, 20, 28, 65, 93 ff., 101–03, 111, 126, 128, 134, 150, 152, 194, 201, 222, 258, 282, 328.
Horace, 6, 10, 15, 17, 22, 54, 77, 251, 252, 261, 297, 306 ff., 319, 323, 325, 326.
hymenaei, 286.
hypocrisis, 105, 112, 114.

iambic, 136–37, 192.
imago, δείκηλον, 27, 58, 89, 179.

infans, 43.
infelix, 10–11, 14, 21, 49–53.
inner space, 64, 84.
insinuatio, 266.
intruded second clause, 182.
ipse (= "le chef"), 39.
irony, 187.
Isocrates, 111.
iterum, iteration, 11, 186, 241, 261, 264, 281, 288, 292, 293, 328, 330.
Iulus / Ascanius, 270 ff.

Jephtha / Idomeneus, 300.
Jesus / Jesin, 135.
Juturna, 134 ff., 200, 203 ff.

κάθαρσις, 112, 322 ff.
Keimentschluß, "seminal decision," 43, 98, 151, 192.
κτίσις, 245, 249 ff.

Labyrinth, 150, 178.
Laomedon, 15, 147, 162, 177, 182, 183, 253–54.
Laudes Italiae, 39.
laughter and the transrational, 314 ff.
Lavinia, 22, 42, 49, 60, 72, 136, 190 ff.
leap into another dimension, 74, 83, 114, 136.
limen, 84, 97.
lists, 207 ff.
Livy *Pompeianus*, 7; on aims of history, 318.
lost children, 202 ff., 267, 274.
Lusus Troiae, 4, 5, 15, 16, 20, 42, 264, 280, 328.
Lycophron, 65.

Maecenatians, 325.
man / bull transformations, 37.
μανία, 318.
Marcellus, 12–13, 20.

marriage and children, 325 ff.
Mars, 6; of Todi, 294.
matres / mater, 46 ff.
Medea, 34, 114, 125, 128, 129, 142, 144, 145, 148, 150, 151, 156, 157, 161, 162, 168, 169, 170.
Medea / Medusa, 140.
medical innuendo, 131.
mental dissociation, 127.
μετάληψις αἰσθήσεως, 115.
metamorphosis, 27, 62, 64, 65 ff.
— and Eros, 68 ff.
metathesis, 107.
mixing of motifs, 133, 169.
monsters, 23–24.
moral universe of *Aeneid*, 318 ff.
Muses, 79–80.
music, 75–76, 212 ff.; Medusa / music theme, 140.

nascor, 31 ff.; *natus*, 32–34.
Nero / Helios (Sol), 334.
nimia pietas, 16, 269, 305.
Nisus and Euryalus, 220 ff.

Octavian as *iuvenis*, 25, 102.
odi et amo, 176, 185.
"one who is to come," 30.
ὁμαλῶς ἀνώμαλον, 114.
ὀνόματα κύρια, 119.
"on that day," 281.
Orpheus, 67, 283, 310.

painting, 275.
Pallas and Turnus, 226 ff.
pantomime, 77, 81 ff., 113, 115, 122, 145, 170, 213, 217.
pario, parens, 42 ff.
Parthenius, 66, 108.
pastoral and Dido, 102.
pater, 44 ff.; *pater* = "sir," 45.

pathetic style, 136.
Pax Augusta, 19.
peace, 7, 20, 26; peace and children, 21, 290 ff.; price of, 301 ff.
peccare, 191.
peepers, women as, 168.
Penthesilea, 231, 299.
Pharsalia, 17.
Pindar, 3, 4, 5, 9, 85, 87, 92, 120, 139, 140, 153, 170, 196, 203, 209, 220, 224, 250, 275, 279, 284, 287, 308, 312, 315, 320, 335, 338.
poetic of silences, 270–71, 312.
pointless repetition, 184.
polyphony, 312.
— of irresolution, 283.
polyprosopic, 100, 145, 170, 328.
present participle nominative singular, dramatic, 47, 128.
principles of circus aesthetic, 83–84.
progenies, 29 ff.
proles, 36 ff., 285.
Prometheus, 214.
propitiatory death, 219.
prosaicisms, 107.
Providence, πρόνοια, 322.
puella, 43.
puer, 43–44; *puer / senex*, 279.

questions, 126 ff., 130, 205, 224, 233.

Racine, 106–07, 121.
racism, 17, 39–40.
recusatio, 92.
reduced laughter, 314.
religious inspiration, 308 ff.
remembering genre, 275.
remotio criminis, 128.
resurrection, 5.
rhetorical decorum, 101 ff.; rhetor's rules, 105 ff.; rhetoric of silences,

Index Rerum et Nominum

107, 113 ff., 118, 125, 157; poetic rhetoric, 106, 108 ff.
Roman aesthetics, 27.

saevus, 72, 147–49, 154, 158.
Sallust, 18, 321.
sambuca, 108.
Sarpedon, 30–31, 215.
satire, 307.
sceleratus, 229–30.
σκιαγραφία, 89.
Seneca *tragicus*, 333–34.
sensibility, 185.
serio-comic, 314.
Shield of Aeneas, 23, 37, 90, 262–63, 295, 299, 316, 323.
sic (= "ohne weiteres"), 39, 77, 114.
Simonides of Ceos, 113.
Simonides of Magnesia, 90–91.
sitting, sacral, 80.
σκευοφόροι, 216.
σκότισον, 312.
snake, 70, 182.
socer generque, 291, 301.
Sophocles, 175.
Sousse Mosaic, 79 ff., 170.
spatium ("lap"), 285.
speaking silence, αὐδήεσσα / φωνήεσσα σιωπή, 113, 116.
spectator sport, 225.
spoudogeloion, 9.
stirps, 37 ff.
subiectio, 110.
Sun-King, 262, 284; see also Alexander, Nero.
suppressed sexuality, 124.

te sine, sacral, 135.
"terrible" as monarchical adjective, 165.
thalamus, 11, 62, 164.

theatre, 76 ff., 121, 292–93.
Theophrastus, 3.
Third Rome, 260–61.
Timanthes of Sicyon, 113.
tragi-comedy, 104 ff.
transrational language, 106, 116, 117.
Troy, last night of, 13 ff.; image of Rome, 15 ff., 253–54.
Truth and Time, 310 ff.
Turnus / Ajax, 45.
Turnus, belt, 10, 165–66, 230 ff., 266.
— death of, 232 ff.
twinning, 55, 56, 58, 171, 259, 264.

utilitas as civic virtue, 94, 307.

Varius *poeta*, 92.
Varro Reatinus, *De Familiis Troianis*, 3.
vates, 76, 77, 80, 89, 94, 99, 117, 119, 120, 154, 156, 194, 283, 306 ff.
Vegio / Vegius, 11, 35, 57, 133, 250, 251, 254, 278–79, 287, 313, 326, 328.
Venus and Juno, 130 ff.
Venus talks like Catullus, 132.
vertical time, 129, 152, 282, 296–97, 311.
Virgil and Callimachus, 94–98.
—and sexuality, 58 ff.
Virgil Etruscan?, 327.
Virgil's Wheel, 119.
virgins, 200 ff.; *virgo*, 190; *virginitas*, 119.

Wisdom of Solomon, 173, 188.
women, role of, 8–9.
— and children, 189 ff.
— as peepers / dreamers, 137, 168.
— rhetoric of, 101 ff., 121 ff.